THE SUFFERING SERVANT

THE SUFFERING SERVANT

Isaiah 53 in Jewish and Christian Sources

Edited by

Bernd Janowski and Peter Stuhlmacher

Translated by

Daniel P. Bailey

WILLIAM B. EERDMANS PUBLISHING COMPANY
GRAND RAPIDS, MICHIGAN / CAMBRIDGE, U.K.

Originally published as *Der leidende Gottesknecht* by Mohr Siebeck, 1996

Wm. B. Eerdmans Publishing Co.
255 Jefferson Ave. S.E., Grand Rapids, Michigan 49503 /
P.O. Box 163, Cambridge CB3 9PU U.K.
www.eerdmans.com

Printed in the United States of America

09 08 07 06 05 04   7 6 5 4 3 2 1

Library of Congress Cataloging-in-Publication Data

Leidende Gottesknecht. English.
    The suffering servant: Isaiah 53 in Jewish and Christian sources /
    edited by Bernd Janowski and Peter Stuhlmacher; translated by Daniel P. Bailey.
        p.   cm.
    Includes bibliographical references and indexes.
    ISBN 0-8028-0845-X (pbk.: alk. paper)
    1. Bible. O.T. Isaiah LIII — Criticism, interpretation, etc. 2. Servant of
Jehovah — Biblical teaching.   I. Janowski, Bernd, 1943- II. Stuhlmacher, Peter. III. Title.

    BS1520.L4513   2004
    224'.1064 — dc22

                                            2004053272

The chapters by Hans-Jürgen Hermisson, Bernd Janowski, Martin Hengel, Peter Stuhlmacher, Otfried Hofius, Jostein Ådna, Christoph Markschies, and Stefan Schreiner previously appeared in *Der leidende Gottesknecht. Jesaja 53 und seine Wirkungsgeschichte*, edited by Bernd Janowski and Peter Stuhlmacher, Forschungen zum Alten Testament 14 (Tübingen: Mohr Siebeck, 1996) and appear in this volume in translation and with additions and revisions by the authors and the translator.

The chapter by Hermann Spieckermann previously appeared as "Konzeption und Vorgeschichte des Stellvertretungsgedankens im Alten Testament," in *Congress Volume: Cambridge 1995*, edited by J. A. Emerton, Supplements to Vetus Testamentum 66 (Leiden: Brill, 1997), pp. 281-95, and appears here in translation.

Contents

Preface

With its idea of the vicarious suffering of the Servant of God, Isaiah 52:13–53:12, the focus of this volume, is one of those leading Old Testament theological texts that have had, and will continue to have, an extraordinary influence or "effective history" (German: *Wirkungsgeschichte*) in Judaism and Christianity. In order to sketch the basic features of this effective history, especially for the postbiblical and early Christian periods, we must have access to the foundational Old Testament text with its tradition and transmission history. Yet the problems begin precisely here. Is the chapter's characteristic category of vicariousness still accessible to modern understanding, or should it not rather be replaced by other categories? Gerhard Friedrich has recommended the latter approach to the interpretation of the death of Jesus (*Die Verkündigung des Todes Jesus im Neuen Testament* [Neukirchen-Vluyn ²1985]). On the other hand W. Pannenberg, after admitting that concepts like sacrifice, vicariousness, and atonement are no longer self-evident to today's people, nevertheless insists that this is insufficient reason to replace the traditional ideas by others. The task of today's interpreter is rather to open up the traditional language and motifs to the understanding of modern readers and so to keep their (original) sense alive (cf. *Systematic Theology,* trans. G. W. Bromiley [Grand Rapids 1994], 2:421-422). Pannenberg concludes: "The problems that people have with ideas like expiation and representation (or substitution) [= a single German term: *Stellvertretung*] in our secularized age rest less on any lack of forcefulness in the traditional terms than on the fact that those who are competent to interpret them do not explain their content with sufficient force or clarity" (422).

The present volume addresses itself to this interpretive task. Seven of its ten main contributions were originally presented in Professor Martin Hengel's graduate and faculty seminar in Tübingen in the Summer Semester of 1991; the essay by

S. Schreiner was written for this volume after 1991 while the one by H. Spiecker-mann appeared in another volume a year after this one in 1997.[1] The essay by D. P. Bailey is specific to the English edition. The essays take up the motif of the Suffer-ing Servant in Isaiah 53 and use interdisciplinary cooperation to expose the com-plex process of interpretation this text has undergone. First, a new text had to be formulated — based on antecedents but also moving beyond them — to explain how the Servant through his sufferings could take the place of "the many" (H. Spieckermann). This text then found its place in the Deutero-Isaianic tradi-tion and received its definitive meaning in this context (H.-J. Hermisson; B. Janowski). Ancient Judaism took up particular statements from Isaiah 53 and applied the whole chapter to Israel, righteous individuals, the prophet Isaiah, and the Messiah (M. Hengel; J. Ådna). The ministry of Jesus of Nazareth caused the Servant Song to be interpreted primarily Christologically in the New Testament (P. Stuhlmacher; O. Hofius). Some church fathers saw the vicariously suffering Je-sus as the basis and cause of the salvation preached by the church, while others saw him as an example of the true Christian (C. Markschies). Justin Martyr stands out as the Christian apologist who made the greatest use of Isaiah 53 in the second cen-tury c.e. (D. P. Bailey). However, from the second century c.e. until the late middle ages, individual Jewish scholars have reacted critically to the Christian reception and interpretation of Isaiah 53 (S. Schreiner). By tracing this effective history we hope that we have presented a differentiated and accurate picture of the theology, historical location, and ongoing influence of this central biblical text that will stimulate further research. An extensive and up-to-date bibliography (W. Hüll-strung, G. Feine, D. P. Bailey) and indexes conclude the volume.

Without energetic and knowledgeable help the appearance of this volume would have been impossible. For work on the German we must thank especially Gerlinde Feine, who converted complicated and heavily reworked manuscripts into texts and achieved editorial uniformity. The English translation was pre-pared by Daniel Bailey, who was a member of the original seminar in Tübingen. In addition to translating the essays he has shaped and expanded the English volume, providing the introductory summaries as well as extra bibliographical and philological notes. Kathrin Liess served as a liaison between the authors and the translator at the proofreading stage. The staff at Eerdmans Publishing Company have done fine work with complicated material.

Bernd Janowski & Peter Stuhlmacher
Tübingen, July 1996; March 2004

---

1. H. Spieckermann, "Konzeption und Vorgeschichte des Stellvertretungsgedankens im Alten Testament," in *Congress Volume: Cambridge 1995*, ed. J. A. Emerton, VTSup 66 (1997) 281-295. Used by permission of E. J. Brill Publishers.

Translator's Preface

With its thoroughly researched and informative essays, this book will doubtless be of interest to professional academics. But I hope that it will also find its way into the hands of pastors, seminary students, and theologians without a formal degree wanting to study this perennially interesting topic: the relationship of the book of Isaiah's traditions about a Suffering Servant to the rest of the Hebrew Bible, its early versions, pre-Christian Jewish texts, the teachings of Jesus and the early church, and postbiblical sources of Judaism and Christianity. I have translated the book especially with this audience in mind. Yet as a former member of the advanced seminar in Tübingen where most of these essays were first presented, I know that they were originally prepared for a different audience: specialists who were either doctoral candidates or professors in one of Germany's most famous universities. I have therefore attempted a translation and adaptation of the original, *Der leidende Gottesknecht: Jesaja 53 und seine Wirkungsgeschichte.*

Major adaptation has not taken place with every essay: those by Professors Spieckermann, Janowski, Stuhlmacher, Hofius, Ådna, and Schreiner are presented essentially unchanged, even though S. R. Driver's 1877 translation of the *Sefer Hizzuk Emunah* had to be substantially adapted for Schreiner's essay. H. Spieckermann's contribution, which first appeared a year after the German volume, is new to this English collection but fits seamlessly with the other essays. Professor Spieckermann co-edits with Professor Janowski the German series in which this volume originally appeared *(Forschungen zum Alten Testament);* his thesis on the prehistory of "vicariousness" or *Stellvertretung* caught my attention when I heard it as a conference paper in Cambridge in 1995.

I have been alert to the possibility of stylistic or editorial changes that might make the volume more accessible to English-speaking readers, and have

proposed such changes to the authors. The first paragraph of H. Spieckermann's essay now includes a block quotation from W. Zimmerli's 1968 essay to
give added concreteness to Spieckermann's summary of Zimmerli's argument.
Such minor editorial enhancements, approved by the authors, are typical and
have been included throughout the volume without special comment.

The summaries introducing each essay are adapted from those I published in an American counterpart to this volume: *Jesus and the Suffering Servant: Isaiah 53 and Christian Origins*.[1] This volume also contains an analysis of
the hermeneutics of two of our essayists, O. Hofius and B. Janowski; see my
"Concepts of *Stellvertretung* in the Interpretation of Isaiah 53" (pp. 231-250). A
positive review of *Der leidende Gottesknecht* by J. Schaper, who has been associated with the Tübingen faculty, is available in *JTS* n.s. 49 (1998) 709-713.

I have been more substantially involved in the final form of three of the
essays, by H.-J. Hermisson, C. Markschies, and M. Hengel. My material additions to the essays by Hermisson and Markschies have been enclosed within
double brackets as the added comments of the Translator: [[(Tr.) . . .]]. This is
unnecessary, however, for my enhancements of Hengel's essay, which are covered by my role as collaborator.

In Hermisson's essay I have translated the originally untranslated Hebrew
and Greek expressions in the text-critical portions of nn. 12-41, sometimes adding bracketed explanations of the origin and meaning of these variant readings.
(Professor Hermisson has reviewed these explanations, but they remain my responsibility.) English-speaking students may be unfamiliar with the practice of
revising the textual tradition based on scholarly judgment without manuscript
evidence — so-called conjectural emendation. I have therefore been careful to
indicate for students which of Hermisson's emendations are conjectural and
which manuscript-based. Occasionally it has been possible to trace out the history of research behind certain readings more fully (e.g. nn. 13, 33 of Hermisson's essay).

C. Markschies's essay on Isaiah 53 in the church fathers was the longest in
the German and is even longer in English because of the need to provide translations of the copiously quoted Greek and Latin sources (from published translations where possible). I have updated the bibliography and provided philological and text-critical help for students, as detailed in n. 1. My own study
following C. Markschies's essay analyzes M. Marcovich's 1997 edition of Justin
Martyr's *Dialogue* as a complement to Markschies's treatment of Justin.

---

1. D. P. Bailey, "The Suffering Servant: Recent Tübingen Scholarship on Isaiah 53," in *Jesus and the Suffering Servant: Isaiah 53 and Christian Origins*, ed. W. Bellinger and W. Farmer (1998) 251-259.

Martin Hengel is well known for his productive practice of involving his research assistants and junior colleagues in the preparation of his prodigious scholarly output.[2] In the essay on "The Effective History of Isaiah 53 in the Pre-Christian Period," I have fulfilled this role by updating and rewriting the two sections that deal with texts from 4Q that had just been made public when Professor Hengel delivered his paper in 1991 and that were the subject of only a few studies when he published it in 1996 — namely *The Aramaic Apocryphon of Levi* 4Q540-541 (below, pp. 106-18) and the *Self-Glorification Hymn* 4Q491c (below, pp. 140-45). Other places in the text and footnotes where I have added philological explanations are listed before the first note.

The essays together constitute an unusually close reading of a well-defined text, and therefore I have wanted to bring out nuances in meaning as clearly as possible. Rather than merely translating the different German words as glosses upon the individual Hebrew or Greek terms, I have usually been able to find existing English translations that mirror rather closely the different nuances being discussed in the German. All references to English Bible versions are therefore my own. I have made frequent use of the RSV, NRSV, NJPS, NAB, NJB, REB, NIV, NASB, and even the KJV, which often is the best starting point for the history of interpretation, as when it renders the disputed Isa 52:15 by "So shall he *sprinkle* (הזי) many nations."

Sub-verses of the Hebrew text of Isaiah 53 are numbered not just as *a* and *b*, but as *aa, aβ, ba, bβ*, etc., in keeping with German practice. The authors are not all consistent in their verse subdivision, but the scheme followed by most of them is set out by H.-J. Hermisson (pp. 22-29). Hermisson provides a translation of the Hebrew text of Isa 52:13-53:12 that can serve as a guide for readers of this volume.

It may be useful to put some of the other works of our authors into their wider context. The works of Martin Hengel are already well known in English translation — so much so that even Tübingen bookstores must stock his works in English, since books such as *The Pre-Christian Paul*, *Paul between Damascus and Antioch*, and *The Johannine Question* (to name only a few) appeared in English before their definitive and more expensive hardback German editions. The work most relevant to the topic of the Suffering Servant, Hengel's *The*

---

2. I think of works produced by Hengel in collaboration with A. M. Schwemer (e.g. *Paul between Damascus and Antioch: The Unknown Years* [1997]), R. Deines (e.g. "Die Septuaginta als 'christliche Schriftensammlung,' ihre Vorgeschichte und das Problem ihres Kanons," in *Septuaginta zwischen Judentum und Christentum*, ed. by M. Hengel and A. M. Schwemer [1994] 182-284; see also below, n. 17, on Hengel and Deines in *JTS* n.s. 46 [1995] 1-70); and C. Markschies (e.g. *The Hellenization of Judaea in the First Century after Christ* [1989]).

Atonement: The Origins of the Doctrine in the New Testament, has appeared in book form only in English.[3]

Peter Stuhlmacher is also frequently translated, and his major *Biblical Theology of the New Testament* is due to appear shortly after the present volume. In addition to the Scripture index of the *Biblical Theology* under Isaiah 53, readers with German may wish to consult Stuhlmacher's essay "Der messianische Gottesknecht," *JBTh* 8 (1993) 131-154, in which he offers a more comprehensive treatment of the Servant — especially in relationship to the Messiah — than could be offered here.

The chief editor of this volume, Bernd Janowski, is known for the world's most detailed study of cultic and non-cultic atonement in the Old Testament associated especially with the Hebrew root *KPR*.[4] Of his work on the atonement only a brief encyclopedia article has appeared in English, and there is a small but significant problem with the translation of the section on Isaiah 53.[5] Janowski's wider views of biblical theology are beginning to become available in English,[6] and they are discussed in a review article by R. E.

---

3. This unusual history of publication has led to a joke among Tübingen students. A future Tübingen professor may some day be able to impress students with the esoteric knowledge of a little-known historical fact: Martin Hengel was actually a German!

4. B. Janowski, *Sühne als Heilsgeschehen. Studien zur Sühnetheologie der Priesterschrift und zur Wurzel KPR im Alten Orient und im Alten Testament,* WMANT 55 ([1]1982; [2]2000). See the reviews by J. Milgrom in *JBL* 104 (1985) 302-304 and C. T. Begg in *CBQ* 47 (1985) 130-131.

5. B. Janowski, "Sühne. 1. Altes Testament und Judentum," *EKL*[3] 4:552-555 = "Atonement. 1. OT and Judaism," *EC* 1:152-154. Section 1.4 of this entry deals with Isa 52:13-53:12. At the first introduction of the Hebrew term *asham* (אָשָׁם) as used in Isa 53:10, the English translator, G. W. Bromiley, adds the gloss "guilt offering" from the NRSV (p. 153). But this is misleading: Janowski leaves the term *asham* untranslated at this point and implicitly disagrees with the NRSV; the German term for the "guilt offering" that Janowski does *not* use would have been *Schuldopfer.* Janowski goes on to explain that in Isa 53:10, the *asham* involves only the obligation to discharge guilt that arises from occasions of human guilt. Therefore, the fact that the Servant makes his life an *asham* to nullify this guilt does not necessarily imply that the Servant is to be compared to the animal *asham*-victim or "guilt offering" in the sense in which *asham* appears in Leviticus. Janowski proposes the term *Schuldgabe,* as distinct from the traditional *Schuldopfer,* to explain how the Servant voluntarily surrenders his innocent life to eliminate the guilt of others — something a typical *asham*-victim cannot be said to have done. Bromiley misses the distinction and translates by "guilt offering." For a more detailed analysis see Janowski's essay below, esp. pp. 65-74.

6. Janowski's inaugural address to mark his appointment to an Old Testament chair in Tübingen dealt with "Der eine Gott der beiden Testamente. Grundfragen einer Biblischen Theologie," *ZTK* 95 (1998) 1-36. This has been translated by C. Helmer in an abbreviated version: B. Janowski, "The One God of the Two Testaments: Basic Questions of a Biblical Theology," *Theology Today* 57 (2000) 297-324.

Murphy,[7] together with the views of Hermann Spieckermann, who originally presented his lecture on this topic in English.[8]

Similarly known for his work on the atonement, especially in Paul, is Otfried Hofius. A reviewer of Hofius's collected essays on this and related topics concludes by describing him as "a scholar who is not afraid to swim against the current, and who swims strongly."[9] Certainly Professor Hofius has lost none of this energy in the present essay. While Hofius's earlier work on the atonement that informs his approach to Isaiah 53 remains untranslated,[10] the seminal work "Die Sühne" (1977) by the Tübingen Old Testament specialist H. Gese (on whom both Hofius and Janowski depend) is translated as "The Atonement."[11] Hofius's views on New Testament atonement are summarized in his article in the *Theologische Realenzyklopädie*.[12]

While Hans-Jürgen Hermisson's studies of Deutero-Isaiah have not previously been translated, fortunately we have a sympathetic English-language review by W. P. Brown of Hermisson's collected essays on prophecy and wisdom — including the essay translated here, plus several others on the Servant and Deutero-Isaiah. Brown considers this to be Hermisson's most original work. He concludes that Hermisson "consistently combines close readings of texts with theological sensitivity" and presents "theological reflections that make his essays enduring for future readers."[13]

Of our three remaining authors, the two youngest, Jostein Ådna and Christoph Markschies, have an increasing number of their studies appearing in

---

7. R. E. Murphy, "Once Again — The 'Center' of the Old Testament," *BTB* 31 (2001) 85-89.

8. H. Spieckermann, "God's Steadfast Love: Towards a New Conception of Old Testament Theology," *Bib* 81 (2000) 305-327. This lecture was delivered on the occasion of the 90th anniversary of the Pontifical Biblical Institute.

9. A. J. M. Wedderburn, review of O. Hofius, *Paulusstudien* (1989), in *JTS* n.s. 42 (1991) 233-235, esp. 235.

10. For the relationship between Hofius's earlier Hartmut Gese–inspired work on atonement — e.g. his "Sühne und Versöhnung: Zum paulinischen Verständnis des Kreuzestodes Jesu" (orig. 1983; repr. in Hofius, *Paulusstudien*, WUNT 51 [1989] 33-49) — and his present work on Isaiah 53, see my "Concepts of *Stellvertretung* in the Interpretation of Isaiah 53" (above n. 1), esp. 237.

11. H. Gese, "Die Sühne," in idem, *Zur biblischen Theologie. Alttestamentliche Vorträge*, BEvT 78 (1977) 85-106 = "The Atonement," in *Essays on Biblical Theology*, trans. K. Crim (1981) 93-116.

12. O. Hofius, "Sühne IV. Neues Testament," *TRE* 32 (2001) 342-347.

13. H.-J. Hermisson, *Studien zu Prophetie und Weisheit. Gesammelte Aufsätze*, ed. by J. Barthel, H. Jauss, and K. Koenen, FAT 23 (1998). Reviewed by W. P. Brown in *RBL* 3 (2001) 196-200, esp. 200, or online at http://www.bookreviews.org.

English, either in translation or original composition.[14] Stefan Schreiner shows his familiarity with (among other things) Polish primary and secondary literature relating to late medieval Judaism, and a few of his many contributions to Jewish studies and Jewish-Christian dialogue have appeared in English.[15]

The Protestant Theological Faculty in Tübingen here shows its strength in collaborative and interdisciplinary work. I believe that this is made possible in part by the fact that all the authors understand themselves to be about the same business — the critical historical study of biblical and extrabiblical Jewish and Christian texts with a view to the identification and evaluation of their theological truth claims. This is not to say that all our authors agree. But it does explain why one finds here a different type of coherence than might be found in the conference proceedings of SBL Seminars or similar North American gatherings, where the institutional settings of the participants and therefore their perceived responsibilities to the profession (and possibly to the church or synagogue) may vary much more widely.

The production of this translation also has a social setting. I would like to thank six women who got me going or kept me going at it. My University of Cambridge mentor Professor Morna Hooker began to earn her reputation in 1959 with her publication of *Jesus and the Servant: The Influence of the Servant Concept of Deutero-Isaiah in the New Testament*. It is she who as *JTS* editor gave me my first translation assignment,[16] and she also got me invited to the 1996 Baylor University Colloquium on Isaiah 53 and Christian Origins (cf. *Jesus and the Suffering Servant*), where I first took up the task of presenting these essays to an English-speaking audience. Near the end of the project I have received a different kind of help from Professor Margaret Mitchell. While not involved di-

---

14. C. Markschies, *Between Two Worlds: Structures of Early Christianity*, trans. J. Bowden (1999); *Gnosis: An Introduction*, trans. J. Bowden (2003); J. Ådna, "Jesus' Symbolic Act in the Temple (Mark 11:15-17): The Replacement of the Sacrificial Cult by His Atoning Death," in *Gemeinde ohne Tempel = Community without Temple*, ed. B. Ego, A. Lange, and P. Pilhofer, WUNT 118 (1999) 461-475; "The Encounter of Jesus with the Gerasene Demoniac," in *Authenticating the Activities of Jesus*, ed. B. Chilton and C. A. Evans (1999) 279-301; "James' Position at the Summit Meeting of the Apostles and the Elders in Jerusalem (Acts 15)," in *The Mission of the Early Church to Jews and Gentiles*, ed. J. Ådna and H. Kvalbein, WUNT 127 (2000) 125-161.

15. S. Schreiner, "'God Has Hidden His Face': The Literary Witness of the Time of the Shoah, or Why So Many Have Written about It," *Christian Jewish Relations* 22 (1989) 68-74; "Why the Dialogue with Judaism Is Indispensable for Christian Theology: Notes on Jewish-Christian Dialogue," in *Breaking Down the Wall Between Americans and East Germans — Jews and Christians through Dialogue*, ed. L. Swidler and L. Dean (1987) 115-130.

16. M. Hengel and R. Deines, trans. D. P. Bailey, "E. P. Sanders' 'Common Judaism,' Jesus, and the Pharisees," *JTS* n.s. 46 (1995) 1-70.

rectly in the translation, she arranged for me to be a Visiting Scholar at the University of Chicago Divinity School and to receive access privileges at the Regenstein Library, where the translation was completed. During an intense phase of revision Dr. Kathrin Liess in the University of Tübingen served as an essential go-between, printing and delivering my emailed translations to the authors and forwarding me their corrections. Jennifer Hoffman, associate managing editor at Eerdmans, showed understanding when the theft of my property set us back another few weeks in an already protracted process. Kathy Blair gave valuable assistance with the indexing. Throughout many months of translation distributed unevenly over several years, moral and sometimes financial support was provided by my mother Marilyn Bailey, who now can be repaid a small part of a huge debt.

Daniel P. Bailey
Chicago, October 2004

Contributors

Jostein Ådna is Professor of New Testament in the Lutheran School of Mission in Stavanger, Norway

Daniel P. Bailey is a Visiting Scholar in the University of Chicago Divinity School and an Adjunct Professor of Biblical Greek at Northern Baptist Theological Seminary and at Garrett-Evangelical Theological Seminary

Martin Hengel is Professor Emeritus of New Testament and Early Judaism in the University of Tübingen

Hans-Jürgen Hermisson is Professor Emeritus of Old Testament in the University of Tübingen

Otfried Hofius is Professor Emeritus of New Testament in the University of Tübingen

Bernd Janowski is Professor of Old Testament in the University of Tübingen

Christoph Markschies is Professor of Early Church History and Patristics at the Humboldt University, Berlin

Stefan Schreiner is Professor of Jewish Studies in the *Institutum Iudaicum* of the University of Tübingen

Hermann Spieckermann is Professor of Old Testament in the University of Göttingen

Peter Stuhlmacher is Professor Emeritus of New Testament in the University of Tübingen

Abbreviations

While a few of the abbreviations below have been coined (e.g. *DSSB, DSSSE*), most have been taken from *The SBL Handbook of Style: For Ancient Near Eastern, Biblical, and Early Christian Studies,* ed. by P. H. Alexander et al. (1999); those not found there may usually be found in the *Theologische Realenzyklopädie: Abkürzungsverzeichnis,* ed. by S. M. Schwertner (²1994).

General

ET	English translation
FS	Festschrift
l., ll.	line(s) in Qumran manuscripts, reference works (e.g. *TWNT*), or modern editions of patristic texts
lit.	literally; literature
mod.	modified
MS, MSS	manuscript(s)
⟦ Tr. ⟧	Translator's note

Bible Versions (Ancient and Modern), Text Types, Manuscripts, and Editions

α′	Aquila, Greek version of (see Ziegler, *Isaias,* Göttingen LXX); also: Aq.
σ′	Symmachus, Greek version of (see Ziegler, *Isaias,* Göttingen LXX); also: Sym.
θ′	Theodotion, Greek version of (see Ziegler, *Isaias,* Göttingen LXX); also: Theod.
1QIsa[a]	Great Isaiah Scroll from Qumran cave 1. Text in M. Burrows, ed., *The Dead Sea Scrolls of St. Mark's Monastery,* Vol. 1: *The Isaiah Manuscript*

	and the Habakkuk Commentary (1950) or in D. W. Parry and E. Qimron, eds., *The Great Isaiah Scroll (1QIsaᵃ): A New Edition,* STDJ 32 (1999)
1QIsaᵇ	Qumran Isaiah Scroll B. Text in E. L. Sukenik, ed., *The Dead Sea Scrolls of the Hebrew University* (1955)
A	Codex Alexandrinus
Aq.	Aquila, Greek version of
ArBib	The Aramaic Bible
ASV	American Standard Version
B	Codex Vaticanus
BHS	*Biblia Hebraica Stuttgartensia*
Brenton	Lancelot C. L. Brenton. *The Septuagint Version of the Old Testament: According to the Vatican Text, Translated into English.* London, 1st ed. 1844. Reprinted: *The Septuagint with Apocrypha: Greek and English.* Grand Rapids, 1972
Chilton	B. D. Chilton. *The Isaiah Targum.* ArBib 11. Wilmington, Del., 1987
DSSB	*The Dead Sea Scrolls Bible.* Translated by M. Abegg, P. Flint, and E. Ulrich. San Francisco, 1999
Field	F. Field. *Origenis Hexaplorum quae supersunt: Veterum interpretum graecorum in totum Vetus Testamentum fragmenta.* 2 vols. Oxford, 1875
Göttingen LXX	*Septuaginta: Vetus Testamentum graecum auctoritate Academiae Scientarum Gottingensis editum*
KJV	King James Version
LXX	Septuagint
MT	Masoretic Text
NA²⁷	*Novum Testamentum Graece,* Nestle-Aland, 27th ed.
NAB	New American Bible
NASB	New American Standard Bible
NEB	New English Bible
NIV	New International Version
NJB	New Jerusalem Bible
NJPS	*Tanakh: The Holy Scriptures: The New JPS Translation According to the Traditional Hebrew Text*
NRSV	New Revised Standard Version
Q	Codex Marchalianus of the Septuagint (6th century). See Ziegler, *Isaias*
Rahlfs	A. Rahlfs. *Septuaginta: Id est Vetus Testamentum graece iuxta LXX interpretes.* 2 vols. Stuttgart, 1935
REB	Revised English Bible
RSV	Revised Standard Version
S	Codex Sinaiticus

Sperber	A. Sperber. *The Bible in Aramaic: Based on Old Manuscripts and Printed Texts.* 4 vols. in 5. Leiden, 1959-1973
Sym.	Symmachus, Greek version of
Syr.	Syriac
Tg.	Targum
Theod.	Theodotion, Greek version of
V	Codex Venetus of the Septuagint (8th century). See Ziegler, *Isaias*
VL	Vetus Latina
Vulg.	Vulgate
Ziegler	J. Ziegler. *Isaias.* Vol. 14 of the Göttingen LXX (see above). 1st ed. 1939. 3d ed. 1983

Reference Works, Journals, and Series

AB	Anchor Bible
ABD	*Anchor Bible Dictionary.* Ed. by D. N. Freedman. 6 vols. New York, 1992
ABR	*Australian Biblical Review*
ABRL	Anchor Bible Reference Library
ACW	Ancient Christian Writers. 1946-
AGJU	Arbeiten zur Geschichte des antiken Judentums und des Urchristentums
AGSU	Arbeiten zur Geschichte das Spätjudentums und des Urchristentums
AJBI	*Annual of the Japanese Biblical Institute*
AKG	Arbeiten zur Kirchengeschichte
AnBib	Analecta Biblica
ANETS	Ancient Near Eastern Texts and Studies
ANF	*Ante-Nicene Fathers*
ANTJ	Arbeiten zum Neuen Testament und Judentum
ArBib	The Aramaic Bible
ASTI	*Annual of the Swedish Theological Institute*
ATA	Alttestamentliche Abhandlungen
ATANT	Abhandlungen zur Theologie des Alten und Neuen Testaments
ATD	Das Alte Testament Deutsch
AUU.HR	Acta Universitatis Upsaliensis. Historia religionum
BASOR	*Bulletin of the American Schools of Oriental Research*
BBB	Bonner biblische Beiträge
BDAG	W. Bauer, F. W. Danker, W. F. Arndt, and F. W. Gingrich. *A Greek-English Lexicon of the New Testament and Other Early Christian Literature.* 3d. ed. Revised and edited by F. W. Danker. Chicago, 2000
BDB	F. Brown, S. R. Driver, and C. A. Briggs. *A Hebrew and English Lexicon of the Old Testament.* Oxford, 1907

BEATAJ	Beiträge zur Erforschung des Alten Testaments und des antiken Judentums
BETL	Bibliotheca ephemeridum theologicarum lovaniensium
BEvT	Beiträge zur evangelischen Theologie
BFCT	Beiträge zur Förderung christlicher Theologie
BFCT.M	Beiträge zur Förderung christlicher Theologie, 2d ser., Sammlung wissenschaftlicher Monographien
BHT	Beiträge zur historischen Theologie
Bib	*Biblica*
BibS(N)	Biblische Studien (Neukirchen, 1951-)
Bijdr	*Bijdragen: Tijdschrift voor filosofie en theologie*
BiLi	*Bibel und Liturgie*
BJRL	*Bulletin of the John Rylands University Library of Manchester*
BJS	Brown Judaic Studies
BK	*Bibel und Kirche*
BKAT	Biblischer Kommentar, Altes Testament
BN	*Biblische Notizen*
BO	*Bibliotheca orientalis*
BR	*Biblical Research*
BRGA	Beiträge zur Religionsgeschichte des Altertums
BSac	*Bibliotheca sacra*
BT	*The Bible Translator*
BTB	*Biblical Theology Bulletin*
BThSt	Biblisch-theologische Studien
BU	Biblische Untersuchungen
BWANT	Beiträge zur Wissenschaft vom Alten und Neuen Testament
BZ	*Biblische Zeitschrift*
BZAW	Beihefte zur Zeitschrift für die alttestamentliche Wissenschaft
CAT	Commentaire de l'Ancien Testament
CBET	Contributions to Biblical Exegesis and Theology
CCSL	Corpus Christianorum: Series latina. Turnhout, 1953-
CDios	*Ciudad de Dios*
CGan	*Collationes Gandavenses*
CH	*Church History*
Christus	*Christus. Cahiers spirituels*
CMech	*Collectanea Mechliniensia*
ConBNT	Coniectanea biblica: New Testament Series
ConBOT	Coniectanea biblica: Old Testament Series
COT	Comentaar op het Oude Testament
CPG	*Clavis patrum graecorum.* Ed. by M. Geerard. 5 vols. Turnout, 1974-1987
*CPL*³	*Clavis patrum latinorum.* Ed. by E. Dekkers. 3d ed. Steenbrugis, 1995
CQR	*Church Quarterly Review*

CSCO	Corpus scriptorum christianorum orientalium. Ed. by I. B. Chabot, et al. Paris, 1903-
CSEL	Corpus scriptorum ecclesiasticorum latinorum
CuBi	*Cultura biblica*
CV	*Communio viatorum*
DBAT	*Dielheimer Blätter zum Alten Testament*
DBSup	*Dictionnaire de la Bible: Supplement.* Ed. by L. Pirot and A. Robert. Paris, 1928-
DCH	*Dictionary of Classical Hebrew.* Ed. by D. J. A. Clines. 5 vols. to date. Sheffield, 1993-
Did(L)	*Didaskalia.* Lisboa, Faculdade de Teologia, Universidade Católica Portuguesa, 1971-
Div	*Divinitas.* Rome
DJD	Discoveries in the Judaean Desert
DSSB	*The Dead Sea Scrolls Bible.* Translated by Martin Abegg, P. Flint, and Eugene Ulrich. San Francisco, 1999
DSSSE	*The Dead Sea Scrolls Study Edition.* By F. García Martínez and E. J. C. Tigchelaar. 2 vols. Leiden and New York, 1997-1998; revised, 2000
DunRev	*Dunwoodie Review*
EBib	Etudes bibliques
EC	*The Encyclopedia of Christianity.* Ed. by E. Fahlbusch. Translated by G. W. Bromiley from *EKL³.* 3 vols. to date. Grand Rapids, 1999-
EdF	Erträge der Forschung
EDNT	*Exegetical Dictionary of the New Testament.* Ed. by H. Balz and G. Schneider. 3 vols. Translation of *EWNT.* Grand Rapids, 1990-1993
EE	*Estudios eclesiásticos*
EECh	*Encyclopedia of the Early Church.* Ed. by A. Di Berardino. Translated by A. Walford from *Dizionario patristico e di antichità cristiane.* 2 vols. New York, 1992
EHPhR	Etudes d'histoire et philosophie religieuses
EK	*Evangelische Kommentar*
EKL³	*Evangelisches Kirchenlexicon.* Ed. by E. Fahlbusch. 4 vols. 3d ed. Göttingen, 1985-1996
ELKZ	*Evangelisch-lutherische Kirchenzeitung*
EncJud	*Encyclopaedia Judaica.* 16 vols. Jerusalem, 1972
ETL	*Ephemerides theologicae lovanienses*
ETR	*Etudes théologiques et religieuses*
ETS	Erfurter theologische Studien
EvErz	*Der evangelische Erzieher*
EvK	*Evangelische Kommentare*
EvQ	*Evangelical Quarterly*
EvT	*Evangelische Theologie*

EWNT	*Exegetisches Wörterbuch zum Neuen Testament.* Ed. by H. Balz and G. Schneider. 3 vols. Stuttgart, 1978-1983
ExpTim	*Expository Times*
FAT	Forschungen zum Alten Testament
FB	Forschung zur Bibel
FC	Fathers of the Church, Washington, D.C., 1947-
FF	*Forschungen und Fortschritte*
FoiTe	*La foi et le temps*
FoiVie	*Foi et vie*
FRLANT	Forschungen zur Religion und Literatur des Alten und Neuen Testaments
FZPhTh	*Freiburger Zeitschrift für Philosophie und Theologie*
GCS	Die griechische christliche Schriftsteller der ersten [drei] Jahrhunderte
GKC	Gesenius' Hebrew Grammar. Ed. by E. Kautsch. Translated by A. E. Cowley. 2d ed. Oxford, 1910
GTT	*Gereformeerd theologisch tijdschrift*
HALAT	*Hebräisches und aramäisches Lexikon zum Alten Testament.* By L. Köhler. Third ed. by W. Baumgartner and J. J. Stamm et al. 5 vols. in 6. Leiden, 1967-1996
HALOT	*The Hebrew and Aramaic Lexicon of the Old Testament.* By L. Köhler, W. Baumgartner, and J. J. Stamm. Translated from *HALAT* under the supervision of M. E. J. Richardson. 4 vols. Leiden, 1994-1999
HAT	Handbuch zum Alten Testament
Hermeneia	Hermeneia: A Critical and Historical Commentary on the Bible
HNT	Handbuch zum Neuen Testament
HTKNT	Herders theologischer Kommentar zum Neuen Testament
HTR	*Harvard Theological Review*
HTS	Harvard Theological Studies
HUCA	*Hebrew Union College Annual*
IBS	*Irish Biblical Studies*
ICC	International Critical Commentary
IJT	*Indian Journal of Theology*
IKaZ	Internationale katholische Zeitschrift
IKZ	Internationale kirchliche Zeitschrift
Interp	*Interpretation*
JBL	Journal of Biblical Literature
JBTh	Jahrbuch für Biblische Theologie
JETS	*Journal of the Evangelical Theological Society*
JJS	*Journal of Jewish Studies*
JNES	*Journal of Near Eastern Studies*
JQR	*Jewish Quarterly Review*
JR	*Journal of Religion*

JSHRZ	Jüdische Schriften aus hellenistisch-römischer Zeit
JSJ	*Journal for the Study of Judaism in the Persian, Hellenistic, and Roman Periods*
JSNTSup	Journal for the Study of the New Testament: Supplement Series
JSNT	*Journal for the Study of the New Testament*
JSOTSup	Journal for the Study of the Old Testament: Supplement Series
JSP	*Journal for the Study of the Pseudepigrapha*
JSS	*Journal of Semitic Studies*
JTS	*Journal of Theological Studies*
Jud	*Judaica*
KAT	Kommentar zum Alten Testament
KD	*Kerygma und Dogma*
KEK	Kritisch-Exegetischer Kommentar über das Neue Testament
KNT	Kommentar zum Neuen Testament. Ed. by T. Zahn
LCC	Library of Christian Classics. Philadelphia, 1953-
LCL	Loeb Classical Library
LD	Lectio divina
LSJ	H. G. Liddell, R. Scott, and H. S. Jones. *A Greek-English Lexicon.* 9th ed. Oxford, 1940. With revised supplement, 1996
LTK	*Lexikon für Theologie und Kirche*
MEOL	Mededelingen en verhandelingen van het Vooraziatisch-Egyptisch Genootschap "Ex Oriente Lux"
MIOF	*Mitteilungen des Instituts für Orientalforschung*
MSR	*Mélanges de science religieuse*
MSU	Mitteilungen des Septuaginta-Unternehmens
MTZ	*Münchner theologische Zeitschrift*
NedTT	*Nederlands theologisch tijdschrift*
NKZ	*Neue kirchliche Zeitschrift*
NovTSup	Novum Testamentum Supplements
NPNF²	*Nicene and Post-Nicene Fathers,* Series 2
NTS	*New Testament Studies*
NTT	*Norsk Teologisk Tidsskrift*
NZSTh	*Neue Zeitschrift für systematische Theologie*
OBO	Orbis biblicus et orientalis
ODCC³	*The Oxford Dictionary of the Christian Church.* Ed. by F. L. Cross. Third edition, by E. A. Livingstone. Oxford and New York, 1997
OECT	Oxford Early Christian Texts
OrChr	*Oriens christianus*
OTEs	*Old Testament Essays.* By the Department of Old Testament, University of South Africa
OTP	*Old Testament Pseudepigrapha.* Ed. by J. H. Charlesworth. 2 vols. New York, 1983
OTS	Old Testament Studies

PAAJR	*Proceedings of the American Academy of Jewish Research*
PEQ	*Palestinian Exploration Quarterly*
PG	Patrologia graeca [= Patrologiae cursus completus: Series graeca]. Ed. by J.-P. Migne. 217 vols. Paris, 1857-1886
PGL	*Patristic Greek Lexicon.* Ed. by G. W. H. Lampe. Oxford, 1968
PGM	*Papyri graecae magicae: Die griechischen Zauberpapyri.* Ed. by K. Preisendanz. Berlin, 1928
PIBA	Proceedings of the Irish Biblical Association
PL	Patrologia latina [= Patrologiae cursus completus: Series latina]. Ed. by J.-P. Migne. 162 vols. Paris, 1844-1864
PO	Patrologia orientalis
PS	Patrologia syriaca. Ed. by R. Graffin. Paris, 1894-
PTA	Papyrologische Texte und Abhandlungen
PTMS	Pittsburgh Theological Monograph Series
PTS	Patristische Texte und Studien
PVTG	Pseudepigrapha Veteris Testamenti Graece
QD	Quaestiones disputatae
RAC	*Reallexikon für Antike und Christentum.* Ed. by T. Klausser et al. Stuttgart, 1950-
RB	*Revue biblique*
RBL	*Review of Biblical Literature*
RevExp	*Review and Expositor*
RevistB	*Revista bíblica.* Buenos Aires, 1939-
RevQ	*Revue de Qumran*
RevScRel	*Revue des sciences religieuses*
RGG³	*Religion in Geschichte und Gegenwart.* Ed. by K. Galling. 7 vols. 3d ed. Tübingen, 1957-1965
RGG⁴	*Religion in Geschichte und Gegenwart: Handwörterbuch für Theologie und Religionswissenschaft.* Ed. by H. D. Betz et al. 6 vols. to date. 4th completely revised edition. Tübingen, 1998-
RivB	*Rivista biblica* [Continues *Rivista biblica italiana*]
RQ	*Revue de Qumran*
RSEHA	*Revue sémitique d'épigraphie et d'histoire ancienne*
RSPT	*Revue des sciences philosophiques et théologiques*
RSR	*Recherches de science religieuse*
RThom	*Revue thomiste*
RTP	*Revue de théologie et de philosophie*
RTR	*Reformed Theological Review*
SANT	Studien zum Alten und Neuen Testaments
SBM	Stuttgarter biblische Monographien
SBS	Stuttgarter Bibelstudien
SBT	Studies in Biblical Theology
SC	Sources chrétiennes. Paris, 1943-

SCH	Studies in Church History
Scr	*Scripture*
ScrTh	*Scripta theologica*
SEÅ	*Svensk exegetisk årsbok*
SEAug	Studia ephemeridis Augustinianum
SémBib	*Sémiotique et bible*
SHAW.PH	Sitzungsberichte der Heidelberger Akademie der Wissenschaften, Philosophisch-Historische Klasse
SHVL	Skrifter utgivna av Kungl. Humanistiska Vetenskapssamfundet i Lund
SJOT	*Scandanavian Journal of the Old Testament*
SJT	*Scottish Journal of Theology*
SMHVL	Scripta minora. Kungl. Humanistiska Vetenskapssamfundet i Lund. Later volumes published under series name: Scripta minora Regiae Societatis Humanarum Litterarum Lundensis
SNT	Studien zum Neuen Testament
SNTSMS	Society for New Testament Studies Monograph Series
SPAW.PH	Sitzungsberichte der Preussischen Akademie der Wissenschaften, Philosophisch-Historische Klasse
SPK	Schriften zur Pädagogik und Katechetik
SQS.NF	Sammlung ausgewählter kirchen- und dogmengeschichtlicher Quellenschriften. Neue Folge
ST	*Studia theologica*
STDJ	Studies on the Texts of the Desert of Judah
StNT	Studien zum Neuen Testament
StPatr	Studia patristica
StPB	Studia post-biblica
Str-B	H. L. Strack and P. Billerbeck. *Kommentar zum Neuen Testament aus Talmud und Midrasch.* 6 vols. Munich, 1922-1961
SUNT	Studien zur Umwelt des Neuen Testaments
SVTP	Studia in Veteris Testamenti pseudepigrapha
SwJT	*Southwestern Journal of Theology*
TB	Theologische Bücherei: Neudrucke und Berichte aus dem 20. Jahrhundert
TBei	*Theologische Beiträge*
TDNT	*Theological Dictionary of the New Testament.* Ed. by G. Kittel and G. Friedrich. Translated by G. W. Bromiley from *TWNT.* 10 vols. Grand Rapids, 1964-1976
TDOT	*Theological Dictionary of the Old Testament.* Ed. by G. J. Botterweck and H. Ringgren. Translated by J. T. Willis, G. W. Bromiley, D. E. Green, and D. Stott from *TWAT.* Rev. ed. 12 vols. to date. Grand Rapids, 1977-
TeKo	*Texte und Kontexte*
TGl	*Theologie und Glaube*

ThA   Theologische Arbeiten
THAT   *Theologisches Handwörterbuch zum Alten Testament.* Ed. by E. Jenni
          and C. Westermann. 2 vols. Munich, 1971-1976
THKNT   Theologischer Handkommentar zum Neuen Testament
ThPh   *Theologie und Philosophie*
ThTo   *Theology Today*
TLG   *Thesaurus Linguae Graecae: Canon of Greek Authors and Works.* By
          L. Berkowitz and K. A. Squitier. 3d ed. New York, 1990
TLOT   *Theological Lexicon of the Old Testament.* Ed. by E. Jenni and
          C. Westermann. Translated by M. E. Biddle from *THAT.* 3 vols.
          Peabody, Mass., 1997
TLZ   *Theologische Literaturzeitung*
TP   *Theologie und Philosophie*
TQ   *Theologische Quartalschrift*
TRE   *Theologische Realenzyklopädie.* Ed. by G. Krause and G. Müller. 35
          vols. to date. Berlin, 1977-
TRu   *Theologische Rundschau*
TS   *Theological Studies*
TSAJ   Texte und Studien zum antiken Judentum
TSK   *Theologische Studien und Kritiken*
TTKi   *Tidsskrift for Teologi og Kirke*
TTZ   *Trierer theologische Zeitschrift*
TU   Texte und Untersuchungen zur Geschichte der altchristlichen
          Literatur. Berlin, 1883-
TUAT   *Texte aus der Umwelt des Alten Testaments.* Ed. by O. Kaiser.
          Gütersloh, 1984-
TWAT   *Theologisches Wörterbuch zum Alten Testament.* Ed. by G. J.
          Botterweck und H. Ringgren. 8 vols. to date. Stuttgart, 1970-
TWNT   *Theologisches Wörterbuch zum Neuen Testament.* Ed. by G. Kittel and
          G. Friedrich. 10 vols. Stuttgart, 1932-1979
TynBul *Tyndale Bulletin*
TZ   *Theologische Zeitschrift*
VC   *Vigiliae Christianae*
VCSup   Supplements to Vigiliae Christianae
VD   *Verbum domini*
VF   *Verkündigung und Forschung*
VL   Vetus Latina: Die Reste der Altlateinischen Bibel. Ed. by the
          Benediktinerkloster Beuron, Germany
VL 1/1   H. J. Frede. *Kirchenschriftsteller: Verzeichnis und Sigel.* VL 1/1 ([4]1995)
VoxEv   *Vox Evangelica*
VT   *Vetus Testamentum*
VTSup   Vetus Testamentum Supplements
WA   M. Luther, *Kritische Gesamtausgabe* (Weimar edition)

WiWei	*Wissenschaft und Weisheit*
WMANT	Wissenschaftliche Monographien zum Alten und Neuen Testament
WO	*Die Welt des Orients*
WTJ	*Westminster Theological Journal*
WUNT	Wissenschaftliche Untersuchungen zum Neuen Testament
YJS	Yale Judaica Series
ZAW	*Zeitschrift für die Alttestamentliche Wissenschaft*
ZKG	*Zeitschrift für Kirchengeschichte*
ZKWL	*Zeitschrift für kirchliche Wissenschaft und kirchliches Leben*
ZNW	*Zeitschrift für die Neutestamentliche Wissenschaft*
ZWKL	*Zeitschrift für Wissenschaft und kirchliches Leben*
ZTK	*Zeitschrift für Theologie und Kirche*
ZWT	*Zeitschrift für wissenschaftliche Theologie*

The Conception and Prehistory of the Idea of Vicarious Suffering in the Old Testament

Hermann Spieckermann

Summary

The concept of "vicariousness" or "vicarious suffering" *(Stellvertretung, stell-vertretendes Leiden)* in the Old Testament is inextricably linked with Isaiah 53. However, since the vicarious role of the Suffering Servant here is unique, it is necessary first to clarify the main characteristics of the idea of vicarious suffering in Isaiah 53 before searching for traditio-historical antecedents. Although the intercession of the one for the sins of the many and the thought of divine initiative are clearly characteristic of the chapter, subordinate themes like the sinlessness of the Servant and his acceptance of his fate remain more difficult to explain. Nevertheless, all these characteristics must guide research into the Old Testament roots of the notion of vicarious suffering. While past studies have sought these roots in the priestly atonement traditions *and* the prophets' intercession for the people, this study focuses on the latter tradition. Further investigation of exemplary texts from Amos, Jeremiah, and Ezekiel shows that the decisive preliminary theological work for the concept of vicarious suffering was accomplished in the seventh and early sixth centuries. Despite the precision of these findings, it is still not possible to reconstruct a self-contained prehistory of the idea of vicarious suffering in Isaiah 53. The prehistory sheds some light on the idea, but not enough to remove the mystery or uniqueness from chapter 53. This lack of predictability provides the best evidence that Isaiah 53 is trying to say something new.

"Konzeption und Vorgeschichte des Stellvertretungsgedankens im Alten Testament." In J. A. Emerton, ed., *Congress Volume: Cambridge 1995*, VTSup 66 (1997), 281-95. Reprinted in H. Spieckermann, *Gottes Liebe zu Israel*, FAT 33 (2001), 141-53.

1

In 1968 W. Zimmerli delivered a paper at the Sixth Congress of the International Organization for the Study of the Old Testament in Rome with the title "Zur Vorgeschichte von Jes. liii" ("On the Prehistory of Isaiah 53"). His thesis ran as follows. First, although the language of "bearing iniquity (or guilt, punishment)," נשׂא עוֹן, was already current at the start of the exilic period, it has been varied with great freedom in the fourth Servant Song (Isa. 52:13–53:12; hereafter Isaiah 53). As Zimmerli notes:

> The language [of bearing iniquity] was by no means used for the first time with reference to the Suffering Servant. It existed previously in other contexts, but now in a novel way it is applied to the Servant and his suffering. To be sure, the original formula נשׂא עוֹן, "to bear iniquity," is varied with great freedom in Isaiah 53. Hence סבל in vv. 4, 11 can replace נשׂא in vv. 4 and 12. Similarly, חלי, "infirmity," in v. 4, מכאב, "disease," in v. 4, and חטא, "sin," in v. 12 can each be substituted for עוֹן, "iniquity," in v. 11. Nevertheless, unmistakably behind all these variations, there still stands a common idea which has a wide range of application in the Old Testament.[1]

Zimmerli then explains that two traditions condition the use of the language of bearing iniquity in Isaiah 53: first, priestly traditions of atonement through the vicarious taking up of guilt and punishment, as in Leviticus 10:17 and 16:22; second, the prophet Ezekiel's symbolic portrayal of the years of Israel's punishment, as reported in Ezekiel 4:4-8. Both traditions have supposedly left their mark on the fourth Servant Song. At the same time the difference between the Servant and Ezekiel cannot be overlooked. Ezekiel's bearing of iniquity for the people had absolutely no atoning effect. Zimmerli therefore concludes that vicarious suffering for "the many" (cf. Isa. 53:11-12) remains the *proprium* of the Servant.

In the following I would like to take up Zimmerli's thesis and modify it in the light of recent research and my own insights. To this end, the concept of vicarious suffering in Isaiah 53 must first be observed more closely (I). Then we must turn our attention to a few texts whose tradition has decisively shaped the profile of the idea of vicarious suffering (II). Finally, we must formulate both the findings and the open questions that result from considering the vicarious event in Isaiah 53 (III).[2]

---

1. Walther Zimmerli, "Zur Vorgeschichte von Jes. liii," in *Congress Volume: Rome 1968*, VTSup 17 (1969), 236-44, quoting 238-39. Reprinted in Zimmerli, *Studien zur alttestamentlichen Theologie und Prophetie* (1974), 213-21.

2. On the fourth Servant Song see W. A. M. Beuken, *Jesaja II B* (1983), 185-241; B. Janowski, "He Bore Our Sins: Isaiah 53 and the Drama of Taking Another's Place" (see below,

I

One important result of recent research on Isaiah 53 which happens to disagree with the perspective of Zimmerli is the recognition that, despite the
NRSV's misleading rendering "an offering for sin," the term אשם in 53:10
should not be understood as signifying a "sin offering," "guilt offering," "atoning sacrifice," or "the doing of penance." Instead it denotes the "obligation
arising from guilt" or the means of "wiping out guilt." The term comes originally not from the cultic but from the legal context, from a situation of guilt
with the resulting obligation to discharge it (e.g., Gen. 26:10; 1 Sam. 6:3-4, 8,
17).[3] The integration of this term into the priestly sacrificial torah (Leviticus
4–5, 7, passim) cannot be presupposed for Isaiah 53, because אשם in verse 10
has no cultic connotations whatsoever; furthermore, the uniqueness of this
wiping out of guilt stands in contradiction to the thought of sacrifice, which
requires repetition.

This last argument shows that there are problems in ascribing to נשא עון
a central function in the understanding of Isaiah 53. One objection is that the
exact phrase does not occur in Isaiah 53; verse 11 contains a synonymous expression סבל עון, but not נשא עון. The formulations in verses 4-5 and 11-12 could
therefore be understood only as a free adaptation of a fixed concept of atonement. Second, it is questionable whether this kind of fixed concept of atonement may be presupposed even for the expression נשא עון. The two passages
that Zimmerli cites, Leviticus 10:17 and 16:22, were in all probability written
later than Isaiah 53, and they associate distinct ideas with the expression נשא
עון that differ both from one another and from Isaiah 53. Hence in Leviticus
10:17 the Aaronic priests, in their role as mediators for the community, take

---

pp. 48-74). The problem of the relationship of the four Servant Songs to one another and to the
Deuteroisaianic corpus need not be discussed here. In any case one would have to give stronger
consideration to the fact that the Servant Songs were never independent literary collections;
from the beginning they belonged to the growing layers of the developing book of Isaiah. For
the current state of the discussion see H.-J. Hermisson, "Israel und der Gottesknecht bei
Deuterojesaja," *ZTK* 79 (1982): 1-24; H. Haag, *Der Gottesknecht bei Deuterojesaja* (1985);
M. Saebø, "Vom Individuellen zum Kollektiven," in R. Albertz, F. W. Golka, and J. Kegler, eds.,
Schöpfung und Befreiung: Für C. Westermann zum 80. Geburtstag (1989), 116-25; R. G. Kratz,
Kyros im Deuterojesaja-Buch (1991), 128-47, 206-17; O. H. Steck, *Gottesknecht und Zion* (1992), 3-
43, 149-72.

3. Cf. R. Knierim, "אָשַׁם," *TLOT* 1 (1997), 191-95 (cf. the comprehensive definition on
p. 193); A. Schenker, "Die Anlässe zum Schuldopfer Ascham," in idem, ed., *Studien zu Opfer und
Kult im Alten Testament* (1992), 45-66 (further literature on pp. 133-35); Janowski, "He Bore Our
Sins," pp. 65-70 below.

away guilt through the proper performance of the sin offering and thereby effect atonement.[4] What happens in Leviticus 16:22 through the scapegoat is different: the ritual elimination of the causes of disaster. This is not representative of the priestly sacrificial theology of Leviticus 10:17, nor does it lead to the idea of vicarious suffering in Isaiah 53.[5]

If we wish to understand the idea of vicarious suffering in Isaiah 53 adequately, there is little point in taking into consideration only one or two important motifs which the tradition has coined and then using them to unlock the theological profile of the entire text. Instead I shall try in this essay to develop the criteria for the idea of vicarious suffering from the text itself in as complete a form as the text allows; only then shall I ask about the traditio-historical background of these criteria.[6]

4. Cf. B. Janowski, *Sühne als Heilsgeschehen* (1982), 239 n. 272:

Even if one understands the collocation נָשָׂא עָוֹן in Lev. 10:17b literally in terms of the "bearing" of iniquity [[i.e., as in the NASB: God gave the sin offering to the priests "to *bear away* the guilt of the congregation," לָשֵׂאת אֶת־עֲוֹן הָעֵדָה, and Moses rebukes the priests Aaron and his two surviving sons for having completely burned the flesh of the goat of the people's sin offering (cf. Lev. 9:15 with 9:11) rather than eating some of it, as the Lord had commanded through Moses (Lev. 6:26; cf. 6:30 with 10:18)]], this does *not* mean that this "bearing" ("putting aside") of guilt happens when the priests eat the חַטָּאת. Rather, because the חַטָּאת has been given to them by God, the priests are appointed as *mediators* to bear the guilt of the congregation of Israel by performing the atonement ritual with the sin offering for the congregation — for this is how the infinitive construct לְכַפֵּר which explains נָשָׂא עָוֹן is to be understood.

Cf. esp. Lev. 10:17: "Why did you not eat the sin offering at the holy place? For it is most holy, and he gave it to you to bear away the guilt of the congregation (לָשֵׂאת אֶת־עֲוֹן הָעֵדָה), to make atonement for them (לְכַפֵּר עֲלֵיהֶם) before the Lord" (NASB). On Lev. 10:16-20 see K. Elliger, *Leviticus* (1966), 131-39; E. S. Gerstenberger, *Leviticus*, ET (1996), 116-22.

5. Cf. B. Janowski, "Azazel und der Sündenbock: Zur Religionsgeschichte von Leviticus 16,10.21f.," in idem, *Gottes Gegenwart in Israel* (1993), 285-302, 336-37; B. Janowski and G. Wilhelm, "Der Bock, der die Sünden hinausträgt: Zur Religionsgeschichte des Azazel-Ritus Lev 16,10.21f.," in B. Janowski, K. Koch, and G. Wilhelm, eds., *Religionsgeschichtliche Beziehungen zwischen Kleinasien, Nordsyrien und dem Alten Testament*, OBO 129 (1993), 109-69.

6. The efforts of T. C. Vriezen tend in the same direction. With reference to Isaiah 53 he writes: "Here prophetic knowledge is the starting point: the mediatorial element *(reconciliatio),* the pedagogical-judicial element (bearing punishment in order to save another), and the radical ethical and faith-oriented sphere of the entire message. The cultic element of *expiatio* remains in the background, merely providing the external framework within which this kerygmatic fullness is summarized" (*Theologie des Alten Testaments in Grundzügen* [1956], 256). Although this judgment is very finely differentiated and rightly emphasizes the dominant role of prophecy in this context, the chosen distinctions hardly seem appropriate to the text. Closer affinity to the text must be sought.

Five criteria seem central to the idea of vicarious suffering in Isaiah 53:

a. *One person intercedes for the sins of others.* This motif is developed in Isaiah 53 in detail. It must first be understood purely descriptively without asking about the initiator or initiators of the vicarious act. In the central section of the fourth Servant Song (53:1-11aα), verses 4a and 5 emphasize that it is precisely the "man of sorrows" (53:3) who has borne *our* griefs and carried *our* sorrows; his "sickness unto death" was for the sake of *our* sins, for *our* peace and *our* healing. He and we are put into a vicarious relationship by the very same factor that prevented a normal relationship from arising between him and us before: the suffering of the Servant that deprived him of human appearance (52:14; 53:2-3). It is this Suffering Servant of whom God says in the closing part of the song (53:11aβ-12): *he* — picking up the emphatic הוא from verses 4-5 in verse 11 — will, through his vicarious act as the righteous one (צדיק), effect righteousness (צדק hiphil) for the many (רבם). That the relationship of God and the Servant is a constituting factor in vicarious suffering is already becoming clear.

b. *The one who intercedes for the sins of the others is himself sinless and righteous.* This motif is represented in the fourth Servant Song in Isaiah 53:9 and 11. In 53:9 no direct connection is made between the sinlessness of the Servant and his vicarious act. But in 53:11 his righteousness, which is important for what he effects vicariously, is bound up with his sinlessness.[7]

c. *The vicarious act of the one occurs once for all.* This criterion is not mentioned explicitly, but it is necessarily presupposed in the presentation of the Servant's fate. The death that he suffers can only be died once. No elements of the text call for the addressees to repeat the event. This is furthermore excluded by the fact that in 53:10-12, this one death is ascribed vicarious force for the future as well. What the nations someday will see and understand is not the exaltation of a whole series of Servants but only of the one Servant of whom Isaiah 53 speaks (cf. 52:13-15).

d. *One intercedes for the sins of others of his own will.* At first glance it would seem that the Servant's decision to act vicariously is not an issue. Impressive above all is the passive language — the language of suffering — in which the

---

7. Perhaps a close connection between sinlessness and the idea of vicarious suffering is also supposed to be hinted at by Isa. 53:9bβ, "and there was no deceit in his mouth." But the syntactical structure of 53:8-9 fails to support this connection. The adversative conjunction עַל at the start of the subordinate clause in 53:9b, which mentions the Servant's sinlessness ("*although* he had done no violence"), clearly refers back to the unjust and dishonorable treatment of one presumed to be *guilty.*

Servant is presented. There seems to be no room for him to make any decisions. The Servant is "despised" and "acquainted" with sickness (53:3); "stricken, struck down by God, and afflicted" (53:4b); "wounded" and "crushed" for our sins (53:5); "oppressed," "afflicted," "led to the slaughter," and "silent" (53:7). This certainly does not sound like a willing acceptance of a vicarious role.

Nevertheless we must not let ourselves be deceived. Three times in the text we meet a variation on the theme that the Servant has borne our sicknesses and sins (53:4a, 11b, 12b). The change to the active voice in verse 4a from the passive language in the surrounding context is particularly important. For the first time the Servant is thrust to the center of attention as the active subject by means of the emphatic הוא: "our infirmities — *he* bore them." In verses 4-5 this Servant makes it clear that taking sins upon himself is *his* act. He thereby creates a relationship with the "we" group — those who until then did not want to know anything about him (53:3b). "Thus his illnesses are healed for those who did not bear them" (cf. 53:5b).[8]

In verse 11, the second variation on the theme of the Servant's taking sins upon himself, we read that his once-for-all act that led to death will remain a vicarious bearing of sins in the future as well. As such it is the foundation for what God regards the Servant as having achieved: as the righteous one, he helps many to attain righteousness (53:11aγ).

The close connection between the Servant's will and God's will already expressed in verse 11 becomes, in the third variation on the theme of taking up guilt in verse 12, almost a fusion of their two intentions. After the initiative of the Servant is brought out perhaps most clearly in verse 12aγ (ערה hiphil with the Servant as the subject: "because he *poured out* himself to death"), in verse 12b we find coupled with this a self-consciously complex formulation that brings the fourth Servant Song to a close. God pronounces that his Servant will intercede for sinners. The surrender to death that has occurred once will remain in force in the future for all sinners. The construction used here, פגע hiphil[9] plus the preposition ל before the object, ולפשעים יפגיע, requires the translation: "and he *interceded* for the transgressors." But we must not lose sight of the fact that the same verb (construed with the preposition ב) has already served a few verses earlier to express God's responsibility for the vicarious event: "But the Lord has *caused* (הפגיע) the iniquity of us all *to fall* on him" (53:6, NASB). By using this one verb differently both of God and of the Servant, the agreement of their wills is made evident.

---

8. H. J. Stoebe, "רפא, to heal," *TLOT* 3 (1997), 1254-59, esp. 1258.

9. On פגע cf. P. Maiberger, "פָּגַע," *TDOT* 11 (2001), 470-76, though Maiberger gives insufficient attention to the semantic connection between Isa. 53:6 and 12 (cf. p. 474 §3a-b).

e. God brings about the vicarious action of the one for the sins of the others inten-tionally. Only in connection with the criterion just dealt with can we properly understand this final criterion for the song's notion of vicarious suffering: *God's* responsibility for the Servant's vicarious act. Already the first part of the song (52:13-15) affirms God's activity in the promise of the Servant's exaltation. In 52:13 the two finite verbs concerned with exaltation, יָרוּם, "he shall be ex-alted," and גָּבַהּ, "he shall be (very) high," consciously frame the central niphal participle נִשָּׂא, "lifted up."[10] This participle must be understood in its funda-mental meaning. It means precisely the Servant's *being borne up* by the same God who requires him to *bear* the guilt of others. Knowledge of this is what is promised to the startled[11] nations (52:15); at the same time it is the concrete form of the "help of our God," which all the ends of the earth shall see (cf. 52:10b).

God's responsibility for the Servant's vicarious role is articulated explic-itly only after the Servant's acceptance of suffering has been established in 53:4a. Two verses in particular have God's responsibility for the vicarious event as their theme: Isaiah 53:6 and 10. Significantly, these verses are similar in form to those that speak of the Servant's active acceptance of suffering. If in the latter the personal pronoun הוּא is put in an emphatic position (v. 4a), so here in 53:6 and 10 the construction וַיהוה stands emphatically at the front. Because compe-tition between God and the Servant regarding who took the initiative in the vi-carious event is excluded, this can only point to the close unity of the wills of both of them.

Special attention is due to the specific theological statements bound up with God's initiative in the vicarious event. I have already mentioned the con-nection of 53:6 to 53:12 that is made by the common use of the verb פגע. The same verb is also used to distinguish the vicarious event that occurs according to God's will from the unsatisfactory understanding of the Servant found in the passive formulation of 53:4b ("stricken, struck down by God, and afflicted"). The dimension of individual fate expressed in verse 4b is transcended but not lost sight of when God "lays" or "causes to fall" (hiphil הִפְגִּיעַ) upon the Servant "the iniquity of us all" (53:6). On the contrary, *individual destiny that is open to others is precisely what stands at the center of the idea of vicarious suffering.* The pronouncement that these others represent "all of us," twice emphasized in

10. [[(Tr.) The form נִשָּׂא in Isa. 52:13 can be parsed either as niphal perfect third mascu-line singular or as niphal participle masculine singular. These two forms, normally distinct, are identical for *lamed-aleph* verbs.]]

11. The verb form יַזֶּה in Isa. 52:15 (KJV: "he shall *sprinkle* many nations") can hardly be understood without the help of the Septuagint's verb θαυμάσονται, followed by the NJB: "many nations will be *astonished*" (cf. NRSV, NJPS: "he shall *startle* many nations").

53:6, needs apparently to be framed by the thought of God's initiative in the vicarious event.[12]

Of great importance is the way that God's role in the vicarious event is formulated in 53:10. Twice it is emphasized that God is *pleased* with the suffering of the Servant (חפץ as a verb and as a noun). The translation of this word by "to plan" or "plan" is unfortunate (cf. NRSV: "the *will* of the Lord"; NJPS: "the Lord *chose*"). God's deep personal involvement in the Servant's fate and work needs to remain audible. Where the Old Testament talks about חפץ, often enough it is love that is at stake. So also in this verse, God's will or "pleasure" in afflicting the Servant is not sadism but rather the manifestation of his loving intention that the wiping out of guilt (אשם) through the Servant's suffering should succeed.

If these five criteria adequately grasp the content of the fourth Servant Song, then it is clear that the main idea behind vicarious suffering is the close community of will between God and the Servant, with the intention of wiping out guilt for the many. The only constellation of ideas that can be relevant to the prehistory of Isaiah 53 must therefore be one that attributes great significance to the personal relationship between God and certain persons who are active on behalf of others. This is the case with the intercession and suffering of certain prophetic figures. The roots of the idea of vicarious suffering in Isaiah 53 lie here.

II

Although some claim that "intercession was one of the original tasks of the prophets,"[13] this is scarcely probable. We must not allow Moses, the intercessor

---

12. One could see the expansion of the circle of addressees by means of the twofold emphatic use of כֻּלָּנוּ at the beginning and end of Isa. 53:6 ("all we . . . us all") as immediately restricted again in 53:8b. In 53:8bβ the MT contains divine direct discourse (a stylistic break) including a strange formulation concerning *God's* initiative in the vicarious event: "[he was] stricken for the transgression of *my* (1QIsaᵃ: *his*) people." Assuming the integrity of the MT textual transmission, it is worth noting that the people, who are mentioned only here, are called the originator of the guilt but not *expressis verbis* the addressees or beneficiaries of the vicarious event. Those who find themselves unconvinced by this argument and with good reason wish to understand the "we" group that speaks in the central part of the song as a group in Israel (so that "all we" would refer to Israel alone) are invited to refer to the larger interpretive context opened up by the "many nations" in the first part of the song and kept open by the "many" in the last part of the song.

13. H. Graf Reventlow, *Gebet im Alten Testament* (1986), 229, cf. 228-64 (literature, pp. 228-29), taking up a view of G. von Rad. For a different view see E. S. Gerstenberger, "פלל,"

par excellence, to deceive us about the age of the idea of intercession. Moses first acquired prophetic features in the Deuteronomic-Deuteronomistic tradition.[14] His frequent intercessions for the people, including the key passages in Exodus 32:7-14 and 30-35, hardly go back to the pre-Deuteronomic period.[15]

Similarly, a solid basis for an older tradition of prophetic intercession cannot be obtained from the first three visions of Amos (Amos 7:1-8). Of the three visions recorded in succession, only the third can make a claim to authenticity in any case. The first two — locusts and fire — are suspect because they appear to be literary topoi, introduced to give Amos an opportunity for intercession.[16]

TDOT 11 (2001), 567-77, esp. 576: "The intercessory function is probably a late accretion to the picture of a prophet."

14. Cf. L. Perlitt, "Mose als Prophet" (1971), in idem, *Deuteronomium-Studien* (1994), 1-19.

15. On Moses as intercessor cf. E. Aurelius, *Der Fürbitter Israels* (1988); J. Van Seeters, *The Life of Moses* (1994), 77-103, 165-207, 220-44, 290-318. However, whether Moses had the function of a "vicarious sufferer" for the sins of the people above and beyond his role as intercessor in the light of Deut. 1:37; 3:23-28; 4:21, as Van Seeters thinks (p. 462), is highly questionable.

On the terminology of prophetic intercession, cf. S. E. Balentine, "The Prophet as Intercessor: A Reassessment," *JBL* 103 (1984): 161-73. For a largely plausible evaluation of the relevant passages, cf. Van Seeters, *Life of Moses,* 171-75.

16. A different view is taken by V. Fritz, "Amosbuch, Amosschule und historischer Amos," in V. Fritz, K.-F. Pohlmann, and H.-C. Schmitt, eds., *Prophet und Prophetenbuch: Festschrift für O. Kaiser,* BZAW 185 (1989), 29-43, who writes about Amos: "The essence of his prophecy consisted of his view of disaster and how to avert it through intercession" (p. 42). Therefore Fritz considers only the first two of Amos's visions in chapter 7 to be authentic. But according to the view presented here, precisely the opposite may be true: the third and fourth visions should by all means be connected with the preaching of the prophet, whereas the linguistic and conceptual content of at least the first two visions point to a later period.

Following several forerunners (A. Weiser, H. W. Wolff, H. Gese), Jörg Jeremias has proposed a thesis about a compositional correspondence between the oracles against the nations in Amos 1–2 and the visions of judgment in chapters 7–8 ("Völkersprüche und Visionsberichte im Amosbuch," in Fritz, Pohlmann, and Schmitt, eds., *Prophet und Prophetenbuch,* 82-97). But this thesis is not without its problems. The proposed approach sheds light on the oracles against the nations but creates a difficulty for the visions, namely, the need to group the first four visions into two pairs of visions: (a) 7:1-3 with 7:4-6; (b) 7:7-9 with 8:1-3. On this basis Jeremias proposes his thesis: "Amos did not become a prophet of disaster of his own will, but only after Yahweh forbade him to intercede for his people" (p. 83; cf. p. 89). But since it is scarcely possible to speak of Amos's free will to preach a message of judgment at any stage of the tradition, it is more probable that a tangible stage of composition can be recognized only in the ordering of the first three visions, which climaxes in the failure of intercession in the third vision after temporary success in the first two. Yet this failure could hardly have happened in the time of Amos. Therefore the preaching of the prophet himself may still be best recognized in the uncompromising message of judgment (cf. R. Smend, "Das Nein des Amos" [1963], in his *Die Mitte des Alten Testaments: Gesammelte Studien 1* [1986], 85-103).

This he does successfully the first time in 7:2 with the word סלח — "forgive" — which does not otherwise occur in preexilic prophecy; and again a second time in 7:5 with the word חדל — "cease" — which only here is addressed to God. God "relents" both times concerning the calamity he had threatened (נחם niphal with על: cf. Amos 7:3, 6). *All* the occurrences of this theologically important idea, including Genesis 6:6-7, point to the exilic period at the earliest (cf. Jer. 18:8, 10; Joel 2:13; Jonah 4:2).[17] God's relenting in Exodus 32:12 and 14, in particular, comes close to his relenting in Amos, because both are the result of intercession. Nevertheless, this closeness of conception did not come about in the eighth century but in the sixth century at the earliest. In the eighth century, intercession for the people would have lain in the power not of the prophets, but of the king. In any case the historically plausible report about Hezekiah's intercession in Jeremiah 26:19 points in the direction of kingly intercession, although it is formulated Deuteronomistically, as is Exodus 32:12, 14.

Beginning with the late preexilic period the intercession of the prophets becomes a standard feature of the prophetic portrait. Accordingly, it is "Yahweh's Servants, the prophets" who, like Moses, warn the nation to repent and simultaneously ensure by their intercession that the nation has the opportunity to repent. The nation, for its part, shows itself unworthy of the chance given it and exposes God's messengers to life-threatening persecution. Prophetic intercession and prophetic suffering therefore belong inseparably together.

In the case of Jeremiah, whose book the Deuteronomists made the charter for their theological program, the tension between prophetic intercession and prophetic suffering is heightened by an important theological accent. As a result of Deuteronomistic redaction, both the futility of calling for repentance and prophetic threats reach their climax when intercession is no longer an option for Jeremiah's prophetic action. Jeremiah mentions intercession one last time in the confession of Jeremiah 18:18-23. Here the complaining prophet reminds God of his futile intercession for the people (18:20). Tellingly, however, Jeremiah's purpose is to deter God from his own atoning activity (18:23)[18] and to move him to bring on the calamity he had planned (cf. also 18:17).

---

17. The necessary exegetical argumentation concerning the passages mentioned above cannot be supplied here. On the idea of God's relenting or changing his mind about his planned punishments, or being sorry about his past actions, see the still useful study of Jörg Jeremias, *Die Reue Gottes* (1975), even though his literary-historical judgments sometimes differ from those presented here; cf. also Aurelius, *Der Fürbitter Israels*, 91-100.

18. The use of the piel of כפר in Jer. 18:23 is also worth noticing. Although usually translated "Do not *forgive* their iniquity" (NRSV), the use of the כפר root (אַל־תְּכַפֵּר) also suggests "Do not *atone for* their iniquity." This shows that it is ultimately up to *God* whether or not to

God, for his part, prohibits Jeremiah from interceding for the people. This prohibition has considerable significance in texts that have Jeremiah's suffering as their consequence or indeed as their theme: Jeremiah 7:16; 11:14; 14:11-12 (with the futile intercession in vv. 13-16); 15:1.[19]

In terms of the prehistory of vicarious suffering, the prohibition of intercession in Jeremiah 7:16 is of special interest. Among the actions forbidden to the prophet here is one that is expressed by פגע qal followed by the preposition בְּ: ". . . and do not *intercede* with me" (וְאַל תִּפְגַּע בִּי).[20] It is the same verb פגע which, in the causative stem (hiphil), is of central importance for the idea of vicarious suffering in the fourth Servant Song (see Isa. 53:6, 12). The verb is an important link between the forbidden intercession and the new idea of vicarious suffering. The complex personal relationship between God and his prophet that characterizes the books of Jeremiah and Ezekiel has, in the concept of vicarious suffering, developed into something deeper: a special partnership between God and his Servant. Out of a rare relationship has developed a unique one. Instead of suffering *because* of the people and *because* of God, we now have the idea of suffering *for* others, according to one's own will as well as God's.

The roots of the idea of vicarious suffering are nevertheless to be found not only in the book of Jeremiah, but also in the book of Ezekiel. Here, too, intercession no longer has a chance. Though it is not rejected by explicit prohibi-

---

make atonement, though this can apparently also be influenced (here negatively) by prophetic intercession. This so-called "atonement" is nevertheless noncultic, without the use of a sacrificial victim. The potential similarity of this idea of atonement and the idea of God's relenting or changing his mind about a planned disaster in Exod. 32:12, 14 and Amos 7:3, 6 deserves further investigation. Might further illumination of the use of אשם in Isa. 53:10 also be possible against this background?

19. Jer. 14:2–15:4 is redactionally structured as one great composition of lament and intercession that can accomplish nothing because the prohibition of intercession is irrevocable: "Do not pray for the welfare of this people" (Jer. 14:11; cf. 7:16). If one recalls the successful (Deuteronomistic) intercession of Moses in Exod. 32:7-14, where the Lord relents or changes his mind about the disaster he had planned to bring on his people (32:14), then Jer. 15:6, הַנָּחֵם נִלְאֵיתִי, "I am weary of relenting," sounds almost like an after-the-fact justification for the failure of the people's lament and petition and for the prohibition of intercession in Jer. 14:2–15:4.

20. 〚(Tr. The verb פגע plus the preposition בְּ is used ironically once again in Jer. 27:18: "If indeed they are prophets, . . . then let them *intercede* (יִפְגְּעוּ) *with* the Lord (בַּיהוָה)."〛 Cf. further the use of פגע in Isa. 47:3 where, however, the sense "to intercede" depends on the grammatical person of the verb, which is textually uncertain. 〚(Tr.) Instead of the MT's first person verb plus direct object, וְלֹא אֶפְגַּע אָדָם, "and *I* will not *spare* a man" (cf. RSV), the *BHS* note at Isa. 47:3 suggests the third person verb in an intransitive use, וְלֹא יִפְגַּע אָדָם, "and *no man* will *intercede*." This is based on the reading of Symmachus, και ουκ αντιστησεται μοι ανθρωπος, "and no man will stand against me" (text in J. Ziegler, *Isaias*, Göttingen LXX, 3rd ed. [1983]) and the Vulgate, *et non resistet mihi homo*.〛

tion, it is nevertheless discouraged by the fact that intercession fails in practice. Although in Ezekiel 9 the prophet is still prepared to intercede (9:8) in order to try to prevent the God-ordained decimation of the Jerusalem populace, he can no longer obtain any reprieve (9:10). By the time we come to the great reckoning with Jerusalem in Ezekiel 22, things have gotten worse: after searching both among the prophets (22:28) and among the people at large, God says that he can no longer find anyone "who would repair the wall and stand in the breach before me on behalf of the land, so that I would not destroy it" (Ezek. 22:30; cf. 13:5 and Ps. 106:23).

In the theological program of the book of Ezekiel, the idea of intercession is effectively limited by the heavy emphasis on individual retribution. In the case of Abraham's intercession for Sodom, ten righteous people would have been enough to rescue the city (Gen. 18:32b-33). In Jeremiah 5:1 a single person who did what is just would have been able to obtain a pardon for the city of Jerusalem. Yet in Ezekiel 14:12-20 not even the exemplary righteous figures Noah, Daniel, and Job are in a position to effect salvation for anyone else. One's own righteousness (צדקה) can save only one's own life.

The major treatment of individual retribution in Ezekiel 18 is also characterized by this conviction. Transfer of guilt is not possible even between fathers and sons. This constitutes a revocation of the Deuteronomistic doctrine of retribution that in explaining the grace formula depicts the iniquity of the fathers as in force to the third and fourth generation.[21] In Ezekiel 18 the impossibility of transferring guilt is tightly bound up with the nontransferability of individually acquired righteousness. What holds between fathers and sons holds generally: "A son shall not bear the guilt (ישא בעון) of his father, and a father shall not bear the guilt of his son. The righteousness of the righteous shall be upon him, and the wickedness of the wicked (רשעת רשע) shall be upon him" (Ezek. 18:20b). Repentance is possible and desirable. But the possibility of the righteous turning to godlessness is contemplated as well: then not even their own former righteousness has any power to compensate (18:21-32; cf. 18:12-20 [and 3:20]).

Because the book of Ezekiel conceives individual responsibility so radically, it is surprising at first that the idea of bearing guilt could be the subject of any symbolic prophetic act. Yet according to Ezekiel 4:4-8, Ezekiel is supposed

---

21. Cf. H. Spieckermann, "Barmherzig und gnädig ist der Herr . . . ," *ZAW* 102 (1990): 1-18, reprinted in idem, *Gottes Liebe zu Israel: Studien zur Theologie des Alten Testaments,* FAT 33 (2001), 3-19. But it is also important to notice that the relationship of the guilt of one's fathers to one's own guilt was already coming under intensive scrutiny in Deuteronomy. The texts Deut. 7:9-10; 5:9-10 = Exod. 20:5-6; 34:6-7 are especially revealing in this regard (Spieckermann, "Baumherzig und gnädig ist der Herr . . . ," 5-10 = *Gottes Liebe zu Israel,* 6-12).

to bear the guilt (נשׂא עון) of Israel and Judah by lying on his left side and then on his right side for a period of time. Because this is supposed to occur while Ezekiel is tied up, the prophet is completely given over to the suffering ordained for him without the possibility that his suffering could function vicariously. The prophet can only painfully illustrate what will afflict the people as a whole. Individual responsibility and collective guilt are not mutually exclusive. Rather, the former brings the latter to light in all its seriousness.[22]

Another aspect of Ezekiel's prophetic suffering is his divinely willed silence (Ezek. 3:26). His silence is formulated with the niphal of אלם, just as is the silence of the Servant in Isaiah 53:7. Nevertheless, this aspect of Ezekiel's suffering still does not have compensatory power for others like the silent suffering in the fourth Servant Song. Ezekiel's silence rather has the function of leaving the people without a prophetic warning. By an intentional compositional device, this silence follows immediately upon Ezekiel's installation in the office of watchman or sentinel for the house of Israel in 3:16-21 (cf. 33:1-20). The prophet is thereby burdened with an almost unbearable responsibility. For he will bear responsibility for the righteous and the wicked at the cost of his own life if he, as their sentinel, does not warn them as charged.

If we consider Ezekiel's post as a sentinel together with the silence God demanded of him, his suffering in all its tension is plain to see. We may recall the shaken confidence in God that a figure like Jeremiah experienced when God failed to protect him in the prophetic office and forbade him to intercede for the people. The parallel for Ezekiel will be his feeling of being torn between the duty of a sentinel and the obligation to remain silent, together with the failure of his intercession in practice. In the hindrances to intercession and in suffering, prophecy found itself in an irresolvable situation in which a new theological alternative — the idea of vicarious suffering — could have been born.

III

If we look once again at the fourth Servant Song and its idea of vicarious suffering against this prophetic background, the theological accomplishment of the new conception becomes clear. *Prophetic suffering acquires a new sense.* It be-

---

22. On the problem of individual responsibility in Ezekiel see P. M. Joyce, "Ezekiel and Individual Responsibility," in J. Lust, ed., *Ezekiel and His Book* (1986), 317-21. I agree with Joyce that the theme of individual responsibility does not dominate Ezekiel. However, above and beyond Joyce's contribution, we still need a clarification of what specific status the undeniable emphasis upon individual responsibility has in the light of the proclamation of judgment against the whole house of Israel.

comes suffering for the guilt of others that is intended by God and the Servant together. At the same time vicarious suffering is limited to and concentrated upon the fate of a single person whose guilt has the power to wipe out guilt once for all. The dimension of prophetic suffering is thereby transcended so decisively that the Servant can no longer be identified with any particular prophetic figure. In the realm of prophecy, the Servant is to a certain extent a "utopian" figure who must remain nameless because no identification can do justice to the claims about vicarious suffering.

The idea of vicarious suffering also overcomes the radically heightened doctrine of individual retribution in the book of Ezekiel. This idea is the mirror image of the intercession that was forbidden in the book of Jeremiah and that failed in practice in Ezekiel. Here as well, the fourth Servant Song risks something new (cf. Isa. 53:11). *By leaving room for one Servant to remain righteous, God makes the Servant's righteousness a part of the vicarious event.* The Servant makes the many righteous and thereby breaks the bounds of previous conceptions of individual retribution and prophetic intercession.

If in the books of Jeremiah and Ezekiel the themes of prophetic suffering, intercession, and individual retribution were oriented strictly to Israel, then in these respects, too, the fourth Servant Song goes a step further. With allusion to what the first three Servant Songs had said about the Servant's office, in Isaiah 53:11-12 the Servant's vicarious act becomes effective for the "many." In the present form of the text, this is hardly to be differentiated from the "many nations" in 52:15. The nations will not only see "the salvation of our God" as this will manifest itself in his return to Zion (52:7-10); they will themselves participate in the wiping out of guilt effected by the Servant.

If the theological accomplishment of the idea of vicarious suffering is beyond question, it also cannot be denied that in the fourth Servant Song the idea is still found *in statu nascendi*. When the point is made about various nations being included in the wiping out of guilt effected by the Servant, it must be understood that those addressed by the vicarious event are not kept in view with constant clarity in the text. The relationship of the "many" to the "many nations" and the relationship of both of these groups to the "we" group who speak pointedly of "us all" (כלנו) in Isaiah 53:6 raise open questions. Does the fourth Servant Song reveal anything about a general development in the scope of the vicarious event's applicability — originally restricted to Israel, then broadening to the nations?

It is also not clear through which type of righteousness the Servant makes many righteous (Isa. 53:11). Isaiah 53 remains in need of clarification precisely in view of the strict doctrine of individual retribution in the book of Ezekiel, with its exact notions of who can be righteous and who cannot. Is the Servant's righteousness to be measured by the standard of Ezekiel? Or does God himself give the Servant his righteousness in order that he might effect righteousness for the many? And if the latter is correct, what theological profile would righteousness have in Isaiah 53:11?

Another problem is the Servant's "namelessness." Just as it is true that a precise identification of the Servant is avoided in view of the prophetic background (no individual prophet fits the bill), so also it is true that the Servant's namelessness could misleadingly imply that the Servant's task can always be taken up afresh by particular persons in the future. Certainly this kind of interpretation does not correspond with the text's original intention. Moreover, the collective consciousness that soon began to develop in the postexilic period — including a collective understanding of the fourth Servant Song — has left no redactional traces in the song itself. Yet we also lack subsequent literary testimony to the original individual understanding. It is therefore not inconceivable that the themes of the uniqueness and finality of the vicarious event could have subsequently been worked out more fully. But apparently a more precise theological profile of the person of the Servant was not an option.

The fourth Servant Song's lack of influence in the Old Testament speaks in favor of this conjecture. Already the introductory question of the "we" group — "who has believed our message?" (Isa. 53:1) — has a skeptical undertone. The prosperity of the Servant is expected in the future, but the most important statements are put in the mouth of God (52:13), who apparently is supposed to create the credibility that the "we" group might hope for but not attain. From a literary standpoint, then, the idea of vicarious suffering cannot be called a success. Even where we might have expected a reception and further development of the thought, namely, in the added literary layers of Third Isaiah, we find nothing — at best a reinterpretation or even an implicit rejection of the idea of vicarious suffering. In Isaiah 59:15-20 it is God himself who takes charge, because he saw that there was no vicarious "intercessor" (מפגיע, hiphil participle, 59:16). It is scarcely imaginable that פגע, the same rare verb as in 53:12, has been used here unintentionally. Rather, the idea of vicarious suffering has now been brought back to the realm of the familiar in prophecy. Prophets and others can indeed take over the function of a mediator; but God always remains the one who does the decisive thing himself.

Thus Isaiah 53 remains a singular text in the Old Testament. It had no "posthistory," and its prehistory left behind nothing "prefabricated." The prehistory simply produced those problems that the new idea of vicarious suffering was supposed to help solve. We do not know to what extent this conception had any success in the Old Testament period. In any case, literary attestation of the development of its theological options is first found outside the Old Testament.

The Fourth Servant Song in the Context of Second Isaiah

Hans-Jürgen Hermisson

Summary

While the Servant in all four Servant Songs (Isa. 42:1-4; 49:1-6; 50:4-9; 52:13–53:12) is presented as a prophetic figure whose experience sums up both past and present experiences of the prophetic office, the universal message of salvation given to the Servant in the fourth song transcends previous conceptions of prophecy. The primary reference in all four songs is to the prophet Second Isaiah himself. Nevertheless, the individual prophetic Servant Second Isaiah cannot fulfill his worldwide mission of being a light to the nations without God's Servant Israel, whom he calls back to God and prepares to be the prime exhibit before the world of God's saving power (cf. 49:5-6). Only through the cooperation of God's two Servants — the prophet who preaches God's word and Israel who receives it — is the Servant role fulfilled. One-sided designations of the Servant as "individual" or "corporate" are therefore too simple, and the text's supra-individual dimensions betray a future to the Servant role not exhausted by the individual prophet. (The songs are not prophecies of Christ, yet no violence is done to them when read in this light.) Although suffering forms no part of the Servant's role in the first two songs and is only a natural consequence of his prophetic ministry in the third, the fourth song makes suffering the means to the accomplishment of his task. The Servant bore vicariously the sins of the "many" in Israel, particularly the sin of unbelief. Therefore, while the Servant's faith may be seen as *representative* of the faith that Israel may one day develop in the future, in the past and in the present time perspective of the text, the individual Servant functions as a *stand-in* or *substitute (Stellvertreter)* — not as a representative *(Repräsentant)* — for the Servant Israel in matters of both faith and suffering. The reward and success of the Servant in his mission becomes the theme linking all four Servant Songs (cf. 42:4; 49:4; 50:7-9 with 52:13).

I. Introduction

Anyone who wants to get involved in the interpretation of Isaiah 53 must realize two things.[1] First, the historical and theological understanding of this great text will remain controversial until kingdom come. Second, one will be able to produce a completely new historical explanation of this text (and of the Servant Songs as a whole) only if one is willing to enter the richly sown field of scholarly oddities. All the interpretations and interpretive elements worth discussing have already been presented, especially in the last 100 years since Bernhard Duhm's Isaiah commentary of 1892, but many of them before then. Likewise, all these interpretations have also been contested at one time or another, because everyone knows how to promote his or her own views against those of others.

Such a perspective at the beginning is no reason for resignation. The existence of different modern explanations should cause no surprise, since there was a history of interpretation already in the development of the book of Second Isaiah and then also in the book of Isaiah as a whole. The best-known example is Isaiah 61 with its appeal to the first Servant Song in Isaiah 42. But there are ideas that appear in several texts of the book of Second Isaiah itself, in its present redactional arrangement, that are even more significant because scholars, in accordance with the rules of proper exegesis, have first directed their attention to the redacted context. If one reads the Servant Songs in their present redactional context, I have no doubt that they[2] are *now* supposed to be understood "collectively" (I use the usual interpretive scheme and terminology, although it does not really do justice to the phenomenon). However, the collective understanding of the Servant is, in my opinion, the interpretation of the third or fourth or even later generation, and it is not without grounds in the

---

1. This essay was first presented to Professor Hengel's New Testament Society on April 19, 1991. Detailed interpretation of Isaiah 53 and a closer examination of the many theses about the Servant were impossible in this setting. Therefore I must refer readers to a few earlier essays — including some of my own, most of which have now been reprinted in my collected essays, H.-J. Hermisson, *Studien zu Prophetie und Weisheit. Gesammelte Aufsätze*, ed. J. Barthel, H. Jauss, and K. Koenen, FAT 23 (1998) — and then also to my ongoing interpretation of the book of Second Isaiah in the forthcoming installments of the *Biblischer Kommentar:* H.-J. Hermisson, *Deuterojesaja*, BKAT 11. Regarding the special adaptation of the text-critical portions of notes 12-41 in this English version see the Translator's Preface, above, p. x.

2. Or at least the first three songs.

texts: it is to a certain extent a legitimate reception and continuation of the first three Servant Songs, although the fourth does not automatically fit in without further ado.

In order to break out of the exegetical stalemate, one must first take the history of redaction seriously as a history of changing perspectives. Beyond this there is enough for us late-born exegetes to do simply to find the *particulae veri* in the rich treasury of earlier explanations — for almost all of them are right at one point or another. We can then try more precisely to ground our own understanding, which grows out of the diverse views of our predecessors.

On the overall problem of the "Servant of the Lord" in Second Isaiah, I can merely outline my own view here, drawing upon other positions only for clarification. First I must sketch the message of Second Isaiah in a few broad strokes.

We can illustrate Second Isaiah's message[3] most readily by starting with the declarative-assertive language of the *salvation sayings* that dominates Second Isaiah. What he has to proclaim here basically takes shape in the first text of the book of Second Isaiah, which presents the prophet's insight into the heavenly scenario and his own calling. A highway is built on which Yahweh leads his liberated people through the desert. This highway naturally leads from Babylon to Jerusalem, as other texts explicitly show. Such great signs and wonders are performed on this highway, as well as at its end, that the whole world is overcome and is being saved, streaming in and confessing the one and only God, the only savior of Israel and the whole world.

This is filled out by many pictures: of shade trees in the desert for the *wandering Jacob* and of abundant, even overabundant water in the wilderness; or of the splendor and multitude of people — in short, of the glorification of *lady Zion*.[4] So far this is simple and seems to require no Servant — or rather

---

3. Cf. on this H.-J. Hermisson, "Jakob und Zion, Schöpfung und Heil: Zur Einheit der Theologie Deuterojesajas," *Die Zeichen der Zeit* 44 (1990): 262-68.

4. Recent attempts at unlocking the tradition of Second Isaiah by means of its redaction history call into question even the unity of the introductory text and the inclusion of the entirety of the Jerusalem-Zion passages in the Deuteroisaianic "foundation document" — so, e.g., the most thorough current investigation of the Deuteroisaianic layers by R. G. Kratz, *Kyros im Deuterojesaja-Buch*, FAT 1 (1991); see somewhat differently the earlier work by K. Kiesow, *Exodustexte im Jesajabuch: Literarkritische und motivgeschichtliche Analysen*, OBO 24 (1979); and finally J. van Oorschot, *Von Babel zum Zion*, BZAW 206 (1993). For the prologue as well as for a series of Zion texts, this seems to me to be unnecessary and at least no longer provable, so that one must begin one's work at the literary level, which is still to a certain degree accessible. The partially observable collective interpretation of the Servant Songs in their present context by means of secondary texts either belongs to a later layer, the "imminent expectation layer" (cf. Kratz's differently delimited "Ebed Israel layer"), or results from the (secondary) composition of the texts. Drawing

only the one Servant, Israel, which joins God on the way and confesses him ju-
bilantly before the whole world.

But the difficulty lies just here. In Second Isaiah's message a real departure from Babylon is at stake, and Israel is no more ready for this than are people of all times under similar circumstances. We need only consider the time
and situation of exiles who are expressly prohibited from returning to their
homeland by their overlord. Whether the prophet had already called for such
an exodus *before* the liberation by the Persian king Cyrus which he expected is a
question that can at least be asked in the light of several texts (cf. 48:20). But
however that may be, it is absurd in the eyes of his audience. Israel is hardly
ready to receive this message and leave Babylon singing hymns. Therefore the
prophet is needed as a second chosen Servant, who gathers Israel around its
God and gets it under way.

One must therefore speak of *both* Servants[5] in order to do justice to the
phenomenon of a Servant who is spoken of both inside and outside the Servant
Songs, with the same predicates applied to figures with different tasks. The prophetic Servant must get Israel under way. This requires not only *assertive*
speech announcing salvation, but also *argumentative* speech. By this distinction
I seek to trace the artful categories of form criticism back to fundamental possibilities of human communication (the hymns would be a third category). But
at this point a difference must be noted. The argumentative speech of the prophetic Servant has two addressees: (1) *Israel* most immediately, in the so-called
discussion sayings; and (2) *the nations* (and indirectly also Israel) in the judgment speeches against foreign nations and their gods. The latter involves theology in its strict sense, namely, the uniqueness of the one God of Israel as the one
and only savior of Israel and the world — for the nations, too, should not simply be amazed but should come to an understanding through reflection. As is
well known, the argumentative basis of this dramatic judicial speech is the "argument from prophecy" or the "proof of prophecy," in which earlier prophecies
are now seen to be fulfilled. It is ultimately not a theoretical but a very practical
argument, whose proof is evident above all in the salvation of Israel itself. Yet
the creative word of Yahweh that brings about this salvation has already been
sent into the world through the prophet; it is an intelligible and therefore a con-
firmable word that is realized in Israel. Once again it is easy to see that both Ser-

---

upon K. Elliger, *Deuterojesaja in seinem Verhältnis zu Tritojesaja*, BWANT 63 (1933), I presented a
provisional attempt at discerning the redaction history at the 1987 Isaiah Congress in Leuven. See
H.-J. Hermisson, "Einheit und Komplexität Deuterojesajas: Probleme der Redaktionsgeschichte
von Jes 40–55," in J. Vermeylen, ed., *The Book of Isaiah — Le Livre d'Isaïe*, BETL 81 (1989), 287-312.

5. Cf. H.-J. Hermisson, "Israel und der Gottesknecht bei Deuterojesaja," *ZTK* 79 (1982): 1-
24.

vants are necessary: the one who makes the creative word of Yahweh accessible beforehand, and the one in whom this word becomes a reality. The latter is no arbitrary figure but the chosen Servant Israel, whom Yahweh created and chose in order to glorify himself in his Servant.

This indicates the general direction, but the argument from fulfilled prophecy also has other elements, one of which has considerable importance for our subject. I pass over the theme of Cyrus, as important as this is in the texts, because this is only the particular way in which Yahweh saves his people. But prior to this, the effectiveness of Yahweh's creative word articulated through the prophets into the world had already been demonstrated in a totally different way: namely, in Israel's destruction in the catastrophe of 587 B.C.E. This is only occasionally hinted at,[6] because it corresponds less closely to the practical goal of the argument from prophecy and plays no role in the future expectation of the prophet Second Isaiah. But it illustrates by example how the ministry of earlier prophets is superseded in the conception of the prophetic Servant.

In short, I understand the Servant Songs as a presentation of the prophetic office that incorporates previous experiences of prophecy. They are therefore reflection texts, though we must immediately add that what is described is the prophetic office as it must look *now*, at this hour of world history, in view of an entirely new initiative of God. Because of this divine plan the prophetic office is inseparably bound up with the office of that other Servant, Israel. The first servant text and the beginning and end of the second describe an effect that only both Servants working together can achieve. But the specific office holder of the Servant Songs is the prophet, the *last* prophet,[7] Second Isaiah, to whom this office is entrusted. We should recall that there would have been little need for this Servant had Israel been ready and willing to get under way. But since Israel is not — or not yet — ready for this, the prophetic Servant as an individual represents Israel, displaying the trust in his God that Israel still refuses to exercise. This becomes especially clear in a particular verse, Isaiah 49:4. Whereas the unbelieving Servant Israel says,

---

6. The answer to this question depends on what is meant by "the former things" (הָרִאשֹׁנוֹת). I believe that the (secondary) passage Isa. 48:3 "the former things . . . suddenly I did them" (הָרִאשֹׁנוֹת . . . פִּתְאֹם עָשִׂיתִי) refers to the events of 587 B.C.E. (cf. H. E. von Waldow, "Anlaß und Hintergrund der Verkündigung des Deuterojesaja," Th.D. dissertation, Bonn [1953], 240-41; Hermisson, *Deuterojesaja*, 226, 228). Above and beyond this, the רִאשֹׁנוֹת may refer to a wide range of past correspondences between the divine announcement and its realization, which admittedly include the announced destruction of Israel as the end of the רִאשֹׁנוֹת (as distinct from the חֲדָשׁוֹת or "new things" of Isa. 42:9; 48:6). On this pair of expressions see Hermisson, *Deuterojesaja*, 130-31, 225-26, 234-35.

7. At least in the view of Second Isaiah.

"My right (מִשְׁפָּט) is disregarded by my God" (Isa. 40:27, RSV),

the prophetic Servant, even in the light of his apparent failure, acknowledges,

"My right (מִשְׁפָּט) is with the Lord" (Isa. 49:4, RSV).[8]

With this I come to the last motif that must be mentioned,[9] because it permeates the first three Servant Songs and carries over into the fourth. It is the motif of the reward and success of the Servant.[10] This is certainly promised him in the first text:

> He will not smolder nor bend
>   until he has established justice in the earth;
>   and the coastlands wait for his teaching. (Isa. 42:4)

The second text contains the Servant's confession of his failure, mentioned just above:

> But I said, "I have labored in vain,
>   I have spent my strength for nothing and vanity;
> yet surely my right [NRSV: *cause*] is with the Lord,
>   and my reward with my God." (Isa. 49:4)

Finally, the third song formulates this more clearly in view of the prophet's opposition and suffering. The experiences of his prophetic predecessors are once again incorporated, especially the experience of the suffering prophet Jeremiah, who was opposed and persecuted in his office. But the one who must now bear the prophetic office and endure opposition does not break down under the strain, as Jeremiah did, for he acknowledges:

> The Lord God helps me;
>   therefore I have not been disgraced;
> therefore I have set my face like flint,
>   and I know that I shall not be put to shame;
>   he who vindicates me is near. . . . (Isa. 50:7-8)

8. See further Isa. 43:22/49:4. ⟦(Tr.) The RSV of Isa. 40:27 and 49:4, quoted above, maintains the parallelism by using the English "my right" in both verses, whereas the NRSV obscures it: "my right" and "my cause." Parallel expressions can also be retained by combining the NJPS and NRSV: "My *cause* is ignored by my God" (40:27, NJPS); "my *cause* is with the Lord" (49:4, NRSV).⟧

9. Naturally there is more to say on the understanding of the Servant Songs: see the theses in part IV at the end of this essay.

10. Cf. H.-J. Hermisson, "Der Lohn des Knechts," in J. Jeremias and L. Perlitt, eds., *Die Botschaft und die Boten: Festschrift für H. W. Wolff zum 70. Geburtstag* (1981), 269-87.

With this sure confession of confidence, the cycle of the first three Servant Songs (which go back to the prophet himself) comes to an end. But it ends with an open question: What became of the reward and success of the Servant, since he obviously did not receive it during his lifetime? And what is the meaning of expressions like "is with my God," "I know . . . ," and "he is near . . ." when the Servant is dead? The answer to this question is provided in the fourth Servant Song which I, with many others,[11] ascribe not to the prophet himself but to one of his pupils. It begins with a citation of a Yahweh Oracle:

> See, my servant shall prosper . . .

It is therefore not a well-thought-out answer nor a clever way of solving a theological problem, but an answer surprising and overpowering even to the author himself — an answer only God can give. The fourth Servant Song reports this answer.

II. Isaiah 52:13–53:12

I need hardly start by complaining about the innumerable difficulties of this text. They begin already with the reconstruction of the text and its translation, so that it will no longer be possible to answer all the questions to our full satisfaction. But once again this is no reason for resignation, for I think it is possible to find a level of understanding at which the text becomes sufficiently clear and the essential controversial questions answerable.

1. Text and Translation

[[*Translator's note:* Hebrew words inserted parenthetically into the translation below represent the text read by Professor Hermisson where it *departs* from the MT; the corresponding English translation is then identified by corner brackets, ⌐as here⌐. (A similar convention is used in the German.) Some of Professor Hermisson's emendations are conjectural; others have manuscript evidence; both types are discussed in the notes. For the sake of English-speaking students, the notes incorporate added philological comments by the translator discussing the standard English translations and other more complicated matters beyond the level of elementary Hebrew — marked [[(Tr.) . . .]]. Each line is given a

---

11. Cf. esp. Elliger, "Deuterojesaja in seinem Verhältnis zu Tritojesaja," 6-27.

Roman and usually also a Greek letter for further identification; for a four-line verse the pattern is typically aα, aβ, bα, bβ. The English translation is based on the NRSV, though this has frequently been modified to reflect Professor Hermisson's understanding of the Hebrew as recorded in his German translation and his more recent suggestions for the English version.]]

13 a　See, my servant shall prosper;

　b　he shall be exalted and lifted up, and shall be very high.

14 a　Just as there were many who were astonished ⌐at him⌐ (עָלָיו)[12]

　bα　— so marred was his appearance, beyond human semblance,

　β　and his form beyond that of mortals —

15 aα　so shall many nations ⌐become agitated⌐ (יִרְגְּזוּ);[13]

　β　kings shall shut their mouths because of him;

　bα　For what was never told them they have seen,

　β　And what they never heard they have understood.[14]

12. The reading עָלָיו, "at him" instead of MT עָלֶיךָ, "at you" (= LXX ἐπὶ σέ) is supported by two Heb. MSS, Syr., Tg., θ′ (επ αυτον). [[(Tr.) Most English versions, including NRSV, NJPS, NJB, NIV, presuppose this variant "at him." NASB follows the MT and tries to make sense of it by a gloss: "at you, *My people*."]]

13. Conjectural emendation יִרְגְּזוּ, "become agitated" *(sich erregen).* Also worth mentioning is the emendation יְזוּחוּ, "get excited" *(sich ereifern),* after the use of the verb זוח in the Hebrew text of Sir. 8:11 (E. Kutsch, *Sein Leiden und Tod — unser Heil: Eine Exegese von Jesaja 52,13–53,12,* BibS[N] 52 [1967], 17); cf. the Syriac זוח, "become agitated" (*HALOT* 1:266 s.v. זוח).

[[(Tr.) On Sir. 8:11 see now P. W. Skehan, *The Wisdom of Ben Sira,* AB 39 (1987), 213: "In v 11a, the verb root זוח, here translated 'Do not (give) ground,' is an Aramaism; in Aram and Syr, it means 'to move, stir, arouse oneself to action.'" The MT reading יַזֶּה (hiphil imperfect of נָזָה), rejected by the conjecture above, is often translated "*he will sprinkle* many nations" (cf. KJV; NASB; NIV; K. Baltzer, *Deutero-Isaiah: A Commentary on Isaiah 40–55,* Hermeneia [2001], 392). Difficulties with this have inspired the conjectural emendations. Kutsch (*Sein Leiden und Tod — unser Heil,* 17) traces the first conjecture, יִרְגְּזוּ (qal imperfect of רָגַז), back to G. F. Moore, "On יזה in Isaiah LII.15," *JBL* 9 (1890): 216-22, esp. 222. The qal of this verb has been translated by various English expressions, including "be agitated" (BDB), "be excited" (Isa. 14:9 [NASB]), "tremble" (Joel 2:1; Ps. 4:5 [NASB; NJPS]), "be disturbed" (Ps. 4:5 [NRSV]), or "be stirred up" (Isa. 28:21 [NASB]).]]

14. Instead of the English perfects "have seen" (רָאוּ) and "have understood" (הִתְבּוֹנָנוּ) (cf. German: *gesehen haben, vernommen haben),* the English future perfect could be used: "they will have seen," "they will have understood" (German: *werden sie gesehen/vernommen haben*). As an explanatory clause (cf. כִּי, "for"), v. 15b describes a future event, even as v. 15a does. [[(Tr.) In agreement with this, the NRSV uses the English future for both the Hebrew imperfect and perfect: "they shall shut" (imperfect יִקְפְּצוּ), "they shall see" (perfect רָאוּ), "they shall contemplate" (perfect הִתְבּוֹנָנוּ). The possibility of the future perfect mentioned above is also supported by Baltzer, *Deutero-Isaiah,* 392: "they will have seen," "they will have understood." Cf. also NJB: "(15a) so many nations will be astonished and kings will stay tight-lipped before him, (15b) *seeing* [in the future] what had never been told them, *learning* [in the future] what they had not heard before."]]

1 a   Who would have believed (*or:* who can believe) what we have just heard?

  b   Upon what sort of figure has the arm of the Lord now been revealed?

2 a α   For[15] he grew up ∟before himself⌐ (לְפָנָיו)/∟before us⌐ (לְפָנֵינוּ)[16] like a young plant,

    β   and like a root out of dry ground;

  b α   he had no form or majesty that we should look at him,[17]

    β   nothing in his appearance that we should desire him.

3 a α   He was despised and rejected[18] by others;

    β   a man of suffering and acquainted with infirmity;

  b α   and as someone from whom one[19] hides the face

---

15. Note the *waw* consecutive form וַיַּעַל. ⟦(Tr.) Accordingly the NRSV translates, "*For* he grew up," (עָלָה) וַיַּעַל). The consecutive form initiates a narrative about the Servant's background, explaining why it is difficult to believe the report of his exaltation that the "we" have heard.⟧

16. MT reads the singular suffix לְפָנָיו, "before *him*," whereas our conjecture above reads the plural לְפָנֵינוּ, "before *us*." The MT's singular suffix can be referred sensibly only to the Servant and not to Yahweh (as it is in the NRSV: "For he grew up before *him*"), yet the translation with reference to the Servant is uncertain: "he grew up *before himself*" (*vor sich hin*); "he grew up *for himself alone*" (*für sich allein*). In this case the Servant's *isolation* is what disqualifies him in the eyes of the "we," but this would not fit well the comparison with the "young plant." If we read "before us," the comparison of v. 2aα gets its negative sense together with v. 2aβ, ". . . out of dry ground."

17. Assuming that it is not to be deleted entirely, וְנִרְאֵהוּ, "that we should look at him" (NRSV), belongs not to v. 2bβ, as in the MT, but to v. 2bα, as above, in view of the parallelism; so also σ′.

⟦(Tr.) We may note the contrast of this line break to that of the MT, LXX, and KJV. These place the expression in question into the next line, v. 2bβ. The MT does so by the accentuation; cf. the conjunctive accent on וְנִרְאֵהוּ and the *athnah* on the preceding word הָדָר, followed by the BHS line spacing. Following this accentuation the KJV reads: "He hath no form nor comeliness; *and when we shall see him,* there is no beauty that we should desire him." Similarly the LXX: "There was neither appearance to him nor glory; *and we saw him,* and he did not have appearance or beauty" (οὐκ ἔστιν εἶδος αὐτῷ οὐδὲ δόξα· καὶ εἴδομεν αὐτόν, καὶ οὐκ εἶχεν εἶδος οὐδὲ κάλλος). Only with Symmachus do we find the now familiar expression: "There was neither appearance to him nor dignity *that we should look at him*" (σ′: ουκ ειδος αυτω ουδε αξιωμα ινα ιδωμεν αυτον; text in Ziegler, *Isaias* [Göttingen LXX]).⟧

18. The sense of the adjective חָדֵל here is not simply descriptive, "the lowest *of* men" (NJB), but passive, "rejected *by* men" (RSV). Others suggest that it was the Servant himself who kept his distance from others, e.g., NEB, "he shrank from the sight of men"; Baltzer, "He . . . forsook human beings" (*Deutero-Isaiah,* 392). But the passive nuance better fits the context.

19. Could this "one" who hides his face from the Servant be Yahweh himself? So among others Elliger, "Deuterojesaja in seinem Verhältnis zu Tritojesaja," 9. See the discussion below, n. 59, with its text.

β   he was despised,[20] and we held him of no account.

4 a α   Surely our infirmities — *he* bore them

　　β   and our diseases — ˪*he*˩[21] (הוּא) carried them;

　b α   yet we accounted him stricken,

　　β   struck down by God, and afflicted.

5 a α   But he was wounded for our transgressions,

　　β   crushed for our iniquities;

　b α   upon him was the punishment that made us whole,

　　β   and by his bruises we are healed.

6 a α   All we like sheep have gone astray;

　　β   we have all turned to our[22] own way,

　b α   and the Lord has laid on him

　　β   the iniquity of us all.

7 a α   He was oppressed, and he bowed down[23]

　　β   and did not open his mouth;

　b α   like a lamb that is led to the slaughter,

　　β   and like a sheep that before its shearers is silent,

　c   so he did not open his mouth.

20. The MT, followed here in our translation of v. 3bβ, reads נִבְזֶה, "despised" (niphal participle masculine singular בָּזָה). By contrast 1QIsaᵃ reads the first person plural imperfect with the third masculine singular objective suffix, ונבוזהו (*DSSB:* "and we despised him"), apparently a dialect form for וְנִבְזֵהוּ or the *waw* consecutive וַנִּבְזֵהוּ. ⟦(Tr.) Cf. *HALOT* 1:117 s.v. בזה at Isa. 53:3b, 1QIsaᵃ, where the proposed vocalization is likewise the qal imperfect נִבְזֶה.⟧ Standing immediately before the perfect וְלֹא חֲשַׁבְנֻהוּ ("and we held him of no account"), the MT's suffixless נבזה in v. 3bβ should be taken as a niphal participle, as in v. 3aα. Stylistically, however, we might have expected the participle's subject to be stated by the pronoun, נִבְזֶה הוּא.

21. Although the MT lacks this restatement in v. 4aβ of the emphatically stated subject הוּא from v. 4aα, the pronoun is literally carried over from v. 4aα into v. 4aβ in several Heb. MSS, Syr., and Vulg. ("vere languores nostros *ipse* tulit et dolores nostros *ipse* portavit"); perhaps it formed part of the original Hebrew text. In any case the emphasis carries over.

22. ⟦(Tr.) The expression אִישׁ לְדַרְכּוֹ פָּנִינוּ in v. 6aβ literally has a *plural* verb (פָּנִינוּ) plus a noun with a *singular* pronominal suffix (לְדַרְכּוֹ), accurately rendered in the RSV: "*we* have turned every one to *his* own way." But of course the pronominal suffix is distributive and means "*our* own way" (NRSV).⟧

23. MT: נִגַּשׂ וְהוּא נַעֲנֶה. The stress on וְהוּא as the subject of the niphal participle נַעֲנֶה ("he bowed down") is not conspicuous, even though the first verb, the niphal perfect נִגַּשׂ, has the same subject. The first verb is a regular passive, the second intransitive, and it is this difference between the two verbs, both niphal, that is made clear by the explicit וְהוּא. Hence the "oppression" comes from outside, but the "bowing down" is the reaction of the Servant. It would contradict the flow of the text to suggest with J. L. Koole (*Jesaja II*, COT [1985]) and others that עָוֹן ("iniquity") from v. 6 is the subject of נגשׂ in v. 7.

8 a α   From oppression[24] and judgment he was taken away.[25]

  β   And his fate[26] — who took care of it?

  b α   For he was cut off[27] from the land of the living,[28]

  β   ⌐stricken to death⌐ (נֶגַע לָמָוֶת)[29] for the transgression of ⌐his people⌐ (עַמוֹ)[30]

24. Or "from imprisonment." [[(Tr.) Cf. KJV, "He was taken from prison."]]

25. Other suggested translations for לֻקָּח include "he was carried away" or "he was taken away" in the sense not of dying, but of being transported, as Elijah was (cf. 2 Kings 2:3, 9-10). But neither fits the context. On "being taken away" in the sense of "dying," as here, see Prov. 24:11; Ezek. 33:6.

26. Other translations include "among his contemporaries." [[(Tr.) Compare RSV "his generation"; also translated "his descendants" (NIV), or even "his abode" (NJPS). Cf. esp. NJB: "Which of his *contemporaries* was concerned at his having been cut off from the land of the living, at his having been struck dead for his people's rebellion?"]]

27. Heb. נִגְזַר. Cf. Ps. 88:5 (MT 88:6), "like those forsaken among the dead, . . . for they are *cut off* (נִגְזָרוּ) from your hand."

28. Cf. Jer. 11:19, "let us *cut him off* (כרת, not גזר as in Isa. 53:8) from the land of the living"; Ps. 52:5 (MT 52:7), "he will *uproot you* (שרש) from the land of the living."

29. Emend MT נֶגַע לָמוֹ to the above נֶגַע לָמָוֶת, cf. 1QIsa^a נוגע and LXX ἤχθη εἰς θάνατον (see translator's note below). MT has מִפֶּשַׁע עַמִּי נֶגַע לָמוֹ, "On account of the transgression of *my* people — a stroke *to him* (לָמוֹ)." The translation "a stroke *for them*" would be more fitting for לָמוֹ but even further removed from the context. It is striking that the traditional Masoretic Text disallows a collective interpretation of the Servant. The expression the "transgression of *my* people" (מפשע עמי) differentiates the people from the Servant, who is without transgression (cf. 53:9), and this expression also finds an exact counterpart differentiating the Servant and the people in v. 5, וחוא מחלל מפשענו, "But *he* was wounded for *our* transgressions" — a fact that Origen took advantage of against Celsus (cf. the contribution of Christoph Markschies in this volume). To the advocates of the collective interpretation, which sees the Servant as Israel, I can offer a conjecture which to my knowledge has not yet been proposed: מִפֶּשַׁע עַמִּים נֶגַע לוֹ [[= "On account of the transgression of the peoples — a stroke to him (i.e., the Servant Israel)" — Trans.]]. This merely requires a bit of "shaking" of the consonantal text. It is not the best Hebrew, but it is better than Lindblom's attempt to extract from the MT the meaning, "For he was cut off from the land of the living because of the rebellion of those to whom my people was a leper" (J. Lindblom, *The Servant Songs in Deutero-Isaiah* [1951], 49, followed by O. Kaiser, *Der königliche Knecht*, FRLANT 70 [1959; 2nd ed., 1962], 85-86).

[[(Tr.) The proposed emendation of MT נֶגַע לָמוֹ to נֶגַע לָמָוֶת involves two changes: נגע is revocalized as נֻגַּע (pual perfect) and ת is supplied to the end of למו. These changes find manuscript support in 1QIsa^a and LXX. First, 1QIsa^a reads נוגע, where the added ו over against the MT represents the pual stem in plene writing; so *HALOT* 2:669 (s.v. נֶגַע): "1QIs^a נוגע = *נוֹגַּע, or rather נוגע pf. pu." Second, LXX ἤχθη εἰς θάνατον, "he was led *to death*," supports the emendation לָמָוֶת. Exactly the same textual assumptions appear to have been made by the NJB: "*struck dead* for *his* people's rebellion." Cf. the translation of 1QIsa^a in *DSSB*, 360: "*he was stricken* for the transgression of *my* [*sic*; read with 1QIsa^a *his*] people." On "*his people*" see the next note.]]

30. Read עַמוֹ. [[(Tr.) עַמוֹ, "*his* people," is attested in 1QIsa^a for MT עַמִּי, "*my* people."]]

9 a α They made his grave with the wicked

β and ⌐his tomb⌐ (בָּמָתוֹ)[31] with the ⌐evildoers⌐ (עֹשֵׂי רַע)[32]

b α although he had done no violence,

β and there was no deceit in his mouth.

10 a α Yet the Lord — whose plan it was to crush him —

β ⌐healed the one who made⌐ (הֶחֱלִים אֶת־שָׂם)[33] his life the means of wiping out guilt.[34]

---

31. Read בָּמָתוֹ in the light of 1QIsaᵃ בומתו (translated *DSSB*, 360: "tomb"). MT reads בְּמֹתָיו, "in his *deaths*" *(sic)*, and although this strange plural form is not unattested (cf. Ezek. 28:10), neither does it fit the parallelism. ⟦(Tr.) The form בָּמָתוֹ is also proposed in *BHS* ("sepulchrum suum") and followed by several modern versions, e.g., NRSV, "tomb"; NJB, "tomb"; and REB, "a burial-place among felons." The term בָּמָה is therefore not used in its most frequent OT sense of a Canaanite "high place" (*HALOT* 1:136 s.v. בָּמָה 4), but in the sense of a tomb or "grave" (*HALOT* 1:136, s.v. בָּמָה 3).⟧

32. Emend to עֹשֵׂי רַע (conjecture), "doers of evil," by adding ע at the end of the consonantal text עָשִׁיר and redividing words. MT's singular אֶת־עָשִׁיר can be understood either individually, "with a rich person" (NRSV margin), or collectively, "with the rich" ⟦= NRSV text; the marginal note conjectures that the literal plural form, i.e., עֲשִׁירִים, may once have stood in the text — Trans.⟧. But it is highly improbable that the tombs of the rich were situated with those of the wicked (plural רְשָׁעִים, v. 9aα).

33. This conjectural expression, הֶחֱלִים אֶת־שָׂם, is perhaps to be read, following the suggestion of J. Begrich, *Studien zu Deuterojesaja*, WMANT 4/25 no. 77 (1938), 58; reprinted in TB 20 (1963), 64. The text is very uncertain at this point; the only certainty is that it deals with Yahweh's intervention on behalf of the Servant.

⟦(Tr.) The history of the proposed conjectural emendation הֶחֱלִים אֶת־שָׂם may be explained. It was hinted at by Elliger, *Deuterojesaja in seinem Verhältnis zu Tritojesaja*, 7-8, before being proposed in its full form by J. Begrich; it is also mentioned in *BHS*. Since the relationship of the conjecture to the MT is complicated, it is best to start with the MT. The MT and the conjecture divide the words and letters differently. The MT includes the first four consonants, החלי, with v. 10aα by its disjunctive accentuation הֶחֱלִי (*zaqeph qaton*). The form is hiphil perfect third masculine singular of חלה I or of its by-form חלא (*HALOT* 1:315, 316-17), "be sick," hiphil "make sick." Hence MT's full expression וַיהוָה חָפֵץ דַּכְּאוֹ הֶחֱלִי means, "Yet it was the will of the Lord to bruise him; *he has put him to grief*" (RSV) or "*he has made him sick*" (RSV margin). Similarly Baltzer: "But it has pleased Yahweh to smite him. He let him become sick" (*Deutero-Isaiah*, 393, translation note 10a). Alternatively, some translations of the MT understand החלי as the noun חֳלִי plus the article modifying the preceding infinitive דַּכְּאוֹ. But these versions are no different with regard to verse division: "to crush him *with pain*" (NRSV; NJB) or "*by disease*" (NJPS; NRSV margin); so also the Vulgate (see below n. 35). Over against all this, the conjectural emendation assumes that the MT and these English and Latin versions are wrong to include החלי in v. 10aα. Rather, these consonants must be included in v. 10aβ. The MT then has the letters החליאמתשׂים. Assuming both (a) that the sequence אם in the middle of this group (which the MT reads as the particle אם, "if") is a transposition of an original מא (Elliger; Begrich) and (b) that the second י is a mistakenly added *mater lectionis* (Elliger), we find the sequence

Or:

10 a α But it was the *Lord's* plan to crush him, ⌐to make him sick⌐ (הֶחֱלִי),[35]

  β yet ⌐he truly made⌐ (אֱמֶת שָׂם)[36] his life the means of wiping out guilt.

  b α He shall see (his) offspring and shall prolong (his) days,

  β and through him the plan of the Lord shall prosper.

11 a α Because of the anguish of his life he shall see ⌐light⌐ (אוֹר);[37]

  β he shall find satisfaction in perceiving him (יִשְׂבַּע בְּדַעְתּוֹ).[38]

  b α ⌐The righteous one⌐[39] My servant shall make righteous the many,

  β and their iniquities — he bears them.

החלימאתשם or הֶחֱלִים אֶת־שָׂם (Begrich). Here הֶחֱלִים is the hiphil perfect of חלם, "to restore to health" (*HALOT* 1:320) and שָׂם the qal perfect of שִׂים, "to put, place, set." Hence: "Yet the Lord . . . *healed the one who made* his life an אָשָׁם." Begrich translates: "Aber Jahwe . . . *heilte den, der* sein Leben zum Schuldopfer *gab*" (italics added).]]

34. On the translation of אָשָׁם (NRSV: "an offering for sin") see below, p. 37 and B. Janowski, "He Bore Our Sins," below, pp. 65-70, who suggests "Schuldtilgung," i.e., the "wiping out of guilt/debt." [[(Tr.) Similarly Baltzer, *Deutero-Isaiah*, 393: "If he gives his life to wipe out debt."]]

35. Instead of the MT's hiphil perfect הֶחֱלִי (חָלָה), "he has made him sick" (RSV margin), the above translation reads the hiphil infinitive construct (א)הַחֲלִי [[(Tr.) The normal pointing of the hiphil infinitive construct of חלה would be הַחֲלוֹת, but הַחֲלִיא is the hiphil infinitive construct of its by-form חלא]]. Alternatively, we may read the noun חֳלִי or delete החלי entirely as a gloss. [[(Tr.) The noun חֳלִי (*HALOT* 1:318) occurs in Isa. 53:3-4 (NRSV: "infirmity") and has been conjectured here in Isa. 53:10 based on the Vulgate (*HALOT* 1:317 s.v. חלה I hiphil). On this reading Yahweh crushes the Servant "with sickness" *(HALOT)*, "by disease" (NRSV margin), or "in infirmity" (NAB); Vulgate: "et Dominus voluit conterere eum *in infirmitate*."]]

36. אֱמֶת שָׂם is a conjectural emendation of the MT's אִם־תָּשִׂים. [[(Tr.) For the adverbial use of the noun אֱמֶת, "truth," in the sense of "truly," as above, see *HALOT* 1:69 s.v. אֱמֶת 6.]]

37. To the shorter MT reading, insert אוֹר, "light," with 1QIsa^a-b, 4QIsa^d (cf. *DSSB*, 360 n. 1178), and LXX (φῶς). [[(Tr.) So most modern versions, including NRSV, REB, NAB, NJB, and NIV, though not NJPS or NASB, which follow the MT.]]

38. We have divided the lines differently from the MT. If, as above, the phrase "he shall find satisfaction" is read in its nonpausal form יִשְׂבַּע with the short vowel *patah* under the *beth* (as in the *BHS* footnote), then יִשְׂבַּע בְּדַעְתּוֹ forms a unit. However, the MT splits up this unit: יִשְׂבָּע is in pause (cf. the long vowel *qamatz* and the disjunctive accent *zaqeph qaton*) and therefore goes with the preceding words, as in RSV: "he shall see the fruit of the travail of his soul *and be satisfied*" (cf. NASB; NIV). This line division may have resulted because of the MT's lack of the word אוֹר, "light"; in any case it leads to difficulties in the length of the lines. [[(Tr.) The above line break is suggested also by the three revisers of the Old Greek, who keep together the ideas of satisfaction and knowledge: "α′ θ′ (α′ σ′ θ′ sec. 86) εμπλησθησεται (σ′ χορτασθησεται Q) εν τη γνωσει αυτου Q 86" (Ziegler, *Isaias* [Göttingen LXX], 323).]]

39. This phrase in the NRSV, "The righteous one," should probably be deleted because the underlying Hebrew term צַדִּיק apparently arose from dittography: יצדיק צדיק.

12 a α Therefore I allot him a portion with the many,

  β and he shall divide the spoil with the numerous;[40]

 b α because he poured out[41] his life to death,

  β and was numbered with the transgressors;

 c α yet he bore the sin of the many,

  β and made intercession for the transgressors.

2. Comments on the Translation

A few more comments are necessary regarding the translation. I can readily pass over the first unresolvable difficulty, in 52:15 (above n. 13), because the context is perfectly clear. The parallelism shows that in place of the MT's term יַזֶּה there must have stood another term, denoting astonishment, wonder, or even excitement, as in most English versions, where the Servant will "startle" (NRSV, NJPS) the nations, or the nations will be "astonished" (NJB) or will "marvel" at him (NIV margin; cf. LXX θαυμάσονται). The popular interpretation of the MT's reading יַזֶּה as suggesting an atonement ritual (KJV, NASB, NIV: the Servant will "sprinkle" many nations) is opposed not only by the linguistic usage[42] and parallelism, but by the whole flow of the text.[43]

The second question concerns 53:1. The alternative I have given in my

---

40. The rendering of v. 12a is contested. The essence of the above translation, including the expressions "*with* the many" (בָּרַבִּים) and "*with* the numerous" (עֲצוּמִים), is followed by most modern versions (e.g., RSV, NRSV, REB, NJB, NASB; cf. NAB, NIV: "among"). This wording is better than that of the NJPS, "Assuredly, I will give him the many as his portion, He shall receive the multitude as his spoil" (or "divide the strong as spoil"), which has considerably greater linguistic difficulties. Against this understanding see Kutsch, *Sein Leiden und Tod*, 37-38; Hermisson, "Israel und der Gottesknecht," 21-23, and further below.

41. "He poured out" = NRSV. Literally "tip out," *HALOT* 2:882 s.v. ערה hiphil = *ausschütten*, *HALAT* 3:834. ⟦(Tr.) The original German text of this essay translates: "dafür, daß er sein Leben dem Tod preisgegeben hat." A similar notion that "pouring out" is equivalent to "surrendering" or "throwing away" is suggested by *HALAT*, "sein Leben dem Tod hingeben" = *HALOT*, "to throw away one's life to death."⟧

42. Against the above translations, the hiphil of נזה followed by an accusative object does not mean "to sprinkle (an implied fluid) on an object," such as the nations (גּוֹיִם), but simply "to sprinkle (the fluid)," where the fluid either stands as the direct object in the accusative (Lev. 16:15; Num. 8:7; 19:21) or, more frequently, follows the partitive מִן ("sprinkle *some of* the blood/oil," etc.). The object *upon which* or *toward which* the fluid is sprinkled is then always preceded by one of the prepositions אל נכח, אל, על or לפני; it never appears as the verb's direct object.

43. See also B. Janowski's essay in this volume, "He Bore Our Sins," pp. 67-68, who claims that Isa. 52:13–53:12 makes no mention of cultic procedures.

translation concerns only the difference between "who *would have* believed" and "who *can* believe what we have heard" and is relatively unimportant. Very different from either of these is Luther's well-known translation, "Wer glaubt aber unserer Predigt?" reflected also in the KJV, "Who hath believed our report?" This stresses what the we-speakers have preached or reported rather than what they have "heard" (NRSV; so most modern versions). The idea of preaching or reporting by the "we" is not excluded by the grammar and vocabulary, but it fails to do justice to the context: what is unbelievable is not the message of the we-speakers, but the message of exaltation in the first Yahweh oracle (52:13-15) when compared with the suffering of the Servant in what follows.

In 53:4 it is necessary to underscore the point made above (see n. 21). Regardless of whether one literally reads the emphatic pronoun "he" (הוּא) in the second line (with Heb. mss; Syr.; Vulg.) as in the first, there is an emphasis on the *Servant's* bearing of suffering in the first line that carries over into the second. One cannot therefore articulate this as R. N. Whybray has done — "He merely shared our sufferings"[44] — in order to interpret the thought of vicarious suffering out of the text.[45]

An important interpretive problem is found in 53:8 (see n. 29), but the emendation נֻגַּע לָמָוֶת ("he was stricken to death") on the basis of the Septuagint's ἤχθη εἰς θάνατον ("he was led to death") seems justified by the context and is in any case to be preferred to the torturous attempts to make sense of the MT. Nevertheless, the popular suggestion that the Servant actually died cannot rely on this uncertain text.

Most difficult of all is 53:10a; all attempts at a resolution are highly hypothetical, yet it is a decisive passage in our text. In order to keep a firm footing, I seek in my interpretation to rely upon the only completely certain expression, "But Yahweh . . . ," and upon the context, which once again is clear. For by verse 10bα, a change has already taken place in the Servant's fortunes ("He shall see his offspring," etc.), which suggests a prior turning point, perhaps in verse 10aβ.

Finally, the first line of 53:12 is another contested case. Since both the translations I have mentioned (cf. n. 40 with its text) as well as others are possible, exegesis must decide which understanding fits better into the overall context.

---

44. Summarizing R. N. Whybray, *Thanksgiving for a Liberated Prophet,* JSOTSup 4 (1978), 29-30.

45. On the theological problem of "vicarious suffering" or *Stellvertretung* see B. Janowski, "He Bore Our Sins" (below, pp. 48-74), as well as the excursus in the present essay, below, part III.

3. Structure and Genre of the Text

If one pays attention to the changing speakers in this text, a clear structure emerges.[46] Isaiah 52:13-15 is a Yahweh speech, as is 53:11b (from יצדק onward) through 53:12. In between stands in 53:1-11a, or at least in 53:1-6, the speech of a majority or "we" group in the first person plural. This central section divides into verses 1-6 and verses 8-11a. Framed by its two occurrences of ולא יפתח פיו ("and he did not open his mouth"), verse 7 takes up a special position between the two parts of the text. Only here is there any mention of the Servant's own independent behavior in response to the suffering inflicted upon him. All other statements of the central section, including those about the Servant's "bearing" infirmities and "carrying" diseases in verse 4,[47] speak only of the fate the Servant must suffer. In verse 7, as in the second half of the central section beginning in verse 8, the majority group that speaks from 53:1 onward ceases to express itself explicitly, although no change of speaker is implied. Instead of the "we," this second subsection uses the more distant expression "ᴸhisᴶ people" (MT: "my people," v. 8b). The two occurrences of the expression ויהוה ("and Yahweh") introducing the conclusions of the two subsections in verses 6b and 10a also affect the structure; it is important for interpretation to note that at least the whole of verse 10 must be included with the preceding subsection (on v. 11a see below).

A proper understanding of the text also requires grasping its time perspective. The text begins not with the first event in the sequence of events, but with the last: "My servant shall prosper." As a historical event this is still future, but as a certainty of Yahweh's oracle it is already present. The first Yahweh speech therefore envisions the moment when the Servant stands over against the entire world of the nations, and the significance of his worldwide office is universally acknowledged. The second Yahweh oracle speaks, as will be seen, of a more narrowly defined cycle of events, but still within the same time perspective.

The two Yahweh speeches at the beginning and end therefore look back upon the period of the Servant's *humiliation* (52:14/53:11b): this is the *past.* And they announce as a *future destiny* the Servant's *exaltation* or the compensation for his previous fate (52:13/53:12).

---

46. On the structure see the thorough study of O. H. Steck, "Aspekte des Gottesknechts in Jes 52,13–53,12," *ZAW* 97 (1985): 36-58, esp. 38-45.

47. There is no hint here of the idea that the Servant took the infirmities and diseases of the "many" upon himself; rather, "*the Lord* has caused the iniquity of us all to fall on Him" (v. 6, NASB). By contrast a different feature dominates the second Yahweh oracle. Here the active aspect of the Servant's behavior appears much more clearly in the context of the statement about the Servant's reward.

Determining the time perspective of the central section is more difficult. The "choir" that speaks here could be a future choir looking back upon the whole event of humiliation and exaltation from the standpoint of the Servant's exaltation. The multitude that speaks here would then begin speaking at that future moment when the Servant's importance is recognized and acknowledged in his exaltation. Starting from this moment of recognition, the group would then present the Servant's entire destiny in hindsight, from the very beginning. But it is much more likely that the whole text looks back from the perspective of the Yahweh oracle that is experienced "now,"[48] and that the earthly realization of the Servant's exaltation is still expected in the future. The unity of time perspective in the text as a whole speaks in favor of this. Also in its favor, despite uncertainties about the temporal significance of the verb forms, is the consistent use of perfects and consecutive imperfects in the verbal clauses in the report about the Servant's humiliation;[49] only in verses 10bα (יַאֲרִיךְ ,יִרְאֶה), 10bβ (יִצְלָח), and 11a (יִשְׂבָּע ,יִרְאֶה) do we have — once again consistently — the plain imperfect for the future destiny of the Servant. Finally, there would be grounds for the idea of a *future* "choir" only if one were to understand 53:1ff. as a quotation of the nations and kings mentioned in 52:15; but that is unlikely because these kings are already said to have "shut their mouths" because of the Servant.

In terms of its *Gattung,* there are only limited possibilities for subsuming the text under the usual forms. The two framing pieces can only very loosely be described as Yahweh oracles because they are not directed to the Servant,[50] but rather say something about him: the actual addressee remains open. The first oracle with its introduction "See, my servant . . ." recalls the presentation saying about the Servant in 42:1ff.; the connection is apparently intentional.

The central section has been compared with a funeral dirge.[51] This would

---

48. Cf. Steck, "Aspekte des Gottesknechts," 42.

49. The exceptions, where only the regular imperfect is used, include the expressions of result, comparison, or condition in v. 2 ("that we should look at him" and "desire him," imperfect), a circumstantial clause in v. 7 ("so he did not open his mouth"), and the rhetorical question in v. 8aβ ("who took care of it?").

50. The second person address in the MT of 52:14aα, "many were astonished *at you* (עָלֶיךָ)," falls completely outside the context and rests on a mere error of copying or reading; the confusion of ו (עָלָיו) for ךָ was especially common in older Hebrew writings. Although this second person ending would be the more difficult reading, the rule of the *lectio difficilior* does not apply to mere scribal errors (so Kaiser, "Der königliche Knecht," 85). Moreover, the change to the second person would also be psychologically unlikely if "the Servant were the actual listener" (ibid.) and the text was formulated in an oral address.

51. Cf. H. Jahnow, *Das hebräische Leichenlied,* BZAW 36 (1923).

be supported by its retrospective on the life and significance of the deceased. But scholars have rightly objected that all praise of the deceased is lacking; his figure appears rather in the most extreme humiliation. When the Servant's great significance is spoken of, it is not from the perspective of the lament over his death, but is indebted to a totally new insight about the Servant and his destiny. This insight rests not upon the comprehension of the Servant's death, but upon the Yahweh oracle. Moreover, the narrative tone of the song does not fit that of the usual funeral dirge. One could consider the report of distress and salvation in the individual thanksgiving hymn as a possible form, except our text is not spoken by the individual who experiences this deliverance.[52]

What is crucial is that the whole Servant Song is spoken at the moment at which the meaning of the Servant's suffering is understood. Regarding the Servant's exaltation the song still speaks prophetically, but this does not mean that the Servant himself is only a figure of the future. The suffering and death of the Servant are already past events for the composer of the text. This suggests that the fate of the prophet Second Isaiah is here seen in its comprehensive significance by the prophet's own students. This fate must have been a violent one, whose precise form we do not know; the text allows only speculation.[53]

Finally, another controversial question concerns the identity of the "we" group that speaks in the central section.[54] If the text is consistently formulated from the time at which the Yahweh oracle is experienced, then the "we" are the author and his group, the disciples of Second Isaiah. This group then speaks representatively for all Israel. The problem is different and more difficult if we have to envision a "choir" that speaks from a future point in time.

This majority group of the central section is not to be separated from the "many," the רַבִּים, who constitute a leitmotif of the two Yahweh oracles (52:14-15/53:11-12). Once again it is contested whether Israel or the world of the nations is meant. In favor of the exclusive reference to the other nations, it is customary to cite the parallelism between the רַבִּים in 52:14 and the גּוֹיִם רַבִּים or "many nations" in 52:15. But rather than indicating limitation or exclusion, the latter

---

52. Therefore Whybray, *Thanksgiving,* 109ff., has to invent the category of the thanksgiving hymn sung by others for the one who is rescued. But this is a mere *ad hoc* construction and not a proper *Gattung.*

53. Isa. 53:8 perhaps speaks of execution; v. 9 of burial with the wicked. One could make sense of this by assuming that the prophet was imprisoned and executed as a rabble-rouser by the Babylonians and buried in a mass grave. If correct, this would be prose; but the text is poetry and uses poetic language to express the actual event in a way that is appropriate but also above and beyond the mere facts. This is why we can no longer see through clearly to the events in the background.

54. Cf. Steck, "Aspekte des Gottesknechts," 40.

expression could instead point to an expanded, universal circle that is evident only at the end, in the Servant's future of which the Yahweh oracle speaks. The "many" who are astonished at the Servant's misery in 52:14 and the "many nations" who are startled by his exaltation in verse 15 (cf. v. 13) are therefore not identical; there is an intensification in the sequence of the text from רַבִּים to גּוֹיִם רַבִּים. By contrast, the astonishment of the "many" in 52:14 clearly goes together with the despising of the Servant by the "we" in 53:1ff.[55] The expression רַבִּים therefore probably designates the larger community from which the Servant was excluded; this means first and foremost Israel. The "we" of 53:1ff. is then a limited group who speak representatively in the name of the many for all Israel. This means that the "we" and the רַבִּים are also not simply identical. The preceding revelation to which 53:1 most closely refers is first made known to a limited circle. This circle shares the same view as the larger society regarding the suffering figure of the past — or rather, they shared it until now; but now, to their surprise, they have been set straight.

4. *The Individual Sections of the Fourth Servant Song*

a. 52:13-15   Like Isaiah 42:1ff. the Yahweh oracle in 52:13-15 begins with Yahweh presenting his Servant: "See, my servant." But whereas the former passage reported only his successful ministry, this text speaks of his exaltation precisely by passing through deep humiliation. When the divine word announces the future exaltation of the Servant before the nations and kings, this must be interpreted within the framework of Second Isaiah's proclamation and in the context of the first three Servant Songs. The time of this future exaltation must then coincide with the great salvific turning point, when the new exodus reaches its goal and the nations also receive a share in salvation.

The Servant's "prosperity" or "success" is also to be understood from this perspective. His success does not simply consist of the fact that the Servant's own suffering acquires some meaning once this end is in view, for it is not his private suffering but the suffering connected with his "office." Rather, it is in the worldwide turning point of salvation that the Servant's ministry reaches its goal, exactly as in 42:4: "He will not grow faint or be crushed until he has established justice (מִשְׁפָּט) in the earth." The universal significance of the Servant's office is thereby confirmed, which shows for the first time that his suffering was not only the unavoidable consequence but also a functional part of his office.

---

55. Cf. also n. 40.

The Servant's exaltation is spoken of with three parallel verbs (52:13) that depict his being lifted up to the highest degree: he is exalted above all nations and kings (52:15) and receives a place very near to God. Once again, as in the first and second Servant songs, traits of the royal tradition have left their mark on the concept of the Servant. His exaltation takes place before the eyes of the whole world, which reacts with utter amazement that such a miserable figure should be so highly exalted.

b. 53:1-11a   Astonishment at the surprising reversal of the Servant's fortune also explains the exclamation in 53:1. In the light of such a discrepancy, who would have believed — or who can believe — what we have heard? And upon what sort of miserable figure has Yahweh's arm, his power, been revealed? So speak those now informed by the Yahweh oracle about the meaning and goal of the Servant's fate of suffering.

At most, a potential problem with this interpretation, which equates the message heard in 53:1a with the Yahweh oracle of 52:13-15, is presented by the formulation of verse 1b. Can the expression "The arm of the Lord has been revealed upon (sc. the Servant)" (cf. NJPS) refer merely to the revelation in words through the oracle? Is this not also intended to include the *visible* demonstration of power, a turn in the fate of the Servant already realized here on earth, which can be seen by "all flesh," as in 40:5, or at least by those who speak here in 53:1ff.? Since such a visible display of God's power has not yet occurred, any "choir" which is supposed to praise it in 53:1ff. would have to be in the first instance a fictive and still future entity. But against the view that requires a visible revelation of the Servant's fate in 53:1b and therefore something more than simply the verbal promise of the Yahweh oracle is first of all the parallelism: the שְׁמוּעָה or message heard in verse 1a is in this context nothing other than the divine message, the oracle that has just been cited.[56] Moreover, the verb גלה, "to reveal," in 53:1b is more often used for a revelation through words,[57] and even though the exact words of the revelation usually appear in the same context as the verb גלה, this is not necessarily so. Therefore in 53:1, the revealed "arm of the Lord," his act of saving power, is the content of the message revealed in the Yahweh oracle. What is said there is already real for Yahweh, even though it is not yet visible to "the eyes of all of the nations," as in 52:10. Second, the imperfects in 53:10b and verse 11aα also speak of a future dimension of the saving event, no matter how the opaque verse 10aα is to be understood; but if we must read there something like the perfect הֶחֱלִים, "he has healed" in verse 10aβ (see

---

56. On this use of שְׁמוּעָה ("message") see also Isa. 28:9, 19.

57. 1 Sam. 2:27; 3:7, 21; Isa. 22:14 (niphal); cf. 1 Sam. 9:15; 2 Sam. 7:27; Amos 3:7 (qal).

our first alternative above, pp. 27-28, with n. 33), then we would once again have the same tension between the fundamental act of salvation that has already occurred with Yahweh and its perceptible earthly effects, which are still expected.

Isaiah 53:2 begins the presentation of the Servant's humiliation. But here it must be noted that the following scenes contain typical expressions of suffering and humiliation that are largely but not entirely determined by the topic of Lamentations. An individual biographical explanation is therefore not possible.[58] An immeasurable degree of suffering and humiliation is expressed, even beyond what is possible in the psalms of lament.

The picture of a root out of dry ground points to the miserable origin of the Servant. There was also nothing attractive in his appearance; rather, he was disgusting and therefore avoided by others, sick, and full of pain — people hid their faces from him out of abhorrence (53:2-3). With K. Elliger and others it is possible to interpret the words "As one from whom one hides the face" (v. 3bα) as suggesting that even God hides his face from the Servant, which would form a connection with the language of the Psalms. Then the questionable logic of divine punishment and human enmity would already be at work as early as verse 3. But that first comes to expression with an explicit mention of God in verse 4b, while the immediate context in verses 2 and 3 speaks only of human contempt for the Servant, so that the hiding of one's face is rather an expression of human disgust.[59] This contempt for the Servant in his society was based on the generally accepted idea that his miserable fate was punishment for his sins: he was struck down and afflicted by God (v. 4b).

Over against this stands the surprising new recognition expressed in verse 4a and verses 5-6: a recognition gained only from the end, from the announcement of the turning point in the Servant's fate. The sickness and suffering were not punishment for his sins; rather, "He has borne our infirmities and carried our diseases" (v. 4a), which means that "the Lord has laid on him," the innocent one, "the iniquity of us all" (v. 6b). Here, too, the same eerie connection between guilt and its consequences that motivated the observers in verses 2-3 is presupposed. But instead of letting the consequential punishment for sins strike the doers, Yahweh piled it upon one individual.

In contrast to the earlier Servant texts it must be noted that this suffering is no longer simply an incidental consequence of prophetic ministry, as in the

---

58. Though it may be possible to interpret the statements about the Servant's death biographically, even here we do not get far beyond speculation; cf. n. 53.

59. So most recently the commentaries by W. A. M. Beuken, *Jesaja,* De Predeking van het Oude Testament 23 (1979, 1983); and J. L. Koole, *Jesaja II,* COT (1985), where a third interpretation, according to which the Servant hides his face "from us," is correctly refuted.

case of Jeremiah and also in the third Servant Song in Isaiah 50:4-9. Rather, it is an integral part of the office, with its own function: it is part of Yahweh's plan, as verse 10 will establish in hindsight.

Isaiah 53:7 presents the Servant's behavior in his appointed suffering. In response to oppression, he bowed down and did not rebel; comparable statements are found in 50:5-6. This is illustrated in the pictorial language of the lamb and the sheep. It must be remembered that this is only a *comparison* that cannot be used as proof of an underlying sacrificial idea.

Scholars have also tried to find evidence for the sacrificial idea in a key word in verse 10: the Servant makes his life an אָשָׁם. This word designates the "guilt offering" in priestly terminology, but it is doubtful whether it is so to be understood here. In a profane sense אָשָׁם can also denote a "restitution" or "indemnity" (so Num. 5:7-8; 1 Sam. 6:3-4, 8, NJPS), and I find this meaning more probable here.[60]

Verses 8 and 9 present the death and burial of the Servant. In verse 8 one could consider the translation "from imprisonment and judgment he was *led away*," which requires us to add, "to the place of execution." But the mere verb לֻקַּח (qal passive of לָקַח, "take") does not yield this meaning, even in this context; therefore the translation "*taken away*"[61] is more probable. Whether עֹצֶר means "imprisonment" (KJV: "he was taken from *prison*") or more generally "oppression" (NRSV) can hardly be decided. The expression is probably intended to leave that open, and only the continuation is capable of suggesting the concrete idea that in the end, the Servant is buried with the wicked and the "doers of evil" (conjecture עֹשֵׂי רַע; cf. n. 32). Once again it is difficult to say to what extent individual traits should be interpreted biographically.[62] But to me it seems certain — even though this is continually debated — that the Servant really died an ignominious death and was shamefully buried. This does *not* then simply involve the common metaphor of the Psalms that severely ill and suffering people already find themselves "in the grip of death."[63] The text explicitly states that this was the death of an innocent person (v. 9b).

---

60. For more detail see B. Janowski's essay below, pp. 68-69.

61. Scholars have also thought of לֻקַּח as a technical term for being "transported" to another realm (see above n. 25). But this would come into consideration here only if one did not need to interpret this expression together with the one about burial.

62. For one possible theory see n. 53.

63. Whybray, *Thanksgiving*, 79-106, here 89, seeks in great detail to prove that the Servant did not die but only came near death. I believe that his very thorough and respectable investigation of the individual expressions ultimately fails to do justice to the subject because it isolates the expressions rather than reading them in their context and flow of thought. Moreover, only partial parallels can be provided from the Psalms.

Verse 10 indicates a turning point. The entire speech of the many is spoken from this point of view: the earlier assurance of this turning point in the first Yahweh oracle was itself enough to set the central section on this course (see above, pp. 33-35). No matter how the text is to be reconstructed in detail, it must have spoken of an act of Yahweh at this turning point.

If one pays attention to the structure of the text, then of the two alternative renderings of verses 10aα-10aβ in my translation above only the first, in which Yahweh "heals" the Servant in verse 10aβ, comes into consideration (at least materially). Although the use of ויהוה, "But Yahweh," at the start of verse 10aα-β picks up the ויהוה that introduced the conclusion to the first part of the central section in verse 6bα-β, a mere repetition of the thought of verse 6bα-β (containing no hint of the Servant's exaltation) would not be enough for verse 10aα-β. For the following positive statement in verse 10bα ("he shall see offspring") does not itself constitute a new beginning, but taken as a continuation of verse 10aα-β it necessarily presupposes a new act of Yahweh on the Servant's behalf.[64] *Materially,* then, verse 10aα-β must speak of this new act of Yahweh, however the original text may have run in point of detail.

With verse 10bβ, "through him Yahweh's plan shall prosper," this part of the text reaches a satisfying conclusion. One could therefore consider making the first half of verse 11, up to and including the expression בְּדַעְתּוֹ in verse 11aβ (rendered above "in perceiving him"), to be part of the final Yahweh speech, even though Yahweh's "I" does not formally appear until the subsequent expression "my servant" in verse 11bα. But in my opinion the personal suffix of בְּדַעְתּוֹ ("in *his* knowledge" or "in the knowledge *of him*") does not refer to the Servant's own knowledge, a subjective genitive, but to his knowledge or percep-

---

64. Accordingly in my first translation of v. 10aα I have rendered the expression חפץ דכאו as an interjected relative clause ("But Yahweh — *whose plan it was to crush him* —") in order to prepare the way for v. 10aβ ("But Yahweh . . . *healed him*") though in the corresponding v. 6bα a construction with a relative clause of course is impossible. This incongruity is avoided by Elliger's proposal (later abandoned) of pointing דכאו as דַּכָּאוֹ (against MT דַּכְּאוֹ) and translating, "But Yahweh took pleasure in his crushed one" (Elliger, *Deuterojesaja in seinem Verhältnis zu Tritojesaja,* 7). However, the use of the same root חפץ in v. 10bβ with reference to the "plan" of the Lord seems to speak against Elliger's meaning "to take pleasure in." Moreover, when it means "to take pleasure in (a person)," as Elliger's view requires, חפץ is construed with בּ plus the person (Koole). However one decides this issue, Elliger at that time correctly stressed that the ויהוה in v. 10aα must introduce the transition from the fatal past of the Servant to his blessed future. Later in *MIOF* 15 (1969), 228ff., Elliger refers the entirety of v. 10aα-β (whose text he reconstructs) to the Servant's suffering: וַיהוָה חָפֵץ דַּכְּאוֹ וְהוּא שָׂם אָשֵׁם נַפְשׁוֹ, "But Yahweh was pleased to crush him, ⌐and he made⌐ himself a guilt offering." But aside from Elliger's substantial alteration of the text, there remains the difficulty of the abrupt transition from this statement to the immediately following change in the Servant's fortunes in v. 10b.

tion of Yahweh, an objective genitive.[65] And since Yahweh does not usually speak of himself in the third person, the final Yahweh oracle begins only in the next phrase in verse 11bα (cf. NJPS, "My righteous servant . . .").

The act of Yahweh in its essence cannot be any other than that announced in the Yahweh oracles at the beginning and end of the song, though even here pictorial expressions appear that obscure the concrete event. The salvific turning point affects even this poor, plagued, struck-down dead Servant, since offspring and length of days (v. 10bα) are the essence of a life blessed by Yahweh. He will see light and find satisfaction in perceiving Yahweh. Finally, Yahweh's plan succeeds through him. This refers to the healing and salvation of the many made possible through the Servant's suffering and death, and furthermore to the universal eschatological turning point of salvation that Yahweh effects through the Servant's ministry.

But how is all this to be understood with respect to the Servant himself, who is dead and buried? One cannot immediately introduce here the thought of a resurrection from the dead — at least there is nothing about this in the text; only our logic seems to demand it. If one respects the largely metaphorical language of the text, then this much can be said: Yahweh will acknowledge his Servant even beyond death and the grave; death imposes no limit upon his fellowship with God; God holds his Servant fast; and the turn of salvation that he helped to effect will also reach him: indeed, God will exalt him to the highest place. How this is to be imagined is not said — here the text is silent to all further questions. Perhaps the subject matter of the text can be more precisely explained in another way. Here two series of statements collide with one another, each correct in itself:

> here is guilt that must lead to death;
> here is righteousness that must lead to life.

Both are necessary conclusions according to the law of deed and consequence, and it becomes an aporia only because Yahweh has exchanged the human subjects of the two statements in verse 6: "But Yahweh. . . ." They therefore appear mutually exclusive. But in between, eliminating that contradiction, stands the second "But Yahweh" in verse 10aα. What exactly is reported here as

---

65. The Servant's knowledge did not previously play any role in the justification of the "many," unless one were to draw a connection with the יַשְׂכִּיל of 52:13 in the sense, "my servant shall *deal wisely*" (ASV) (cf. also LXX συνήσει, "he shall *understand*"). But יַשְׂכִּיל in 52:13 has — in correspondence with יִצְלָח "(through him the plan of the Lord) *shall prosper*" in 53:11 — the prevalent meaning of "he shall prosper."

the act of Yahweh remains hidden from us because of the condition of the text and the metaphorical language; even "healing" in verse 10aβ is a metaphorical expression (assuming that I have correctly reproduced the sense of the original). But "metaphorical" does *not* mean not real! It is a real divine act that eludes human imagination and therefore also the direct grasp of language.

c. 53:11b-12   The concluding divine speech sums up once again the office and reward of this Servant. He has brought the many back into a right relationship with God by surrendering his life for the sins of the many. Therefore Yahweh says: "I shall give him a portion with the many, and he will share the booty with the mighty" (NJB) — all of a sudden the Servant is no longer isolated! In order to understand this we must recall an experience from Israel's psalms of thanksgiving and lament. It is precisely the suffering one who is isolated, excluded from the society of the many. But whenever the sufferer is saved by Yahweh, he is also reintegrated and absorbed into this society. This seems to be precisely the point of the text, that the one who in view of his wretched, isolated, and fateful role was avoided by all now receives a share of salvation together with the many.[66]

This interpretation admittedly poses the problem of how to relate the Servant's integration into his society to his extraordinary exaltation in the first Yahweh oracle. We must not play them off against each another, since each statement should be understood on its own in its individual context: the deepest humiliation corresponds to the highest exaltation, and isolation to renewed integration. But beyond this, the incongruence is consciously accepted; one could even say that it is precisely as the representative of the many that the Servant is so highly exalted in the first oracle. Therefore with regard to the Servant's *future*, the "collective" interpretation contains a certain amount of truth, since Yahweh carries out his saving work through Israel *and* the Servant, and since the difference that "now" exists in the text between the two Servants will eventually lose its meaning when Israel exhibits the same trust as the prophetic Servant (cf. Isa. 49:4; 50:4-9 over against 40:27).[67] But this is not true in the text's "present" — at the time of Isaiah 53's original composition by a disciple or disciples of the prophet (as distinct from later redactional understandings represented in the "final form"; cf. part I, Introduction) — nor is it true of Isaiah 53's view of the past. For in the present and in the past the individual prophetic Servant is strictly differentiated from corporate Israel; in matters of faith and trust as well as in the bearing of guilt, the prophetic Servant is the *substitute* or

---

66. Cf. Hermisson, "Lohn," 285-87; "Israel und der Gottesknecht," 23-24.
67. Cf. Hermisson, "Israel und der Gottesknecht," 15-16.

stand-in (*Stellvertreter*) for God's Servant Israel, not Israel's *representative* (*Repräsentant*). But again one must remember that the old alternative between "collective" and "individual" falls hopelessly short, when for example the Servant *as an individual* represents the true Israel: "He said to *me*, '*You* (singular אַתָּה) are my servant, Israel, in whom I will be glorified'" (49:3).[68]

If, then, the second Yahweh oracle of the fourth song (except for the saying about the "spoil") concentrates more than the first oracle upon the Servant's relationship to *Israel*, this is in keeping with the tendency of the preceding three Servant Songs, which progress from the universal horizon of the first two texts to the inner-Israelite horizon of the third, without giving up the universal horizon.

The "spoil" or "booty" of 53:12 is nothing other than the Servant's reward, which he receives together with the many. But the Servant's reward is the success of Yahweh's saving will or plan, spoken of in verse 10bβ and introduced in the first two Servant Songs. This plan involves the divine conquest of the world (49:2) and the establishment of a salutary order in the world of nations (42:1, 4), in order that — as Yahweh informs his own Servant — "my salvation may reach to the end of the earth" (49:6).

How is this supposed to happen? Here I must pass over the somewhat complicated exegesis of the last two verses, especially v. 12a,[69] but the result is very simple. The Servant will have success when Israel finally comes to understand the suffering and death of this miserable figure; when it grasps, agrees, believes: for Yahweh has exalted precisely this suffering one, who by his vicarious suffering bore the sin — that is, the unbelief — of the "many."

The guilt of the many: This may include more than unbelief, but the dominant perspective of the text seems to me not to be devoted to various antisocial behaviors or moral offenses or the breaking of the commandments. Rather it is the sin of not turning to Yahweh, of unbelief, as already in First Isaiah (e.g., 30:15). Therefore:

> All we like sheep have gone astray;
> we have all turned to our own way (Isa. 53:6)

— where "turning to our own way" for the exiles means turning to their own miserable and resigned, but time-tested, procedure of trying to find their way as best they could in the exile instead of gathering around Yahweh (49:5).

---

68. This interpretation of "Israel" in Isa. 49:3 is not completely certain, but the alternative would be to suppose that "Israel" is an interpolation subsequently added in order to reinterpret the text.

69. Cf. Hermisson, "Lohn," 285-87.

Yahweh arranges for this עָוֹן (53:5, 6, 11), this "iniquity" with its necessary consequence of disaster, to strike the one instead of the many. But this presupposes that the many who have now come to insight and faith are not "all nations," but Israel. Yet the other nations are not forgotten. When Yahweh's plan through the Servant succeeds, then the nations come to salvation by noticing what happens to an Israel that has found its way to faith through the suffering, death, and exaltation of the Servant.

Admittedly, this exaltation of the Servant and that insight of Israel is still a future event, but it is already certain because Yahweh has said it.

Let us return in conclusion to the larger context of the last Servant Song. That this Servant stands in for the Servant Israel because the Servant Israel does not do what is expected of it is also evident elsewhere, above all in the great similarity of the predicates of both Servants. Both are "called" and "chosen," and if for Israel this means primarily the certainty of salvation, such certainty still needs to be *accepted*. Israel should constitute itself as the nation certain of its salvation and should gather around Yahweh, in order by so doing to bear witness to him. Because Israel does not and cannot do this on its own, it needs that special Servant who through his word and fate first bears witness before Israel to the God who, as the only God, wants to be the savior of Israel and thereby also of the world. Israel's inability to accept the message of salvation once again recalls the prophetic experience of the past. The sum total of this experience confronts us already in the fundamental anthropological insight of Jeremiah and requires for the eschatological future an entirely new solution: the new covenant, the new heart. Naturally the experience of past prophets repeats itself forcefully in Second Isaiah's experience of his contemporaries' rejection of his message — although now the issue is no longer the nation's ability to do good, but merely the ability to believe Yahweh's word. Yet the question about faith as the criterion for Israel is not entirely new. It was already the favorite theme of the great prophet Isaiah in the eighth century.

On the basis of such experiences, the older prophets or their school (as in the case of the new covenant of "Jeremiah") formulated various expectations, which always expressed in their different ways how Yahweh would repair such damage. But the way in which Second Isaiah and his school expect the coming of salvation is entirely different and leads far beyond those expectations. For now salvation is no longer effected only by a future change in humanity or a coming figure or a still outstanding act of God in Israel. Rather, it occurs in the suffering and death of a contemporary messenger of God through whom Israel is supposed to come to knowledge and faith. Naturally there remains a need for a future act of God, his exaltation of his Servant, which awakens Israel's insight. What the author of the last Servant Song concretely had in mind by this we do not know, because the text obscures it, speaking in pictures and well-known categories of death and life, humiliation and exaltation. But the author also did not have to say it any more precisely: it was Yahweh's coming work, whose significance was adequately described by the well-known categories. Interpreters often correctly stress that nothing is said about the resurrection of the dead; but whether it was conceptually *possible* to speak about this in the sixth century is a completely different question and not so easy to deny. In any case it was not *necessary* for the author to speak so concretely, nor was it possible, because it remained Yahweh's miracle. And if a future miracle of Yahweh is needed, then even here it is strictly and necessarily and materially related to the suffering and death of a contemporary figure, God's messenger. He proclaimed God's salvation and thereby experienced suffering, but took this suffering upon himself as God's delegate and in the certainty of reward.

III. Excursus: The Traditio-Historical Problem of Vicarious Suffering[70]

Scholars often have wished to derive the statements of the last Servant Song from Babylonian tradition. For example, the cult of the dying and rising vegetation god Tammuz with his liturgies is sometimes thought to stand in the background. But this thesis fails because, according to recent investigations, Tammuz descended into the underworld but never came up again.[71] Scholars have also found a paradigmatic example of vicarious or substitutionary suffering in the "suffering" of the king in the Babylonian New Year ritual or in the Babylonian custom of the substitute king, who in circumstances of threatened disaster had to take the real king's place. But as J. Scharbert has helpfully shown,[72] none of these comes seriously into consideration as a pattern for Isaiah 53.

If one asks about the prehistory of the office depicted here, one is rather referred to the Old Testament traditions.[73] There are primarily two lines of tra-

---

70. For a thorough treatment of *Stellvertretung* or "vicarious suffering" see the essay of B. Janowski in this volume.

71. Cf. O. R. Gurney, "Tammuz Reconsidered: Some Recent Developments," *JSS* 7 (1962): 147-60.

72. J. Scharbert, "Stellvertretendes Sühneleiden in den Ebed-Jahwe-Liedern und in altorientalischen Ritualtexten," *BZ* 2 (1958): 190-213.

73. On the following see G. von Rad, *Theologie des Alten Testaments* vol. 2, 4th ed. (1965), 2:285-90 = ET, *Old Testament Theology*, 2 vols. (1965), 2:273-77, as well as the essay in this volume by H. Spieckermann, "The Conception and Prehistory of the Idea of Vicarious Suffering in the Old Testament," above, pp. 1-15.

dition. One comes from the prophet's office as a mediator who intercedes before Yahweh. This is old and can be observed as early as Amos; Moses also appears in this role in Numbers 14, although this is perhaps later. The other line of tradition is characterized by the experience of prophetic suffering, which increasingly — especially in the case of Jeremiah — becomes a non-negotiable part of the prophetic office. Jeremiah's suffering still remained without any function of its own; it is simply what befalls him, a trial, a consequence of his ministry, to be suffered but not to be understood. Yet in Jeremiah's confessions both lines of tradition are combined, because here the prophet's suffering is provoked precisely by his office as mediator.

Both models also come together in the picture of Moses in Deuteronomy. Moses is a prophetic figure — the mediator who intercedes for the people before Yahweh — but also a suffering one, with hints that he even suffers vicariously for the people. The thought of vicarious suffering is therefore not completely new; in the cultic realm it is already existent with the scapegoat that is sent away into the desert on the Day of Atonement (Leviticus 16).

Nevertheless, the figure of the Suffering Servant, the one who takes away the sin of the many and atones for it through his suffering and death, is not simply to be derived from all of this. The tradition only provides the means to facilitate an expression that far transcends all that is traditional (so also H. Spieckermann).

That such vicarious atonement of the one for the many is an integral part of the turning point of salvation is not said anywhere else in Second Isaiah. Outside Isaiah 53 Yahweh himself sets sin aside on his own initiative or, as he himself says, "for my own sake" (e.g., Isa. 43:25). In interpreting Second Isaiah's fate, this text goes beyond Second Isaiah.

IV. Appendix: Theses on the Servant in Isaiah

1. The office of the Servant described in the Servant Songs of Second Isaiah is a prophetic office.

2. As a prophetic office the Servant role is characterized by a series of royal features, certainly in the first two songs, and then partially at the beginning of the last servant text. But the suffering of the Servant is not part of this.

2.1. The possibility of taking up royal elements into the prophetic office is already present in the tradition: a similar connection is already found in the report of Jeremiah's call. The significance of this report is that it shows that the universal sphere of activity that belongs to the prophet belongs to him as Yahweh's delegate. The scope of his office is comparable to that of the king according to the Jerusalem royal tradition, but in contrast to the king, the prophet exercises his office only through the word entrusted to him.

2.2. However, the transfer of statements of royal status to the office of the prophet must be seen within a larger theological context in Second Isaiah. Even if there is no room for an expected Messiah as the ruler of the age of salvation, nevertheless the prophet took up the messianic tradition — to the extent that it is already existent — or in any case he took up the royal tradition and by an original interpretation he distributed it among three entities: the people of Israel, Cyrus, and the Servant.[74] Each of these three entities is given a function in the eschatological turning point of salvation, and each in its own way plays a part in effecting universal salvation: *Cyrus* in world conquest and the subjection of the nations, and therefore in a temporally limited kingdom; *Israel* as Yahweh's passive witness, the object of his saving activity; and the *Servant* as his active witness, who through his proclamation establishes Yahweh's salutary order to the ends of the earth.

2.3. It follows from this that the Servant of the Servant Songs cannot carry out his office without the Servant Israel. His worldwide ministry essentially consists of the fact that he calls and empowers Israel for its office of Servant by leading it back to Yahweh. Beyond this, the correlation of the prophetic Servant and the Servant Israel is absolutely necessary in another way, as illustrated by the proof from prophecy: Yahweh's creative word of salvation for Israel, which dealt with Cyrus's victory on behalf of Israel and Israel's salvation, was brought into the world through the prophet, publicly proclaimed, and realized in Israel. Through the cooperation of the two Servants, it becomes evident to the world that Yahweh alone is the saving God. And so the nations also come to salvation through their acknowledgment of the only saving God, an acknowledgment based on the fulfillment of the salvific word already realized in Israel.

2.4. Even if we see here more of an "indirect" effect of the prophetic Servant upon the nations (since the procedure gets into gear only by the gathering of Israel to Yahweh), nevertheless the second Servant Song and above all a text like 45:22-23 (as well as the judgment speeches against the foreign nations) show an immediate ministry of the prophetic Servant to the nations. He has a saving word to proclaim to them in Yahweh's name, which invites all and certainly will bring all to Yahweh — as surely as Yahweh's oath is valid and he does what he says (45:22-23).

3. The bearer of the royal prophetic office of the Servant Songs is the

---

74. Cf. O. H. Steck, "Deuterojesaja als theologischer Denker" (1969), reprint in idem, *Wahrnehmungen Gottes im Alten Testament: Gesammelte Studien,* TB 70 (1982), 204-20, esp. 213 n. 12.

prophet Second Isaiah himself. In view of the statements of the fourth Servant Song, this presupposes that the text was composed not by the prophet but in the circle of his pupils.

3.1. This specific prophetic Servant is occasionally spoken about outside the Servant Songs, for example, in 43:10, once again in correlation to the Servant Israel as Yahweh's witness, then also in 44:26, in the self-predication of Yahweh as the one "who confirms the word of his (prophetic) servant."

3.2. The interpretation of the Servant as applying to the prophet himself can be attested also with a text like Isaiah 44:21. This is an admonitory word with which the prophet accomplishes exactly that which, according to 49:5, is the task of the Servant: namely, to bring Israel to the Yahweh who creates salvation. Finally the so-called proof from prophecy, which is central to the proclamation of Second Isaiah, presupposes the correlation of both Servants (see above §2.3).

3.3. The interpretation advocated here is nevertheless not simply "individual" or even "autobiographical." It seeks to do justice to the collective and supra-individual traits in the Servant Songs and to the correspondence between the two Servants. The prophet represents in part the "true Israel." He understands his role in connection to his society and as the summation of previous prophecy, through which Yahweh now as always sends his creative word into the history of Israel. The prophetic Servant cannot accomplish this task alone, but only in connection with the Servant Israel.

3.4. The special feature of these texts — their floating, metaphorical, tradition-bound expressions — allows no biographical interpretation in detail. The whole tradition of the prophetic office, the experience of many prophets, has flowed into the presentation of this office. Therefore it is correct to say that the texts have in mind the prophetic office as such. But they are not simply a summary of the tradition. The unusually heightened dimensions of this office correspond to the universal dimension of the turn of salvation. Therefore it is absurd to accuse this prophet of overestimating himself or to use this argument to nullify the interpretation that applies the text to the prophet. He is the bearer of the office as it must present itself now, at the salvific turning point.

3.5. Accordingly the texts are — except for a part of the last one — not prophecy. Rather their supra-individual feature as well as their overly large dimension is simultaneously their future dimension: they are not finished with their reference to that concrete prophet; their truth is not thereby exhausted. They are not prophecies of Christ, but no violence is done to them when they now, after the fact, are used to open up a correct understanding of the Christ event. They can appropriately be used to express the Christ event because they speak of God's eschatological work of salvation toward Israel and the world, and so in the final analysis, they speak of the *same God*. To the extent that he is a figure in whom God's eschatological work comes to expression, the Servant of the Servant Songs is a "type" of the Servant Jesus Christ.

4. The task of the Servant develops at various levels. Even if his task is at first only the limited one of "bringing Israel back" in the spiritual and political sense of the word (49:5-6), nevertheless this task becomes one that is extended to the nations: through the Servant's ministry they receive a share in salvation. Once again we need not ask whether Second Isaiah first became aware of his task to Israel and then of his task to the nations. Rather, in the sequence hinted at in Isaiah 49, there is theological reflection about how the salvation of the world of nations is related to the salvation of Israel, and how all this relates to the office of the Servant. It is precisely in Yahweh's active deliverance of Israel that the nations will recognize and acknowledge Yahweh and so become a part of the plan of salvation. If in the third song the prophet's suffering belongs to his office as the self-evident consequence of prophetic ministry, in the fourth song it becomes something more: the immediate content of the ministry that Yahweh imposed on the Servant. It is precisely through his suffering — the one for the many — that the Servant will fulfill his task.

5. The traditional sequence of the texts outwardly displays a clear progression of events and is therefore to be retained. After the Servant's presentation before Yahweh's throne and the declaration of his mission to the nations in 42:1-4, Yahweh's delegate appears before the nations in a proclamation of his empowerment and installation into office (49:1ff.). The third text speaks of suffering as the necessary consequence of his ministry, while the fourth speaks finally of the suffering, death, and future exaltation in which the meaning of the Servant's suffering will become clear.

5.1. The overall context becomes even more clear in another motif that appears in its own way in all four texts: namely, the certainty of success, of reward, of the justification or vindication of the Servant. Hence 42:4 says that he will not grow faint or be crushed until he has established the justice (מִשְׁפָּט) of Yahweh upon the earth. In 49:4 and 50:7-9 the Servant himself expresses such certainty in a word of trust and a confession of confidence. And this is exactly what stands at the beginning and end of the last text, which begins, "See, my servant shall prosper" (52:13), and in so doing connects back to the first text. But now there lies in between the public failure of the Servant: his suffering to the point of a shameful death. What the "many" considered to be only the wretched end of a miserable figure lay precisely within Yahweh's saving plan: God acknowledges his failed Servant, and through this failure, God will bring the many to salvation and success and reward to the Servant — that is the certainty of the last Servant text.

He Bore Our Sins: Isaiah 53 and
the Drama of Taking Another's Place

Bernd Janowski

For Hans Walter Wolff

Summary

A drama of delayed recognition in Isaiah 53 provides an alternative to Immanuel Kant's narrow understanding of representation or "taking another's place"
(German *Stellvertretung*), which insists that no person can represent or take
the place of another in matters of personal guilt. In this passage, the "we" figures (who stand for all Israel) do eventually come to see themselves and their
guilt represented in the fate of another — the Servant whom they formerly despised and who had already borne their sins by making his life an *asham*, the
means of wiping out guilt. Yet this recognition of the Servant's representative,
vicarious suffering is delayed until after the innocent death of the Servant, here
identical with the prophet Second Isaiah himself. Prior to the Servant's death,
Israel wrongly assumed that his sufferings were the result of *his own* guilt, according to traditional understandings of actions and their consequences (the
so-called "action-consequences connection"). Hence they kept their distance
from this "man of sorrows" (v. 3), accounting him "stricken, struck down by
God, and afflicted" (v. 4). Yahweh's oracle about the Servant's success (52:13-
15) was therefore needed to help the "we" recognize that it was *their* sin that
he was bearing (53:4-6; cf. vv. 11b-12). Only when the "we" see this can they

---

Originally an inaugural lecture at the University of Heidelberg on July 1, 1992, this essay
has been expanded for publication by the addition of the footnotes. It first appeared in
German in *ZTK* 90 (1993): 1-24. The terminology of *Stellvertretung* or "place-taking" has
been specially adapted and explained in the English version (see below, pp. 52-54, passim).
The translator has also updated the bibliographic entries in nn. 11, 14. For simplicity's sake
the designation "Isaiah 53" refers to Isa. 52:13–53:12 as a whole.

acknowledge their guilt as well as its cancellation, becoming changed in the process.

I. The Problem

Few religious texts of antiquity have been so influential yet puzzling as the biblical stories of the "suffering righteous."[1] What they have in common with comparable texts from Mesopotamia and Egypt[2] is a particular, decidedly strange view of righteousness: the righteous live by their faithfulness and suffer *because* they are righteous. That is a paradox in the true sense of the word. It contradicts another, more traditional view of reality in which every consequence relates back to a corresponding action and all deeds come back upon their doers either for good or for evil. This circular, or rather reciprocal, structuring of activity is deprived of its force in the suffering righteous tradition. For wherever suffering is understood as a consequence of guilt — as it is, for example, when viewed from the perspective of the *Tun-Ergehen-Zusammenhang* or "action-consequences connection"[3] — the sufferer cannot be one of the righteous. Ex-

1. See L. Ruppert, *Der leidende Gerechte: Eine motivgeschichtliche Untersuchung zum Alten Testament und zwischentestamentlichen Judentum*, FB 5 (1972); K. T. Kleinknecht, *Der leidende Gerechtfertigte: Die alttestamentlich-jüdische Tradition vom "leidenden Gerechten" und ihre Rezeption bei Paulus*, 2nd ed., WUNT 2/13 (1988); and finally G. Barth, *Der Tod Jesu Christi im Verständnis des Neuen Testaments* (1992), 28ff. A four-stage "typology of the suffering righteous" has been proposed by H.-J. Klimkeit, "Der leidende Gerechte in der Religionsgeschichte: Ein Beitrag zur problemorientierten 'Religionsphänomenologie,'" in H. Zinser, ed., *Religionswissenschaft: Eine Einführung* (1988), 164-84, following a suggestion by H. H. Schmid. See more recently H. H. Schmid, "Alttestamentliche Voraussetzungen neutestamentlicher Christologie," *JBTh* 6 (1991): 33-45, esp. 38ff.

2. For Mesopotamia see the representative collection of texts by W. von Soden, "'Weisheitstexte' in akkadischer Sprache," *TUAT* 3/1 (1990): 110-88. For Egypt see J. Assmann, "Der 'leidende Gerechte' im alten Ägypten: Zum Konfliktpotential der ägyptischen Religion," in C. Elsas and H. G. Kippenberg, eds., *Loyalitätskonflikte in der Religionsgeschichte: Festschrift für Carsten Colpe* (1990), 203-24.

3. The German technical term *Tun-Ergehen-Zusammenhang* (or *Tat-Ergehen-Zusammenhang*, "deed-consequence connection") was first coined by K. Koch in his dissertation "Die israelitische Sühneanschauung und ihre historischen Wandlungen," D. Habil., Erlangen, 1956. The term reflects a particular view of the connection between deed and consequence that interprets all consequences as the result of deeds and sees God as the active guarantor of this connection. See the overview by K. Koch and J. Roloff, "Tat-Ergehen-Zusammenhang," in K. Koch et al., eds., *Reclams Bibellexikon*, 4th ed. (1987), 493-95, and further H.-D. Preuss, *Theologie des Alten Testaments*, vol. 1 (1991), 209-20 ("Der Tun-Ergehen-Zusammenhang") = ET, *Old Testament Theology*, trans. L. G. Perdue, vol. 1 (1995), 184-94 ("The

pressions about righteousness cannot even be used: the "righteous" cannot suffer; those who suffer cannot be called "righteous." Correlation of righteousness and suffering becomes plausible only in a context where traditional understandings of the relationship between actions and consequences have broken down.

Although they all share this context, the *passio iusti* texts from Mesopotamia, Egypt, and Israel also display significant differences among them. In comparison with Egypt, for example, Israel has gone its own way by associating the suffering of the righteous with the hope of being rescued by God: "Many are the afflictions of the righteous, but the Lord rescues them from them all" (Ps. 34:20 [ET 19]). But the problem acquires its most marked contours — outside of Job — in Isaiah 53 and its idea of vicarious suffering. P. Volz believes that this idea gave Jewish theodicy a completely new appearance:

> Only when we sympathize with the pressures that lay upon the pious in that ancient period can we understand the wonderful feeling of liberation expressed in Isaiah 53. The new solution topples the old theory that allowed suffering to be taken as evidence of guilt even in the case of the most pious — the terrible, tyrannical theory under which Job suffered so miserably. . . . We are at the historical source from which the idea of vicarious suffering sprang.[4]

Today the formula of vicarious suffering is as familiar to us as it is difficult for us to explain. Ever since Kant's work on religion of 1793, it has been asserted repeatedly that the idea of vicarious suffering is no longer comprehensible because guilt, as an "intrinsic personal feature,"[5] is nontransferable. Guilt, according to Kant, is

---

Connection between Deed and Consequence"). In English see also K. Koch, "Is There a Doctrine of Retribution in the Old Testament?" (German: "Gibt es ein Vergeltungsdogma im Alten Testament?" [1955]), trans. T. H. Trapp in J. L. Crenshaw, ed., *Theodicy in the Old Testament* (1983), 57-87, esp. 58-64 (cf. 68, 73, 80: "Action-Consequences-Construct"). Whether Koch's view is tenable in all respects cannot be discussed here; see the critical inquiries in J. Assmann, "Vergeltung und Erinnerung," in *Studien zu Religion und Sprache Ägyptens: Festschrift für W. Westendorf* (1984), 687-701; idem, *Ma'at: Gerechtigkeit und Unsterblichkeit im Alten Ägypten* (1990), 60ff., 177ff., 253-54, 283ff.; idem, *Das kulturelle Gedächtnis: Schrift, Erinnerung und politische Identität in frühen Hochkulturen* (1992), 232ff.; and B. Janowski, "Der Tat kehrt zum Täter zurück: Offene Fragen im Umkreis des 'Tun-Ergehen-Zusammenhangs,'" *ZTK* 91 (1994): 247-71.

4. P. Volz, "Jesaja 53," in K. Marti, ed., *Karl Budde zum siebzigssten Geburtstag am 13. April 1920*, BZAW 34 (1920), 180-90, esp. 185-86.

5. German: "unveräußerliches Persönlichkeitsmerkmal."

not a *transmissible* liability which can be made over to somebody else, in the manner of a financial debt (where it is all the same to the creditor whether the debtor himself pays up, or somebody else for him), but the *most personal* of all liabilities, namely a debt of sins which only the culprit, not the innocent, can bear, however magnanimous the innocent might be in wanting to take the debt upon himself for the other.[6]

The difficulties with the idea of vicarious suffering come in this case from a particular view of humanity, namely, from the axiom of the *nonrepresentability of the subject:* as long as the subject sets the standard for his own responsibility, guilt, too, remains his alone and cannot be taken away by anything or anyone. "Guilt is always one's own, because it is attached to the ego, and no one can give anyone else his ego."[7] However, before we accept uncritically this subject-centered theory of guilt, which makes the sinner merciless toward himself and blind to the "other"[8] who might be more accommodating toward him, and be-

---

6. Immanuel Kant, "Religion within the Boundaries of Mere Reason," in idem, *Religion and Rational Theology,* trans. and ed. A. W. Wood and G. Di Giovanni (1996), 113 (at 6:72). (A fuller citation of this passage from Kant is included within the present volume by O. Hofius in his n. 27.) Kant's German runs: "[Die Schuld] ist keine *transmissible* Verbindlichkeit, die etwa, wie eine Geldschuld (bei der es dem Gläubiger einerlei ist, ob der Schuldner selbst oder ein anderer für ihn bezahlt), auf einen anderen übertragen werden kann, sondern die *allerpersönlichste,* nämlich die Sündenschuld, die nur der Strafbare, nicht der Unschuldige, er mag auch noch so großmütig sein, sie für jenen übernehmen zu wollen, tragen kann." Text: "Die Religion innerhalb der Grenzen der bloßen Vernunft" (1st ed., 1793; 2nd ed., 1794) in *Kants gesammelte Schriften,* ed. Königlich Preußischen Akademie der Wissenschaften, vol. 6 (1907), 72. For a criticism of this idealistic thesis about persons being "irreplaceable" and therefore (!) "unrepresentable" see D. Sölle, *Stellvertretung: Ein Kapitel Theologie nach dem "Tode Gottes,"* 2nd ed. (1982), 30-40 (pp. 35-47 in the 1st ed. of 1965) = ET, *Christ the Representative: An Essay in Theology after the "Death of God,"* trans. D. Lewis (1967), 31-38. Sölle proposes the counter-thesis that people are "irreplaceable" *(unersetzlich)* but nevertheless "representable" *(vertretbar)* (pp. 44-54 = ET 43-50). On Kant's understanding of vicarious suffering see G. Wenz, *Geschichte der Versöhnungslehre in der evangelischen Theologie der Neuzeit,* vol. 1 (1984), 223ff., esp. 226-27.

7. G. Friedrich, *Die Verkündigung des Todes Jesu im Neuen Testament,* 2nd ed., BThSt 6 (1985), 151. For criticism of this axiom see K. Lehmann, "'Er wurde für uns gekreuzigt': Eine Skizze zur Neubesinnung in der Soteriologie," *TQ* 162 (1982): 298-317, esp. 311ff.; W. Breuning, "Wie kann man heute von Sühne reden?" *BK* 41 (1986): 76-82, esp. 79-80; and C. Link, "'Für uns gestorben nach der Schrift,'" *EvErz* 43 (1991): 148-69, esp. 148ff., 165ff.

8. Both Lehmann "'Er wurde für uns gekreuzigt,'" 315-16, and Breuning, "Wie kann man heute von Sühne reden?" 79-80, refer in this connection to the category of the "other" as described by E. Lévinas, "La trace de l'autre," in *En découvrant l'existence avec Husserl et Heidegger,* 4th ed. (1982), 195ff., where tellingly Lévinas speaks about Isaiah 53 on p. 196 (unfortunately this essay is not included in the English version, *Discovering Existence with Husserl,* trans. R. A. Cohen and M. B. Smith [1998]). See also Lévinas, "La substitution," *Revue philosophique de Louvain*

fore we follow scholars like G. Friedrich in consigning the idea of vicarious suffering to theological meaninglessness,[9] we should reflect more intensively about other possible understandings. A text like Isaiah 53 provides a good place to start.

In order to give at least a hint of the direction in which the following reflections are headed, I begin with a few remarks on the concept of vicarious suffering or "vicariousness" — what we in German call simply *Stellvertretung*, "place-taking" or "taking another's place," though the German is conventionally translated into English by either "representation" or "substitution" (usually two different ideas).[10] The German abstract noun "place-taking" first came into being rather late, in the course of the eighteenth century and in the context of Socinian criticism of the doctrine of satisfaction within Old Protestant orthodoxy.[11] Luther did not yet use the noun; but he did use verbal paraphrases for

66 (1968): 487-508, esp. 499-504 = ET, "Substitution," in A. T. Peperzak, S. Critchley, and R. Bernasconi, eds., *Emanuel Levinas: Basic Philosophical Writings* (1996), 79-95, esp. 89-93. In German see Lévinas, *Die Spur des Anderen: Untersuchungen zur Phänomenologie und Sozialphilosophie*, trans. and ed. W. N. Krewani (1983), 222ff., 315ff. On this topic see also C. Gestrich, *Die Wiederkehr des Glanzes in der Welt: Die christliche Lehre von der Sünde und ihrer Vergebung in gegenwärtiger Verantwortung* (1989), 342-49 = ET, *The Return of Splendor in the World: The Christian Doctrine of Sin and Forgiveness*, trans. D. W. Bloesch (1997), 305-10.

9. See Friedrich, *Die Verkündigung des Todes Jesu im Neuen Testament*, 150-51, and Barth, *Der Tod Jesu Christi im Verständnis des Neuen Testaments*, 3, 68, although the latter sees the problem in more nuanced terms (cf. pp. 37ff., 68ff., 158-59).

10. For the following see Sölle, *Stellvertretung*, 17ff. = ET, *Christ the Representative*, 17ff.; E. Jüngel, "Das Geheimnis der Stellvertretung: Ein dogmatisches Gespräch mit Heinrich Vogel" (1984), reprinted in idem, *Wertlose Wahrheit: Zur Identität und Relevanz des christlichen Glaubens: Theologische Erörterungen III*, BEvT 107 (1990), 243-60; and H.-R. Reuter, "Stellvertretung: Erwägungen zu einer dogmatischen Kategorie im Gespräch mit René Girard und Raymund Schwager," in J. Niewiadomski and J. Palaver, eds., *Dramatische Erlösungslehre: Ein Symposion*, Innsbrucker theologische Studien 38 (1992), 179-99. With the help of a general structural formula for the place-taking relationship, Weiss elsewhere develops a typology of the material accomplishments of place-taking. See J. Weiss, "Stellvertretung: Überlegungen zu einer vernachlässigten soziologischen Kategorie," *Kölner Zeitschrift für Soziologie* 36 (1984), 43-55, esp. 45ff.

11. According to K.-H. Menke, *Stellvertretung: Schlüsselbegriff christlichen Lebens und theologische Grundkategorie* (1991), 82ff., the earliest known occurrence of the term *Stellvertretung* is to be found in the work of the Erlangen mediating theologian G. F. Seiler, *Über den Versöhnungstod Jesu Christi*, 2 vols. (1778-79) (referred to also by Reuter, "Stellvertretung," 181 n. 6); cf. Jüngel, "Geheimnis der Stellvertretung," 250 n. 12. On the problem in the history of theology see Wenz, *Geschichte der Versöhnungslehre in der evangelischen Theologie der Neuzeit*, vol. 1, 119ff. On *Stellvertretung* (rendered in the following English translations by "representation" [Sölle; Pannenberg, *Theology*]; "substitution" [Pannenberg, *Jesus*]; or "substitutionary action" [Gestrich]) as a central Christian category see Sölle, *Stellvertretung*, 54-61 = ET, *Christ the Representative*, 51-56; Gestrich, *Die Wiederkehr des Glanzes in der Welt*, 320-75 = ET, *The Return of Splendor in the World*, 285-337; W. Pannenberg, *Grundzüge der Christologie*, 3rd ed. (1969),

the idea it represents, for example: "Jesus Christ, God's Son, came *in our stead*" ("an unserer Statt," WA 35:443 line 21). We may therefore suspect that when the German word for *place-taking* came into use, its task was to bring a concept previously formulated with *verbs* to expression as a technical *term*.[12] The German abstract noun must therefore actually be read as a *noun of action*, fully in accordance with the biblical traditions that have preserved the originally verbal structure of place-taking. Thus in the New Testament the idea of place-taking is expressed with the help of verbs qualified by the prepositions ἀντί, διά, περί, and especially ὑπέρ, as well as by prepositionally augmented nouns like ἀντάλλαγμα, ἀντίλυτρον, περικάθαρμα, and others. These terms say that one person has done or suffered something "instead of" *(anstatt)* or "in place of" *(an Stelle)* other persons. "And because that which was done or suffered 'instead of' or 'in place of' others is a negative event that is thereby spared them, these terms have at the same time the positive meaning 'for' or 'on behalf of.'"[13] The Old Testament means something similar when it formulates the idea of place-taking with the help of prepositionally qualified verbs like נָתַן תַּחַת, "to give *in place of/for*" (e.g., Isa. 43:4) or with the help of the expressions סבל or נשׂא plus a term for sin or sickness, "to bear sin(s)/sickness(es)" (e.g., Isa. 53:4, 11-12).[14] It always means that one person, by some action or suffering, takes the

---

265-77 ("Der Tod Jesu als Stellvertretung") = ET, *Jesus — God and Man,* trans. L. L. Wilkins and D. A. Priebe (1968), 258-69 ("Jesus' Death as Substitution"); Pannenberg, *Systematische Theologie,* vol. 2 (1991), 460, 461-83 ("Stellvertretung als Form des Heilsgeschehens") = ET, *Systematic Theology,* trans. G. W. Bromiley, vol. 2 (1994), 415, 416-37 ("Representation as the Form of the Salvation Event"). See now also C. Gestrich, *Christentum und Stellvertretung: Religionsphilosophische Untersuchungen zum Heilsverständnis und zur Grundlegung der Theologie* (2001), G. Röhser, *Stellvertretung im Neuen Testament,* SBS 195 (2002), and the five-part article on "Stellvertretung" in *TRE* 32 (2001), 133-53, with contributions by P. Gerlitz, H. Spieckermann, C. Thoma, G. Röhser, C. Gestrich, and T. Hüttenberger.

12. Cf. Jüngel, "Geheimnis der Stellvertretung," 250-51.

13. Jüngel, "Geheimnis der Stellvertretung," 251. On the relevant expressions and especially the ὑπέρ formula see now Barth, *Der Tod Jesu Christi im Verständnis des Neuen Testaments,* 41ff. (lit.) and further Reuter, "Stellvertretung," 179, who describes what these expressions have in common as follows: "First, they express that one person has done or suffered something 'in place of' *(anstelle)* another. Secondly, they say that the deed or suffering of that person has resulted 'because of' *(wegen)* the sin or guilt of other persons. Thirdly, they express that the deed or suffering of that one person has taken place 'on behalf of' *(zugunsten)* all other persons."

14. Unfortunately there is no monograph devoted to the Hebrew words associated with the idea of place-taking in the Old Testament. But of course there are individual analyses of the terms mentioned above or of similar expressions. See, for example, R. Knierim, *Die Hauptbegriffe für Sünde im Alten Testament,* 2nd ed. (1967), 50ff., 114ff., 193ff., 203ff., 217ff., and W. Zimmerli, "Zur Vorgeschichte von Jes 53" (1969), reprinted in idem, *Studien zur alttestamentlichen Theologie und Prophetie,* TB 51 (1974), 213-21. As the picture of the symbolic "bearing" of Israel's guilt in

"place"[15] of others who are not willing or able to take it up themselves. According to the definition of the social ethicist H.-R. Reuter, place-taking ultimately points to the "idea of an intercession of one person for all others as a reality that is already given to reason."[16] The fourth Servant Song is about this reality.

The general horizons of the theme "Isaiah 53 and the Drama of Taking Another's Place" have now been defined. The problem is that on the basis of Isaiah 53, no one-dimensional answer can be given to the question, Who ultimately is the subject who has brought about the Servant's vicarious action or suffering? Was it the Servant himself, Israel (the "we"),[17] or God?[18] Isaiah 53 presents a "dramatic" event that involves several "actors." We shall approach it first through its wider context. This includes the question of the relationship of Isaiah 53 to the rest of the Servant Songs (II/1) as well as the question of the Servant's identity (II/2). After these questions have been answered, Isaiah 53 itself must have its say (III).

II. The Context of Isaiah 53

1. *Isaiah 53 and the First Three Servant Songs*

It is highly significant for interpretation that Isaiah 52:13–53:12 has many connections with the other Servant Songs.[19] (The first three Servant Songs are Isa-

---

Ezek. 4:4-8 shows (see Zimmerli, "Zur Vorgeschichte," 217ff), a proper analysis of place-taking would have to deal with the topic of the "symbolic actions" of the prophets. (See now the essay of H. Spieckermann in the present volume, pp. 1-15.) Also relevant are prophetic or priestly "intercession" and the representation of God or the divine through an "image" (Gen. 1:26ff., etc.). On intercession see R. Le Déaut, "Aspects de l'intercession dans le Judaïsme ancien," *JSJ* 1 (1970): 35-57. On the problem of images see K.-H. Bernhardt, *Gott und Bild: Ein Beitrag zur Begründung des Bilderverbotes im Alten Testament*, ThA 2 (1956), 61ff.; S. Schroer, *In Israel gab es Bilder: Nachrichten von darstellender Kunst im Alten Testament*, OBO 74 (1987), 322ff. Finally on place-taking or substitution in the history of religion see G. Lanczkowski, "Stellvertretung," *RGG*[3] 6 (1962), 356-57; P. Gerlitz, "Stellvertretung I," *TRE* 32 (2001), 133-35.

15. On the "local" dimension of place-taking see Gestrich, *Die Wiederkehr des Glanzes in der Welt*, 327-28 = ET, *The Return of Splendor in the World*, 291, who speaks of the different "places" people can occupy.

16. H.-R. Reuter in W. Huber and H.-R. Reuter, *Friedensethik* (1990), 272.

17. On the role of the "we" see below.

18. Cf. Reuter, "Stellvertretung," 179, who asks similar questions regarding the subject who caused Christ to suffer in place of others.

19. For the following see especially H.-J. Hermisson, "Israel und der Gottesknecht bei Deuterojesaja," *ZTK* 79 (1982): 1-24; idem, "Der Lohn des Knechts," in Jörg Jeremias and

iah 42:1-4; 49:1-6; and 50:4-9.) Thus in Isaiah 52:13a — "Behold, my servant shall prosper" — the fourth Song is introduced by a formulation that reaches back explicitly to 42:1-4, the first Servant Song. The Servant is there introduced with the formula, "Behold my servant, whom I uphold, my chosen, in whom my soul delights!" (42:1a). This Servant is given a task with respect to the nations — the task of bringing מִשְׁפָּט and תּוֹרָה to the nations and coastlands (42:1bβ, 3b, 4aβ, b). This linking of the fourth with the first Song raises the question of the function of the second and third Songs that stand in between. Although this question can be answered only at the level of the book of Second Isaiah as a whole, it is nevertheless not difficult to see that both between the first and second and between the second and third Songs, connections exist that operate by means of particular keywords and motifs.

Thus the connection between 42:1-4 and 49:1-6, the first and second Songs, is established by means of the motif of the *nations*. In 49:1 the call to the "coastlands" (אִיִּים) and "peoples" or "nations" (לְאֻמִּים) to pay attention connects with the motif of the nations in 42:1bβ and 4b (גּוֹיִם and אִיִּים). This shows that the second Servant Song is designed to be an explanation of the task already given the Servant, that of being a "light to the nations": "I give you as a light to the nations (אוֹר גּוֹיִם), that my salvation may reach to the end of the earth" (49:6b).

By contrast, the connection between 49:1-6 and 50:4-9, the second and third Songs, is formed by means of the motif of *complaint* and *trust*. It is striking that in 50:4-9 the complaint of 49:4a is lacking and is replaced in 50:5aβ-6 by

---

L. Perlitt, eds., *Die Botschaft und die Boten: Festschrift für H. W. Wolff* (1981), 269-87; O. H. Steck, "Aspekte des Gottesknechts in Deuterojesajas 'Ebed-Jahwe-Liedern'" (1984), reprinted in idem, *Gottesknecht und Zion: Gesammelte Aufsätze zu Deuterojesaja*, FAT 4 (1992), 3-21; idem, "Aspekte des Gottesknechts in Jesaja 52,13–53,12," in idem, *Gottesknecht und Zion*, 22-43. Our present concern is the primary meaning of the four Songs and their relationship to each other from the perspective of the problem of place-taking, which is only one (albeit important) part of the overall topic. The Servant Songs were freshly appropriated and productively updated in the course of their reception over three centuries, in which their primary meaning further developed and changed. On this see the summary by O. H. Steck, "Gottesvolk und Gottesknecht in Jes 40–66," *JBTh* 7 (1992): 51-75, but also R. G. Kratz, *Kyros im Deuterojesaja-Buch: Redaktionsgeschichtliche Untersuchungen zu Entstehung und Theologie von Jes 40–55*, FAT 1 (1991), 144ff.; O. H. Steck, "Die Gottesknechts-Texte und ihre redaktionelle Rezeption im Zweiten Jesaja," in idem, *Gottesknecht und Zion*, 149-72. On the difference between the primary meaning and secondary interpretations see above all M. Weippert, "Die 'Konfessionen' Deuterojesajas," in R. Albertz, F. W. Golka, and J. Kegler, eds., *Schöpfung und Befreiung: Festschrift für C. Westermann* (1989), 104-15, and M. Saebø, "Vom Individuellen zum Kollektiven: Zur Frage einiger innerbiblischer Interpretationen," in *Schöpfung und Befreiung: Festschrift für C. Westermann* (1989), 116-25.

a confession of confidence. The third Song is recited wholly on the basis of the confidence of 49:4b, 5b and is marked by the motif of trust: "He who vindicates me is near: who will contend with me? Let us stand up together!" (50:8a).

Finally, the connection between 50:4-9 and 42:1-4, the third and first Songs, is established by means of the הֵן formula ("behold"). The double "behold" of 50:9 (cf. RSV) that brings the first three Songs to an emphatic close may be a backward reference to the "behold" of 42:1a. At the same time it may mark a break before the "behold" of 52:13. The Servant's future is thereby left totally in the hands of God, who will help him get justice in the face of all his enemies: "[Behold,] the Lord God helps me; therefore I have not been disgraced" (50:7a); or again, "Who will declare me guilty?" (50:9a).

The first three Songs therefore describe the Servant's way into the world of Israel and the nations. This way leads from the Servant's presentation at the heavenly council and his being given a universal task for the nations (first Song), through the proclamation of his installation in office before the nations coupled with his difficult task of gathering Israel (second Song), on to his painful encounter with Israel (third Song) — an Israel that opposes the Servant to the point that he is humanly isolated and radically dependent on Yahweh's help (50:4-9). If the Servant was fully with Yahweh at the beginning of the first Song — "Behold my servant, whom I uphold" (42:1a) — so is he also at the end of the third Song: "Behold, the Lord God helps me" (50:9aα). But the change in perspective is nevertheless telling. It is the change from the presentation of the chosen one to the attacks of the suffering one; from closeness to God to the enmity of people made "bearable" only by the certainty of God's nearness.[20]

---

20. In Isa. 50:8 the motif of the "justification" or "vindication" of the Servant by Yahweh, who is called מַצְדִּיקִי, "my vindicator," in v. 8aα (an expression predicated of God only here in the OT), leads directly to the two מִי questions, "Who will contend with me?" and "Who is my adversary?" (8aβ//8b, RSV). In Isa. 53:11aβ this motif is taken up and transformed into an active quality of the Servant: "By his knowledge [of God] the righteous one, my Servant, will justify the many (בְּדַעְתּוֹ יַצְדִּיק צַדִּיק עַבְדִּי לָרַבִּים)." Cf. Steck, "Aspekte des Gottesknechts in Jesaja 52,13–53,12," 38; Kleinknecht, *Der leidende Gerechtfertigte,* 45ff., esp. 46-47; H. Niehr, *Herrschen und Richten: Die Wurzel* שפט *im Alten Orient und im Alten Testament,* FB 54 (1986), 259-60. In Isa. 50:8 the three forensic terms צדק hiphil, "vindicate" (with Yahweh as subject; contrast רשע hiphil, "condemn" or "declare guilty," in 50:9aβ, with the Servant's enemies as the subject), ריב, "contend," and מִשְׁפָּט "judgment" (lit., בַּעַל מִשְׁפָּטִי "the master of my accusation," NIV: "my accuser"; RSV: "my adversary") all combine to show that the "legal case" of the Servant is at issue. In the first Song of Isa. 42:1-4 the Servant is given the task of spreading the divine מִשְׁפָּט throughout the world of the nations (42:1bβ, 3b, 4aβ; cf. תּוֹרָה, "his teaching," in 42:4b), yet in 49:4bα his own מִשְׁפָּט or "cause" (NRSV) is left with Yahweh (cf. the contrasting expression applied to Jacob/Israel in 40:27, "My cause [מִשְׁפָּטִי] is ignored by my God," NJPS). On the connections between these passages see esp. Hermisson, "Lohn des Knechts," 274-75, 278ff., 282-83;

In material terms as well, the third Servant Song ends with an open question. Has the Servant, whose future lies entirely in Yahweh's hands, failed in his mission of restoring Israel and making them a "light to the nations" (49:5-6; cf. 42:1-4)? Or has he been vindicated in his existence and function? And what might this vindication look like? It would have to be more in any case than simply a confirmation of his individual certainty of salvation; it must comprehend not only his person but also his task, because the two belong together. This open question at the end of the third Servant Song is one of the impulses that will have given rise to the fourth Song.[21]

2. The Servant inside and outside the Servant Songs

But who composed the fourth Servant Song, and what answer can be derived from it to the open question of the third Song? Here we touch upon the problem of the collective or individual interpretation of Isaiah 53, which is in any case more complex than the simple alternative collective versus individual suggests. When one asks about the figure of the Servant inside and outside the Servant Songs,[22] the facts present themselves briefly as follows.

Outside the Servant Songs there are texts in the book of Second Isaiah that speak of Jacob/Israel as the "servant of Yahweh": 41:8-9; 44:1-2; 44:21-22; 45:4;

Kleinknecht, *Der leidende Gerechtfertigte,* 53ff.; further Jörg Jeremias, "מִשְׁפָּט im ersten Gottesknechtslied (Jes XLII 1-4)," *VT* 22 (1972): 31-42 (cf. Hermisson, "Lohn des Knechts," 282 n. 27), and R. Kilian, "Anmerkungen zur Bedeutung von מִשְׁפָּט im ersten Gottesknechtslied," in J. J. Degenhardt, ed., *Die Freude an Gott — unsere Kraft: Festschrift für O. B. Knoch* (1991), 81-88.

21. Following H.-J. Hermisson, "Einheit und Komplexität Deuterojesajas," in J. Vermeylen, ed., *The Book of Isaiah,* BETL 81 (1989), 287-312, esp. 309ff.; Kratz, *Kyros im Deuterojesaja-Buch,* 144ff.; Steck, "Aspekte des Gottesknechts in Jesaja 52,13–53,12," 33 n. 39; idem, "Gottesknechts-Texte," 152ff., and others, I assume that the Servant Songs were composed independently of the book of Second Isaiah and were collected successively (Servant Songs I-III + Servant Song IV) before being worked into the formative book of Second Isaiah. Another model of origins has been proposed by T. N. D. Mettinger, *A Farewell to the Servant Songs: A Critical Examination of an Exegetical Axiom,* SMHVL 1982-1983:3 (1983), 18ff., and followed by F. Matheus, *Singt dem Herrn ein neues Lied: Die Hymnen Deuterojesajas,* SBS 141 (1990), 104ff. On this see H.-J. Hermisson, "Voreiliger Abschied von den Gottesknechtsliedern," *TRu* 49 (1984): 209-22; B. Janowski, review of Mettinger, *WO* 20-21 (1989-90): 304-7; and J. A. Emerton, review of Mettinger, *BO* 48 (1991): 626-32.

22. On this see above all Hermisson, "Israel und der Gottesknecht," 3ff., 11ff.; idem, "Einheit und Komplexität Deuterojesajas," 307; cf. Kratz, *Kyros im Deuterojesaja-Buch,* 80 n. 286; Steck, "Gottesknechts-Texte," 153. On the history of research see D. Michel, "Deuterojesaja," *TRE* 8 (1981): 521ff. (510-30), and E. Rupprecht, "Knecht Gottes," *EKL*³ 2 (1989), 1315-17 with forthcoming ET under "Servant" or "Servant of the Lord" in *EC.*

and 48:20. Beside these stand texts in which by "servant" a figure *different from* Jacob/Israel is meant: 43:10 and 44:26. Who is this Servant? Isaiah 44:21-22 helps with the answer. For although this word of the Lord speaks of Jacob/Israel as the Servant, read in conjunction with 49:5-6, it sheds light on the special Servant figure who is differentiated from Jacob/Israel. According to 49:5-6 the Servant's task is to "bring back" Jacob to Yahweh and to "gather" Israel to him (v. 5a), or again to "raise up" Jacob and to "bring back" Israel to him (v. 6a) — in other words, to do for Jacob/Israel precisely what the speaker of the word of the Lord in Isaiah 44:21-22 has called for:

21 Remember these things, O Jacob,
      and Israel, for you are my servant;
    I formed you, you are my servant;
      O Israel, you will not be forgotten by me.
22 I have swept away your transgressions like a cloud,
      and your sins like mist;
    turn back to me (שׁוּבָה אֵלַי), for I have redeemed you.

(Isaiah 44:21-22)

5   And now the LORD says,
      who formed me in the womb to be his servant,
    to bring Jacob back to him (לְשׁוֹבֵב יַעֲקֹב אֵלָיו),
      and that Israel might be gathered to him,
    for I am honored in the sight of the Lord,
      and my God has become my strength —
6   he says,
    "It is too light a thing that you should be my servant
      to raise up the tribes of Jacob
    and to bring back the survivors of Israel (וּנְצוּרֵי יִשְׂרָאֵל לְהָשִׁיב);
    I will give you as a light to the nations,
      that my salvation may reach to the end of the earth."

(Isaiah 49:5-6)

If we relate these two texts to one another, then 44:21-22 says implicitly the same thing as 49:5-6: the Servant is supposed to "bring back" Jacob/Israel to Yahweh (שׁוב polel, 49:5a; hiphil, 49:6a) by calling them to "turn back" to Yahweh (שׁוב qal, 44:22). One may call this activity the Servant's work of leading the people back. "He leads people to Yahweh by calling them to turn back."[23]

---

23. Hermisson, "Israel und der Gottesknecht," 11.

That is precisely what Second Isaiah did in his preaching. We may therefore conclude that the Servant who appears outside the Servant Songs and who is differentiated from Jacob/Israel is the prophet himself.

Within the Servant Songs as well, the problem presents itself in a subtle form, because the first three Songs must be differentiated from the fourth. According to the first three Servant Songs, the Servant's task is to get Jacob/Israel to turn back to Yahweh and to make it an active Servant dedicated to Yahweh and the world of the nations. But because Israel refuses this role, even though it has been chosen and called as a "servant" (41:8-9, passim),[24] the prophetic Servant represents "true Israel" from the first Servant Song onward. The role that this Servant thereby acquires over against empirical Israel lies beyond the simple alternative of collective versus individual:

> He represents not his own but Yahweh's cause, and so his vindication cannot be separated from the success of this cause. Conversely, Yahweh helps him achieve vindication by bringing his cause to fruition — through the Servant. "His cause" is here the cause of Yahweh *and* of his Servant: the two belong together.[25]

In the light of this, it also becomes clear that the Servant's vicarious role begins not in the fourth Servant Song but already with Yahweh's choice of the Servant in the first Song. "Vicariousness" or "representation" consequently has a double meaning. The prophetic Servant represents Yahweh's מִשְׁפָּט in all its consequences before the nations (first and second Songs) and before Israel (third Song), and he thereby brings the "servant" Israel back to Yahweh, though Israel acknowledges this only after the fact (Isa. 53:4-6; cf. the closing oracle in 53:11aβ-12).

Both outside and inside the Servant Songs, then, various Servants appear — outside the Songs the Servant Jacob/Israel and the Servant "Second Isaiah"; within the first three Songs a Servant who is identical with the prophetic Servant outside the Songs. The problem is different once again in the fourth Servant Song, which tells of this prophetic Servant's vicarious surrender of life, thus taking a position *post mortem servi Dei*. For the prophetic Servant to represent "true Israel" by actively and resolutely testifying to Yahweh's מִשְׁפָּט while the rest of Israel persists in passivity[26] would be understandable but unaccept-

---

24. See the overview by Hermisson, "Israel und der Gottesknecht," 11-12.

25. Hermisson, "Lohn des Knechts," 280.

26. Israel's passivity is expressed both inside (cf. Isa. 50:4) and outside (cf. Isa. 40:27-31, esp. vv. 29-30) the Servant Songs by the metaphor of the "weary one" (יָעֵף) who is strengthened by the God who never grows weary (40:28-29) or sustained by the word of the Servant (50:4-5aα); cf. the Servant's similar ministry to the "bruised reed" and the "dimly burning wick" in

able after the collapse of 587 B.C.E. That matters did not stay that way was due to the behavior of the Servant and its narrative recollection in Isaiah 52:12–53:13. In him it became clear to the people of Israel that their own salvation was the *undeserved fruit of another's deed:* "Surely *our* sicknesses — *he* bore them" (53:4aα). This unassuming sentence is one of the keys to understanding the dramatic event to which we now turn.

III. The Text of Isaiah 53

1. The Composition of the Fourth Servant Song

We have seen that the double "behold" that concludes the first three Servant Songs in 50:9 points back to the "behold" of 42:1a and also marks the break over against the "behold" of 52:13a. With the help of this keyword technique, Isaiah 52:13–53:12 is related back to the first three Songs and is seen as an answer to the open question of 50:4-9. The open question of the third Song is whether the Servant, whose future lies entirely in Yahweh's hands, has failed in the eyes of Israel and the nations. If one takes the view of the group of persons who begin to speak in the first person plural in 53:1 (the "we" group), then the Servant actually has failed:

> 2   For he grew up before us [lit., "him"] like a young plant,
>   and like a root out of dry ground;
>   he had no form or majesty that we should look at him,
>   nothing in his appearance that we should desire him.
> 3   He was despised and rejected by others;
>   a man of pains and acquainted with sickness;
>   and as one from whom others hide their faces,
>   he was (so) despised that we held him of no account.
>
> (Isaiah 53:2-3)

But that is only half the truth. For the fourth Servant Song does not begin with the address of these "we" figures but with Yahweh's oracle that speaks of the Servant's future "success" and "exaltation":

42:3 (referring to the nations). See also G. F. Hasel, "עָף, etc.," *TWAT* 3 (1982), 710-18, esp. 717-18 = *TDOT* 6 (1990), 148-56, esp. 155-56; Hermisson, "Lohn des Knechts," 281; Steck, "Aspekte des Gottesknechts in Jesaja 52,13–53,12," 37 n. 46; Weippert, "Die 'Konfessionen' Deuterojesajas," 111-12; and on 40:27-31 K. Elliger, *Deuterojesaja*, BKAT 11/1 (1978), 93ff.

See, my servant shall *succeed;*
he shall be *exalted* and lifted up, and shall be very high. (Isaiah 52:13)

The fourth Servant Song thus begins with *God's perspective* and returns to it at the end in 53:11aβ-12. This perspective says that the Servant has not failed before Yahweh; Yahweh rather proclaims his future "success," as the Servant had hoped but never experienced (see 50:7-9). This commitment of Yahweh to his Servant above and beyond his violent fate, as disclosed in the oracle of 52:13-15 and its proclamation in 53:1, provides the turning point to the new view of the "we" group[27] that they themselves introduce emphatically in 53:4 with the particle אָכֵן, "nevertheless":

Nevertheless, our sicknesses — he bore them,
and our pains — [he] took them upon himself;
yet we accounted him as one afflicted,
as one stricken by God and bowed down. (Isaiah 53:4)

On the basis of the transition from the Yahweh address to the "we" address at the beginning and the return to the Yahweh address at the end, the fourth Servant Song acquires a concentric structure. At the center stands the "we" address (53:1-11aα), which is framed by the two Yahweh addresses in 52:13-15 and in 53:11aβ-12. The subject that speaks in this central section is identical with the "many" who appear in the framing sections.[28] Who are these "many"? Are they the "many nations" and "kings" of 52:15 and therefore the representatives of the whole world of nations, or are they the whole of a particular society and therefore empirical Israel? If one proceeds from the songs of individual complaint and thanksgiving as the relevant background texts, as I think we must,[29] then the answer is clear. The "many" refers to the empirical

---

27. As claimed already by E. Kutsch, "Sein Leiden und Tod — unser Heil: Eine Auslegung von Jesaja 52,13–53,12" (1967), reprinted in idem, *Kleine Schriften zum Alten Testament: Festschrift für E. Kutsch,* ed. L. Schmidt and K. Eberlein, BZAW 168 (1986), 169-96, here 178: "What has brought about this swing in the judgment of the Servant's suffering? By themselves the 'many' would never have come to this. Apparently the saving significance of this suffering for the many was the content of that message which was so unbelievable in 53:1a. The fact that God with this suffering had intervened savingly in their own destiny had to be 'revealed' to them (53:1b)." Cf. also Steck, "Aspekte des Gottesknechts in Jesaja 52,13–53,12," 24.

28. See esp. Steck, "Aspekte des Gottesknechts in Jesaja 52,13–53,12," 25ff.

29. Following Hermisson, "Israel und der Gottesknecht," 23-24; idem, "Lohn des Knechts," 286; and Steck, "Aspekte des Gottesknechts in Jesaja 52,13–53,12," 26-27. On the combination of "the one" and "the many" and the inclusive use of רַבִּים, "many" (designating the whole of a society), in the fourth Servant Song and in the songs of individual thanksgiving or

Israel that cruelly isolates the praying person or Servant in his need — as for example in Psalm 31:12-14 — and that also appeals to God in so doing, as in Psalm 3:2-3:

> 2   O LORD, how *many* are my foes!
>   *Many* are rising against me!
> 3   *Many* are saying of me,
>   "There is no help for him in God." (Psalm 3:2-3 [ET 1-2])

> 12   I am the scorn of all my adversaries,
>   a horror to my neighbors,
>   an object of dread to my acquaintances;
>   those who see me in the street flee from me.
> 13   I have passed out of mind like one who is dead;
>   I have become like a broken vessel.
> 14   For I hear the whispering of many —
>   terror all around! —
>   as they scheme together against me,
>   as they plot to take my life. (Psalm 31:12-14 [ET 11-13])

The disregard and threats articulated here also marked the behavior of the "we" toward the Servant during his lifetime according to Isaiah 53:2-3. What a revolutionary effect there is, by contrast, in the knowledge with which the "we" look back upon this stage in verses 4-6!

2. Confession of Guilt and Surrender of Life in the Fourth Servant Song

a. Israel's Confession of Guilt   In its framing sections in Isaiah 53:2-3 and 53:10aβ-11aα, which read like the "prologue" and "epilogue" of the prophet's biography,[30] the "we" speech designates the extremes of a long, hard road: life cut

---

complaint see J. Jeremias, "πολλοί," *TWNT* 6 (1959), 536-45, esp. 537-38 = *TDNT* 6 (1968), 536-45, esp. 537-38; Kutsch, "Sein Leiden und Tod — unser Heil," 176, 191-92; H. Ringgren, "רב etc.," *TWAT* 8 (1990), 294-320, esp. 315 (*TDOT* 13 [2004], 272-98, esp. 293); O. Keel, *Feinde und Gottesleugner: Studien zum Image der Widersacher in den Individualpsalmen*, SBM 7 (1969), 22, 141, 168, 206ff.

30. "Biography" here refers not to a literary genre but to a description of the life of the Servant reduced to core statements. It consists of "before and after" perspectives in 53:2-3 and 53:10aβ, 11aα, and a "path of suffering" in 53:8-9, including the stages of rejection and persecu-

off by Israel (vv. 2-3); life promised by Yahweh (vv. 10aβ-11aα). However, this radical *change from death to life* does not occur by itself; it is caused by the proclamation of the Yahweh oracle in 52:13-15 and 53:1, which initiates a far-reaching process of recognition with the "we."

At the level of the *text* of verses 2-6, this process of recognition is described by juxtaposing two points of view, but these are separated by a "before" and a "now" at the level of the actual *events*. The "we" could have believed the Servant earlier, but they did not do so. Verses 2-6 go back to this stage *before* the pronouncement of the Yahweh oracle in 52:13-15 and treat the role of the "we" by contrasting their earlier with their present view. How is this to be understood?

The *earlier view* of the "we" (vv. 2-3, 4b, 6a) is based on the logic of the "action-consequences connection."[31] Each deed comes back upon the doer as a corresponding consequence and determines the doer's fitness or unfitness for society. Such a model of understanding is present in numerous psalms in which the suffering of the praying person appears to others as the consequence of his own guilt. Trusted friends become enemies who consistently marginalize the one they used to esteem. The depiction of need in one song of individual complaint, Psalm 41,[32] may serve as an example of this form of "social death":

6   My enemies (אוֹיְבַי) say of me in malice:
       "When will he die, and his name perish?"

7   And when one comes to see me, he utters empty words,
       while his heart gathers mischief;
       when he goes out, he tells it abroad.

8   All who hate me (שֹׂנְאַי) whisper together about me;
       they imagine the worst for me.

9   They say, "A deadly thing has fastened upon him,
       he will not rise again from where he lies."

---

tion by the "we," a violent end, and a disgraceful burial. K. Baltzer, *Die Biographie der Propheten* (1975), 171ff., esp. 176-77 has sought to characterize the Servant Songs as parts of an "ideal biography," while Weippert, "Die 'Konfessionen' Deuterojesajas," 104ff., accepts only the two "I" texts in 49:1-6 and 50:4-9 as biographical in the strict sense and considers them comparable to the "confessions" of Jeremiah: "they have grown out of the reflections of the prophet Second Isaiah on his 'calling'" (p. 112).

31. German: "Tun-Ergehen-Zusammenhang." On this "action-consequences connection" see the references above in n. 3.

32. Cf. J. Begrich, *Studien zu Deuterojesaja*, ed. W. Zimmerli, TB 20 (1963), 63ff., and Steck, "Aspekte des Gottesknechts in Jesaja 52,13–53,12," 39-40, with further references.

10 Even my bosom friend (אִישׁ שְׁלוֹמִי) in whom I trusted,
who ate of my bread (אוֹכֵל לַחְמִי), has lifted the heel against me.[33]
(Psalm 41:6-10 [ET 5-9], RSV)

The behavior of the "we" toward the Servant was that of such "enemies." They considered this unsightly "man of sorrows" (Isa. 53:3a) to be one "stricken, struck down by God, and afflicted" (v. 4b), and they distanced themselves from him.

The *present view* of the "we" (see vv. 4-6) is based on the breakdown of this logic. The "we" were wrong and had all, in their blind self-centeredness, turned to their own way: "All we like sheep have gone astray; we have all turned to our own way" (v. 6a). They now realize that the Servant's suffering was the consequence not of his but of their actions, the actions of others. This is indicated by the causative formulations with מִן in verse 5a: "pierced *because of* our transgressions, crushed *because of* our iniquities." By coming to their present view by means of the Yahweh oracle in 52:13-15, the "we" can finally face up to the disastrous consequences of their actions. That is the beginning but also the condition of change.

While this insight of the "we" into the true state of affairs is liberating, it is strange by contrast to think of God himself as actively involved in this event. The passage in verses 4-6 conveys this in the offensive statement that Yahweh "caused the iniquity of us all to strike (הִפְגִּיעַ) him" (v. 6b).[34] Even more offensive is the picking up of this idea in verse 10aα, where it says pointedly, "But

---

33. This lament in Psalm 41 (cf. Job 19:13-22) contains a comprehensive description of the enemies that runs from the אוֹיְבִים or "enemies" (Ps. 41:6, general enmity) to the שֹׂנְאִים or "haters" (v. 8, faithless friends) and finally to the אִישׁ שְׁלוֹמִי, "my bosom friend" (= "the one with whom I live in שָׁלוֹם") // אוֹכֵל לַחְמִי, "the one who ate my bread" (v. 10, the neighbor). On the individual designations of the enemies see L. Ruppert, *Der leidende Gerechte und seine Feinde: Eine Wortfelduntersuchung* (1973), 7ff., 34ff., 85ff., 104, 105, 108-9. The activities of these enemies are also comprehensively described, including both *words* ("speak malice," v. 6; cf. vv. 7-9) and *actions* ("lift the heel," v. 10).

34. On the text-critical problems of vv. 6b, 12bβ see K. Elliger, "Textkritisches zu Deuterojesaja," in H. Goedicke, ed., *Near Eastern Studies in Honor of W. F. Albright* (1971), 115-16, 119 (113-19) (reconstruction of v. 6b: "But Jahweh let 'our iniquity' strike him"); idem, "Nochmals Textkritisches zu Jes 53," in J. Schreiner, ed., *Wort, Lied und Gottesspruch: Festschrift für J. Ziegler*, FB 2 (1972), 143-44 (137-44) (Elliger reads in v. 12bβ the niphal of פגע, "to be struck"). On the question of whether the hiphil of פגע denotes a verbal intercession of the Servant, see the provisional answers of E. Haag, "Das Opfer des Gottesknechts (Jes 53,10)," *TTZ* 86 (1977): 97 (81-98); B. Janowski, "Sündenvergebung 'um Hiobs willen': Fürbitte und Vergebung in 11QtgJob 38,2f. und Hi 42,9f. LXX," *ZNW* 73 (1982): 251-80, esp. 275; and Steck, "Aspekte des Gottesknechts in Jesaja 52,13–53,12," 31 n. 38.

Yahweh *planned* (חָפֵץ) to crush him"![35] What kind of God is it, we ask ourselves, who surrenders his "chosen one" (42:1) and delivers him to the power of his foes? It is not enough that the text provokes this question with the formulation of verse 6; it insists on it by presenting Yahweh's procedure as something "according to plan" in verse 10aα. What kind of "plan" is it that leads Yahweh to surrender the life of his chosen one?

b. The Surrender of the Life of the Servant (vv. 7-10a)   While the first half of the central part of the "we" address (vv. 4-6) is spoken from the perspective of the "we," the second half (vv. 7-10a) has the Servant's suffering in the foreground. A case was brought against him; he was tormented to death and finally given a grave with the wicked. That is the ignominious end to a life that began so differently and was also meant so differently. The Servant accepted the things imposed upon him without resistance: this agrees with his peaceful and truthful way of life (compare v. 7a with v. 9b). As we all know from other contexts, meekness and truthfulness can arouse aggression and force those who exemplify them into the role of *victims*. The pictures of a lamb or a sheep led to be slaughtered or sheared speak a clear language (v. 7b). Not so clear, by contrast, is whether the Servant's passion is to be thought of in terms of a ritual sacrifice.[36] The statement in verse 10a, toward which everything flows, has something else in view in my opinion:

> But Yahweh planned to crush him [. . .];
> and he made his life the means of wiping out guilt.[37] (Isaiah 53:10a)

35. On this text see below. The basic meaning of the root חפץ cannot be determined with certainty; see G. J. Botterweck, "חָפֵץ, חֵפֶץ," *TWAT* 3 (1982), 100-116, esp. 102 = *TDOT* 5 (1986), 92-107, esp. 93. Nevertheless, the main idea can be approximated by "like" or "want"; cf. Elliger, *Deuterojesaja*, 286. The translations "to plan, want" for חָפֵץ and "plan, (saving) will" for חֵפֶץ highlight the aspect of the will (as over against the emotional aspect of the expressions "like," "take pleasure in") that comes to the fore in the occurrences of these terms in Isaiah 40-55. Cf. Elliger, *Deuterojesaja;* Botterweck, "חָפֵץ, חֵפֶץ," 114-15 = ET 105-6; and Steck, "Aspekte des Gottesknechts in Jesaja 52,13–53,12," 30 n. 33.

36. See below.

37. With regard to textual criticism, I assume that the MT's הֶחֱלִי at the end of Isa. 53:10aα (RSV: "he has put [him] to grief") was absent from the original text, while in v. 10aβ, instead of the MT's אִם־תָּשִׂים אָשָׁם נַפְשׁוֹ I read וְהוּא שָׂם אָשָׁם נַפְשׁוֹ (שָׂם, qal participle of שִׂים, also read by H. Hermisson, n. 36 in his essay in this volume). On the text of Isa. 53:10aα-10aβ see the proposed emendations by Kutsch, "Sein Leiden und Tod — unser Heil," 185-86, and K. Elliger, "Jes 53,10: alte crux — neuer Vorschlag," *MIOF* 15 (1969): 228-33; cf. idem, "Textkritisches zu Deuterojesaja," 137; H. Haag, *Der Gottesknecht bei Deuterojesaja*, EdF 233 (1985), 179-80; D. Barthélemy, *Critique textuelle de l'Ancien Testament*, vol. 2: *Isaïe, Jérémie, Lamentations*, OBO

That is the central statement of the fourth Servant Song; it summarizes the Servant's entire task of suffering and explains it by the terms חָפֵץ, "to will, to plan," and אָשָׁם, the "discharging/wiping out of guilt." If we add the immediately following passage — as suggested by the parallel expressions "Yahweh planned" (יְהוָה חָפֵץ) in verse 10a and "the plan of Yahweh" (חֵפֶץ יְהוָה) in verse 10b — then while the riddle of Yahweh's plan is not solved, a possibility of understanding it is nevertheless opened up:

He shall see his offspring, and shall prolong his days;
and Yahweh's plan — through him it shall succeed. (Isaiah 53:10b)

We must read this sentence against the background of the first three Servant Songs. According to 42:1-4, Yahweh has set his Servant on a course that has him take the place of others step by step: that is his "plan."[38] In his actions and suffering the Servant takes up an "alien" fate that has its full effect on him. Yet why this dramatic "role reversal" that brings with it the rejection, suffering, and death of the innocent? It is in order to release others from the evil consequences of their evil actions,[39] or more concretely, to "bring Israel back" to Yahweh after the catastrophe of 587 B.C.E. (49:5-6; cf. 44:21-22). Any other way — such as that followed by preexilic judgment prophecy with its proclamation of disaster — was apparently no longer viable for the Deuteroisaianic tradition, for it would have driven Israel even deeper into despair. Therefore the Servant's suffering is, at its core, about the *salvation* of Israel and — in the context of the Servant Songs — about the *salvation* of the nations.[40]

59/2 (1986), 400ff. (with the strange interpretation: "Le Seigneur a agréé [cf. the technical use of חָפֵץ of the Lord's taking pleasure in sacrifices, e.g., Isa. 1:11; Ps. 40:7; 51:18, 21] son broyé, qu'il avait mis à mal," p. 402; the French is similar to the NASB, "But the Lord was pleased to crush him, putting him to grief," or the NJB: "It was Yahweh's good pleasure to crush him with pain"); and finally Steck, "Aspekte des Gottesknechts in Jesaja 52,13–53,12," 26 n. 28. Kutsch concludes: "Even if no certainty has been reached to this day regarding the original text, at least one thing is certain: the Servant's life has been made an אָשָׁם" ("Sein Leiden und Tod — unser Heil," 186). On אָשָׁם see below.

38. Cf. Hermisson, "Lohn des Knechts," 285, and also Botterweck, "חָפֵץ, חֵפֶץ," 114-15 = ET 105-6.

39. Cf. Steck, "Aspekte des Gottesknechts in Jesaja 52,13–53,12," 42-43: "Yahweh is the one who assigns the Ebed a fate in which the connection between the iniquity of others and its consequences [German: *Vergehen-Ergehen-Zusammenhang anderer*] takes full effect upon the Ebed, which can only mean freeing the others completely from that connection" (p. 42).

40. This is the "success" that the Servant will have according to the Yahweh oracle in Isa. 52:13-15; see Hermisson, "Lohn des Knechts," passim. On "suffering" as the particular form of experience in the exilic period see Preuss, *Theologie des Alten Testaments*, vol. 2 (1992), 149-55, esp. 154; cf. 324-26, esp. 326 = *Old Testament Theology*, 2 (1996), 141-46, esp. 145-46; cf. 303-5, esp. 305.

But salvation of the many at the expense of the one? Did Yahweh actually "sacrifice" the Servant to save Israel? The various answers to this question all revolve around the second key term of verse 10a, namely, אָשָׁם, which I have translated above as a means of "wiping out guilt." But that is not the usual interpretation. As a rule, the translations "guilt offering," "sin offering," "atoning sacrifice," or the "doing of penance" are preferred (cf. NIV: "guilt offering"; NJPS: "offering for guilt"; NJB: "sin offering"; REB: "sacrifice for sin"; NRSV: "offering for sin"),[41] supported by references to the law of the guilt offering in Leviticus 5:14-26 or the "scapegoat" ritual of Leviticus 16:10, 20-22. The guilt-offering interpretation is held emphatically by G. Fohrer, who equates killing the Servant with making a sacrifice:[42]

[אָשָׁם] designates the sacrifice that an individual has the priest offer when he has unwittingly transgressed one of the divine commands. The blood ritual, in which the blood of the sacrificial animal is dashed all around on the altar, was the most important act in the sacrificial procedure. Now the blood of the "Servant of Yahweh" was also shed in his execution, and this execution is equated with the sacrificial procedure in Isa. 53:10. The Servant was the sacrificial animal that God, as the officiating priest, "struck," that is, slaughtered, because this "pleased" him — in other words, because he accepted the Servant as suitable for sacrifice.[43]

The equation of the Servant with a sacrificial animal leads in my opinion to a dead end, for in Isaiah 52:13–53:12 there is no mention of the (shed) blood of the Servant, nor is the Servant seen in the role of a sacrificial animal ritually slaughtered by a priestly official. The verb דכא, "to strike" (NRSV "to crush,"

---

41. See the brief overviews by Kutsch, "Sein Leiden und Tod — unser Heil," 186-87, and Haag, *Der Gottesknecht bei Deuterojesaja*, 192-93.

42. G. Fohrer, "Stellvertretung und Schuldopfer in Jes 52,13–53,12" (1969), reprinted in idem, *Studien zu alttestamentlichen Texten und Themen (1966-1972)*, BZAW 155 (1981), 24-43; cf. idem, *Theologische Grundstrukturen des Alten Testaments* (1972), 27-28. Another scholar who thinks of a ritual sacrifice in Isa. 53:10 is Haag, "Das Opfer des Gottesknechts," who speaks of "the mediator's giving of his life, understood as an atoning sacrifice" (p. 96). Haag continues: "For tellingly the 'qualification' of this unique sacrifice uses the same terminology that is used in cultic regulations (and known also to the critics of the cult) to indicate the acceptance or rejection of a sacrifice: Yahweh 'delights' (רצה) in his Servant (Isa 42:1) and 'approves of' (חָפֵץ) his suffering (Isa 53:10)" (pp. 96-97). Cf. also L. Ruppert, "Schuld und Schuld-Lösen nach Jesaja 53," in G. Kaufmann, ed., *Schulderfahrung und Schuldbewältigung: Christen im Umgang mit Schuld* (1982), 17-34, esp. 27-28 with n. 27; 28-29 with n. 30. However, on the understanding of חָפֵץ in Isa. 53:10a see above, n. 35 with its text.

43. Fohrer, "Stellvertretung," 41; cf. idem, "Theologische Grundstrukturen," 27.

v. 10a piel; cf. v. 5a pual), is not a sacrificial term,[44] and cultic vocabulary is also lacking in the rest of Isaiah 52:13–53:12.[45] Similarly the second model, which appeals to Leviticus 16:10, 20-22 and comes up periodically in exegesis,[46] is of no further help. According to this model, the Servant is supposed to take Israel's guilt upon himself like the scapegoat and overcome it through his substitutionary "atoning" death.[47] Virtually everything speaks against this, but the most serious objection — next to the absence of the term אָשָׁם in Leviticus 16 (the scapegoat in Lev. 16:10, 20-22 is not given any technical term in the Hebrew Bible, except to say that it is "for Azazel"; later patristic writers termed it the goat that is "sent away," ἀποπομπαῖος [cf. *PGL*, 205 s.v.]) — is the incomparability of a scapegoat ritual for the elimination of disaster[48] with the Servant's vicarious surrender of life. In Isaiah 52:13–53:12 Israel's guilt is not "gotten rid of" by a scapegoat in some remote area; it is rather endured, *borne* by the Servant.

My alternative to the models just reviewed runs as follows. The term אָשָׁם comes originally not from the cult, but from contexts in which — as in Genesis 26:10 and 1 Samuel 6:3-4, 8, 17, etc. — guilt-incurring encroachments and their

---

44. See H. F. Fuhs, "דכא," *TWAT* 2 (1977), 207-21 = *TDOT* 3 (1978), 195-208. The expressions for "to slaughter" are rather זבח, טבח, and שחט. Isa. 53:7bα-bβ presents a picture that compares the Servant with a lamb led to the "slaughter" (טֶבַח) and to a sheep that before its shearers is silent. The point of the comparison is the *patient acceptance* of a violent fate (see also v. 7aβ; further Jer. 11:19; Ps. 38:14), not the identification of that fate with a *ritual sacrifice*. See also C. Westermann, *Das Buch Jesaja Kapitel 40–66*, 5th ed., ATD 19 (1986), 213.

45. Cf. Kutsch, "Sein Leiden und Tod — unser Heil," 186-87. For critical inquiries into Fohrer's thesis see Ruppert, "Schuld und Schuld-Lösen nach Jesaja 53," 28 n. 29, and Steck, "Aspekte des Gottesknechts in Jesaja 52,13–53,12," 29 n. 29.

46. As for example with Ruppert, "Schuld und Schuld-Lösen nach Jesaja 53," 27ff., 33-34, and Mettinger, *A Farewell to the Servant Songs,* 41. See the criticism by Hermisson, "Voreiliger Abschied," 221-22. Fohrer discusses Lev. 16:10, 20-22 in this context but rejects it as "a preliminary form for the vicarious suffering in the life of the 'Servant of Yahweh'" ("Stellvertretung," 38-39).

47. [[(Tr.) Professor Janowski places quotation marks around the word "atoning" (or rather the whole German expression *Sühnetod*, "atoning death") in order to indicate that the scapegoat ritual does not effect that positive type of cultic "atonement" which alone is designated by the word *Sühne* in Tübingen exegesis since H. Gese's essay on "Die Sühne" (in idem, *Zur biblischen Theologie: Alttestamentliche Vorträge*, BEvT 78 [1977], 85-106). The scapegoat is not a positive ritual but a negative "elimination ritual"; and it is not a cultic (i.e., blood) sacrifice. Therefore, any explanation of the Servant based on the scapegoat could only be considered as "atonement" improperly so called.]]

48. On the "scapegoat ritual" in Lev. 16:10, 21-22 see now B. Janowski and G. Wilhelm, "Der Bock, der die Sünden hinausträgt: Zur Religionsgeschichte von Lev 16,10.21f," in B. Janowski, K. Koch, and G. Wilhelm, eds., *Religionsgeschichtliche Beziehungen zwischen Kleinasien, Nordsyrien und dem Alten Testament: Internationales Symposion Hamburg 17.-21. März 1990*, OBO 129 (1993), 109-69.

reparation are the theme.[49] From there the term made its way, after several intermediate stages and *after the composition of Isaiah 53*, into the priestly sacrificial torah (Leviticus 4–5, 7, passim). Its meaning is determined by the *situation of obligation arising from guilt*, in which the guilty person must provide material compensation to discharge this guilt. Furthermore, in contrast to חַטָּאת, "sin," the term אָשָׁם is "not a term for trespass, transgression"; it always relates "only to a particular type of *consequence* of transgressions"[50] of which the doer is aware and for which he or she must take responsibility. An appropriate paraphrase for אָשָׁם would therefore be "the obligation to discharge guilt that arises from a situation of guilt."[51]

If we apply this basic meaning of אָשָׁם to Isaiah 53:10a, then the statement there about the surrender of life as a means of "wiping out guilt" acquires a precise sense. Israel, which is in no position to take over the obligation arising from its guilt, must be released from this obligation in order to have any future. This liberation comes from an innocent one who surrenders his life according to Yahweh's "plan" (v. 10a, b) and as a consequence of his own ministry (vv. 7-9). "Surrender of *one's own life* as a means of wiping out guilt" is therefore identical with "taking over the consequences of *others' actions*." As I see it, the expression about the vicarious "bearing" of the guilt of others (v. 4a; cf. vv. 11b, 12b) means to say nothing other than this.

Thus in 53:10a and its key term אָשָׁם we find the same structure of vicarious suffering that is evident in the fourth Servant Song as a whole.[52] The main aspects of this structure may now be summarized briefly.

1. The consequences of the actions of the "we" speakers, which they should have borne themselves but did not, are loaded onto another. The initia-

---

49. See above all R. Knierim, "אָשָׁם," *THAT* 1, 2nd ed. (1975), 251-57, esp. 254 = *TLOT* 1 (1991), 191-95, esp. 192-93; D. Kellermann, "אָשָׁם etc.," *TWAT* 1 (1973), 463-72, esp. 465 = *TDOT* 1 (1977) 429-37, esp. 430-31; A. Marx, "Sacrifices de Réparation et Rites de Levée de Sanction," *ZAW* 100 (1988): 183-98; and H. J. Stoebe, "Schicksal Erkennen — Schuld Bekennen: Gedanken im Anschluß an Lev 5,17-19," in R. Liwak and S. Wagner, eds., *Prophetie und geschichtliche Wirklichkeit im alten Israel: Festschrift für S. Herrmann* (1991), 385-97, esp. 387ff. On the difference between אָשָׁם and חַטָּאת and the meaning of אָשָׁם in Leviticus 4–5 and Leviticus 6–7 etc. see most recently J. Milgrom, *Leviticus 1–16*, AB 3 (1991), 319ff., 339ff.; R. Rendtorff, *Leviticus*, BKAT 3/2-3 (1990-92), 152-53, 192, 194-95, 199ff., 208-9, 209ff., 214ff.; and A. Schenker, "Die Anlässe zum Schuldopfer Ascham," in idem, ed., *Studien zu Opfer und Kult im Alten Testament*, FAT 3 (1992), 45-66.

50. Knierim, "אָשָׁם," 253 (italics added).

51. Cf. Knierim, "אָשָׁם," 254.

52. Cf. also Rendtorff, *Leviticus*, 214-15, who claims that the understanding of אָשָׁם in Isa. 53:10 "depends for the most part upon the interpretation of the difficult text Isa. 52:13–53:12 as a whole."

tive for this proceeds from Yahweh (vv. 6b, 10aα).[53] He allows an *alien "action-consequences connection" to come back full circle upon the Servant* so that the truly guilty — namely, Israel — find themselves in the position of the saved, while the same connection breaks the Servant.

2. When the "we" recognize this, they acknowledge the guilt borne by the Servant as their own. The recognition of guilt accomplished in the confession of verses 4-6 is the presupposition for Israel's future, because it brings with it not only a guilt-free Israel but an Israel that has been *changed by this recognition*. Only this Israel will return to the community of Yahweh as the Servant's "offspring" (vv. 10-11).

3. The fourth Servant Song does not begin with the address of the "we" but with the proclamation of the Yahweh oracle. This oracle produces a *double insight* among the "we." On the one hand they have an insight into the Servant's innocence; on the other they have the insight that their own guilt has been wiped out by the Servant's suffering. The Servant's "success," prophesied by the two framing Yahweh addresses (52:13-15; 53:11-12), is closely tied up with this double insight: Israel turns back to Yahweh only because it has "understood" the meaning of this death and thereby its own situation.[54]

IV. The Reality of Place-Taking

"I see the depths, but I cannot get to the bottom"[55] — this is what Augustine once said with the ocean before his eyes. This saying can easily be applied to Isa-

---

53. Therefore it is hardly correct, in my opinion, when W. Vogler claims that "the subject who has handed over this Servant to death is not God, but the Servant himself. He interceded for the sins of the 'many' on his own initiative (53:11-12). Of his own free will he sacrificed his life as a guilt offering for them" ("Jesu Tod — Gottes Tat? Bemerkungen zur frühchristlichen Interpretation des Todes Jesu," *TLZ* 113 [1988]: 481-92, esp. 489 n. 7). Over against this, the composition of Isa. 52:13–53:12 and especially the relationship between v. 6b and 10aα-aβ shows that the Servant's activity *corresponds to* Yahweh's activity. Cf. also Steck, "Aspekte des Gottesknechts in Jesaja 52,13–53,12," 41ff., who rightly speaks of the "active-passive form of Israel's Servant task" (p. 43). However, this also heightens the problem, because it bears upon the question of God. On this see also R. Girard, *Des choses cachées depuis la fondation du monde* (1979), 177-81 = ET, *Things Hidden Since the Foundation of the World*, trans. S. Bann and M. Metteer (1987), 154-58; K.-P. Jörns, "Der Sühnetod Jesu Christi in Frömmigkeit und Predigt: Ein praktisch-theologischer Diskurs," in E. Jüngel, ed., *Die Heilsbedeutung des Kreuzes für Glaube und Hoffnung des Christen*, ZTK Beiheft 8 (1990), 70-93, esp. 79-80; and Link, "'Für uns gestorben nach der Schrift,'" 166-67. See further n. 62 below.

54. Cf. Hermisson, "Lohn des Knechts," 287.

55. A. Augustinus, Sermo 28:7, *PL* 38:182, as cited by Jüngel, "Das Geheimnis der Stellvertretung," 247.

iah 53. The bottomless depth of this text is reflected in the vicarious event: an innocent one bears the guilt of others, perishes by it, and will nevertheless have "success." "What a strange victory," writes C. Mesters in his interpretation of the Servant Songs along the lines of liberation theology:

> It simply does not fit our way of thinking. We cannot properly classify it among our ideas. What we can imagine is a victory of the great over the small, and also of the small over the great. We can imagine a draw. But a defeat that is a victory? That is something that "has never happened before!" (Isa 52:15).[56]

The reason we cannot imagine this is connected with our style of thinking. I pointed out at the beginning that modern difficulties with place-taking stem from the axiom of the nonrepresentability of the subject.[57] Admittedly — so runs the objection — another can preserve my place in society by representing me over against others as a guardian, as a lawyer, or, in the context of the state, as a representative. All these are relationships in which others "take our place" daily in private and public affairs. But place-taking in matters of *guilt* breaks down because guilt attaches to the ego and no one can let another have his or her ego. It seems, then, as though the criticism of the theological use of the idea of place-taking has the last word.

About the rightness or wrongness of this criticism we need not decide here, for this would require examining the view of persons here presupposed.[58] We need only see that the biblical tradition goes another way and poses the problem differently.[59] In the Bible,

> a person becomes guilty by that which he or she does, and this guilt is uncovered by God. Guilt is not a failure to meet the demands and expectations that particular conventions place upon me. It is not a moral problem, but rather . . . the result of attempting to live in contradiction to the creation.[60]

---

56. C. Mesters, *Die Botschaft des leidenden Volkes* (1982), 100; see the entire context from pp. 91ff.

57. See above, pp. 50-52.

58. But see the references given above in n. 8.

59. For the following see Link, "'Für uns gestorben nach der Schrift,'" 148ff., 165ff. According to Link, place-taking or representation occurs "'in time' (i.e., in order to make time for us and to grant us new time, a future); since the process of representation depends on those who are represented, it is only conceivable as *entrance* into their history and therefore as a representation of their existence. However, because one cannot act responsibly, let alone love unreservedly, without falling into the fellowship of human *guilt,* Jesus became — as God's love made him to be — *guilty*" (p. 166).

60. Link, "'Für uns gestorben nach der Schrift,'" 152.

The biblical experience of guilt is the poverty of not being able to go on under one's own power, because the guilt which keeps the guilty living in the past is too heavy and makes life unbearable. Here the problem of place-taking comes up. The question is not

> whether guilt is transferable or not, whether it can be compensated or gotten rid of through an accomplishment external to me, as if it were "something" attached to me like an unpaid bill or a sickness. The question is rather whether there is someone who identifies himself with us in this situation, who steps in between us and our past and makes us once again bearable for God and the world — and therefore also for ourselves — "not . . . in order that we might in some indefinite future be so far along as to take this place ourselves, but rather that we might never fall into this place again."[61]

Isaiah 53 has unfolded this procedure of place-taking in all its drama and has disclosed its troubling as well as its liberating side. It is *troubling,* because an innocent one lets himself be struck without striking back and takes all the violence upon himself in order to break its power. The principle that violence breeds violence exhausts itself on this one who is unconditionally ready for peace; it thus leads *ad absurdum.* This is a reality that is no longer rationally comprehensible but nevertheless exists.[62] Yet this procedure is also *liberating,*

---

61. Link, "'Für uns gestorben nach der Schrift,'" 153. The citation within the citation is from H. Gollwitzer, *Von der Stellvertretung Gottes* (1967), 43.

62. This is also the way to understand H.-R. Reuter's definition of taking another's place (see above n. 16 with its text). "Place-taking" refers to the thought of the intercession of the one (who is innocent) for others (who are guilty) as a reality "which is already a given to reason" and can be "taken in" only by knowledge. Nevertheless, there is still a remainder that cannot be grasped rationally because it touches upon the dark side of this procedure. The taking of the place of others described in Isaiah 53 consists of three related elements: God lets his chosen one bear Israel's sin (v. 6b; cf. v. 10aα); the Servant makes his life an אָשָׁם in accordance with Yahweh's activity and "plan" (v. 10aβ); and the others, the "we," resort to violence (vv. 7-9). On this complexity of Isaiah 53, which is only heightened by the addition of other relevant concepts (such as Mesopotamian substitute king rituals, prophetic intercession, etc.), see also Steck, "Aspekte des Gottesknechts in Jesaja 52,13–53,12," 41 n. 62. Girard, *Des choses cachées depuis la fondation du monde,* 160ff., has sought to unlock the complex connections with the help of his theory of a "scapegoat mechanism" that sees the Servant as a "human scapegoat." This model makes sense in so far as it requires the element of violence to be taken seriously. But some scholars have been irritated by Girard's vague use of the term "scapegoat," usually limited to more particular phenomena in the study of religions. For criticism see M. Herzog, "Religionstheorie und Theologie René Girards," *KD* 38 (1992): 105-37, esp. 127ff.; Reuter, "Stellvertretung," 179ff., esp. 183ff. For clarification of Girard's position see N. Lohfink, "Der gewalttätige Gott des Alten Testaments und die Suche nach einer gewaltfreien Gesellschaft," *JBTh* 2 (1988): 106-36, esp. 113ff.,

because it is not simply left as it stands: the "we" recognize their own guilt by it. The guilty recognize that they are guilty: that is the beginning of change.[63] But no one is able to recognize this on their own. Such recognition requires an impulse "from outside" to make *theoretical* knowledge *practical*. Isaiah 53 describes this as well. The reality of place-taking is disclosed to the "we" not simply through reflection or resolution but rather by confessing the word that Yahweh speaks in the introductory oracle about his Servant's success (52:13-15). This word triggered for the "we" the process of recognition: "Surely our sicknesses — he bore them!" (53:4aα).

Ever since the famous question of the Ethiopian eunuch to Philip in Acts 8:34 — "About whom, may I ask you, does the prophet say this [sc. Isa. 53:7-8], about himself or about someone else?" — and Philip's no less famous reaction in Acts 8:35 — "Then Philip began to speak, and starting with this scripture, he proclaimed to him the good news about Jesus" — the Christ event has been interpreted again and again in the light of the Servant Songs, especially Isaiah 53.[64] If the Christological interpretation of the Servant Songs is no longer self-evident today but rather must be made plausible by the circuitous route of historical reasoning,[65] this does not mean that there is no connection between the

---

and R. Girard, *Le Bouc émissaire* (1982), 163-80, esp. 170ff. = ET, *The Scapegoat*, trans. Y. Freccero (1986), 112-24, esp. 117ff.

63. Cf. Mesters, *Die Botschaft des leidenden Volkes*, 111: "Only those who acknowledge their guilt can be forgiven. Oppressors must acknowledge that they are oppressors. Otherwise they cannot receive forgiveness. Knowledge of guilt is the beginning of change. Forgiveness conquers injustice at its roots and leads the oppressor to become a comrade, the enemy to become a brother or sister." On the problem of knowledge see also J. Fischer, "Vom Geheimnis der Stellvertretung," *EK* 21 (1988): 165-67, esp. 167, and idem, *Glaube als Erkenntnis: Studien zum Erkenntnisproblem des christlichen Glaubens*, BEvT 105 (1989), 76ff., esp. 89-90. Fischer concludes his reflections with the following statement regarding Christ's taking the place of others: "The question of whether Christ's taking the place of others in his death is still comprehensible for people today is synonymous with the question of whether people today are still capable of such practical knowledge in the realm of their faith. We must be clear here: If the answer is No, then every understanding of Jesus' death and all faith and all theology is soteriologically irrelevant, because through it nothing, absolutely nothing, is changed in human reality" ("Vom Geheimnis der Stellvertretung," 167).

64. Still relevant here is H. W. Wolff, *Jesaja 53 im Urchristentum* (1942; 4th ed. reprinted in 1984 with an introduction by P. Stuhlmacher), 7-11.

65. Cf. Kutsch, "Sein Leiden und Tod — unser Heil," 195-96, and Hermisson, "Israel und der Gottesknecht," 2-3. Historical reasoning must clarify among other things whether Koch is right to characterize Isaiah 53 as an "erratic block" which continued on in the stream of tradition "without being understood even into the New Testament period" (K. Koch, "Sühne und Sündenvergebung um die Wende von der exilischen zur nachexilischen Zeit" [1966], reprinted in idem, *Spuren des hebräischen Denkens: Beiträge zur alttestamentlichen Theologie: Gesammelte*

Songs and the earliest Christian proclamation of the death of Jesus. On the contrary. But it does mean that the Old Testament texts do not first derive their truth from the New Testament.[66] That would be totally out of keeping with the spirit of Acts 8:34-35. For Philip did not answer, "This word [sc. Isa. 53:7-8] is fulfilled in Jesus!" or "The Servant of Isaiah 53 is Jesus Christ!" Rather, he took Isaiah 53:7-8 as the starting point of his proclamation, which in turn led him beyond this Scripture passage. "His preaching about Jesus the Christ is, so to speak, a continuation of the book of Isaiah."[67]

The common view of both Testaments that the suffering and death of the righteous does not coincide with failure and meaninglessness[68] explains why the New Testament witnesses took up the tradition of the vicarious suffering of the righteous despite the problem of tradition history — namely, "in order to grasp the meaning of the death of Jesus more pointedly by means of this typology."[69] For the Ethiopian eunuch and many others, Isaiah 53 was a decisive aid to understanding.

Aufsätze Band 1, ed. B. Janowski and M. Krause [1991], 184-205, esp. 203). On the other hand, there may be intermediate developments linking Isaiah 53 to the New Testament. See most recently C. Breytenbach, *Versöhnung: Eine Studie zur paulinischen Soteriologie*, WMANT 60 (1989), 205ff.; Barth, *Der Tod Jesu Christi im Verständnis des Neuen Testaments*, 56ff.; and P. Stuhlmacher, *Biblische Theologie des Neuen Testaments*, vol. 1 (1992), 125ff., esp. 129-30. The fact that the history of the reception of the Servant Songs begins as early as Isaiah 40-44 and then extends over a period of three centuries in the books of Second and Third Isaiah is also, I believe, of considerable importance for this problem. Cf. Steck, "Gottesvolk und Gottesknecht in Jes 40–66," 51ff.; idem, "Gottesknechts-Texte," 149ff.

66. Cf. E. Zenger, *Das Erste Testament: Die jüdische Bibel und die Christen* (1991), 123ff.

67. Zenger, *Das Erste Testament*, 128; cf. Steck, "Gottesvolk und Gottesknecht in Jes 40–66," 53, 75.

68. Cf. Steck, "Gottesvolk und Gottesknecht in Jes 40–66," 53: "The Servant Songs allow the Christ event to be understood as God's act, and vice versa. In retrospect, the Christ event discloses the ultimate meaning of that act of God which was sketched out in the formulations of the Servant Songs."

69. H. W. Wolff, *Anthropologie des Alten Testaments*, 5th ed. (1990), 176. I understand "type" and "typology" in the sense described more precisely by Kutsch, "Sein Leiden und Tod — unser Heil," 195-96.

The Effective History of Isaiah 53 in the Pre-Christian Period

Martin Hengel
with the collaboration of Daniel P. Bailey

For Frieder Mildenberger on his 65th birthday with deepest gratitude

Summary

Did Isaiah 53 have any significant pre-Christian influence? Or is this mainly the invention of a few conservative exegetes? This essay takes a middle position. The reception and further development of Isaiah 53 can indeed be detected in a wide variety of pre-Christian Jewish writings — including Hebrew and Aramaic texts as well as original Greek texts and translations: even the LXX of Isaiah 53 shows important interpretive tendencies. The widespread assumption that Isaiah 53 was without much influence therefore needs modification. The passage was not only read and interpreted; it was apparently also interpreted *messianically* (so, e.g., in 1QIsaᵃ). Nevertheless, the passage's influence in early Judaism is not all of the same type, nor all of the type that would necessarily support the preaching of early Christianity regarding a *suffering, atoning figure* who bears the sins of others *vicariously*. With the exception of the Hebrew (both MT and 1QIsaᵃ) and Greek texts of Isaiah 53 — and perhaps Daniel

---

The English version of this essay has been updated and expanded by the translator, Daniel P. Bailey, in consultation with the author. This is most evident in section 7 below on the *Aramaic Apocryphon of Levi* (4Q540-541), where there are several pages of added material; similar updating takes place in section 10 on the *Self-Glorification Hymn* (4Q491c) and elsewhere throughout the text. Philological arguments, which are now accompanied by references to multiple English translations, have been expanded and made more accessible to those without an advanced knowledge of Hebrew and Greek, for example in the text of the discussions of the book of Daniel (below §4) and LXX Isaiah 53 (below §8), and especially in the notes. These include nn. 30, 36, 37, 38, 40, 52, 67-70, 73, 87, 91, 99, 118, 135, 162, 175, 176, 184, 185, 193, 199, 200, 204, 216, 217.

11–12, the *Aramaic Apocryphon of Levi* 4Q540-541, and the *Testament of Benjamin* 3:8 — the motif of vicarious suffering tends to recede into the background in the Jewish tradition, especially where the savior's exaltation or his role as judge is prominent (e.g., *1 Enoch; Self-Glorification Hymn* 4Q491). Nevertheless, the demonstrated uses and echoes of this text are enough to suggest that traditions of suffering and atoning eschatological messianic figures were current in Palestinian Judaism, and that Jesus and the earliest Church *could* have known and appealed to them. This would explain how first Jesus and then his disciples could assume that their message of the Messiah's vicarious atoning death would be comprehensible to their Jewish contemporaries.

1. Preliminary Observations

After the two self-contained, well-rounded, and knowledgeable presentations that we have heard in the first couple of meetings of our seminar,[1] today I can provide you — to adopt a Markan turn of phrase — only κλάσματα, "broken pieces" or indeed only ψιχία, "crumbs." This lies in the nature of the case. For it is debated whether the text that is engaging us this semester, the so-called fourth Servant Song of Second Isaiah, had any "effective history" (German: *Wirkungsgeschichte*) at all worthy of the name during the pre-Christian period. Might these "effects" not rather be mainly the product of the wishful thinking of a few conservative exegetes? The danger becomes especially acute when in searching for traces of this text, one concentrates upon the problem of a potential "messianic" savior figure who suffers or dies vicariously for others, and whose picture is supposed to have been influenced by this text — in other words, when one tries to prove that there are hints of a "suffering Messiah" bearing the stamp of Isaiah 53 already in the pre-Christian period. Yet the wish of so-called critical interpreters to reject this kind of tradition history from the start before examining the complex details of the case is no less suspect. Historical reality never follows our wishes. It would indeed be strange if this unique text, Isaiah 53, had left no tangible effects over a period of more than 500 years during which the Jewish people were beset by heavy sufferings.[2]

---

1. The reference is to the essays by H. J. Hermisson and B. Janowski in the present volume; the first essay, by H. Spieckermann, was not part of the original German volume *Der leidende Gottesknecht.*

2. The impact of Isaiah 53 on pre-Christian Jewish texts has never been thoroughly researched as far as I can tell. See the all too brief overview by H. Haag, *Der Gottesknecht bei Deuterojesaja,* EdF 23 (1985), 34-36, and J. W. van Henten, ed., *Die Entstehung der jüdischen Martyrologie,* StPB 38 (1989), especially the contribution to the discussion by L. Ruppert: "I used

In the Christian period it is entirely different. From the second century C.E. onward we possess in Judaism scattered references to a Messiah figure who suffers for a short time and who could be described by passages from Isaiah 53 and elsewhere. We even find a Messiah ben Joseph or Messiah from Ephraim who ultimately dies, though in the background stands not Isaiah 53 but rather Zechariah 12:10-14 (in addition to Deut. 33:16-17); see the Baraita in *b. Sukkot* 52a.[3] The origin of this one "anointed for war," who according to later traditions dies in the battle against Gog and Magog or the "Antichrist" Armilos, remains opaque. I do not believe with Billerbeck that we need to see him as "merely the product of Jewish scriptural erudition."[4] But since a pre-Christian origin of this idea is only possible, not provable, we must leave it to one side for the moment, remembering at the same time that given the fragmentary and accidental nature of our sources, the argument from silence is the most questionable of all arguments. Hence there could be for example an ancient connection between Isaiah 53 and Zechariah 12:10-14 and 13:7 (see below §3). The rise of the idea of a Messiah ben Joseph may coincide with the three great national catastrophes between 66 and 135 C.E., but it could also be significantly older. Yet at its best, this idea forms part of the effective history of Isaiah 53 only indirectly, helped along by Zechariah 12:10ff. and the Armenian version of the *Testament of Benjamin* 3:8. The latter is an especially controversial text, upon which J. Jeremias laid great weight and to which we must briefly return.[5]

Several other texts are excluded from our survey. These include the reference to the death of the Messiah after a 400-year reign of his messianic kingdom found in *4 Ezra (2 Esdras)* 7:29. This may speak of the Servant (assuming that *filius meus Christus* = παῖς θεοῦ or Χριστός), but not of his atoning sufferings. Also excluded on temporal grounds alone are the later rabbinic reports of the suffering (not the death) of the Davidic Messiah already mentioned.[6]

---

to consider the diptych (in Wisdom 2 and 5) and the Daniel passages in 11:33ff. and 12:2-3 to be the earliest effects of Isaiah 53, but regarding the Daniel passages I am no longer so certain" (p. 251). But we will have to reckon with more of these "effects." The often confused work of E. Ruprecht, "Die Auslegungsgeschichte zu den sogenannten Gottesknechtliedern im Buche Deuterojesaja unter methodischen Gesichtspunkten bis zu Bernhard Duhm," Ph.D. dissertation, University of Heidelberg, 1972, is completely unsatisfactory.

3. R. Dosa, around 180; see Str-B 2:293, 299. Cf. also O. Skarsaune, *The Proof from Prophecy,* NovTSup 56 (1987), 395ff., on Justin Martyr immediately after the Bar-Kochba Revolt.

4. Str-B 2:294. On Armilos see Str-B 3:638ff., esp. 639.

5. In §9 below. On this see M. de Jonge, "Test. Benjamin 3,8 and the Picture of Joseph as 'a good and holy man,'" in van Henten, *Die Entstehung der jüdischen Martyrologie,* 204-14.

6. On this see G. Dalman, *Der leidende und sterbende Messias der Synagoge im ersten christlichen Jahrtausend* (1888); Str-B 2:274-92; J. J. Brière-Narbonne, *Le Messie souffrant dans la littérature rabbinique* (1940).

Finally, elsewhere in this volume Jostein Ådna deals with the special problems of the *Targum of Isaiah* on our text against the background of the rabbinic parallels, while for later medieval rabbinic interpretation of Isaiah 53, I may refer to the study of my colleague Stefan Schreiner.

I shall also pass over the question of the interpretation of Isaiah 53 in the various post-Christian Jewish versions. These include the Greek translations of the Old Testament by Theodotion, Aquila (listed in this order first by Irenaeus,[7] who thereby hints at their correct chronological sequence), and the Jewish Christian Symmachus, whose background is admittedly debated,[8] as well as the Syriac Peshitta version. All these versions have been investigated in detail, though with uncertain results, by Harald Hegermann.[9] Yet I shall set them aside because of their relative unproductivity, especially since in the case of the Christian Symmachus (assuming that he really was one), an interpretation in terms of God's Servant Jesus is naturally to be presupposed. The same goes for the Peshitta. Recent research has shown that we cannot certainly establish its supposed origins from a pre-Christian Jewish Targum from the Jewish regions of north Mesopotamia (i.e., Adiabene), as suspected by P. Kahle and, in dependence on him, J. Jeremias and Hegermann. Thus according to A. van der Kooij, *Die alten Textzeugen des Jesajabuches* (1981), the Peshitta of Isaiah originated in east Syria in the second half of the second century, from a Syrian Jewish Christian who used the Hebrew text and the LXX but was uninfluenced by an older Palestinian Targum.[10] The existence of a Jewish, pre-Christian *Vetus Syra* cannot be maintained according to van der Kooij. In any case we find ourselves on such uncertain ground that we do better to set aside this problem. In the case of the Peshitta the danger is too great that we presuppose an older Jewish Targum, but in reality draw our results from the interpretation of a Syrian (Jewish) Christian. In other words, we shall limit ourselves to the Jewish texts that are *clearly* pre-Christian.

7. Irenaeus, *Haer.* 3.21.1. See on this M. Hengel with R. Deines, "Die Septuaginta als 'christliche Schriftensammlung', ihre Vorgeschichte und das Problem ihres Kanons," in M. Hengel and A. M. Schwemer, eds., *Die Septuaginta zwischen Judentum und Christentum,* WUNT 72 (1994), 205 n. 71 = M. Hengel, *The Septuagint as Christian Scripture: Its Prehistory and the Problem of Its Canon,* trans. M. E. Biddle (2002), esp. 43 with n. 59.; M. Harl, G. Dorival, and O. Munnich, *La Bible Grecque des Septante* (1988), 142ff., 150ff.

8. Hengel, "Die Septuaginta," 205 = ET, *The Septuagint,* 43. Symmachus is first mentioned by Eusebius, *Hist. eccl.* 6.16 in connection with Origen's *Hexapla;* cf. 6.17 for the claim that Symmachus was an Ebionite. D. Barthélemy suspects on the basis of rabbinic reports that Symmachus was a Samaritan converted to Judaism: "Qui est Symmaque?" (1974), reprinted in idem, *Études d'histoire du texte de l'Ancien Testament,* OBO 21 (1982), 307-21.

9. H. Hegermann, *Jesaja 53 in Hexapla, Targum und Peschitta,* BFCT 56 (1954).

10. A. van der Kooij, *Die alten Textzeugen des Jesajabuches,* OBO 35 (1981), 258-98. The translator could have inserted Jewish (or Jewish Christian) interpretive traditions.

Greek Minor Prophets Scroll from Nahal-Hever[15] — with the constant influence of corrective Palestinian recensions upon the original Septuagint translation. Paul sometimes used a Greek text revised according to the Hebrew, as in his citation of Isaiah 52:7 in Romans 10:15, though in his immediately following citation in Romans 10:16 of Isaiah 53:1 he once again follows the Septuagint version.[16] Palestinian and Hellenistic Jewish texts and interpretive traditions cannot be so neatly separated. Therefore one will hardly be able to say with Jeremias that "following the LXX, Hellenistic Judaism referred [the Servant passages of Deutero-Isaiah, including Isaiah 42:1 and Isaiah 53] to the people Israel," thus interpreting them "collectively," while "Palestinian Judaism takes [them] to be wholly Messianic."[17] Individual messianic and collective interpretations seem to have stood together as possibilities from the start, though depending on the situation, the emphasis could be placed on one side or the other. Under certain circumstances the two possibilities could be viewed simultaneously as different aspects of the text, because a messianic figure is always at the same time a representative of the whole people.

This still holds even in early Christianity, where ecclesiology is completely grounded in Christology. The messianic eschatological expectation was also at home in the Egyptian diaspora, as a comparison of Balaam's oracle (Num. 24:7ff., 17ff.) in the LXX and the MT shows.[18] The Old Greek version of the LXX from the third century B.C.E. here shows close points of contact with the later Targum and Palestinian tradition, and the same holds true for its history of interpretation up through Philo and the *Sibylline Oracles*. The disastrous revolt of the Jews in Egypt and the Roman province of Cyrenaica in 115-117 C.E. was messianically inspired, as was the slightly later revolt of Bar-Kochba in Judea. Theodotion, who according to Jeremias and Hegermann offers messianic interpretations in his recension of the LXX, was not a Palestinian Jew but a proselyte from Ephesus; Aquila came from Pontus, and the Jewish scholars who in-

---

the motherland; cf. I. L. Seeligmann, *The Septuagint Version of Isaiah*, MEOL 9 (1948), and further below, §8.

15. D. Barthélemy, *Les devanciers d'Aquila*, VTSup 10 (1963); E. Tov et al., *The Greek Minor Prophets Scroll from Nahal Hever (8 Hev XIIgr)*, DJD 8 (1990).

16. See D. A. Koch, *Die Schrift als Zeuge des Evangeliums*, BHT 69 (1986), 66-67, 81-82, 243. Isaiah 53:1 LXX = John 12:38 represents a pre-Pauline "standard Christian formula." Cf. Justin, *Dial.* 42.2; 114.2. According to Skarsaune, *Proof from Prophecy*, 94, 116, Justin here is directly dependent on Romans.

17. Jeremias, *TWNT* 5:682 ll. 13-23 = *TDNT* 5:683 l. 24–684 l. 8.

18. M. Hengel, "Messianische Hoffnung und politischer 'Radikalismus' in der jüdisch-hellenistischen Diaspora," in D. Hellholm, ed., *Apocalypticism in the Mediterranean World and the Near East* (1980), 655-86, esp. 679-80.

formed Origen of the collective interpretation of our text (*c. Cels.* 1.55) did so presumably in Palestinian Caesarea (*Contra Celsum* is from the end of Origen's life, shortly before the Decian persecution). It is true that the Greek παῖς allows for an interpretation in the sense of God's "son" or "child" more readily than does the Hebrew עֶבֶד.[19] But already in Palestinian Judaism, the designation "Son of God" can be applied collectively to Israel, to the Messiah, and to the individual godly, pious, or wise person.[20] This will hardly have been different for the designation "Servant of God."

2. The Eschatological Interpretation of the Whole Book of Isaiah

We encounter the book of Isaiah as a unity probably as early as the time of 2 Chronicles 32:32, that is, in the early Hellenistic period, because here the material concerning Hezekiah in 2 Kings 18–20 (= Isaiah 36–39) is already assumed to be part of the "vision of Isaiah," חֲזוֹן יְשַׁעְיָהוּ (2 Chron. 32:32 and Isa. 1:1), or ὅρασις in Greek (ὅρασις in Isa. 1:1, though προφητεία in 2 Chron. 32:32; cf. ὅρασις Sir. 48:22). 2 Chronicles 20:20 already cites the wordplay about "believing and being established" in Isaiah 7:9b, while 2 Chronicles 20:7 presumably cites the wordplay in Isaiah 41:8.[21] The book's unity is clearly attested by Ben Sira around 200 B.C.E. in his "Hymn of the Fathers" (Sir. 44:1–51:24), where Isaiah, the most important of the writing prophets, is called "a great man *trustworthy in his vision*," πιστὸς ἐν ὁράσει αὐτοῦ (Sir. 48:22 NJB, against the NRSV's plural "visions").[22] Ben Sira continues:

19. J. Jeremias, *Abba* (1966), 193-94, 196ff.

20. Cf. M. Hengel, *The Son of God: The Origin of Christology and the History of Jewish-Hellenistic Religion* (ET, 1976).

21. "The seed of Abraham your/my friend," זֶרַע אַבְרָהָם אֹהֲבֶךָ or אֹהֲבִי; van der Kooij, *Die alten Textzeugen des Jesajabuches,* 15-19. There is no support for the hypothesis expressed by H. Greßmann, *Der Messias* (1929), 333-34, and others who claim on the basis of 2 Chron. 36:22 and Ezra 1:1 that Isaiah 40–55 was originally attributed to Jeremiah, an idea now taken up once again by Ruprecht, "Auslegungsgeschichte," 6-7. The fulfillment of "the word of the Lord spoken by Jeremiah" mentioned in these passages refers rather to the seventy years of exile prophesied in Jer. 25:11; 29:10; cf. Zech. 1:12.

22. Sir. 48:22: "For Hezekiah did what is pleasing to the Lord, and was steadfast in the ways of David his father, enjoined on him by the prophet Isaiah, a great man trustworthy in his vision" (NJB). Although this verse is lacking, presumably by accidental omission, in the only Hebrew manuscript of Sirach extant for this text (B), it must be presupposed there to complete the sense, since the expression "he saw the last things" (εἶδεν τὰ ἔσχατα = חֹזֶה אַחֲרִית) in v. 24 is true only of Isaiah, not of Hezekiah.

In the power of the spirit [Isaiah] saw the last things

(אחרית = τὰ ἔσχατα)

and comforted the mourners in Zion.

He revealed the future things (נהיות = τὰ ἐσόμενα) to the end of time

(עד עולם = ἕως τοῦ αἰῶνος)

and the hidden things (נסתרות = τὰ ἀπόκρυφα) long before they

happened. (Sirach 48:24-25, NJB modified)

These last sentences refer clearly to the prophecies of Deutero- and Trito-Isaiah, while the phrase "he comforted the mourners in Zion," παρεκάλεσεν τοὺς πενθοῦντας ἐν Σιων, refers to texts like Isaiah 40:1. In the prayer in Sirach 36 about the eschatological salvation of the people of God, there are allusions to Isaiah 60:22b;[23] 47:8b = 47:10c;[24] 41:26; 48:16;[25] and other passages. The conclusion "all who are on the earth will know that you are the Lord, the God of the ages" (Sir. 36:22 NRSV; v. 17 LXX) is a typical Deuteroisaianic formulation.[26]

In Sirach 48:10 the task given to Elijah (cf. Sir. 48:1, 4) is "to turn the heart of the father to the son, and to restore the tribes of Jacob" (RSV, following LXX; Heb. reads "Israel").[27] Here Ben Sira has taken up language originally applied to the Servant in Isaiah 49:6, "to raise up the tribes of Jacob and to restore the survivors of Israel," and has combined it in a slightly modified form with a saying from Malachi 4:6 (MT 3:24) about Elijah, who will "turn the hearts of fathers to their sons," in order to speak about the Elijah *redivivus* who is to come at the appointed time. Isaiah 49:6 has therefore been given "a messianic or at least an *individual* interpretation"[28] and has been associated with Elijah, though it remains questionable whether Ben Sira wished to identify the Servant *directly* with Elijah *redivivus*.

23. Compare Sir. 36:10 (v. 7 LXX), "Hasten the day, and remember the appointed time" (NRSV) with Isa. 60:22b, "I am the Lord; in its time I will accomplish it quickly" — challenged by the ungodly in Isa. 5:19, "Let him make haste, let him speed his work."

24. Compare Sir. 36:12 (v. 9 LXX), "Crush the heads of hostile rulers who say, 'There is no one but ourselves'" (NRSV) with Isa. 47:8b = 47:10c, "I am, and there is no one besides me." This entire verse in Sirach, with its allusion to Num. 24:17 ("a star shall come out of Jacob, and a scepter shall rise out of Israel; it shall *crush* the borderlands of Moab"), is directed against the Hellenistic ruler cult.

25. Compare Sir. 36:20 (v. 14 LXX), "Bear witness to those whom you created in the beginning, and fulfill the prophecies spoken in your name" (NRSV) with Isa. 48:16, "From the beginning I have not spoken in secret, from the time it came to be I have been there."

26. Cf. Isa. 40:28; 41:5, 9; 43:6; 45:22; 48:20; 49:6; 52:10; 62:11.

27. Compare Sir. 48:10 Hebrew ל[בטי ישרא] שׁ ולהכין . . . להשׁיב with LXX καταστῆσαι φυλὰς Ἰακωβ and Isa. 49:6: לְהָקִים אֶת־שִׁבְטֵי . . . יִשְׂרָאֵל לְהָשִׁיב.

28. Haag, *Gottesknecht*, 35; cf. Ruprecht, "Auslegungsgeschichte," 10ff., who draws too far-reaching conclusions.

Since the beginning of the early Hellenistic period at the latest, the book of Isaiah was interpreted as a whole (and eschatologically) and exerted its influence as such. Our modern divisions of the text can therefore not be presupposed for the early period. For one thing, the distinction of sense units can vary from manuscript to manuscript. Hence while in the Qumran Isaiah Scroll A (1QIsaᵃ) a new column begins at Isaiah 52:13, and the rest of the line is left blank at the end of 52:12, in Scroll B we find only the normal distance between words separating 52:12 and 13, but a larger distance, indicating a sense division, between 52:10 and 11. On the other hand, the writer of Scroll A begins Isaiah 40:1 with the last line of a column, seeing here no significant new beginning. In post-Christian Jewish manuscripts there was a clear sense division at Isaiah 54:1, because there began the *haftara* readings from the Prophets to complement the Torah reading from Genesis 16:1. But the immediately preceding *haftara* began at Isaiah 52:3 and originally included only this verse according to *t. Meg.* 3:18 (cf. *b. Meg.* 24a). Later the reading was extended to 52:5 or 52:10, and finally Isaiah 53:4 and 5 were added as a messianic supplement.[29] Our *Biblia Hebraica*, which here follows Codex Leningradensis, still makes these developments partly visible, though admittedly it sees 52:13–53:12 as a unit in its own right.

Nevertheless, already with Ben Sira it is clear that as early as the beginning of the second century B.C.E., that is, still in the pre-Maccabean period, people were applying Isaiah's *whole* work to the eschatological future. Ben Sira's grandson, who translated his original Hebrew work, renders אחרית by τὰ ἔσχατα (Sir. 48:24), an expression that first appears in a temporal, eschatological sense of "the last things" in Second Isaiah (Isa. 41:22; 46:10; 47:7).[30] Also on the basis of the fragments of the Isaiah *pesharim* A-D from 4Q (4Q161-165) one can assume that this important prophetic work was interpreted almost entirely with reference to the "last days," that is, in Qumran, also with reference to the present time "at the end of days."[31] This will also hold true for Isaiah 53 with its

---

29. J. Mann, *The Bible as Read and Preached in the Old Synagogue,* vol. 1 (1940), lv, 298-99, 566 n. 71.

30. The expression τὰ ἔσχατα translates אחרית also in LXX Ps. 72:17 (MT 73:17); 138:9 (MT 139:9); Job 42:12, but without Isaiah's temporal *and* eschatological sense. In LXX Ps. 138:9 the sense is spatial rather than temporal (τὰ ἔσχατα τῆς θαλάσσης = "the *farthest limits* of the sea"), while in Job 42:12, ὁ δὲ κύριος εὐλόγησεν τὰ ἔσχατα Ιωβ, "the Lord blessed the *latter days* of Job," the sense is temporal but not eschatological. Only in LXX Ps. 72:17 may an eschatological sense begin to creep in: ἕως εἰσέλθω εἰς τὸ ἁγιαστήριον τοῦ θεοῦ καὶ συνῶ εἰς τὰ ἔσχατα αὐτῶν, "until I go into the sanctuary of God and understand their *latter end*."

31. Heb. באתרית הימים (or ל־); see the index under 4QpIsa in Allegro, DJD 5:92. Cf. also 1QpHab 2:6; 9:6 and other examples from the exegesis of the prophets; see J. H. Charlesworth, *Graphic Concordance to the Dead Sea Scrolls* (1991), 134-35.

numerous future-tense statements. The only question is where and how this happened.

3. The Effects of Isaiah 53 upon Zechariah 12:9–13:1 and 13:7-9

First we must look back from Sirach to two older texts which reflect the military catastrophes of the early period of the Diadochi immediately following Alexander the Great and perhaps belong together with the conquest of Jerusalem after the battle of Gaza in 312 B.C.E. (or after Ipsos in 301) by Ptolemy I Soter.[32] They are among the latest canonical prophetic texts: Zechariah 12:9–13:1 (esp. 12:10-14) and 13:7-9.

Both passages speak of the violent death of a (messianic?) leader. The first seems to be about a Davidide, and this is also probably true in the second passage, since the "shepherd" (Zech. 13:7) was one of the most important metaphors for a ruler. In the case of the anonymous continuation of the prophetic books, we must assume that the unknown authors of these prophetic oracles, which were already apocalyptically colored, knew the older prophetic literature — here once again supremely Isaiah — extremely well. Countless interpreters of Zechariah have therefore suspected, I believe correctly, the influence of the Suffering Servant Song of Isaiah 53. W. Rudolph sees a reference to the Messiah in the shepherd chapter of Zechariah 11:4-17 and in the related passage in 13:7-9 about the death of the shepherd and the refining of the remnant (which Rudolph places directly after 11:17): "On God's behalf, the prophet recalls the Messiah's task."[33] This offensive "pessimism of the prophet, that even the Messiah would suffer such a terrible fiasco with Yahweh's approval in 13:7," is best explained by the fact that "the prophet had

---

32. See M. Hengel, *Juden, Griechen und Barbaren*, SBS 76 (1976), 33-35 = ET, *Jews, Greeks and Barbarians*, trans. J. Bowden (1980), 18-20; O. H. Steck, *Der Abschluß der Prophetie im Alten Testament*, Biblisch-theologische Studien 17 (1991), 37-55, 99-105, whose date for Zechariah between 240 and 226 B.C.E. seems to me to be too late. By the time of Ben Sira around 200 B.C.E. the prophetic canon is already fixed. On this see M. Hengel, "'Schriftauslegung' und 'Schriftwerdung' in der Zeit des Zweiten Tempels," in M. Hengel and H. Löhr, eds., *Schriftauslegung im antiken Judentum und Urchristentum*, WUNT 73 (1994), 1-72, esp. 24ff., 34-35, 38ff.

33. W. Rudolph, *Haggai — Sacharja 1–8 — Sacharja 9–14 — Maleachi*, KAT 13/4 (1976), 206. On Zech. 13:7: "This can only be about the first shepherd, in whom we recognize the Messiah." A direct connection of 13:7 with 11:17 has been championed by many interpreters since Ewald. See also T. H. Robinson and F. Horst, *Die zwölf kleinen Propheten*, HAT I/14 (1964), 253-54.

before him the figure of the Servant in Deutero-Isaiah."[34] As Rudolph explains,

> Just as the prophet Second Isaiah learned that the Messiah's demise at human hands could not alter God's saving plan (Isa 53:10), so our prophet in Zechariah received the divine message that Yahweh would take this human guilt into his saving plan. At the same time he deals freely with the Servant Song. In Isaiah, the fate of the Ebed stands center stage; his death is not punishment for his own sins but is vicarious suffering. . . . Zech 13:7-9, by contrast, is first and foremost about the fate of the people. The severity of their punishment corresponds to the severity of their guilt, but this also serves simultaneously to refine them, so that in the end the ideal relationship between God and his people is established.[35]

Close linguistic points of contact with Isaiah arise from the use of the verb נָכָה, "strike," in Zechariah 13:7b. This is understood in the MT as a command of Yahweh to his own sword to "strike the shepherd," הַךְ אֶת־הָרֹעֶה, where הַךְ is the hiphil imperative of נָכָה.[36] However, some textual critics, guided in part by the first person future πατάξω, "I will strike," in a few Septuagint manuscripts (cf. Matt. 26:31; Mark 14:27),[37] have suggested that the original Hebrew may have read the first person hiphil imperfect אַכֶּה, "I will strike" (cf. Zech. 12:4),[38] parallel to the first person וַהֲשִׁבֹתִי (*"I will turn* my hand") at the end of the verse. This would then express not Yahweh's command but his fixed

---

34. Rudolph, *Sacharja 9–14*, 213; cf. K. Elliger, *Das Buch der zwölf kleinen Propheten*, vol. 2, ATD 25 (1980), 166: "There can be no doubt but that the author has before him a Messiah figure."

35. Rudolph, *Sacharja 9–14*, 213-14. Rudolph refers in this context to P. Lamarche, *Zacharie IX–XIV, Structure littéraire et messianisme* (1961), 139-47, see especially pp. 144-45, with reference to older literature.

36. The short imperative הַךְ in Zech. 13:7b is found a total of seven times in the OT (e.g., Amos 9:1), though it can also be spelled more regularly as הַכֵּה (Ezek. 6:11).

37. For the LXX manuscripts see *Duodecim prophetae*, ed. J. Ziegler (Göttingen LXX), 322 on Zech. 13:7: πατάξω, "I will strike," is read by V-538, 46-86ᶜ-711ᶜ, 106, 233′, etc., against the text's imperative πατάξατε, "strike!"

38. Against the MT's short form of the imperative הַךְ, "strike!", the note in *BHS* at Zech. 13:7 mentions both אַכֶּה, "I will strike," and הַכֵּה, "strike!" as plausible conjectures for metric reasons (*metri causa*). It may be possible to think of a textual evolution from an original imperfect אַכֶּה (cf. Zech. 12:4) to the imperative הַכֵּה (cf. Ezek. 6:11) to the MT's short imperative הַךְ. The first person imperfect אַכֶּה is also favored by Elliger (*Das Buch der zwölf kleinen Propheten*) and Robinson and Horst, *Die zwölf kleinen Propheten*, 252: "Wahrlich *ich* schlage den Hirten" (Zech. 13:7). Possibly the Hebrew textual tradition found the first person "*I* will strike" to be offensive and softened it. On the other hand, Zech. 13:7b as cited in the Damascus Document CD-B 19:8 (see *DSSSE* 1:566-67) appears exactly as in the MT, reading הך.

purpose. Either way it is about God's judgment of the one he describes as "my shepherd" (רֹעִי), "the man who is my associate" or "who stands next to me" (גֶּבֶר עֲמִיתִי) (Zech. 13:7a, NRSV and RSV, respectively)[39] — a designation that comes relatively close to "my Servant." In Isaiah 53:4b the Servant is described by the same verb "to strike" as one who is מֻכֵּה אֱלֹהִים, "struck down by God."[40] The "scattering of the sheep" in Zechariah 13:7 recalls Isaiah 53:6, "All we like sheep have gone astray; we have turned every one to his own way" (RSV). However, Isaiah 53:5-6 presents the retrospective view of the congregation, whereas Zechariah 13:7 presents God's direct activity. Salvation in Zechariah is not granted through vicarious suffering that effects atonement. Instead, a remnant is saved by passing through the fire of judgment, giving God the glory (Zech. 13:8-9). The judgment upon the shepherd who stands close to God appears as the beginning of this refining judgment.

In Zechariah 12:10-14 a comparable event is presented from a very different angle. The many sentences in the chapter beginning with the "apocalyptic" introductory formula "on that day" express alternatively the deadly threat to Judea and Jerusalem from the nations and the saving care of their God.[41] Zechariah 12:9 as a transitional verse brings together the events of looming destruction and of salvation. From 12:10 the passage "presents how after a heroic struggle a great cultic festival of mourning is held."[42]

As a sign of the dawning of the age of salvation God himself pours out "a spirit of compassion and supplication on the house of David" (Zech. 12:10a), which alone makes possible an insightful lament worthy of this event. This fundamental insight means that the residents of Jerusalem "look on the one whom they have pierced" (12:10b),[43] while the "spirit of compassion and supplication"

---

39. Similar to the RSV (cited above), L. Koehler, W. Baumgartner, and J. J. Stamm in *HALAT* 1:199 s.v. גֶּבֶר translate גֶּבֶר עֲמִיתִי in Zech. 13:7 by "der Mann, der mir nahe steht," though the English version reads simply "male companion" (*HALOT* 1:176 s.v. גֶּבֶר I).

40. In Isa. 53:4, instead of the MT's מֻכֵּה אֱלֹהִים, "struck down by God" (hophal participle of נָכָה), the LXX speaks only of one who is ἐν πληγῇ, "in suffering" or perhaps "wounded." According to Field *(Origenis Hexaplorum)*, Aquila and Theodotion expand this by ἐν πληγῇ ὑπὸ θεοῦ, "wounded by God." However, in Ziegler's edition (*Isaias*, Göttingen LXX), an alternative reading, which Field attributes only to Symmachus, is attributed to all three revisers: πεπληγότα ὑπὸ θεοῦ, "smitten by God" (cf. τοῦ ἀνθρώπου τοῦ πεπληγότος, Num. 25:14, perfect participle of πλήσσω).

41. Zech. 12:4, 6, 8, 9; 13:1-4; cf. 14:1, 6.

42. H. Gese, "Anfang und Ende der Apokalyptik dargestellt am Sacharjabuch," reprinted in idem, *Vom Sinai zum Zion*, BEvT 64 (1974), 202-30, esp. 225-26 (originally in *ZTK* 70 [1973]: 20-49, esp. 43-44).

43. On the text and translation of Zech. 12:10b, see Robinson and Horst, *Die zwölf kleinen Propheten*, 254. Cf. Elliger, *Das Buch der zwölf kleinen Propheten*, 2:158, 160-61: "the text can just as well contemplate the death [of the pierced one] at the hands of the besiegers assembled for

brings with it the knowledge of their own guilt over against the pierced one. The various clans mentioned in the lament (12:12-14) add vividness to the ideal picture of Jerusalem at the time of David. At the same time this lament recalls the perpetual lament that Jeremiah composed for the legal reformer Josiah, who died at Megiddo.[44] One can furthermore ask whether the comparison with the lament or mourning for the dying and rising Hadad-rimmon in the plain of Megiddo in Zechariah 12:11 is not already a veiled reference to the apocalyptic possibility of a resurrection of the dead, which we encounter in Isaiah 26:19, a roughly contemporary text.[45] Of this puzzling text in Zechariah 12:10 Karl Elliger asks, "Has this figure already flowed together with the figure of the Deutero-Isaianic Servant, revealing the figure of a martyr Messiah or a messianic forerunner who suffers for the sins of the people?" Elliger answers this question in the affirmative by referring to the statement of the shepherd in Zechariah 13:7 and the concluding promise of 13:1 that the "fountain shall be opened for the house of David and the inhabitants of Jerusalem, to cleanse them from sin and impurity" (NRSV).[46] A messianic reference in Zechariah 12:10 is also maintained decisively by W. Rudolph, who identifies "the one whom they have pierced" with the shepherd or Messiah of Zechariah 11:4ff. and 13:7, claiming that "the prophet is under the influence of Isaiah 53, where the verbs חלל and דכא in 53:5 are synonymous with the verb דקר [in Zech. 12:10]."[47]

---

the final battle as death at the hands of his comrades in arms" (161). See also M. C. Albl, *"And Scripture Cannot Be Broken": The Form and Function of the Early Christian* Testimonia *Collections*, NovTSup 96 (1999), 253-65, who includes a study of the versions of Zech. 12:10 and its use in the New Testament and early Christian literature.

44. Jer. 22:10; cf. esp. 2 Chron. 35:24-25: "All Judah and Jerusalem mourned for Josiah. Jeremiah also uttered a lament for Josiah, and all the singing men and singing women have spoken of Josiah in their laments to this day. They made these a custom in Israel; they are recorded in the Laments." The book of Chronicles and Zechariah 12–14 stand chronologically close to one another.

45. Elliger, *Das Buch der zwölf kleinen Propheten*, 2:162: "although with the mention of Hadad-Rimmon the mystery of the resurrection is strangely also touched upon — but just touched upon — the idea of the resurrection of the martyr seems far from the author's mind." By contrast, a positive reference to resurrection is seen in Zech. 12:10-11, correctly in my opinion, by H. Gese, "Death in the Old Testament," in idem, *Essays on Biblical Theology* (1981), 56-57.

46. Elliger, *Das Buch der zwölf kleinen Propheten*, 2:171-72. By contrast Gese, "Anfang und Ende der Apokalyptik," 227-28, interprets the text in terms of "the collective of the fallen Jews who have suffered the martyrdom of the end time," although Zech. 13:7 shows the possibility of a messianic interpretation in terms of the "Davidic king of the end time, who together with his people goes through a martyrdom caused by Yahweh himself." On Zech. 13:7 cf. Gese, "The Messiah," in *Essays on Biblical Theology*, 151.

47. Rudolph, *Sacharja 9–14*, 223-24. Both Rudolf and Gese correctly exclude a direct reference to a historical person; the text is about an "apocalyptic vision of the future."

This supposition of a connection between Zechariah 12:10 and the fourth Servant Song is supported by three additional facts. First, the context of Zechariah 12:9–13:1 relates the wonderful victory over the peoples of the world, which one could have read about in Isaiah 52:13-15.[48] Second, Isaiah 53:1-9 also presents a spirit-inspired collective lament that does not hesitate to relate the community's own failure, which the mourners do not properly "see" or know in its true depth until after the death of the Servant. Finally, at the end in Isaiah 53:10-12, sin and guilt are overcome for those afflicted by them. I also ask myself whether in the later (unknown) interpretive tradition of this puzzling text in Zechariah the immediate comparison of the "house of David" with "God" or the "angel of Yahweh" in 12:8 could have been carried over to the "only child" or the "firstborn" or "pierced one" in 12:10.

Admittedly, a "messianic" interpretation of Zechariah 12:10 first appears again in earliest Christianity and then with the Messiah ben Joseph in Judaism. The Septuagint's distorted translation ἐπιβλέψονται πρός με ἀνθ' ὧν κατωρχήσαντο ("they shall look upon me, because they have mocked [me]") and the *Targum Jonathan* show that people no longer interpreted the text with reference to a suffering savior figure, and in the case of the Targum, one will be able to say in Zechariah as in Isaiah 53 that people no longer wanted to interpret it this way.[49] In view of the extremely rare traces of a pre-Christian suffering Messiah figure, we should not forget that, apart from Qumran, we have only a few clearly pre-Christian "messianic texts," and that even in the messianically interpreted Old Testament texts, the motif of the end-time victor and judge predominates. After all, the end-time hope was directed toward the reestablishment and liberation of the people of God. The suffering of an end-time representative could therefore appear only in connection with concrete historical experiences and as a preparation for salvation. Traditions of messianic suffering had to play a necessarily marginal role in the end-time expectation. A collective interpretation lay much closer to hand, whether it applied to the persecuted

---

48. On the motif of victory or exaltation in the Septuagint of Isaiah 53 see below §8; on the same motif in the Targum see the essay by J. Ådna in this volume.

49. For the original text see A. Sperber, *The Bible in Aramaic*, vol. 3: *The Latter Prophets According to Targum Jonathan* (1962), 495, where Zech. 12:10b is completely twisted. Possible translations include "and they will entreat me for those who went into exile" or "will entreat me for him on whose account they went into exile" — possibilities mentioned by Str-B 2:538, as noted in K. J. Cathcart and R. P. Gordon, *The Aramaic Bible*, vol. 14: *The Targum of the Minor Prophets* (1989), 218 n. 28. They themselves translate, "and they shall entreat me because they were exiled." This reinterpretation is to be understood as anti-Christian polemic. Codex Reuchlinianus (f6) has here a long passage about the death of the Messiah bar Ephraim outside the gates of Jerusalem in the battle against God. A lament is held for him (on this see above, §1).

true Israel during the time of the messianic woes immediately before the dawn of the age of salvation, or paradigmatically to the suffering righteous.

4. Traces of Isaiah 53 in the Book of Daniel

About 150 years after Third Isaiah, between Ben Sira and the Qumran *pesharim,* lies the book of Daniel. It originated in 165/164 B.C.E. at the time of the desecration of the temple and at the height of the associated persecution under Antiochus IV Epiphanes. In the minds of contemporaries, this was a catastrophe that exceeded even the destruction of the temple in 587 B.C.E., and it was understood as the essence of the "end-time woes," which could be followed only by the immanent appearance of the kingdom of God.[50] The older commentators have already pointed out the manifold points of contact between the conclusion to the book of Daniel and the book of Isaiah.[51] The unknown author of Daniel lived in the certainty, as did the translator of the LXX of Isaiah and the Teacher of Righteousness in Qumran with his disciples a little later, that the prophetic promises would be fulfilled in the present. The relationship of Daniel to Zechariah 11–14 should also not be overlooked here.

In Daniel 12:2 the formulation "many of those who sleep in the dust of the earth *will awake*" (וְרַבִּים מִיְּשֵׁנֵי אַדְמַת־עָפָר יָקִיצוּ) comes from Isaiah 26:19, יָקִיצוּ וְירַנְּנוּ שֹׁכְנֵי עָפָר, "the dwellers in the dust *will awake* and *shout for joy*" — reading here the two imperfects יקיצו וירננו with 1QIsaᵃ, as the author of Daniel appears to have done, instead of the MT's imperatives הָקִיצוּ וְרַנְּנוּ ("awake and shout for joy!").[52] Then in Daniel 12:2b, "some [will awake] to

---

50. Cf. Dan. 12:1, NRSV: "There shall be a time of anguish, such as has never occurred since nations [RSV *a nation;* NJPS *the nation;* Heb. גּוֹי] first came into existence." Contrary to the NRSV, I believe that the singular גּוֹי refers not to the "nations" and hence to the overall history of the world, but rather, in keeping with the whole context, to the one "nation" chosen by God, Israel. The anguish will therefore be greater than any in the history of Israel from the oppression in Egypt before the exodus until the time of the book of Daniel (cf. Exod. 9:18; Deut. 4:32). Note however the supersession of this statement in Mark 13:19; cf. Joel 2:2.

51. E.g., R. H. Charles, *The Book of Daniel* (1913), and others. On the influence of Isaiah (and other prophetic texts) on Daniel 9–12 see M. Fishbane, *Biblical Interpretation in Ancient Israel* (1985), 482-99, esp. 493 on the "wise" (מַשְׂכִּלִים) in Dan. 12:3, 10; Haag, *Gottesknecht,* 35; and U. Kellermann, "Das Danielbuch und die Märtyrertheologie der Auferstehung. Erwägungen," in van Henten, *Die Entstehung der jüdischen Martyrologie,* 51-75, esp. 52ff.; see also 59ff., 67-68 for the influence of Isaiah 53 on Daniel 7.

52. See further A. van der Kooij, "Zur Theologie des Jesajabuches in der Septuaginta," in H. Graf Reventlow, ed., *Theologische Probleme der Septuaginta und der hellenistischen Hermeneutik* (1997), 9-25, esp. 22-24, and D. P. Bailey, "The Intertextual Relationship of Daniel

shame and everlasting *abhorrence*" (cf. NJPS), the word for "abhorrence," דְּרָאוֹן, found here in the construction דְּרָאוֹן עוֹלָם, occurs elsewhere in the Old Testament only in Isaiah 66:24c, the last phrase in the book: "they shall be an *abhorrence* to all flesh" (NRSV).

Another generally recognized connection exists between Daniel 12:3, about "the wise (מַשְׂכִּלִים) who will shine like the brightness of the sky" and "like the stars forever and ever," who are moreover described as "those who lead many to righteousness" (מַצְדִּיקֵי הָרַבִּים), and Isaiah 53:11b, "The righteous one, my servant, shall make the many righteous" (יַצְדִּיק צַדִּיק עַבְדִּי לָרַבִּים). Montgomery[53] points out that in both passages, the hiphil of צדק does not have its usual sense of "declaring innocent" but rather means "to make the many righteous." Furthermore, to P. Volz's question as to whether the Daniel passage "talks about vicarious suffering or a *thesaurus meritorum*,"[54] Montgomery replies that "the ref(erence) . . . to the propitiatory value of the sufferings of martyrs is not impossible." One could appeal to the second part of the parallelism in Isaiah 53:11 MT, which Daniel has not explicitly mentioned: "The righteous one, my servant, shall make many righteous, and *he shall bear their iniquities*." Isaiah 53 is not so much about the imparting of instruction that makes others righteous as it is about vicarious suffering. H. L. Ginsberg[55] points to the whole complex of "the wise" (מַשְׂכִּלִים) and their relationship to "the many" (רַבִּים) that begins as early as Daniel 11:33: "The wise among the people shall give understanding to the many (וּמַשְׂכִּילֵי עָם יָבִינוּ לָרַבִּים); for some days, however, they shall fall (נִכְשְׁלוּ) by sword and flame, and suffer cap-

---

12:2 and Isaiah 26:19: Evidence from Qumran and the Greek Versions," *TynBul* 51 (2000): 305-8. Against F. Field, *Origenes Hexaplorum,* both van der Kooij (p. 23) and Bailey (p. 306) align the LXX future ἐγερθήσονται, "they will rise," primarily with the second verb קוּם (MT and 1QIsa^a יְקוּמוּן) in Isa. 26:19 rather than with the third verb קיץ (MT הָקִיצוּ 1QIsa^a יקיצו), so that this Greek future tense does not necessarily attest to the Qumran imperfect יקיצו in the Septuagint translator's *Vorlage* (though as van der Kooij points out, the translator could have intended ἐγερθήσονται to cover both קוּם and קיץ, since they are synonyms). Yet because the following imperfect וירננו of 1QIsa^a, "they will shout for joy," apparently stood in the *Vorlagen* of all the Greek versions — as suggested by the futures εὐφρανθήσονται (LXX), αἰνέσουσιν (Aquila), ἀγαλλιάσονται (Symmachus), and ἀλαλάξουσιν (Theodotion) — we have additional though indirect evidence that the text of Isa. 26:19 read by the author of Daniel probably contained the imperfect יקיצו (cf. Bailey, p. 308).

53. J. A. Montgomery, *A Critical and Exegetical Commentary on the Book of Daniel,* ICC (1927), 47-48.

54. P. Volz, *Jüdische Eschatologie von Daniel bis Akiba* (1903), 12 = *Eschatologie der jüdischen Gemeinde im neutestamentlichen Zeitalter* (1934), 14.

55. H. L. Ginsberg, "The Oldest Interpretation of the Suffering Servant," *VT* 3 (1953): 400-404.

tivity and plunder" (NRSV [mod.]). The author of Daniel can identify Isaiah's Servant with "the wise" (מַשְׂכִּלִים) because the fourth Servant Song begins by saying הִנֵּה יַשְׂכִּיל עַבְדִּי, "See, my servant will act *wisely*" (Isa. 52:13, NIV). Ginsberg therefore wants to see Daniel 11:33–12:10 as "the oldest interpretation of the suffering servant,"[56] a view Lacocque follows in his commentary.[57] To be sure, the vicarious suffering of Daniel's מַשְׂכִּלִים is not clearly mentioned but is at best only alluded to, because the interpretation of Daniel 11:35 is disputed:

> And some of the wise (מַשְׂכִּלִים) will fall (יִכָּשְׁלוּ), to refine (לִצְרוֹף)[58] among them — or *through them* (בָּהֶם)? — and to purge and to cleanse until the time of the end.

The question here concerns the referent of the expression בָּהֶם, "them" or "among them." This may refer back to the "many" in the preceding verse,[59] a possible understanding of the RSV: "And *many* shall join themselves to them [sc. the wise] with flattery; and some of those who are wise shall fall, to refine and to cleanse *them* [i.e., the many] and to make *them* [the many] white" (Dan. 11:34-35). In this case the wise מַשְׂכִּלִים suffer vicariously as martyrs for the many. But בָּהֶם could also refer to the wise themselves. These could be the wise who have fallen, thereby purifying *themselves*,[60] as in the NRSV (cf. NJPS): "Some of the wise shall fall, so that *they* may be refined," etc. Or they could be the rest of the wise who did not fall but who benefit from the suffering of those who did, as in the NAB: "Of the wise men, some shall fall, so that *the rest* may be tested, refined, and purified" (Dan. 11:35). Here the wise do indeed suffer vicariously, but only for other wise men, not for the many.

Here I must add a few remarks about the *martyr's death* and *vicarious suffering and death*.[61] The Old Testament does not yet know the concept of the

---

56. Ginsberg, "Interpretation," 402: "Undoubtedly our author has identified the Many of Isa LII 13–LIII 12 with the masses in the time of the Antiochian religious prosecution, and the Servant with the minority of steadfast antihellenizers."

57. A. Lacocque, *Le Livre de Daniel*, CAT 15b (1976), 170 =ET, *The Book of Daniel* (1979), 230.

58. For לִצְרוֹף cf. כִּצְרֹף, "as one refines [silver]," in Zech. 13:9.

59. So Montgomery, *Daniel;* Lacocque, *Daniel.*

60. So A. Bentzen, *Daniel* (1952); O. Plöger, *Das Buch Daniel* (1965).

61. See on this the collected essays on the origin of Jewish martyr theology edited by van Henten, *Entstehung,* especially the introduction by van Henten and B. Dehandschutter, 1-19. On Daniel see the contribution by U. Kellermann, 51-75; see further H. S. Versnel, "Quid Athenis et Hierosolymis: Bemerkungen über die Herkunft von Aspekten des 'Effective Death,'" 162-96. More recently see J. W. van Henten and F. Avemarie, *Martyrdom and Noble Death: Selected Texts from Graeco-Roman, Jewish, and Christian Antiquity* (2002). I have already treated some of these

glorification of martyrs or heroes who sacrifice their life for their people or for God and his law.[62] Vicarious atonement outside the legally regulated sacrificial cult in the sanctuary, for example through the surrender of human life, is likewise foreign to the Old Testament. This is precisely why the only real exception, Isaiah 53, is called an "erratic block" in the oft-cited formulation of K. Koch.[63] Over against this we have many examples in Greece since the archaic period, such as the widespread *pharmakos* motif or the sacrifice of the virgin (Iphigenia). Later, especially in the context of the Persian Wars, we find the heroizing of warriors who die for the *polis* and its holy laws. The nearest Old Testament analogies are found in the early period with Jephthah's daughter, Samson, or the Song of Deborah.[64] Child sacrifice was widespread precisely among the West Semites, Canaanites, and Phoenicians and was therefore bitterly rejected in Israel. In ancient Israel, as far it can be recovered from the Old Testament texts, every person dies because of his or her own sin according to the traditional connection between deeds and consequences. Therefore the violent death of the prophets cannot be transformed hagiographically. Such incidents are briefly reported but not glorified or elaborated.[65]

But all this changed suddenly with the religious crisis under Antiochus IV and the Maccabean revolt. In the three men in the fiery furnace in Daniel 3, we encounter for the first time Jewish martyrs who "disobeyed the king's command and yielded up their bodies rather than serve and worship any god except their own God" (Dan. 3:28, Aramaic).[66] The accompanying *Prayer of Azariah*

---

themes in M. Hengel, *The Atonement: The Origins of the Doctrine in the New Testament,* trans. J. Bowden (1981).

62. This is in fact one of the arguments for the Jewish origin and antiquity of the *Lives of the Prophets,* where the motifs of the martyr and atonement remain in the background despite the violent death of many prophets. See A. M. Schwemer, *Studien zu den frühjüdischen Prophetenlegenden Vitae Prophetarum,* 2 vols., TSAJ 49 (1995), TSAJ 50 (1996).

63. K. Koch, "Sühne und Sündenvergebung um die Wende von der exilischen zur nachexilischen Zeit," *EvT* 26 (1966): 217-39, esp. 237.

64. Judg. 5:18; 9:17; 12:3; 16:28-29; cf. also 1 Sam. 28:21.

65. Typical of this reserve is the presentation, which already belongs to the early Hellenistic period, of the murder of the prophet Zechariah son of Jehoiada in 2 Chron. 24:17-22; on this see Schwemer, *Studien,* 2:288ff. The narrative is still completely determined by the Deuteronomistic scheme of the violent fate of the prophets. See O. H. Steck, *Israel und das gewaltsame Geschick der Propheten,* WMANT 23 (1967), 16 n. 4, 162-64, 252-54. Moreover, the issue involved in the violent fate of the prophets is always the sin of Israel, which brings divine visitation and punishment.

66. On this see E. Haag, "Die drei Männer im Feuer nach Dan 3,1-30," in van Henten, *Entstehung,* 20-50. It is significant that the three young men do not die but are miraculously saved.

included in the Greek Additions to Daniel (between Dan. 3:23 and 3:24 MT) provides a theological comment in Daniel 3:40 (= Pr. Azar. 3:17 in Protestant versions of the Apocrypha), though the precise reading depends on which of the two Greek texts one takes as a basis. The text traditionally attributed to Theodotion is the basis for example of the NRSV Apocrypha:

> οὕτως γενέσθω θυσία ἡμῶν ἐνώπιόν σου σήμερον
> καὶ ἐκτελέσαι ὄπισθέν σου,
> ὅτι οὐκ ἔσται αἰσχύνη τοῖς πεποιθόσιν ἐπὶ σοί. (Pr. Azar. 3:40,
> Theodotion)

> Such may our sacrifice be in your sight today [sc. like burnt offerings of rams, etc.],
> *and may we unreservedly follow you,*
> for no shame will come to those who trust in you. (Pr. Azar. 3:17, NRSV)

The NRSV margin notes that the meaning of the middle line is uncertain. But more important for our purposes is the older, pre-Hexaplaric Septuagint version of the same passage, as attested in the second- or early-third-century c.e. Papyrus 967:

> οὕτω γενέσθω ἡμῶν ἡ θυσία ἐνώπιόν σου σήμερον
> καὶ ἐξιλάσαι[67] ὄπισθέν σου,
> ὅτι οὐκ ἔστιν αἰσχύνη τοῖς πεποιθόσιν ἐπὶ σοί,
> καὶ τελειῶσαι ὄπισθέν σου. (Daniel 3:40, LXX)[68]

> So let our sacrifice be in your sight today [sc. like burnt offerings of rams, etc.],

---

67. ἐξιλάσαι and τελειῶσαι are aorist optative. For discussion of another proposed accentuation, ἐξιλάσαι, see below n. 70. ἐξιλάσαι stands in place of Theodotion's ἐκτελέσαι and is probably the earlier reading; cf. J. W. van Henten, "The Tradition-Historical Background of Romans 3.25: A Search for Pagan and Jewish Parallels," in Martinus C. de Boer, ed., *From Jesus to John: Essays on Jesus and New Testament Christology in Honour of Marinus de Jonge,* JSNTSup 84 (1993), 101-28, esp. 114.

68. Text in J. Ziegler, ed., *Septuaginta: Vetus Testamentum Graecum Auctoritate Societatis Litterarum Gottingensis editum,* vol. 16/2: *Susanna, Daniel, Bel et Draco* (1954), 123-24. The text is a combination of the readings of Papyrus 967 and 88-Syh, because 967 lacks ὄπισθέν σου after ἐξιλάσαι and σου after τελειῶσαι ὄπισθέν. The last line καὶ τελειῶσαι ὄπισθέν σου is a doublet, apparently added by a copyist to the original Greek composition, since it is not attested in Theodotion and is marked by the obelus (÷) in the Syrohexapla. See further Ziegler, 16; W. Hamm, *Der Septuaginta-Text des Buches Daniel Kap. 3–4 nach dem kölner Teil des Papyrus 967,* PTA 21 (1977), 302-3.

and may it make atonement before [lit., *behind*] you,
for there is no shame to those who trust in you,
and may it be perfect before [lit., *behind*] you.[69]

While the grammar of this version is very difficult and its translation uncertain,[70] its developing language of *atonement* is of the greatest interest.

---

69. Translated by D. P. Bailey. See the similar translation of *Prayer of Azariah* v. 17 = LXX Dan. 3:40 by C. A. Moore, *Daniel, Esther, and Jeremiah: The Additions,* AB 44 (1977), 55 at v. 17: "So may our 'sacrifice' be in your sight today and make atonement before you" (cf. also Moore's notes, p. 59). Our German translation runs: "So soll unser Opfer (θυσία) vor dir heute geschehen und dir gegenüber Sühne wirken (καὶ ἐξιλάσαι ὄπισθέν σου)" (M. Hengel, "Zur Wirkungsgeschichte von Jes 53 in vorchristlicher Zeit," in B. Janowski and P. Stuhlmacher, eds., *Der leidende Gottesknecht,* FAT 14 [1996], 49-91, esp. 62).

70. Uncertainties arise in LXX Dan. 3:40 for several reasons. While the term accented ἐξιλάσαι (ἐξιλάσκομαι) could technically be either aorist active infinitive or aorist active optative 3rd singular, its parallel term τελειῶσαι (τελειόω) must be optative, as in Jdt. 10:8, where it parallels the optative δῴη, since the infinitive is differently accented, τελειῶσαι, as in Exod. 29:29, where it parallels another infinitive, χρισθῆναι. The optative of wish is frequent in Septuagintal prayers and blessings, e.g., Gen. 28:3, ὁ δὲ θεός μου εὐλογήσαι σε καὶ αὐξήσαι σε καὶ πληθύναι σε; Ps. 19:5, δῴη and πληρώσαι. Only when accented on the antepenult, ἐξίλασαι, can the form in question be an imperative: aorist middle-deponent imperative 2nd singular; cf. Lev. 9:7; Num. 7:11. (Verb-forms with a long penult, e.g., παιδευσαι, have three possible parsings according to accent: παίδευσαι aorist middle imperative 2nd singular; παιδεῦσαι aorist active infinitive; παιδεύσαι aorist active optative 3rd singular. But with the short penult, as in ἐξιλάσαι, the infinitive and optative are identical.) The imperatival accent ἐξίλασαι was assumed in an earlier analysis by J. W. van Henten, who has since changed his mind to the optative (personal correspondence with D. P. Bailey on 26 February 2003). This earlier analysis suggests that the form in LXX Dan. 3:40 "can only be a second person singular middle imperative of ἐξιλάσκομαι" — so van Henten, "The Tradition-Historical Background of Romans 3.25," in De Boer, ed., *From Jesus to John,* 114. Van Henten translates: "Let our sacrifice be as such before You this day. And let Yourself *be atoned* [ἐξίλασαι] (from) behind You . . . and consecrate [τελείωσαι] (from) behind You" (van Henten, "The Tradition-Historical Background of Romans 3.25," 112; cf. 111 n. 4 on the accentuation). Reaccenting the verbs as the imperatives ἐξίλασαι and τελείωσαι would have the merit of giving the former the middle-deponent voice that ἐξιλάσκομαι is otherwise known to have. But the proposed translation would still raise questions: ἐξίλασαι does not convey the passive sense "be atoned" (i.e., propitiated, conciliated), and the active sense required by the deponent fails to fit the context: this imperative asks *God* to make atonement, leaving no room for the "sacrifice" of the martyrs. God is not otherwise the subject of ἐξιλάσκομαι in the LXX; it is humans and their sacrifices that expiate or make atonement for sins. Moreover, the presumed imperative τελείωσαι would be a true middle, otherwise unattested for τελειόω in the LXX. Accordingly, the third person optative parsing of ἐξιλάσαι and τελειῶσαι is assumed in our English and German translations. This optative is also suggested by Plöger's translation, "So *möge* unser Opfer vor dir gelten, und *dich versöhnen*" ("Zusätze zu Daniel," in W. G. Kümmel, ed., *Historische und legendarische Erzählungen,* JSHRZ 1/1 [1973], 72,

1 Maccabees gives a prominent place to the theme of the heroic death for God's commands and people and for the hero's own fame, often in almost Greek-sounding formulas.[71] Yet in keeping with its Sadducean tendency, it acknowledges no vicarious atonement or resurrection of the dead, a hope which only the glorification of the martyr properly justifies. However, both atonement and resurrection confront us in 2 Maccabees 7 (and still more clearly in the later 4 Maccabees):

> I, like my brothers, give up body and life for the laws of our ancestors, appealing to God to show mercy soon to our nation . . . and through me and my brothers to bring to an end the wrath of the Almighty that has justly fallen on our whole nation. (2 Maccabees 7:37-38)

Because the ideas introduced are new, they are at first only cautiously hinted at.[72] Isaiah 53, as a unique text in the Old Testament, may have helped this development along, though at first the collective understanding stood in the foreground, and only certain aspects of the whole text exerted an influence. It also needs to be remembered, as already said, that the pre-Christian Apocrypha and Pseudepigrapha contain almost no literal scriptural citations. We can therefore conduct only a very cautious search for traces.

Let us now return with these presuppositions to the conclusion of the book of Daniel. The glorification of the מַשְׂכִּלִים, the "wise" or "insightful" (NRSV; NASB; hiphil participle of שָׂכַל, "be prudent"), through their exaltation after the resurrection (cf. 12:2) and their heavenly splendor in Daniel 12:3 וְהַמַּשְׂכִּלִים יַזְהִרוּ כְּזֹהַר הָרָקִיעַ ("Those who are wise shall shine like the brightness of the sky") could point back to Isaiah 52:13, "See, my servant shall have *success* or *insight* (יַשְׂכִּיל); he shall be exalted and lifted up, and shall be very

---

italics added). However, our German translation in terms of *Sühne* or "atonement" (see n. 69) is preferable to Plöger's, since sacrifice or burnt offering in biblical literature is never directly said to "propitiate" or "conciliate" God, as suggested by Plöger's *versöhnen* plus object. Somewhat problematically, our accentuation ἐξιλάσαι gives the normally middle-deponent ἐξιλάσκομαι an active ending where we might have expected the middle ἐξιλάσαιτο; this fits its active sense but is otherwise unattested. The active voice of τελειῶσαι also presents an anomaly. The only meaning that makes sense here, the intransitive idea of being or becoming "perfect," is normally expressed by the passive voice, as in *Didache* 16:2 (cf. BDAG 996 s.v. τελειόω 2e). Finally, the preposition ὄπισθεν, often used in the sense of following *after* or *behind* someone, here means something like "*before* you" (cf. "*vor* dir").

71. 1 Macc. 2:50-51, 64; 6:44; 9:10; cf. 11:23; 13:27-30; 14:29; 2 Macc. 2:21; 13:14; 14:18. See on this Hengel, *The Atonement*, 145ff., 151, 155-56.

72. J. W. van Henten, "Das jüdische Selbstverständnis in den ältesten Martyrien," in idem, *Entstehung*, 127-61, esp. 141ff.

high." The verb יַשְׂכִּיל can be interpreted in either sense, of having insight or having success. The LXX of Isaiah translates this a little later by συνήσει, "he shall understand," and Aquila, by ἐπιστήμων ἰστήσεται, "he shall be wise *or* insightful."[73] The מַשְׂכִּלִים are the insightful ones, who in the end also enjoy success. In 52:13b יָרוּם וְנִשָּׂא וְגָבַהּ מְאֹד ("he shall be exalted and lifted up, and shall be very high") recalls for Second Isaiah God's "high and lofty" (רָם וְנִשָּׂא) throne in Isaiah 6:1, while at the same time forming the reversal of the high-as-heavens presumption of the king of Babylon who, having skidded down to the underworld, is looked upon there with satisfaction by the kings of the nations (Isa. 14:9ff.). For the Servant, by contrast, humiliation unto death leads to incomparable exaltation. In Daniel, the king of Babylon becomes the pattern for the self-apotheosis and fall of Antiochus IV (Dan. 8:25). By contrast, the מַשְׂכִּלִים are led through their martyrdom to resurrection and ascension, that is, to fellowship with God. At the same time the scene in Daniel 7:9-15 becomes vivid, in which the true Israel (i.e., the martyrs and those faithful to the law) appears "like a son of man" (כְּבַר אֱנָשׁ) before God the judge and his heavenly

73. The patristic evidence (there is no direct evidence in biblical manuscripts) gives Aquila's form as a single word, ἐπιστημονισθήσεται. See Eusebius of Caesarea, *Commentary on Isaiah* 2.42 on Isa. 52:13, ed. J. Ziegler, GCS *Eusebius Werke*, vol. 9, *Der Jesajakommentar*, 333 ll. 18-19 (cf. l. 25): κατὰ τὸν Ἀκύλαν ἰδοὺ· ἐπιστημονισθήσεται ὁ δοῦλός μου, and Procopius of Gaza, *Commentarii in Isaiam*, PG 87.2:2516 ll. 37, 55, as well as the editions of the Hexaplaric fragments by F. Field, *Origenis Hexaplorum*, vol. 2 (1875), 533 and Ziegler, *Isaias*, 320. As Hegermann points out (*Jesaja 53 in Hexapla, Targum und Peschitta*, 28-29 with 28 n. 1), this future passive ἐπιστημονισθήσεται, which is to be understood intransitively, "he shall *be* wise" (not causatively, "shall *be made* wise"), suggests that the adjective ἐπιστήμων, "wise" (cf., e.g., James 3:13), which Aquila uses elsewhere when translating this verb שׂכל (e.g., 1 Sam. 18:14, for מַשְׂכִּיל), has apparently been used by Aquila in Isa. 52:13 to form a new verb, ἐπιστημονίζω. According to Hegermann, this is unattested in other writers (as a *TLG* search confirms) but parallels Aquila's use of the synonomous verb ἐπιστημονέω, likewise unique to Aquila. However, because the results are phonetically almost identical, by replacing θ by τ one could also interpret the -ίζω suffix plus the future passive ending combined in the letters "ισθήσεται" as an independent word, ἰστήσεται, the future middle (intransitive) of ἴστημι, as in the original German of this essay, ἐπιστήμων ἰστήσεται (p. 63). (We might note that the τ has similarly fallen out from Eusebius's spelling of τι(τ)θιζόμενον; see below, n. 200). Although ἰστήσεται itself is not attested in *TLG* sources and the classical form of the future middle is simply στήσεται, ἰστήσεται would be the natural spelling of the future middle of the regularized -ω verb ἰστάω (cf. also ἰστάνω), attested as a later collateral form of ἴστημι (cf. LSJ; BDAG). This follows the analogy of other older -μι verbs like ἀφίημι and συνίημι, which in the Koine period developed the regular -ω verb endings ἀφίω and συνίω. Aquila could have construed ἰστήσεται with the predicate adjective ἐπιστήμων with the meaning, "he shall be wise," because in intransitive senses, ἴστημι is "freq. merely a stronger form of εἶναι, *to be*" (LSJ, s.v. ἴστημι B). While both expressions, ἐπιστημονισθήσεται and ἐπιστήμων ἰστήσεται, are unusual, they are essentially identical in meaning.

court. The "startling" of many nations in Isaiah 52:15 (so NRSV; cf. LXX θαυμάσονται, "they will be amazed *or* astonished," reading perhaps יִרְגְּזוּ, "they will tremble," instead of MT's יַזֶּה, "he will sprinkle," hiphil of נָזָה), together with the mention of the kings who must shut their mouths, would then have to be understood as a manifestation of judgment (cf. Dan. 7:10ff.).[74]

The resurrection from the "dust of the earth" in Daniel 12:2 would correspond to the overcoming of the grave in Isaiah 53:9 and 10. The phrase "to everlasting life" in Daniel 12:2 would find its equivalent in "he shall prolong his days" (יַאֲרִיךְ יָמִים) in Isaiah 53:10, while the statement in 53:11, "he shall see *light*" (יִרְאֶה אוֹר, so NRSV; NJB; NIV) — attested in 1QIsa[a], 1QIsa[b], 1QIsa[d], and the LXX (δεῖξαι αὐτῷ φῶς) over against the MT (which lacks "light") — is reflected in the vision of the מַשְׂכִּלִים who have been exalted to be with God according to Daniel. The success of the divine plan in 53:10, "through him the will of the Lord shall prosper" (וְחֵפֶץ יְהוָה בְּיָדוֹ יִצְלָח), as well as the mention of "receiving the multitude as his spoil" (NJPS) in 53:12 can be related either to the judgment of the kings and their many peoples or to the establishment of God's kingdom according to Daniel 7:9-28. Therefore, in rereading our text, the author of Daniel 11 and 12 (and 7) *could* perhaps have understood it *in a collective sense* as a promise which is to be fulfilled now in the end-time. There is even room for the possibility of vicarious atonement — cautiously alluded to — in Daniel's reference to the suffering of the מַשְׂכִּלִים and their function as "those who lead many to righteousness" (מַצְדִּיקֵי הָרַבִּים, Daniel 12:3). But the exceptional reserve of the texts at precisely this point needs to be respected.

Individual motifs that allude to Isaiah 52:13ff. and Daniel 12:3 also had separate effects in other texts, as in the heavenly exaltation of Israel according to the *Testament of Moses* 10:9-10: "And God will raise you to the heights and fix you firmly in the heaven of the stars. . . . And you will behold from on high and see your enemies on the earth" (*Et altavit te deus et faciet te h[a]erere caelo stellarum . . . et conspicies a summo et vides inimicos tuos in terram*). It is telling that here, in contrast to Daniel 11 and 12 and in keeping with the tendency of the later *Targum of Isaiah,* only the suffering of Israel's enemies as part of the collective exaltation of (the Servant) Israel is mentioned.

---

74. The points of contact between Daniel 7 and Isaiah 53 have been highlighted especially by U. Kellermann, "Das Danielbuch und die Märtyrertheologie der Auferstehung," in van Henten, *Entstehung,* 50-75, esp. 59ff. He speaks of "strong, dramatic points of contact with the fourth Servant Song." "The Song stresses the exaltation of this martyred and executed man" (67-68).

5. Influence upon the Similitudes of *1 Enoch*

It has long been recognized that the mysterious figure of "the Son of Man" in the Similitudes of *1 Enoch* (Ethiopic Apocalypse of Enoch, chaps. 37–71) also shares some of the traits of the Servant of Deutero-Isaiah.[75] The collectively interpreted "one like a son of man" (כְּבַר אֱנָשׁ) in Daniel 7:13 has here become a "messianic-heavenly" savior figure who has been concealed with God. Admittedly, one must immediately add that even here, there is no mention of a "*suffering* Son of Man." The puzzling and controversial text of the Similitudes contains the most interesting parallels to New Testament Christology but is most certainly not Christian. Chronologically the text may be placed about 130-220 years after the book of Daniel, between the Parthian invasion of 40 B.C.E. and the Jewish War of 66 C.E. There is no mention of the catastrophe of the destruction of Jerusalem, and the identification of the Son of Man with Enoch makes it absurd to presuppose a Christian origin. Although the Gospel of Matthew and later Tertullian seem to know the Similitudes,[76] this text still has nothing to do with the Christian kerygma. Whether its original language was Greek or Aramaic remains unclear. Even its Palestinian origin is not entirely certain.

The relationship of *1 Enoch* to the Servant motif concentrates upon the first two Songs in Isaiah 42:1-3 and 49:1-7. By contrast, the third Servant Song plays no role at all and the fourth only a marginal one. The connection of *1 Enoch* to the fourth Song is limited on the one hand to the fact that the expression "the Righteous One" referring to the Son of Man occurs relatively frequently with "the Elect One" or "the Chosen One" (e.g., *1 Enoch* 53:6), which points to Isaiah 42:1. This could derive above all from the expression "the righteous one, my servant" in Isaiah 53:11,[77] next to other passages such as Zechariah 9:9. Another possible point of contact is found in the various versions of the theme of the judgment of the kings and the powerful. However, there is no mention of their being "silenced"

---

75. See M. Black, "The Messianism of the Parables of Enoch: Their Date and Contributions to Christological Origins," in J. Charlesworth, ed., *The Messiah: Developments in Earliest Judaism and Christianity* (1984), 145-68, esp. 160, 167-68 on Isaiah 53.

76. Tertullian, *De cultu feminarum* 3.1-3.

77. M. Black, *The Book of Enoch or 1 Enoch: A New English Edition*, SVTP 7 (1985), 195. This suggestion goes back to P. Billerbeck, "Hat die alte Synagoge einen präexistenten Messias gekannt?" *Nathanael* 19 (1903): 97-105; 21 (1905): 89-150. Billerbeck points to a large number of "similarities between the Similitudes and the Servant Songs." A selection of the most important is provided by J. Theisohn, *Der auserwählte Richter*, SUNT 12 (1975), 115. Compare *1 Enoch* 39:6 with Isa. 50:6-10; 53:9, 11; *1 Enoch* 39:7; 62:7 with Isa. 49:2 (hiddenness or concealment); *1 Enoch* 46:6 with Isa. 50:11; *1 Enoch* 48:3 with Isa. 49:1 (being given a name); *1 Enoch* 48:4 with Isa. 42:6; 49:6 (the light of the Gentiles); *1 Enoch* 62:5 with Isa. 52:15 (confrontation with the kings).

before the Son of Man, as in Isaiah 52:15. The most probable place where we could suspect an allusion to Isaiah 52:13 and 15 is in *1 Enoch* 62:5:

> One half of them shall glance at the other half; they shall cast down their faces . . . when they see that Son of Man sitting on the throne of his glory.[78]

When people look at each another in alarm and lower their gaze in shame, they also tend to fall silent.

Nickelsburg admittedly sees in *1 Enoch* 62:1-16 and 63:1-11 very many more correspondences to Isaiah 53. They begin with the address from God and the exaltation of the Son of Man as judge, where there is an allusion to Isaiah 11:4. What follows is recognition by his enemies, who must see the exalted one and react with terror. Sharp pain seizes them (Isaiah 13:8; 21:3; 26:17). They must confess their sins — as in Isaiah 53:1-6 — and acclaim him. The parallels between *1 Enoch* 62–63 and Wisdom 5, where the righteous one and the ungodly meet in the judgment, are especially clear, yet the fourth Servant Song seems so distant that we may well ask how much the composer of the Similitudes still had Isaiah 53 in view. The suffering of the righteous is completely suppressed by him, unless one finds it collectively in the few references to the persecution of the righteous and chosen ones.[79] In *1 Enoch* 47:1, 4 the "blood of the righteous" that is "avenged (*or* admitted [*OTP*]) before the Lord of the Spirits" is nevertheless to be interpreted collectively, despite the considerations of M. Black,[80] with Theisohn and Sjöberg.[81] One could at best point to the fact that the "righteous and elect *ones*" (e.g., *1 Enoch* 62:12, 13, 15) here join the Righteous and Elect *One* and unite themselves with him in the end. Collective and individual interpretations could go together here, as they often do elsewhere. Another important aspect of the scriptural usage of the Similitudes is that a whole series of Old Testament messianic motifs and texts are bound up with the figure of the end-time judge and redeemer. Next to Daniel 7:9-15, the most important texts are Isaiah

78. This is immediately preceded in *1 Enoch* 62:4 by an allusion to the birth pangs of Isa. 13:8.

79. G. W. E. Nickelsburg, Jr., *Resurrection, Immortality and Eternal Life in Intertestamental Judaism*, HTS 26 (1972), 71ff. Nickelsburg also presents the parallels between the Similitudes of *1 Enoch* and Wis. 5:1-8. Cf. also H. C. C. Cavallin, *Life After Death*, ConBNT 7/1 (1974), 206-7, 209 n. 20 for a review of literature on the exaltation or resurrection of the suffering Servant; 210-11 on Isaiah 53.

80. M. Black, *The Book of Enoch* (1985), 209: "Isa 53.11 lies as certainly behind this passage as it does Wis 2.12-18"; we should not exclude "a deliberate allusion to 'the Righteous One' par excellence of [*1 Enoch*] 38.2; 53.6."

81. See Theisohn, *Der auserwählte Richter*, 33f., 217 n. 9, who refers in this connection to E. Sjöberg, *Der Menschensohn im äthiopischen Henochbuch*, SMHVL 41 (1946), 129. Sjöberg's work was directed against an unpublished lecture by J. Jeremias in Uppsala in 1938.

11:1ff.; 42:1ff.; 49:1ff.; Psalm 110:1; Proverbs 8:23ff.; and Psalm 90:2. It also needs to be pointed out that the collective figure in Daniel 7:13 has become an individual, though one admittedly difficult to fit into the traditional messianology. Naturally there is no room for the vicarious suffering of this heavenly judge himself. The Son of Man of the Similitudes shares traits of the Servant, but only by functioning as the righteous judge of the ungodly, never by discharging human guilt through vicarious suffering. This complete absence of his vicarious suffering also speaks *decisively* against a Christian origin; it corresponds rather to the Jewish tendency in the interpretation of the Servant.

6. The Two Qumran Isaiah Scrolls

Before we look for traces of an interpretation of Isaiah 53 in Greek texts (below, §8), we must deal in more detail with the two Isaiah Scrolls from 1Q[82] and with a recently published Aramaic text from 4Q (see below §7). Here above all the Isaiah Scroll A (1QIsa[a]), which originated in the middle or latter half of the second century b.c.e., contains not a few partly intentional changes that can no longer be explained simply as scribal errors. They rather point to conscious interpretation and should be understood in part, especially in Deutero-Isaiah, as truly messianic. Yet in point of detail these interpretations remain very uncertain. For example, in Isaiah 51:5 the Masoretic Text reads:

> My righteousness is near, my salvation has gone out. *My arms* will judge the peoples; the coastlands will wait for *me*, and in *my* arm they will hope. (Isaiah 51:5, MT)

After beginning the same way, 1QIsa[a] reads the third person forms:

> *His arm* will judge the peoples; the coastlands will wait for *him*, and in *his* arm they will hope.[83] (Isaiah 51:5, 1QIsa[a])

The third person suffixes here in 51:5 which suddenly replace the first person could refer to the Servant mentioned in the third person in Isaiah 50:10,

---

82. For the text of 1QIsa[a] see Millar Burrows, ed., *The Dead Sea Scrolls of St. Mark's Monastery,* vol. 1: *The Isaiah Manuscript and the Habakkuk Commentary* (1950) or the new edition by D. W. Parry and E. Qimron, eds., *The Great Isaiah Scroll (1QIsa[a]): A New Edition,* STDJ 32 (1999). For 1QIsa[b] see E. L. Sukenik, ed., *The Dead Sea Scrolls of the Hebrew University* (1955).

83. The English translation of 1QIsa[a] is from M. Abegg, P. Flint, and E. Ulrich, *The Dead Sea Scrolls Bible: The Oldest Known Bible Translated for the First Time into English* (1999), 267-381, here p. 355 (hereafter *DSSB*). This edition also provides marginal notes to other Qumran readings.

parallel to Yahweh: "Who among you *revere*[84] the Lord, obeying[85] the voice of his servant?" (1QIsa^a). Scholars have therefore suspected that the third singular references in 1QIsa^a at Isaiah 51:5 might constitute another Servant saying that should be interpreted messianically. Nevertheless, van der Kooij prefers to believe that the third person suffix here refers to Cyrus.[86]

In the fourth Servant Song it is striking that the text of Scroll A differs significantly from that of Scroll B, which follows the Masoretic Text much more closely and takes fewer interpretive freedoms. The most important variant that Scrolls A and B have in common (see also 4QIsa^d) is the phrase יראה אור ("he will see *light*") in 53:11, attested also in the LXX.[87] But interpretation of this verse is also affected by the frequent addition of the *waw* copula in Scroll A. In Isaiah 52:13–53:12 alone, Scroll A supplies a *waw* nine times over against the MT, providing interpretive help and strengthening the impression of connections or sequences.[88] It omits the *waw* in this section only once over against the MT (cf. כרחל in 53:7). Overall, Scroll A supplies the *waw* over 200 times, while Scroll B has only 70 such additions, though Scroll A also omits the *waw* some 70 times over against the MT.[89]

This discrepancy over against the MT is pronounced in 1QIsa^a, since late Hebrew at the time of the production of the scroll tended to avoid the asyndeton that would arise from a missing "and" and hence supplied it (though by contrast the *waw* consecutive with verbs was no longer used in this period and gave way to the *waw* conjunctive).[90] This is especially clear in verse 11: "Out of the suffering of his soul he will see *light, and* find satisfaction" (1QIsa^a additions over against the MT in italics). Then begins a new sentence, over against the LXX and MT: "*And*

---

84. 1QIsa^a reads the qal participle masculine plural construct יִרְאֵי יְהוָה, lit., "*fearers of* Yahweh" (cf. Mal. 3:16); MT reads the singular יְרֵא "*fearer of* Yahweh."

85. MT and 1QIsa^a read the qal participle שֹׁמֵעַ, "hearing" (i.e., obeying), whereas the *Vorlage* of the Septuagint's imperative ἀκουσάτω, "let him hear" (followed also by the Syriac), apparently read the imperfect יִשְׁמַע, "he shall hear" (cf. *BHS*).

86. Van der Kooij, *Die alten Textzeugen des Jesajabuches.*

87. LXX: δεῖξαι αὐτῷ φῶς (Isa. 53:11). Isa. 53:10b-11 reads: καὶ βούλεται κύριος ἀφελεῖν ἀπὸ τοῦ πόνου τῆς ψυχῆς αὐτοῦ, δεῖξαι αὐτῷ φῶς καὶ πλάσαι τῇ συνέσει, "And the Lord desires to take away from the anguish of his soul, to show him light, and to form/fill [him] with understanding." Taking κύριος rather than the Servant as the subject, the LXX has apparently read the hiphil causative forms of the first two verbs of v. 11, i.e., יַרְאֶה (cf. Isa. 30:30) and יַשְׂבִּעַ or יַשְׂבִּיעַ (cf. Job 9:18; Ps. 105:40), instead of the MT's consonantally identical qal forms יִרְאֶה and יִשְׂבָּע. The Hebrew causative meanings "to make [him] see light" (i.e., to show him light) and "to satisfy *or* fill [him] with understanding" are reflected in our translation of the Greek. See below §8.

88. E. Y. Kutscher, *The Language and Linguistic Background of the Isaiah Scroll (1QIsa^a)* (1974), 420: see Isa. 52:13; 53:3 twice, 4, 5 twice, 10, 11 twice.

89. For these statistics see Kutscher, *Language*, 422, 426, 427.

90. See Kutscher, *Language*, 351-52, 422, 424.

through his knowledge *his* [MT: *my*] servant, the righteous one, will make many righteous." The MT, however, includes this "knowledge" in the preceding line as the means of the Servant's satisfaction.[91] Hence in 1QIsa[a], God's Servant justifies the many through the knowledge he gained when he saw the light and found satisfaction. His exaltation precedes his justification of the many more clearly in 1QIsa[a] than it does in the MT. Because 1QIsa[a] lacks the MT's first personal "*my* servant" in verse 11, God's first-person address does not begin in this manuscript until verse 12, לכן אחלק לו ברבים (= MT): "Therefore I will allot him a portion with the great."

There are two other important changes in 1QIsa[a] that are probably to be interpreted messianically in the widest sense (see Isaiah 52:14; 53:10). Yet we must remember that in the second century B.C.E., we do not yet possess any fixed Jewish doctrine of the Messiah — there basically never was one — but must rather deal with various ideas of anointing and the Anointed One. In Qumran, not only the Davidic Messiah but also the eschatological high priest and the prophets are considered "anointed ones." Most difficult here is the puzzling divine address in Isaiah 52:14b, which according to 1QIsa[a] reads:

כאשר שממו עליכה רבים
כן משחתי מאיש מראהו ותוארו מבני האדם (Isaiah 52:14, 1QIsa[a])

The first line agrees with the MT (though the MT's עָלֶיךָ is here spelled with the final ה *mater*) and may be translated "Just as many were astonished at you." But in the second line, instead of the MT's unclear *hapax legomenon* מִשְׁחַת or מַשְׁחֵת, "marring," "disfigurement," 1QIsa[a] suffixes a *yod* to read the qal perfect first singular מָשַׁחְתִּי, "I have anointed."[92] To the last word אָדָם, 1QIsa[a] furthermore adds the article: "*the* human." We may therefore translate:[93]

---

91. Cf. NRSV: "he shall find satisfaction through his knowledge" (53:11). Whereas the LXX version of Isa. 53:11 completely transforms its Hebrew *Vorlage*, the minor Greek versions of Aquila, Symmachus, and Theodotion follow the MT in that they preserve the sense and asyndetic relationship of the first two verbs יִרְאֶה יִשְׂבָּע, lack the word "light," and connect knowledge with satisfaction: ἀπὸ τοῦ πόνου τῆς ψυχῆς αὐτοῦ ὄψεται, ἐμπλησθήσεται (Sym. χορτασθήσεται) ἐν τῇ γνώσει αὐτοῦ = "Out of the anguish of his soul he shall see; he shall be filled (Sym. satisfied) with his knowledge." Compare the NJPS translation of the MT: "Out of his anguish he shall see it; He shall enjoy it to the full through his devotion."

92. The other possible pointing of the Qumran consonants as a substantive, מִשְׁחָתִי, "my anointing *or* ointment," makes no sense here. *DSSB*, 359, has a completely different interpretation: "so was *he marred* in his appearance," adding the footnote, "Possibly, my marring 1QIsa[a]. Literally, *marring of* MT" (n. 1152).

93. Abegg, Flint, and Ulrich in *DSSB* offer a different translation of 1QIsa[a] at Isa. 52:14: "Just as many were astonished *at you* — so was *he marred* in his appearance, more than any human, and his form beyond that of the sons of humans."

Just as many were astonished at you,[94]
so have I anointed his appearance beyond that of any (other) man,
and his form beyond that of the sons of humanity [lit., of the human].
(Isaiah 52:14, 1QIsaᵃ)

The Servant's unique exaltation and his anointing by God correspond to one another. Barthélemy, who proposed a similar translation as early as 1950,[95] finds this form of the text to be better and less violent than that of the MT. He points to Leviticus 21:10 — "The priest who is exalted above his fellows, on whose head the anointing oil has been poured" — and Exodus 30:31-32 — the holy anointing oil that belongs to Yahweh alone "shall not be poured upon the flesh of (any ordinary) man (עַל־בְּשַׂר אָדָם)." Such a (priestly) anointing would also make more understandable the equally mysterious כֵּן יַזֶּה גּוֹיִם רַבִּים in 52:15 (KJV: "So shall he *sprinkle* many nations," cf. NASB), which Aquila and Theodotion translate by ῥαντίσει, "he will sprinkle." Like a priest, the Servant will sprinkle "many nations" to purify them from sin.[96]

The same introductory כֵּן in the second line (עַל־כֵּן, "therefore") plus the collocation of מָשַׁח ("to anoint") with an exclusive comparative מִן (here "beyond") attested in Isaiah 52:14 occurs also in Psalm 45:8:

אָהַבְתָּ צֶּדֶק וַתִּשְׂנָא רֶשַׁע
עַל־כֵּן מְשָׁחֲךָ אֱלֹהִים אֱלֹהֶיךָ שֶׁמֶן שָׂשׂוֹן מֵחֲבֵרֶיךָ

You love righteousness and hate wickedness;
therefore God, your God, has anointed you
    with the oil of gladness beyond your companions. (Psalm 45:8)

The preceding verses in Psalm 45 present the enthronement of a royal figure in mythical hues. Finally we may refer to the anointing of the eschatological prophet (or priest)[97] in Isaiah 61:1:

---

94. This "you" addresses the true Israel, just like the תָּשִׂים of 53:10, "When *you make* his life an offering for sin" (NRSV).

95. Barthélemy, *RB* 57 (1950): 546ff. = *Études d'histoire du texte de l'Ancien Testament*, OBO 21 (1978), 17ff.

96. LXX reads: οὕτως θαυμάσονται ἔθνη πολλά, "so shall many nations marvel," perhaps from יִרְגְּזוּ? Symmachus reads ἀποβαλεῖ.

97. A priestly interpretation is held by A. Grelot, "Sur Isaïe LXI: La première consécration du grand-prêtre," *RB* 97 (1990): 414-31. See also É. Puech, "Fragments d'un apocryphe de Lévi et le personnage eschatologique: 4QTestLéviᶜ⁻ᵈ(?) et 4QAJa," in J. Trebolle Barrera and L. Vegas Montaner, eds., *The Madrid Qumran Congress*, vol. 2, STDJ 11/2 (1992), 449-501, esp. 496.

רוּחַ אֲדֹנָי יְהוִה עָלָי יַעַן מָשַׁח יְהוָה אֹתִי

The spirit of the Lord God (1QIsaᵃ lacks אֲדֹנָי) is upon me,
because the Lᴏʀᴅ has anointed me. (Isaiah 61:1)

Returning to Isaiah 52:14, I should stress that I do not wish to go as far as Barthélemy. He championed מָשַׁחְתִּי ("I anointed") as the original reading and wanted to erase the *hapax legomenon* מִשְׁחַת ("disfigurement") from the Hebrew lexica, thereby encountering spirited opposition. Nevertheless, I do believe that this interesting variant in 1QIsaᵃ could be based on a conscious interpretation of Isaiah 52:14 in Qumran. Barthélemy points additionally to Leviticus 16:32: "*The* priest (הַכֹּהֵן) who is anointed and consecrated as priest in his father's place shall make atonement."

A second important change in 1QIsaᵃ concerns the textually corrupt verse 53:10. The MT reads וַיהוָה חָפֵץ דַּכְּאוֹ הֶחֱלִי, "But the Lᴏʀᴅ was pleased to crush Him, putting [Him] to grief" (NASB). Yet in place of the last word, where the MT reads הֶחֱלִי, the hiphil causative of חָלָה ("he has made him sick," RSV margin), and where 1QIsaᵇ has a gap, 1QIsaᵃ reads ויחללהו. This is the *waw* consecutive imperfect of the verb חלל with an object suffix: "he pierced him."[98] This verb also appears in the passive in Isaiah 53:5, והואה מחולל מפשעינו: "But He was *pierced through* for our transgressions" (NASB; 1QIsaᵃ = MT except for the plene writing).[99] I wonder whether this twofold usage of the language of "piercing" might not in fact suggest a connection with the "pierced one" of Zechariah 12:10, "they will look on me whom they have *pierced*," though here as well as in Zechariah 13:3 ("they will *pierce* him through," referring to the false prophet), the idea of piercing is expressed not by the verb חָלָל but by its synonym דָּקַר (BDB 201; *HALOT* 1:230). However that may be, the sometimes striking departures of 1QIsaᵃ particularly in Isaiah 52:13–53:12 suggest that this text received more attention in Qumran than scholars today commonly assume.

---

98. Once again Abegg, Flint, and Ulrich in *DSSB* offer a different translation, which does not essentially differ from the MT, "Yet the Lord was willing to crush him, *and he made him suffer*" (Isa. 53:10, 1QIsaᵃ).

99. Grammatically, the above language of "piercing" assumes that 1QIsaᵃ ויחללהו in Isa. 53:10 is the piel imperfect and that 1QIsaᵃ מחולל = MT מְחֹלָל in Isa. 53:5 is the polal participle of the verb which is numbered חלל II in *HALOT* (1:320), חלל I in BDB (p. 319), and חלל III in *DCH* (3:325-26). This is preferable to an analysis in terms of the pual participle of the *HALOT* homonym חלל I, "to profane" (= BDB חלל III; *DCH* חלל I), which *HALOT* suggests as a "conjecture" for Isa. 53:5 in the light of Ezek. 36:23: "pu. pt. מְחֻלָּל profaned . . . Ezk 36:23 cj. Is 53:5 for מְחֹלָל."

7. The *Aramaic Apocryphon of Levi* 4Q540-541

Portions of a text called the *Aramaic Testament of Levi (i)* have been preserved in 4Q213-214 (4QLevi^a-f ar) as well as in 1Q21 (1QTLevi ar).[100] However, here we are concerned only with a similarly named text or pair of texts that G. Vermes and K. Beyer have called the *Aramaic Testament of Levi (ii)*,[101] but that is now called not a "testament" but an "apocryphon" in E. Tov's comprehensive manuscript list,[102] followed by F. García Martínez and E. J. C. Tigchelaar in their *Dead Sea Scrolls Study Edition* (*DSSSE* 2:1078-81) and in the definitive critical edition by É. Puech in DJD 31 (see below). Our focal documents are therefore *4QApocryphon of Levi^a (?) ar* (4QapocLevi^a? ar) and *4QApocryphon of Levi^b (?) ar* (4QapocLevi^b? ar) — in other words, Qumran manuscripts 4Q540 and 541.

The publishing history and sigla of these documents must first be explained.[103] Although Abbé Starcky, to whose lot of Aramaic texts these originally belonged, had referred to them as early as 1963, his notices did not receive much attention among theologians.[104] In 1992 É. Puech published a preliminary edition of these texts, then still designated as a "testament," under the title "Fragments d'un apocryphe de Lévi et le personnage eschatologique. 4QTestLévi^c-d(?) et 4QAJa," in *The Madrid Qumran Congress*, volume

---

100. See briefly G. Vermes, *The Complete Dead Sea Scrolls in English* (1997), 524-25, "Testament of Levi (i)" = 4Q213-214 and 1Q21. More complete texts and translations are available in F. García Martínez and E. J. C. Tigchelaar, *The Dead Sea Scrolls Study Edition*, 2 vols. (1997, 1998; rev. ed., 2000), 1:446-55, including 4Q213-214b (six texts). For 1Q21 see *DSSSE* 1:56-59.

101. Vermes, *Complete Dead Sea Scrolls*, 526-27: "Testament of Levi (ii)" = 4Q537 and 4Q540-541; K. Beyer, *Die aramäischen Texte vom Toten Meer: Ergänzungsband* (1994), 78-82: "Das Testament Levis II" = 4Q540-541 (herafter *Ergänzungsband*).

102. See E. Tov, "Appendix F: Texts from the Judean Desert," in P. H. Alexander, et al., eds., *The SBL Handbook of Style for Ancient Near Eastern, Biblical, and Early Christian Studies* (1999), 176-233, esp. 206 under 4Q540-541.

103. See also the detailed explanation by G. J. Brooke, "4QTestament of Levi^d(?) and the Messianic Servant High Priest," in de Boer, *From Jesus to John*, 83-100, esp. 83-86. The older designation 4QTestament of Levi^d(?) refers to 4Q541.

104. J. Starcky, "Les quatre étapes du messianisme à Qumran," *RB* 70 (1963): 481-505, esp. 492. However, Abbé Starcky kindly gave me a copy of fragment 9 of 4Q541 in 1977 with permission to cite from it, and my colleagues and I have been able to refer to it on several occasions. See M. Hengel, "Der stellvertretende Sühnetod Jesu II," *IKZ* 9 (1980), 136-37 (135-47); *The Atonement*, 58-59; *La Crucifixion dans l'Antiquité et la Folie du Message de la Croix* (1981), 184-85; "Christological Titles in Early Christianity," in J. H. Charlesworth, ed., *The Messiah* (1992), 445 n. 69 (425-48). See also P. Stuhlmacher, *Biblische Theologie des Neuen Testaments*, vol. 1: *Grundlegung. Von Jesus zu Paulus* (1992), 129. My colleague H. Gese has also produced a translation which highlights the thoroughly poetic structure of the text.

2.[105] Puech's definitive edition of 4Q540-541 and other Aramaic texts has now appeared in DJD, volume 31, *Qumrân Grotte 4: XXII: Textes Araméens, Première Partie, 4Q529-549* (2001), and reflects the new designation as an apocryphon: "4Q540-541. 4QApocryphe de Lévi[a-b]? ar" (pp. 213-56). Since the preliminary publications by Puech and Starcky are the source of some earlier, obsolete sigla (Starcky's siglum 4QAhA below stands for 4QAh[aronique]), we may summarize the sigla from the earliest to the most recent:

MSS No.	Starcky 1963 (RB)	Puech 1992 (Madrid II)	Puech 2001 (DJD 31); Tov; García Martínez & Tigchelaar (DSSSE)	DJD 31 pages	DJD 31 plates
4Q537	—	4QAJa	4QTJacob? ar	171-90	11
4Q540	4QAhA bis	4QTestLévi[c](?)	4QapocLevi[a]? ar	217-23	12
4Q541	4QahA	4QTestLévi[d](?)	4QapocLevi[b]? ar	225-56	13-14

4Q541 is most important for our purposes. It consists according to Puech of twenty-four fragments, though only eleven of these preserve larger portions of text.[106] To this Puech added two related documents, 4Q540, consisting of three fragments and presumably belonging likewise to an apocryphon of Levi,[107] and 4Q537, from a Testament of Jacob, with 25 fragments.[108]

Puech's attempts at textual restoration of 4Q541 result in portions of at least seven columns from an original document of at least eight or nine columns, ordered in a hypothetical textual sequence. García Martínez and Tigchelaar likewise present seven self-contained though partly fragmentary portions of text, following Puech in the arrangement of fragments, though with a few variant readings of individual words (*DSSSE* 2:1078-81). By contrast, K. Beyer does not attempt to piece together the fragments or to order them into any overall sequence, preferring to translate fourteen individual fragments, ordered according to length (hence Beyer's fragment 1 is fragment 9

---

105. Hereafter Puech, "Fragments," in J. Trebolle Barrera and L. Vegas Montaner, eds., *The Madrid Qumran Congress*, vol. 2, STDJ 11/2 (1992), 449-501. Although Puech's definitive edition in DJD 31 supersedes this, we have given the page numbers of both editions for common material. References to Puech's "Fragments" also remain where this offers commentary not found in DJD 31 (e.g., below, nn. 148-59). Differences in Puech's two editions are duly noted, e.g., below, nn. 122, 123, 127. Another preliminary publication of the text is R. H. Eisenman and M. Wise, *The Dead Sea Scrolls Uncovered* (1992), 142-45.

106. Text in DJD 31:230-52.

107. Text in DJD 31:219-23.

108. Text in DJD 31:175-90.

in the other editions).[109] Analysis of the handwriting leads both Puech and Beyer to date 4Q540 and 541 near the end of the second century, perhaps around 100 B.C.E.[110]

Below I have selected aspects of 4Q541 most pertinent to our theme. The basic translation is from *The Dead Sea Scrolls Study Edition* by García Martínez and Tigchelaar (2:1078-81), supplemented by notes of alternative textual readings or translations from the other editions.[111] The largest fragment, fragment 9 (made available to me by Starcky in 1977), is also the most interesting, though it receives further illumination from the other fragments. The poetical nature of this text is seen clearly in its parallelism.

4QapocLevi[b]? ar (4Q541), Fragment 9 column i = Fragment 1 (Beyer)[112]

1 [. . .] . . . [. . .] the sons of his generation [. . .] . . . [. . .]
   2 [. . .] his [wi]sdom
And he will atone (ויכפר) for all the children of his generation,
   and he will be sent to all the children of 3 his [people].[113]
His word is like the word of the heavens,
   and his teaching, according to the will of God.
His eternal sun (שמש עלמה)[114] will shine
   4 and its fire will burn (ויתזה)[115] in all the ends of the earth;

---

109. Beyer, *Ergänzungsband,* 78-82, esp. 79, fragment 1. I would like to thank Professor Beyer for sending me his page proofs prior to their publication.

110. Puech, DJD 31:227 (4Q541), 217 (4Q540) (= Puech, "Fragments," 452, 480); Beyer, *Ergänzungsband,* 78.

111. In addition to the works by E. Puech, K. Beyer, G. Vermes, F. García Martínez and E. J. C. Tigchelaar, and G. Brooke already mentioned, see the detailed analysis of all the important fragments of 4Q541 by J. Zimmermann, *Messianische Texte aus Qumran: Königliche, priesterliche und prophetische Messiasvorstellungen in den Schriftfunden von Qumran,* WUNT 2/ 104 (1998), 247-77.

112. For texts and translations, see DJD 31:241-45; *DSSSE* 1080-81; Vermes, *Complete Dead Sea Scrolls,* 527; Beyer, *Ergänzungsband,* 79; Brooke, "4QTestament of Levi," 87; Zimmermann, *Messianische Texte aus Qumran,* 255-56.

113. Line 3 beginning, Puech in DJD 31:241-42 reads [ע]מֹּה, "son *[peu]ple*"; *DSSSE* likewise [עמ]ה, "his [people]"; Vermes, "his [peo]ple"; but Beyer reads [נצ]בֹּה, literally נִצְבָּה, "planting," although he translates similarly to the others, "seines Geschlechtes."

114. Another possible translation: "the sun of his age."

115. Like the above translation from *DSSSE,* Puech traces ויתזה to the root אזה ("to heat"), as in Dan. 3:19, 22, and translates, "et son feu sera brûlant." But the itaff'al of נזה is also worth mentioning: וְיַתֵּזֶה (suggestion of H. Gese; see also Puech, DJD 31:243 = "Fragments," 468). This would be a Hebraism that could be connected to Isa. 52:15: "to be sprinkled (forth)" as purifying fire. Cf. Vermes, *Complete Dead Sea Scrolls,* 527: "his fire will *spring forth*

above the darkness it will shine.[116]
Then, darkness will vanish 5 [fr]om the earth,
    and gloom from the dry land.
They will utter many words against him,
    and an abundance of 6 [lie]s;
they will fabricate fables against him,
    and utter every kind of disparagement against him.
His generation (דרה) will be evil and changed 7 [and . . .] will be,[117]
    and its [better: his][118] position (מקמה) of deceit and of violence.
[And] the people will go astray in his days
    and they will be bewildered. . . .

An indication of this figure's suffering can be seen below in fragment 6 and perhaps also in fragment 4 column ii. Puech and the editors of *DSSSE* have pieced these two fragments together, with fragment 4 column ii supplying the beginnings of the lines. However, Beyer presents fragment 6 (= fragment 8 in his numbering [*Texte*, 81]) on its own and shows how it might make sense as a unit. Each fragment can be examined separately below:[119]

---

to all the ends of the earth" (italics added). See also the discussion in Brooke, "4QTestament of Levi," 93.

116. Cf. 1Q27 col. i 5-7; *T. Levi* 4:3; 18:3ff.; John 1:5; 8:12; 9:5; 1 John 2:8.

117. Translation of *DSSSE*; text: להוה [. . . ו] ואפיך באיש דרה (so also Beyer). Puech reads a *yod* at the beginning of the third word and restores the lacuna differently and more fully: להוה [די דחה] יאפיך באיש דרה (DJD 31:241). Puech translates: "Sa génération, le mal pervertira [*de sorte que rejeté*] il sera."

118. *DSSSE* = ". . . *its* position"; text: מקמה וחמס שקר ודי. The pronominal suffix of the last word, מקמה, "*its* position," could refer, as it does above in *DSSSE*, to the situation of deceit and violence in which the "*generation*" (דר; with suffix, דרה; for דר see Dan. 3:33; 4:31) in the preceding line will find itself. This has the virtue of parallelism: "His generation . . . and *its* position/situation." Similarly Beyer: "Seine *Generation* wird böse und verkehrt [und . . .] sein, und *ihre* Stellung aus Lüge und Unrecht bestehen" (*Ergänzungsband*, 79, frag. 1, ll. 6b-7a, italics added). But the suffix of מקמה might more plausibly be applied to "*his* [own] position/situation/existence" under conditions of falsehood and violence, referring to the text's main character, since he is further alluded to in the next line in the expression ביומוהי, "in his days." So Puech, DJD 31:242: "Sa génération, le mal pervertira [*de sorte que rejeté*] il sera, et que mensonge er violence (sera) son existence." See also Vermes, *Complete Dead Sea Scrolls*, 527: "Evil will overturn *his* generation [because . . .] will be, and because lies and violence will (fill) *his* existence, and the people will go astray in *his* days and will become perplexed" (italics added). This has the advantage of maintaining the same reference of the pronominal suffix throughout.

119. Text and translation according to *DSSSE* 1080-81; the text is reconstructed slightly differently in DJD 31:238, e.g., *DSSSE* בשבי frag. 4 ii 5 = DJD 31:238 בטבי (cf. p. 235).

4QapocLevi[b]? ar (4Q541)

Frag. 4 col. ii

ו[ארעא]	and] the earth [
לבר יו[סף]	to the son of Jo[seph
לכא מ]ן	here . . .[
דמכה]	your blood [
בשבי מ]ן	for the captives from [
מן הי]ן	of . . .[

Frag. 6

[ומכאבין עלמ]	] those smitten for . . .[[120]
ד]ינכה ולא תהוה חי]ב	your [ju]dgment and you will not be gui[lty
[נגדי מכאוביכה ד]י	] the blows of your pains (?) wh[ich
[לא גועלונכה וכול]	]. . . your deposit and all [
[ית לבכה מן ק]ן	]. . . your heart from . . .[

As can be seen, the references to suffering are concentrated in fragment 6, though the expression "your blood"[121] in fragment 4, line 4 adds to the picture.

The textual restorations and translations of the various scholars diverge sharply in 4Q541 fragment 24 column ii (= Beyer fragment 5). The important issues of interpretation will arise naturally from a comparison of these translations. Controversy surrounds especially lines 4b-5a, though it may be best to give lines 3-6 in their entirety, with underlining of words disputed for either text-critical or translational reasons:[122]

3 מ[פריקן או שגיא]ן [מסן]כ[תרן]כ[מה די להוי]ן שגיאן מגליאן וא[ל]
צ[דיקא יבריככה]

---

120. Text: [. . .]מ ומכאבין עלמ. Puech translates: "et ceux qui *sont* (?) frappés à cause de/par . . ." (DJD 31:237). Beyer has a different word division, [. . .]ומכאבין על מן, and translates: "und Leiden auf" (*Ergänzungsband*, 81, frag. 8).

121. [. . .]דמכה, "your blood" ("ton sang"), is read here, although not without a question mark, by Puech, DJD 31:236. Beyer has: "dein Blut (oder: schlafende)" (*Ergänzungsband*, 81, frag. 13 l. 4).

122. Text in Puech, DJD 31:252 (a significantly different text, especially in line 3, was published earlier in Puech, "Fragments," 475). For another restoration of the text see Beyer, *Ergänzungsband*, 80, frag. 5. Outside of the term וֹתֹלֹיא in line 4 we have not consistently reproduced Puech's text-critical symbols for uncertain letters: see his edition. Beyer cannot clearly make out the ת in this word and leaves it untranslated; similarly García Martínez and Tigchelaar in *DSSSE*. The fifth word in line 4 (Puech: יונא, "dove" or "agitator") Beyer reads as זֹיונא, "brilliant appearance" *(strahlendes Aussehen)*. See below.

4 בקר ובעי ודע מא <u>יונא</u> בעה ואל [123]תמחולהי ביד <u>שחפא ו֯תֿליא</u>
כ[די]ן֯ אל תדין]

5 <u>וצצא</u> אל תקרוב בה ותקים לאבוכה שם חדוא ולכול אחיכה יסוד מבחן

6 ת{צ}ו<ע>א ותחזה בנהיר עלמא ולא תהוה מן שנאא

Different translators sometimes give completely different senses to these lines. For example, García Martínez and Tigchelaar translate (*DSSSE* 2:1081, italics added):

> 3 [And] God will establish many [. . .] many [. . .] will be revealed, and [. . .]
> 4a Examine, ask and know what the *dove* (**יונא**) has asked; 4b and do not
> punish it by the *sea-mew* (**שחפא**) and (**ליא**[. . .]ו, left untranslated). . . . 5a
> do not bring the *night-hawk* (**צצא**) near it. 5b And you will establish for
> your father a name of joy, and for your brothers you will make a [tested]
> foundation 6 rise. 6a You will see and rejoice in eternal light. 6b And you
> will not be of the enemy. (4QapocLevi[b]? ar [4Q541], fragment 24 column ii)

The translation "dove" in line 4a is adopted also by Vermes,[124] Brooke,[125] and Zimmermann[126] and goes back to Puech's "colombe" in his earlier 1992 translation (now removed from his 2001 translation). It is based on the reading of **יונא** in the sense of Hebrew **יוֹנָה**. If the "dove" is the right reading — Puech later retranslates this same word as "agitator"[127] — Puech suggests that it could allude to a vision or revelation, in which the dove could be a symbol of Israel (cf. *L.A.B.* 39:5).[128] Yet the reference above to the two other birds, the "sea-mew" and the "nighthawk," is unique to the translation of García Martínez and Tigchelaar, though Puech mentions the birds in his commentary as lexical if not contextual possibilities.[129]

---

123. The reading **תמחולהי** in DJD 31:252 supersedes the earlier reading **תמחי להי** in Puech, "Fragments," 475; see discussion in DJD 31:254.

124. Vermes, *Complete Dead Sea Scrolls,* 527: "Search and seek and know what is sought by the *dove.*"

125. Brooke, "4Q Testament of Levi," 90: "Search and seek and know what the *dove* has sought."

126. Zimmermann, *Messianische Texte aus Qumran,* 264: "Forsche und erkenne, was die *Taube* (?) sucht."

127. Compare Puech, DJD 31:253 — "Cherche et demande et sache ce que demande *l'agitateur*" — with Puech, "Fragments," 476 — "Scrute et recherche et connais ce qu'a demandé *la colombe.*" See DJD 31:255 for justification of the change.

128. Puech, "Fragments," 476; cf. DJD 31:254.

129. Cf. Puech, "Fragments," 477; DJD 31:255. **שחפא** can mean "mouette" (gull or mew); while **צצא**, if understood as defective writing of **ציצא**, can mean "autruche/vautour" (ostrich/vulture); cf. also Puech, "Fragments," 478 n. 23.

Interestingly, however, García Martínez's earlier Spanish translation of fragment 24 column ii, lines 4b-5a (as represented below in the English translation of the Spanish by W. G. E. Watson) has virtually the same meaning as Puech's 1992 French translation, except it lacks Puech's reference to "hanging," that is, crucifixion (see below). It will be seen that the other translators basically follow Puech:

4Q541 Fragment 24 ii 4b-5a:

Puech (1992):
4b et ne châtie pas un affaibli au moyen d'épuisement (שחפא) et de pendoir/pendaison (תליא) (?) t[out *le jour* (?)] 5a et de clou (וצצא) (?) n'approche pas de lui.[130]

García Martínez (1992/1994):
4b and do not punish one weakened because of exhaustion (שחפא) and from being uncertain (תליא) a[ll . . .] 5a do not bring the nail (וצצא) near him.[131]

Brooke (1993):
4a and do not chastise the one tired with consumption and hanging a[ll] 5a And a diadem/nail/purity do not bring near to him.[132]

Zimmermann (1998):
4b und schlage nicht einen Schwachen durch Auszehrung und Aufhängen(?) al[lle . . .] 5a Und den Nagel(?) nähere ihm nicht.[133]

Vermes (1997):
4b and do not smite one who is exhausted with consumption and troubles . . .[134]

With the exception of Vermes, who does not translate verse 5a, these translators all follow Puech in referring to the וצצא in line 5a as a "nail" (*clou, Nagel*), although García Martínez later opts for the translation "night-hawk" (see above), and Brooke offers three alternatives: "diadem/nail/purity." Puech's translation of תליא as *pendaison*, "hanging," understood as a possible reference

---

130. Puech, "Fragments," 476; we have added the Aramaic glosses for clarity.

131. F. García Martínez, *The Dead Sea Scrolls Translated*, trans. by W. G. E. Watson from *Textos de Qumrán* (orig. 1992; ET 1994), 270.

132. Brooke, "4Q Testament of Levi," 90.

133. Zimmermann, *Messianische Texte aus Qumran*, 264.

134. Vermes, *Complete Dead Sea Scrolls*, 527.

to crucifixion, is also picked up by Brooke and Zimmermann, though Vermes has more generally "troubles" and García Martínez "and from being uncertain," which he later leaves untranslated in his revised edition (*DSSSE*, above) because of the textual uncertainty of the letters לי[. . .]ו. The notion of "hanging" as "crucifixion" is made explicit in Puech's revised translation of 2001:

> 4a Cherche et demande et sache ce que demande l'agitateur, 4b et ne le *repousse*/l'*affaibis* pas au moyen d'épuisement/*bâton* (שחפא) et de pendaison/crucifixion (תליא) comme *[pein]e* [(capitale) ne *prononce pas*(?)] 5a et de clou (צצא) n'approche pas de lui. (4Q541 Fragment 24 ii 4-5, DJD 31:253)

> Seek and ask and know what the agitator is asking, and do not repel him/do not enfeeble him by means of exhaustion/a rod and hanging/crucifixion as [(capital) punishment do not pronounce these (?)],[135] and do not bring the nail near to him.

However, before we examine this striking thesis, another very different translation calls for attention. Beyer translates:

> 4a Examine and search and know what our *brilliant appearance* (זִיונא) requires, 4b and do not weaken it through consumption. And (ו[תֿ]ליא, left untranslated). . . . 5a and the *frontlet* (צצא) [of the high priest]. Do not touch it/him, 5b so you will establish for your father a name of joy and for all your brothers make a tested foundation 6 rise.[136]

The translation of line 5b is uncontroversial. But in lines 4a and 5a, Beyer offers a pair of alternative readings, "brilliant appearance" and "the frontlet" (on the high priest's forehead), which tend to reinforce one another.

In line 4a of fragment 24, at the beginning of Puech's consonants יונא

---

135. Puech's translation is apparently intended to indicate that our text proscribes both the rod (i.e., beating) and hanging or crucifixion as means of (capital) punishment. Compare his comments in his introduction to 4Q540-541 in DJD 31. Puech says that the eschatological high priest who is the subject of these texts will be rejected by his generation and perhaps by his own family. Nevertheless, according to 4Q541 frag. 24 ii 4-5, "he should not be avenged and condemned to punishments which appear proscribed: beating/exhaustion, שחפא, and crucifixion, ותליא, צצא" = "batonnade/épuisement . . . et crucifixion" (DJD 31:216).

136. Beyer, *Ergänzungsband*, 80, italics added. Original German: "4 Forsche nach und suche und erkenne, was unser strahlendes Aussehen benötigt! Und schwäche es nicht durch Schwindsucht! Und . . . [. . .] 5 und das Stirndiadem (des Hohepriesters). Berühre ihn/es nicht, so wirst du für deinen Vater einen Freudennamen aufrichten und für alle deine Brüder ein erprobtes Fundament 6 hervorgehen lassen."

("dove"), Beyer restores an admittedly unclear *zayin* to read the noun זיו, "splendor,"[137] which, when combined with the first person plural pronominal suffix נא-
available in the undisputed consonants, yields זיונא, "our splendor" or "our brilliant appearance." However, it is not clear whether this is supposed to apply to the
high priest, as implied by Beyer's reading of line 5a, or to God, mentioned in line 3.

In line 5a of fragment 24, Beyer reads the same consonants as Puech but
suggests a different etymology. Beyer by his translation "Stirndiadem (des
Hohenpriesters)" understands צצא as an Aramaized form of the Hebrew ציץ,
that is, as a defectively written ציצא.[138] In the Bible ציץ designates the engraved
golden plate or frontlet on the high priest's turban (Exod. 28:36; 39:30; Lev. 8:9),
variously termed in English as the "plate" (RSV; NIV; NAB), "rosette" or "orna-
ment" (NRSV), "flower" (NJB), "frontlet" (NJPS), or "medallion" (REB) —
Greek πέταλον.[139] This allows Beyer to supply an allusion to the high priest:
"the frontlet (of the high priest)."

However, as we have already seen above, Puech traces צצא in line 5a of
fragment 24 to the Syriac word *ṣṣ'*, "nail."[140] This might be part of an allusion to
crucifixion or torture: "the sense of 'nail' is better understood after the mention
of שחפא ותליא ביד and could allude to crucifixion."[141] A related term תלה (cf.
the noun תליא, "hanging"), whose Hebrew counterpart תָּלָה appears in the
statement "anyone *hanged* is a curse of God" (Deut. 21:23, NJB), *might* be attested in another part of this document, fragment 2 column ii, line 1, ותלה.[142]
Puech translates "and is suspended/crucified,"[143] while Zimmermann similarly
speaks of being "hanged."[144] However, García Martínez and Tigchelaar regard
the word as too textually uncertain to incorporate into their translation.

---

137. Cf. BDB 1091 s.v. זיו. This is translated "brilliance" in Dan. 2:31 and "splendor" in
Dan. 4:33 (NRSV 4:36). In the plural, it applies to a person's "brightness of countenance" in Dan.
5:6, 9, 10; 7:28.

138. See also the summaries of the discussion in Brooke, "4QTestament of Levi," and
Zimmermann, *Messianische Texte aus Qumran*, 264-65, translation note g.

139. Beyer's priestly understanding of צצא may be partly supported by Puech's discussion ("Fragments," 487) of the high priest's πέταλον in *T. Levi* 8:2, τὸ πέταλον τῆς πίστεως (mis-
translated in *OTP* 1:791 as "the *breastplate* of faith").

140. Payne-Smith, *Thesaurus Syriacus*, 3436: "clavus," cited by Puech, "Fragments," 477
n. 21; DJD 31:255 n. 26. See also the discussion of the two alternatives "nail" and "diadem" in
Puech, DJD 31:214 (= "Fragments," 487).

141. "Le sens de 'clou' se conçoit mieux après les mentions de שחפא ותליא ביד et
pourrait faire allusion à la crucifixion" (Puech, "Fragments," 478 = DJD 31:255).

142. 4Q541 2 ii 1, Puech DJD 31:231.

143. "et (est?) (sus)pendu/crucifié," 4Q541 2 ii 1, Puech DJD 31:232.

144. "hängen/aufgehängt," Zimmermann, *Messianische Texte aus Qumran*, 250. Cf. p. 251
translation note g; p. 264 translation note f; and Brooke, "4QTestament of Levi," 91 n. 2.

Finally, 4Q541 fragment 2 ii 3 reads [י]מכאבב תסב, "you will take the smitten" (*DSSSE*, 2:1079), an expression we have seen before in the first line of fragment 6, על ומכאבין, "those smitten for." Nevertheless, the overall context of these statements about suffering remains unclear. Moreover, Beyer's alternative interpretation in terms of the "brilliant appearance" and "frontlet" or "diadem" of the high priest does not make bad sense.

Our other document in this section, 4Q540 fragment 1 = 4QapocLevi[a]? ar, also contains expressions of suffering. The text, relatively full but very puzzling, is offered below in the translation of García Martínez and Tigchelaar:[145]

> 1 [. . .] Again distress will come upon him, and the little one will lack goods and will . . . [. . .] 2 [After?] 52 [weeks?]. Again, a loss will come to it, and he will lack goods [. . .] 3 [. . .] and he will not resemble anyone <lacking> good, but instead like the great sea [. . .] 4 [. . .] he will lea[ve] the house in which he was born, and anoth[er] dwelling [. . .] 5 [. . .] serving [. . .] his . . . a sanctuary [. . .] he will consecrate [. . .][146]

As early as 1963, Starcky suspected that these portions of 4Q540 and 541 (or 4QAhA bis and 4QAhA in his nomenclature) "seem to evoke a suffering Messiah in the perspective opened up by the Servant Songs."[147] In the largest fragment (frag. 9 of 4Q541), Jacob presumably is addressing his son Levi, to whom he reveals "an eschatological figure, who is certainly the High Priest of the messianic era." A reference to the Teacher of Righteousness is not convincing. The figure is rather to be identified as "the Servant of Yahweh, whose wisdom will be known by all the earth and who will offer his life as expiation for the people; he will have appeared identical to him (i.e., the author) to the Messiah of Aaron." Yet Starcky notes that "none of the expressions used in 4QAhA [= 4Q541] indicates that the sufferings of this Messiah have redemptive value," a reservation which we encounter also in other Jewish texts that allude to Isaiah 53.

Puech basically follows Starcky but suspects that the document is to be identified as a *Testament* (or *Aprocryphon*) *of Levi* with a messianic out-

---

145. Translation modified from *DSSSE* 2:1079, incorporating a suggestion about the fifty-two "weeks" (?) in l. 2 from Puech, DJD 31:220 (= "Fragments," 481); cf. Beyer, *Ergänzungsband*, 79-80, frag. 3.

146. Puech's restoration of l. 5 is slightly fuller than the above. He translates: "[. . . et (il) (re)bâtira(?), (comme?)] ministre de Di[eu, avec] ses [bie]ns, le sanctuaire [après] qu'[(ils) l'] aur[ont] dévasté(?)[. . .]" (DJD 31:220; text p. 219). By contrast, Beyer can discern with certainty only the word "sanctuary" (*Ergänzungsband*, 80, frag. 3 l. 5).

147. For the following see Starcky, "Les quatre étapes du messianisme à Qumran," 492.

look.[148] An important parallel is the Greek *Testament of Levi* 18 with its presentation of the end-time messianic high priest, who shines like the sun and drives away darkness, spreads the light of knowledge and makes peace.[149] At the end of his impressive edition of the text, Puech ventures a research hypothesis which he considers more promising. The text apparently is about a revelation of an angel to Levi (or Jacob), presenting apocalyptic, cultic, and wisdom motifs in the first few fragments and then a universal teacher of wisdom, the end-time high priest, in fragment 9. He is a messenger invested with divine glory who acts according to God's will, but is simultaneously viciously attacked by people dominated by evil and injustice.

Puech presents this figure in three aspects as "a sage, a priest, and a despised servant."[150] The last aspect is naturally most interesting to us. Puech refers to the prophetic word "I have given you as . . . a light to the nations" in Isaiah 42:6 (cf. 49:6) and furthermore to Isaiah 51:4-5. The Qumran text is also reminiscent of the idea of the Servant "seeing light" (Isaiah 53:11, 1QIsa[a-b], LXX).[151] The light is sent into the darkness (cf. 50:10), with the call to leave it behind. The Servant is the bearer of God's word (Isa. 42:1-4; cf. *Tg. Isa.* 42:1; 49:2; 50:4-5; 53:5b). Puech seeks to show that this understanding of motifs from the Servant Song is already on its way to the understanding of these motifs in the Targum (cf. also Isa. 53:11b). Like the Servant, this eschatological priest is "sent to all the children of his people" (4Q541 frag. 9 i 2-3). Both the Servant and he "will be despised, mocked, rejected, the object of all sorts of slander, Isa 50:6-8; 53:2-12 and 4Q541 frag. 9 i 5-6."[152] Even the occurrence in this Aramaic text of the Hebraism מכאוביכה/מכאובין ("smitten for"/"pains") twice in the opaque fragment 6 and once in fragment 5 is no accident. Of the total of sixteen occur-

---

148. Puech, "Fragments," 487 = DJD 31:214. In "Fragments," 489-91, Puech cites an expanded edition of a text, now numbered 4Q537, that had been published by J. T. Milik as a Testament of Jacob ("Écrits préesseniens de Qumrân," in M. Delcor, ed., *Qumrân: Sa piété, sa théologie et son milieu*, BETL 46 [1978], 91-106, esp. 103-5) and by K. Beyer as 4QGen(esis)Ap(okryphon) (*Die aramäischen Texte vom Toten Meer* [1984], 186-87). See now 4Q537 *4QTestament of Jacob(?) ar* in DSSSE 2:1074-77 and DJD 31:171-90, esp. 175-76. Jacob says that he has read on a tablet received from an angel "all my troubles (כל עקתי) and all that was to happen to [me]" (4Q537 frag. 1 l. 4). Suffering plays an important role even for the patriarch.

149. Puech, "Fragments," 493: "It is striking that *T. Levi* 18:2-6, 9 presents in a completely similar way the arrival of the new Priest"; cf. p. 497, with reference to *T. Levi* 18:7-8. The *Apocryphon of Levi* 4Q54-541 makes it unlikely that *T. Levi* as a whole is of Christian origin. We can at most reckon with an early Christian reworking at certain points.

150. Puech, "Fragments," 492; cf. 492-99.

151. Puech, "Fragments," 497.

152. Puech, "Fragments," 498.

rences of מַכְאוֹב in the OT, two come from Isaiah 53:3-4; the Servant is the אִישׁ מַכְאֹבוֹת or "man of sorrows" par excellence.

According to Puech the atonement effected by this end-time priest should be understood cultically. It occurs in the rebuilt or reconsecrated sanctuary to which 4Q540 and the *Targum of Isaiah* 53:5 refer. According to the *Targum of Isaiah* 53:11b and 12, the Servant will "beseech concerning the sins" of the many. Whereas in the Targum and in rabbinic interpretation the Servant's suffering and vicarious atonement for the sins of the people fade completely into the background, fragment 9 gives evidence of cultic atonement and repudiates the abuse of the end-time priest. Nevertheless, no vicarious surrender of life is evident in the fragments, though one could associate the יכפר ("he will atone") of fragment 9 line 2 with the אָשָׁם (NRSV "an offering for sin") of Isaiah 53:10. Fragment 10 *might* perhaps refer to a scene such as is depicted in Daniel 3:40 LXX in the Greek Additions to Daniel (see above §4; cf. also the Aramaic Dan. 3:28 = LXX 3:95).[153]

Even "a violent death of the 'Priest-Servant'" is not unthinkable for Puech.[154] He refers here to the admittedly very uncertain fragment 24 with its occurrences of terms for suffering, torture, or execution, and then to analogous expressions in the *Targum of Isaiah,* since a connection between fragments 9 and 24 cannot be excluded. Puech even mentions crucifixion, which was known in Palestine already in the Hellenistic period.[155] But here we find ourselves on very uncertain ground. Puech admits this himself in his conclusion: "the interest in these fragments is great, even though at several essential points they hardly allow us to ask questions or to catch a glimpse of answers."[156] He nevertheless believes that the author of the text clearly had the Suffering Servant of Isaiah in view "as background for his presentation of the future priest." "This Servant Messiah will fulfill the function of a priest and not that of a king. . . . He will be rejected and scorned by his own people, who will wonder and be perplexed."[157] Because the most important fragment (frag. 9) breaks off, the result of this individual's mission and the possibility of his atoning sufferings for the people remain uncertain, while his priestly function comes clearly to the fore. We are faced with a similar uncertainty about this figure as we are about the angel prince Melchizedek in *11QMelchizedek* (11Q13), with whom he may have some connection.

153. Puech, "Fragments," 499.
154. Puech, "Fragments," 499.
155. Puech, "Fragments," 499 with n. 59; DJD 31:216, 253, 255 with n. 28.
156. Puech, "Fragments," 499. Several of these comments in the conclusion of Puech's "Fragments" are not incorporated into the text edition in DJD 31.
157. Puech, "Fragments," 500.

For Puech — and we can hardly contradict him here, despite all the remaining uncertainties — our text contains "the first and oldest midrashic exploitation of the Servant Songs of Isaiah interpreted in terms of an individual, in a current of Palestinian Judaism which more or less dates from the second century B.C.E. at the latest."[158] At the same time the text sheds new light on previously disputed texts such as the *Testament of Levi* 4 and 18, the *Testament of Benjamin* 3:8 (see below §9), and the Similitudes of *1 Enoch*, but also on the *Targum of Isaiah*, which may in fact have a pre-Christian history that is unknown to us. This is suggested by "the sapiential coloring of the Servant figure"[159] in both 4Q541 and the *Targum of Isaiah*, though this is also found in the Synoptic Gospels, above all in Q.[160] I believe that it would be worth considering whether the interpretation of Isaiah 53 in the Targum, which is oriented around the Pharisaic-rabbinic messianic expectation of the king from the house of David, might not have suppressed an older interpretation oriented around the priestly Messiah, whose wisdom-didactic features and motif of intercession for sinners the Targum retains.

In the years of the first bloom of Qumran research, scholars including Dupont-Sommer, M. Black, and others sought to connect the Suffering Servant with the Teacher of Righteousness and to find allusions to the Isaiah text in the *Hymns* or *Hodayot*. But this attempt has been so clearly refuted by J. Carmignac and G. Jeremias that we no longer need to deal with it again here.[161] The *Hodayot* show no more allusions or points of contact to the Servant texts than they do to other passages from the Prophets or Psalms. Moreover, the suffering of the Teacher does not occur vicariously for others, but only for his own purification and instruction.

---

158. Puech, "Fragments," 500. Similarly Brooke, "4QTestament of Levi," 95: "we may have in this text [4Q541] the earliest individualistic interpretation of the Isaianic servant songs in a particularly cultic direction."

159. Puech, "Fragments," 501.

160. Cf. Mark 6:2; 1:22, 27; Matt. 11:19 = Luke 7:35; Matt. 11:25-26 = Luke 10:21f.; Matt. 12:42 = Luke 11:31f.; Matt. 23:34-36 = Luke 11:49-51, etc., as well as the Johannine missionary or "sending" Christology. 4Q541 also shows, as do many other Qumran texts, that "wisdom" and "apocalyptic" cannot be torn apart. Such texts undermine the entire anti-apocalyptic Q speculation that thrives especially in America and wishes to situate the original form of Q in close proximity to the Cynic *chreia* collections. The Q specialists in Claremont should pay closer attention to 4Q541 and other Qumran parallels. Precisely from the wisdom material of Qumran we may expect a few more surprises.

161. J. Carmignac, "Les Citations de l'Ancien Testament et spécialement des Poèmes du Serviteur dans les Hymnes de Qumran," *RevQ* 2 (1960): 357-94; G. Jeremias, *Der Lehrer der Gerechtigkeit*, WUNT 2 (1963), 299-307. Jeremias finds the only points of contact between the Qumran Teacher of Righteousness and Isaiah's Servant in the citations of Isa. 50:4 in 1QH 7:10 (= 15:10 in *DSSSE*, 177 [Sukenik col. 7]) and 8:35-36 (= 16:35-36 in *DSSSE*, 183 [Sukenik col. 8]).

8. The Septuagint Translation of Isaiah 53
and the *passio iusti,* Including Wisdom 2 and 5

Our impression concerning the lack of vicarious suffering in the Jewish sources is strengthened by the Septuagint translation of Isaiah 53.[162] As its telling contemporary allusions show, the Greek version of the book of Isaiah originated at a time when the threat against Judea by Antiochus IV had been rebuffed and the Maccabean freedom struggle had proved successful. Isaiah 19:16-25 and other texts indicate that the work originated in Egypt, when Onias IV had founded the temple in Leontopolis with its extensive Jewish military settlements. Seeligman concludes on the basis of Isaiah 23:10 that the translation was made shortly after the destruction of Carthage in 146 B.C.E., though van der Kooij dates it somewhat later, shortly after 141 B.C.E., after the conquest of Selucid Babylon by the Parthian king Mithridates I.[163]

In any case Isaiah was not translated into Greek until after the book of the Twelve Minor Prophets,[164] at a time when the idea of the end-time fulfillment of the prophetic predictions in the present had achieved wide currency. The writer of the translation, a scribe, possessed a good knowledge of the older translations.[165] Like Ben Sira in the Hymn to the Fathers (Sirach 44:1–51:24), the composer of Daniel, and the scribe who wrote 1QIsaᵃ, the translator of this book related Isaiah's prophecies in manifold ways to the events of his time as signs of the (immanent) eschatological fulfillment.

162. On the Septuagint of the Servant Songs see now E. R. Ekblad, *Isaiah's Servant Poems According to the Septuagint,* CBET 23 (1999), esp. pp. 167-266 on Isaiah 52:13–53:12. Although this appeared after the German version of this essay (1996) and could not be fully taken into account here, our English translations of the Septuagint often rely on Ekblad's renderings. See especially his parallel translation of the MT and LXX on pp. 173-77 and the slightly different translations he offers in his verse-by-verse commentary, pp. 178-266.

163. Seeligmann, *The Septuagint Version of Isaiah,* 70ff., 90ff.; van der Kooij, *Die alten Textzeugen des Jesajabuches,* 70ff. On the strong Egyptian coloring of the translation's language and milieu see J. Ziegler, *Untersuchungen zur Septuaginta des Buches Isaias,* ATA 12/3 (1934), 175-212. The translator, who admittedly knew Aramaic and Greek better than Hebrew, may nevertheless — like Ben Sira's grandson around the same time — have come from the Palestinian motherland. For a detailed discussion of the problem see M. Harl, G. Dorival, and O. Munnich, *La Bible Grecque des Septante* (1988), 94f., 102f., 111.

164. In Codices B, A, V, and in Athanasius, Cyril of Jerusalem, Epiphanius, and others, the book of the Twelve Minor Prophets stands before Isaiah. The reversal of this order by Sinaiticus, Melito, and Origen rests upon the influence of the Hebrew "canon." See the overview in H. B. Swete, *An Introduction to the Old Testament in Greek* (1902), 201ff. For the dependence of LXX Isaiah upon the LXX of the Twelve Prophets and other Septuagintal texts see also Ziegler, *Untersuchungen zur Septuaginta des Buches Isaias,* 104-5.

165. Cf. van der Kooij, *Die alten Textzeugen des Jesajabuches,* 62-63 on Isa. 33:18.

I shall take Ziegler's Göttingen edition of Greek text as the basis of my observations.[166] In contrast to Euler, who constantly reckons with Christian interpolations,[167] our received Septuagint text of the fourth Servant Song seems to be a relatively reliable witness to the Old Greek. Euler does not consider the time and situation of the translator. Instead, he proceeds from the vague fiction of a general Septuagintal piety, which never existed in this form, since the Septuagint is anything but a unified work. Rather, it is a collection of writings whose origins stretched over a period of 300 years.[168] The translation of Isaiah was apparently prepared by an individual who was at times uncertain about the frequently difficult text.[169] Therefore he sometimes rendered by means of an interpretive and actualizing paraphrase rather than an exact translation. But on the whole it is not a bad translation; one can judge it both philologically and theologically to be a considerable "hermeneutical" achievement. At the same time, given its many departures from the MT, it is difficult to say whether the translator possessed a different Hebrew original, or took these freedoms himself.

That the translator regards the present as the time of fulfillment is seen by his relatively clear use of tenses, which is less ambiguous than in the MT, where it sometimes is not clear whether we have the *waw* copulative or *waw* consecutive. The Hebrew scroll 1QIsaᵃ similarly shows that scribes were no longer consistent in this regard, and also that they no longer understood the prophetic

---

166. Ziegler, *Isaias* (Göttingen LXX), 3rd ed. (1983). The text by A. Rahlfs (*Septuaginta* [1935]) is adequate for most purposes, differing little from Ziegler, though see below on Ziegler's emendation ἀνέτειλε μέν (for ἀνηγγείλαμεν) in Isa. 53:2. The readings of the later Greek versions by Aquila, Theodotion, and Symmachus are more fully presented in Ziegler's second Greek apparatus than they are in F. Field, *Origenis Hexaplorum*, 2 vols. (1867, 1875). See also the very helpful comparative table of texts of Isaiah 53 (MT, LXX, Targum, Peshitta, Aquila, Theodotion, Symmachus) that appears as an appendix in Hegermann, *Jesaja 53 in Hexapla, Targum und Peschitta*.

167. K. F. Euler, *Die Verkündigung vom leidenden Gottesknecht aus Isa 53 in der griechischen Bibel*, BWANT 66 (1934). For the older literature see A. Zillessen, "Isa 52,13–53,12 hebräisch nach Septuaginta," *ZAW* 25 (1905): 261-84. Appearing in the same year as Euler's work is the thorough study of Ziegler, *Untersuchungen zur Septuaginta des Buches Isaias*. See also Venantius de Leeuw, *De Ebed Jahweh-Profetieen* (1956), 9-17; Ruprecht, "Auslegungsgeschichte."

168. Harl, Dorival, and Munnich, *La Bible Grecque des Septante*, 83ff. passim; M. Hengel and R. Deines, "Die Septuaginta als 'christliche Schriftensammlung,' ihre Vorgeschichte und das Problem ihres Kanons," in M. Hengel and A. M. Schwemer, eds., *Die Septuaginta zwischen Judentum und Christentum*, WUNT 72 (1994), 182-284 = M. Hengel, *The Septuagint as Christian Scripture* (ET 2002).

169. On translation technique see also D. A. Baer, *When We All Go Home: Translation and Theology in LXX Isaiah 56–66*, JSOTSup 318 (2001).

perfect. The divine oracle in 52:13-15 points to a future — which the translator regards as already dawning or soon to be fulfilled — in which the wonderful exaltation of the Servant to God will be revealed. This exaltation presupposes the granting of divine knowledge to the Servant. The often observed wisdom or apocalyptic coloring of interpretation in contemporary texts shows itself again here. The translator presupposes the expectation of the resurrection of the dead, as in Isaiah 26:19: ἀναστήσονται οἱ νεκροί, καὶ ἐγερθήσονται οἱ ἐν τοῖς μνημείοις, καὶ εὐφρανθήσονται οἱ ἐν τῇ γῇ, "The dead will resurrect, and those in the graves will rise (passive intransitive), and those in the ground will rejoice."

In Isaiah 52:13 the translator draws together the three Hebrew verbs "he will be exalted" (יָרוּם) and "be lifted up" (נִשָּׂא) and "be very high" (גָּבַהּ מְאֹד) into a two-verb Greek formula: ὑψωθήσεται καὶ δοξασθήσεται, "he will be exalted and glorified." Or, to be more exact, the translator renders יָרוּם by ὑψωθήσεται, omits נִשָּׂא, and uses δοξασθήσεται for גָּבַהּ. Both Greek verbs are divine passives. The translator loves this two-verb formula of ὑψόω and δοξάζω, having a special fondness for δόξα ("glory") and cognates.[170] We see the formula as early as 4:2, where he renders very freely:

Τῇ δὲ ἡμέρᾳ ἐκείνῃ ἐπιλάμψει ὁ θεὸς ἐν βουλῇ μετὰ δόξης ἐπὶ τῆς γῆς τοῦ ὑψῶσαι καὶ δοξάσαι τὸ καταλειφθὲν τοῦ Ισραηλ.

In that day, God shall shine with glory in counsel on the earth, to exalt and glorify the remnant of Israel.

Therefore Isaiah 4:2 and 52:13 can be interpreted in the light of one another. The Servant is either the remnant of Israel itself (cf. Daniel 12) or Israel's representative. Collective and individual interpretations need not be mutually exclusive. They are two aspects of the same thing. The collocation of the two verbs ὑψόω and δοξάζω occurs again in 5:16; 10:15; and 33:10. While 10:15 is not strictly relevant,[171] in 33:10-11 we find this language applied to Yahweh himself, combined with a statement of eschatological judgment: νῦν ἀναστήσομαι, λέγει κύριος, νῦν δοξασθήσομαι, νῦν ὑψωθήσομαι· 11 νῦν ὄψεσθε, νῦν αἰσθηθήσεσθε, "'Now I will

170. L. H. Brockington, "The Greek Translator of Isaiah and His Interest in DOXA," *VT* 1 (1951): 23-32, esp. 26ff. He points to Isa. 52:14; 53:2. In 60:1 "light and glory" are "symbols of salvation" (p. 28 n. 1). This usage is a theological idiosyncrasy of the translator, and in my opinion it has no apocalyptic background. On δόξα in the LXX see C. C. Newman, *Paul's Glory-Theology*, NovTSup 69 (1992), 134-53 (literature).

171. But see Isa. 5:16, ὑψωθήσεται κύριος σαβαωθ ἐν κρίματι, καὶ ὁ θεὸς ὁ ἅγιος δοξασθήσεται ἐν δικαιοσύνῃ, "The Lord of hosts will be exalted by justice, and the Holy God will be glorified by righteousness."

arise,' says the Lord, 'now I will be glorified, now I will be exalted; now you will see, now you will perceive'" (cf. ὄψονται and συνήσουσιν, "they will see," "they will consider," in Isa. 52:15). The text continues: "Then nations will be burned up; like a thorn in the field, cast out and burnt up. Those far off will hear what I have done; those who draw near will know my strength" (Isa. 33:11-12, LXX). Comparing this with 52:13-15, we see that God's own end-time activity and that of his exalted Servant become almost interchangeable. In this divine oracle in 33:10-12, which has been built on a similar pattern to Isaiah 52:13-15, the translation is likewise very free. We can recognize the Hebrew text only fragmentarily. The expression δοξασθῆναι as a divine passive appears in Deutero-Isaiah also in 43:4, where it applies to Israel as "precious in [God's] sight and *glorified*," while Israel is similarly glorified in 44:23 as an aspect of its salvation: "God has redeemed Jacob, and Israel *will be glorified*" — against the MT, where it is God who will be glorified *in* Israel. So again in 49:3, God himself is glorified in Israel, though in 49:5, by contrast, Israel is gathered and glorified by God.

In Isaiah 52:14-15 the amazement of the many (cf. ἐκστήσονται, future of ἐξίστημι) and the astonishment of many nations (cf. θαυμάσονται; the two verbs appear together also in Jer. 4:9 and Acts 2:7) combine with the shutting of kings' mouths to form a statement of judgment. The verb ἐξίστημι is likewise a favorite word of the translator. He uses it twelve times for eight different Hebrew equivalents. The expression θαυμάζω in 52:15 recalls 52:5 in the immediate context, θαυμάζετε καὶ ὀλολύζετε, "wonder and howl," once again against the Hebrew text. At the final judgment, the pagan nations and their kings will see him invested with divine glory, whom they once dishonored and considered insignificant (v. 14: οὕτως ἀδοξήσει ἀπὸ ἀνθρώπων τὸ εἶδός σου καὶ ἡ δόξα σου ἀπὸ τῶν ἀνθρώπων, "So shall your face be without glory from men and your glory [disregarded] by men"). In verse 14, the LXX *hapax legomenon* ἀδοξέω combined with δόξα — itself a questionable translation of תֹּאַר ("form") — appears to be a deliberate wordplay on the δοξασθήσεται σφόδρα of verse 13.

The second divine oracle in the Greek version of the song begins not at the end in 53:11-12, as it does in the Hebrew, but somewhere in between, in verses 8 and 9. Following upon the first divine oracle in 52:13-15, the confession of the congregation (the "we" group) is introduced in the first person plural in 53:1-7. Here the Servant's vicarious suffering is presented and the people's own misunderstanding and guilt lamented. The second divine speech apparently began for the Greek translator with the turning point in verse 8.[172] His expression "for the lawless deeds of *my* people" (ἀπὸ τῶν ἀνομιῶν τοῦ λαοῦ μου) in verse 8

---

172. P. Grelot, *Les Poèmes du Serviteur*, LD 103 (1981), 106-7: "most probable is that the speech of God begins again in Isa 53:8a."

suggests that his *Vorlage* read the first person suffix עַמִּי, "*my* people," with the MT and 1QIsa[b][173] but against 1QIsa[a] (עמו = "*his* people")[174] and the assumption of many present-day interpreters.

God alone can introduce this turning point by his word. Therefore in 53:9, instead of translating the MT's third person singular consecutive imperfect וַיִּתֵּן, "*he made* his grave with the wicked" (KJV), which merely describes the situation, the translator uses the Greek equivalent of the Hebrew first person imperfect וְאֶתֵּן with the simple copulative rather than the consecutive *waw*, yielding the future δώσω, "I will give," understood as a promise. Hence "instead of" (cf. ἀντί) the Servant being given his own grave with the wicked and being with the rich in his death, as in the Hebrew text of verse 9 (cf. NJPS), the Lord promises to hand over both the wicked and the rich to judgment: "And I [the Lord] will give/hand over (δώσω) the wicked instead of (ἀντί) his grave, and the rich instead of (ἀντί) his death."[175] Perhaps this means that the Servant himself has already been installed as their judge. The kings and nations of 52:15 would then be speechless and confused, precisely because they will have been handed over for judgment *to him* who was killed but has been exalted to be with God; in other words, we must essentially supply to δώσω an αὐτῷ, "I will hand [them] over *to him*," that is, to the Servant.[176]

In this way, the Septuagint explains a development toward the idea of judgment that culminates in *1 Enoch* 62–63 and Wisdom 5.[177] Jewish interpreta-

---

173. For the Septuagint (and MT) reading τοῦ λαοῦ μου or "*my* people" in Isa. 53:8 see also *Tg. Isa.* ("the sins which *my* people sinned he will cast on to them"), the Peshitta, and Aquila, Theodotion, and Symmachus.

174. This is missed in the translation of 1QIsa[a] in Abegg et al., *DSSB*, which gives the usual MT reading "for the transgression of *my* [not *his*] people" as the reading of 1QIsa[a].

175. Translation of Isa. 53:9 LXX from D. A. Sapp, "The LXX, 1QIsa, and MT Versions of Isaiah 53," in W. H. Bellinger and W. R. Farmer, eds., *Jesus and the Suffering Servant: Isaiah 53 and Christian Origins* (1998), 183; similarly Ekblad, *Isaiah's Servant Poems According to the Septuagint*, 236: "I will give the wicked in place of his burial and the rich in place of his death."

176. Grelot, *Les Poèmes du Serviteur*, 107: "the prophetic announcement of judgment here supplements that of salvation." The notion of God handing over the wicked to the *Servant* as judge in the sense of δώσω (sc. αὐτῷ) has recently been questioned by Ekblad, *Isaiah's Servant Poems*, 237 with n. 281 (responding to the German version of this essay). Nevertheless, Ekblad agrees in part with the view taken here, namely that the LXX of Isa. 53:9 expresses the thought of final judgment by God.

177. Compare by analogy the reversal of the MT's וַיִּתֵּן in *Tg. Isa.* 53:9: "and *he* will hand over the wicked to Gehenna"; Peshitta, רשיעא קברה, "Es gab ein Gottloser sein Grab" = "There was a grave for the godless" (Hegermann, *Jesaja 53 in Hexapla, Targum und Peschitta*, 104); and Aquila, Theodotion, and Symmachus: δώσει τοὺς ἀσεβεῖς ἀντὶ τῆς ταφῆς αὐτοῦ, "*he* will give the wicked in place of his burial."

tion sharpens the tendency toward a statement of judgment at the end of the song and can completely suppress the idea of vicarious suffering. This is shown by Theodotion in the last phrase of 53:12. Against the Septuagint's expression of vicariousness, in which the Servant "was delivered up on account of their sins" (see below) (καὶ διὰ τὰς ἁμαρτίας αὐτῶν παρεδόθη), Theodotion reads *et impios torquebit*, "and he will *torture* the impious."[178] The Septuagint is still a long way from this complete reversal of the thought. The Servant receives his authority to act as judge precisely "*because* he did not do wrong, nor was deceit found in his mouth" (ὅτι ἀνομίαν οὐκ ἐποίησεν οὐδὲ εὑρέθη δόλος ἐν τῷ στόματι αὐτοῦ, v. 9). The motif of the innocent and righteous sufferer is therefore even clearer in the Septuagint than in the MT.

To the divine promise "I will give/hand over" (δώσω) in verse 9a corresponds the promise in verse 12, part of the *concluding prophetic speech based on God's revelation* in verses 10-12: "Therefore he will inherit many and divide the spoils of the mighty" (διὰ τοῦτο αὐτὸς κληρονομήσει πολλοὺς καὶ τῶν ἰσχυρῶν μεριεῖ σκῦλα, v. 12a). This is best understood as a promise of dominion (cf. Dan. 7:14). The victor takes possession of and divides the spoils. The basis for this is the Servant's vicarious death for the sins of the many, his "atoning death" according to God's will, mentioned at the end of verse 12, which is once again very freely translated: "he was delivered up [sc. by God: divine passive] on account of their sins" (διὰ τὰς ἁμαρτίας αὐτῶν παρεδόθη; cf. also 53:5). Although the motif of vicarious atoning suffering which effects salvation is weakened at a few points in the LXX over against the MT, it remains unambiguous. Already in the lament in verse 4 it says clearly that "he bears our sins and is pained for us" (οὗτος τὰς ἁμαρτίας ἡμῶν φέρει [נָשָׂא] καὶ περὶ ἡμῶν ὀδυνᾶται; cf. v. 11d: τὰς ἁμαρτίας αὐτῶν αὐτὸς ἀνοίσει [יִסְבֹּל]). Verse 5 carries the thought forward, "But he himself was wounded on account of our lawless deeds and he became sick because of our sins" (αὐτὸς δὲ ἐτραυματίσθη διὰ τὰς ἀνομίας ἡμῶν καὶ μεμαλάκισται διὰ τὰς ἁμαρτίας ἡμῶν), while the second half of the verse seals it: "by his wounds we were healed" (τῷ μώλωπι αὐτοῦ ἡμεῖς ἰάθημεν). The Servant's vicarious suffering cancels the guilt of sin and brings salvation to his people who confess their sins. Verse 7, "he was led like a sheep to the slaughter" (ὡς πρόβατον ἐπὶ σφαγὴν ἤχθη), associates his death with the slaughter of an animal victim at the altar.

---

178. On Theodotion's translation of Isa. 53:12, see Hegermann, *Jesaja 53 in Hexapla, Targum und Peschitta*, 52. Cf. Symmachus καὶ τοῖς ἀθετοῦσιν ἀνέστη, "and he stood up against the rebellious" (cf. ἀνθιστάνω/ἀνθίστημι, ἀθετέω) (Hegermann, 65-66); similarly the Peshitta, ובעולא פגע, "und den Sündern entgegentrat" = "and he stood up against the sinners" (Hegermann, 106-8), where פגע apparently has the negative sense of "encountering" an opponent (cf. Hegermann, 108 n. 2). Perhaps this is based on a Jewish interpretive tradition.

This decisive motif is once again strengthened at the end of the song in 53:11c and 12d. An interpretation of the Servant's fate is found in verses 10 and 11, at the beginning of the concluding prophetic speech of verses 10-12. Like verse 12, this interpretation is connected to the divine words in verse 8 and explains the opaque statements about the turning point in verse 8a.

Verse 10 is governed by the two uses of the verb βούλεται, "to will, want, desire" in verse 10a, d. Both depend on the subject κύριος, and they correspond respectively to the verb חָפֵץ, "to be pleased," and the noun חֵפֶץ, "pleasure."[179] Hence in verse 10a, the translator writes, "The Lord desires to purify him of the plague" (καὶ κύριος βούλεται καθαρίσαι αὐτὸν τῆς πληγῆς), instead of the MT: "But the Lord was pleased to crush him (דַּכְּאוֹ), making [him] sick (הֶחֱלִי)." The two words πληγή and καθαρίζω could suggest leprosy,[180] but in fact they are only meant metaphorically. One can only guess what the translator's Hebrew text will have been. Perhaps he read זַכּוֹ, "he made him clean" (piel of זכה with object suffix) instead of דַּכְּאוֹ, "to crush him," and מֵחֳלִי, "from my sickness" instead of הֶחֱלִי, "he made [him] sick."[181]

Verse 10b-c follows with an exhortation to the congregation: "If you [= the members of the congregation] make a sin offering (περὶ ἁμαρτίας),[182] your souls will see a long-lived posterity" (ἐὰν δῶτε περὶ ἁμαρτίας, ἡ ψυχὴ ὑμῶν ὄψεται σπέρμα μακρόβιον). In other words, the congregation — the "we" group of verses 1-7 — will participate in the eternal life of the Servant. This verse, which departs sharply from the MT, is very difficult to understand in the context. In close connection with the Hebrew, the Greek text of verses 5-6 and verses 11-12 emphasizes that the Servant's vicarious suffering for the sins of the people atones for and cancels this sin. Therefore in the MT of verse 10, the *Servant himself* gives his life as an אָשָׁם or "guilt offering" (NASB; NIV; cf. NJPS), that is, an atoning sacrifice. By contrast, the Greek conditional sentence ἐὰν

179. Both Aquila and Symmachus match the Greek parts of speech in Isa. 53:10 (verb and noun) more exactly with the Hebrew than the LXX does. Aquila: ἐβουλήθη (10a) and βούλημα (10d); Symmachus: ἠθέλεσεν and θέλημα. See the second apparatus in Ziegler's edition (*Isaias*, Göttingen LXX) and the discussion in Hegermann, *Jesaja 53 in Hexapla, Targum und Peschitta*, 42-43, 62.

180. Cf. Isa. 53:3: ἄνθρωπος ἐν πληγῇ ὤν, "being a man in a plague"; 53:4: ἐλογισάμεθα αὐτὸν εἶναι . . . ἐν πληγῇ, "we considered him to be . . . in a plague." In the LXX πληγή translates מַכְאֹב, "pain," only in Isa. 53:3; in 53:4 πληγή translates מֻכֶּה (hofal participle of נכה).

181. See Euler, *Die Verkündigung vom leidenden Gottesknecht*, 79.

182. The expression περὶ (τῆς) ἁμαρτίας rarely translates אָשָׁם (which in Leviticus usually means "guilt offering"); see 2 Kings 12:16 (MT 12:17), ἀργύριον περὶ ἁμαρτίας = כֶּסֶף אָשָׁם, "the money from the guilt offerings"; cf. Lev. 5:7. Otherwise περὶ (τῆς) ἁμαρτίας is above all the translation of חַטָּאת, "sin offering."

δῶτε περὶ ἁμαρτίας in verse 10b requires a "sin offering" from the members of the *congregation* who previously went astray and who were guilty in relationship to the Servant, in order that they might receive their share of the salvation promised to the Servant. Should their recognition of God's dealings through the Servant and their consequent acknowledgment of their own guilt perhaps be interpreted as their "spiritual sin offering"?[183]

The statement about the congregation's seed or posterity in verse 10c (see above) corresponds to the Servant's "generation" in verse 8b, which is so large that nobody can "declare" it (τὴν γενεὰν αὐτοῦ τίς διηγήσεται;). The restoration of the true Israel through the resurrection of the dead is presupposed. That the Servant himself has received a share in God's eternal life may already be hinted at in verse 8c, ὅτι αἴρεται ἀπὸ τῆς γῆς ἡ ζωὴ αὐτοῦ, "for his life is *taken up* (removed) from the earth." The use of the same verb αἴρω in verse 8a may indicate that God himself has nullified the legal judgment against him: "in humiliation his judgment was *taken away* (nullified)" (ἐν τῇ ταπεινώσει ἡ κρίσις αὐτοῦ ἤρθη).

After the mention of the congregation's posterity in verse 10c comes the detailed presentation of the Servant's future or already-realized salvific destiny in the prophetic speech beginning in verse 10d. This completely changes the syntax of the Hebrew. The subject of all the Greek verbs from verse 10d through the first part of verse 11d — from βούλεται through δικαιῶσαι (cf. יַצְדִּיק) — is the Lord. Parallel to the expression καὶ κύριος βούλεται (וַיהוָה חָפֵץ) καθαρίσαι αὐτὸν in verse 10a, where the Greek and Hebrew verbs correspond, the translator in verse 10d renders the nominal expression וְחֵפֶץ יְהוָה, "and the will of the Lord," by the same Greek verb once again in the present tense, καὶ βούλεται κύριος, "and the Lord wills or desires." Each of the following four Greek infinitives in verses 10-11, ἀφελεῖν, δεῖξαι, πλάσαι, and δικαιῶσαι, is dependent upon this second occurrence of βούλεται:

βούλεται κύριος	The Lord wills/desires
<u>ἀφελεῖν</u> 11 ἀπὸ τοῦ πόνου	*to take away* from the anguish
τῆς ψυχῆς αὐτοῦ,	of his soul,
<u>δεῖξαι</u> αὐτῷ φῶς,	*to show* him light,
καὶ <u>πλάσαι</u> τῇ συνέσει,	and *to form* [him] with understanding,

---

183. Cf. Euler, *Verkündigung vom leidenden Gottesknecht,* 120-21, who refers to Isa. 5:5-6 and to the promises made to Abraham after his binding of Isaac (Gen. 22:17 LXX). Grelot, *Les Poèmes du Serviteur,* 108, suspects that the translator may have read the second person plural verb תָּשִׂימוּ, "if *you (plural) make* his life as an אָשָׁם" instead of the MT's second person singular תָּשִׂים. I cannot understand why Ruprecht, "Auslegungsgeschichte," 34-35, wishes to deny the notion of atoning sacrifice in principle. Here the widespread aversion to the idea of sacrifice in Germany comes to light.

δικαιῶσαι δίκαιον   *to justify/vindicate* the righteous one
εὖ δουλεύοντα πολλοῖς.   serving many well.

These statements reflect a complicated translation procedure. To arrive at his first infinitive, ἀφελεῖν, the translator read not the MT's יִצְלָח, "it shall prosper," as in "the will of the Lord shall prosper" (NRSV), but rather יַצִּיל, "he will deliver" (hiphil of נצל). This the translator refers not back to the Lord's will (as in MT), but forward to מֵעֲמַל נַפְשׁוֹ = ἀπὸ τοῦ πόνου τῆς ψυχῆς αὐτοῦ, with the sense, "to deliver [him] from the anguish of his soul."

For his second infinitive δεῖξαι, instead of the MT's qal form יִרְאֶה, "he will see," the translator presupposed the causative hiphil vocalization of the same consonants, יַרְאֶה, with the sense, "to *make* [him] see," and hence "to *show* [him]" = δεῖξαι. This is in fact the almost invariable translation of the hiphil of ראה throughout the LXX.[184] The word "light" (אוֹר) is included as the object of the Hebrew verb in 1QIsaᵃ and 1QIsaᵇ (though not in MT), and was apparently also in our translator's *Vorlage*, hence δεῖξαι αὐτῷ φῶς, "to show him light."

The basis for the infinitive πλάσαι in the third expression καὶ πλάσαι τῇ συνέσει, "and to form [him] with understanding," remains unclear. Perhaps the translator found the Hebrew meaning "to be satisfied" or "filled" (יִשְׂבָּע) to be inappropriate and instead inserted his favorite word πλάσσω, "to form."[185] This he uses nine times in Deutero-Isaiah between Isaiah 43:1 and our verse, eight times for יצר ("to form"),[186] and here in 53:11 instead of שׂבע. As elsewhere,

---

184. There are sixty-two occurrences of the hiphil of ראה in the MT. Usually these are translated by "to show" in the NRSV (exceptions include Gen. 48:11; Deut. 34:4; Josh. 5:6; 2 Sam. 15:25; Song 2:14 "let me/you/them see"; Isa. 30:30 "cause to be seen"; Nah. 3:5; Ps. 59:10 "let nations/me look"; Hab. 1:3; Ps. 71:20 "make me see"; Ps. 4:6 "that we might see"; Esth. 1:4 "he displayed"; cf. also Ps. 60:3). By the same token, all but five of these sixty-two hiphils are translated by a form of δεικνύω in the LXX. The five exceptions are Josh. 5:6 (ἰδεῖν); Judg. 13:23 (ἐφώτισεν); Isa. 39:4 (εἴδοσαν); Jer. 11:18 (εἶδον); and Mic. 7:15 (ὄψεσθε).

185. Alternatively, the reading πλάσαι (aorist infinitive of πλάσσω) in our Septuagint manuscripts might be a scribal misreading of an original πλῆσαι, aorist infinitive of πίμπλημι (for the form cf. ἐμπλῆσαι in Gen. 42:25 [ἐμπίμπλημι]) — hence πλῆσαι τῇ συνέσει, "to *fill* [him] with understanding." This would be somewhat closer to the Hebrew, and πίμπλημι is certainly a common Septuagintal word (116 occurrences). On the other hand, the essentially synonymous composite form ἐμπίμπλημι is more common in Isaiah (23 occurrences; cf. esp. Isa. 11:2-3, πνεῦμα σοφίας καὶ συνέσεως . . . ἐμπλήσει αὐτὸν, "the spirit of wisdom and understanding . . . will fill him," referring to the rod from the root of Jesse) than is simple πίμπλημι (only 4 occurrences), so that we might expect the translator to have used ἐμπίμπλημι, had this been his original meaning. See also the related composite ἐπιπίμπλημι (not in LXX; cf. LSJ 651) in Aquila and Theodotion, ἐπιπλησθήσεται, "he shall be filled" (for the form cf. πλησθήσεται [πίμπλημι], e.g., Lev. 19:29).

186. Isa. 43:1, 7; 44:2, 9, 10, 21, 24; 49:5; cf. also Isa. 27:11; 29:16 (twice). The textual variant καὶ ἔπλασά σε in 49:8 (cf. 44:21) occurs without corresponding יצר.

πλάσσω here expresses God's creative (and elective) activity toward the Servant.[187]

The boldest translation is found in the last member of this sequence. Here the translator read the consonants of עַבְדִּי ("my servant") without the *yod* suffix as the participle עֹבֵד, "serving," resulting in his translation δικαιῶσαι δίκαιον εὖ δουλεύοντα πολλοῖς, "to justify/vindicate the righteous one *serving many well.*" This striking rhetorical figure δικαιῶσαι δίκαιον, which repeats members of the same word group in different forms (πολύπτωτον in Greek rhetoric; Eng. *polyptoton*), may perhaps be dependent upon the Greek translation of Solomon's prayer of dedication at the temple in 1 Kings 8:32 (= 2 Chron. 6:23). Solomon asks God, in response to oaths of innocence that may be sworn before the temple's altar, to differentiate between the guilty and the innocent, and then in the case of the latter, τοῦ δικαιῶσαι δίκαιον δοῦναι αὐτῷ κατὰ τὴν δικαιοσύνην αὐτοῦ, "to justify/vindicate the righteous one, giving to him according to his righteousness" (1 Kings 8:32). Here lies the root of the New Testament idea of the resurrection as the justification or vindication of the crucified one (1 Tim. 3:16; John 16:10; cf. also Rom. 4:25).

The result of this translation procedure in 53:10d-11d is a thoroughly impressive presentation of the Lord's dealings with and through his Servant. The will of the Lord is to deliver the Servant from the anguish and pain of death; to show him light, that is, eternal life in communion with God; to grant him superhuman understanding — indeed, to make him a "new creation." The expression "to form [him] with *understanding,*" πλάσαι τῇ συνήσει (53:11), relates back to the exaltation of the Servant at the start of the song: ἰδοὺ συνήσει ὁ παῖς μου, "Behold, my servant will *understand*" (52:13). God, as the truly just one, will achieve justice for the one who "served many well" through his death. The "justification" of 53:11 is the justification of the one who, although considered ungodly in the eyes of sinners, was in fact the only truly righteous one. It is therefore the precondition of the justification of the real sinners, which the Servant effects through his vicarious death.

Only after this fourfold description of God's dealings with his Servant is there a change of the subject from God to the Servant. In the latter part of 53:11d, the expression εὖ δουλεύοντα πολλοῖς, "who serves the many well," describes the righteous one, God's Servant. His "servitude" (δουλεύειν) over against the "many" consists of his having borne and thereby canceled their sins: "and he shall bear their sins," καὶ τὰς ἁμαρτίας αὐτῶν αὐτὸς ἀνοίσει (53:11e).

But who is this "righteous one" in the eyes of the translator? A one-sided

---

187. Cf. Isa. 44:2, 21, 24; 49:5, 8 (var.). Cf. 43:1, "I who formed you, *Israel,*" yet without explicit mention of the "Servant."

collective interpretation referring to Israel seems to me hardly possible.[188] Israel must be identified rather with the confession of the "we" group, which can hardly refer to the Gentile nations, since the Gentiles have no "report" to proclaim, as in 53:1 (ἀκοὴ ἡμῶν). Nor are the Gentiles healed by his "wounds" or "bruises" (53:5: μώλωψ); this can only apply to the people of God. The Servant will rather judge the kings and the nations, the wicked and the rich (Isa. 52:15; 53:9, 12). "The many" in 53:11-12 are the same as the "we" who make their confession in the first person plural in verses 1-7. They represent the doubting, straying Israel, for which the Servant has sacrificed himself. If the people of Israel repent, acknowledging and confessing their sins — which is perhaps their spiritual "sin offering" (cf. ἐὰν δῶτε περὶ ἁμαρτίας, 53:10) — then on the basis of the Servant's vicarious atoning suffering, they may share his exalted destiny.

These phenomena are commonly explained by reference to the notion of the *suffering righteous one* or the *passio iusti*.[189] This certainly comes to the fore more clearly at certain points in the Septuagint (especially 53:11d, δικαιῶσαι δίκαιον) than it does in the Hebrew text, and it plays an important role for the translator throughout the book. L. Ruppert suspects that the translator may have related the puzzling sentence in Isaiah 3:10, Δήσωμεν τὸν δίκαιον ὅτι δύσχρηστος ἡμῖν ἐστιν ("Let us bind the righteous one, for he is burdensome to us"), to Isaiah 53:11.[190]

Further explanation can be sought in the intensive reworking of the Septuagint of Isaiah 53 together with other motifs from Isaiah in the Wisdom of Solomon 2:10–5:23, particularly 2:12-20 and 5:1-6.[191] Here the righteous one's suffering, death, and exaltation above the wicked in the judgment take center stage. Countless authors have already seen here the striking relationships to the

---

188. This is pointed out by Grelot, *Les Poèmes du Serviteur*, 109ff., even though he himself espouses a collective interpretation of the Servant Songs in the LXX: "the identification of the Servant with the community of Israel is much less obvious in the fourth song (52:13–53:12) than in the first and second songs" (109). "The personification of this group (i.e., 'the group of the suffering righteous who undergo their punishment in the place of the culprits') leads to a strongly individualized description" (110). "The last Servant Song . . . opened up a new way at this point" (111).

189. L. Ruppert, *Der leidende Gerechte: Eine motivgeschichtliche Untersuchung zum Alten Testament und zwischentestamentlichen Judentum*, FB 5 (1972), 59-62 on Isaiah 53 LXX; idem, "Der leidende Gerechte," in van Henten, *Entstehung*, 76-87, esp. 78-82.

190. Ruppert, *Der leidende Gerechte*, 62, cf. 59. See also Wis. 2:10 and Justin, *Dial.* 17.2; 136.2; 137.3.

191. Ruppert, *Der leidende Gerechte*, 70-105; idem, *Jesus als der leidende Gottesknecht*, SBS 59 (1972), 23-24; K. T. Kleinknecht, *Der leidende Gerechtfertigte*, 2nd ed., WUNT 2/13 (1988 [1984]), 104-10. See already the early study of M. J. Suggs, "Wisdom 2:10-5: A Homily Based on the Fourth Servant Song," *JBL* 76 (1957): 26-53.

Servant Songs, especially the fourth.[192] To this end they can refer to Wisdom 2:13, where the righteous one calls himself παῖς κυρίου, "the Servant of the Lord," to his condemnation to a shameful death in 2:20, and then above all to Wisdom 5:1-6 (RSV):[193]

1	τότε στήσεται ἐν παρρησίᾳ πολλῇ ὁ δίκαιος	Then the righteous man will stand with great confidence
	κατὰ πρόσωπον τῶν θλιψάντων αὐτὸν	in the presence of those who have afflicted him,
	καὶ τῶν ἀθετούντων τοὺς πόνους αὐτοῦ.	and those who make light of his labors.
2	ἰδόντες ταραχθήσονται φόβῳ δεινῷ	When they see him, they will be shaken with dreadful fear,
	καὶ ἐκστήσονται ἐπὶ τῷ παραδόξῳ τῆς σωτηρίας·	and they will be amazed at his unexpected salvation.
3	ἐροῦσιν ἐν ἑαυτοῖς μετανοοῦντες	They will speak to one another in repentance,
	καὶ διὰ στενοχωρίαν πνεύματος στενάξονται καὶ ἐροῦσιν	and in anguish of spirit they will groan, and say,

192. The older literature is available in C. Larcher, *Études sur le livre de la Sagesse*, EBib (1969), 91-92, who nevertheless rightly warns against an exaggeration: "The Servant Songs are thus not detached from their context and they do not seem to have taken a particular stamp." He understands Isaiah as a unit, of which chapters 40–56 admittedly come to the fore. Cf. E. Haag, "Die drei Männer im Feuer nach Dan. 3,1-30," in van Henten, *Die Entstehung der jüdischen Martyrologie*, 20-50, esp. 44ff.

193. We must cite the RSV here, since the plural pronouns in the NRSV, presumably inserted mainly in the interests of inclusive language, also prematurely decide the case in favor of a collective interpretation of the "righteous one" (ὁ δίκαιος) in Wis. 5:1-6 and obscure its verbal connections with Isaiah 53: "Then the righteous [ones] will stand with great confidence in the presence of those who have oppressed *them* and those who make light of *their* labors. When the unrighteous see *them,* they will be shaken with dreadful fear, and they will be amazed at the unexpected salvation of the righteous [ones]." In response the unrighteous say: "These are *persons* whom we once held in derision and made a byword of reproach" (Wis. 5:1-2, 4, NRSV). However, at the level of translation, we should leave open at least the possibility that a representative righteous *individual* is in view, even though a collective interpretation may commend itself for other reasons. Elsewhere in Wisdom, the expression "a/the righteous *man*" is used even in the NRSV to translate δίκαιος when it alludes to a specific though unnamed figure from the biblical story, including Noah, Abraham, Lot, Jacob, and Joseph (cf. Wis. 10:4, 5, 6, 10, 13). Although the reference in Wisdom 5 is necessarily more generic, the possibility of an allusion to a particular scriptural passage or an ideal figure should not be dismissed from the start. Note also that ὁ δίκαιος is translated as singular by the NRSV in Wis. 2:10, 12, 18.

4 Οὗτος ἦν, ὃν ἔσχομέν ποτε εἰς γέλωτα

καὶ εἰς παραβολὴν ὀνειδισμοῦ
οἱ ἄφρονες·
τὸν βίον αὐτοῦ ἐλογισάμεθα μανίαν
καὶ τὴν τελευτὴν αὐτοῦ ἄτιμον.

5 πῶς κατελογίσθη ἐν υἱοῖς θεοῦ

καὶ ἐν ἁγίοις ὁ κλῆρος αὐτοῦ
ἐστιν;
6 ἄρα ἐπλανήθημεν ἀπὸ ὁδοῦ ἀληθείας,

καὶ τὸ τῆς δικαιοσύνης φῶς οὐκ
ἐπέλαμψεν ἡμῖν,
καὶ ὁ ἥλιος οὐκ ἀνέτειλεν ἡμῖν·

"This is the man whom we once
held in derision
and made a byword of reproach —
we fools!
We thought that his life was
madness and that his end was
without honor.
Why has he been numbered
among the sons of God?
And why is his lot among the
saints?
So it was we who strayed from the
way of truth,
and the light of righteousness did
not shine on us,
and the sun did not rise upon us."

Here there are numerous verbal and conceptual parallels with the Greek text of Isaiah 53. The "amazement" (cf. ἐκστήσονται) of his unrighteous persecutors at the unexpected salvation of this righteous man in Wisdom 5:2b recalls the similar amazement (again ἐκστήσονται) of "the many" at the Servant's unexpected salvation and exaltation in Isaiah 52:14. The fact that the unrighteous here do not repent (cf. Wis. 5:3) or recognize their guilt over against the righteous one (cf. 5:4) until *after* his exaltation is structurally parallel to the behavior of the "we" group in Isaiah 53:3-5 (cf. 53:12). The destiny of the unrighteous is contrasted with that of the righteous in Wisdom 5:5. The righteous one has been numbered among the sons of God and has his lot among the ἅγιοι. This is translated as the "saints" in the RSV, NRSV, and NAB (cf. "God's people," REB), but it probably refers to the "holy ones" (NJB) — that is, the angels. In Wisdom 5:6, the persecutors' confession of error, "it was we who strayed" (ἐπλανήθημεν), could recall the two references to going astray, both corporate and individual, in Isaiah 53:6, "All of us like sheep have *gone astray;* each of us has *gone astray* in his own way" (πάντες ὡς πρόβατα ἐπλανήθημεν, ἄνθρωπος τῇ ὁδῷ αὐτοῦ ἐπλανήθη). Finally, the lament that "the light of righteousness did not shine on us" (τὸ τῆς δικαιοσύνης φῶς οὐκ ἐπέλαμψεν ἡμῖν, 5:6) forms a clear contrast with the Servant's destiny of being shown the light in Isaiah 53:11 (cf. δεῖξαι αὐτῷ φῶς).

Yet despite these close connections with the fourth Servant Song, we must agree with the objection that even in Wisdom the Servant Songs are not separated from the rest of the book of Isaiah. Like the authors of the *Aramaic*

Apocryphon of Levi (4Q540-541) and Daniel 11–12, the author of Wisdom saw the work of the prophet Isaiah as a whole. Furthermore, other texts, including Jeremiah, Daniel, and above all the Psalms contribute almost as much to the theme of the suffering righteous and the wicked as Isaiah does. The *passio iusti* became almost a commonplace between the Maccabean period and the second century C.E. The book of Wisdom therefore presents a universally applicable religious experience, which it supports by manifold allusions to the Scriptures, not least to (Deutero-) Isaiah. But Isaiah 53 loses its unique traits almost completely. Moreover, it should be stressed that the motif of *vicarious* suffering to overcome the guilt of others is entirely absent. Wisdom deals only with the basically conventional idea of the justification of the righteous and the punishment of the wicked, and even the immanent eschatological expectation essential to Daniel, Qumran, and the Septuagint of Isaiah 53 falls away. Since Wisdom is a relatively late text, coming from the Egyptian diaspora around the beginning of the first century C.E., I believe its significance for the formation of the earliest Christology, which occurred in Palestine, has been overestimated. It is more a matter of sharing isolated terminological analogies than the same subject. By the same token, the earliest passion reports in Mark should not be made too heavily dependent on the simple *passio iusti* conception. Mark's theme is rather the unique and unparalleled atoning sufferings of the Messiah and Son of God, Jesus of Nazareth.[194] The *passio iusti*, combined with the motif of the death of the devout martyr, first comes more clearly to the fore with the God-fearing Greek writer Luke.

Let us return, then, to the Septuagint of Isaiah 53. The translator in Egypt in the middle of the second century B.C.E. hardly had a general, religious, wisdom-oriented "truth" like the author of Wisdom about 100 to 150 years later. We cannot therefore simply attribute to him a general collective interpretation in terms of the *passio iusti*.

Euler suspects an allusion to the fate of the prophet himself, referring to the *Martyrdom and Ascension of Isaiah* chapter 5,[195] according to which Isaiah

---

194. See on this M. Hengel, "Probleme des Markusevangeliums," in P. Stuhlmacher, ed., *Das Evangelium und die Evangelien*, WUNT 28 (1983), 221-65, esp. 239-40 = ET, "Literary, Theological, and Historical Problems in the Gospel of Mark," in P. Stuhlmacher, ed., *The Gospel and the Gospels* (1991), 209-51, esp. 227-28; Hengel, *The Atonement*, 35ff., 39ff.: "The Messiah alone is the righteous and sinless one par excellence" (41).

195. Euler, *Die Verkündigung vom leidenden Gottesknecht*, 128ff., who admittedly mentions only the early Christian Ascension of Isaiah. On the older, originally Jewish life of Isaiah in the *Lives of the Prophets* see Schwemer, *Studien zu den frühjüdischen Prophetenlegenden Vitae Prophetarum*, 1:92 on the *Martyrdom and Ascension of Isaiah*, 1:98-99 on Isaiah 53. No clear connection can be detected between the LXX of Isaiah 53 and this text. Ruppert, *Der leidende*

was sawn in two. Yet the late sources of this tradition that have come down to us — *Lives of the Prophets,* the *Ascension of Isaiah,*[196] Justin,[197] and rabbinic legends[198] — lack any reference to the idea of vicarious suffering. And nothing suggests that the translator of Isaiah already knew these legends.

It therefore needs to be asked whether the translator does not in fact have in view the concrete suffering of an individual person and his glorification, with the suffering in the past and the eschatological glorification still in the future, but already being prepared for in the eyes of the translator. This twofold division is suggested by a very clear use of tenses. Whereas the future tense is used to express the Servant's exaltation and glorification in 52:13 (συνήσει, ὑψωθήσεται, δοξασθήσεται) as well as the shock or amazement of the kings and nations understood as judgment in verses 14-15 (ἐκστήσονται [contrast the perfect שָׁמְמוּ], θαυμάσονται, συνέξουσιν, ὄψονται, συνήσουσιν), the congregation's confession in 53:1-7, which reports both their own failure and the Servant's vicarious suffering, is expressed almost entirely in the aorist tense. The congregation therefore appears to look back upon the death of an exemplary pious person.

The future tenses begin once again with the presentation of the turning point in verses 8-9. The future occurs in the divine address with the question concerning the future of the Servant's person and work, τὴν γενεὰν αὐτοῦ τίς διηγήσεται, "Who will describe his generation?" (cf. Acts 8:33). It occurs again in the divine promise in verse 9, δώσω, "I will give" the wicked and the rich, which points to victory and judgment, as does the statement in verse 12, κληρονομήσει πολλοὺς καὶ τῶν ἰσχυρῶν μεριεῖ σκῦλα ("he will inherit the many and will divide the spoils of the strong"). The future expression τὰς ἁμαρτίας αὐτῶν αὐτὸς ἀνοίσει, "he will bear their sins" (v. 11), shows the fruit of his death for the many, which will be revealed to all.

Gerechte, 62-63 also inclines toward the interpretation of Euler, who additionally appeals to Isa. 57:1. He is followed by Haag, *Gottesknecht,* 46.

196. Cf. *Martyrdom of Isaiah* 5 (English translation in *OTP* 2:163-64). That Isaiah did not cry out when martyred but rather "spoke with the Holy Spirit" (5:14) clearly contradicts the Servant's "silence" in Isa. 53:7.

197. Justin, *Dialogue with Trypho* 120.5. On this see M. Hengel, "Die Septuaginta als von den Christen beanspruchte Schriftensammlung bei Justin und den Vätern vor Origenes," in J. D. G. Dunn, ed., *Jews and Christians: The Parting of the Ways* A.D. *70 to 135,* WUNT 1/66 (1992), 49 n. 39; 62 n. 89 = American reprint with new translations, "The Septuagint as a Collection of Writings Claimed by Christians: Justin and the Church Fathers before Origen," in *Jews and Christians,* 2nd ed. (1999), 48 n. 39; 61 n. 89. Cf. also Heb. 11:37, ἐπρίσθησαν, "they were sawn in two."

198. Cf. *y. Sanh.* 10:2 28c ll. 44-48; *b. Yebam.* 49b; without details in *b. Sanh.* 103b.

That our passage *could* be about a person with an eschatological saving function can be seen most easily from 53:2, where Ziegler in his Göttingen edition conjectures that the translator originally wrote ἀνέτειλε μέν, "for *he rose/ sprang* up before him as a child," instead of the incoherent ἀνηγγείλαμεν (lit., "*we announced* before him as a child") attested in all the major Septuagint manuscripts and patristic writers. He justifies this unusual text-critical decision against the entire manuscript tradition by referring to the "frequent confusion of ἀναγγέλλειν and ἀνατέλλειν, especially in Isaiah."[199] Ἀνατέλλω appears fourteen times in Isaiah for eight different Hebrew words. The Hebrew text has וַיַּעַל, "and he grew up"; Aquila and Theodotion similarly καὶ ἀναβήσεται, "and he will rise up"; Symmachus καὶ ἀνέβη, "and he rose up"; *Targum Jonathan* ויתרבא, "and he shall grow up" (Stenning) or "be exalted" (Chilton); while the Peshitta — once again against the LXX manuscripts and with the MT — reads *seʿlaq*, "for he grew up" (G. Lamsa). By contrast, a Hebrew *Vorlage* of the Septuagint reading ἀνηγγείλαμεν cannot be identified. Presumably we are dealing

---

199. Ziegler, *Isaias* (Göttingen LXX), 99. Cf. Euler, *Verkündigung*, 53-56, esp. 53: Because "a misreading of a Hebrew text is excluded," this textual variation "must be a matter of an inner-Greek mistake. We should probably think of a form of ἀνάγειν or ἀνατέλλειν [as original]." Euler refers to J. Fischer, *In welcher Schrift lag das Buch Isaias den LXX vor?* BZAW 56 (1930), 13 on Isa. 42:9; 45:8; and 53:2, where ἀναγγέλειν has displaced an original ἀνατέλλειν. In the light of this and similar findings W. Zimmerli, "παῖς θεοῦ," *TWNT* 5 (1954), 675 = *TDNT* 5 (1967), 676 asks "whether there may not be discerned in the LXX trans. a Messianic understanding," which he takes as a serious possibility. For a different view favoring the received manuscript reading ἀνηγγείλαμεν in Isa. 53:2 see Ekblad, *Isaiah's Servant Poems*, 199-201, who finds Ziegler's conjectural emendation ἀνέτειλε μέν to be "not at all convincing" (199), in part because ἀνηγγείλαμεν is the *lectio difficilior*. Ekblad understands the LXX translator's change in person and sense from the MT's "And he went up" to the first-person plural "We announced" to be "an intertextual exegetical move that sought to *deliberately* read this text in the light of scriptures expressing Israel's missionary vocation" (200, italics added). Somewhat problematically, Ekblad equates the παιδίον in 53:2, which he renders "little servant," not, as expected, with the Suffering Servant but with the "we," the "announcing community," in the sense: "*We* announced before him [αὐτοῦ = the Servant] like a *little servant* or παιδίον [which we are]." Hence: "The description of the servant and pronouns in 53:2bff [= οὐκ ἔστιν εἶδος αὐτῷ, etc.] in fact clearly identifies the [suffering] servant as the αὐτοῦ before whom the 'little servant' announces" (201). Ekblad concludes: "A remembrance of the rejected, persecuted servant and a constant reference to his paradoxical life serves as a reference for the announcing community, defining and orienting them in their vocation as the Lord's servant" (201). But since the collective understanding of Israel as the servant uses παῖς rather than παιδίον, which rather recalls the "child" of Isa. 9:5 (ET 9:6), it is more natural to take both the pronoun and noun in ἀνηγγείλαμεν ἐναντίον αὐτοῦ ὡς παιδίον as referring to the Suffering Servant. Ekblad's interpretation of ἀνηγγείλαμεν as the translator's self-conscious reflection upon Israel's missionary vocation may still commend itself without the problematic identification of Israel as the παιδίον

with a very early copying error. There are 250 years for such an error to occur between the original translation of Isaiah and Clement of Rome, the earliest Christian witness to the reading ἀνηγγείλαμεν. Therefore we cannot exclude the possibility that a modern editor may need to correct a corrupted text by conjectural emendation. Such conjectures are immeasurably more common in the classical texts that have come down to us.

The restored reading of Isaiah 53:2, ἀνέτειλε μὲν ἐναντίον αὐτοῦ ὡς παιδίον, ὡς ῥίζα ἐν γῇ διψώσῃ, "For he *sprang up* before him as a child, as a root in parched [lit., *thirsting*] ground," would then recall Isaiah 11:1, καὶ ἐξελεύσεται ῥάβδος ἐκ τῆς ῥίζης Ιεσσαι, καὶ ἄνθος ἐκ τῆς ῥίζης ἀναβήσεται — to which Aquila, Theodotion, and Symmachus allude by using the same verb in Isaiah 53:2 (ἀναβήσεται, ἀνέβη) — "And a rod/shoot will come forth from the root of Jesse, and a blossom will *come up* from this root" (Isa. 11:1). In 11:2 this rod or shoot is granted the spirit of wisdom and σύνεσις, anticipating Isaiah 52:13 (ἴδου συνήσει) and 53:11 (πλάσαι τῇ συνέσει). But the unusual use of ὡς παιδίον in Isaiah 53:2 to render כַּיּוֹנֵק (NJB "sapling"; NRSV "young plant"; NASB, NIV "tender shoot") could rather point back to the messianic child in Isaiah 9:5 (ET 9:6) and 7:14-16. Aquila and Theodotion are similar to the Septuagint's παιδίον with their two different expressions — τιτθιζόμενον, θηλάζον — suggesting an unweaned child.[200] A cognate noun to ἀνατέλλω, namely, ἀνατολή, "branch," translates צֶמַח in Jeremiah 23:5; Zechariah 3:8; 6:12, referring in each case to the

---

200. Isa. 53:2, Aquila: καὶ ἀναβήσεται ὡς τιτθιζόμενον (Aq. ὡς τιτθιζόμενον, manuscript Q) εἰς πρόσωπον αὐτοῦ (according to Eusebius). Theodotion: καὶ ἀναβήσεται ὡς θηλάζον (Theod. ὡς θηλάζον Q) ἐνώπιον αὐτοῦ (Eusebius). For the texts and witnesses see Ziegler, *Isaias* (Göttingen LXX). Theodotion's form θηλάζον, as the substantival neuter participle of θηλάζω, denotes a nursing child. For the equivalent attributive expression see τὸ παιδίον τὸ θηλάζον in 1 Kings 3:25; cf. the masculine substantival participle τὸν θηλάζοντα, Num. 11:12. Aquila's τιτθιζόμενον is more difficult to identify. Eusebius's form τιτθιζόμενον (found only in Eusebius in TLG sources) suggests a verb τιτθίζω or τιτθίζομαι, not otherwise attested. However, LSJ p. 1799 defines the variant form τιτθιζόμενον given for Aquila in manuscript Q (Codex Marchalianus) as the passive of τιτθίζω, *suckle,* hence *suck,* here *suckling child* (cf. τιτθός, a woman's *breast,* not used in biblical Greek). C. Markschies's onomatopoetic interpretation of initial letters of Eusebius's form "τιτθι," as the baby sound "Ti-Ti" in the German version of his essay (*Der leidende Gottesknecht,* 239 with n. 277) is therefore unneccessary: "He [the Servant] will grow up like a nursing child who cries 'Ti-Ti' [= *ein 'Ti-Ti' rufender Säugling*]." For further analysis of Aquila's use of τι(τ)θιζόμενον see Hegermann, *Jesaja 53 in Hexapla, Targum und Peschitta,* 35. In addition to these two forms, Field (*Origenis Hexaplorum*) reads τιθηνιζόμενον. Although there is no attested verb τιθηνίζω or τιθηνίζομαι in LSJ, related words including τιθηνέω, τιθηνία, τιθηνός (attested in the LXX; cf. also τιθηνεύω, τιθήνημα, τιθήνησις, τιθηνητήριος) all suggest once again a nursing child. For a grammatically parallel expression involving the substantival passive participle of τιθηνέω see οἱ τιθηνούμενοι (ἐπὶ κόκκων), "those nursed (in scarlet)," Lam. 4:5.

future Messiah. He is called "my servant, the Branch" in Zechariah 3:8 (using δοῦλος rather than παῖς), while in 6:12 the etymological wordplay of the Hebrew is preserved in the Greek: צֶמַח יִצְמָח = Ἀνατολὴ ἀνατελεῖ = "the Branch will branch out" (or spring up). The same verb ἀνατέλλω occurs again in Isaiah 60:1 to express the eschatological dawning of the Lord's glory, καὶ ἡ δόξα κυρίου ἐπὶ σὲ ἀνατέταλκεν, "and the glory of the Lord has risen upon you."[201]

F. Hahn comments tersely on our text, "A messianic interpretation cannot be recognized even in the Septuagint version of Isaiah 53."[202] I cannot be so certain after the analysis above. At least the possibility of a messianic interpretation must be kept open, though as the Qumran texts now show, in the second century B.C.E. the concept of what was "messianic" was not yet as clearly fixed on the eschatological saving king from the house of David as it was later to become in the post-Christian rabbinic tradition. We must not allow the narrow concept of the Messiah in the post-Christian rabbis to regulate the diverse pre-Christian messianic ideas.

If we wish to draw a connection between the Servant in the Septuagint version of Isaiah 53 and a concrete historical figure, we *could* — very hypothetically — think of Onias III, the last legitimate Zadokite high priest. In 2 Maccabees 4:2 he is praised as "the man who was the benefactor of the (holy) city, the protector of his compatriots, and a zealot for the laws." He also saved the life of the wicked Heliodorus by his intercession (2 Macc. 3:33). Relieved of his high priestly duties at the time of the succession of Antiochus IV Epiphanes and replaced first by his own brother Jason (4:7) and then by the Jewish usurper Menelaus (4:24), Onias was killed at Menelaus's instigation after being lured out of his place of sanctuary at Daphne near Antioch (4:32-34) — an unjust murder which grieved and displeased not only Jews, but also many of other nations (4:35).

Daniel 9:26 mentions the murder of Onias as an end-time event: "After the sixty-two weeks, an anointed one (מָשִׁיחַ) shall be cut off." The expression וְאֵין לוֹ which follows (NRSV: "and shall have nothing") is a *crux interpretum*. Possibly it should be expanded "and he was without guilt, defence, or disciple."[203] Another suggestion is to interpret his death as vicarious: "but not for himself."[204] Daniel 11:22 once again alludes to his death: "the prince of the cove-

---

201. ἡ δόξα κυρίου ἐπὶ σὲ ἀνατέταλκεν (זָרַח).

202. F. Hahn, *Christologische Hoheitstitel*, 2nd ed., FRLANT 83 (1964), 154 n. 1. Unfortunately this is not included in the ET, *The Titles of Jesus in Christology: Their History in Early Christianity*, trans. H. Knight and G. Ogg (1969), 146 with 201 n. 108, where the original German note of twenty-eight lines has been reduced to two lines.

203. J. A. Montgomery, *Daniel*, ICC (1927), 381.

204. A. Lacocque, *Le Livre de Daniel*, CAT 15b (1976), 145. Cf. ET, *The Book of Daniel*, trans. D. Pellauer (1979), 196. Here the English phrase "but not for himself" translates "mais pas

nant also will be utterly broken." Reference to the violent death of Onias is probably also made in *1 Enoch* 90:8. In 2 Maccabees 15:12 and 14 the murdered Onias appears to Judas Maccabeus in a dream or vision. Once again he is presented in hagiographic fashion: "a noble and good man, of modest bearing and gentle manner, one who spoke fittingly and had been trained from childhood in all that belongs to excellence," who moreover "was praying with outstretched hands for the whole body of the Jews" (2 Macc. 15:12). He is accompanied by a second figure, whom he introduces to Judas as the martyr-prophet Jeremiah. Evidently Onias III was held in the highest regard in pious Jewish circles, not least in the Jewish military colonies founded by his son Onias IV in Egypt — precisely that milieu in which the translator of Isaiah was situated, who alludes to the founding of a new sanctuary in Leontopolis.[205]

If however the Septuagint text can already be related to an end-time figure whom we can call "messianic" in the widest sense, then this is all the more true for Aquila und Theodotion, whose revisions originated in the second century c.e., when the idea of a suffering messiah is clearly attested in Judaism.

9. *Testament of Benjamin* 3:8

The Armenian version of the *Testament of Benjamin* 3:8,[206] which is closer to the original than the surviving Greek version (see below),[207] presents Jacob addressing his son Joseph as follows:

---

pour lui-même," which Lacocque attributes to the French *La Bible de Jérusalem,* whose 1975 edition reads: "et il n'y a pas pour lui." The notion of vicariousness is not clearly present in the English *Jerusalem Bible,* which indicates the interpretive problem by an ellipsis: "an anointed one will be cut off — and . . . will not be for him — the city and the sanctuary will be destroyed by a prince who will come." The NJB is even more radical with its broken sentence: "And after the sixty-two weeks an Anointed One put to death without his . . . city and sanctuary ruined by a prince who is to come."

205. Seeligmann, *The Septuagint Version of Isaiah,* 91ff., rightly emphasizes the connection of LXX Isaiah with the Onias temple. Following Seeligmann (p. 84), van der Kooij, *Die alten Textzeugen des Jesajabuches,* 50ff., refers Isa. 8:7-8 to the deposition of Onias III. Could we not perhaps connect this text with statements such as Isa. 3:10; 52:13–53:12; and 57:1? See also van der Kooij, pp. 52ff. on Isa. 19:18 and Leontopolis.

206. For a survey of the discussion of *T. Benj.* 3:8 since R. H. Charles, J. Jeremias, and E. Lohse, see now de Jonge, "Test. Benjamin 3:8 and the Picture of Joseph as 'a good and holy man,'" in van Henten, *Entstehung,* 204-19, esp. n. 3 for an overview of the various opinions.

207. On the Armenian text see R. H. Charles, *The Greek Versions of the Testaments of the Twelve Patriarchs* (1908, reprinted 1960), xiiff., esp. xvi: "the Christian interpolations are present in a much less degree in A . . . specially . . . in the last two Testaments." With special reference to

In you [Joseph] will be fulfilled the heavenly prophecy which says that the spotless one will be defiled by lawless men and the sinless one will die for the sake of impious men. (*Testament of Benjamin* 3:8, Armenian)[208]

This is preceded by Joseph's urging his father Jacob "to pray for his brothers, that the Lord would not hold them accountable for their sin which they so wickedly committed against him" (*T. Benj.* 3:6). This highly controversial text in 3:8 could very well be of Jewish origin, since a Christian redactor would hardly have applied this prophecy to Joseph but rather to Judah, the ancestor of David and Jesus of Nazareth. Only the Greek version of the *Testament of Benjamin* 3:8 contains the types of expansions that Christians found missing in the Jewish original version:

In you [Joseph] will be fulfilled the heavenly prophecy *concerning the Lamb of God, the Savior of the world,* because the unspotted one will be *betrayed* (παραδοθήσεται) by lawless men and the sinless one will die for impious men *by the blood of the covenant for the salvation of the gentiles and of Israel and the destruction of Beliar and his servants.* (*Testament of Benjamin* 3:8, Greek)[209]

In contrast to de Jonge, I am convinced that the *Testaments of the Twelve Patriarchs* is not of early Christian origin, but was merely reworked by Christians in the second century C.E. The Qumran parallels discussed above confirm this assumption, and the situation is similar for the *Lives of the Prophets,* the Jewish *Sibylline Oracles,* and comparable writings.[210] The synonymous parallel-

---

T. Benj. 3:8 see now A. Hultgård, "L'eschatologie des Testaments des Douze Patriarches I und II," *AUU.HR* 6-7 (1977-82): 2:39-40: "The Armenian version is shorter, but it is not secondary, because it is difficult to understand why precisely the Christological assertions would have been removed by the Armenian texts." For a detailed earlier study see J. Becker, *Untersuchungen zur Entstehungsgeschichte der Testamente der zwölf Patriarchen,* AGJU 8 (1970), 51-56.

208. *OTP* 1:826, right column at *T. Benj.* 3:8.

209. *OTP* 1:826, left column at *T. Benj.* 3:8 (italics added). The retroverted Greek text is available in M. de Jonge, *The Testaments of the Twelve Patriarchs: A Critical Edition of the Greek Text,* PVTG 1/2 (1978), 169-70; see earlier Charles, *The Greek Versions of the Testaments of the Twelve Patriarchs,* 218-19.

210. Cf. de Jonge, "Test. Benjamin 3:8 and the Picture of Joseph as 'a good and holy man,'" 206: "The Testaments as a whole have to be approached as a witness to the continuity in thought and ideas between Judaism (in particular Hellenistic Judaism) and early Christianity." This possibility of "continuity" must also apply to the "Christological" texts. See now the objections to the hypothesis of a Christian origin of the *Testaments* in D. Mendels, *The Land of Israel as a Political Concept in Hasmonaean Literature,* TSAJ 15 (1987), 89, who illuminates the Hasmonean political background, while Maren Niehoff, *The Figure of Joseph in Post-Biblical Lit-*

ism "the spotless one will be defiled by lawless men and the sinless one will die for the sake of impious men" has its next real parallel in Isaiah 53 (cf. vv. 5b, 9b, 12b). Nevertheless, whom this prophecy refers to remains a question. Possibly the dying Messiah ben Joseph (or Ephraim) is meant; this depends on when the final editing of the text took place and how old the tradition is. We have found fragments of individual testaments like those of Levi, Naphtali, Judah, and perhaps Joseph in the Cairo Genizah and in Qumran, but the existence of the complete work *Testaments of the Twelve Patriarchs* is first attested by Origen and Jerome, and its manuscript tradition begins even later.[211] Because the Christian revised edition presupposes the Fourth Gospel, this edition is best placed in the second half of the second century c.e.[212] But it is very probable that there were always other versions in circulation. The redaction of the *Testaments of the Twelve Patriarchs* as a whole is today commonly dated to the late Hasmonean period, before the Roman invasion in 63 b.c.e., but parts of the work could have been added later. The rise of the concept of a dying Messiah ben Joseph *perhaps* goes together with the fact that the selling of Joseph by his brothers was regarded in Judaism as the great sin, next to the later production of the golden calf.[213] The patriarch Joseph would then be promised a future savior figure from his own line, who would make atonement for the sin of his brothers or his people. But this remains sheer speculation.

Finally, from Josephus we know of a whole series of political or eschatological-prophetic "savior" figures (who actually brought disaster) that died as "martyrs," but we hardly know anything about their message, the reli-

---

erature, AGJU 16 (1992), points out the numerous relationships to Jewish haggadah from Josephus until *Tg. Pseudo-Jonathan;* see the index p. 176 under "Testaments of the Twelve Patriarchs." A Christian of the second century could never have written such a work.

211. E. Schürer, *The History of the Jewish People in the Age of Jesus Christ: A New English Version,* rev. and ed. G. Vermes and F. Millar (1973-87), vol. III/2, 775-76.

212. For attestation of the Fourth Gospel in the second century see M. Hengel, *Die johanneische Frage,* WUNT 67 (1993), 9-75, or (in a shorter form) idem, *The Johannine Question* (1989), 1-16; Schürer, *History,* III/2, 775-76. Hyppolytus, too, appears to have presupposed an early Christian edition of the *Testaments.* See M. de Jonge, "Hippolytus' 'Benedictions of Isaac, Jacob and Moses, Testaments of the Twelve Patriarchs,'" *Bijdr* 46 (1985): 245-60.

213. The sin of the sale of Joseph into slavery by his brothers is the negative counterpart of Abraham's "Binding of Isaac" (עקדת יצחק). Already in *Jub.* 34:18-19 the sacrifice of the "young kid" on the Day of Atonement on the tenth day of the tenth month is appointed on account of the sin of Joseph's brothers; see K. Berger, *Das Buch der Jubiläen,* JSHRZ II/3 (1981), 494-95; E. Urbach, *The Sages* (1975), 1:521-22; 2:920-21 nn. 43-47. In later legend this crime of selling Joseph is atoned for by the death of the ten martyrs at the time of Hadrian; see chapter 10 of this story in the edition by G. Reeg, *Die Geschichte von den zehn Märtyrern,* TSAJ 10 (1985), 61-63 (translation of chap. 10), 10*-17* (Hebrew text).

gious hopes of their followers, their origin, or the reactions to their violent death.[214] The puzzling and horizon-expanding text *Testament of Benjamin* 3:8 is therefore one index among others of the diversity of Jewish expectations for the future and of interpretations of suffering in the centuries around the turn of the era — a diversity about which we know only the tip of the iceberg, and which therefore forbids us in New Testament scholarship from using the primitive, constantly misused argument from silence as an exclusively negative argument. Simply sticking this text with the label "Joseph as the suffering righteous one" does not explain its uniqueness as a "heavenly prophecy" and testimony to vicarious atonement. Moreover, Joseph himself is not sinless, nor does he die for his brothers.

The expectation of an eschatological suffering savior figure connected with Isaiah 53 cannot therefore be proven to exist with absolute certainty and in a clearly outlined form in pre-Christian Judaism. Nevertheless, a lot of indices that must be taken seriously in texts of very different provenance suggest that these types of expectations could *also* have existed at the margins, next to many others. This would then explain how a suffering or dying Messiah surfaces in various forms with the Tannaim of the second century c.e., and why Isaiah 53 is clearly interpreted messianically in the Targum and rabbinic texts.[215]

10. The *Self-Glorification Hymn* (4Q491 Fragment 11 Column i = 4Q491c)

As an example of this *diversity*, which is not taken seriously enough, I wish in addition to the *Aramaic Apocryphon of Levi* 4Q540-541 (see above §7) to introduce by way of conclusion another relatively unknown text, which M. Baillet published in DJD 7 in 1982 as fragment 11 column i of 4Q491, a collection of fragments that bears the overall title *4Q Milhama A* (4QM[a]) or *4QWar Scroll[a]*. Baillet entitled our particular text "The Song of Michael and of the Just."[216] In

---

214. M. Hengel, *The Zealots* (1989), 256-71. According to Acts 5:36-37 the death of these savior figures was a sign of their failure. But see the speculations about the murder of the messianic pretender Menahem in Josephus, *J.W.* 2.442-48; on this cf. A. M. Schwemer, "Elia als Araber," in R. Feldmeier and U. Heckel, eds., *Die Heiden*, WUNT 70 (1994), 108-57.

215. On the *Targum of Isaiah* 53 see the essay by J. Ådna below.

216. "Cantique de Michel et Cantique des Justes." For the text see M. Baillet, *Qumrân Grotte 4, III (4Q482-4Q520)*, DJD 7 (1982), 12-44, esp. 26-29 with plate VI. The Hebrew text, including a few alternative reconstructions over against Baillet, is also available in *DSSSE* 2:978-81 and in the first of the following two works by M. Smith, "Ascent to the Heavens and Deification in 4QM[a]," in L. H. Schiffman, ed., *Archaeology and History in the Dead Sea Scrolls: The New York*

the meantime it has been questioned whether this hymnic text belongs to the *4QWar Scroll,* and it has been likened instead to certain *4QHodayot* fragments (e.g., 4Q427 frag. 7 col. 1 and 9; 4Q471b).[217] The designation 4Q491c now differentiates it from the other fragments of 4Q491.[218]

What is striking about this poetic text is that an unknown figure presents his own exaltation to the status of God and the angels almost in the form of an aretalogy. Accordingly 4Q491c is entitled *4QSelf-Glorification Hymn[b]* (*DSSSE* 2:978-81), with the similar title *4QSelf-Glorification Hymn[a]* reserved for 4Q471b (*DSSSE* 2:952-53). Morton Smith in his new reconstruction of 4Q491c has worked out the poetic character of the hymn and suspects that it does not in fact deal with the archangel Michael. Rather, the speaker must be a human figure who has been enthroned in the heavenly world with God and his angels. The question is nevertheless *who* is speaking here. Unfortunately the readings of the fragmentary text are uncertain in many places. The language is no longer classical Hebrew but contains several Aramaisms and late Hebrew words.

Conference in Memory of Yigael Yadin, JSPSup 8 (1990), 181-88; idem, "Two Ascended to Heaven — Jesus and the Author of 4Q491," in J. H. Charlesworth, ed., *Jesus and the Dead Sea Scrolls,* ABRL (1992), 290-301, esp. 295-99 (though the consequences that Smith draws from this text, following one of his favorite themes, are admittedly absurd). For other interpretations see J. J. Collins, "A Throne in the Heavens: Apotheosis in Pre-Christian Judaism," in J. J. Collins and M. Fishbane, eds., *Death, Ecstasy, and Other Worldly Journeys* (1995), 43-58; revised and reprinted, "A Throne in the Heavens," chap. 6 in Collins, *The Scepter and the Star: The Messiahs of the Dead Sea Scrolls and Other Ancient Literature* (1995), 136-53 (references below are to this revised edition); M. G. Abegg, "Who Ascended to Heaven? 4Q491, 4Q427, and the Teacher of Righteousness," in C. A. Evans and P. W. Flint, eds., *Eschatology, Messianism, and the Dead Sea Scrolls* (1997), 61-73; Zimmermann, *Messianische Texte aus Qumran,* 285-310; E. Eshel, "The Identification of the 'Speaker' of the Self-Glorification Hymn," in D. W. Parry and E. Ulrich, eds., *The Provo International Conference on the Dead Sea Scrolls,* STDJ 30 (1999), 619-35; I. Knohl, *The Messiah before Jesus: The Suffering Servant of the Dead Sea Scrolls* (2000), 15-20, 23-26, 77.

217. On these texts related to 4Q491c see E. Schuller, "A Hymn from a Cave Four Hodayot Manuscript 4Q427 7 i + ii," *JBL* 112 (1993): 605-28, and the works of Collins in the preceding note. The *4QSelf-Glorification Hymn[b]* 4Q491 frag. 11 (4Q491c) has close connections with the *4QHodayot[a]* 4Q427 frag. 7 (*DSSSE* 2:896-97) and the *4QSelf-Glorification Hymn[a]* 4Q471b (*DSSSE* 2:952-53). Collins ("A Throne in the Heavens," 138) suspects that these are copies of the same text because of their sometimes verbal overlaps. However, there remain some unparalleled elements in 4Q491 11, including the mention of a "mighty throne in the congregation of the gods." See J. J. Collins and D. Dimant, "A Thrice-Told Hymn," *JQR* 85 (1994): 151-55, esp. 153-54. See further D. Dimant, "A Synoptic Comparison of Parallel Sections in 4Q427 7, 4Q491 11 and 4Q471B," *JQR* 85 (1994): 157-61; E. Eshel, "4Q471[b]: A Self-Glorification Hymn," *RevQ* 17 (1996): 175-203 (with discussion of other manuscripts of the hymn including 4Q491 11).

218. For further description of the 4Q491 fragments see Abegg, "Who Ascended to Heaven?" 62.

References to this text have been complicated by the differing line numbers used by the various editors. M. Baillet's *editio princeps* of 4Q491 fragment 11 column i in DJD, volume 7, pages 26-27, begins with line 8 (and runs from lines 8 to 23; line 24 preserves only a single letter) because of its alignment with column ii, whose upper portion extends to line 1 (see plate 6 in DJD 7). But in the meantime this two-column alignment has been questioned,[219] and column i has been renumbered (keeping Baillet's line breaks) from lines 1 to 16, as in the editions of García Martínez and Tigchelaar (*DSSSE* 2:980) and Eshel.[220] Smith adopts an entirely different procedure, using the apparent metrical structure of column i to produce a poetic text of 37 (or 38) lines.[221]

Baillet has produced a French translation (DJD 7:28-29); Zimmermann a German translation.[222] English translations are provided by Smith[223] (followed by J. J. Collins[224]), Vermes,[225] Eshel,[226] and García Martínez and Tigchelaar (*DSSSE* 2:981).[227] The presentation below uses the translation of García Martínez and Tigchelaar (with their line numbers in boldface), but lays out the lines according to metrical structure and line numbering of Smith (see the numbering in the left margin). Some of Smith's unique readings are commented upon below.

4Q491c *Self-Glorification Hymn^b* (Baillet 4Q491 Fragment 11 Column i)

11 **4** [+ Smith: El 'Elyon gave me a seat among] the perfect ones of
   5 [. . . et]ernal;
   a mighty throne in the congregation of the gods
13 above which none of the kings of the East shall sit,
   and their nobles no[t . . .] silence (?) [+ Smith: come near it].
15 **6** [. . .] my glory is in[comparable]
   and besides me no-one is exalted, nor comes to me,
17 for I reside in [. . .], in the heavens,
   and none **7** [+ Smith: find fault with me].
19 I am counted among the gods
   and my dwelling is in the holy congregation;

219. Cf. Eshel, "Identification of the 'Speaker,'" 621 n. 7.
220. Eshel, "Identification of the 'Speaker,'" 621-22.
221. Smith, "Ascent to the Heavens," 183-84.
222. Zimmermann, *Messianische Texte aus Qumran*, 287.
223. Smith, "Ascent to the Heavens," 184-85.
224. Collins, "A Throne in the Heavens" (rev. ed.), 136-37 with 149 n. 3.
225. Vermes, *Complete Dead Sea Scrolls*, 185.
226. Eshel, "Identification of the 'Speaker,'" 622.
227. Abegg, "Who Ascended to Heaven?" 63, also offers an apparently independent English translation of Smith's ll. 12-20 (= Baillet's ll. 12-14).

21 [my] des[ire] is not according to the flesh,
   [but] all that is precious to me is in (the) glory (of) **8** [. . .] the
      holy [dwel]ling.

23 [W]ho has been considered despicable on my account?
   And who is comparable to me in my glory?

25 Who, like the sailors, will come back
   and tell? [+ Smith: of my equivalent?]

27 **9** [. . .] Who bea[rs all] sorrows like me? [Smith: laughs at griefs . . .]
   And who [suffe]rs evil like me? There is no-one.

29 I have been instructed,
   and there is no teaching comparable **10** [to my teaching . . .]

31 And who will attack me when [I] op[en my mouth]?
   And who can endure the flow of my lips?

33 And who will confront me and retain comparison with my judgment?
   11 [. . . friend of the king, companion of the holy ones . . .
      incomparable,

35 f]or among the gods is [my] posi[tion,
   and] my glory is with the sons of the king.

37 To me (belongs) [pure] gold, and to me, the gold of Ophir.[228]

Following are a few remarks about the interpretation of this text and its
points of contact with the third and fourth Servant Songs.[229]

1. In common with the fourth Servant Song is the motif of the exaltation
of the text's main figure and his opposition to the kings and nobles in lines 13-14.
The "kings of the east" could refer to the Parthians, who were victorious in the
east from the second half of the second century B.C.E.[230] If Smith is right in his
reconstruction and translation of lines 23-24,[231] then these could be aimed at the

---

228. The text continues with the lines that Baillet called "Cantique des justes," ll. 19-23 in
his edition or ll. 12-16 in *DSSSE* 2:981: "12 [blank] 13 [. . . exult,] just ones, in the God of [. . .] in
the holy dwelling, sing for h[im . . .] 14 [. . . p]roclaim during the meditation jubilation [. . .] in
eternal happiness; and there is no . . . [. . .] 15 [. . .] to establish the horn of [his] Mess[iah . . .] 16
[. . .] and to make known his power with strength." See also Knohl, *The Messiah before Jesus*, 23;
Eshel, "Identification of the 'Speaker,'" 622.

229. For additional comparisons between Isaiah 53 and the various versions of the Self-
Glorification Hymn see Knohl, *The Messiah before Jesus*, 11-26.

230. Smith's reading אדומי ("Edomite") at the start of his l. 15 (i.e., the last word of
Baillet's l. 12 = *DSSSE* l. 5) and his reference to the Edomite Herod is questionable, because in
the photograph there is a clear space between the *aleph* and the *daleth*. Baillet reads א דומיׄ and
translates the last word by "silence," followed by *DSSSE*.

231. However, Smith's reconstruction here is regarded as "highly speculative" by Collins
and Dimant, "A Thrice-Told Hymn," 151-55, esp. 152.

Seleucids as well as the Hasmoneans: "[The status of a holy temple,] not to be violated, has been attributed to me, and who can compare with me in glory?"

2. The threefold stress upon this figure's "glory" (כבוד) in lines 15, 24, and 36 recalls the Septuagint translation of Isaiah 53. In line 16, as in Isaiah 52:13, the uniqueness of his exaltation is emphasized: "and besides me no one is exalted" (ולוא ירומם זולתי), where the piel imperfect ירומם may be compared with the qal imperfect יָרוּם ("he shall be exalted") of Isaiah 52:13.

3. The suffering of the exalted one is briefly hinted at in lines 27-28: "Who bea[rs all] sorrows like me? And who [suffe]rs evil like me?" In line 27 instead of Smith's מיא ישחק לצערים כמוני ("who laughs at griefs as I do?") I would read מיא ישא רב צערים כמוני ("who bears great sorrows like me?") or something similar, because the rising stroke of the *lamed* in לצערים is not visible in the photograph (cf. also כול צערים in *DSSSE*). This would yield a better parallelism to line 28: ומיא לסבול רע הדמה ביא (*DSSSE* reads יסבול). The use here of the verbs נשא and סבל recalls Isaiah 53:4, 12.

4. Special *wisdom* is attributed to this figure in one of the possible reconstructions of the text, which would then recall the יַשְׂכִּיל in Isaiah 52:13 (ASV: "my servant shall *deal wisely*") and 11:2ff. In lines 29-30 I would propose against Baillet and Smith: ואין נשניתי והוריה לוא תדמה חכמתי (or something similar): "I was not instructed; (human) teaching is not comparable to my wisdom." Or: "When I was instructed, (human) teaching was not comparable to my wisdom."

5. The speaker's sinlessness could be alluded to in line 18 if Smith is correct in his restoration of מחייבים: "and none [find fault with me]."

6. The situation of a legal battle recalls the third Servant Song. The expression מזל שפתי ("the flow of my lips") in line 32 is reminiscent of לְשׁוֹן לִמּוּדִים ("the tongue of a teacher") in Isaiah 50:4. Moreover, the threefold question of Isaiah 50:8-9,

> Who will contend with me?
> Who is my adversary?
> Who will declare me guilty?

finds its counterpart in the analogous questions of lines 31 and 33-34 (translated by Smith):

> Who will attack me . . . ?
> Who will call me into court . . . ?
> In my legal judgment[232] [none will stand against] me.

---

232. "Judgment" here is singular, משפטי (cf. Isa. 50:8b, מִי־בַעַל מִשְׁפָּטִי), against Smith's plural "judgments." Cf. also Rom. 8:23-24.

7. The justification or vindication by God of Isaiah 50:8 ("he who vindicates me is near") and Isaiah 53:11 LXX (δικαιῶσαι δίκαιον) occurs here through the exaltation to the heavenly "mighty throne" in the congregation of the angels, which can also be understood as the judgment seat in the heavenly court of judges (cf. Dan. 7:9-14). The eschatological-dualistic context indeed presupposes a situation of judgment. Especially in the Similitudes of *1 Enoch*, but also in Matthew 25:31 and 19:28, enthronement and judgment go hand in hand.[233]

Who this figure is — the true Israel embodied through the Essene community, or the messianic high priest, the Teacher of Righteousness exalted to the status of God — remains unclear. However, after repeated reading I myself begin to wonder again about Morton Smith's theory: Could Michael not in fact be in view here as the representative of Israel, exalted above the throngs of angels of the nations who are contending with each other like satraps? But why would he then compare himself with earthly rulers? Perhaps a collective interpretation lies closest to hand, possibly represented by a patriarchal figure. Basically we can only guess, more so here than in the other text, 4Q541 *Aramaic Apocryphon of Levi*, which bears a number of similar traits (see above §7). This confirms once again the oft-made observation that the boundary between the individual and the collective appears fluid; the exemplary individual embodies the community, as conversely the community can be represented in an ideal individual figure.

11. Summary

Searching for traces of the influence of Isaiah 53 has led us, despite diversity and ambiguity, to many interesting passages. Let us then summarize the very provisional result once again as an overview.

The passage Isaiah 52:13–53:12, designated today as the fourth Servant Song, was not entirely without influence within the framework of Jewish interpretation of Isaiah in the pre-Christian period. Yet this influence is anything but unified.

The strongest influence upon other texts is exerted by the motif of exaltation in Isaiah 52:13-15 together with 53:11. This motif is applied collectively to the true Israel or the righteous ones in Daniel 11–12 (see above §4), allusively in the

---

233. On the enthronement motif and 4Q491 see M. Hengel, "'Setze dich zu meiner Rechten!' Die Inthronisation Christi zur Rechten Gottes und Psalm 110,1," in M. Philonenko, ed., *Le Trône de Dieu*, WUNT 69 (1993), 108-94, esp. 175ff. = ET, "'Sit at My Right Hand!': The Enthronement of Christ at the Right Hand of God and Psalm 110:1," in M. Hengel, *Studies in Early Christology* (1995), 119-225, esp. 201ff.

Testament of Moses 10:9-10 (see §4), clearly in Wisdom 2 and 5 (see §8), and possibly in the *Self-Glorification Hymn* 4Q491 (see §10). Here and elsewhere, the Servant's exaltation can be combined with the judgment of the kings and pagan nations. This is especially true of the Similitudes of *1 Enoch*. The elect and righteous Servant is identified with the Son of Man of Daniel 7:13 and the Messiah of Isaiah 11. He therefore appears on the scene not as a collective figure but as savior and judge, though the "righteous" and "elect" ones are still most closely united with him. Whereas in the collective interpretation in Daniel 11–12 and Wisdom 2, the motif of suffering comes clearly to the fore, it is almost completely suppressed in the Similitudes, where suffering affects only the righteous and elect *ones*.

The Isaiah Scroll 1QIsaᵃ (see §6) is evidence, in my opinion, of a messianic interpretation, probably applied — as the *Aramaic Apocryphon of Levi*ᵇ (4Q541) suggests — to the end-time high priest. This could possibly also be true of the *Self-Glorification Hymn* (4Q491), though admittedly the suffering is only hinted at. An individual eschatological interpretation is also present in the Septuagint of Isaiah (see §8), which likewise refers to a suffering individual of the dawning end-times, perhaps to Onias III. Finally, the *Testament of Benjamin* 3:8 could very well be pre-Christian and dependent on Isaiah 53.

The motif of vicarious atoning death in the Hebrew text of Isaiah 53 recedes more or less into the background in the other pre-Christian texts. It is perhaps hinted at in Daniel 11–12, is completely absent in the Similitudes and Wisdom, but appears clearly by contrast in the Septuagint of Isaiah 53, despite the strengthened motif of the *passio iusti*. It perhaps plays a role in the *Aramaic Apocryphon of Levi*ᵇ (4Q541), but it is not visible at all in the *Self-Glorification Hymn* (4Q491). Finally, it is interesting that already in the Septuagint and the *Aramaic Apocryphon of Levi*ᵇ, a tendency comes to the fore that is fully developed in the likewise individual messianic interpretation of the *Targum of Isaiah*.

Basically, we can say that wherever the motif of the judge is prominent, the motif of vicarious suffering disappears. On the whole only traces of this motif are visible, most clearly where there is a need to translate the text more or less faithfully in the Septuagint. Nevertheless, I believe we are not entirely without grounds for the hypothesis that already in the pre-Christian period, traditions about suffering and atoning eschatological messianic figures were available in Palestinian Judaism (as well as in the Diaspora; the two cannot be strictly separated), and that Jesus and the Early Church *could* have known and appealed to them. This would explain how first Jesus himself and then his disciples after Easter could presuppose that their message of the vicarious atoning death of the Messiah (cf. 1 Cor. 15:3-5) would be understood among their Jewish contemporaries.

Isaiah 53 in the Gospels and Acts

Peter Stuhlmacher

For Luise Abramowski on her 65th birthday, July 8, 1993

Summary

The New Testament's Christological interpretation of Isaiah 53 goes back to Jesus' own understanding of his mission and death, here explored by a traditio-historical argument. Jesus' understanding, in turn, depends upon a demonstrable early Jewish messianic interpretation of Isaiah 53, into which Jesus also incorporated passages such as Isaiah 43:3-4; 52:7 and 61:1-2. By making one of the first applications of the whole Servant text, including its suffering motif, to an individual historical figure (cf. also the *Aramaic Aprocryphon of Levi,* 4Q541), Jesus and his disciples after Easter extended the early Jewish interpretation independently. Messianic interpretations of the chapter, both ancient Jewish and early Christian, are commonly attributed to an "individualistic" understanding of the servant, as opposed to the "corporate" understanding favored in much recent scholarship. The dichotomy is, however, a false one. In Judaism the individual figure of the Servant-Messiah is the prince appointed by God, a prince who rules over the people of God and simultaneously represents them before God. So also with Jesus. He is the Son of God who leads the people of God; yet that people also constitutes his body. One can call this understanding "individual" only so long as one also remembers the collective aspect and refuses to oppose the two conceptions.

The topic of Isaiah 53 in the Gospels and Acts is often discussed and extremely complicated and can therefore be treated here only partially in a brief sketch.[1]

---

1. There is another reason why only a sketch is possible: Jesus developed his understanding of his mission not only from Isaiah 53 but also from Isa. 43:3-4; 52:7 (cf. Mark 1:14-15) and

The ancient source material discussed elsewhere in this volume by J. Ådna, M. Hengel, H.-J. Hermisson, O. Hofius, B. Janowski, C. Markschies, and S. Schreiner need not be surveyed once again, but can be presupposed. This includes the important fragments from Qumran Cave 4 (especially 4Q540-541) that E. Puech has now finally published and commented upon in a definitive scholarly edition.[2]

This source material must constantly be kept in mind. So must J. Jeremias's correct observation that in early Judaism we can neither presuppose that the ancients had a "concept of *the* Ebed as understood in modern research" (especially since B. Duhm's *Das Buch Jesaja, übersetzt und erklärt* [1892])[3] nor assume that they encountered the Servant Songs as discrete textual units. The proposition to be refuted here is a different one: the *communis opinio* of recent New Testament scholarship that "the application of the Servant conception to Jesus was the work of the early church with very limited influence."[4] Rather, as scholars including J. Jeremias,[5] H. W. Wolff,[6] O. Betz,[7] L. Goppelt,[8] and others

---

61:1-2 (cf. Luke 6:20; 7:22 par.). Obviously the reception of the entire Isaianic tradition in Jesus' preaching and the Gospels and Acts cannot be investigated here.

2. We now have the definitive edition of the Aramaic texts 4Q529-549: E. Puech, ed., *Qumrân Grotte 4. XXII: Textes Araméens, Première Partie, 4Q529-549*, DJD 31 (2001). A preliminary edition of 4Q540-541 and other texts was also published: E. Puech, "Fragments d'un apocryphe de Lévi et le personnage eschatologique: 4QTestLévi^{c-d}(?) et 4QAJa," in J. T. Barrera and L. V. Montaner, eds., *The Madrid Qumran Congress: Proceedings of the International Congress on the Dead Sea Scrolls, Madrid, 18-21 March, 1991*, 2 vols., STDJ 11 (1992), 2:449-501. M. Hengel has commented on the significance of these textual fragments briefly in his essay "Christological Titles in Early Christianity," in J. H. Charlesworth, ed., *The Messiah: Developments in Earliest Judaism and Christianity* (1992), 425-48, esp. 445 n. 67. More fully see §7 of Hengel's essay in the present volume. See also below, nn. 43-44.

3. J. Jeremias, "παῖς θεοῦ," *TWNT* 5 (1954), 676-713, esp. 681 ll. 14-15 = *TDNT* 5 (1967), 677-717, esp. 682 ll. 26-27. Jeremias reworked the New Testament part of his article and republished it in his essay collection *Abba: Studien zur neutestamentlichen Theologie und Zeitgeschichte* (1966), 191-216.

4. H. Haag, *Der Gottesknecht bei Deuterojesaja* (1985), 78.

5. Cf. J. Jeremias, *Neutestamentliche Theologie I*, 2nd ed. (1973), 283-84 = ET, *New Testament Theology*, trans. J. Bowden (1971), 298-99, as well as Jeremias's article "παῖς θεοῦ."

6. H. W. Wolff, *Jesaja 53 im Urchristentum*, 4th ed. (1984), with an introduction by P. Stuhlmacher.

7. O. Betz, "Die Frage nach dem messianischen Bewußtsein Jesu," in idem, *Jesus — Der Messias Israels: Aufsätze zur biblischen Theologie*, WUNT 42 (1987), 140-68; idem, *Was wissen wir von Jesus?* (1991), 106-8 (this section is absent from the original 1964 German version and hence from its ET, *What Do We Know about Jesus?* [1968]).

8. L. Goppelt, *Theologie des Neuen Testaments I*, ed. J. Roloff (1975), 243-44 = ET, *Theology of the New Testament*, vol. 1, trans. J. E. Alsup (1981), 195-96.

have long since realized, it is the other way around: the Christological interpretation of Isaiah 53 that comes to the fore in Romans 4:25; 1 Corinthians 15:3b-5; 1 Peter 2:22-25; Hebrews 9:28, and so forth was not first and foremost the fruit of post-Easter faith; its roots lie rather in Jesus' own understanding of his mission and death. He himself adopted the general messianic interpretation of Isaiah 53 current in early Judaism,[9] but he understood his sufferings quite independently of the prevailing tradition in the light of the word of God given to him from Isaiah 43:3-4 and 53:11-12. After the completion of Jesus' mission in the cross and resurrection, the song of the Suffering Servant was applied in early Christianity consistently for the first time to a historical individual whose fate made the whole text transparent.

I

The view suggested above in thesis form is confirmed when one situates the debated texts within the formative process behind the synoptic tradition, as it has been newly explained over the last thirty years by H. Schürmann, B. Gerhardsson, M. Hengel, and R. Riesner. According to this new view, the decisive origins of the synoptic tradition lie in the "school" of Jesus, who taught as the "messianic teacher of wisdom" (so M. Hengel). The παραδόσεις or traditions of this school were transmitted to the primitive church in Jerusalem by the μαθηταί whom Jesus himself had called. These traditions then formed an essential part of the "teaching of the apostles" (διδαχὴ τῶν ἀποστόλων) mentioned in Acts 2:42.[10] Since a carefully maintained continuity of tradition existed between Jesus' disciples and the Jerusalem church, and since the apostolic guarantors of the Jesus tradition remained alive until the outbreak of the first Jewish war, synoptic texts may be spoken of as subsequent "formulations of the Church" only when it can be shown exactly who created them, when, why, and for what recipients they were created, and under what circumstances they were accorded equal authority with the Jesus tradition backed by the apostles. When one cannot provide the answers to these questions, one must reckon with authentic tradition in the Synoptics.

Another factor comes into play. F. Lang in his essay "Observations on the

---

9. Cf. above all the text fragments from 4Q published by Puech (above, n. 2 and below, nn. 43-44) as well as the variant reading of 1QIsa^a at Isa. 52:14, מָשַׁחְתִּי, "I have anointed," instead of the MT's מִשְׁחַת, "marring" (cf. M. Hengel in §6 of his essay above). Here too belong the statements in *1 Enoch* 38:2; 46:4; 62:3, which I believe are to be dated not in the later Christian era but at the beginning of the first century C.E.

10. On this see my *Biblische Theologie des Neuen Testaments*, vol. 1 (1992), 18-19, 44-46.

Eschatological Preaching of John the Baptist"[11] has shown that the "more powerful one" (ὁ ἰσχυρότερος) announced by John in Mark 1:7 and parallels betrays "a close relationship to that Enoch-like figure for whom a connection between Daniel 7; Isaiah 11; 42:6; and 52:15 already exists and to whom the motif of 'coming' in Dan 7:13 properly belongs."[12] If this is correct, then we can assume that the Baptist confronted Jesus with the expectation of the soon-to-come messianic Son of Man and Judge of the World, and that Jesus had to relate his own mission to this expectation. He did so by understanding himself as the messianic Son of Man from the beginning of his public preaching and by decisively modifying John's expectation regarding the "more powerful one" to come, so that Jesus understood his own witness, which led to his death after many disputes, from the perspective of Isaiah 43:3-4 and 53:11-12. Jesus taught his disciples this understanding of his messianic mission and sufferings in private in various settings. Testimony to such private instruction is found above all in Mark 9:31 par.; 10:45 par.; 14:22, 24 par.; and also in Luke 22:35-38.

In the context of the Synoptic Gospels, the so-called *passion predictions* of Jesus (Mark 8:31-33 par.; 9:31-32 par.; 10:32-34 par.) are developed into advance hints of the passion intended to prepare readers in three steps for reading and understanding the passion story. However, this literary framing of the texts in no way denies that they incorporate authentic Jesus tradition. Above all, as J. Jeremias has shown,[13] one may regard the enigmatic saying of Mark 9:31, ὁ υἱὸς τοῦ ἀνθρώπου παραδίδοται εἰς χεῖρας ἀνθρώπων ("The Son of Man is going to be betrayed into the hands of men"), as the Jesuanic foundation of the passion predictions. Here the passive παραδίδοται is to be read (as in Rom. 4:25) as a divine passive, and the betrayal of the "man" or rather the Son of Man by God is best understood from the perspective of Isaiah 43:3-5 and 53:5-6, 11-12.[14] Jesus saw himself as the "man" or Son of Man whom God in his love willed

---

11. F. Lang, "Erwägungen zur eschatologischen Verkündigung Johannes des Täufers," in G. Strecker, ed., *Jesus Christus in Historie und Theologie: Neutestamentliche Festschrift für H. Conzelmann zum 60. Geburtstag* (1975), 459-73.

12. Lang, "Erwägungen," 471.

13. Jeremias, *Neutestamentliche Theologie I,* 267-68, 280ff. = *New Testament Theology,* 281-82.

14. Notice the striking verbal agreement between the Greek ὁ υἱὸς τοῦ ἀνθρώπου παραδίδοται ("the Son of Man is delivered up") and the articular Hebrew construction of 1QIsa[a] 43:4b: אתן האדם תחתיך, "I give *the* man in exchange for you" (overlooked in the translation of 1QIsa[a] in *DSSB:* "I give *people* in your stead"). The MT has only the anarthrous noun "man" in a generic or collective sense, וְאֶתֵּן אָדָם תַּחְתֶּיךָ (cf. NJPS: "I give *men* in exchange for you"). As I mentioned at the beginning, Mark's double reference in 9:31 to Isaiah 43 and 53 is explained by the fact that the Servant Songs of Second Isaiah were read in early Judaism not as discrete units, but in the context of the whole book of Isaiah.

to deliver up for Israel's salvation, and the ὑπακοή or "obedience" of Jesus praised in Philippians 2:8 consisted of his submitting to this will of God (cf. Mark 14:41 par.).

The much-discussed *ransom saying* of Mark 10:45 (Matt. 20:28) points in the same direction. As W. Grimm has pointed out[15] and as I have already shown elsewhere,[16] this logion represents a "dissimilar" or "nonderivable" and hence an authentic word of Jesus. It interprets Jesus' mission and suffering from the perspective of Isaiah 43:3-4 and 53:11-12 and belongs materially with Mark 8:37 and its parallels (cf. Ps. 49:8-9). According to this logion, Jesus understood himself as the "man" or Son of Man whom God had sent to save Israel and whose life he had designated as a "ransom" (Heb. כֹּפֶר; Greek λύτρον, ἀντίλυτρον, or ἀντάλλαγμα) to redeem the existence of "the many" (Israel: cf. Isa. 53:11-12) from the final judgment, since their existence was forfeited by their guilt.

As I have learned from my former student J. Ådna and from the materials he has worked with, the ransom saying of Mark 10:45 and its parallels coheres surprisingly closely with Jesus' so-called temple cleansing (Mark 11:15-17 par.).[17] This symbolic messianic act presented the temple priesthood with an alternative — either to continue to carry out the sacrificial cult without reference to Jesus and his message and thereby to become separated from God once and for all, or to face up to this message and together with Jesus to approach "the temple established by God's own hands" in the βασιλεία (cf. Mark 14:58 par. with Exod. 15:17-18).[18] With this incredibly provocative act Jesus knowingly risked his life, and this was "in fact the occasion for the definitive official action against him."[19] Jesus' action against the sellers of sacrificial animals and the money changers in Solomon's Portico was equivalent to an attempt to under-

15. W. Grimm, *Die Verkündigung Jesu und Deuterojesaja*, 2nd ed. (1981), 231ff.

16. Cf. my essay "Existenzstellvertretung für die Vielen: Mk 10,45 (Mt 20,28)," in P. Stuhlmacher, *Versöhnung, Gesetz und Gerechtigkeit: Aufsätze zur biblischen Theologie* (1981), 27-42 = ET, "Vicariously Giving His Life for Many, Mark 10:45 (Matt. 20:28)," in idem, *Reconciliation, Law, and Righteousness: Essays in Biblical Theology*, trans. E. Kalin (1986), 16-29. See also my *Biblische Theologie des Neuen Testaments I*, 120ff.

17. See J. Ådna, *Jesu Stellung zum Tempel: Die Tempelaktion und das Tempelwort als Ausdruck seiner messianischen Sendung*, WUNT 2/119 (2000).

18. On the relationship of this saying in Mark 14:58 about a temple "not made by [human] hands" to the early Jewish understanding of Exod. 15:17-18 ("the sanctuary, O Lord, that your hands have established") see A. M. Schwemer, "Irdischer und himmlischer König: Beobachtungen zur sog. David-Apokalypse in Hekhalot Rabbati §§ 122-126," in M. Hengel and A. M. Schwemer, eds., *Königsherrschaft Gottes und himmlischer Kult*, WUNT 55 (1991), 309-59, esp. 356.

19. Jeremias, *Neutestamentliche Theologie I*, 266 = *New Testament Theology*, 279.

mine the entire buying and selling of sacrificial animals as well as the payment of obligatory contributions in the Tyrian temple currency. These contributions paid among other things for the twice-daily *tamid* sacrifice (Heb. תָּמִיד; cf. Exod. 29:38-46; Num. 28:3-8) by which Israel could be redeemed from its guilt morning and evening (cf. *Jub.* 6:14; 50:11; *Pesiqta of Rab Kahana* 55b; cf. Str-B 2:247 n. 1). If one assumes that Jesus anticipated the priesthood's negative reaction to his deed, then from Mark 10:45 and its parallels it can be concluded that he himself was ready to take the place of the sacrifices offered in vain by the priests for Israel and to redeem the people of God from its guilt before God once for all with his life. The close connection between Mark 10:45 par. and the temple cleansing provides documentary proof that Jesus entered the final disputes in Jerusalem decisively and ready to suffer.

The Last Supper tradition also attests to this. The most difficult (and therefore the oldest) version of the words of institution may be found in Mark 14:22, 24 (and not in Luke 22:19-20 or 1 Cor. 11:24-25). The wording of 1 Corinthians 10:16-17 shows that Paul knew not only the pre-Lukan "cult etiology" which he cited in 1 Corinthians 11:23-25, but also the form of the *verba testamenti* reproduced by Mark.[20] Whether the Markan bread saying in Mark 14:22 was formulated with reference to Isaiah 53 is difficult to say, but the Lukan addition τὸ ὑπὲρ ὑμῶν διδόμενον ("which is given for you," Luke 22:19) recalls Isaiah 53:6, 12 (παραδίδωμι). The *cup saying* in Mark 14:24 takes up both Exodus 24:8 and Isaiah 53:10-12 and by means of this double allusion shows that the Suffering Servant's passion was understood as an event of atonement, even as it was by Jesus himself. According to Isaiah 53:10 the Servant's life was made an אָשָׁם, that is, a "means of wiping out guilt,"[21] which gives Israel a new life before God. This wiping out of guilt occurs when Jesus as God's Servant vicariously suffers the violent death which lay before him and makes atonement for "the many" by his blood, thus inaugurating them into the (new) "covenant" that guarantees them forgiveness of their sins (cf. Mark 14:24) and places them in fulfillment of God's will (cf. Exod. 24:8 with Jer. 31:31-34).

If one contemplates the sequence of Jesus sayings in Mark 9:31 par.; 10:45 par.; and 14:22, 24, all of which have been formulated with a view to Isaiah 53 (and Isa. 43:3-4), then the figurative saying about the *two swords* in the Lukan special tradition, Luke 22:35-38, can be counted among the genuine sayings of Jesus based on the criterion of coherence. In Luke 22:37, Isaiah 53:12 is cited not

---

20. For the tradition-historical connections of these passages see my *Biblische Theologie des Neuen Testaments I*, 130ff.

21. This translation of אָשָׁם has been proposed in the essay in this volume by B. Janowski, "He Bore Our Sins: Isaiah 53 and the Drama of Taking Another's Place," above, pp. 65-67.

according to the Septuagint but according to the Hebrew text: "He was numbered with transgressors" (μετὰ ἀνόμων = אֶת־פֹּשְׁעִים). The formulation of the saying is only partly Lukan,[22] and in it Jesus submits to the will of God revealed to him in Isaiah 53 no less obediently than he does in the other sayings just mentioned. He was ready to let himself (and his faithful followers) be "numbered with the transgressors" and to end his life as God, through his word in Scripture, had determined for him.[23]

From the Jesus sayings examined up to this point it is safe to draw the following conclusion: *The earthly Jesus himself understood his witness and his approaching death in the light of the tradition already given to him in Isaiah about the (vicariously suffering) Servant of God. He understood the suffering laid upon him as an event in which God's will was fulfilled.*

II

On the basis of the Easter events the former disciples of Jesus led by Peter founded the Early Church in Jerusalem shortly after Jesus' death and resurrection. Because according to Acts 1:12-26 the core of the Early Church was formed by the circle of the Twelve (supplemented only by the eyewitness Matthias) which Jesus "created,"[24] by members of Jesus' own family, and by women from Jesus' home area, the teachings of Jesus known to these men and women and their recollections of his person and story were transmitted to the Early Church. Together with the earliest confessions and the kerygmatic stories of Jesus' passion, burial, and appearances formulated after Easter, these first-hand recollections constituted an essential part of the διδαχὴ τῶν ἀποστόλων (Acts 2:42).

In the light of the experience that Jesus' prophecies about his own death based on Isaiah 43 and 53 had been fulfilled by his crucifixion, burial, and resur-

---

22. According to J. Jeremias, *Die Sprache des Lukasevangeliums* (1980), 292-93, "the singular τὸ γεγραμμένον used as a designation of a Bible verse occurs in the New Testament only in Luke 20:17; 22:37 and in 2 Cor 4:13. This expression is consistent with Luke's fondness for the substantival participle." On the other hand, the presence of non-Lukan tradition in Luke 22:37 is suggested by several expressions, including λέγω γὰρ ὑμῖν ὅτι, δεῖ ("it *must* be") used in the context of the passion, the divine passive τελεσθῆναι, "to be fulfilled" (sc. according to the plan of God), and τὸ περὶ ἐμοῦ, as well as by the citation of Isa. 53:12, which follows not the LXX but the MT.

23. On this understanding of the saying see Jeremias, *Abba*, 214-15, and I. H. Marshall, *The Gospel of Luke*, 2nd ed. (1979), 826-27.

24. Cf. the formulation of Mark 3:14: καὶ ἐποίησεν δώδεκα κτλ.

rection, Jesus' sacrifice and resurrection were interpreted on the basis of Isaiah 53 with full conviction in the "school" of the apostles. One can see this best in the *traditional texts* that Paul quotes in his letters. After his spectacular call, the apostle was made familiar with the διδαχή of the apostles by the Christians of Damascus, Jerusalem, and Antioch, and he cites in his letters a few of the didactic texts which he learned in this way.

The two-line *Christological formula* in Romans 4:25 interprets Jesus' passion and exaltation as the work of God. In agreement with Jesus' own teaching (see above), it says that God handed over "Jesus our Lord" to death διὰ τὰ παραπτώματα ἡμῶν and raised him from the dead διὰ τὴν δικαίωσιν ἡμῶν. Behind this formulation stood above all the Hebrew text of Isaiah 53:5, 11. By contrast, if the Septuagint of Isaiah 53:5-6, 11-12 had been the basis of the formula in Romans 4:25, it would have suggested speaking of ἁμαρτίαι, "sins," instead of παραπτώματα, "transgressions" (which goes back to the "transgressors," פֹּשְׁעִים, of Isa. 53:12), and of the justification of the Servant himself (cf. 1 Tim. 3:16) instead of the justification of the many.[25]

The confessional formula that Paul cites in 1 Corinthians 15:3b-5 probably presents a summary of the teaching of the gospel that is constitutive for faith. It has been prepared for easy memorization in religious instruction by a fourfold ὅτι and by a twofold (generalizing) use of κατὰ τὰς γραφάς. Paul learned it himself and then passed it on in his missionary teaching (e.g., in Corinth: cf. 1 Cor. 15:1). This catechetical text calls Jesus Χριστός, thus taking up Jesus' messianic confession before the Sanhedrin in Mark 14:61-62.[26] It is based on Jesus' own predictions of his death and summarizes the passion and Easter traditions known in Jerusalem (and Antioch). It is therefore not to be understood in isolation from these traditions or even as an alternative to them (as is usually done), but with reference to them and in connection with them.

---

25. In Isa. 53:11 LXX the expression δικαιῶσαι δίκαιον εὖ δουλεύοντα πολλοῖς speaks not of the Servant justifying the many, but rather of the Servant himself being given the rights that his enemies wish to deny to him. On the differences between the Hebrew and Greek texts of Isa. 53:11 see now D. Sapp, "The LXX, 1QIsa, and MT Versions of Isaiah 53 and the Christian Doctrine of Atonement," in W. H. Bellinger and W. R. Farmer, eds., *Jesus and the Suffering Servant: Isaiah 53 and Christian Origins* (1998), 170-92, esp. 173-76, 186-89, and E. R. Ekblad, *Isaiah's Servant Poems According to the Septuagint*, CBET 23 (1999), 249-60.

26. On the authenticity of this text I have already commented in my *Biblische Theologie des Neuen Testaments I*, 115ff., and in my essay "Der messianische Gottesknecht," *JBTh* 8 (1993): 131-54. M. Hengel also assumes that the earthly Jesus made messianic claims in his two essays "Jesus der Messias Israels," in I. Grünwald et al., eds., *Messiah and Christos: Studies in the Jewish Origin of Christianity, Festschrift for D. Flusser* (1992), 155-76 and "Christological Titles in Early Christianity."

1 Corinthians 15:3b takes up the ὑπέρ from the Last Supper tradition (Mark 14:24 par.) and speaks of the death of Christ ὑπὲρ τῶν ἁμαρτιῶν ἡμῶν. The κατὰ τὰς γραφάς suggests that we should think above all of the fulfillment of Isaiah 53:5, 10-12. In 1 Corinthians 15:4a the burial of Jesus is spoken of with reference to the burial traditions; this could have been understood as the fulfillment of Isaiah 53:9. 1 Corinthians 15:4b confesses Jesus' resurrection on the third day "according to the scriptures." The date corresponds to the finding of the empty tomb on the third day after Jesus' crucifixion, but the appended expression κατὰ τὰς γραφάς is presumably intended to point to the fulfillment of Hosea 6:2[27] and could also refer to Isaiah 52:13 and 53:10-11. In 1 Corinthians 15:5 the confession of the resurrection of Jesus is followed (much as it is in Luke 24:34) by a mention of Jesus' appearances to Peter and the Twelve. Whether these appearances were understood in the light of Isaiah 53:10-12 cannot be said with certainty. Nevertheless, because the Twelve led by Peter were destined to become rulers and judges over the end-time Israel (i.e., "the many"; cf. Luke 22:30) and were newly established in Jerusalem in order to represent the people of God there, one can see in the appearances of Jesus to Cephas and the Twelve a fulfillment of Isaiah 53:12: God will give the exalted Servant "a portion with the many."

In sum, from the catechetical summary of 1 Corinthians 15:3b-5 and from Romans 4:25, we see by examples how the interpretation of the passion from Isaiah 53 advanced by Jesus himself provided Christians after Easter with clear and precise soteriological terms for speaking about Jesus' death on the cross and his resurrection.

III

Soteriological discourse about Jesus' death and resurrection was not limited to confessional or faith formulas in early Christianity. Rather, the faith-knowledge expressed in these formulas combined with the teachings of Jesus and with memories of his deeds and destiny to form a new entity when the gospel traditions were fixed. It is to this that we owe the narrative testimony to the ministry and death of Jesus as God's Servant.

27. The formulation of Hos. 6:2 LXX, ἐν τῇ ἡμέρᾳ τῇ τρίτῃ ἀναστησόμεθα, "on the third day we shall rise," has points of contact with 1 Cor. 15:4 that extend to the very wording. In early Judaism Hos. 6:2 was related to the end-time resurrection of the dead (cf. Str-B 1:747). Therefore, the κατὰ τὰς γραφάς of 1 Cor. 15:4 could express the faith conviction that with the resurrection of Jesus, the end-time resurrection of all the dead has begun (Rom. 1:3-4 says the same thing). Paul apparently understood 1 Cor. 15:4 this way, judging by what he says in 1 Cor. 15:20-22.

In Luke 24:6-7, 44-46, the Evangelist has programmatically shown how an understanding of the saving significance of Jesus' suffering, death, and resurrection was first opened up to the New Testament witnesses by the mouth of God's heavenly messengers and the interpretation of the Holy Scriptures by the risen Christ. The retelling of Jesus' passion along the lines of the psalms of suffering, Psalms 22, 69, and Psalm 31 (cf. Luke 23:46), rests upon this faith perspective just as surely as does the development of Jesus' passion predictions into passion summaries (i.e., Mark 8:31-33 par.; 9:30-32 par.; 10:32-34 par.). Jesus' prophecies of his death based on Isaiah 43 and 53 are thereby once again shown to their best advantage (see above). In Luke 17:25 the first of these summaries is repeated. A saying of Jesus represented in only a part of the textual tradition of Luke 23:34, "Father, forgive them, for they do not know what they are doing" (πάτερ, ἄφες αὐτοῖς, οὐ γὰρ οἴδασιν τί ποιοῦσιν), has clearly been formulated with reference to the Hebrew text of Isaiah 53:12, "He made intercession for the transgressors." This saying provided the pattern for Acts 7:60 (Stephen: "Lord, do not hold this sin against them") and is therefore a genuine part of the Lukan tradition.[28]

The old-fashioned language in Acts about Jesus as God's anointed Servant or παῖς θεοῦ (Acts 3:13, 26; 4:27, 30), humiliated and put to death by his enemies according to God's will but exalted by God and invested with divine authority, refers back to Isaiah 61:1 and 52:13; 53:11. Parallel to this, Jesus is called ὁ δίκαιος, the Righteous One, in Acts 3:14; 7:52; 22:14 (cf. Isa. 53:11 and *1 Enoch* 38:2; 53:6). Whether such expressions merely take up individual motifs from the Servant tradition or rather present a more comprehensive picture of Jesus' ministry, suffering, and exaltation as God's Servant is a question that can be answered by two considerations. First, the two titles predicated of Jesus are certainly pre-Lukan and must therefore be considered not apart from but together with the Jerusalem formulaic texts Romans 4:25 and 1 Corinthians 15:3b-5 (see above). Moreover, Luke has used them not independently of his passion story but only in conscious connection with it (cf. Acts 3:13-16; 4:27-28; 7:52). Both considerations suggest that in the figure of Jesus a holistic concept of God's Servant has been realized. Without such a larger concept it would be impossible to understand the language of the forgiveness of sins that came through Jesus' mission as the παῖς θεοῦ, which Luke repeats almost stereotypically (cf. Acts 3:13, 19 with 2:38; 5:31; 10:43, etc.). But the intercessions in Luke 22:32 and 23:34 together with Isaiah 53:12 explain this language quite well. The exalted Christ will continue the "intercession for transgressors" which

---

28. On the textual criticism of Luke 23:34 see B. M. Metzger, *A Textual Commentary on the Greek New Testament*, 2nd ed. (1994), 154.

he began on earth, and even in the final judgment he will bring them forgiveness of sins through his vicarious death for sinners.[29]

In Acts 8:26-39 Luke reports about the baptism of the Ethiopian eunuch (taking up an older Philip tradition). In 8:32-33 the Septuagint text of Isaiah 53:7-8 is cited. The question of this "court official" (δυνάστης, 8:27) in 8:34 about whether the text refers to the prophet or to someone else is understandable when we consider that in early Judaism the Servant could be understood "collectively" as well as "individually" (see below) and that the tradition of the martyrdom of the prophet Isaiah was current among Jews and Christians.[30] The content of the gospel Philip preached to the official starting with this Scripture (cf. Acts 8:35) is not further explained in the text; all that is clear is that Philip applied the Isaiah text to Jesus and thus interpreted it Christologically. The reader of Acts (and of the Gospel of Luke) can and should understand Philip's message on the analogy of the Lukan passages already mentioned.

Matthew's summary of Jesus' healing ministry in Matthew 8:16 is expanded by the Evangelist in 8:17 by a retrospective citation of Isaiah 53:4. Matthew presupposes the Hebrew text of this passage; even Jesus' messianic healings should be understood as the work of the Servant. Whether an isolated motif of the text has thereby been taken up in a merely "atomistic," early Jewish manner,[31] or whether Matthew has extended the interpretation of Jesus' sufferings already known to him (cf. Matt. 16:21-23; 17:22-23; 20:17-19, 28; 26:26-28, 45, 54; 27:14 [cf. Isa. 53:7]; 27:19 [cf. Isa. 53:11]) to encompass Jesus' mission and healing ministry as a whole can be decided only after the fulfillment citation of Isaiah 42:1-4 in Matthew 12:17-21 has been considered.

---

29. On the Old Testament and early Jewish motif of the forgiveness of sins based on the intercession of the suffering righteous, cf. B. Janowski, "Sündenvergebung 'um Hiobs willen': Fürbitte und Vergebung in 11QtgJob 38,2f. und Hi 42,9f. LXX," *ZNW* 3 (1982): 251-80. O. Hofius deals with the same motif in *Tg. Isa.* 53 in an essay that unfortunately remains unpublished: "Kennt der Targum zu Jes 53 einen sündenvergebenden Messias?" in *Freundesgabe für Prof. P. Stuhlmacher zum 50. Geburtstag* (manuscript, 1982), 215-54.

30. Cf., e.g., *Lives of the Prophets* 1 (translation in *OTP* 2:386; Greek text in A. M. Denis, *Concordance greque des pseudépigraphes d'Ancien Testament* [1987], 868). Further references are given by A. Strobel in P. Rieger, ed., *Das Kreuz Jesu: Theologische Überlegungen* (1969), 113, including Heb. 11:3; Justin, *Dial.* 120; Tertullian, *De patientia* 14; Josephus, *Ant.* 10.38; *b. Yeb.* 49b; *Martyrdom and Ascension of Isaiah* 5:1-14.

31. U. Luz, *Das Evangelium nach Matthäus, Bd. 2: Mt 8–17* (1990), 19 = ET, *The Gospel According to Matthew*, vol. 2, trans. J. E. Crouch, Hermeneia (2001), 14: "In contrast to 12:18-21, the word παῖς θεοῦ ("servant of God") does not occur here. Precisely that part of Isa 53:3-5 is used here [in Matt 8:17] that does not speak of the suffering of God's servant. Our quotation is an example of the way early Christian exegesis, like the Jewish exegesis of the time, sometimes quotes individual words of scripture without any regard for their context."

U. Luz rightly considers this old-fashioned citation in Matthew 12:17-21, which goes back to the Hebrew text, to be highly significant. He ascribes it to "a pre-Matthean christological *testimonium* that late in the process was connected, perhaps by Matthew himself, with the summary of Mark 3:7-12,"[32] which Matthew takes up himself in 12:15-16. The formula quotation "opens the eyes of Matthew's readers to the entirety of the story of Jesus," which is "a story of gentleness, of mercy, of nonviolence, and of love."[33] If one considers the fact that the so-called fourth Servant Song was available to early Judaism and Christianity only in the context of the book of Isaiah and the Deuteroisaianic sayings about the Servant as a whole, then one will no longer be able to play off the messianic understanding of Isaiah 42:1-4 and its use in Matthew 12 against an understanding of Jesus' sacrifice based on Isaiah 53. One must rather combine the two. It would appear, then, that in the Gospel of Matthew, the understanding of Jesus' mission on the basis of the Deuteroisaianic tradition of the (suffering) Servant has been extended from Jesus' passion predictions and the passion story to encompass the whole story of Jesus.[34] The messianic Immanuel proclaimed by Matthew, who will save the people of God from their sins (cf. Matt. 1:21-23) and who, as the exalted one, will be with his missionary messengers until the end of the age (cf. Matt. 28:20), is none other than the Servant appointed by God for the salvation of his people (and the Gentiles) who proclaims the εὐαγγέλιον τῆς βασιλείας (cf. Matt. 4:23; 9:35). His ministry as the authoritative yet humble Messiah in word and deed,[35] as well as his passion, may be comprehended as events of messianic fulfillment from the perspective of Isaiah 42:1-4; 52:7; 52:13–53:12; and 61:1-2.[36]

32. Luz, *Das Evangelium nach Matthäus*, 2:246 = ET, *The Gospel According to Matthew*, 2:192.

33. Luz, *Das Evangelium nach Matthäus*, 2:250 = *The Gospel According to Matthew*, 2:195, 196.

34. According to A. Schlatter, *Der Evangelist Matthäus*, 6th ed. (1963), 283, by means of the scriptural citation that Matthew supplies from Isa. 53:4 in Matt. 8:17 ("He took our infirmities and bore our diseases"), the Evangelist does not want to correct Jesus' self-understanding as Suffering Servant, but to demonstrate that Jesus found even more meaning in Isaiah 53. J. Schniewind, *Das Evangelium nach Matthäus,* 12th ed. (1968), 112, evaluates the citation the same way: "Up until this point Jesus' miracles appeared as signs of unlimited power. Now they are described as part of the suffering of God's Servant. He takes our diseases upon himself as *passion* (cf. John 11:33, 38; Mark 1:41D [[ὀργισθείς — Trans.]]). That Matthew intends his citation of the prophetic passage to be taken this way is shown by the further use of Isaiah 53 and of Second Isaiah generally by Matthew (12:17ff.; 11:15) and by the early church (Acts 8:32f.; 1 Pet 2:22ff.)."

35. For this formulation see Schniewind, *Matthäus*, 8, 37, 106.

36. The Qumran fragment 4Q521, *Messianic Apocalypse*, has recently become available. See E. Puech in DJD 25 (1998), 1-38, plates I-III; *DSSSE* 2:1044-47; G. Vermes, *The Complete Dead*

IV

The interpretation of Isaiah 53 in the *Gospel of John* (and in the Johannine letters) is not easy to ascertain, because the Johannine gospel tradition after Easter emanated from the "school" of John in a long and complicated process involving both the adoption of old apostolic tradition and the independent rereading and supplementation of the Synoptic tradition. Moreover, outside John 12:38 there are no citations of Isaiah 53 in the Johannine corpus, but only allusions to the Servant Song by means of words and motifs.[37] If one assumes with M. Hengel[38] that both the Johannine letters and the Fourth Gospel go back to the πρεσβύτερος John, then the letters were composed during the lifetime of this "elder" according to 2 John 1 and 3 John 1, whereas the Gospel in John 21:23 already has in view the death of the Beloved Disciple (in whom the elder saw himself embodied). It is therefore necessary to approach our problem by way of the letters.

In 1 John 2:1-2 the exalted Christ is called first the "righteous one" (δίκαιος) and second an "advocate" (παράκλητος), which is grounded, third, in the fact that he is the "means of atonement for our sins" (ἱλασμὸς περὶ τῶν ἁμαρτιῶν ἡμῶν). All three expressions can be understood very well against the background of a Christological interpretation of Isaiah 53:4-6, 10-12.[39] The same goes for 1 John 4:10: "God loved us and sent his Son to be the means of

---

Sea Scrolls in English (1997), 391-92. This fragment provides a wonderful parallel to Matt. 11:2-6 and makes it clear that the Qumran Essenes already had very concrete ideas about the fulfillment of Isa. 35:5-6 and 61:1-2 by God's Messiah. On this text see O. Betz and R. Riesner, *Jesus, Qumran und der Vatikan* (1993), 111-15 = ET, *Jesus, Qumran and the Vatican*, trans. J. Bowden (1994), 90-93, and my essay "Der messianische Gottesknecht."

37. The book of Revelation also forms part of the tradition of the Johannine school. But only in Rev. 14:5 is there possibly a direct citation of Isaiah 53 (cf. 53:9) or more probably of Zeph. 3:13. According to Rev. 14:4-5, the 144,000 "have been redeemed from humankind as first fruits for God and the Lamb, and in *their* mouth no lie was found (ἐν τῷ στόματι αὐτῶν οὐχ εὑρέθη ψεῦδος); they are blameless" (NRSV). Yet as Wolff, *Jesaja 53 im Urchristentum*, 105, rightly emphasizes, "in Rev 14:5 it is not Isaiah 53 that appears, but Zephaniah 3:13." Wolff believes that the difference between the singular "*his* mouth" in Isa. 53:9 (οὐδὲ εὑρέθη δόλος ἐν τῷ στόματι αὐτοῦ) and the plural "*their* mouth" in Zeph. 3:13 (οὐ μὴ εὑρεθῇ ἐν τῷ στόματι αὐτῶν γλῶσσα δολία) is significant, and that this difference "ties Rev 14:5 [which also has the plural] firmly to Zeph 3:13" rather than to Isa. 53:9 (Wolff, 105 n. 456).

38. M. Hengel, *The Johannine Question* (1989).

39. H.-J. Klauck, *Der erste Johannesbrief,* EKKNT 23/1 (1991), 106ff., does not mention Isaiah 53 in his explanation of 1 John 2:1-2. He points only to cultic atonement and the intercession of the aged martyr Eleazar in 4 Macc. 6:28-29. However, in the context of the Johannine preexistence Christology, the intercession motif is better explained by Isa. 53:12.

atonement for our sins" (ἱλασμὸς περὶ τῶν ἁμαρτιῶν ἡμῶν). On the basis of these passages one may also interpret John 3:16 and the discourse about the (voluntary) surrender of life by the good shepherd for his sheep (10:11, 15, 17, 18) against the background of Isaiah 53.

In John 1:29, 36 John the Baptist calls Jesus ὁ ἀμνὸς τοῦ θεοῦ ὁ αἴρων τὴν ἁμαρτίαν τοῦ κόσμου, "the Lamb of God who takes away the sin of the world." In the context of the Fourth Gospel, this designation refers first and foremost to the vicarious atoning death of Jesus as the end-time paschal lamb (cf. John 1:36 with 1 Cor. 5:7) and only in its depth-dimension to Isaiah 53:7. However, since the expression about "taking away the sin of the world" can be explained only by Isaiah 53:4, 11-12 and not by the tradition of the paschal lamb, the Suffering Servant tradition certainly stands behind the designation of Jesus as ἀμνὸς τοῦ θεοῦ as well.[40]

These passages from 1 John 2:1-2; 4:10 and John 1:29, 36 show that Jesus' mission, passion, and exaltation were understood from the perspective of Isaiah 53 in the "school" of John despite the absence of direct citations. Moreover, in the two "fulfillment" citations in John 12:37-40, the stubbornness and unbelief of the Jews in the face of Jesus' σημεῖα is interpreted as the fulfillment of God's will by references to Isaiah 53:1 (LXX) and 6:10 (MT). Paul argues the same way in Romans 10:16. If one proceeds from the assumption that all the Johannine passages are coherent, then one need not see this citation of Isaiah 53:1 in John 12:38 as proof of the atomistic exegesis of Isaiah 53 in early Christianity.[41] Rather, we may assume with H. W. Wolff "that the evangelist has cited it here out of his deep insight into the whole prophecy 'Behold, my servant shall prosper.'"[42]

V

Looking back, the thesis mentioned at the beginning is once again established: *Jesus' appearance in history and his messianic understanding of his mission, which*

---

40. Once one sees these connections it is no longer necessary to follow the complicated procedure of Jeremias, *Abba*, 194f., who traces the expression ὁ ἀμνὸς τοῦ θεοῦ back to an Aramaic טליא דאלהא, which in turn is supposed to point to an עבד יהוה.

41. Cf. R. Schnackenburg, *Das Johannesevangelium, II. Teil*, HTKNT 4/2 (1971), 516 = ET, *The Gospel According to St John*, vol. 2, trans. C. Hastings et al. (1980), 414: "The fact that the passage is part of the last Servant Song, which talks about the Servant's expiatory suffering, does not justify the conclusion that Is 53 had a strong influence on John. The remark is only an aside on the part of the prophet, and does not bring in the Servant."

42. Wolff, *Jesaja 53 im Urchristentum*, 84.

was oriented toward Isaiah 52:13–53:12 (as well as Isa. 43:3-4; 52:7; 61:1-2), present a decisive new development in the history of the interpretation and influence of Isaiah 53. Given Jesus' own understanding, the Easter witnesses were able for the first time to relate the whole Suffering Servant text to an individual historical figure and to interpret Jesus' sufferings soteriologically from this text. However, this Christological interpretation of Isaiah 53 in the post-Easter texts of the New Testament is not primarily or only an expression of the faith-knowledge opened to the Christian church by Easter; it is also an answer and a reaction to Jesus' own prophecies of his death, which appeared to the witnesses to have been confirmed (by God) in the light of Easter.

As Jesus applied Isaiah 43 and 53 to himself and his sacrifice and as early Christianity interpreted the Suffering Servant Christologically, they connected with the messianic exposition of the Servant tradition in early Judaism and extended it independently. To be sure, the early Jewish messianic interpretation of Isaiah 53 and the messianic application of Isaiah 53 to Jesus which is dependent on it are often ascribed to an "individual" understanding of the Servant according to our current terminology, over against which the "collective" understanding (known to every reader of Isaiah from 49:3) is then juxtaposed. But historically, this alternative is skewed and clarifies neither the Jewish nor the New Testament position. The Servant is understood messianically in early Jewish texts such as the *Aramaic Apocryphon of Levi* (4Q540-541),[43] the *Aramaic Testament of Jacob* (4Q537),[44] *1 Enoch* 38:2; 46:4; 62:3, and then later in the *Targum of Isaiah* 53. He is thus viewed as priest, righteous man, son of man, or God's chosen one, but never without reference to the people of God. The Servant is the "prince" (נשׂיא) appointed by God who rules over God's people and, in so doing, simultaneously represents them before God.

Matters are no different in the New Testament. Jesus in his messianic mission as Son of God and Son of Man always saw himself as belonging to the end-time Israel. He founded the circle of the Twelve to gather up and represent the end-time people of the twelve tribes (cf. Mark 3:14-19; Luke 12:32; 22:28-30). He gathered the Twelve around himself as representatives of this people at the Last (Passover) Supper in order to give "the many" a share in his atoning death (cf. Luke 21:14-16). He took the way of sacrifice in order to effect a "substitution of existence" *(Existenzstellvertretung)* for Israel according to God's will, and it is

---

43. For the texts of 4Q540-541 and a French translation see Puech in DJD 31:213-56. For the same texts with an English translation see *DSSSE* 2:1078-81; cf. Vermes, *The Complete Dead Sea Scrolls in English,* 526-27. Further on these texts see §7 in M. Hengel's essay in the present volume.

44. See DJD 31:171-90; *DSSSE* 2:1075-76; Vermes, *Complete Dead Sea Scrolls,* 526.

no accident that when Jesus publicly confessed himself to be the Messiah, he was already on the way to his death (cf. Mark 14:61-62 par.). Early Christianity's confession of the Χριστός whose death and resurrection become soteriologically transparent from Isaiah 53 was likewise about the Son of God who leads the people of God, has this people as his "body," and represents the members of his body before God in prayer. One can call this understanding "individual" only to the extent that one simultaneously takes up the collective aspect and refuses to play them off against each other.

When matters are seen in this way, it becomes clear that in their interpretation of Isaiah 53, Jesus and early Christianity by no means robbed Israel of the Isaiah texts first addressed to it. But historically speaking, they did irrevocably confront Israel with the question of whether and how the Deuteroisaianic statements about the Servant can be interpreted more appropriately than they have been in the New Testament. By the same token the Old Testament, Jewish interpretive tradition confronts New Testament scholars with the responsibility of not glossing over the biblical and early Jewish traditions in their interpretation of the relevant texts, but of taking them fully into account in their discourse about Jesus as the Suffering Servant.

The Fourth Servant Song
in the New Testament Letters

Otfried Hofius

For Hans-Jürgen Hermisson on his 60th birthday

Summary

A nuanced view of the various ways in which one person may be said to *take another's place* is essential to understanding the reception and development of Isaiah 53 in the New Testament. In the original passage the Servant has taken the place of the speakers or onlookers in the "we" sections. They are in effect outside or *excluded from* the Servant's fate: "*he* has borne our infirmities and carried our diseases" (v. 4); "*he* shall bear their iniquities" (v. 11); "*he* bore the sin of many" (v. 12). Substitution and transference of guilt have therefore occurred — a taking of another's place that exempts or *excludes* the other party (hence "exclusive place-taking" in the recent German parlance). However, while such notions from Isaiah 53 may have been applied to Jesus without much reflection by those responsible for some of Christianity's earliest formulaic sayings, the writers of the New Testament letters, who preserve these sayings, are more conscious of the need to interpret them. Christ always takes the place of others in a way that still *includes* them as persons, thus affecting their very being. Sins are not here viewed as detached or detachable from persons. This "inclusive" understanding of *place-taking* in the New Testament provides the pattern into which the authors integrate Isaiah 53, thereby placing it in a new light.

This essay was originally a main paper delivered at the 47th meeting of the Society for New Testament Studies in Madrid on July 29, 1992 in the Aula Magna of the El Escorial monastery. It first appeared in German as "Das vierte Gottesknechtslied in den Briefen des Neuen Testamentes," *NTS* 39 (1993): 414-37.

The Christological and soteriological statements of the New Testament letters contain multiple clear references to the fourth Servant Song of Second Isaiah, chapters 52:13–53:12.[1] My aim in making these references the topic of the following reflections is not simply to convey the statistics of passages that prove that the Servant Song has been applied to Jesus. Nor is it to make a philological decision as to whether the respective New Testament texts owe their wording to the Hebrew of Isaiah 53, to the Septuagint or some other Greek version, or even to an Aramaic Targum. My interest lies rather in another direction, in the question, *How* is the fourth Servant Song taken up in the New Testament letters? In what *theological* sense and with what *theological* understanding has it been received?

I. Isaiah 53: "Exclusive Place-Taking" (Substitution)

I believe the Servant Song itself requires that we ask these questions. For it contains at its core a statement that poses very serious problems for theological reflection about truth claims. I have in mind the astonishing claim that one person has *taken the place* of others. This is expressed several times in the passage and should undoubtedly be seen as its dominant and central theme. The Servant's unheard of debasement comes to expression in the "we" address of Isaiah 53:2-6 (cf. vv. 4-6):

4 a α   Surely our sicknesses — *he* bore (נשא) them,
  a β   and our pains — *he* suffered (סבל)[2] them.
  b   Yet we considered him as one (justly) stricken,
         as one struck down by God and afflicted.
5 a   But he was pierced for our transgressions,
         and crushed for our iniquities.

---

1. From the literature I mention W. Zimmerli and J. Jeremias, "παῖς θεοῦ," *TWNT* 5:653-713 = *TDNT* 5:654-717; J. Jeremias, "Παῖς (θεοῦ) im Neuen Testament," in idem, *Abba: Studien zur neutestamentlichen Theologie und Zeitgeschichte* (1966), 191-216; H. W. Wolff, *Jesaja 53 im Urchristentum*, 3rd ed. (1952; reprinted with an introduction by P. Stuhlmacher, 4th ed., 1984); M. D. Hooker, *Jesus and the Servant: The Influence of the Servant Concept of Deutero-Isaiah in the New Testament* (1959); P. Grelot, *Les Poèmes du Serviteur: De la lecture critique à l'herméneutique*, LD 103 (1981), 138-89.

2. The verb סבל does not mean "to take upon oneself" but rather "to bear"; it is therefore a full synonym of the verb נשא that appears in v. 4aα. The sense of the second line, v. 4aβ, is misrepresented by common translation "he took them [sc. our pains] upon himself" or "he loaded them on himself." In v. 11bβ (see below) I translate סבל with "to bear," but in v. 4aβ I vary the translation of the same word, choosing "he suffered them [sc. our pains]" to avoid reusing "he bore them" from v. 4aα. The sense of v. 4aβ could also be captured like this: "and our pains — they lay (weighed) upon him."

b   The punishment[3] for our salvation lay upon him,[4]
      and by his wounds, healing came to us.

6 a   We all have strayed like sheep,
      each of us has turned to his own way.

b   But Yahweh has caused to fall on him
      the iniquity of us all.

What is formulated here as a *confession* is expressed once again as a *fact* in the Yahweh address that concludes the Song (Isa. 53:11b-12):

11 bα   The righteous one, my servant, makes righteous the many,
   bβ   for their iniquities — *he* bears (סבל) them.[5]

and

12 cα   Yet he bore (נשׂא) the sin of many
    cβ   and he interceded for the transgressors.[6]

In the sentences just quoted, the verbs נשׂא and סבל each appear twice as synonyms meaning "to bear."[7] Both are construed with terms or metaphors for sin.[8] In Isaiah 53:4aα and 12cα the expression נשׂא plus a term for sin[9] has a

---

3. מוסר, "discipline," "chastening," is here used in the sense of "punishment" (NRSV). Cf. Isa. 26:16; Jer. 30:14. See also the piel of the related verb יסר, used of penal discipline or chastisement in Ps. 6:2; 38:2; 39:12; Lev. 26:18, 28.

4. The meaning is better captured if we formulate, in dependence on Luther's translation, "Die Strafe lag auf ihm, auf daß wir Frieden hätten," "The punishment lay on him so that we might have peace" (Isa. 53:5b).

5. On the translation of the verb סבל see above, n. 2.

6. The expression פגע hiphil with ל of the person (= "to intercede for") in v. 12cβ does not mean intercession through prayer, but rather a substitution of one existence for another (*Existenzstellvertretung*). This involves substitutionarily taking over guilt and substitutionarily bearing suffering. See C. Westermann, *Das Buch Jesaja: Kapitel 40–66*, 5th ed., ATD 19 (1986), 217.

7. נשׂא in Isa. 53:4aα, 12cα; and סבל in 53:4aβ, 11bβ. The Vulgate conveys the synonymy appropriately through its choice of the verbs *ferre* for נשׂא and *portare* for סבל. See also the Peshitta.

8. Terms for sin: "to bear sin" = נשׂא + חטא (Isa. 53:12cα); "to bear iniquities" = סבל + עונת (53:11bβ). Metaphors for sin: "to bear sicknesses" = נשׂא + חלים (53:4aα); "to suffer pains" = סבל + מכאבים (53:4aβ).

9. On the expression נשׂא plus a term for sin and its possible meanings see W. Gesenius and F. Buhl, *Hebräisches und aramäisches Handwörterbuch über das Alte Testament*, 17th ed. (1915 [reprinted 1962]), 524 s.v. נשׂא qal 2b (נשׂא עון, etc.), "Schuld auf sich laden und tragen"; qal 3b (נשׂא עון), "die Schuld jem. wegnehmen, d.i. aufheben"; cf. the modified translation of an earlier

meaning well attested in the Old Testament: "to bear guilt," which more precisely means "to have to bear the punitive consequences of one's guilt."[10] The same meaning is to be presupposed for the synonymous expression סבל plus a term for sin in Isaiah 53:4aβ and 11bβ.[11] What is unusual in the fourth Servant Song is the *use* of the expression נשׂא with a term for sin and accordingly of its synonym סבל with a term for sin. Elsewhere in the Old Testament the expression with נשׂא usually appears only where persons must "bear" the penal consequences of their *own* guilt — that is, in cases where they must "do penance" for the evil that they themselves have committed and that now comes back upon them as a disaster.[12] Here in Isaiah 53 by contrast — and only here — there is talk of one person "bearing" *substitutionarily* (German: *stellvertretend*) the guilt of *other* persons; he thus suffers the penal consequences of *alien* guilt. That which according to the so-called "action-consequences connection" or *Tun-Ergehen-Zusammenhang* ought to have struck the guilty has now struck the innocent and righteous Servant.[13] His indescribable suffering, but above all his violent death, are to be explained from this perspective:

> 8 b He was cut off from the land of the living,[14]
>   stricken to death for the transgression of his people.[15]

---

edition of Gesenius in BDB 671 s.v. נשׂא qal 2b, "*bear* guilt, or punishment"; qal 3c, "*take away* guilt, iniquity, transgression." See further *HALOT* 2:726 s.v. נשׂא qal 15, "to bear (or share) guilt and punishment"; qal 17, "to carry away, to take"; Str-B 2:363-67; W. Zimmerli, "Die Eigenart der prophetischen Rede des Ezechiel: Ein Beitrag zum Problem an Hand von Ez. 14,1-11," in idem, *Gottes Offenbarung: Gesammelte Aufsätze zum Alten Testament*, TB 19 (1963), 148-77, esp. 157-61; K. Elliger, *Leviticus*, HAT I 4 (1966), 73 n. 38; 221-22 with n. 11; 229 n. 33; 259 n. 38; R. Knierim, *Die Hauptbegriffe für Sünde im Alten Testament*, 2nd ed. (1967), 50-54, 114-19, 193, 202-4, 217-22, 226; F. Stolz, "נשׂא," *THAT* 2:109-17, esp. 113-14 §§3f-g = *TLOT* 2:769-74, esp. 772 §§3f-g.

10. *TLOT* 2:772 §3f (punctuation modified). For references see below, n. 12.

11. Outside of Isaiah 53, the expression סבל plus a term for sin occurs only *once* in the whole Old Testament, in Lam. 5:7.

12. נשׂא עון: Lev. 5:17; 7:18; 17:16; 19:8; 20:17, 19; Num. 5:31; 14:34; 18:23; 30:16; Ezek. 14:10; 44:10, 12; נשׂא חטא: Lev. 20:20; 24:15; Num. 9:13; Ezek. 23:49 (cf. also 23:25). In other texts these and similar expressions indicate not substitutionary punishment but joint liability: Num. 14:33, וְנָשְׂאוּ אֶת־זְנוּתֵיכֶם ("they shall bear your whoredoms"); Ezek. 18:19-20 (נשׂא עון). The symbolic act of Ezek. 4:4-6 does not involve vicarious or substitutionary suffering, but the symbolic suffering of the prophet, intended to point out the guilt of the house of Judah; cf. G. Fohrer, *Ezechiel*, HAT 1/13 (1955), 30-31; W. Eichrodt, *Der Prophet Hesekiel: Kapitel 1–18*, ATD 22/1 (1959), 28-29.

13. On the Servant's innocence see Isa. 53:9b as well as the צדיק of 53:11b.

14. On this expression see Ps. 52:7; Jer. 11:19; cf. also Ps. 88:6.

15. In v. 8bβ the following text should be read: מפשע עמו נגע למות (cf. the *BHS* textual notes as well as the essay by H.-J. Hermisson in the present volume, "The Fourth Servant Song in the Context of Second Isaiah," nn. 29-30).

It is important to notice that *Yahweh* is ultimately the one at work behind the Servant's fate. *He "caused* to fall (hiphil) on him the iniquity of us all" (53:6b);[16] it was *his* "plan" — that is, *his* will — "to crush him" (53:10a). Yahweh himself thus redirects the due punishment from the guilty by discharging it upon the innocent Servant. At the same time it is true that the Servant submitted himself to Yahweh's plan in free obedience and therefore in deliberate self-surrender "gave up his life to death" (53:12b). The same state of affairs is described in the statement that the Servant "made his life an אָשָׁם" (53:10aβ).[17] The word אָשָׁם must not be translated as "guilt offering,"[18] nor is something like "cultic atonement" in view.[19] The word comes rather from the legal realm and denotes "the obligation, the duty, the liability, that results from incurring guilt."[20] Therefore אָשָׁם in Isaiah 53 acquires the sense "resolution of guilt," "discharge of guilt," "wiping out of guilt."[21] Verse 10aβ therefore says that the Servant made his life the means of "discharging" or "wiping out guilt." Accordingly the Servant takes the place of the guilty in such a way that he takes responsibility for their guilt with his own life.[22] He takes over the guilt of the many and therefore also the responsibility for this guilt; and he pays a debt that is not his

16. Another translation: "But Yahweh has *allowed* to fall on him the guilt of all of us" (K. Baltzer, *Deutero-Isaiah: A Commentary on Isaiah 40–55,* Hermeneia [2001], 392, italics added). This sentence must be interpreted against the background of the following statements: Num. 32:23: "be sure your sin will find you out"; Ps. 40:13: "my iniquities have overtaken me"; Exod. 32:34 LXX: ἐπάξω ἐπ' αὐτοὺς τὴν ἁμαρτίαν αὐτῶν, "I will bring upon them their sin."

17. Instead of the MT's תָּשִׂים, we should read יָשִׂים; cf. H. W. Wolff, *Jesaja 53 im Urchristentum,* 28 n. 61; G. Fohrer, "Stellvertretung und Schuldopfer in Jesaja 52,13–53,12 vor dem Hintergrund des Alten Testaments und des Alten Orient," in idem, *Studien zu alttestamentlichen Texten und Themen (1966-1972),* BZAW 155 (1981), 24-43, esp. 28, 41-42.

18. So, e.g., Fohrer, "Stellvertretung und Schuldopfer," 28, 32-33, 34-35, 41-42; D. Kellermann, "אָשָׁם," *TWAT* 1:463-72, esp. 470 §3 = *TDOT* 1:429-37, esp. 435 on Isa. 53:10.

19. For another view see e.g. W. Zimmerli, *Das Gesetz und die Propheten: Zum Verständnis des Alten Testamentes* (1963), 143. The thought of atonement is *not* present in the fourth Servant Song.

20. R. Knierim, "אָשָׁם, guilt," *TLOT* 1:193 §3c. Cf. the somewhat fuller definition in the German original, "Die aus einem Schuldiggewordensein resultierende Verpflichtung, die Schuldpflicht, Schuldverpflichtung, das Schuldverpflichtetsein oder die Haftpflicht" ("אָשָׁם, Schuldverpflichtung," *THAT* 1:254 §3c).

21. Cf. Knierim, "אָשָׁם," 255-56 §3e, "Schuldableistung" = *TLOT* 1:194 §3e, "resolution of guilt." In agreement with this Baltzer, *Deutero-Isaiah,* 393, translates Isa. 53:10, "If he gives his life to wipe out debt (guilt)," though he offers as an alternative the cultic interpretation rejected above, "as an offering for sin (guilt)."

22. The thought of vicariousness lies not in the term אָשָׁם as such nor in the expression שִׂים אָשָׁם נַפְשׁוֹ as such. This expression gains its vicarious character only in the overall context of Isaiah 53.

own by giving his life over to death. Through substituting his existence for that of others (German: *Existenzstellvertretung*), the Servant clears the guilty of guilt. He secures them the acquittal that makes possible their continued life (53:11b)[23] and therefore the "healing" of their broken relationship with God, the restoration of their שָׁלוֹם (53:5b).

The ideas of substitution or place-taking (German: *Stellvertretung*) sketched above are simply outrageous — the speakers[24] in our Servant Song realized that fully themselves. The opening section (52:13-15) speaks about things previously "never told" and "never heard" (v. 15b). But this is hardly to be limited to the Servant's unique fate: it relates directly to the substitution of existence that occurs in that fate.[25] Exegesis concerned with the truth of texts faces here the problem of whether the existential substitution described in the Song can be thought at all *possible*. Is it conceivable that one person should be able to suffer substitutionarily the punishment justly due others? Are guilt and punishment transferable between persons?[26] Certainly our legal thinking poses this question. In the legal realm personal guilt is nontransferable; the punishment to be borne by any given person can *under no circumstances* be substitutionarily taken over and atoned for by another person.[27] Yet biblical-theological considerations pose this question as well. Is

---

23. The servant shall "make righteous" (יַצְדִּיק) the many. On the hiphil of צדק in Isa. 53:11bα cf. P. Volz, *Jesaja II*, KAT 9 (1974 [1932]), 180: "The term must be understood in a forensic-religious sense. The Ebed effects not uprightness but acquittal, justification."

24. I have in mind the circle of pupils of the unknown prophet whom we call Second Isaiah. H.-J. Hermisson suspects that the fourth Servant Song was composed by a pupil of Second Isaiah who was intimately acquainted with his teacher's proclamation. See H.-J. Hermisson, "Der Lohn des Knechts," in Jörg Jeremias and L. Perlitt, eds., *Die Botschaft und die Boten, Festschrift für H. W. Wolff* (1981), 269-87, esp. 283.

25. That there are no real parallels to Isaiah 53 has been convincingly shown by Fohrer, "Stellvertretung und Schuldopfer," 35-39, 39-41.

26. On this problem see the section on "Christ for Us" in O. Weber, *Grundlagen der Dogmatik*, 2 vols. (1962), 2:232-36 = ET, *Foundations of Dogmatics*, trans. D. L. Guder, 2 vols. (1983), 2:203-7. ⟦(Tr.) The hard-to-translate term *Stellvertretung* is often rendered by Guder by the combination of two English terms, "'representation' or 'substitution.'" Still, this comprehensive concept remains inadequate according to Weber: "But what about 'substitution' or 'representation' (German: *Stellvertretung*) where guilt is atoned for? This is impossible as long as the individual isolation of man, the polarity of I to I, is not broken up. My guilt can be taken away only by One who, so to speak, frees me of my very self" (*Foundations of Dogmatics*, 206). Weber then proceeds to recommend the concept of *inklusive Stellvertretung* or "inclusive substitution," that is, "inclusive place-taking" in the present essay.⟧

27. On this problem from a *philosophical* standpoint see for example I. Kant, "Die Religion innerhalb der Grenzen der bloßen Vernunft" (1st ed., 1793; 2nd ed., 1794) in *Kants*

it theologically possible that *God* transfers the guilt of one person to another person or persons?

To begin with there are two Old Testament texts that, theologically speaking, raise this question. Exodus 32:30-34 reports Moses' intercession for God's people, who had forfeited their existence by setting up and worshiping the golden calf. Moses' intercession concludes with the following words: "And now, if you could only forgive their sin! But if not, blot me out of the book that you have written!" (Exod. 32:32). These words are not to be understood as Moses' offer to surrender his life vicariously in exchange for the life of the people. They are rather his declaration of the deepest solidarity with them: if Yahweh refuses to forgive the guilty, then the innocent one is prepared to suffer the same fate as they.[28] Yahweh's answer is highly significant: "Only the one who has sinned against me will I blot out of my book" (v. 33). The same notion that only the guilty and not the innocent may be punished is emphasized in the second relevant text, a saying of Yahweh from Ezekiel 18:

> Only the person who sins shall die. A son shall not bear the guilt of his father, and a father shall not bear the guilt of his son. The righteousness of the righteous shall be upon him (exclusively), and the godlessness of the godless shall be upon him (exclusively). (Ezekiel 18:20)

The two texts just cited emphatically exclude the possibility that an innocent party could be held responsible for guilt *together with* the guilty party.[29] How much more, then, must we exclude from the *interpersonal* realm

---

gesammelte Schriften, ed. Königlich Preußischen Akademie der Wissenschaften, vol. 6 (1907), 72 = ET, "Religion within the Boundaries of Mere Reason," in Kant, *Religion and Rational Theology,* trans. and ed. A. W. Wood and G. Di Giovanni (1996), 113 (at 6:72): "Moreover, so far as we can judge by our reason's standards of right, this original debt, or at any rate the debt that precedes whatever good a human being may ever do (this, and no more, is what we understood by *radical* evil; cf. the first Section), cannot be erased by somebody else. For it is not a *transmissible* liability which can be made over to somebody else, in the manner of a financial debt (where it is all the same to the creditor whether the debtor himself pays up, or somebody else for him), but the *most personal* of all liabilities, namely a debt of sins which only the culprit, not the innocent, can bear, however magnanimous the innocent might be in wanting to take the debt upon himself for the other." See also n. 6 in B. Janowski's essay in this volume.

28. Cf. J. J. Stamm, *Erlösen und Vergeben im Alten Testament: Eine begriffsgeschichtliche Untersuchung* (1940), 60; B. Janowski, *Sühne als Heilsgeschehen: Studien zur Sühnetheologie der Priesterschrift und zur Wurzel KPR im Alten Orient und im Alten Testament,* WMANT 55 (1982), 143-44.

29. Cf. also Jer. 31:30: "But everyone will die (only) for his own iniquity."

a *substitutionary* נשׂא עון or "bearing of sin" in which the guilty party himself goes away scot-free. The logic becomes even more compelling when we compare the understanding of sin behind the two texts cited above with that of the fourth Servant Song. The idea of substitution or place-taking evident in Isaiah 53 could be described as "one party taking the place of another in such a way that the guilty party is *excluded* from that obligation or fate." For convenience we may term this "*exclusive* place-taking" (German: "*exkludierende* Stellvertretung"). This concept presupposes a relationship with God that is already intact *in itself:* it can be damaged, but after it is damaged it can also be restored. Guilt and sin are thus essentially viewed from the perspective of *deeds* and *doing,* and in keeping with the concept of the action-consequences connection they are understood as something disastrous that necessarily comes back upon the doer. As such guilt and sin are indeed a life-threatening "burden" to people, but this burden can nevertheless be detached and distanced from their own persons. That is why it can be thought and said that the Servant takes away from the guilty what burdens them. "Exclusive place-taking" in the sense we have been describing can no longer be contemplated, however, in cases where deeper insight has been gained into the essence of sin and thus into the essence of being a sinner. Such insight, which may already lie behind the two texts Exodus 32:30-34 and Ezekiel 18:20, is also encountered in Israel's great prophets[30] — including Second Isaiah![31] — and then especially impressively in Psalm 51. This may serve as our leading example. The one praying this Psalm "knows that one's being in its basic relationship to God is under the dominance of sin":[32]

> Surely I was born in guilt;
> I was in sin when my mother conceived me. (Psalm 51:5 [MT 51:7])

30. See O. Hofius, "'Rechtfertigung des Gottlosen' als Thema biblischer Theologie," in idem, *Paulusstudien,* WUNT 51, 2nd ed. (1994), 121-47, 133-42.

31. I need only point to Isa. 48:8 and 43:22-26. One cannot avoid the impression that sin in its essence is seen more deeply by Second Isaiah himself than by his circle of pupils. To this corresponds what Isa. 43:22-25 (cf. 44:22) says about "wiping out" or "blotting out" sin: The one who steps in between God and his people is not a third party, who must bear sin vicariously, but God himself, who takes the place of guilty Israel. On this see the profound meditation on Isa. 43:22-26 by H. J. Iwand, *Predigt-Meditationen,* vol. 1 (1963), 380-85. Iwand impressively traces the lines that lead from *this* text to the New Testament's testimony about the vicariously atoning act of God in Christ's death on the cross.

32. H. Gese, "Die Herkunft des Herrenmahls," in idem, *Zur biblischen Theologie: Alttestamentliche Vorträge,* 3rd ed., BEvT 78 (1989 [1977]), 107-27, esp. 120 = ET, "The Origin of the Lord's Supper," in *Essays on Biblical Theology,* trans. K. Crim (1981), 117-40, esp. 132.

These words are enough for us to recognize that the one praying here understands sin as *"personal sin."*[33] "Personal sin" means that sin is not "something" *about* a person. It is not simply or primarily deeds and actions, not merely misbehavior or failure — in short, it is not a quantity that can be detached from persons themselves. Sin reaches rather into the *center of a person*. As a corruption that marks out and permeates humanity from the start, sin conditions the human constitution, the fundamental direction of human existence.[34] If it is true that sin forms no part of the structure of human beings as originally created and therefore in no sense constitutes the essence of humanity, it is just as true that sin completely dominates and conditions humanity. That sin thus understood could simply be taken away from a person would be absolutely unthinkable for the one praying Psalm 51. What is thinkable — and therefore requested in the Psalm — is only a comprehensive "cleansing" from sin through the miracle of a complete new creation. The only conceivable solution is "removal" of sin's *reality* itself. I cite verses 1-2 and 10 (MT 3-4, 12):

1 Be gracious to me, O God,
>   according to your steadfast love;
> according to your abundant mercy
>   blot out my transgressions.
2 Wash me thoroughly from my iniquity,
>   and cleanse me from my sin.[35]
10 Create in me a clean heart, O God,
>   and put a new and right spirit within me.

God the creator must himself step in and intercede for the sinner so that he or she becomes a "new creature" and *in this way* becomes free from his or her sin. The psalm's insight into the essence of sin and of being a sinner is confirmed most emphatically in the New Testament. Paul and John, the authors of Colossians and Ephesians, and also the second Evangelist and the author of Hebrews know of the *total* and *radical* fallenness of all humanity. They know sin only in its strict sense as "personal sin" and therefore as something that marks

---

33. *"Person-Sünde."* On the term and its meaning see Weber, *Grundlagen der Dogmatik,* 1:654 = ET, *Foundations of Dogmatics,* 1:592: "Sin is 'personal sin.' It is not 'something' about man, neither a defect nor an attribute nor an act performed by man. It is the comprehensive qualification of his being, in that it defines his direction."

34. Cf. H.-J. Kraus, *Psalmen 1,* 5th ed., BKAT XV/1 (1978), 544, 548.

35. See further Ps. 51:9 (ET v. 7), "Purge me with hyssop, and I shall be clean; wash me, and I shall be whiter than snow."

the *being* of *every* person. From this perspective it must be acknowledged that sin is no more removable or transferable than death is.[36] In the situation of sin, as in the situation of death, people are "unrepresentable." Just as it is impossible for people to die the death of others, so it is impossible for them, being sinners *themselves,* to make the sin of others their own. When this is acknowledged it also forces a conclusion about the fourth Servant Song. What this song says about the Servant's substitutionary death is theologically incomprehensible as it stands and as it is meant. This holds independently of the answer to the heavily contested question, *Who* is meant by "the servant" according to the Old Testament text? Whether it deals with the prophet Second Isaiah himself, or collectively with faithful Israel, or with a future messianic figure, in any case we must conclude: being freed up from sin and guilt through *human* substitution is theologically simply unthinkable![37]

II. The New Testament: "Inclusive Place-Taking"

When we now turn to the reception of the fourth Servant Song in the New Testament, we encounter a highly remarkable state of affairs. We must reckon with the possibility that in some of the early *traditional formulas* that may be reconstructed from the New Testament letters, certain of the song's statements were at first applied to Jesus in a relatively unreflected way. *The authors of the letters themselves,* by contrast, proceed in a thoroughly reflected way when referring to Isaiah 53. They did not simply take up the song or certain of its sayings and apply it to Jesus. Rather, in receiving the Old Testament text Christologically, they simultaneously set it in a completely new light. This happened as the Servant Song was integrated into a new view of the Christ event that sees it as an event

36. Cf. H. J. Iwand, *Gesetz und Evangelium,* Nachgelassene Werke 4 (1964), 100-110. Iwand rightly declares: "Everyone must die his own death, everyone knows his sin as his own, as non-transferable" (p. 101).

37. One may indeed question whether this full-blown concept of substitution has made its way into the Septuagint version and the rendering of the Targum. According to the Septuagint, the Servant's vicarious action does *not* prevent the many from making their *own* sin offering: ἐὰν δῶτε περὶ ἁμαρτίας, ἡ ψυχὴ ὑμῶν ὄψεται σπέρμα μακρόβιον, "If you (plural) give a sin offering, your soul shall see a long-lived seed" (Isa. 53:10 LXX). The Targum interprets the expressions נשא or סבל plus a term for sin to apply to the *intercession* of the Servant (i.e., the Messiah), which effects God's forgiveness only for those who turn from sin to obedience to the Torah: cf. *Tg. Isa.* 53:4-6, 11-12: "he will beseech concerning our sins and our iniquities for his sake will be forgiven" (v. 4); "he subjected rebels to the law; yet he will beseech concerning the sins of many, and to the rebels it shall be forgiven for him" (v. 12) (translation according to B. D. Chilton, *The Isaiah Targum,* ArBib 11 [1987], 104-5).

of "*inclusive* place-taking" (German: *inkludierende Stellvertretung*). Christ takes the place of sinners in such a way that he does not displace them (as in the substitutionary model) but rather encompasses them as *persons* and affects them in their very being.[38]

The Christ event, understood as an event of "inclusive place-taking," involves four essential aspects whose elements are sketched below.

1. Fundamental and decisive for this view as a whole is the conviction that in Jesus Christ, not a man but *God himself* has interceded for sinners. The man Jesus of Nazareth, whose genuine, complete, and individual humanity the New Testament authors presuppose, is according to this conviction not a "purus homo" — that is, not a man in the sense that he is in origin and being "one of us." He is in his origin and being rather "qualitatively other" than all other human beings;[39] he is the "Son of God," who belongs completely on the side of God, "*one* with God the Father and therefore *himself God*."[40] As this eternal and preexistent Son of God he has, in the miracle of his incarnation, *stepped over* to the side of humanity and thus has *become* "one of us." In Christ's being a *divine* person in this sense stands or falls the saving significance of his work. For if he were, like the Servant of Second Isaiah (cf. Isa. 42:1-4), one called out of the people's midst and selected for a special work, then the same thing must apply to him that held true of the Servant: in the situation of sin there neither is nor can be any *human* way of taking another's place. But because Christ is the preexistent and incarnate Son of God, *he* is able to take our place "where no other person can take our place."[41]

2. Inextricably bound up with this idea is another: the existential taking of another's place that Christ exercises is not to be separated from his human existence as such and thus from his person. In contrast to the Servant of Isaiah 53, he does not assume a certain task only within the bounds of history. Rather, his vicarious death for sinners is the meaning and goal of his coming into the world and of his being in the world. It is enough to recall here the sending formulas of Romans 8:3; Galatians 4:4; and 1 John 4:9-10. These formulas say that

---

38. [[(Tr.) The English translation here draws upon the language of K.-H. Menke, *Stellvertretung: Schlüsselbegriff christlichen Lebens und theologische Grundkategorie* (1991), 17, to fill out the definition of "Stellvertretung" or "place-taking." For further explanation of Professor Hofius's understanding of "inclusive place-taking," see D. P. Bailey, "Concepts of *Stellvertretung* in the Interpretation of Isaiah 53," in W. H. Bellinger and W. R. Farmer, eds., *Jesus and the Suffering Servant: Isaiah 53 and Christian Origins* (1998), 223-50, esp. 241.]]

39. K. Barth, *Die kirchliche Dogmatik IV: Die Lehre von der Versöhnung I* (1953), 174; cf. 176-77 = ET, *Church Dogmatics* IV/1:160: "qualitatively different from all other men"; cf. 161-62.

40. Barth, *Die kirchliche Dogmatik* IV/1:186 = *Church Dogmatics* IV/1:170.

41. Iwand, *Gesetz und Evangelium*, 101.

Christ's "whole existence on earth is a vicarious existence," that "his whole life from first to last is characterized by the 'for you.'"[42]

3. The relationship between God and Christ by no means took the same form that is presented as existing between God and the Servant in Isaiah 53. Whereas God there deals with the Servant and *by means of* him, such that the Servant appears as his tool, God's dealings here are *in* Christ as the one who himself is the saving "praesentia Dei." If God according to Isaiah 53 makes the sin of the many the Servant's problem, then God in Christ makes the sin of all *his own* problem. To be sure, the fourth Servant Song knows how to talk about a unity of action between God and his Servant, but nevertheless it differentiates very clearly between the activity of God and that of the Servant. In the understanding of the Christ event, on the other hand, the exclusive "solus Deus" is identical with the exclusive "solus Christus," as is demonstrated, for example, by the alternating of God and Christ as the subject of many otherwise identical soteriological statements.[43]

4. Jesus' death in our place is an event of atonement in the sense that has recently come to be associated with the expression "sanctifying atonement."[44] What is important here is not the cultic aspect as such, but rather the *truth* that is expressed by means of cultic terms and concepts. Christ has not simply come alongside the sinner in order to take away something — namely, guilt and sin; he has rather become identical with the sinner,[45] in order through the surrender of his life to lead sinners into union with God and thus to open to them fellowship with God for the first time. Christ thus dies not only "in place of" *(anstelle)* the sinner; he dies "for" him in such a way that his death is as such the sinner's death and his resurrection is as such the sinner's "coming to God."[46] Therefore no restitution takes place here, but rather new creation — not the restoration of an integral condition that once existed, but rather the

42. Iwand, *Gesetz und Evangelium,* 102.

43. This can be illustrated from Paul: God delivers his Son to death (Rom. 4:25; 8:32), and the Son delivers himself up to death (Gal. 1:4; 2:20). God's delivering up of the Son is grounded in God's "love" (Rom. 5:5; cf. 8:39) just as it is in Christ's love (Gal. 2:20; cf. Rom. 8:35). The vicarious death of God's Son demonstrates both the "grace" of God (Rom. 3:24; 5:15) and the "grace" of Christ (2 Cor. 8:9).

44. On the terminology and subject matter of "sanctifying atonement" see H. Gese, "Die Sühne," in *Zur biblischen Theologie,* 85-106 = ET, "The Atonement," in *Essays on Biblical Theology* (1981), 93-116; O. Hofius, "Sühne und Versöhnung: Zum paulinischen Verständnis des Kreuzestodes Jesu," in idem, *Paulusstudien,* 33-49.

45. See especially 2 Cor. 5:21 and Gal. 3:13.

46. See 2 Cor. 5:14b: "one died for all, therefore all died." [[(Tr.) The language about the atonement as "a coming to God," "ein Zu-Gott-Kommen," goes back to Gese, "Die Sühne," 104 = ET, "The Atonement," 114. See below n. 98.]]

constituting of wholeness in a *new* being that the sinner never before possessed.[47]

As these points show, what is at issue in "inclusive place-taking" is the fundamental recognition that only God the creator is able to free sinners from their sin; he does this by making sin and indeed sinful people themselves his own problem in all seriousness. "Inclusive place-taking" is not human but *divine* place-taking. The letter to Diognetus expresses this well when it declares in view of Christ's death (9:2): "God took our sins upon himself" (αὐτὸς τὰς ἡμετέρας ἁμαρτίας ἀνεδέξατο).[48] The Christological and soteriological statements that speak of inclusive, *divine* place-taking in *this* sense are the decisive ones in the New Testament. They provide the framework into which the fourth Servant Song's statements about one person's taking the place of others have been integrated, as I shall argue below.

III. Paul's Letters

I begin with the letters of the Apostle Paul. That Paul found in the fourth Servant Song the message of the crucified and risen Christ is one of the conclusions I think we can safely draw from Romans 10:14-17 and Romans 15:20-21. In the context of Romans 10:14-17, Paul explains that the rejection of the gospel by the overwhelming majority of Israel has already been prophetically announced in the complaint of Isaiah 53:1: "Lord, who has believed our message?" (Rom. 10:16). In Romans 15:20-21 Paul provides grounds for his practice of not preaching the gospel "where Christ has already been named" (v. 20) with an explicit reference to Isaiah 52:15: "Those who have never been told of him [i.e., the Servant] shall see [him], and those who have never heard [of him] shall come to know [him]" (v. 21). Accordingly the gospel of Jesus Christ is the message about the Servant who has been killed for the many and raised by God.[49] Now this

---

47. Adam was not ἐν Χριστῷ!

48. See also the whole context of Diognetus 9:2-5.

49. I consider the argument on this point by D.-A. Koch, *Die Schrift als Zeuge des Evangeliums: Untersuchungen zur Verwendung und zum Verständnis der Schrift bei Paulus*, BHT 69 (1986), 234-39, to be in no way compelling. Koch advances the thesis "that Paul does not yet know Isaiah 53 as a theologically fruitful text for interpreting the passion" (234). He finds confirmation for this not least in Rom. 15:3b, "The insults of those who insult you have fallen on me." About this verse he writes: "Paul wishes here to interpret the suffering of Christ with the help of a scriptural citation. Nevertheless, he appeals not to Isaiah 53 but to a depiction of suffering from one of the psalms of lament (Ps 68:10b LXX) — this despite the fact that after Rom 15:3a (cf. also 14:15: ὑπὲρ οὗ Χριστὸς ἀπέθανεν!) a citation formulating the vicarious character of the

crucified Servant is in Paul's view by no means a "purus homo"; he is the κύριος τῆς δόξης (1 Cor. 2:8) and the κύριος πάντων (Rom. 10:12).[50] He is the preexistent Son of God; as the preexistent one "in the form of God" and "equal to God," he became man in freely chosen *kenosis* in order to die a death on the cross for humanity.[51] The fundamental text 2 Corinthians 5:14-21 goes to great lengths to present this death on the cross as an event of "*inclusive* place-taking" and therefore as God's own deed that makes atonement and reconciliation. Other texts in Paul's letters either state this directly or presuppose it unambiguously.[52] But this subject, which I have discussed elsewhere,[53] is not the theme here. We need rather to ask how Paul received the fourth Servant Song's statements about taking another's place and then fitted them into his view of the Christ event. In this connection I have in mind above all the traditional formulas already available to the apostle. I will consider first only those two formulaic texts whose dependence on Isaiah 53 cannot be doubted: 1 Corinthians 15:3b-5 and Romans 4:25.[54]

---

death of Jesus from Isaiah 53 would have been much more appropriate" (234-35). But Koch has neglected to ask for what *reason* Paul cites precisely Ps. 68:10b, which he interprets as an utterance that the suffering Christ addressed to God. The answer is not difficult: Paul does not merely wish to express "the vicarious character of the death of Jesus," as Koch says, but also the fact that Christ died for God's "enemies" (Rom. 5:10) and took upon himself the fatal consequence of their "enmity against God" (Rom. 8:7). *This* could not have been said with a citation from Isaiah 53.

50. Both expressions are divine titles. On ὁ κύριος τῆς δόξης or "Lord of glory" see *1 Enoch* 22:14; 25:3, 7; 27:3, 5; 36:4; 40:3; 63:2; 75:3; 83:8; *Martyrdom and Ascension of Isaiah* 9:32; *Apocalypse of Elijah* 1:3 (in *OTP* 1:735). On κύριος πάντων or "Lord of all" see Job 5:8 LXX; Esth. 4:17c; 1QapGen ar 20:13; but also the non-Jewish sources in BDAG 578 s.v. κύριος 2bγ (Pindar; Plutarch; *PGM*) as well as Iamblichus, *Vita Pythagorica* 137.

51. Phil. 2:6-8; Rom. 8:3; Gal. 4:4.

52. I mention only Rom. 3:22b-26; 5:6-10; 6:1-11; 7:4-6; 8:3-4; 1 Cor. 1:30; Gal. 2:19-20.

53. See my essay "Sühne und Versöhnung."

54. A reference to Isaiah 53 may also be present in the παρεδίδετο ("on the night when *he was betrayed*") of the Lord's Supper tradition in 1 Cor. 11:23b-25 (here v. 23b) as well as in the surrender formula of Rom. 8:32, with God as subject of παραδίδωμι ὑπέρ plus a term for persons: ὑπὲρ ἡμῶν πάντων παρέδωκεν αὐτόν, "[God] delivered him up for us all." On the other hand I am skeptical about a reference to Isaiah 53 in the self-surrender formulas with Christ as subject of παραδίδωμι (or δίδωμι) ἑαυτὸν ὑπέρ plus either a term for sins, as in Gal. 1:4, or more frequently a term for persons, as in Gal. 2:20; Eph. 5:2, 25; 1 Tim. 2:6; Titus 2:14. A reference to the idea of the self-surrender of one's life in the MT of Isa. 53:10aβ (שִׂים נַפְשׁוֹ, see above n. 17) is not necessarily excluded from these texts, but it cannot be conclusively proven. However, I do not see *any* reference to Isaiah 53 in the statement about Christ's intercession in Rom. 8:34.

1 Corinthians 15:3b-5

In 1 Corinthians 15:3b-5 Paul cites a four-member catechetical summary[55] which, according to his own statement (v. 3a), he had "received" from Church tradition:

ὅτι Χριστὸς ἀπέθανεν ὑπὲρ τῶν ἁμαρτιῶν ἡμῶν κατὰ τὰς γραφάς
καὶ ὅτι ἐτάφη
καὶ ὅτι ἐγήγερται τῇ ἡμέρᾳ τῇ τρίτῃ κατὰ τὰς γραφάς
καὶ ὅτι ὤφθη Κηφᾷ εἶτα τοῖς δώδεκα.

The controversial question of whether an original Aramaic version lies behind the Greek text can hardly be answered with certainty.[56] It is also impossible to come to a certain conclusion as to whether all four members of the summary go back to the fourth Servant Song — as I suspect they do — with the twofold κατὰ τὰς γραφάς thus pointing decisively to Isaiah 53.[57] On the other hand there can be no doubt that the statements in the first member about one person taking the place of others — Χριστὸς ἀπέθανεν ὑπὲρ τῶν ἁμαρτιῶν ἡμῶν κατὰ τὰς γραφάς — must be referred to Isaiah 53.[58] The reference to a *sin-*

---

55. On the *designation* of 1 Cor. 15:3b-5 as a "catechetical summary" see P. Stuhlmacher, *Das paulinische Evangelium I: Vorgeschichte*, FRLANT 95 (1968), 266-82. On the *demarcation* of this unit and its non-Pauline expressions see J. Jeremias, *Die Abendmahlsworte Jesu*, 4th ed. (1967), 95-96 = ET, *The Eucharistic Words of Jesus*, trans. N. Perrin (1966), 101-2; H. Conzelmann, *Der erste Brief an die Korinther*, 4th ed., KEK 5 (1969), 296-303. On the unit's *structure* see the important essay by F. Mussner, "Zur stilistischen und semantischen Struktur der Formel 1 Kor 15,3-5," in R. Schnackenburg et al., eds., *Die Kirche des Anfangs, Festschrift für H. Schürmann*, ETS 38 (1977 [reprinted 1978]), 405-15.

56. Cf. C. Wolff, *Der erste Brief des Paulus an die Korinther: Zweiter Teil: Auslegung der Kapitel 8–16*, THKNT 7/2 (1982), 156-57.

57. I believe that the following points of contact are evident between Isaiah 53 and the four members of the catechetical summary in 1 Cor. 15:3b-5:

I. ἀπέθανεν ὑπὲρ τῶν ἁμαρτιῶν ἡμῶν, "[Christ] died for our sins": Isa. 53:4a, 5, 6b, 8b, 11b, 12b-c.

II. ἐτάφη, "he was buried": Isa. 53:9a.

III. ἐγήγερται, "he was raised": Isa. 53:10b, 11a (on "seeing light" as a metaphor for "living" see below n. 68); also 52:13 (the Servant's exaltation).

IV. ὤφθη, "he appeared": Isa. 52:15b; 53:1 (the report about the victory won by the Servant and his unique exaltation).

58. C. Wolff, *1 Korinther II*, 160 rightly remarks: "Only this Old Testament passage deals with dying for others." It must furthermore be noted that the expression ὑπὲρ τῶν ἁμαρτιῶν ἡμῶν (1 Cor. 15:3b) represents a linguistic variation of διὰ τὰς ἁμαρτίας ἡμῶν in Isa. 53:5aβ (cf. n. 64).

gle Scripture passage thereby presupposed is by no means contradicted by the plural κατὰ τὰς γραφάς. As in the overwhelming number of cases in the New Testament,[59] so also in 1 Corinthians 15:3b and 4b, the plural denotes the Scripture as a whole,[60] so that the meaning "according to the Scripture" results from κατὰ τὰς γραφάς. And the fact that reference to the γραφαί can have in view a single Scripture passage is sufficiently illustrated by Mark 12:24 = Matthew 22:29 on the one hand, and by Matthew 21:42 on the other.[61]

But if there is a reference to Isaiah 53 in the sentence Χριστὸς ἀπέθανεν ὑπὲρ τῶν ἁμαρτιῶν ἡμῶν, then the words ὑπὲρ τῶν ἁμαρτιῶν ἡμῶν correspond to the expressions מעונתינו/מפשענו ("for our transgressions"/"for our iniquities") in Isaiah 53:5a MT or διὰ τὰς ἁμαρτίας ἡμῶν in Isaiah 53:5aβ LXX. Now if the statement about place-taking in 1 Corinthians 15:3 is understood in terms of these expressions, then the ὑπέρ must be interpreted causally and translated: "Christ died *for the sake of (because of)* our sins." Comparison with an Old Testament text whose Septuagint rendering also uses the expression ἀποθνῄσκειν ὑπὲρ τῶν ἁμαρτιῶν shows how this would have to be understood in the context of Isaiah 53. In 1 Kings (LXX 3 Kingdoms) 16:18-19 it is said about Zimri: ἀπέθανεν ὑπὲρ τῶν ἁμαρτιῶν αὐτοῦ, ὧν ἐποίησεν = "he died *for* the sins he had committed." In agreement with the Hebrew *Vorlage*,[62] these words depict Zimri's death as the penal consequence of his sins, and they thereby depict Zimri's sins as the reason and cause of his death. The sin-death connection thereby invoked is also the issue in the remaining Old Testament passages where the expression "to die for sin(s)" appears.[63] The figure ἀποθνῄσκειν ὑπὲρ τῶν ἁμαρτιῶν in the sense "to die for the sake of (because of) *one's own* sins"[64]

59. Mark 12:24; 14:49; Matt. 21:42; 22:29; Luke 24:32, 45; John 5:39; Acts 17:2, 11; 18:24, 28; Rom. 1:2; 15:4.

60. This corresponds to the usage in the rabbinic literature, where the *determinate* plural הכתובים can designate the Holy Scriptures as a whole, in which case it is synonymous with the determinate singular הכתוב; cf. W. Bacher, *Die exegetische Terminologie der jüdischen Traditionsliteratur*, 2 vols. (1899, 1905 [reprinted 1965]), 1:92; 2:94-95.

61. In the light of the quotation "I am the God of Abraham, the God of Isaac, and the God of Jacob" in Mark 12:26, the expression "the Scriptures" in Mark 12:24 most nearly refers to this particular scripture, Exod. 3:6 (cf. similarly Matt. 22:29, 32). Matthew 21:42 quotes a single passage, Ps. 118:22-23, as an example of what one reads "in the Scriptures." As a rabbinic example see, e.g., *Lev. Rab.* 9:9 on Lev. 7:12.

62. וימת על־חטאתיו אשר חטא (on the textual criticism see *BHS* at 1 Kings 16:18-19).

63. Num. 27:3; Josh. 22:20; Jer. 31:30; Ezek. 3:18-20; 18:17-18, 24, 26; 33:8-9, 13, 18; 2 Chron. 25:4.

64. On the causal sense of ὑπέρ with the genitive of a term for sin see also Ps. 38:12 LXX, ἐν ἐλεγμοῖς ὑπὲρ ἀνομίας ἐπαίδευσας ἄνθρωπον, "With rebukes *for* sin (i.e., *because of* sin) you chastened a man"; Diod. Sic. 10.21.2, ἡ ὑπὲρ τῶν ἁμαρτημάτων τιμωρία, "the punishment which

corresponds materially with the expression סבל/נשא with a term for sin in the sense "to have to carry the penal consequences of *one's own* guilt." Just as the Hebrew expression in Isaiah 53 is used to describe the *substitutionary* "bearing" of *alien* guilt, so also in 1 Corinthians 15:3b — read in the light of Isaiah 53! — there is the language of *substitutionary* death for the sake of *alien* sin.

Thus understood, the first line of the summary describes Christ's death as the penal consequence of "our" sins, and "our" sins as the reason and cause of his dying. Christ's death would thereby be interpreted as an instance of substitutionarily taking over guilt and punishment. Christ has taken the place of the guilty, who are liable to death because of their sin, and by surrendering his own life to death, he has freed them from the "burden" and thereby from the fatal consequences of their sin. Place-taking in this substitutionary sense — still understood completely along the lines of Isaiah 53 — *could* be what is meant within the framework of the *pre*-Pauline formula. *Paul himself,* by contrast, certainly did *not* have this understanding. Paul rather wanted the statement of 1 Corinthians 15:3b to be understood in terms of his conception of "inclusive place-taking." The meaning of the ὑπέρ is to be found in a theology of *atonement;* therefore the expression must be translated, "Christ died *to make atonement for* our sins."[65]

That Paul understood the statement about place-taking as an *atonement theology* in this sense is a conclusion that arises necessarily from the argumentation in 1 Corinthians 15:12-22. On the basis of the summary cited in verses 3b-5 and with clear recourse to these statements, Paul here explains that Christ's resurrection provides the basis for the resurrection of the dead and has this resurrection as its necessary consequence, so that it must be said conversely, "If there is no resurrection from the dead, then Christ has not been raised" (v. 13). Thus it says in the context of verses 12-19: "If the dead are not

---

is meted out *for* guilty acts" (LCL 4:89). This same causal sense of ὑπέρ with the genitive of a term for sin is found in the LXX with other expressions, including those involving διά with the accusative (so, e.g., Lev. 26:39; Num. 27:3; Isa. 64:6; Jer. 13:22; 2 Macc. 7:32 and the statements about vicarious suffering in Isa. 53:5a, 12c) and περί with the genitive (so 1 Kings 15:30; 16:13; Lam. 1:22; Tob. 3:5; 4 Macc. 11:3).

65. This use of ὑπέρ with genitive plus a term for sin conveying a theology of *atonement* for sins is also found elsewhere, e.g., Heb. 5:1; 7:27; 9:7; 10:12; see further *Barn.* 7:3-6; Ignatius, *Letter to the Smyrnaeans* 7:1; Polycarp, *Letter to the Philippians* 1:2 as well as LXX Mic. 6:7b; 1 Esdras 7:8; 9:20. The construction περί with genitive plus a term for sin is used in the same sense: 1 John 2:2; 4:10. The idea of *atonement* in these texts results from the context, not simply from the use of ὑπέρ or περί as such. As for Gal. 1:4, τοῦ δόντος ἑαυτὸν ὑπὲρ (var. περὶ) τῶν ἁμαρτιῶν ἡμῶν ("who gave himself for our sins"), *Paul* will have understood this admittedly traditional formula in terms of "inclusive place-taking"; cf. Gal. 2:19-20.

raised, then Christ has not been raised. But if Christ has not been raised . . .
you are still in your sins" (vv. 16-17). The plural "your sins" (v. 17), untypical
for Paul, shows that the Apostle is referring here explicitly to the summary.
The denial of the resurrection from the dead implies the denial of Christ's resurrection and thereby also the negation of the sentence Χριστὸς ἀπέθανεν
ὑπὲρ τῶν ἁμαρτιῶν ἡμῶν. This conclusion is compelling only when the summary is understood in terms of the idea of atonement — that is, when Christ's
death and resurrection, which are indissolubly connected, are grasped as "inclusive place-taking," as an event into which all who belong to Christ[66] have
been drawn from the start. According to verses 20-22, the risen Christ is the
ἀπαρχὴ τῶν κεκοιμημένων (v. 20). This means that in *his* resurrection as such,
the resurrection of the dead is settled decisively, so that the saying holds, "as in
Adam all die, so in Christ will all be made alive" (v. 22). Again, this statement
follows strictly from the summary only if the summary is interpreted in terms
of "inclusive place-taking." If, on the other hand, the summary were understood along the lines of Isaiah 53, the argumentation would be in no way con-
clusive. We may, then, confidently conclude that Paul interpreted afresh the
summary of 1 Corinthians 15:3b-5 and therefore also Isaiah 53 itself in terms of
the idea of *atonement*.

Romans 4:25

The same findings result from the traditional formula in Romans 4:25, where it
is said of Christ:

> παρεδόθη διὰ τὰ παραπτώματα ἡμῶν
> καὶ ἠγέρθη διὰ τὴν δικαίωσιν ἡμῶν.

This is a summary of the fourth Servant Song distilled to essentials. The
first line (παρεδόθη διὰ τὰ παραπτώματα ἡμῶν) is very closely related to Isaiah
53:12cβ LXX — διὰ τὰς ἁμαρτίας αὐτῶν παρεδόθη — but at the same time it
also recalls Isaiah 53:5a LXX: ἐτραυματίσθη διὰ τὰς ἀνομίας ἡμῶν καὶ
μεμαλάκισται διὰ τὰς ἁμαρτίας ἡμῶν. By contrast, the *second* line (ἠγέρθη διὰ
τὴν δικαίωσιν ἡμῶν) directs our attention to the *Hebrew* text of Isaiah 53:11: "After the anguish of his life he shall see light;[67] . . . the righteous one, my servant,

---

66. 1 Cor. 15:23, οἱ τοῦ Χριστοῦ, "those who are Christ's" or "those who belong to Christ";
cf. also the ἐν Χριστῷ of 1 Cor. 15:18-19.

67. The MT must be supplemented by the word "light" (אור) according to 1QIsa[a-b] and
the LXX (φῶς).

shall make many righteous."[68] The questions of whether the traditional formula goes back to an original Hebrew or Aramaic formula, and which textual form of the fourth Servant Song it is indebted to, can hardly be answered satisfactorily.[69] In terms of what the formula *says*, there are in principle two interpretive possibilities. If one reads the formula strictly from the perspective of the fourth Servant Song, then the διά in the first line must be taken to indicate the cause; the διά in the second line by contrast the end or purpose in view:

He was handed over [to death] *for the sake of/because of* our trespasses, and raised *for* our justification.

On this reading, the first line says that Christ in his death bore substitutionarily the penal consequences of our trespasses. The second line adds, fully in accordance with the sense of Isaiah 53:11, that the death of the Servant whom God has raised has given us a once-again intact relationship with God. I do not wish to exclude the possibility that the original meaning of the formula Paul has cited might be appropriately summarized in this way. Nevertheless, *Paul himself* understands the formula in terms of his concept of atonement, so that in accordance with his understanding, the lines must be translated:

He was handed over [to death] *to atone for* our trespasses,[70] and raised *for* our justification.

On this understanding the δικαίωσις mentioned in the second line is not — as in the pre-Pauline formula itself — simply the restoration of our relation-

---

68. The expression "see light" is a metaphor for "live"; see Ps. 36:10; 49:20; Job 3:16; 33:28-30 (cf. also Ps. 56:14). Therefore the statement in Isaiah 53:11aα could be interpreted as the granting of new life to the dead Servant and therefore as his resurrection from the dead.

69. The correspondence between ὃς παρεδόθη διὰ τὰ παραπτώματα ἡμῶν, "who was handed over for our trespasses," in Rom. 4:25 and אתמסר בעויתנא in *Tg. Isa.* 53:5, which is said not of the Servant but of the temple ("And he will build the sanctuary which was profaned for our sins, *handed over for our iniquities*), may be purely accidental. If the forms παρεδόθη and ἠγέρθη in Rom. 4:25 are both supposed to be divine passives, so that ἠγέρθη here is exceptionally the true passive "be raised (by God)" rather than the intransitive passive "rise," then the possibility of a Semitic *Vorlage* would be excluded from the start, for neither in Hebrew nor in Aramaic does the corresponding verb קום form a true passive meaning "be raised."

70. The in itself causal expression "*because of* our trespasses" (διά with accusative: διὰ τὰ παραπτώματα ἡμῶν) here acquires the meaning, "to atone *for* our trespasses." In statements about the saving significance of the death of Jesus, διά with the accusative can correspond to ὑπέρ with the genitive; cf. 1 Cor. 8:11 with Rom. 14:15, where a person "for whom" Christ died can be referred to as either δι' ὅν or ὑπὲρ οὗ.

ship with God. It is rather the δικαίωσις ζωῆς — the "justification that brings life" — of Romans 5:18. This is the justification through which the person reconciled with God is transferred into a new *being*, into the ἐν Χριστῷ εἶναι. There are good reasons, both in the broader and narrower contexts of Romans 4:25, for believing that Paul interpreted it in terms of atonement theology. As for the *broader* context, it is enough to recall that Romans 4 must be read in the same "key" as Romans 3:21-31 and the statement there developed about *atonement* (see vv. 22b-26).[71] And in the *narrower* context of Romans 4 itself, it must be remembered that the "justification of the ungodly" (v. 5) and the forgiveness of sins (vv. 7-8) are explicitly designated as miracles: *giving life to the dead* and *new creation* (v. 17).

If we draw conclusions at this point, the following must be said. In the citations of the traditional formulas in 1 Corinthians 15:3b-5 and Romans 4:25 there is indirect but nevertheless unmistakable reference to the fourth Servant Song. Because we do not know the original context of the two formulas, we cannot exclude the possibility that their view of the death of Jesus remained totally within the framework of the substitutionary thinking of Isaiah 53. But about the Pauline understanding of the two formulas there cannot be the slightest doubt. By integrating the traditional texts that had come down to him into his own theological conception, Paul reinterpreted the statements of the fourth Servant Song in essential ways.

Direct References

The same picture as above can be confirmed — though it can only be hinted at here — in cases where Paul makes *direct* reference to Isaiah 53. In Romans 5:15-19 he explains that the saving act of Jesus Christ, his vicarious death for the sinners and ungodly (Rom. 5:6, 8), brings "justification" to "many" — a saving acquittal that constitutes new being and brings life (vv. 16b, 17b, 18b, 19b).[72] The mention of "the many" (οἱ πολλοί) may be indebted to Isaiah 53; the words δίκαιοι κατασταθήσονται οἱ πολλοί (v. 19b) will be based on Isaiah 53:11b directly.[73] In

---

71. On the idea of atonement or "inclusive substitution" within the complex of Rom. 3:21–8:32 see also 5:6-11; 5:12-21; 6:1-11; and 8:3.

72. The δικαίωμα ("justification") of Rom. 5:16b is the antonym of κατάκριμα ("condemnation") in v. 16b and a synonym of δικαίωσις (also translated "justification") in v. 18b. The expressions δικαίωμα (v. 16b), δικαιοσύνη (v. 17b), δικαίωσις (v. 18b), and δίκαιος καθίστασθαι ("to be made righteous," v. 19b) all refer to the same subject matter.

73. Paul must have before him a text of Isa. 53:11b that departs from the LXX and agrees with the Hebrew.

noticing this, however, it must not be forgotten that the Adam-Christ typology in Romans 5:12-21 speaks of Christ's death as an event that *includes* "the many," so that the words δίκαιοι κατασταθήσονται οἱ πολλοί for Paul imply without a doubt the aspect of new creation. The same theological connections are fully evident in the fundamental text already mentioned above, 2 Corinthians 5:14-21. From the thesis of a "place-taking that includes others" in verse 14b (εἷς ὑπὲρ πάντων ἀπέθανεν, ἄρα οἱ πάντες ἀπέθανον), there follows the statement of new creation in verse 17:

> εἴ τις ἐν Χριστῷ, καινὴ κτίσις·
> τὰ ἀρχαῖα παρῆλθεν, ἰδοὺ γέγονεν καινά.

> If anyone is in Christ, there is a new creation:
> everything old has passed away; see, everything has become new!

Again, this statement is supported by the statements about atonement and reconciliation in verses 18-21, which conclude with a sentence that takes up Isaiah 53 but at the same time transcends it in an amazing way (v. 21):[74]

> τὸν μὴ γνόντα ἁμαρτίαν ὑπὲρ ἡμῶν ἁμαρτίαν ἐποίησεν,
> ἵνα ἡμεῖς γενώμεθα δικαιοσύνη θεοῦ ἐν αὐτῷ.[75]

> For our sake he made him to be sin who knew no sin,
> so that in him we might become the righteousness of God.

This sentence describes most impressively the miracle of the *new creation* accomplished in Christ's death. The sinful person who is identified with the crucified one has become "in Christ" a "new creation" — a person qualified in his or her being by God's saving "righteousness." That Paul thereby says something *more* and indeed something *different* from what the fourth Servant Song had given him is obvious.

---

74. In my view this bold statement in 2 Cor. 5:17 is not a tradition Paul inherited but, like Gal. 3:13, is one that he formulated. What J. A. Bengel, *Gnomon Novi Testamenti*, 3rd ed., ed. P. Steudel (1773; reprinted 1887) has said about Gal. 3:13 also applies to 2 Cor. 5:17: "Quis auderet sine blasphemiae metu sic loqui, nisi apostolus praeiret?" = "Who would dare without the fear of blasphemy so to speak, if the apostle had not led the way?" (translated by C. T. Lewis and M. R. Vincent, Bengel's *Gnomon of the New Testament*, 2 vols. [1860], 2:355 at Gal. 3:13).

75. The relationships between 2 Cor. 5:21 and Isaiah 53 are as follows: τὸν μὴ γνόντα ἁμαρτίαν = ἀνομίαν οὐκ ἐποίησεν (Isa. 53:9b LXX); ὑπὲρ ἡμῶν ἁμαρτίαν ἐποίησεν = κύριος παρέδωκεν αὐτὸν ταῖς ἁμαρτίαις ἡμῶν (Isa. 53:6b LXX); ἵνα ἡμεῖς γενώμεθα δικαιοσύνη θεοῦ ἐν αὐτῷ = MT, "The righteous one, my servant, shall make many righteous" (Isa. 53:11b, see n. 73).

IV. Non-Pauline Letters

In the last stage of our investigation we must ask about the reception of the fourth Servant Song in the non-Pauline letters of the New Testament. Only two letters need be considered: Hebrews and 1 Peter.[76]

Hebrews

The only reference to the fourth Servant Song in the letter to the Hebrews is found in 9:28:

ὁ Χριστὸς ἅπαξ προσενεχθεὶς εἰς τὸ πολλῶν ἀνενεγκεῖν ἁμαρτίας . . .

Christ, having been offered once to bear the sins of many . . .

In view of the clause εἰς τὸ πολλῶν ἀνενεγκεῖν ἁμαρτίας, there can be no doubt that Isaiah 53:12cα LXX, αὐτὸς ἁμαρτίας πολλῶν ἀνήνεγκεν, has been taken up here.[77] In accordance with the LXX text, the verb ἀναφέρειν has the meaning "to bear"; it can hardly have the meaning "to take away."[78] This formulation makes it sound as though Hebrews 9:28 is saying, fully in keeping with the sense of Isaiah 53, that Christ bore the penal consequences of sin substitutionarily for the many.[79] However, such an understanding of the clause taken from Isaiah 53 is excluded by the preceding and more important statement that Christ "was offered (as a sacrifice)." The sacrificial terminology (προσενεχθείς, from προσφέρεσθαι[80]) shows clearly enough that the expression from Isaiah 53:12cα LXX has been incorporated into the big picture of Hebrews

---

76. In my view there is *no* direct reference to Isaiah 53 in 1 John 3:5: ἐκεῖνος (i.e., ὁ υἱὸς τοῦ θεοῦ) ἐφανερώθη, ἵνα τὰς ἁμαρτίας ἄρῃ, καὶ ἁμαρτία ἐν αὐτῷ οὐκ ἔστιν, "he was revealed to take away sins, and in him there is no sin."

77. Cf. the similar uses of φέρω or ἀναφέρω plus a term for sin in Isa. 53:11bβ LXX — καὶ τὰς ἁμαρτίας αὐτῶν αὐτὸς ἀνοίσει — and 53:4aα LXX — οὗτος τὰς ἁμαρτίας ἡμῶν φέρει.

78. Ἀναφέρειν actually means to "take upon oneself" or "lay upon oneself" (cf. BDAG 75 s.v. ἀναφέρω 4, Heb. 9:28, "he *assumed* the sins of the many") and could indeed be used in this sense in LXX Isa. 53:11bβ and 12cα. But since it is the translation of סבל or נשׂא, we may accept the meaning "bear," as in Num. 14:33 LXX, ἀνοίσουσιν τὴν πορνείαν ὑμῶν, "they shall *bear* your fornication."

79. The interpretation of Heb. 9:28 as penal substitution is represented for example by E. Riggenbach, *Der Brief an die Hebräer*, 3rd ed., KNT 14 (1922; reprinted 1987), 289-92.

80. On προσφέρειν, to "offer" a sacrifice, cf. Heb. 7:27; 8:3; 9:14, 25; 10:12; see also προσφορά, "offering," Heb. 10:10, 14.

— that is, into the overall teaching about the self-sacrifice of Christ the high priest. The author understands this self-sacrifice as an event of atonement that sets aside the reality of sin and grants access to God.[81] But Jesus' death on the cross effected "purification of sins"[82] precisely because Jesus is not a "*purus homo*," but rather the preexistent divine "Son"[83] who *became* human in incredible condescension in order to die as such for the people of God.[84]

1 Peter

1 Peter does not use the term "Son of God" for Jesus and also never speaks explicitly about the preexistence and incarnation of Christ. But the idea of preexistence is presupposed in 1 Peter 1:10-11 when the Spirit of *Christ* is said to have "testified in advance" to the Old Testament prophets regarding "the sufferings of Christ and the subsequent glory."[85] That the writer of the letter is thinking here primarily of the fourth Servant Song is made clear by the texts 2:21-25 and 3:18. The statements in 1 Peter 2:21-25, in part clearly recognizable as well-formed traditional Christological material,[86] make multiple reference to statements from the Septuagint version of the fourth Servant Song, as the following notes show:[87]

21b Χριστὸς ἔπαθεν ὑπὲρ ὑμῶν
    ὑμῖν ὑπολιμπάνων ὑπογραμμὸν
    ἵνα ἐπακολουθήσητε τοῖς ἴχνεσιν αὐτοῦ,
22   ὃς ἁμαρτίαν *οὐκ ἐποίησεν*

---

81. On this see Heb. 2:10-18; 5:7-10; 8:1–10:18; 10:19-22.

82. See Heb. 1:3c: καθαρισμὸν τῶν ἁμαρτιῶν ποιησάμενος, "When he had made purification of sins."

83. See Heb. 1:1-14 with its fundamental divine titles or prerogatives for the Son in vv. 3, 8, 10: "He is the *reflection* of God's *glory* (ἀπαύγασμα τῆς δόξης) and the exact *imprint* of God's very *being* (χαρακτὴρ τῆς ὑποστάσεως αὐτοῦ)" (v. 3); "But of the *Son* he says, 'Your throne, O God (ὁ θεός), is forever and ever'" (v. 8); "In the beginning, *Lord,* you founded the earth," σὺ κατ' ἀρχάς, κύριε, τὴν γῆν ἐθεμελίωσας — said of the Son (v. 10).

84. See Heb. 2:5-18; 5:5-10; 10:5-10.

85. 1 Pet. 1:20 also presupposes the preexistence of Christ. That Christ belongs on the side of *God* is shown for example by the fact that he is the object of faith (1 Pet. 1:8; 2:6-7), just as is God himself (1:21).

86. See the commentaries on this passage as well as R. Deichgräber, *Gotteshymnus und Christushymnus in der frühen Christenheit: Untersuchungen zu Form, Sprache und Stil der frühchristlichen Hymnen,* SUNT 5 (1967), 140-43.

87. I reproduce the text in the κατὰ-κῶλα arrangement of Nestle/Aland, 26th ed.

οὐδὲ εὑρέθη δόλος ἐν τῷ στόματι αὐτοῦ,[88]

23 ὃς λοιδορούμενος οὐκ ἀντελοιδόρει
πάσχων οὐκ ἠπείλει,[89]
παρεδίδου δὲ τῷ κρίνοντι δικαίως·

24 ὃς τὰς ἁμαρτίας ἡμῶν αὐτὸς ἀνήνεγκεν[90]
ἐν τῷ σώματι αὐτοῦ ἐπὶ τὸ ξύλον,
ἵνα ταῖς ἁμαρτίαις ἀπογενόμενοι
τῇ δικαιοσύνῃ ζήσωμεν,
οὗ τῷ μώλωπι ἰάθητε.[91]

25 ἦτε γὰρ ὡς πρόβατα πλανώμενοι,[92]
ἀλλὰ ἐπεστράφητε νῦν ἐπὶ τὸν ποιμένα
καὶ ἐπίσκοπον τῶν ψυχῶν ὑμῶν.

Despite the constant reference to Isaiah 53, Christ's death is seen in these sentences not as the substitutionary bearing of the penal consequences of our sin, but as an event of sanctifying atonement. That is shown, on the one hand, by the formulation that departs from Isaiah 53 in verse 24a — Christ "carried up our sins in his body[93] to the tree" (NRSV margin)[94] — then, on the other hand, by the immediately following purpose clause in verse 24b: "so that, free from sins, we might live for righteousness." This says that through Christ's death on the cross, the reality of sin itself is wiped out and nullified; those for whom Christ died have been drawn into the Christ event, with the result that a new life-reality is open to them through Christ's death

88. Citation of Isa. 53:9b: ὅτι ἀνομίαν οὐκ ἐποίησεν, οὐδὲ εὑρέθη δόλος ἐν τῷ στόματι αὐτοῦ.

89. "When he was abused, he did not return abuse; when he suffered, he did not threaten" (NRSV). Perhaps this alludes to Isa. 53:7, "He was oppressed, and he was afflicted, yet he did not open his mouth; like a lamb that is led to the slaughter, and like a sheep that before its shearers is silent, so he did not open his mouth."

90. "He himself carried up our sins in his body to the tree" (NRSV margin). This alludes to several statements in Isaiah 53 that speak of "bearing" sins, Isa. 53:4aα: οὗτος τὰς ἁμαρτίας ἡμῶν φέρει, 53:11bβ: καὶ τὰς ἁμαρτίας αὐτῶν αὐτὸς ἀνοίσει, 53:12cα: καὶ αὐτὸς ἁμαρτίας πολλῶν ἀνήνεγκε.

91. "By his wound you were healed." A free citation of Isa. 53:5bβ, τῷ μώλωπι αὐτοῦ ἡμεῖς ἰάθημεν.

92. "For you were going astray like sheep." An allusion to Isa. 53:6aα: πάντες ὡς πρόβατα ἐπλανήθημεν.

93. "*in* his body," ἐν τῷ σώματι αὐτοῦ, could also be translated "*with* his body." On the role of Christ's body in redemption see Col. 1:22; Heb. 10:10.

94. On ξύλον as an expression for the wood of the *cross* see Acts 5:30; 10:39; 13:29; Gal. 3:13.

and resurrection.[95] Already in 1:18-19 the author had characterized the new being of the letter's recipients in a similar way: Christ, "through his precious blood" — that is, through his atoning death — has freed them from the previously inescapable bondage to sin and has thereby transferred them into a new, God-oriented life.[96] Vicarious atonement is also in view in 1 Peter 3:18, where the reference to Isaiah 53 (especially 53:11) is unmistakable:

a   Χριστὸς ἅπαξ περὶ ἁμαρτιῶν ἔπαθεν,
       δίκαιος ὑπὲρ ἀδίκων,
b   ἵνα ὑμᾶς προσαγάγῃ τῷ θεῷ
       θανατωθεὶς μὲν σαρκὶ
       ζῳοποιηθεὶς δὲ πνεύματι.

At first sight one might be tempted to interpret these words from the perspective of Isaiah 53. In that case the expression περὶ ἁμαρτιῶν would have to have a causal meaning, "for the sake of sins." In other words, verse 18a would say that Christ in his death bore substitutionarily the penal consequences of sin on behalf of the "unrighteous." However, the purpose clause of verse 18b tells decisively against this interpretation. According to this half-verse, Christ "brought" sinners "to God." This presents the Christ event as an event of atonement[97] in exactly the same way that the Old Testament understands cultic atonement: "Cultic, sanctifying atonement is . . . a coming to God that consists in passing through the death sentence."[98] Therefore the words περὶ ἁμαρτιῶν in verse 18a must be interpreted in terms of atonement theology. The result is that 1 Peter 3:18 as a whole must be translated:

Christ died (lit., suffered)[99] once for all to make atonement for sins,
    the righteous for the unrighteous,
in order to bring you to God —
    he who was put to death in the flesh,
    but made alive in the spirit.

95. On 1 Pet. 2:24b see Rom. 6:11, 18 and indeed the whole of Romans 6. In my opinion these points of contact with Romans 6 exclude the possibility of interpreting the purpose clause of 1 Pet. 2:24b as paraenesis and thereby merely ethically.

96. Cf. also the reference to Christ's atoning death in 1 Pet. 1:2.

97. Cf. on this Heb. 10:19-22 and 2:10.

98. "Die kultische, die heiligende Sühne ist . . . ein Zu-Gott-Kommen durch das Todesgericht hindurch," Gese, "Die Sühne," 104 = ET, "The Atonement," 114 (mod.).

99. To "suffer," πάσχειν, here means to "die," as in Luke 22:15; 24:46; Acts 1:3; 3:18; 17:3; Heb. 9:26.

The idea of place-taking from Isaiah 53 is taken up here; yet at the same time — as in Paul and in Hebrews — it is placed in an entirely new light.

V. Hermeneutical Reflections

If we look back upon what we have discovered from the New Testament letters, we may safely conclude that there is not a single passage where the fourth Servant Song has been taken up in its original sense. The statements of the Song have rather always been drawn into a more profound view of the person and work of Jesus Christ and thus interpreted afresh. Jesus Christ, in his person and in his work, is not merely and not primarily explained by Isaiah 53: Isaiah 53 is rather explained *by him.* The fourth Servant Song by no means provides the hermeneutical key for understanding Jesus and for interpreting his death on the cross; this then provides a leading example to illustrate the truth of what Hans Joachim Iwand once described as follows:

> The Old Testament is understood anew from the New Testament's procla-
> mation of Christ. . . . The Old Testament is not taken over by Christianity
> "simply"; rather, from the perspective of Jesus Christ, the crucified and
> risen one, it is opened afresh! . . . The Old Testament experiences in the
> New Testament its decisive Renaissance.[100]

These words may not and must not be understood as though the Old Testament texts — and therefore particularly also the fourth Servant Song — had an *excess* of meaning that remained concealed from the original authors and bearers of the tra- dition, only to be discovered by the New Testament authors and brought to light by means of the Christological interpretation. Rather, by being received Christologically, the fourth Servant Song acquires a sense that was *not* originally its own, one that changes it in content and meaning so that we must talk in certain re- spects about a *new* text. Once the name of the Son of God, Jesus Christ, is entered for the words "my servant" — which point to a mere human — the coordinates of the fourth Servant Song as a whole are changed. For now Christ's death and resur- rection determine the meaning of *sin, being a sinner,* and *existential place-taking for sinners.* That the Old Testament text was open for such a Christological reception is surprising enough. Yet at the same time it needs to be said: only through the Christological reception does this text become theologically affirmable and there- fore a text for which we can take responsibility in the preaching of the Church.

---

100. Iwand, *Predigt-Meditationen,* 693.

The Servant of Isaiah 53 as Triumphant and Interceding Messiah: The Reception of Isaiah 52:13–53:12 in the Targum of Isaiah with Special Attention to the Concept of the Messiah

Jostein Ådna

Summary

The departures of the Targumic Aramaic translation of Isaiah 52:13–53:12 from the wording of the Hebrew text — beginning with "Behold, my servant, *the Messiah,* shall prosper" in 52:13 — are well known. What they reveal of the translator's procedure and theology is, however, a debated matter. This study claims that the translator's changes in favor of a triumphant rather than a suffering Messiah cannot be traced to any conscious anti-Christian motive. Neither can the translator's procedure fairly be labeled as arbitrary reinterpretation or atomistic exegesis. Rather, the Targumist provides a unified and consistent interpretation of Isaiah 53 that does not differ substantially from his treatment of other parts of the book. Working between 70 and 135 C.E. and starting from the possible identification of the Lord's *Servant* with the Messiah (cf., e.g., Zech. 3:8 and *Tg. Zech.* 3:8), the Targumist becomes convinced that the prosperous and exalted figure in Isaiah 52:13 can be none other than the Messiah. The change in the Hebrew text from the third person singular in 52:13 to the second person singular in verse 14 ("many were astonished at *you*") further persuades him that all statements of suffering and death in 52:14 and 53:3-9 must apply to others than the Servant-Messiah (the Gentiles, the wicked in Israel, etc.). Hence, he is able to render Isaiah 52:13–53:12 in keeping with the typical Jewish view of a triumphant Messiah, who judges the peoples and the wicked and rules over God-fearing and law-keeping Israel. The Targumist emphasizes the Messiah's roles as temple builder (cf. v. 5: "he will build the sanctuary"), teacher of the law (cf. v. 5: "by his teaching the peace will increase upon us"), and intercessor for Israel (cf. vv. 4, 11, 12). As an intercessor the Messiah follows the example of Moses to the point of being willing to surrender his life vicariously (cf. v. 12: "he handed over his soul to the death . . . , yet he will beseech concerning the sins of many," with Exod. 32:30-34). In thus uniting a multiplicity of eschatological roles in a single mediator figure, the Targumist proceeds by a way that has analogies in the New Testament, even though there the authors conceive the messianic office very differently.

1. Anti-Christian Polemic?

Even a superficial reading of Isaiah 52:13–53:12 in the Hebrew Bible and the *Targum of Isaiah* (a part of the *Targum Jonathan to the Prophets*)[1] reveals considerable differences between the Hebrew and Aramaic versions.[2] In the Tar-

---

1. I would like to thank the translator, Daniel P. Bailey, for adding interesting philological material (marked [(Tr.) . . .] in nn. 80, 107) and for making my linguistic arguments more accessible to English-speaking readers, both by incorporating new references to *HALOT*, Jastrow, and Sokoloff (e.g., nn. 57, 70) and by referring to various English Bible translations (e.g., nn. 48, 57, 70). As text editions I presuppose K. Elliger and W. Rudolph, *Biblia Hebraica Stuttgartensia = BHS*, 4th ed. (1990) and A. Sperber, *The Bible in Aramaic*, vol. 2: *The Former Prophets According to Targum Jonathan* (1959); vol. 3: *The Latter Prophets According to Targum Jonathan* (1962), esp. 107-9 for Isa. 52:13–53:12. The Aramaic text of the Targum of Isaiah 53 can also be found in G. Dalman, *Aramäische Dialektproben*, 2nd ed. (1927; reprinted 1978), 10-11; J. F. Stenning, *The Targum of Isaiah* (1949; reprinted 1953), 179, 181; and H. Hegermann, *Jesaja 53 in Hexapla, Targum und Peschitta*, BFCT 2/56 (1954), appendix.

2. The basic English translation of the *Targum of Isaiah* in this essay is that of B. D. Chilton; alternative translations are discussed in the notes. See B. D. Chilton, *The Isaiah Targum: Introduction, Translation, Apparatus and Notes*, ArBib 11 (1987), 103-5, for *Tg. Isa.* 52:13–53:12. Chilton's translation presents "the innovative wording of the Targum in italics, while the more straightforward rendering of the Hebrew text by the meturgeman is presented in roman type" (ibid., xxxiii) — a convention retained here. For other English translations see Stenning, *The Targum of Isaiah*, 180, 182, reprinted in C. K. Barrett, ed., *The New Testament Background: Selected Documents*, rev. ed. (1987), 314-15; J. Jeremias, "παῖς θεοῦ, C. παῖς θεοῦ in Later Judaism in the Period after the LXX," *TDNT* 5:677-700 (esp. 692-95 on the *Targum of Isaiah*, translation of 52:13–53:12 on pp. 693-94); R. Syrén, "Targum Isaiah 52:13–53:12 and Christian Interpretation," *JJS* 40 (1989): 201-12, esp. 201-2. German translations may be found in Str-B 1:482-83; P. Seidelin, "Der 'Ebed Jahwe und die Messiasgestalt im Jesajatargum," *ZNW* 35 (1936): 194-231, esp. 206-9; J. Jeremias, *TWNT* 5:691-93; H. Haag, "Der 'Gottesknecht' bei Deuterojesaja im Verständnis des Judentums," *Jud* 41 (1985): 23-36, esp. 27-29; and integrated into the discussion in Hegermann, *Jesaja 53 in Hexapla, Targum und Peschitta*, and K. Koch, "Messias und Sündenvergebung in Jesaja 53 — Targum: Ein Beitrag zu der Praxis der aramäischen Bibelübersetzung," *JSJ* 3 (1972): 117-48. Although unpublished, a good German translation with extensive linguistic analysis is offered by O. Hofius in a private Festschrift for the 50th birthday of Professor Peter Stuhlmacher on January 18, 1982: see Hofius, "Kennt der Targum zu Jes 53 einen sündenvergebenden Messias?" 215-54, esp. 216-19 (notes pp. 239-44).

gum, the Suffering Servant has become a triumphant Messiah who is elevated above all suffering. The suffering and blows which strike the Servant according to the original Hebrew, culminating in his shameful death, are redirected in the Targum to other groups and entities, including the Gentiles, the whole house of Israel or Israel's wicked, and the temple.[3]

In the light of this stark contrast between the presentations in the Hebrew Bible and the Targum, it is no surprise that some scholars have wondered about possible earlier stages of the version available to us in the *Targum to the Prophets,* in which the elements of suffering in the life and death of the Servant were not yet fully suppressed. The main exponent of this approach is Harald Hegermann. In his 1954 monograph *Jesaja 53 in Hexapla, Targum und Peschitta,* Hegermann claims to have discovered an older version of the Targum hidden behind the present one.[4] Hegermann believes that this older version spoke of a suffering Messiah already in pre-Christian times. By contrast, the presently available Targum text is supposed to have come into being only after the New Testament period by means of a thorough revision.[5] This may be understood largely as a polemical reaction to the Christian interpretation of Isaiah 53 as a prophecy of the passion of Jesus of Nazareth.

Opinions differ about whether and to what extent this earlier stage, which is supposed to have spoken of the Servant's sufferings, shines through in the present Targum text.[6] Nevertheless, the present Targum version is fre-

---

3. Cf. R. A. Aytoun, "The Servant of the Lord in the Targum," *JTS* 23 (1921-22): 172-80, esp. 173-74.

4. Hegermann, *Jesaja 53 in Hexapla, Targum und Peschitta,* 66-94, 115-26.

5. Cf. in particular the discussion of the most important passages in Hegermann, *Jesaja 53 in Hexapla, Targum und Peschitta,* 115-22. For details see the meticulous analysis of the Targum text on pp. 66ff., e.g., 71f., 75, 77, 79f., 83, 87, 88, 92.

6. Thus for example Jeremias, "παῖς θεοῦ," *TDNT* 5:695, claims that "the statements about the sufferings of the servant of God are so radically eliminated [in *Tg. Isa.* 53] that only at two points do weak traces remain," namely, in *Tg. Isa.* 53:3, 12 (ibid., 695 n. 302). Yet even in *Tg. Isa.* 53:3 the presence of this trace is a matter of textual criticism involving the difference between the letters י and ו. A Suffering Servant is in view only if we read the second verb in this verse as the aphel וְיַפְסֵיק, "he will cause to cease," rather than as the peal or qal וְיִפְסוּק, "it will cease." As Jeremias explains, "The two readings presuppose different subjects. In the first (יַפְסֵיק) the Messiah is the subj.: 'Then *he* [sc. the Servant] will be despised and will cause to cease the glory of all kingdoms.' . . . In the second (יִפְסוּק) the subj. is 'the glory of all kingdoms' and the transl. is: 'Then *the glory of all kingdoms* will turn to shame and will cease'" (ibid., 694 n. 296, italics added). Although the aphel form with the *yod* has the better external attestation, I disagree with Jeremias and favor וְיִפְסוּק with the *vav* as the original reading (cf. also Chilton's translation: "*Then the glory of all the kingdoms will be for contempt* and *cease*"). The letters *vav* and *yod* can easily be confused in manuscript transmission. Moreover, because v. 3 as a whole has to do with the fate of the Gentile nations and בְּסִירִין ("despised") at the end of the verse

quently seen as anti-Christian polemic. Joachim Jeremias offers a representative view:

> [T]here is only one possible explanation for this violent wresting of the chapter in the Tg., with its consistent reversal of the meaning, namely, that we have here an instance of *anti-Christian polemic*. From the 2nd cent. at the latest Judaism sought in various ways to rescue Is. 53 from its use by Christians as a Christological proof from Scripture. The curious version of Is. 53 in the Tg. shows with what consistency this end was pursued.[7]

I believe that we should be skeptical about such attempts to discern in the present Isaiah Targum earlier stages of an Aramaic text supposedly nearer to the original Hebrew than the final version. Claims about textual layers often rest on a negative assessment of the final version as an artificial, tendentious reinterpretation, as atomistic exegesis, and so on. As an example I cite the judgment of Hans Walter Wolff from his famous monograph *Jesaja 53 im Urchristentum*: "The complete reversal that the Targum Pseudo-Jonathan [*sic*] undertakes in its 'rewriting' of Isaiah 53 is deplorable."[8]

---

picks up יְהֵי לְבוּסְרָן ("will be for contempt") at the beginning, the qal or peal form which has "the glory of all kingdoms" as its subject is in my opinion the more probable. But even assuming the aphel form, the verse says only that the Gentile nations will begin to despise the Servant and that he in turn will deprive their kingdoms of glory. This is no "trace of the Messianic passion" (*contra* Jeremias, 694 n. 296) or "remainder of the Messianic passion" (*contra* Hegermann, *Jesaja 53 in Hexapla, Targum und Peschitta*, 75). On this whole topic see Hofius, "Kennt der Targum zu Jes 53 einen sündenvergebenden Messias?" 241 n. 29. On the presumed "trace of suffering" in *Tg. Isa.* 53:12 see below, pp. 219-22.

7. Jeremias, "παῖς θεοῦ," *TDNT* 5:695 (italics from German original). See among others also Hegermann, *Jesaja 53 in Hexapla, Targum und Peschitta*, 121: "The Targum's revision may be directed above all against the Christian interpretation of Isaiah 53, perhaps additionally against similar opinions that grew up in broader Jewish circles, for example as a result of Christian-Jewish discussions." Barrett is more cautious in his *New Testament Background*, 315 note on ll. 4-5: "[T]he variations that the translator has made . . . may have been made because the Christians had made their own use of the Song of the Suffering Servant, and it was found necessary to counter their interpretation with another."

8. H. W. Wolff, *Jesaja 53 im Urchristentum*, 4th ed. (1984), 52. Similarly Hegermann, *Jesaja 53 in Hexapla, Targum und Peschitta*, 116: "*Tg. Isa.* 53 combines a strict grounding in the original text with a method of translation that is in part highly artificial and tendentious, altering the sense. But not all parts of Isaiah 53 are equally affected by such misinterpretation of the sense; only the sayings about the Servant's lowliness or suffering are dismissed and bypassed in this way." For further statements of this sort see Hegermann, 68, 76, 80, 84, 87, 89, 118-19. See also G. Dalman, *Jesaja 53, das Prophetenwort vom Sühnleiden des Gottesknechtes mit besonderer Berücksichtigung der jüdischen Literatur*, 2nd ed. (1914), 7; P. Seidelin, "Der 'Ebed Jahwe," 211, 214, 216; and Jeremias, "παῖς θεοῦ," *TDNT* 5:695 n. 304.

However, we are not well served by such characterizations of the final version of the *Targum of Isaiah*. They bar the way to an appropriate appreciation of the extant Targum text and predispose us to a materially negative judgment.[9] I believe that *Targum of Isaiah* 53 presents us with a unified and consistent interpretation of the underlying Hebrew text that does not differ nearly as much as has been claimed from the translator's procedure in other portions of the text of Second and Third Isaiah.[10] In this connection Klaus Koch has done us a great service in his 1972 study, "Messias und Sündenvergebung in Jesaja 53–Targum." Koch reminds us of important but long-neglected observations of the Jewish scholar Pinkhos Churgin about the general translation principles of the *Targum to the Prophets,* and then he demonstrates that these apply to Isaiah 52:13–53:12 as well. Koch concludes that

> the Targumist in this chapter did nothing but follow the same translation principles that guided him elsewhere, in order to provide his readers with a completely clear and simple Holy Scripture. In contrast to widespread opinion, his translation has nothing to do with midrash or sermonic "paraphrase." The Hebrew text is followed word for word, though often for the sake of translation or clarification two or more Aramaic words are necessary where only one stands in the Hebrew.[11]

The text does not invite speculation from literary criticism or transmission history regarding earlier layers, in comparison with which the present version of the *Targum of Isaiah* 53 would show itself to be a reworking.[12] Rather,

9. See on this the balanced judgment of O. Betz, "Die Übersetzungen von Jes 53 (LXX, Targum) und die Theologia Crucis des Paulus," in idem, *Jesus, Der Herr der Kirche: Aufsätze zur biblischen Theologie II,* WUNT 52 (1990), 197-216, esp. 201-2.

10. So Jeremias, "παῖς θεοῦ," *TDNT* 5:695: "By reason of its freedom of paraphrase, which is unusual in the translation technique of the Tg., the section Tg. Is. 52:13–53:12 stands alone in the total context of Tg. Is. 40–66, which elsewhere keeps much more closely to the Heb." See also Aytoun, "The Servant of the Lord in the Targum," 172, 179; Stenning, *The Targum of Isaiah,* xv; Hegermann, *Jesaja 53 in Hexapla, Targum und Peschitta,* 22; A. van der Kooij, *Die alten Textzeugen des Jesajabuches: Ein Beitrag zur Textgeschichte des Alten Testaments,* OBO 35 (1981), 208.

11. Koch, "Messias und Sündenvergebung," 147. On the Targumist's translation principles see Koch, 121-23; for detailed demonstration, 123ff. Koch draws upon P. Churgin, *Targum Jonathan to the Prophets,* Yale Oriental Series — Researches XIV (1927), 78ff. This work has been reprinted by KTAV, bound together with *Studies in Targum Jonathan to the Prophets,* by L. Smolar and M. Aberbach (1983).

12. Cf. Koch, "Messias und Sündenvergebung," 147: "A thoroughgoing revision that profoundly alters the original text (like Hegermann maintains) can nowhere be grasped with certainty." Syrén, "Targum Isaiah 52:13–53:12," 205-10, provides a good history-of-research overview

what is expected and demanded from us is to offer an interpretation of the text of the *Targum of Isaiah* 52:13–53:12 as a well-rounded unit. Naturally its connections with the rest of the *Targum of Isaiah* and to other parts of *Targum Jonathan* must not be ignored. Although I make no attempt to analyze the text's transmission history, I should immediately add that I have no objection to traditio-historical questions involving possible incorporations of or allusions to historically preexisting motifs and theologoumena.

2. Dating the Text

If it is impossible in the Targumic tradition of Isaiah 53 to differentiate between the present version and an earlier one dealing with a suffering Messiah and then to assign them to the pre– and post–New Testament periods, then the question of dating poses itself afresh. According to Peter Schäfer, all that can be said about *Targum Jonathan* as a whole is that it originated in Palestine and underwent a final, unifying redaction in Babylon between the third century and fifth century C.E., and that "the dating will hardly get beyond the determination of a *terminus a quo* in the pre-Christian period and a *terminus ad quem* in the Arabian period."[13] Because there are hardly any historically reliable external statements of witnesses about the origin of *Targum Jonathan*,[14] we must rely for a precise historical orientation upon internal findings such as potential references and allusions to circumstances and events already known from other sources.

Churgin did important pioneering work in this area as well. Through an extensive sifting of the data,[15] he arrived at the conclusion that *Targum Jonathan* contains materials that reflect the conditions both in Palestine during the

---

of various answers to the questions about the Targumist's translation method and his possible anti-Christian motivation. Syrén's own view is that "there is nothing in it [sc. *Tg. Isa.* 52:13–53:12] needing to be accounted for as a reaction against the Christian exposition of the passage. . . . Accordingly, the reasons for the targumic intrusion upon the text can safely be sought within Jewish theology and messianology" (210).

13. P. Schäfer, "Bibelübersetzungen, II: Targumim," *TRE* 6 (1980): 216-28, esp. 223. Cf. also E. Schürer, *The History of the Jewish People in the Age of Jesus Christ (175 B.C.–135 A.D.)*. A New English Version, rev. and ed. G. Vermes and F. Millar, vol. 1 (1973), 101-2.

14. On the tradition of *b. Meg.* 3a, according to which Jonathan ben Uzziel is supposed to have written the *Targum of the Prophets* under the supervision of the prophets Haggai, Zechariah, and Malachi, see B. D. Chilton, *The Glory of Israel: The Theology and Provenience of the Isaiah Targum*, JSOTSup 23 (1983), 1-3.

15. Churgin, *Targum Jonathan*, 9-51.

Tannaitic period, and in Babylonia during the Amoraic period. This result, which testifies to a complex history of origin, applies equally to the Isaiah portion of *Targum Jonathan*. Today's leading expert on the *Targum of Isaiah*, Bruce D. Chilton, takes Churgin's view, and in his works he identifies many references in the *Targum of Isaiah* to historical circumstances over several centuries, beyond those already cited by Churgin.[16]

The historically most readily comprehensible passages of this sort may be those that refer to the Jerusalem temple. Thus, on the one hand, the criticism of the high priest in the *Targum of Isaiah* 28:1-4 (*"the wicked one of his sanctuary,"* vv. 1, 4) presupposes that the Jerusalem temple is still standing; this text must therefore be dated before 70 c.e.[17] On the other hand, the destruction of the temple is viewed as a past event, explicitly in the *Targum of Isaiah* 32:14 (*"the sanctuary is desolate"*) and indirectly in the *Targum of Isaiah* 30:20 (*"he* will not any more *take up his Shekhinah from the sanctuary"*).[18]

Chilton also thinks that the centuries-long history of origin of the *Targum of Isaiah* expresses itself in two different theological tendencies.[19] Some passages deal with the present state of disaster, whose effects include the disobedience of Israel, the desolation of the sanctuary, and the absence of the *Shekhinah;* here salvation is consistently future and eschatologically conceived. Other passages, by contrast, are dominated by a "theoretical" viewpoint, as Chilton calls it, according to which the *Shekhinah* and the sanctuary are already present in heaven. Israel is designated not as a people but as a "congregation,"

---

16. See Chilton, *Glory of Israel,* 109-10, 160 n. 25; idem, *The Isaiah Targum,* xxiii: "Is it plausible to argue that the Targum as we know it emerged substantially over the rabbinic generations between first century Palestine and fourth century Babylon? The classic contribution of Pinkhos Churgin (1927) was intended to show precisely that such a prolonged period of formation must be reckoned with. . . . The Notes in the present volume give many more examples of references to conditions in both the Palestinian and Babylonian phases of the Targum's emergence."

17. Churgin, *Targum Jonathan,* 23-24; Chilton, *Glory of Israel,* 20, 23; idem, *The Isaiah Targum,* 54-55.

18. Chilton, *Glory of Israel,* 20; idem, *The Isaiah Targum,* 63: "Indeed, [*Tg. Isa.* 32] vv. 12-14 make it quite plain that 'the sanctuary' and 'the cities' around it have already been destroyed. The perspective of the passage is quite clearly of the period after A.D. 70." On the removal of the Shekhinah from the sanctuary in *Tg. Isa.* 30:20 as an indirect reference to the temple's destruction see below, p. 211. Additionally Chilton, *Glory of Israel,* 23, points to *Tg. Isa.* 25:2 as a statement that is to be placed chronologically between 70 c.e. and the Bar-Kochba revolt in 132-135.

19. In *Glory of Israel,* Chilton develops and supports this thesis by means of an "Analysis of Characteristic Terms or Phrases" in chapter 2, which comprises 65 percent of the book (pp. 13-96 with notes on pp. 127-58, or 116 out of 178 total pages). An introduction to Chilton's view can be found either in *Glory of Israel,* chapter 3, "Conclusion," 97-111, or more conveniently in his *The Isaiah Targum,* xiv-xx.

an entity without national political ambitions, and the conversion of Israel is already under way, thanks to God's activity.

While these two "levels" of the *Targum of Isaiah*, the "eschatological" and the "theoretical," do not contradict one another according to Chilton,[20] they nevertheless remain for him signs of chronological differences that are to be divided into the Tannaitic and Amoraic periods.[21] Yet even apart from the question of the appropriateness of this type of differentiation between theological tendencies in the *Targum of Isaiah*, there is good reason to question such subtle distinctions as reliable criteria of dating.[22]

---

20. Chilton, *The Isaiah Targum*, xx: "Distinctions of emphasis among the characteristic terms and phrases . . . suggest that there are two levels of meaning within the overall theological orientation of the Targum. The first level is practical and national. Within its perspective, the Messiah, repentance, and Shekhinah are all urgently desired: only their realization can bring about the restoration of the sanctuary and the return of the house of Israel from exile. The second level is more settled in outlook. Within its perspective, the Messiah and the Shekhinah already exist in God's sight, repentance has begun and even the sanctuary is already present, albeit in heaven. Despite the theoretical existence of all that, however, there appears to be a certain acknowledgment that Israel is much more a gathered community waiting upon God than a national unit. The two levels do not contradict one another; it is just that the first is rather more eschatological than the second, and the second rather more theoretical or abstract in its understanding of divine realities than the first. What they have in common is a hope in the messianic vindication of Israel. At the first level, that hope involves the military victory of the Messiah and the actual rebuilding of the Temple. At the second level, it involves waiting for God, of whose power the Messiah is witness; God alone guards the contents of restoration in heaven."

21. Chilton, *The Isaiah Targum*, xxiii: "In our description of the levels of meaning within the overall theology of the Targum, we distinguished between the national, eschatological perspective of one level, and the more settled, theoretical orientation of another. The first appears to suit the Tannaitic phase of the Targum's development, and the second its Amoraic phase." Sometimes the older, Tannaitic level can itself be further divided into two different strata. See Chilton, *Glory of Israel*, 103: "[O]ur analysis has not isolated a single framework, but the work of framework interpreters at two levels (Tannaitic and Amoraic), with the earlier level distinguished into two strata (before and after the destruction of the Temple)."

22. The need for caution regarding these sorts of theological distinctions as dating criteria is urged by the juxtaposition of both present and future eschatological understandings of the kingdom of God in Qumran as well as the New Testament. In Qumran, compare the present understanding of God's kingly reign in the Songs of the Sabbath Sacrifice, 4Q400-407; 11Q17 (cf. A. M. Schwemer, "Gott als König und seine Königsherrschaft in den Sabbatliedern aus Qumran," in M. Hengel and A. M. Schwemer, eds., *Königsherrschaft Gottes und himmlischer Kult im Judentum, Urchristentum und in der hellenistischen Welt*, WUNT 55 [1991], 45-118) with the future eschatological understanding for example in the War Scroll (1QM) and the Habakkuk Commentary (1QpHab). In the New Testament compare the present participation in heavenly existence in Eph. 2:6 (referring back to 1:20) and the heavenly worship already under way in Revelation with the many future eschatological statements both in Revelation and elsewhere in the New Testament.

Even if attempts to differentiate between older levels and the final version of the *Targum of Isaiah* fail to help us date the text, more general studies of the origin of *Targum Jonathan* and its Isaiah portion have nevertheless shown that the age of its various textual units varies greatly. In view of the reservations just expressed about dating texts based on their theological tendencies, it is less than persuasive when Chilton relies on these criteria to include chapters 52 and 53 among those passages that "appear in their present orientation to reflect more the Tannaitic level of thinking."[23] Nevertheless, chapter 53 does seem to contain allusions to historical conditions that likewise point to the Tannaitic period and perhaps even enable a precise dating. For *Targum of Isaiah* 53:5, 8 assume that the Jerusalem temple is destroyed and that the holy land is occupied by Gentiles, while at the same time these two verses and many other statements in the text seem to be carried along by the glowing messianic expectation that this state of disaster will soon come to an end. This probably dates *Targum of Isaiah* 53 to the period shortly before the Bar-Kochba revolt in 132-135 C.E.[24]

3. The Targumist's Translation Technique

Let us now turn to the text of the *Targum of Isaiah* 52:13–53:12 to illustrate the Targumist's translational and interpretive technique by means of some exam-

---

23. Chilton, *The Isaiah Targum*, xxiv.

24. I do not understand how Aytoun, "Servant of the Lord in the Targum," 176, can use *Tg. Isa.* 53:8 to fix the year 50 B.C.E. as the *terminus a quo* for the Targum text and 30 C.E. as the *terminus ad quem*. Moreover, Koch's understanding of *Tg. Isa.* 53:5 must also be called into question: "The weakening of the Hebrew 'crushed' *(dk')* to 'handed over' *(msr)* [predicated in the Targum not of the Servant but of the temple] can be explained only by assuming that the Jerusalem temple is not yet destroyed at the time of the Aramaic translation, although it is in the wrong hands" ("Messiah und Sündenvergebung," 136). By contrast, Hofius correctly explains what the Aramaic expression אִתְמְסַר, "handed over," means, when applied to the temple: handed over "to destruction by enemies" (Hofius, "Kennt der Targum zu Jes 53 einen sündenvergebenden Messias?" 242 n. 37, referring back to p. 217). For this understanding of the statement about the temple in *Tg. Isa.* 53:5 see also L. Smolar and M. Aberbach, *Studies in Targum Jonathan*, 200 with n. 464; similarly Churgin, *Targum Jonathan*, 26: "V. 5 points clearly to Bar Kochba," and Chilton, *Glory of Israel*, 130 n. 11: "Such confidence [that the destroyed sanctuary would be renewed: cf. ibid., 20-21] was grist for the Bar Kokhba mill, whose revolt this passage apparently antedates." See further Chilton, *Glory of Israel*, 93-94; idem, *The Isaiah Targum*, 105; S. H. Levey, *The Messiah: An Aramaic Interpretation: The Messianic Exegesis of the Targum*, HUCM 10 (1974), 67. Here we may also mention those scholars who rather one-sidedly associate the whole Isaiah Targum with the school of Rabbi Akiba and the Bar Kokhba revolt: van der Kooij, *Die alten Textzeugen*, 192ff., and Smolar and Aberbach, *Studies in Targum Jonathan*.

ples. The first striking difference between *Targum of Isaiah* 52:13–53:12 and its Hebrew *Vorlage*, which also becomes decisive for understanding the whole text, is the equation of the Servant with the Messiah in the first verse: "Behold, my servant, *the Messiah*, shall prosper, he shall be exalted and *increase*, and shall be very *strong*." This identification is by no means self-evident. For in most of the passages in Deutero-Isaiah containing the term עֶבֶד, which usually occurs in the form עַבְדִּי, "my servant," the Targum applies it, as does the book of Isaiah itself, to the people of Israel.[25] Within the so-called Servant Songs this is true of the second song, Isaiah 49:1ff.: see especially verses 3 and 6 in the Targum: "you are my servant, Israel" (Tg. = Heb.); "you *are called my* servant*s*" (plural Tg.).[26] The third song, Isaiah 50:4ff., also uses the term "servants" in the plural, but equates them with the prophets: "his servant*s the prophets*" (*Tg. Isa.* 50:10).[27] Whether the Targum of the first song, Isaiah 42:1ff., identifies the Servant with the Messiah, as the fourth song clearly does, is debated, since the term מְשִׁיחָא in *Targum of Isaiah* 42:1 ("my servant, *the Messiah*") is not attested in all manuscripts.[28] Therefore next to *Targum of Isaiah* 52:13, there is only one certain passage in the whole of the *Targum of Isaiah* equating the Servant with the Messiah, namely, *Targum of Isaiah* 43:10.

The *Targum of Isaiah* speaks of the Messiah for the first time in 4:2, where the Hebrew Bible's promised appearance of the צֶמַח יהוה, "the branch of the

---

25. See the overview in Jeremias, "παῖς θεοῦ," *TDNT* 5:680 n. 176.

26. Similarly in *Tg. Isa.* 49:8a the Hebrew's second person singular is replaced by the Targum's second person plural. Cf. Seidelin, "Der 'Ebed Jahwe," 202: "Although there are several ambiguities [in *Tg. Isa.* 49:1-9], on the whole the Targumist probably understood the passage as dealing with Israel." According to H. Haag, *Der Gottesknecht bei Deuterojesaja*, EdF 233 (1985), 36 n. 4, E. Ruprecht in his unpublished dissertation, "Die Auslegungsgeschichte zu den sogenannten Gottesknechtsliedern im Buch Deuterojesaja unter methodischen Gesichtspunkten bis zu Bernhard Duhm," Ph.D. dissertation, Heidelberg, 1972, to which I have not had access, concludes that the Targum understands both the second and third (cf. n. 27) Servant Songs "not as prophecies but as the prophet's discourse about himself as the one who prepares the people for the messianic age, thereby including all the other prophets as well" (cited by Haag from Ruprecht, 18). With the proviso that I have not been able to see Ruprecht's argumentation, it seems to me that the above-mentioned features in *Tg. Isa.* 49:3, 6a, 8a clearly show that here, as in the majority of cases elsewhere in the Isaiah Targum (cf. n. 25), the Servant is to be equated with the people of Israel.

27. Cf. Seidelin, "Der 'Ebed Jahwe," 202-6.

28. I believe that the word "Messiah" in *Tg. Isa.* 42:1 is a secondary addition because it is lacking in the most important textual witnesses. The same judgment is reached by Stenning, *The Targum of Isaiah*, 140, 141, and Chilton, *The Isaiah Targum*, 80, 81. By contrast Jeremias, "παῖς θεοῦ," *TDNT* 5:693 n. 292, argues for the reading including מְשִׁיחָא. Seidelin, "Der 'Ebed Jahwe," 196-200, does not go into the text-critical problem and assumes the messianic interpretation of *Tg. Isa.* 42:1-7 as self-evident; so apparently also Koch, "Messias und Sündenvergebung," 123.

Lord," is rendered by the Aramaic מְשִׁיחָא דַיוי, "*the Messiah* of the Lord." This messianic interpretation of the Lord's Branch has a clear precedent in the Old Testament, for example in Jeremiah 23:5 (cf. also Jer. 33:15):

> The days are surely coming, says the Lord, when I will raise up for David a righteous Branch, and he shall reign as king and deal wisely, and shall execute justice and righteousness in the land. (Jeremiah 23:5 NRSV)

Similarly in Zechariah 3:8 the term "branch," צֶמַח, stands in apposition to God's "servant," עַבְדִּי, with a messianic sense: "I am going to bring my servant the Branch." As expected, the Targum of this passage speaks explicitly of "my servant, *the Messiah*." Because the Isaiah Targumist already understands the Branch as the Lord's Messiah in *Targum of Isaiah* 4:2, the equation of the Lord's Servant with the messianic Branch in Zechariah 3:8 makes it possible for him to identify the Servant with the Messiah even where the Bible text has only עַבְדִּי. Yet as already seen, this identification is by no means automatic but is made sparingly in only two passages, *Targum of Isaiah* 43:10 and 52:13. It seems that the Targumist here makes use of the possibility in the tradition of identifying the Servant with the Messiah, because he is convinced that the statement of the future glorious exaltation of the Servant can be true of no figure other than the Messiah. One of the Targumist's fundamental translational principles is that general lexemes are made more precise, and that is exactly what happens here.[29] The prosperous, strong, exalted Servant is none other than the Messiah.

One might think that Isaiah 52:13 on its own deals with a purely triumphant and exalted figure. But do not matters look different when the following verses are included? How can the Servant of 52:13 be understood as the Messiah in the light of the suffering described in verses 14ff.? I believe we should follow Otto Betz in his view that on the basis of 52:13, which speaks of the Servant's success, the Targumist concluded that the statements of suffering and death (52:14 and 53:3-9) must apply to others. He found this understanding confirmed in the change of person present in the Hebrew text from the third person in Isaiah 52:13, "my servant," to the second person in verse 14, "many were astonished at *you* (עָלֶיךָ)."[30] Therefore, against a widespread assumption (found for exam-

---

29. Cf. Koch, "Messias und Sündenvergebung," 123: the addition of the word "Messiah" in *Tg. Isa.* 52:13 "may be explained by the fact that the mere translation of the title ʿabdî did not seem clear enough, since the following prophecy clearly had to apply to the future saving king." Syrén, "Targum Isaiah 52:13–53:12," 203, points to certain verbal agreements between *Tg. Isa.* 52:13 and the description of David in *Tg. 1 Sam.* 18 (see esp. v. 30) to provide additional support for the messianic interpretation of *Tg. Isa.* 52:13.

30. Cf. Betz, "Die Übersetzungen von Jes 53," 202.

ple in the *BHS* apparatus), not only the translator of the Septuagint,[31] but also the Targumist read עָלֶיךָ in his Hebrew *Vorlage,* in accordance with 1QIsa[a][32] and the Masoretic Text.[33]

Although the addition of מְשִׁיחָא in *Targum of Isaiah* 52:13 is determinative for the overall understanding of *Targum of Isaiah* 52:13–53:12, it appears to be only a tiny change to the *Vorlage* compared to the Targumist's rendering of many other statements in this text. But can we then still affirm Koch's claim cited above that the translation is not arbitrary but that "the Hebrew text is followed word for word" (see above, p. 193)? I choose a few examples to show that in my opinion, Koch is right.

Isaiah 53:3b in the MT reads: וּכְמַסְתֵּר פָּנִים מִמֶּנּוּ נִבְזֶה וְלֹא חֲשַׁבְנֻהוּ, "and as one from whom others hide their faces he was despised, and we held him of no account." This is rendered in the Targum as: וּכְמָא דַהֲוֵית מְסַלְקָא אַפֵּי שְׁכִינְתָּא מִנַּנָא בְּסִירִין וְלָא הֲשִׁיבִין, "and as when *the* face *of the Shekhinah was*

31. For the LXX text see either J. Ziegler, ed., *Isaias: Septuaginta, Vetus Testamentum Graecum auctoritate Academiae Litterarum Gottingensis editum,* 2nd ed., vol. 14 (1967), or A. Rahlfs, ed., *Septuaginta* (1935; reprinted 1979). Where the MT changes from speaking *to* the Servant in the second person in Isa. 53:14aα to speaking *about* him in the third person in v. 14aβ-b ("many were astonished at *you* — so marred was *his* appearance," etc.), the LXX retains the second person address throughout the verse: ὃν τρόπον ἐκστήσονται ἐπὶ σὲ πολλοί, οὕτως ἀδοξήσει ἀπὸ ἀνθρώπων τὸ εἶδός σου καὶ ἡ δόξα σου ἀπὸ τῶν ἀνθρώπων, "as many shall be astonished at *you,* so deglorified from among men will be *your* appearance and *your* glory from among these men" (trans. E. R. Ekblad, *Isaiah's Servant Poems According to the Septuagint* [1999], 175, italics added).

32. 1QIsa[b] unfortunately has a textual gap at this point. See E. L. Sukenik, *The Dead Sea Scrolls of the Hebrew University* (1955), plate 10, col. 8, l. 11.

33. *Tg. Isa.* 52:14aα reads: כְּמָא דְסַבָּרוּ לֵיהּ בֵּית יִשְׂרָאֵל יוֹמִין סַגִּיאִין, "*Just as the house of Israel hoped for him many days,*" instead of the Hebrew, "Just as many were astonished at you." From this several scholars have concluded that the Targumist read in his *Vorlage* עָלָיו, "at him" rather than the MT's עָלֶיךָ, "at you," including Stenning, *The Targum of Isaiah,* xix; Hegermann, *Jesaja 53 in Hexapla, Targum und Peschitta,* 67; Koch, "Messias und Sündenvergebung," 125. But by simply inferring from the Aramaic סַבָּרוּ לֵיהּ the Hebrew שָׁמְמוּ עָלָיו, these exegetes fail to consider the Targumist's basic thought about the text's overall meaning. It is tempting to charge *them* with "atomistic exegesis" of the Targum! Hegermann, 68, admits that it is unclear to him "how the Targum arrived at the translation of שָׁמְמוּ [*were astonished*] by סַבָּרוּ [*hoped*]" and concludes that it must be a "free translation." But much more plausible is our explanation that סַבָּרוּ is not directly derived from שָׁמְמוּ but rather goes back to the Targumist's knowledge that the suffering and despised house of Israel described in v. 14 sets its hope upon the Messiah presented in v. 13. Nevertheless, the *BHS* apparatus may be right to suggest that the Targumist's הֲוָו חֲשׁוּךְ corresponds to a reading of מְשָׁחַת or מָשְׁחָת in the Hebrew text of v. 14aβ (cf. Hegermann, 67 n. 3). In any case the Targum's messianic interpretation of Isa. 52:13–53:12 did not originate from the reading משחתי in 1QIsa[a], which can be read as מָשַׁחְתִּי, "I have anointed."

taken up from us, they are despised and not esteemed." At first glance this appears to have little to do with the Hebrew *Vorlage,* as Chilton's italics show. But if one realizes that the absolute term פָּנִים in the Hebrew text is taken by the Targumist as an anthropomorphism for the divine face and that he consistently refers to this as "the face of the (my, your) *Shekhinah,*"[34] then everything looks different. The third person singular suffix of the Hebrew מִמֶּנּוּ, referring to the one "from whom" others hide their faces, is referred by the Targumist to the first person plural, which is certainly possible grammatically.[35] The text then says that God's face veils itself *from us.* Moreover, the Hebrew particle כְּ before מַסְתֵּר shows that a comparison is involved. It is clear to the Targumist from the context that the focus of the comparison is the state of the Gentile kingdoms: it is as bad as Israel's state was when God withdrew his Shekhinah from them.

If *Targum of Isaiah* 53:3bα is understood this way, then the meaning of verse 3bβ follows almost as a matter of course: like many of the words in the text, the Hebrew נִבְזֶה, "he was despised," is understood as a collective singular and is therefore rendered in the Aramaic translation by the plural בְּסִירִין, "*they are* despised." The last phrase of the Hebrew text, הֲשַׁבְנֻהוּ, must be parallel to נִבְזֶה. Perhaps the Targumist read the same consonants but vocalized differently from the MT, reading the word as the substantive חֶשְׁבֹּן with the uncontracted suffix *ᵉhû,* i.e., "and his reckoning was not," which he once again appropriately renders as וְלָא חֲשִׁיבִין, "and they are not esteemed." If this analysis of *Targum of Isaiah* 53:3b is correct, then we cannot accuse the translator of arbitrariness.[36]

As a further example let us turn to the first part of Isaiah 53:7. The Hebrew reads: נִגַּשׂ וְהוּא נַעֲנֶה, "He was oppressed, and he was afflicted." The Targum reads totally differently: בָּעֵי וְהוּא מִתּוֹתַב, "He *beseeches,* and he *is answered.*" But even here the Targumist follows the original text very closely. For the last letter of the first Hebrew word, נגש, he apparently read שׁ rather than שׂ, yielding נִגַּשׁ or נִגָּשׁ, the niphal perfect third singular or the niphal participle of נגשׁ, meaning "he approached" or "he drew near."[37] God is understood as the one approached, and therefore drawing near to him amounts to petition or beseeching. The Targumist reads the last Hebrew term, נַעֲנֶה, exactly as it stands in the MT. However, instead of deriving it from the root ענה II (*HALOT*; BDB ענה III) in the sense "to be bowed down, afflicted," he has derived it from the

---

34. As a parallel see *Tg. Isa.* 59:2; cf. 8:17; 54:8; 64:6 (Chilton 64:7) and elsewhere in *Targum Jonathan,* e.g. *Tg. Jer.* 33:5; *Tg. Ezek.* 7:22; 39:23-24, 29; *Tg. Mic.* 3:4.

35. Cf. GKC §103, 2c.

36. This analysis is for the most part taken from Koch, "Messias und Sündenvergebung," 133.

37. W. Gesenius, *Hebräisches und aramäisches Wörterbuch über das Alte Testament,* 17th ed. (1962), 485; BDB 620 s.v. נָגַשׁ.

much more common root עָנָה I with the niphal meaning "to be provided with an answer."[38] The Targumist's ithapal participle מְתּוֹתַב, from the root תוב,[39] corresponds to this niphal participle נַעֲנָה. Therefore here too in verse 7 we can discern a translation technique oriented to the actual words of the Hebrew text.

These two examples should suffice to illustrate the Targumist's translation technique.[40] Almost everywhere in the *Targum of Isaiah* 52:13–53:12 it is possible to show how he arrived at his translation without any arbitrary procedures. The Targumist is convinced that this Bible text deals with the glorification and exaltation of the Messiah (see above on 52:13) and furthermore that the Messiah is not a suffering one, which he finds confirmed in the change of third to second person from 52:13 to 52:14.[41] Armed with this fundamental conviction as a hermeneutical key, the translator goes about his work. The material changes over against the Hebrew *Vorlage* can all be explained by this hermeneutical principle. The Targumist offers a theologically reflected and consistent interpretation of Isaiah 53 and is able thereby to retain an impressive proximity to the smallest components of the Bible text. His Aramaic translation of the fourth Servant Song really does constitute "a respectable accomplishment," as Otto Betz has said.[42]

4. Structure, Content, and Parallels

4.1. In the original Hebrew version of Isaiah 52:13–53:12 there is an alternation of speaker between Yahweh and a group of persons who speak in the first person plural. The passage is both introduced (52:13-15) and concluded (53:11aβ-12) by Yahweh speeches, while the material in between (53:1-11aα) is a "we" speech. Whereas the Yahweh speeches announce the *future* exaltation of the Servant, the "we" speech focuses for the most part on the new view the "we" group has gained from the first Yahweh speech into the *past* suffering and death of the Servant, which has now replaced their earlier view of the same topic. Only in

38. *HALOT* 2:852 s.v. עָנָה I, niphal; cf. Gesenius, *Wörterbuch*, 603-4.

39. G. Dalman, *Grammatik des jüdisch-palästinischen Aramäisch*, 2nd ed. (1905; reprinted 1978), 326 § 70.11.

40. For further examples see below nn. 51, 57, 70.

41. Cf. Chilton, *Glory of Israel*, 91-92, who in discussing whether anti-Christian polemic played a role in the Targum's reception of the prophetic text rightly remarks: "[O]ne may think that no tendency is evident but the primitive motif of a victorious messiah in whom suffering would be anomalous" (91). "It is far more plausible [than the assumption of anti-Christian polemic] to suppose that the meturgeman, who was unperturbed by Christian claims, was influenced by primitive messianology as he rendered the MT" (92).

42. Betz, "Die Übersetzungen von Jes 53," 201.

the last sentences, verses 10aγ-b and 11aα, does the "we" speech turn to describing the Servant's future as the Yahweh speech does: "he shall see his offspring, and shall prolong his days; through him the will of the Lord shall prosper. Out of his anguish he shall see light and find satisfaction."

The translation of the text in the *Targum of Isaiah* takes over this structure only in part. The framing Yahweh speeches, *Targum of Isaiah* 52:13-15 and 53:12 (which is now shorter than the second Yahweh speech in the Hebrew), are still maintained, but the center piece (53:1-11) now appears as the speech of the prophet, which also partly allows the repentant Israelites of the messianic age to express themselves in the first person plural in *Targum of Isaiah* 53:4-6. The narrative present is understood to be the desperate situation of Israel depicted in *Targum of Isaiah* 52:14, against which the rest is to be seen as *future events*.[43] Koch proposed the thesis that these future events in *Targum of Isaiah* 52:13–53:12 are divided into five chronologically ordered scenes. A drama of the messianic age is depicted, running from the Messiah's accession to his reign in 52:13-15 through several "clearly marked stations"[44] up to the final dividing of the spoil and the subjecting and forgiving of the rebels in 53:12.[45] But Koch's view leads inevitably to strained exegesis of individual statements in the text,[46] and it also cannot be supported by the use of the Aramaic particle בְּכֵין in verses 3, 4, 12 as he claims.[47] The Targumist presents not a chronological sequence of scenes but only different aspects of the messianic age.

43. Cf. Hofius, "Kennt der Targum zu Jes 53 einen sündenvergebenden Messias?" 216, 239 nn. 12, 14, for this understanding of the Targum text.

44. Koch, "Messias und Sündenvergebung," 147.

45. See especially Koch's overview, "Messias und Sündenvergebung," 147.

46. Thus, for example, Koch's position shows signs of tension when on the one hand he must understand the Targum's rendering of Isa. 53:11aα as a backward temporal reference, "because the [Hebrew] original allows no other possibility" ("Messias und Sündenvergebung," 143), while on the other hand he must dispute that the idea of the Messiah declaring others innocent described in the rest of the verse should be "referred to the messianic judgment," since this judgment is supposedly already past according to vv. 8-9. Rather, Koch believes that the idea of making others righteous should be referred to "granting other people the ability to follow the will of God" (ibid., 144).

47. Koch, "Messias und Sündenvergebung," 131, 134, 145, thinks that the Aramaic term בְּכֵין in *Tg. Isa.* 53:3, 4, 12, which Stenning and Chilton translate simply as "then," serves "to announce a new scene" (131), and therefore Koch translates it with a stronger temporal sense as *danach*, "after this," "afterwards," "thereafter" (though somewhat differently in *Tg. Isa.* 53:12; see Koch 145 with n. 1). But this view is not supported by the use of בְּכֵין elsewhere in the *Targum of Isaiah* (cf., e.g., *Tg. Isa.* 1:18; 10:4; 16:5; 60:5). The particle must be translated more neutrally as "then." Each use of בְּכֵין in *Tg. Isa.* 53 has the function of introducing another aspect of the messianic age (rather than different ages or stages). See Hofius, "Kennt der Targum zu Jes 53 einen sündenvergebenden Messias?" 241 n. 28; cf. also 243 n. 58.

4.2. The messianic age is preceded by a condition of degradation and crisis in Israel (*Tg. Isa.* 52:14). Hence Gentiles rule Israel's land (53:8), the temple is destroyed (v. 5), and the Israelites themselves are partly enslaved in their own land by Gentile rulers (v. 11), partly scattered among the Gentiles as exiles (vv. 6, 8). The Targumist sees this dire situation as caused by Israel's own sin (vv. 4-6, 8, 10-12) and as God's punishment of the people (v. 4). As argued above, this description of Israel's situation seems applicable to the beginning of the second century C.E. (see p. 197). But it is also so general that the same description can readily be applied to many other historical situations as a type of the crisis created by the sins of God's people.

Into this situation there now comes a prophetic message of good tidings, a בְּסוֹרְתָא (*Tg. Isa.* 53:1).[48] The Messiah so passionately hoped for and expected by suffering Israel (*Tg. Isa.* 52:14) will soon appear in holy brilliance (53:2), which in its stark contrast to the despised degradation of Israel will stun the Gentile peoples into silence (52:15). The glory of the Gentile kingdoms will turn to contempt and cease (v. 3). The Messiah will free the land of Israel from foreign rulers (v. 8), scatter (52:15) and destroy (vv. 7-8) the Gentile peoples, and give their treasure to the Israelites as spoil (vv. 11-12). For Israel the appearance of the Messiah signals the moment of truth. He will hand over the "wicked" (רַשִׁיעַיָא) among them to Gehenna and eternal condemnation (v. 9), while the "righteous" (צַדִּיקַיָא [v. 2]) among them he will acquit as innocent (v. 11).[49] Contrite Israelites who formerly belonged to the wicked but now

---

48. By its translation in 53:1 of the Hebrew שְׁמֻעָתֵנוּ (RSV, NRSV, NJB, NJPS, "what we have heard"; cf. KJV, "our report"; NASB, "our message") by בְּסוֹרְתַנָא, "our report" or "message" (cf. Stenning, *The Targum of Isaiah*, "tidings"), the Targum creates a connection to the מְבַשֵּׂר, "messenger," of Isa. 52:7 (= מְבַסַּר in *Tg. Isa.* 52:7) who announces the dawning of the kingdom of God. As a translation of שְׁמוּעָה, the expression בְּסוֹרְתָא in *Targum Jonathan* can stand, as it does here, for the message of salvation, but also for the message of judgment, as for example in *Tg. Ezek.* 21:12, where the "tidings" of coming destruction cause hearts to melt (trans. S. H. Levey, *The Targum of Ezekiel*, ArBib 13 [1987], 66). Cf. P. Stuhlmacher, *Das paulinische Evangelium, I: Vorgeschichte*, FRLANT 95 (1968), 131-33.

49. I construe the expression יְזַכֵּי זַכָּאִין in *Tg. Isa.* 53:11 in the same way as do Chilton, *The Isaiah Targum*, 105 ("he [shall] make *innocents* to be accounted *innocent*"), Jeremias, "παῖς θεοῦ," TDNT 5:694 ("he will pardon the innocent"), Hegermann, *Jesaja 53 in Hexapla, Targum und Peschitta*, 90-91, and Hofius, "Kennt der Targum zu Jes 53 einen sündenvergebenden Messias?" 232-33. Unlike Seidelin, "Der 'Ebed Jahwe," 215, 224, and Koch, "Messias und Sündenvergebung," 144, I do not apply this pardon or acquittal of the "innocent" to the immediately following "many" who are to be made into servants of the law (see below, n. 52). Rather, I understand this declaring innocent as applying only to the righteous (cf. *Tg. Isa.* 53:2) who have not sinned but have kept the law with a perfect heart (cf. *Tg. Isa.* 7:3; 26:2).

repent[50] will gain a share in salvation through the Messiah's ministry; he will "beseech" or make intercession for their sins (vv. 4, 11, 12),[51] which will be forgiven them for his sake (vv. 4, 6, 12). Israel, once again gathered in their own land after the Messiah has brought back the exiles (v. 8), will throng around the Messiah to be taught the law by him; he will make them truly subject to the law (vv. 11, 12),[52] by which they receive forgiveness of sins (v. 5). In a land freed of foreigners which was in need of a Messiah (v. 2), the people, now refined, cleansed, and obedient (v. 10), will see the kingdom of their Messiah (v. 10), which will be characterized by inexpressible wonders (v. 8). The Messiah will lavish on them the plunder of the Gentile peoples (vv. 11-12) and build for them a new sanctuary in place of the old desecrated and destroyed temple (v. 5). This briefly summarizes the content of *Targum of Isaiah* 52:13–53:12.

4.3. Many features of the picture sketched in *Targum of Isaiah* 53 also appear elsewhere in the *Targum of Isaiah*. Hence *Targum of Isaiah* 11:10 says that the Gentiles and their kingdoms will be obedient to the Messiah, while 16:1 says that they will pay him tribute. According to 10:27 and 14:29, the Messiah will shatter and punish them. The Messiah is depicted as a righteous judge in 11:3-4; 28:6, and as bringing back the exiles in 11:11-12. The Messiah's own fear of the Lord

---

50. Hofius, "Kennt der Targum zu Jes 53 einen sündenvergebenden Messias?" 220-23 (cf. also the pertinent notes on pp. 245-46), has proved in detail that the *Targum of Isaiah* differentiates consistently between the "righteous," the "wicked," and the "repentant" in Israel (cf., e.g., 10:21-23; 33:13-14; 57:19-20) and that these three groups are represented also in our text. In Chilton's remarks on "Repentance" (*Glory of Israel*, 37-46), the problem with his distinction between different, chronologically sequential theological "levels" (cf. above, p. 196) becomes evident, because he attributes the language of the repentance of wicked individuals only to the Amoraic stage, while he thinks that the notion of the collective-national repentance of Israel is to be found at the older Tannaitic stage to which he assigns Isaiah 53 (cf. above nn. 23, 24).

51. The Targumist has not imported the idea of the Messiah's intercession in *Tg. Isa.* 53:4, 11, 12 from outside the text. Rather, he uses the words בְּעֵי עַל חוֹבִין, "to beseech concerning sins" (Chilton), to translate the following Hebrew expressions: נָשָׂא חֳלָיִים (v. 4aα) (the חֳלָיִים or "infirmities" [NRSV] are similarly understood as "sins," ἁμαρτίαι, in the LXX and 1 Pet. 2:24), סָבַל עֲוֹנוֹת (v. 11b), and נָשָׂא חֵטְא (v. 12bα). Therefore he understood these idioms not as statements about the Servant's bearing sins in the sense of vicariously suffering the penalty of sin, but as statements about his intercession for sinners in petition before God. Cf. Hofius, "Kennt der Targum zu Jes 53 einen sündenvergebenden Messias?" 225; also Hegermann, *Jesaja 53 in Hexapla, Targum und Peschitta*, 78.

52. On this understanding of שַׁעְבֵּיד לְאוֹרָיְתָא see J. Bowman, *The Gospel of Mark: The New Christian Jewish Passover Haggadah* (1965), 71-72, and Hofius, "Kennt der Targum zu Jes 53 einen sündenvergebenden Messias?" 234: this expression "need not denote a violent act of the Messiah; it can just as well mean that by his instruction, the Messiah makes the unrepentant into 'servants of the Torah,' those who 'do the Torah' (עָבְדֵי אוֹרָיְתָא)."

and its extension over the whole earth is spoken of in 11:2-3, 9. His kingdom will be characterized by glory and joy and peace for Israel according to several texts (4:2; 9:5; 11:1, 6, 10; 28:5).

These traits of the Messiah attested in various passages of the *Targum of Isaiah*[53] also appear in early Jewish texts outside the Targum, such as the famous *Psalms of Solomon* 17. According to this text, presumably from the first century B.C.E.,[54] the Messiah on the one hand will likewise drive the Gentiles out of the holy land and the holy city, punishing and destroying them (*Pss. Sol.* 17:22-24, 29-30, 35-36). On the other hand he will gather Israel as a holy people in their land (vv. 26-28) and rule them as a righteous, sinless, and God-instructed king (vv. 32, 35-36). This rule will be characterized by blessing, longevity, and glory grounded in the Messiah's fear of God and righteousness (vv. 37ff.). Notable is the outstanding role of the Messiah's words in *Psalms of Solomon* 17, comparable with *Targum of Isaiah* 53:5:

> His words will be purer than the finest gold, the best. . . . His words will be as the words of the holy ones, among sanctified peoples. Blessed are those born in those days to see the good fortune of Israel which God will bring to pass in the assembly of the tribes. (*Psalms of Solomon* 17:43-44, trans. *OTP* 2:668-69)

The Messiah's words also play a role in judgment according to verse 35: "He will strike the earth with the word of his mouth forever."

Targum of Isaiah 53 presents the Messiah as judge of the peoples and the wicked and as ruler of the God-fearing and law-keeping Israel in its glorious *shalom* existence, thereby exhibiting many connections to other statements about the Messiah in the *Targum of Isaiah* and generally in early Judaism. Next to these frequently occurring features *Targum of Isaiah* 53 also offers details that are less widespread and therefore draw more attention to themselves. These seem to deal with matters that have not necessarily been dictated by the general messianic ideas of the time, but rather have been taken specifically from the translated biblical text, Isaiah 52:13–53:12. These include the statements about the Messiah as intercessor for Israel (vv. 4, 11, 12), about the forgiveness of sins granted Israel for his sake (vv. 4, 6, 12), about his ministry as teacher of the law (vv. 5, 11, 12),[55] and about the Messiah as the builder of the new temple (v. 5). These statements raise the question whether there is an inner theological con-

---

53. On the Messiah in the Targumim other than the *Targum of Isaiah* see Levey, *The Messiah*, and Chilton, *Glory of Israel*, 112-17.

54. Cf. R. B. Wright, "Psalms of Solomon," *OTP* 2:640-41.

55. On Isa. 53:11-12 see above n. 52.

nection between the Messiah's erecting of the new temple, his teaching in the law, and the forgiveness of sins effected through his intercession.

5. The Portrait of the Messiah

5.1. The Messiah as Teacher of the Law

Targum of Isaiah 53:5 reads:

> And he *will build the sanctuary which was profaned* for our *sins, handed over* for our *iniquities; and by his teaching the* peace[56] *will increase* upon *us,* and in *that we attach ourselves to his words our sins will be forgiven* us.

The idea of the Messiah as a teacher of the law that here clearly comes to expression[57] corresponds to *Targum of Isaiah* 11:5 (cf. *Tg. Onq.* Gen.

---

56. Chilton's translation, modified. Although Chilton correctly renders "*his* peace" based on the reading שְׁלָמֵיה accepted by most interpreters, the alternative reading שְׁלָמָא, "*the* peace," is to be preferred based on the parallel statements in *Tg. Isa.* 9:5 (Chilton 9:6); 11:6 (cf. also 38:17) about *the* peace "in the days of the Messiah" (cf. *Tg. Isa.* 53:8). Cf. Hofius, "Kennt der Targum zu Jes 53 einen sündenvergebenden Messias?" 242 n. 38.

57. The language of the Messiah's "teaching," אֻלְפָנֵיה, in *Tg. Isa.* 53:5 comes about because the Targumist has understood the word מוּסָר in the Hebrew not as moral "discipline" (BDB) — that is, "chastisement" (KJV; NJPS) or "punishment" (NRSV; NJB) — but as "instruction" or "teaching," a meaning found, for example, in Prov. 1:8; 4:1, where we may compare NRSV "instruction" with NJPS "discipline." (Moreover, a text like Sir. 30:1-13 shows how close together these two meanings lay in educational and pedagogical practice.) Similarly the Targumist has interpreted the Hebrew expression חֲבֻרָתוֹ (NRSV "his bruises") not in terms of its biblical meaning "wound, slash" (*HALOT* 1:285, s.v. חַבּוּרָה or its hypothetical form *חֲבוּרָה), but in the light of a later meaning "company, association, party, . . . the colleagues at school" (M. Jastrow, *A Dictionary of the Targumim, the Talmud Babli and Yerushalmi, and the Midrashic Literature* [1903], 1:416, s.v. חֲבוּרָה I, as distinct from חַבּוּרָה, "wound"). Hence the Targumist understands the Hebrew בַּחֲבֻרָתוֹ as meaning "in his company" or "in association with him." This may in turn have been suggested by the identity of the later Hebrew meaning with the Aramaic meaning "group, party, collegium of disciples" (M. Sokoloff, *A Dictionary of Jewish Palestinian Aramaic of the Byzantine Period* [1990], 184 s.v. חֲבוּרָה). The Targumist then interprets or "decodes" this company or association as a *learning* community and speaks of the people "gathering around his words." (For "decoding" or *Entschlüsselung* and its application in *Tg. Isa.* 53:5 compare Koch, "Messias und Sündenvergebung," 123 item 4 with 136 ll. 15-18.) This analysis goes back to Seidelin, who explains: "[The Targumist] understood חבורה in its late Hebrew sense: 'company, association.' 'His company' in the Jewish way of thinking must naturally mean: 'when we gather around his words,' i.e. in synagogues and lecture halls of the messianic age, where the Messiah himself will appear as teacher" ("Der 'Ebed Jahwe," 213). See also Hofius, "Kennt der

49:11);[58] 12:3; and also 42:7, despite the uncertain transmission of the term "Messiah" next to "Servant" in 42:1 (see above, p. 198). The expectation that the Messiah will minister as a teacher of the law is not attested elsewhere in the *Targum of the Prophets*,[59] but it is common in other Targumim[60] and also occurs both in the rabbinic literature[61] and occasionally in pre-Christian Jewish texts.[62]

The consequence of the repentant Israelites "attaching" themselves to the instructive words of the Messiah in *Targum of Isaiah* 53:5 is the forgiveness of their sins. Koch thinks that the Messiah speaks a "forgiving" or "redeeming" word "which applies to those who turn to him in faith."[63] He therefore understands the Messiah to be the subject who forgives.[64] But because פִּתְגָמוֹהִי, "his words," stands parallel to אֻלְפָנֵיה, "his teaching," the expression "his words" here refers to nothing other than his teaching of the law. The idea of devotion or attachment to the words of the Messiah as the foundation of the forgiveness of sins is the same in the *Targum of Isaiah* as the return of the repentant wicked to the law (cf., e.g., *Tg. Isa.* 1:16-18; 26:10; 31:6; 57:19). By this teaching the Messiah "subjects" them to the law (vv. 11-12),[65] so that they become true עַבְדֵי אוֹרָיְתָא, "servants of the law," who will prosper in the Lord's pleasure in the messianic kingdom (cf. *Tg. Isa.* 53:10). As teacher of the law the Messiah leads the repentant to obey the law, but the forgiveness that they need he cannot pronounce; this is for God alone.[66] We must therefore disagree with Koch when he

---

Targum zu Jes 53 einen sündenvergebenden Messias?" 231; Betz, "Die Übersetzungen von Jes 53," 207. Finally, it is a sign of the Targumist's skill that despite his not retaining the root *msr* in his translation of מוּסָר by אֻלְפָן, he is able to do so in using the verb אִתְמְסַר, *"handed over"* (cf. Chilton, *The Isaiah Targum*, 104).

58. *Tg. Onq.* Gen. 49:11: *"the righteous shall be round about him* [sc. the Messiah]; *and they that carry out the Law shall be with him in study"* (trans. B. Grossfeld, *The Targum Onqelos to Genesis*, ArBib 6 [1988], 158). The Aramaic text may be found in A. Sperber, *The Bible in Aramaic*, vol. 1: *The Pentateuch According to Targum Onkelos* (1959), 85, and Dalman, *Aramäische Dialektproben*, 7.

59. Cf. Chilton, *Glory of Israel*, 116.

60. Cf. *Tg. Onq.* Gen. 49:11 (above n. 58); see further *Tg. Ps.* 45:10-11 and *Tg. Cant.* 8:1-2.

61. Cf. R. Riesner, *Jesus als Lehrer: Eine Untersuchung zum Ursprung der Evangelien-Überlieferung*, 3rd ed., WUNT 2/7 (1988), 327-29.

62. Such as *Pss. Sol.* 17:43-44 (cited above, p. 206), although this does not expressly mention the Messiah's teaching of the law. On *1 Enoch* 49:1-4 and 51:3 see Riesner, *Jesus als Lehrer*, 323-24.

63. Cf. Koch, "Messias und Sündenvergebung," 136.

64. Koch's view is taken up by Haag "Der 'Gottesknecht,'" 31.

65. See above n. 52.

66. For God as the subject of the forgiveness of sins in *Tg. Isa.* 53 see below, p. 218.

claims to find "the idea of a Messiah who forgives sins in word and deed"[67] attested in *Targum of Isaiah* 53.[68]

5.2. The Messiah as Builder of the Temple

The statement about the temple, "the house of the sanctuary" (בֵּית מַקְדְּשָׁא), in *Targum of Isaiah* 53:5 is not an arbitrary insertion into the text,[69] but is based upon the understanding of וְהוּא מְחֹלָל מִפְּשָׁעֵנוּ in the Hebrew *Vorlage* as "he was *desecrated/profaned/polluted* for our transgressions."[70] That the sin

---

67. Koch, "Messias und Sündenvergebung," 148.

68. For a refutation of Koch see above all Hofius, "Kennt der Targum zu Jes 53 einen sündenvergebenden Messias?" 229-32. See further Chilton, *Glory of Israel*, 93, 157 n. 17; B. Janowski, "Sündenvergebung 'um Hiobs willen': Fürbitte und Vergebung in 11QtgJob 38,2f. und Hi 42,9f. LXX," *ZNW* 73 (1982): 251-80, esp. 276 n. 126; C.-H. Sung, *Vergebung der Sünden: Jesu Praxis der Sündenvergebung nach den Synoptikern und ihre Voraussetzungen im Alten Testament und frühen Judentum*, WUNT 2/57 (1993), 143.

69. So Hegermann, *Jesaja 53 in Hexapla, Targum und Peschitta*, 79.

70. Compare with this interpretation the usual English translations of Isa. 53:5: "But he was *wounded* (KJV, NRSV, NJPS, NJB)/*pierced through* (NASB) for our transgressions." The difference between the Targum and the familiar interpretation comes about because two Hebrew homonyms חלל are involved. According to *HALOT* (1:319-20), the root חלל I is most frequent in the piel, where its common meaning is "to profane." It is also frequent in the hiphil, which can mean "to allow to be profaned" (Ezek. 39:7) but usually means "to begin." The second root, חלל II, occurs much less frequently; in the polel it means "to pierce" (Isa. 51:9; Job 26:13). The MT of Isa. 53:5 contains the corresponding polal participle (passive of the polel) of this less frequent verb: "he was wounded" (*HALOT*) or "pierced through" (NASB). It is attractive to assume that the Targumist read מחלל as מְחֻלָּל, the pual participle of חלל I, translated "profaned," as in Ezek. 36:23; *HALOT* conjectures that this may have been the original Hebrew reading in Isa. 53:5. But it is not necessary to assume that the Targumist derived מחלל from חלל I, because חלל II is also attested in the pual participle (Ezek. 32:26). Whichever Hebrew root is involved, the next word מִפְּשָׁעֵנוּ with the prefixed preposition מִן gives the cause: "But he was wounded [or profaned] *because of* our sins" (NJPS); cf. BDB, 580, s.v. מִן 2.f. Aquila's Greek translation of והוא מחלל מפשענו also understands מחלל in the sense of profanation or ritual defilement, but applies it to the Servant rather than the temple: καὶ αὐτὸς βεβηλωμένος ἀπὸ ἀθεσ(μ)ιῶν ἡμῶν, "and he was profaned because of our lawless deeds" (text in Ziegler's second apparatus [*Isaias*, 321]; for similar examples of the perfect passive participle βεβηλωμένος, -η, -ον, cf. Lev. 21:7, 14; 1 Macc. 4:38, 44; for the causative use of ἀπό, cf. BDAG, 106, s.v. ἀπό 5.a.). Koch explains the Targum's application of the term מחלל to the temple as follows ("Messias und Sündenvergebung," 135-36): "The phrase 'that which/he who was profaned by our transgressions' can be applied much more easily to the temple than to a human being. It shows that the Targumist disapproves so strongly of the present state of the temple that he regards Israel's religious center — as the Qumran community does — as profaned and delivered up to destruction (cf. *Tg. Isa.* 28:1-4)."

of Israel defiles the Lord's temple in Jerusalem is a fact well known to the Targumist from the Old Testament.[71] Reference should be made above all to Ezekiel 8–11, where the practice of foreign cults in the Jerusalem temple (cf. particularly Ezek. 8:10-17) brings judgment upon Israel. All the apostates will be killed (9:1ff.) and the sanctuary will be defiled by their corpses (9:7). The judgment culminates in the departure of God's glory, his כָּבוֹד, from the temple (10:18-19; 11:22-23).[72] The Targumist expresses not only here in *Targum of Isaiah* 53:5 but also in other passages in the *Targum of Isaiah* that Israel's sins have profaned the temple (cf. *Tg. Isa.* 5:1-4; 28:9-13). The consequence of this profaning is that God takes up his Shekhinah from the temple (*Tg. Isa.* 5:5).[73] This corresponds naturally to the withdrawal of the כָּבוֹד in Ezekiel,[74] and as in Ezekiel, it also brings with it the destruction of the temple (*Tg. Isa.* 5:5; 32:14; 63:17-18).[75] It also follows that the language about the temple in *Targum of Isa-*

71. The rabbis too could attribute the destruction of the temple to particular sins of Israel; cf. *b. Yom.* 9b; *b. Shabb.* 119b.

72. That these events properly are to be classified as a desecration of the sanctuary is confirmed by the explicit statements in Ezekiel where Israel or groups within Israel, such as the priests, are the subject of the piel form of the verb "to profane" (חלל I), with Yahweh's sanctuary as the object: Ezek. 22:26; 23:39; 44:7. God's judgment of the sanctuary is expressed in similar language: הִנְנִי מְחַלֵּל אֶת־מִקְדָּשִׁי, "Behold, I will *profane* my sanctuary (Ezek. 24:21). For the prohibition of profaning the sanctuary see Lev. 21:12, 23.

73. The close connection of the Shekhinah with the sanctuary in Targumic thought is evident in the frequent designation of the temple as בֵּית שְׁכִינְתָּא, "house of the Shekhinah" (e.g., in *Tg. Isa.* 17:11; 26:21; 38:11; 48:15; 56:5). Cf. also *Tg. Jer.* 7:15; 15:1; 52:3, where the Aramaic expression אֲרַע בֵּית שְׁכִינְתִי or אֲרַע בֵּית שְׁכִינְתֵיהּ, "the land of the house of my/his Shekhinah," corresponds to the Hebrew פָּנַי or פָּנָיו, "my face" or "his face" (the suffix here obviously refers to God). For the translation of Hebrew פָּנִים by Aramaic Shekhinah see above n. 34 with its main text. The localization of the Shekhinah on Zion is clearly expressed in *Tg. Isa.* 8:18: שְׁכִינְתֵיהּ בְּטוּרָא דְצִיּוֹן, "his Shekhinah is on Mount Zion" (cf. also *Tg. Isa.* 28:10; *Tg. Hab.* 2:20; *Tg. Joel* 4:17, 21). The same close connection is attested by the sayings in *Tg. Isa.* 4:5; 30:20; 52:8; 60:13 that announce the future return of the Shekhinah to the sanctuary on Zion. Yet this is not to deny that the Shekhinah according to the *Targum of Isaiah* also transcends the earthly temple on Mount Zion (cf., e.g., *Tg. Isa.* 32:15; 37:16; 38:14; 40:22; 45:15). That there is a connection between the presence of the Shekhinah on Zion and in heaven is clear from *Tg. Isa.* 6:1-6; cf. the repeated phrase "in the heavens of the height." On this whole topic see Chilton, *Glory of Israel*, 69-75, 100.

74. This analogy holds despite the fact that the Hebrew כָּבוֹד is consistently translated by יְקָרָא in the Targums (so also *Tg. Ezek.* 10:18-19; 11:22-23). Cf. G. Kittel, "δόξα, E: כָּבוֹד and יְקָרָא in Palestinian Judaism," *TDNT* 2:245-47.

75. According to Ezek. 8:1, Ezekiel's great vision of judgment in Ezekiel 8–11, including the departure of God's glory from the temple, takes place in the sixth year of the exile of King Jehoiachin, i.e., in 592 B.C.E. (cf. Ezek. 1:2 for the counting of the years and below, n. 86). The prophet is informed about the fall of Jerusalem and with it the destruction of the temple only in the twelfth year of the exile, from an eyewitness who had escaped from the city (Ezek. 33:21; cf.

iah 53:5 is anticipated by the statement in verse 3 that *"the Shekhinah was taken up from us."*[76] To be sure, verse 3 involves a comparison to the contemptible condition of the Gentile kingdoms, yet this comparison is not to be understood as unreal,[77] but rather speaks of a previous event or of a previous and ongoing condition: it will soon be as bad for these glorious kingdoms as it is at the moment for Israel, oppressed in its own land and fainting in the exile, living without the temple, that is, without the presence of the Shekhinah, the gracious presence of God.[78] This crisis situation will come to an end only when the Messiah builds a new temple to replace the old one, which was profaned for Israel's sins and handed over to destruction for their iniquities. This new temple is the subject of the promises of the renewed and never-ending presence of the Shekhinah: "And the LORD will give you *the possessions* of *the adversary* and *the plunder* of *the one who distresses,* and *he* will not any more *take up his Shekhinah from the sanctuary,* but your eyes will see *the Shekhinah in the sanctuary"* (*Tg. Isa.* 30:20; cf. 4:5; 52:8).[79]

If according to the *Targum of Isaiah* Israel's crisis consists of the absence of the Shekhinah, and a renewed presence of the Shekhinah depends on a new temple, then one might think that when describing the Messiah's saving ministry, the Targumist was simply forced to ascribe the erecting of the new temple to him, because the eschatological salvation of Israel without the Shekhinah presence of Yahweh is simply unthinkable. One could then ask whether the lan-

---

24:26). That Jerusalem's desolation is not a coincidental stroke of fate but the fulfillment of Yahweh's judgment foretold by the prophet becomes clear among other things from the fact that Yahweh opens the mouth of the prophet whom he had previously silenced (cf. Ezek. 24:15-27) and enables him once again to proclaim the Lord's word (33:22, cf. 23ff.). Now Israel can and must recognize that Ezekiel's proclamation of judgment, which they so far have ignored or related to a remote future (cf. Ezek. 12:21-28), was from the Lord and applies to them, for as the Lord promises Ezekiel, "On that day your mouth shall be opened to the one who has escaped, and you shall speak and no longer be silent. So you shall be a sign to them; and they shall know that I am the Lord" (Ezek. 24:27).

76. Cf. the remarks above, pp. 200-201. The departure of God's glory in *Tg. Isa.* 53:3 is correctly seen as an indirect statement about the temple's destruction by several interpreters, including Koch, "Messias und Sündenvergebung," 133; van der Kooij, *Die alten Textzeugen,* 171, and Hofius, "Kennt der Targum zu Jes 53 einen sündenvergebenden Messias?" 241 n. 31.

77. Cf. the unreal condition in Jeremias's German translation of *Tg. Isa.* 53:3: "wie wenn die Schekina das Gesicht von uns gewendet *hätte*" ("παῖς θεοῦ," *TWNT* 5:692, italics added), though this uncertainty is removed in Bromiley's English translation: "as when the *shekinah* turns its face from us" (*TDNT* 5:694). Similar to Jeremias is Haag, "Der 'Gottesknecht,'" 28.

78. Cf. *Tg. Isa.* 57:17; 59:2.

79. Statements about the presence of the Shekhinah in the age of salvation in the *Targum of Isaiah* once again correspond to statements about God's כָּבוֹד in Ezekiel; cf. Ezek. 43:1ff.

guage about the Messiah as builder of the temple in verse 5 is merely an isolated statement that of necessity resulted from the exegesis of the prophetic text Isaiah 53. Many of the early Jewish texts that speak of an eschatological temple would at first seem to confirm this conclusion, for they make no mention of the Messiah's work in building the temple.[80] But while these texts prove that in early Judaism people could very well imagine the construction of the new temple without the work of the Messiah, it would nevertheless be premature to conclude that the Messiah has nothing to do with it. For there are further examples which show that the ministries that the Messiah performs according to

---

80. According to 11QTemple (11Q19) 29:8-9 ("I shall make my glory reside over it until the day of creation, when I shall create my temple"; trans. *DSSSE*, 1251) and *Jub*. 1:29 ("until the day of the new creation . . . until the sanctuary of the Lord is created in Jerusalem upon Mount Zion"), God will bring forth a new temple by an act of new creation; *Jub*. 1:17 speaks of God "building" his sanctuary (cf. v. 27). In the Animal Apocalypse of *1 Enoch* 85:1–90:38, the metaphor of a "house" usually stands for Jerusalem and is distinguished from the "tower" as the actual metaphor for the temple (cf. *1 Enoch* 89:50 [*OTP* text: "building"; margin: "tower"], 54, 56, 66-67, 72-73; in 89:36 the "house" is a metaphor for the wilderness tabernacle). Nevertheless, the "house" whose pillars and columns are pulled out and replaced by new ones in *1 Enoch* 90:28-29 may include both the temple and the new Jerusalem in which it is located. If so, then this passage simply says that God replaces the old sanctuary by a new one in the eschatological Jerusalem; the book speaks about the Messiah only after this transformation has already taken place (90:37). According to the Apocalypse of Weeks in *1 Enoch* 93:1-10; 91:11-17, in the eighth week of the world the righteous will acquire "houses" (or "great things," *1 Enoch* 91:13a; cf. Isa. 65:21-22), and "a house shall be built to the Great King in glory for evermore" (91:13b; from the perspective of 93:7-8 this clearly refers to the future temple). The variation between the active and the passive within this single verse, 91:13, perhaps shows that the righteous are actively involved in acquiring their own houses but not in building the temple. An analogous distinction may be present in Tob. 14:5b: "After this they all will return from their exile and will rebuild (οἰκοδομήσουσιν) Jerusalem in splendor; and in it the temple of God will be rebuilt (οἰκοδομηθήσεται), just as the prophets of Israel have said concerning it." Whether the passive "will be rebuilt" intends to designate God as the builder of the new, eternal temple (as in *Jub*. 1:17) is hard to say, especially since the plural οἰκοδομήσουσιν, "*they* will rebuild," in this verse is used both of Jerusalem and of "the house" (τὸν οἶκον), presumably referring to "the temple *of God*" (NRSV). However that may be, there is no special role for the Messiah as the builder of the temple in these texts. [[(Tr.) In Tob. 14:5, the NRSV combines the right interpretation with potentially misleading textual criticism. The genitive τοῦ θεοῦ belongs textually in the expression ὁ οἶκος τοῦ θεοῦ . . . οἰκοδομηθήσεται in v. 5b, but not in οἰκοδομήσουσιν τὸν οἶκον in v. 5a, where the addition of τοῦ θεοῦ, effectively assumed by the NRSV ("they will rebuild the temple *of God*"), is attested in only a single Greek manuscript, minuscule no. 46. The translators have assimilated the two expressions in the context, presumably without meaning to suggest that this has strong manuscript support. For the text and variants see R. Hanhart, ed., *Tobit*, Septuaginta: Vetus Testamentum Graecum Auctoritate Academiae Scientiarum Gottingensis editum 8/5 (1983), 178-79.]]

some texts are ascribed directly to God and his activity in other texts.[81] Within early Judaism, then, *Targum of Isaiah* 53:5 is not a unique and completely isolated statement about the Messiah as the builder of the new temple.

Targum of Isaiah 53:5 finds its nearest parallel in *Targum of Zechariah* 6:12-13a:

> Thus speaks the Lord of hosts, saying, Behold, the man whose name is *Anointed will be revealed, and he shall be raised up,* and shall build the temple of the Lord. He shall build the temple of the Lord and he shall assume majesty and shall sit and rule upon his throne.[82]

The Masoretic Text of the same passage runs:

> Thus says the Lord of hosts: Here is a man whose name is Branch: for he shall branch out in his place, and he shall build the temple of the Lord. It is he that shall build the temple of the Lord; he shall bear royal honor, and shall sit and rule on his throne. (NRSV)

In this case there are already two clear references to the building of the temple in the Hebrew *Vorlage*.[83] The person depicted in this Yahweh oracle receives the name Branch, צֶמַח. It has already been shown above that the Targumist consistently understands the Branch in the Hebrew text as the Messiah (see p. 199), and he does so here as well. This is an interpretation that is fully in agreement with the proclamation of the prophet Zechariah. For צֶמַח occurs a total of two times in Zechariah (3:8; 6:12), both times in sayings addressed to the high priest Joshua (cf. 3:8aα; 6:11b-12aα), and it is clear that by the Branch a person other than the high priest Joshua himself is meant. Both the

---

81. For example, it is God himself who brings back the exiles according to Bar. 2:34; Tob. 14:5a; *Jub.* 1:15 and 11QTemple (11Q19) 59:11-12, whereas the same activity is ascribed to the Messiah in *Tg. Isa.* 11:11-12; 53:8. The close connection between God's bringing back the exiles and his raising up his Messiah (or Memra) as his instrument for liberating Israel is illustrated by *Tg. Jer.* 30:1-11, esp. vv. 8 and 11: "[The people of Israel] *shall obey the Anointed, the son of* David, their king whom I will raise up for them"; and "*my Memra is at your assistance*, says the Lord, to redeem you" (trans. R. Hayward, *The Targum of Jeremiah*, ArBib 12 [1987], 128).

82. *Tg. Zech.* 6:12-13a, trans. R. P. Gordon, in K. J. Cathcart and R. P. Gordon, *The Targum of the Minor Prophets*, ArBib 14 (1989), 198. Text in Sperber, *Bible in Aramaic*, 3:485, and Dalman, *Aramäische Dialektproben*, 12:

כִּדְנָן אֲמַר יוי צְבָאוֹת לְמֵימַר הָא גַבְרָא מְשִׁיחָא שְׁמֵיהּ עֲתִיד דְּיִתְגְּלֵי וְיִתְרַבֵּי וְיִבְנֵי יָת הֵיכְלָא דַיוי

הוּא יִבְנֵי יָת הֵיכְלָא דַיוי וְהוּא יְטוֹל זִיו וְיִתֵּיב וְיִשְׁלוֹט עַל כּוּרְסוֹהִי

83. On Zech. 6:12-13 and *Tg. Zech.* 6:12-13 see Seidelin, "Der 'Ebed Jahwe," 212-13.

context in Zechariah (chapter 4) and the preaching of the contemporary prophet Haggai show clearly that the Branch must be meant to refer to Zerubbabel, governor of Judah.[84] According to a word of Yahweh to the prophet in Zechariah 4:8-9, Zerubbabel had laid the foundation of the new temple and would also complete it,[85] which agrees with the statement about the Branch in Zechariah 6:12-13. According to 1 Chronicles 3:17-19 Zerubbabel is a grandson of Jeconiah (Jehoiachin) and therefore a Davidide.[86] We can therefore refine this description of the Branch and the equation of the Branch with the Messiah by the Targumist by saying that this "Branch-Messiah" comes from the line of David, just as in the relevant Branch promises in Jeremiah (cf. Jer. 23:5; 33:15). The *Targum of Isaiah* also clearly identifies the Messiah as David's offspring or, in dependence upon the Hebrew *Vorlage* in Isaiah 11:1, 10, as the offspring of David's father Jesse (1 Sam. 16:11-12): see *Targum of Isaiah* 11:1, 10; 14:29. Therefore according to *Targum of Isaiah* 53:5 and *Targum of Zechariah* 6:12-13 it is the Davidic, royal Messiah who builds the new temple.[87]

5.3. The Messiah as Intercessor

As already mentioned, the question of the forgiveness of sins takes a central place in *Targum of Isaiah* 53, which is clear already from the frequent use of the root שבק,[88] once in the peal with the meaning "forgive" (v. 6), and three times in the ithpeel with the meaning "be forgiven" (vv. 4, 5, 12). Koch suspects that there is a close functional relationship in *Targum of Isaiah* 53 between the forgiveness of sins and the erecting of the new temple by the Messiah:

---

84. See the juxtaposition of Zerubbabel the governor and Joshua the high priest as the two leading figures in Jerusalem at the time of the rebuilding of the temple: Hag. 1:1, 12, 14; 2:2 (so also in the work of the Chronicler, e.g., Ezra 3:2; Neh. 12:1).

85. Cf. also Hag. 2:1-9.

86. Jehoiachin succeeded his father Jehoiakim on the throne in Jerusalem during Nebuchadnezzar's first campaign against Judah (2 Kings 24:6), and just three months later (24:8), he was taken captive to Babylon (24:15), where he remained until he was released from prison thirty-seven years later (25:27-30). Zerubbabel is called the "son of Shealtiel" by the Chronicler and Haggai (e.g., Ezra 3:2; Neh. 12:1; Hag. 1:1), and this Shealtiel is a son of Jehoiachin according to 1 Chron. 3:17.

87. Cf. J. Ådna, *Jesu Stellung zum Tempel: Die Tempelaktion und das Tempelwort als Ausdruck seiner messianischen Sendung*, WUNT 2/119 (2000), 50-87, for a detailed treatment of the Messiah as builder of the temple in the Old Testament and early Judaism, esp. 76-86 with regard to the Targumim.

88. On the use of the Aramaic root שבק, cf. Janowski, "Sündenvergebung," 266-68.

Because in the opinion of the late Israelite period a functional sanctuary and a celebration of the rite of the Day of Atonement are indispensable for true forgiveness of sins, the messianic forgiveness of sins[89] can come about only through the erecting of the new sanctuary.[90]

Since the forgiveness of sins occurs moreover on the basis of the Messiah's intercession (cf. "he will beseech," vv. 4, 11, 12) and "for his sake" (בְּדִילֵיהּ, vv. 4, 6, 12),[91] Koch sees the Messiah in *Targum of Isaiah* 53 in the role of a priest,[92] even mentioning the possibility that the Messiah performs the end-time Day of Atonement ritual as high priest.[93] But this assumption is very unlikely, and not only because *Targum of Isaiah* 53 is silent about priestly-cultic functions of the Messiah. The book of Zechariah is tradition-historically important for the Messiah's ministry as temple builder, and this book with its reception in *Targum of Zechariah*, as well as *Targum Jonathan* as a whole, differentiate precisely between the competencies of the Messiah and those of the high priest or the priests. Zechariah 6:12-13a, cited above, continues in verse 13b according to the Hebrew: "There shall be a priest by his throne, with peaceful understanding between the two of them" (NRSV).[94] This peaceful coexistence fits the picture Zechariah draws of the

89. For criticism of Koch's thesis of a Messiah who forgives sins in *Tg. Isa.* 53, see above, pp. 208-9 with nn. 63-68.

90. Koch, "Messias und Sündenvergebung," 136. Koch believes that the Messiah's erecting of the temple qualifies him for his role as the forgiver of sin, adding: "After building the temple, the Messiah is able to speak a redeeming word" (ibid.). For the decisive role of the temple in the forgiveness of sin in Israel, Koch refers in the same context (136 n. 1) to his essay, "Sühne und Sündenvergebung um die Wende von der exilischen zur nachexilischen Zeit," *EvT* 26 (1966): 217-39, reprinted in idem, *Spuren des hebräischen Denkens: Beiträge zur alttestamentlichen Theologie: Gesammelte Aufsätze I*, ed. B. Janowski and M. Krause (1991), 184-205.

91. Although Sperber's text reads לֵיהּ as the last word of *Tg. Isa.* 53:12, the reading should probably be בְּדִילֵיהּ, given the strong manuscript support in Sperber's apparatus: cf. *The Bible in Aramaic*, 3:109.

92. Cf. Koch, "Messias und Sündenvergebung," 144: "The Messiah to a large extent takes on priestly functions." Cf. ibid., 137, 138, 141-42, 148.

93. Thus, for example, Koch asks concerning the transfer of Israel's sins to the Gentiles in *Tg. Isa.* 53:8: "Is this perhaps an act similar to the activity of the high priest with the scapegoat in Lev 16:20-21?" ("Messias und Sündenvergebung," 140; cf. 134, 144).

94. The collocation translated above by the NRSV as "peaceful understanding," עֲצַת שָׁלוֹם (lit., NASB: "counsel of peace"), has also been interpreted as "peaceable agreement" (*HALOT* 2:867, s.v. עֵצָה I, definition 3) or "agreement in plans" ("Übereinstimmung in Plänen," Gesenius, *Wörterbuch*, 610). On the eschatological harmony and agreement between the king and the priests see Jer. 33:14-22.

relationship between the Davidic governor Zerubbabel and the high priest Joshua.[95]

In Zechariah's fourth night vision, Zechariah 4:1-6aα, 10b-14,[96] Zerubbabel and Joshua are presented equally next to one another as two olive trees and are called שְׁנֵי בְנֵי־הַיִּצְהָר, "the two anointed ones," literally "the two sons of oil." Accordingly for Zechariah the high priest stands as a "son of oil" or anointed one next to the royal Davidic ruler. This view is retained in *Targum of Zechariah* 6:13b: "And there shall be a *high* priest beside his throne, and there shall be peaceful understanding between the two of them."[97] This distinction between the two different figures is confirmed by other passages in *Targum Jonathan,* according to which God will also raise up priests next to the Messiah, who will perform their service before God (*Tg. Jer.* 33:21-22)[98] or God's Messiah according to God's will (*Tg. 1 Sam.* 2:35).[99] The power of the Messiah's intercession to effect forgiveness of sins therefore does not rest on a priestly ministry which he supposedly exercises in a new temple, as Koch assumes.[100] If anything can be said about the reason for

---

95. In the list of the high priests from Aaron to the exile in 1 Chron. 6:1-15 (6:1-15 NRSV = 5:27-41 MT), it is Jehozadak the father of Joshua (cf. Hag. 1:1, 12, 14; 2:2) who stands in last place; by implication, Joshua himself continues the high priestly line from the exile to the second temple.

96. See on this H. Gese, "Anfang und Ende der Apokalyptik, dargestellt am Sacharjabuch" (1973), reprinted in idem, *Vom Sinai zum Zion: Alttestamentliche Beiträge zur biblischen Theologie,* 1st ed., BEvT 64 (1974; 3rd ed., 1990), 202-30, esp. 210-11.

97. Trans. R. P. Gordon in Cathcart and Gordon, *The Targum of the Minor Prophets,* 198. Text in Sperber, *The Bible in Aramaic,* 3:109, and Dalman, *Aramäische Dialektproben,* 12: וִיהֵי כָהֵין רַב עַל כּוּרְסוֹהִי וּמַלְכָּא דִשְׁלָמָא יְהֵי בֵין תַּרְוֵיהוֹן. It is no accident that Gordon's rendering of מַלְכָּא דִשְׁלָמָא in *Tg. Zech.* 6:13 by "peaceful understanding" is exactly the same as the NRSV translation of the corresponding Hebrew עֲצַת שָׁלוֹם (see n. 94), since מֵלֵךְ/מִלְכָּא or מַלְכָּא in Aramaic is the usual Targumic rendering of the Hebrew עֵצָה (cf., e.g., *Tg. Isa.* 11:2; 14:26; 19:11, 17). As rightly indicated by Gordon's italics, the only novelty in the Targum over against the Hebrew is its designation of the priest beside the throne as a "*high* priest."

98. מְשַׁמְּשִׁין קֳדָמָי.

99. וִישַׁמֵּישׁ קֳדָם מְשִׁיחִי. Cf. also Chilton, *Glory of Israel,* 96. On the evaluation of the priests in *Tg. Isa.* 22:15-15 see Chilton, *The Isaiah Targum,* 45 with note.

100. A connection between sacrifice and the intercession that effects forgiveness of sins is found in a very interesting comparative text, Job 42:7-10. Here it is reported how at God's request, Job intercedes for his friends Eliphaz, Bildad, and Zophar, against whom God's wrath is kindled because unlike Job, they have not spoken of God what is right. The Masoretic Text requires Job's friends to sacrifice a burnt offering and Job to offer a prayer of intercession (v. 8), but the LXX version attributes more of the activity to Job, who not only prays but also sacrifices the burnt offering (v. 8). The LXX also emphasizes much more Job's person and intercession as the absolute prerequisite for the forgiveness of his friends, for in a plus over against the MT, God explains to the friends why only Job can intercede: Ἰωβ δὲ ὁ θεράπων μου εὔξεται περὶ ὑμῶν, ὅτι εἰ μὴ πρόσωπον αὐτοῦ λήμψομαι· εἰ μὴ γὰρ δι᾽ αὐτόν, ἀπώλεσα ἂν ὑμᾶς, "And Job my

the effectiveness of the Messiah's intercession, the answer must be sought in the Messiah's fear of God and his perfect obedience to the law (cf. *Tg. Isa.* 9:5; 11:2-3). The one who intercedes for the sins of Israel is none other than the one who, as teacher of the law, leads back to the law the repentant wicked, whose sins will be forgiven them for the sake of their obedience to the law.[101]

The effect of the Messiah's intercession is the forgiveness of sins granted to repentant sinners in Israel for his sake (*Tg. Isa.* 53:4, 12). I have already shown that the subject of the forgiveness expressed in *Targum of Isaiah* 53:5 by the ithpeel of the verb שבק is not the Messiah (see above, pp. 208-9). Moreover, in the two other verses in *Targum of Isaiah* 53 where this verb occurs in the ithpeel, there is in contrast to verse 5 an explicit mention of the Messiah's "beseeching" or intercession (cf. vv. 4, 12),[102] so that the Messiah here cannot be the subject

---

servant will pray for you, because I will accept him [lit., his face]; *for were it not for his sake, I would have destroyed you*" (v. 8). Moreover, in v. 9 where the MT is satisfied with saying that "the Lord accepted Job," the LXX speaks more explicitly of the Lord forgiving the friends' sin *for Job's sake:* καὶ ἔλυσεν [sc. ὁ κύριος] τὴν ἁμαρτίαν αὐτοῖς διὰ Ιωβ, "And [the Lord] pardoned them their sin for Job's sake." That it is Job's intercession that effects this forgiveness is clear from the next verse: ὁ δὲ κύριος ηὔξησεν τὸν Ιωβ· εὐξαμένου δὲ αὐτοῦ καὶ περὶ τῶν φίλων αὐτοῦ ἀφῆκεν αὐτοῖς τὴν ἁμαρτίαν, "And the Lord prospered Job; and when he prayed also for his friends, he forgave their sin" (Job 42:10a). From this vantage point the previous statements that God would have annihilated the friends were it not for Job (LXX v. 8) and that God forgave them their sins for Job's sake (v. 9) can be made more precise: because of Job's intercession, his friends are spared annihilation and are granted forgiveness. An Aramaic translation of our text, particularly of Job 42:9b, 10, is found in 11Q *Targum of Job* (11Q10), col. 38, ll. 2-3. Unfortunately because of textual gaps we do not know whether this Targum spoke of a burnt offering and, if so, whether it understood the sacrificer to be the friends, as in the MT, or Job, as in the LXX. In any case the preserved portion remains very interesting. Corresponding to v. 9b in the MT ("and the Lord accepted Job"), the 11Q Targum of Job reads: אלהא ושמע אל[ה]וא בקלה די איוב ושבק (3) להון חטאיהון בדילה, "and G[o]d heard Job's voice and forgave them their sins on his account" (text and translation from *DSSSE*, 1200-1201). The Aramaic terms are exactly as in *Tg. Isa.* 53: the peal of שבק for "to forgive," and בדילה for "on his account/for his sake." For a detailed discussion of Job 42:7-10 in the MT, the LXX, and 11QtgJob see Janowski, "Sünden-vergebung."

101. Cf. Betz, "Übersetzungen," 207-8: "Forgiveness of sins occurs for the sake of the Servant, who intercedes for his own. But effective intercession and forgiveness presuppose a life of Torah observance. Therefore the Servant (עֶבֶד) becomes 'one who makes servants' of others (מְשַׁעֲבֵד), in that he 'subjects the rebels to the law'; only then is his intercession for their sins legitimate (*Tg. Isa.* 53:12b)." Cf. ibid., 212. On the idea of the intercessor's own merits as an essential prerequisite for his effective intercession see *Tg. Isa.* 59:16; 63:5. See further R. le Déaut, "Aspects de l'intercession dans le Judaïsme ancien," *JSJ* 1 (1970): 35-57, esp. 49-50, and Bowman, *Gospel of Mark*, 72: "the Messiah, because of his merit is efficacious in prayer as was Moses, and many of the Hasidim."

102. *Tg. Isa.* 53:4: בְּכֵין עַל חוֹבָנָא הוּא יִבְעֵי וַעֲוָיָתָנָא בְּדִילֵיהּ יִשְׁתַּבְקָן, "*Then he will beseech concerning our sins, and our iniquities for his sake will be forgiven.*" 53:12: וְהוּא עַל חוֹבֵין

who forgives sins. Rather, it is explicitly said that forgiveness occurs "for his sake" (בְּדִילֵיה). This indirect connection between the forgiveness of sins and the Messiah is confirmed by verse 6, where next to שבק in the peal with God as subject, the sins are the object, and there is a separate reference to the Messiah ("for his sake"): "*before* the LORD *it was* a *pleasure* to forgive the *sins* of us all *for his sake*."[103] It follows that the uses of the ithpeel of שבק in verses 4, 5, 12 are to be understood as divine passives, circumlocutions for God's activity. This is further confirmed by the fact that the statements in verses 4 and 12 about the Messiah's intercession and the consequent forgiveness[104] are formulated in correspondence to the so-called נִסְלַח + כִּפֶּר formula of Leviticus 4–5 and Numbers 15. The formula runs: "The priest shall make atonement (כִּפֶּר) for him/them, and it shall be forgiven (נִסְלַח) to him/them."[105] The change from the active piel form כִּפֶּר with the priest as the subject to the passive niphal form נִסְלַח shows that not the priest but God is the subject of forgiveness.[106] The same holds by analogy for the statements of forgiveness in *Targum of Isaiah 53*. When it says that forgiveness occurs "for his sake" (vv. 4, 6, 12), this is to be understood as a reference to his intercession, which here corresponds to the priestly atonement ritual in Leviticus 4–5 and Numbers 15.[107]

סַגִּיאִין יְבְעֵי וּלְמָרוֹדַיָּא יִשְׁתְּבִיק בְּדִילֵיה, "yet he *will beseech concerning* the *sins* of many, and *to the rebels it shall be forgiven for him.*"

103. *Tg. Isa.* 53:6: לְמִשְׁבַּק חוֹבֵי כֻלָּנָא בְּדִילֵיה.

104. Cf. n. 102.

105. וְכִפֶּר עָלָיו/עֲלֵיהֶם הַכֹּהֵן וְנִסְלַח לוֹ/לָהֶם. The basic formula, which then appears in certain variations, is found in Lev. 4:31b: וְכִפֶּר עָלָיו הַכֹּהֵן וְנִסְלַח לוֹ (concerning the sin of one of the "ordinary people" who is not a priest or ruler). Cf. also Lev. 4:20, 26, 35; 5:10, 13, 16, 18; 19:22, 26; Num. 15:25, 28. For orientation see B. Janowski, *Sühne als Heilsgeschehen: Traditions- und religionsgeschichtliche Studien zur Sühnetheologie der Priesterschrift*, 2nd ed., WMANT 55 (2000), 249ff.

106. Cf. Janowski, *Sühne als Heilsgeschehen*, 251-52: "Since the passive נִסְלַח ["it will be forgiven"] is doubtless a circumlocution for the divine subject, a clear difference is made between the subject of atonement [sc. the priest] and the subject of forgiveness."

107. Hofius, "Kennt der Targum zu Jes 53 einen sündenvergebenden Messias?" 224-25, points out that the Targum's way of relating intercession and forgiveness has an exact parallel in the Vulgate's translation of the נִסְלַח + כִּפֶּר formula. In dealing with this formula the Vulgate consistently renders כִּפֶּר — usually rendered in English by "to make atonement" (e.g., NRSV) — by *rogare*, "to ask, beg, solicit," or by *orare*, "to pray, beg, beseech, entreat" someone for something. [[(Tr.) Compare or contrast the other Latin terms used to translate the piel כִּפֶּר elsewhere in the Pentateuch, such as *expiare/expiatio*, "to expiate/expiation" (e.g., Exod. 29:36; Lev. 1:4; 6:30; 16:16, 27, 30, 32-33; 17:11, etc.), *deprecare*, "to ward off or avert, to intercede for the averting of evil, to obtain pardon for transgression" (e.g., Exod. 30:10; Lev. 9:7; Num. 6:11), or *placare*, "to assuage, appease, pacify, placate; to reconcile or cause to be reconciled" (e.g., Exod. 30:10).]] Therefore Hofius concludes: "The Vulgate sees the granting of forgiveness as God's answer to

In the concluding divine speech in *Targum of Isaiah* 53:12 the Servant's being rewarded with the treasures of the Gentiles is justified by an attention-grabbing clause which seems to stand close to the statement of the Servant's suffering in the Hebrew *Vorlage:* "Then[108] I will divide him *the plunder of* many *peoples,* and he shall divide the spoil, *the possessions of* strong *fortresses;* because he *handed over* his soul to the death," חֲלָף דִּמְסַר לְמוֹתָא נַפְשֵׁיה. According to Hegermann, "here a statement of suffering is translated in accordance with the Hebrew text."[109] In Jeremias's opinion it probably refers, in accordance with the original Hebrew text, "to death (or danger of death) from maltreatment, cf. Is. 53:7f."[110] Although Koch holds, with reservations, that "the Aramaic text is open to an interpretation in terms of the actual death of the Messiah,"[111] it must be concluded from the otherwise multiply attested meaning of מְסַר נַפְשָׁא as "to put oneself in danger"[112] that the Targum says only that the Messiah put himself in danger of death, not that he actually died. Several interpreters refer the statement thus understood to violent military

---

the priest's intercession. The Targum of Isaiah 53 sees the connection between Messiah's intercession and Yahweh's forgiveness no differently" (ibid., 225). Cf. also Janowski, "Sündenvergebung," 275 with n. 123, and le Déaut, "Aspects de l'intercession," 56 and 47 n. 3. However, le Déaut sees the Messiah's intercession not only as a correspondence or parallel to the priest's making of atonement, but, rather like Koch, he sees the Messiah's intercession as *priestly intercession.* For the more precise sense of "for the Messiah's sake" as meaning "for his intercession's sake," see the individual contexts in *Tg. Isa.* 53:4, 6, 12. In vv. 4 and 12, the term בְּדִילֵיה, "for his sake," refers back to his intercession (Chilton, *The Isaiah Targum,* speaks of the Messiah's "beseeching"). In v. 6, the same term בְּדִילֵיה points forward to the Messiah's intercession in v. 7. See further above, n. 100.

108. Cf. above n. 47.

109. Hegermann, *Jesaja 53 in Hexapla, Targum und Peschitta,* 92. Because of its remaining trace of a Suffering Servant, Hegermann considers this portion of *Tg. Isa.* 53:12 to be "a piece of the old text that has been preserved" (ibid.), that is, a piece of Hegermann's proposed older version of *Tg. Isa.* 53 (see above, p. 191).

110. Jeremias, "παῖς θεοῦ," *TDNT* 5:694 n. 301.

111. Koch, "Messias und Sündenvergebung," 146. Nevertheless, Koch assumes that "the Targumist himself is presumably not yet reckoning with the violent death of the prophesied Servant" (ibid., 148). At the same time Koch states that the notice of the Messiah's death in 4 Ezra (2 Esdras) 7:29 ("After those years my son the Messiah shall die," NRSV) could be understood as an interpretation of the statement in *Tg. Isa.* 53:12. Aytoun, "The Servant of the Lord in the Targum," 177, concludes, without further analysis, from *Tg. Isa.* 53:12 "that though the Targum elsewhere does away with the Suffering of the Servant-Messiah, it actually leaves a statement that the Messiah had submitted to death."

112. Hofius, "Kennt der Targum zu Jes 53 einen sündenvergebenden Messias?" 253 nn. 171, 178, and Syrén, "Targum Isaiah 52:13–53:12," 210, mention among others the following references: *Tg. Onq.* Deut. 24:15; *Tg. Ps.-J.* Num. 31:5; *Tg. Judg.* 9:17 and *Tg. Ps.* 99:6.

conflicts which the Messiah must confront.[113] Chilton says more generally "that the Messiah risked his very life for the sake of his ministry"[114] and thereby rightly refuses to limit the danger of death to military conflicts. Syrén considers a connection to the *Aqedah:*[115] "Perhaps, then, the Messiah's 'risking' of his life is . . . to be regarded in this light: in the mode of Isaac, he will do his utmost — if God so asks of him — to fulfil his God-given assignment."[116] However, in my opinion the idea that was central in connection with the *Aqedah* of the merits of the fathers benefiting later generations[117] plays no role in *Targum of Isaiah* 53,[118] and it is also not obvious and understandable how Isaac should be a type of the Messiah in *Targum of Isaiah* 53 who puts himself in danger of death.

When we ask about a typological pattern for the Messiah's readiness to risk death for his ministry, it is rather Moses who comes into consideration,

113. Cf. Seidelin, "Der 'Ebed Jahwe," 215: "Where this danger to life lies cannot be determined from the text; but since the beginning of the verse points to war, one may probably assume that there is an allusion to the dangers of the war that will precede the Messianic age." This is also mentioned as a possibility by Jeremias, "παῖς θεοῦ," *TDNT* 5:694 n. 301 (though see n. 110 above, with its text, for Jeremias's preferred option), and Hegermann, *Jesaja 53 in Hexapla, Targum und Peschitta,* 92, for the present — to their mind revised — form of the text. By contrast, Koch, "Messias und Sündenvergebung," 146, refers the statement about the Messiah's handing over his soul to death in *Tg. Isa.* 53:12 to the last part of the verse, which talks about subjecting the rebels to the law, and concludes in favor of "the motif of a violent encounter of the Messiah with rebels."

114. Chilton, *The Isaiah Targum,* 105.

115. Syrén, "Targum Isaiah 52:13–53:12," 212: "An expression such as 'putting one's life at stake' indeed suggests a background in martyrological vocabulary, so it would seem possible that the Targumist did see the Messiah of Is. 53 in association with the Aqedah." (The Aqedah or "binding of Isaac," עֲקֵדַת־יִצְחָק, refers to the haggadic interpretation of Genesis 22.) Syrén, 211, refers to the tradition of the Palestinian Targumim on Genesis 22 and cites in particular *Tg. Neof.* Gen. 22:14 (in addition to Syrén's translation see now M. McNamara, *Targum Neofiti 1: Genesis,* ArBib 1A [1992], 118-19). A synopsis of the various Palestinian Targumim on Genesis 22 in German translation is available: P. Naumann, *Targum — Brücke zwischen den Testamenten I: Targum-Synopse ausgewählter Texte aus den palästinischen Pentateuch-Targumen,* Bibel-Kirche-Gemeinde vol. 34 (1991), 126-39 (cf. commentary, 140-49).

116. Syrén, "Targum Isaiah 52:13–53:12," 212.

117. Cf. Syrén, "Targum Isaiah 52:13–53:12," 211: "The Targumist [in *Tg. Isa.* 53] may have been inspired also by other figures and other complexes," including "the idea of the merits of the Fathers benefiting their descendants." Syrén continues: "The 'binding' of Isaac is central in this context."

118. This is not to suggest that this concept plays no role elsewhere in the *Targum of Isaiah;* the Targumist certainly knows and accepts the concept of the merits of the fathers (e.g., *Tg. Isa.* 62:6).

since like the Messiah of *Targum of Isaiah* 53 he is an intercessor for Israel.[119] Exodus 32:30-34 records his intercession for Israel after the people had sinned a "great sin" (חֲטָאָה גְדֹלָה) with the Golden Calf (cf. vv. 30-31).[120] In this connection Moses says to God: "But now, if you will only forgive their sin — but if not, blot me out of the book that you have written" (v. 32). As intercessor Moses enters a "zone of special endangerment, where the issue is not just any fate for the guilty individuals or the guilty people, but their very demise or survival."[121] To be sure, in the original context, Moses' request to be blotted out of God's book in case the people are not forgiven is not an offer by him to suffer substitutionary punishment to atone for Israel's sin. It is rather his expression of his solidarity with the people, that he wants to be destroyed along with them in case they are not forgiven.[122] Nevertheless, as Otfried Hofius has shown, the Jewish interpretive tradition on Exodus 32:32 in part understands this request by Moses precisely as this sort of readiness to take the punishment for sin upon himself vicariously:

> And so you also find (in the Scripture) that the patriarchs and the prophets offered their lives in behalf of Israel (נתנו נפשם על ישראל). As to Moses, what did he say: "Yet now, if thou wilt forgive their sin; and if not blot me, I pray Thee, out of the book which Thou hast written" (Ex. 32.32). (*Mekilta,* pisha 1 on Exodus 12:1)[123]

119. Cf. Exod. 32:9-14, 30-34; 34:8-9; Num. 14:10-20; Deut. 9:18-19, 25ff.; 10:10; Ps. 106:23. Scholars who rightly point to Moses as an example of intercession include Bowman, *The Gospel of Mark,* 69, 72 (cf. above n. 101), and Betz, "Die Übersetzungen von Jes 53," 210.

120. On this text see Janowski, *Sühne als Heilsgeschehen,* 142-44.

121. Janowski, *Sühne als Heilsgeschehen,* 150-51. Cf. also 150: "According to the basic structure of intercession, the intercessor is a *mediator who vicariously stands in the 'breach'* [Ps. 106:23] *between God and humanity arising from moral, religious, or legal guilt.* . . . By 'stepping in' between the two parties, the mediator aims 'to turn away God's wrath from' the people (חֵמָה מִן הֵשִׁיב: Num. 25:11; Jer. 18:20; Ps. 106:23), thus making possible a restored relationship between God and humanity."

122. So Janowski, *Sühne als Heilsgeschehen,* 144, and Hofius, "Kennt der Targum zu Jes 53 einen sündenvergebenden Messias?" 235. Moreover, Hofius refers to the midrash *Exodus Rabbah* 46:1 on Exod. 34:1 to show that the Jewish interpreters later understood Exod. 32:32b in this way. For a translation see H. Freedman and M. Simon, eds., *Midrash Rabbah,* vol. 3: *Exodus,* trans. by S. M. Lehrman, 3rd ed. (1983), 526-28, esp. 527: "When he [Moses] realised that there was no future hope for Israel, *he linked his own fate with theirs* and broke the Tables, saying to God: 'They have sinned; well, I have now also sinned in breaking the Tables. If Thou wilt forgive them, forgive me also'" (italics added).

123. Hebrew text and translation from J. Z. Lauterbach, *Mekilta de-Rabbi Ishmael,* vol. 1 (1933; reprinted 1961), 10 l. 106 (Hebrew). For the Jewish history of interpretation concerning Exod. 32:32b, I am dependent on Hofius, who also cites *b. Ber.* 32a and *b. Sot.* 14a as further refer-

Hofius to my mind argues convincingly that the causal clause in *Targum of Isaiah* 53:12 should be understood analogously as an expression of the Messiah's readiness to die:

> The Targumist knows how to speak of a final, deep struggle of the Messiah for the salvation of the sinners of Israel who justly have fallen under the sentence of death. For the salvation of their forfeited life the Messiah will offer his own life to God. . . . On the basis of this readiness for vicarious surrender of life, God will open to the "rebels" the possibility of repentance. This is realized when those who previously have despised Yahweh's Torah are "subjected to the Torah" by the Messiah's teaching, being trained and led back to Torah obedience by him.[124]

As the intercessor for Israel the Messiah does not hesitate to jump into the "breach" between sinners and God that resulted from their guilt. God allows his readiness for vicarious death to benefit him; according to verse 12 he rewards him with the plunder and possessions of the Gentile peoples. The death necessary to remove the reality of sin strikes precisely these Gentile peoples instead of Israel or the Messiah according to verse 8.[125]

5.4. Conclusion: The Davidic Messiah as the Sole Mediator of Salvation

Although I do not share Klaus Koch's view of the connection between the cultic and intercessory ministries of the Messiah in *Targum of Isaiah* 53 (see above, p. 215), I too would like to argue for a theologically conscious connection between the roles of the Messiah as temple builder and as intercessor, together with other functions attributed to the Messiah in the text, for example, his role as teacher of the law. There were groups within early Judaism whose eschatol-

---

ences for the idea of "the declared readiness of the intercessor before God to suffer death vicariously in order to atone for the sin of Israel" ("Kennt der Targum zu Jes 53 einen sündenvergebenden Messias?" 236).

124. Hofius, "Kennt der Targum zu Jes 53 einen sündenvergebenden Messias?" 236.

125. See *Tg. Isa.* 43:3-4. Furthermore, several rabbinic texts clearly connect Isa. 43:3-4 to the final judgment, in which Israel's salvation will be made possible by a ransom in the form of the life of the nations. See *Mekilta*, tractate Nezikin 10 on Exod. 21:30 (Lauterbach, *Mekilta de-Rabbi Ishmael*, 3:87-88); *Exod. Rab.* 11:2 on Exod. 8:19 (*Midrash Rabbah*, 3: *Exodus*, 139); *Sipre* 333 on Deut. 32:43 (*Sifre to Deuteronomy: An Analytical Translation*, 2 vols., trans. J. Neusner, BJS 98, 101 (1987), 2:382 at *Sipre* 333.V.2). See also W. Grimm, *Weil ich dich liebe: Die Verkündigung Jesu und Deuterojesaja*, 2nd ed., ANTJ 1 (1981), 245-46.

ogy reckoned with a plurality of saving mediator figures, including the Qumran community, which according to 1QS 9:11, 4QTestimonia (4Q175) 1-20, and other texts appears to have reckoned with three end-time figures, namely, the prophet, the Messiah of Aaron, and the Messiah of David. In such an eschatological conception the functions were distributed among the various figures.

Targum of Isaiah 53 focuses on the traditional Davidic-royal functions that fall naturally to the Davidic Messiah, such as the overthrowing of Gentile oppressors and the liberation of Israel from the exile and within the holy land. As shown above, the building of the new temple also belongs to the realm of the Davidic Messiah. But when the Targumist in *Targum of Isaiah* 53 presents the Davidic Messiah, who here appears alone, also as a teacher of the law and an intercessor, he ascribes to him roles that in a division of functions belong to the priestly Messiah and especially the prophet. In the Qumran writings the priestly Messiah is given the names "Teacher of Righteousness," יוֹרֵה הַצֶּדֶק (CD-A 6:11; *DSSSE* 1:559, "he who teaches justice")[126] and "the Interpreter of the law," דּוֹרֵשׁ הַתּוֹרָה (CD-A 7:18; 4QFlor [4Q174] 1:11), while the branch of David (צֶמַח דָּוִד) or the future king of Israel is directed to let himself be instructed by the priests (4QpIsa^a [4Q161] frags. 8-10 col. iii 22-24; 11QTemple [11Q19] 56:20-21; 57:12-14).[127] The "office" of intercessor is designated as prophetic according to the tradition;[128] this also holds true for the figure of Moses, which provides a typological foundation for the interceding Messiah of *Targum of Isaiah* 53 (cf. above, pp. 220-21).[129]

126. In his capacity as a teacher, specifically a teacher of righteousness, the *future* priestly Messiah is to be differentiated from the *historical* Teacher of Righteousness mentioned, for example, in CD-A 1:11 (*DSSSE*, 551); 1QpHab 5:10; 7:4 (*DSSSE*, 15, 17); and 4QpPs^a 3:15 on Ps. 37:23-24 (*DSSSE*, 345); this is shown explicitly by the clarification added to the title in CD-A 6:11 (*DSSSE*, 559): "the Teacher of Righteousness *at the end of days*," יוֹרֵה הַצֶּדֶק בְּאַחֲרִית הַיָּמִים. For a detailed discussion of this passage see G. Jeremias, *Der Lehrer der Gerechtigkeit*, SUNT 2 (1963), 275-89.

127. Cf. A. S. van der Woude, "χρίω κτλ., C.IV. Qumran," *TDNT* 9 (1974), 517-21, esp. 518-19; Riesner, *Jesus als Lehrer*, 308. Even if Riesner is right about his dating and interpretation of a few additional Qumran fragments, which "may point to a later revaluation of the Davidic Messiah, since they seem to attribute a teaching ministry to him" (309; cf. 309-11), on the whole the priestly anointed one remains superior to the royal anointed in teaching as well as in other aspects. Matters are similar with the *Testaments of the Twelve Patriarchs*, which are not always easy to fit into a single tradition-historical scheme because of Christian revisions (cf., e.g., T. Reu. 6:8; T. Levi 8:17; 18:2ff.; see Riesner, ibid., 312-14).

128. Cf., e.g., 1 Sam. 7:5-9; 12:19-23 (about Samuel); Jer. 18:20; 42:1-4; Ezek. 9:8; 11:13.

129. On Moses as a prophet see Deut. 18:15, 18. For the designation of Moses as a "prophetic intercessor" see Janowski, *Sühne als Heilsgeschehen*, 142, with additional authors in n. 194. Although priests could occasionally appear as intercessors in the Old Testament (on Ps. 106:30a,

In his picture of the eschatological turning point sketched on the basis of the prophecy in Isaiah 53, the Targumist finds room for only a single saving figure, the Messiah, who then unites all the eschatological roles discussed above in himself. It is not any arbitrary or accidental juxtaposition of various functions such as temple building, instruction in the law, and intercession — a product of atomistic exegesis — that meets us in this text. We are rather dealing with a conscious theological conception developed and unfolded by the Targumist in his explanatory translation of the prophetic text from Hebrew into Aramaic. Inasmuch as it takes up all the eschatological mediator functions in itself, the picture of the Messiah in *Targum of Isaiah* 53 presents an analogy to that of the New Testament, though it must immediately be added that the New Testament description of the Messiahship of Jesus Christ places the accent on very different features.

cf. B. Janowski, "Psalm CVI 28-31 und die Interzession des Pinchas," *VT* 33 [1983]: 237-48) and increasingly played this role in early Judaism as intercession extended to wider circles (cf. le Déaut, "Aspects de l'intercession," 38-48), Koch's designation of the Messiah's intercession in *Tg. Isa.* 53 as a priestly or high-priestly activity is to be rejected for reasons already outlined above on pp. 215-22.

Jesus Christ as a Man before God:
Two Interpretive Models for Isaiah 53 in the Patristic Literature and Their Development

Christoph Markschies

Summary

Isaiah 52:13–53:12 is not a central text in the Church Fathers, but it is an important text. This essay traces two ways in which the Fathers understood it — as an "exemplary" model and as a "Christological" model. In the former the Servant is viewed as an example of the true Christian, and the text is taken as ethical instruction. In the latter model Isaiah 53 speaks of a unique event of salvation in Christ that cannot be imitated, only believed. Although the boundaries between these two interpretive models are fluid, generally the Christological model comes to predominate. The exemplary model thrives only in the early period, for example, in 1 Clement (ca. 96 C.E.) and in the second-century acts of the martyrs. Here Isaiah 53 has already become Hellenized along the lines of a hero cult. Hellenization of a different kind takes place with the Christological model. Initially a genuinely Jewish framework is maintained, especially in literature of Jewish-Christian debate, for example, Justin Martyr, Aphrahat the Persian Sage, and later Adversus Judaeos literature. In the later phases, however, characteristically Greek resistance to the idea that the divine nature in Christ could have suffered affects the great Isaiah commentaries and doctrinal works of Origen, Eusebius, and Hilary. Patristic exegesis of Isaiah 53 thus diverges gradually not only from the original Old Testament sense of the passage, but also from its original Christian sense. Today we can interpret the text properly only by having both Jewish and patristic exegesis as conversation partners, without repeating their errors.

I. Preliminaries: Statistical Study of Citations; Two Models

It is hardly necessary to begin by complaining about the difficulties of the present investigation,[1] such as the widespread dissemination of Isaiah 53 (i.e., Isa. 52:13–53:12) in early patristic literature, the diversity of the ancient authors and their purposes beneath the surface of this single text, or the mass of primary and secondary literature.[2] Anyone who has flipped through the relevant pages

1. The text of my lecture in Professor Hengel's seminar on July 5, 1991, was expanded for its German version by additions in the footnotes. It has been revised and augmented once again for the English version by the translator, Daniel P. Bailey. While most of the essay is a straightforward translation, Dr. Bailey has sometimes written out my argument in the text in a fuller style for the general reader (without separate notation). Extended use has been made of published English translations of patristic texts, or of Bailey's translations for a few works, such as Eusebius of Caesarea's *Commentary on Isaiah* (see below, §IV.2). Occasionally, Dr. Bailey has taken material from my notes (e.g., German nn. 212, 225, 298) and has moved it to the text, sometimes in expanded form. See especially pp. 277-78 below on Anastasius the Sinite's quotation of material from Melito of Sardis, *Peri Pascha* 96. Here, instead of the original two lines between nn. 174 and 175 on p. 225 of the German *Der leidende Gottesknecht,* there now stand 28 lines between these two notes, spelling out the implications of material originally found in my n. 175 (the new n. 175 is also expanded). Similarly the three-point excursus on Justin Martyr's understanding of Isa. 53:8, "Who shall declare his generation?" now consists of 66 lines on pp. 262-64, expanded from just eight lines in the original text (p. 217). In the footnotes, Dr. Bailey has checked the citations, provided selected bibliographic entries since 1991, and written additional philological, text-critical, or background notes for the primary sources. In a few cases where there is a thorough mix of the original and the translator's new material in a footnote, there is no effort to differentiate them, and the entire note is simply headed by [[Expanded by translator]]. Otherwise, many of the additions have simply been enclosed with double brackets and attributed to the translator: [[(Tr.) . . .]] Other less significant expansions, corrections, and additions —either of new secondary literature, or of actual quotations (or fuller quotations) from primary or secondary literature previously cited — have been made by the translator *without* the symbol [[(Tr.) . . .]].

2. Important secondary studies include G. T. Armstrong, "The Cross in the Old Testament according to Athanasius, Cyrill of Jerusalem and the Cappadocian Fathers," in C. Andresen and G. Klein, eds., *Theologia Crucis — Signum Crucis: Festschrift für E. Dinkler zum 70. Geburtstag* (1979), 17-38; D. D. Bundy, "The Interpretation of Isaiah 53 in East and West," in M. Schmidt with C. F. Geyer, eds., *Typus, Symbol, Allegorie bei den östlichen Vätern und ihre Parallelen im Mittelalter,* Eichstätter Beiträge 4 (1982), 54-73; G. M. De Durand, "'Sa génération, qui la racontera?' Is. 53,8b: L'éxegèse des Pères," *RSPT* 53 (1969): 638-57; E. Fascher, *Jesaja 53 in christlicher und jüdischer Sicht* (1958); W. H. C. Frend, "The Old Testament in the Age of the Greek Apologists A.D. 130-180," *SJT* 25 (1973): 129-50, reprinted as chapter 3 in idem, *Religion, Popular and Unpopular in the Early Christian Centuries: Collected Studies* (1976); R. Gelio, "Isaia 52,13–53,12 nella Patrologia Primitiva I," in *Sangue e Antropologia Biblica nella Patristica,* Centro Studi Sanguis Christi, Roma, 23-28 Novembre 1981, a cura di Francesco Vattioni (1982), 119-54; H. Haag, "Der Gottesknecht bei Deuterojesaja im Verständnis der alten Kirche," *FZPhTh* 31

of the seven currently available index volumes of biblical citations in the patristic literature *(Biblia Patristica)* already has an idea of the difficulties and knows the limits of any attempt not simply to survey the 713 indexed references[3] but also to examine their context — especially since this figure includes neither Athanasius nor Cyril of Alexandria and John Chrysostom.

In view of this great mass of material, no attempt will be made to provide an overview of the exegesis of this passage.[4] Instead, I shall present in exemplary fashion two interpretive models and their history up to shortly after the Nicene Council of 325 C.E. However, before we meet these models, we must engage with a more fundamental question: What should we conclude from the great number of references about the *significance* or relevance of this Scripture passage in Early Church theology?

The statistics might at first give the impression that the Song of the Servant of God was one of the central Bible passages in the scriptural argumentation of the Early Church. But is this preunderstanding correct? The statistics themselves provide part of the answer:

The first three volumes of the *Biblia Patristica* index on Isaiah 52:13–53:12 record 317 references in seven pages for the period from the end of the first century to the end of the second century (the third century is more difficult to analyze because of the currently incomplete coverage of the *Biblia Patristica*). Compared with the number of references to the Johannine Prologue during the same period — to

---

(1984): 343-77; C. R. North, *The Suffering Servant in Deutero-Isaiah*, 2nd ed. (1956); E. Ruprecht, "Die Auslegungsgeschichte zu den sogenannten Gottesknechtsliedern im Buch Deuterojesaja unter methodischen Gesichtspunkten bis zu Bernhard Duhm," Ph.D. dissertation, Heidelberg University (1972); Arthur Freiherr von Ungern-Sternberg, *Der traditionelle alttestamentliche Schriftbeweis "de Christo" et "de Evangelio" in der alten Kirche bis zur Zeit des Eusebs von Cäsarea* (1913).

3. *Biblia Patristica: Index des Citations et Allusions Bibliques dans la Littérature Patristique*, seven volumes to date. The 713 citations of or allusions to Isa. 52:13–53:12 are distributed among the seven volumes as follows: from the beginnings of early Christian literature (i.e., Apostolic Fathers) to Clement of Alexandria and Tertullian, there are 154 references in four pages (vol. 1: *Des origines à Clément d'Alexandrie et Tertullien* [1975], 153-56); for the third century excluding Origen, there are 66 references covering a little more than a page (vol. 2: *Le troisième siècle (Origène excepté)* [1977], 156-57); for Origen, there are 97 references in a little more than one column (vol. 3: *Origène* [1980], 125-26); in volume 4, there are 208 references in three columns (vol. 4: *Eusèbe de Césarée, Cyrille de Jérusalem, Épiphane de Salamine* [1987], 118-20); in volume 5, there are 58 references in a little less than one column (vol. 5: *Basile de Césarée, Grégoire de Nazianze, Grégoire de Nysse, Amphiloque d'Iconium* [1991], 191-92); in volume 6, there are 111 references in slightly less than two columns (vol. 6: *Hilaire de Poitiers, Ambrose de Milan, Ambrosiaster* [1995], 85-86); and in volume 7, there are 19 references (vol. 7: *Didyme d'Alexandrie* [2000], 69).

4. For a brief overview see Haag, "Gottesknecht."

choose one clear example — this number is actually rather small. The same three index volumes offer 1,444 references covering twenty pages for this text.[5] Moreover, if one also takes into account the 542 references to the Prologue in the fourth volume,[6] one can speak of a growing interest in this text, something one cannot say of the fourth Servant Song. Therefore, we must begin by recognizing that when the whole patristic corpus is overviewed, Isaiah 53 is not a *central* text, though of course it is also not completely unimportant. My impression is that it is "upper middle class," if I may introduce such a category. But the statistics say precious little about the value of the patristic arguments concerning Isaiah 53 in their particular contexts.

Even a superficial survey of the patristic references to Isaiah 53 shows that they are concentrated in *individual* authors. Among the 154 references in the patristic literature up to Clement of Alexandria and Tertullian,[7] there are only seven longer citations of three or more verses.[8] Moreover, these are distributed among only *three* of the twenty authors: Justin, Irenaeus, and Clement. Among them, Justin takes pride of place in view of the frequency and fullness of his appeals to the passage.[9] These observations, which could be continued into the other volumes of the *Biblia Patristica,* illustrate not only the historical gaps in the documentary record (Justin's *Apology* is fully preserved, but not Melito's; Justin's *Dialogue,* but not that of Aristo of Pella), but also the fact that frequency of the citation of the fourth Servant Song depended upon a particular literary-theological situation: Justin disputed with Jews; Eusebius wanted in his *Demonstration of the Gospel* to prove individual topics of Christian dogma; Origen commented upon the Old Testament as a Christian.

---

5. *Biblia Patristica* 1:379-86 (409 references); 2:322-27 (265 references); 3:309-14 (770 references).

6. *Biblia Patristica* 4:257-61 (542 references).

7. *Biblia Patristica* 1:153-56 (154 references).

8. *Biblia Patristica* 1:153: (1) Isa. 52:10–54:6 see Justin, *Dial.* 13.2-9; (2) Isa. 53:12 plus 52:13–53:8a see Justin, *1 Apol.* 50.2-11; (3) Isa. 52:13-15 see Irenaeus, *Dem.* 68; (4) Isa. 53:1-12 see Clement of Rome, *1 Clem.* 16.3-14; (5) Isa. 53:2, 3, 9, 5, 7 see Justin, *Dial.* 32.2; (6) Isa. 53:8b-12 see Justin, *1 Apol.* 51.1-5. [[(Tr.) Here we must also include material from Justin that the *Biblia Patristica* has failed to identify as a longer citation: (7) *Dialogue* 89.3. This contains a chain of indirect quotations of phrases from Isa. 53:8d + 3 + 4 + 12 + 8b; cf. M. Marcovich, *Iustini Martyris Dialogus cum Tryphone,* p. 225 ll. 11-13. Although *Dial.* 89.3 and 32.2 (no. 5 above) are very similar, the *Biblia Patristica* treats *Dial.* 32.2 as a single longer citation under Isa. 53:2-9 (even though this is not a connected citation, but contains isolated phrases from Isa. 53:2-3 + 8b + 9 + 5 + 7), while it separately indexes the elements of *Dial.* 89.3 under Isa. 53:3 (skipping v. 4), 7, 8b, 8d, 12, thus obscuring the chain citation. For details see §4.1 of the following essay by D. P. Bailey, esp. pp. 339-43.]]

9. See below, part III. "Christological Model I: Early Developments, 1. Jewish-Christian Dialogue on Isaiah 53, I: Justin," pp. 245-68, and for Justin's *Dialogue,* the following study in this volume by D. P. Bailey, pp. 324-417, esp. 343-45 (overview).

Our ancient Church authors generally assume the same verse limits for the fourth Servant Song as today's Old Testament scholars do: Isaiah 52:13–53:12. But there are a few exceptions. The author of the *Acts of Peter* cites Isaiah 53:8b (τὴν γενεὰν αὐτοῦ τίς διηγήσεται;) and 53:2 one after the other, but ascribes them to two different prophets.[10] Nevertheless, this scholarly slip is more characteristic of the genre of folk literature than it is of ancient Christianity's engagement with the Song as a whole. Otherwise, when less than the full text is cited, the reasons are usually clear: *1 Clement* has very particular reasons for leaving out the last three verses of Isaiah 52, as we shall see.[11] By contrast, Justin cites the whole text, framing it in a way that suggests that he would find the modern delimitation of the Song to be appropriate.[12] Citation of the text recedes somewhat in the third century (even though a substantial amount of Christian literature has been preserved),[13] and therefore there are no complete citations. Nevertheless, Origen does cite a long portion of the text at this time (Isa. 52:13–53:8),[14] while a complete citation is found once again in the fourth century in Eusebius.[15]

An important, but not a central passage — this impression is confirmed by the biblical index of the first volume of Alois Grillmeier's *Christ in Christian*

---

10. *Actus Petri cum Simone* 24; text in R. A. Lipsius, ed., *Acta Apostolorum Apocrypha*, vol. 1 (1891; reprinted 1972), 71 l. 30-72 l. 1. Ruprecht, "Auslegungsgeschichte," 57, considers this a typical example of the "atomistic use of Scripture."

11. See below part II. "The Exemplary Model, 1. First Clement," pp. 234-41.

12. Justin cites the final verse of the passage, Isa. 53:12, at the beginning of his citation in *1 Apology* 50-51 and then once again at the end, as if to show that he knows precisely where the fourth Servant Song starts and finishes and where its climax is. See the unbroken citation of Isa. 53:12 plus Isa. 52:13–53:8a in *1 Apol.* 50.3-11, followed after a brief comment in *1 Apol.* 50.12 by the rest of the passage, Isa. 53:8b-12 (thus repeating v. 12), in *1 Apol.* 51.1-5. Justin includes an even longer citation, Isa. 52:10–54:6, in his *Dialogue with Trypho* 13.2-9.

13. The *Biblia Patristica* bibliography contains twenty-seven pages of primary sources for the first and second centuries until Clement of Alexandria and Tertullian (*Biblia Patristica* 1:19-45) and thirty-three pages for the third century excluding Origen (2:23-55).

14. Isa. 52:13–53:8 is cited in Origen, *c. Cels.* 1.54 (text: GCS *Origenes Werke* 1 [1899], 105 ll. 11-106 l. 2, ed. P. Koetschau; or *Contra Celsum libri VIII*, VCSup 54 [2001], 55 l. 13-56 l. 2, ed. M. Marcovich), followed by a discussion of contemporary Jewish interpretation of Isaiah 53 in *c. Cels.* 1.55. See below part IV. *Christological Model II: Later Developments*, 1. Origen.

15. Eusebius, *Eclogae propheticae* 4.27 (PG 22:1241 l. 40-1244 l. 36). [[(Tr.) Like Justin's long citation of Isa. 52:10–54:6 in *Dial.* 13.2-9, the citation in Eusebius, *Eclogae propheticae* (= ἐκλογαὶ προφετικαί, *Prophetic Extracts*) 4.27 covers Isa. 52:10–54:1, and is separated by only a few lines of Eusebian commentary from the preceding citation of Isa. 52:5b-7. These *Prophetic Extracts*, mostly messianic prophecies, constitute books 6-9 of a larger ten-volume work of Eusebius called Ἡ τοῦ καθόλου στοιχειώδης εἰσαγωγή or "General Elementary Introduction," cataloged as *CPG* 2, no. 3474. See further A. von Harnack, *Geschichte der altchristlichen Literatur bis Eusebius*, 2 vols. in 4, 2nd ed. (1958), 1/2:579-80.]]

Tradition,[16] which shows clearly that our passage falls far short in significance of the "purple passages" of creation and Christology, such as Genesis 1:1, 26; Psalm 110:1 (LXX and Vulgate, 109:1);[17] the Johannine Prologue (esp. John 1:14); or the Philippian and Colossian Hymns — a finding confirmed also by the *Biblia Patristica.*

If one wished to add a personal observation — though one which might sound heretical in a volume devoted to Isaiah 53 — one would have to confess that precisely on account of the unanimous patristic interpretation of this text in terms of Christ's suffering and death, already presupposed in the New Testament, Isaiah 52:13–53:12 is not one of the most exciting texts by which to study the history of interpretation.[18] Moreover, Adolf von Harnack showed already in 1926 that outside of a few prayers and other liturgical texts, the central title of our text, παῖς θεοῦ, "Servant of God," by no means played the central role among the titles of Christ that one might expect:

> From the beginning of the history of Christianity, the Ebed Yahweh of Isaiah has been interpreted as a prophecy of Christ. One therefore might expect that "Ebed Yahweh" (παῖς θεοῦ) was also a common designation of Jesus. But this is not the case. In all the preserved Christian literature from about A.D. 50 to 160, the phrase παῖς θεοῦ as a designation of Jesus is transmitted to us only 14 times in 4 writings. This is a *tiny* number compared with the designations Χριστός, κύριος, and υἱὸς τοῦ θεοῦ, which are transmitted to us more than 2000 times in this period. παῖς θεοῦ was therefore not a common name for Jesus at this time.[19]

16. A. Grillmeier, *Christ in Christian Tradition,* trans. J. Bowden, 2nd ed., vol. 1 (1975), index, 590-93; cf. the more recent German edition, Grillmeier, *Jesus der Christus im Glauben der Kirche,* vol. 1 (1979), index, 787-93.

17. On this see C. Markschies, "'Sessio ad Dexteram': Bemerkungen zu einem altchristlichen Bekenntnismotiv in der christologischen Diskussion der altkirchlichen Theologen," in M. Philonenko, ed., *Le Trône de Dieu,* WUNT I/69 (1993), 252-317.

18. So also Ruprecht, "Auslegungsgeschichte," 57, but see the objection of Haag, "Gottesknecht" 343: "Scholars generally rest content with the finding — buttressed by selective citations of individual authors — that the fathers interpreted the pericopae unanimously as applying to Christ. What fails to become clear is the degree to which individual fathers employed the Servant Songs as a weapon in the christological and trinitarian disputes of their time."

19. A. von Harnack, "Die Bezeichnung Jesu als 'Knecht Gottes' und ihre Geschichte in der alten Kirche," *SPAW.PH* (1926), 212-38, esp. 233-34, reprinted in idem, *Kleine Schriften zur Alten Kirche: Berliner Akademieschriften 1908-1930,* 2 vols., ed. J. Dummer, Opuscula 9 (1980), 2:730-56, esp. 751-52. This finding is repeated with approval by Haag, "Gottesknecht," 345; cf. also J. T. Brothers, "The Interpretation of παῖς θεοῦ in Justin Martyr's Dialogue with Trypho," *StPatr* 9/3 = *TU* 94 (1966): 127-38.

The subtitle of my presentation claims that the great majority of the ancient references to our passage can be systematized into "Two Interpretive Models for Isaiah 53 in the Patristic Literature." I believe that we must differentiate between (a) an *exemplary model* and (b) a *Christological model.* I shall seek to demonstrate this in what follows. In the *first* model the Servant is taken as an example of the true Christian and the text is taken, so to speak, as instruction in ethical behavior. In the *second* model Isaiah 53 is understood as a statement about a singular saving act of Christ — one that cannot be imitated, but only believed in, so as to gain its benefits. As always, the boundaries are fluid: the exemplary model does not strictly exclude the Christological model, and the Christological implies no radical "No" to the exemplary. Rather, several different nuances are hidden under the general heading "Christological model."

In the following I shall seek to present the development of these models as far as possible chronologically. This fits the subject matter, since the exemplary model actually comes up in the first Early Church document that cites the fourth Servant Song, the letter of *1 Clement.* From there the exemplary motif is found above all in the acts of the martyrs; finally it for the most part fades into the background. In itself this model already presupposes a kind of Hellenization, since a text originally conceived very strongly against the background of Jewish sacrificial theology is here opened to the influence of hero and martyr cults, including those of Hellenistic-Jewish stamp. The Hellenization of the second model occurs more gradually and may be regarded as a different type of Hellenization, since I would like to use this often diffusely used term "Hellenization" more particularly with reference to the steadily growing Hellenistic influence of the axiom of God's impassibility or *apatheia* (ἀπάθεια).[20] This latter development will be traced through the presentation of four chosen authors: Justin (who provides a baseline because he does *not* Hellenize the text in this sense), Origen, his academic grandson Eusebius, and Hilary (see parts III.1 and IV below). Occasionally other authors will also be taken into account (see parts III.2-4 below).

II. The Exemplary Model

Although it is well known that the ancient Church universally applied our text to Christ and that this interpretation was uncontested among Christians, reactions from the Jewish and pagan sides tell a different story. Non-Christians thought that the Christian practice of taking this text, originally dealing with an Israelite

---

20. On the axiom of divine "impassibility" see below, nn. 173, 207, 310.

prophet of the eighth century B.C.E., and reapplying it to a messianic pretender of the first century C.E. was a daring and inappropriate move. We can see this in the polemic of the middle platonic philosopher Celsus around 178 C.E.,[21] who was opposed by Origen in his *Contra Celsum*. Origen tells us that this pagan philosopher had a very negative reaction to the first known literary dialogue, dated around 140 C.E., between a Jewish Christian and a Jew, the "Dialogue (or Disputation) between Jason and Papiscus concerning Christ," by Aristo (Ariston) of Pella.[22] Perhaps then Aristo had already made a Christian use of the prophetic text in Isaiah 53.[23] Origen credits Celsus with the following harsh words:

21. P. Merlan, "Celsus," *RAC* 2 (1954): 954-65.

22. Title: Ἰάσονος καὶ Παπίσκου ἀντιλογία περὶ Χριστοῦ, *CPG* no. 1101, *Disputatio Iasonis et Papisci*. In general see "Aristo of Pella (*c.* 140)," *ODCC*, 3rd ed., 101; V. Zangara, "Aristo of Pella," *EECh* 1:73; Harnack, *Geschichte der altchristlichen Literatur*, 2/1:268-69; and B. R. Voss, *Der Dialog in der frühchristlichen Literatur*, Studia et Testimonia Antiqua 9 (1970), 23-25. The *Dialogue* and its authorship by "Ariston" (= Ἀρίστων) of Pella is mentioned in a scholion of John of Scythopolis (died after 532), which was formerly attributed to Maximus the Confessor; see the scholion (including this false attribution) in O. Stählin, ed., GCS *Clemens Alexandrinus* 3 (1909), 199 ll. 1-4. However, A. Resch in his *Außercanonische Paralleltexte zu den Evangelien*, TU 10/1 (1906), 453-55, identifies the dialogue's author with Jesus' disciple Ἀριστίων or "Aristion." In fact, MS δ of Jerome's *Vir. ill.* 18.2, which incorporates Fragment 7 of Papias mentioning this disciple, reads his name as "Ariston" rather than "Aristion," opening the possibility that Papias's "Ariston" and Ariston of Pella might be the same person. (See the textual apparatus of Jerome, *Vir. ill.* 18.2 in A. Ceresa-Gastaldo, ed., *Gli uomini illustri = De viris illustribus*, Biblioteca patristica 12 [1988], text p. 110: "Aristion"; apparatus p. 111: "Ariston δ.") However, against Resch's identification of the *Dialogue*'s author Ariston with the disciple Aristion known to Papias see Harnack, *Geschichte der altchristlichen Literatur*, 2/1:269, and U. H. J. Körtner, *Papias von Hierapolis: Ein Beitrag zur Geschichte des frühen Christentums*, FRLANT 133 (1983), 125 with 288 n. 11 (lit.). ⟦(Tr.) Papias's statement about Aristion, which classifies him as a "disciple" after the Twelve and alongside the presbyter John, Ἀριστίων καὶ ὁ πρεσβύτερος Ἰωάννης, τοῦ κυρίου μαθηταί, is also available in Eusebius, *Hist. eccl.* 3.39.4; see GCS *Eusebius Werke*, vol. 2: *Die Kirchengeschichte*, ed. E. Schwartz, 3 parts, vol. 2/1 (1903), 286 l. 19; K. Lake, ed., LCL *Eusebius: The Ecclesiastical History*, vol. 1 (1926), 292 l. 8. But since Eusebius separately mentions Ariston of Pella in *Hist. eccl.* 4.6.3, he perhaps does not consider Ariston and Papias's Aristion to be identical. This Aristion has sometimes been claimed as the author of the longer ending of Mark. See the most recent survey in J. A. Kelhoffer, *Miracle and Mission: The Authentication of Missionaries and Their Message in the Longer Ending of Mark*, WUNT 2/112 (2000), 20-23, 25-26, 28-29.⟧

23. Although Aristo's use of Isaiah 53 in his *Dialogue* is not certain, it would be strange if he did not use it, since one of Aristo's presumed exemplars in the dialogue genre, the dialogue between Philip and the Ethiopian Eunuch in Acts 8:26-40, is precisely about the interpretation of the fourth Servant Song (so also Voss, *Der Dialog*, 318). The analogy between Luke and Aristo goes further: both dialogues conclude with a baptism. We know this for Aristo's *Dialogue* from the description of its contents in Celsus's preserved Latin preface to his now-lost Latin translation of the *Dialogue*. This preface, known as *Ad Vigilium episcopum de Iudaica incredulitate*, is

At any rate, the allegories which seem to have been written about them [sc. the books of the law] are far more shameful and preposterous than the myths, since they connect with some amazing and utterly senseless folly ideas which cannot by any means be made to fit. (Origen, *Contra Celsum* 4.51)[24]

A little later Celsus says:

I know a work of this sort, a Controversy between one Papiscus and Jason, which does not deserve ridicule but rather pity and hatred. (Origen, *Contra Celsum* 4.52)[25]

Origen defends against this charge by referring to the grand masters of allegory, Philo and Aristobulus, whose interpretations are "so successful (ἐπίτευγμα) that even Greek philosophers would have been won over by what they say" (*c. Cels.* 4.51).[26] Celsus could have objected that these exegetes did not interpret Isaiah 53 or any other comparable passage in the Old Testament Christologically; one expects Origen to have more concrete reasons, but his assumptions have taken over his arguments. The self-evident nature of these assumptions can hardly be explained other than by reference to the already established application of the text to Jesus Christ in the New Testament. Nevertheless, the protest of a figure like Celsus shows that in the ancient world not everything was as self-evident as Aristo and Origen took it to be.

---

available in W. Hartel, ed., *S. Thasci Caecili Cypriani Opera omnia*, CSEL 3/3 (1871), 119-32, here 128 l. 9-129 l. 6, esp. 128 ll. 18-19. [[(Tr.) This authentic preface of Celsus, *Ad Vigilium* etc., is described by H. J. Frede as "the preface of Celsus to his non-extant translation of the *Dialogue* of Aristo of Pella," with a third-century date in Africa (H. J. Frede, *Kirchenschriftsteller: Verzeichnis und Sigel*, 4th ed., VL 1/1 [1995], 425; hereafter: *Kirchenschriftsteller*). Nevertheless, it is available only in collections of Cyprian's works, as above, attributed to Pseudo-Cyprian, and hence Frede classifies it under the siglum PS-CY Vig (p. 425). It is also designated as *CPL*, 3rd ed., no. 67° (p. 20), i.e., as one of the spurious works of Cyprian discussed immediately *after* no. 67 (which is a totally different work). Cf. also *CPG* no. 1101, *Disputatio Iasonis et Papisci*, note (a), *Praefatio*.]]

24. Trans. H. Chadwick, *Contra Celsum* (1st ed., 1953; 2nd ed., 1965), 226. Text, *c. Cels.* 4.51: αἱ γοῦν δοκοῦσαι περὶ αὐτῶν ἀλληγορίαι γεγράφθαι πολὺ τῶν μύθων αἰσχίους εἰσὶ καὶ ἀτοπώτεραι, τὰ μηδαμῆ μηδαμῶς ἁρμοσθῆναι δυνάμενα θαυμαστῇ τινι καὶ παντάπασιν ἀναισθήτῳ μωρίᾳ συνάπτουσαι (GCS *Origenes Werke*, 1:324 ll. 8-11, ed. P. Koetschau).

25. Trans. Chadwick, *Contra Celsum*, 226-27. Text, *c. Cels.* 4.52: οἵαν δὴ καὶ Παπίσκου τινὸς καὶ Ἰάσονος ἀντιλογίαν ἔγνων, οὐ γέλωτος ἀλλὰ μᾶλλον ἐλέους καὶ μίσους ἀξίαν (GCS 1:325 ll. 5-7, ed. Koetschau).

26. Trans. Chadwick, *Contra Celsum*, 226; text Koetschau, GCS *Origenes* 1:324 ll. 11-16. Moreover, Origen accuses Celsus of not even having read Aristo's *Dialogue* (*c. Cels.* 4.52 = GCS 1:325 ll. 15-21).

1. First Clement (ca. 96 C.E.)

Because the New Testament offers no full citation,[27] the natural starting point for our investigation is the first full literal citation of the entire chapter Isaiah 53 (excluding the introduction in 52:13-15) in early Christian literature, namely, chapter 16 of the *First Letter of Clement*.[28] In contrast to the "atomistic citation" (P. Stuhlmacher) of Isaiah 53 in the New Testament, we find here at the end of the first century the whole fourth Servant Song, or at least the whole of chapter 53 as we define it today, so that we need not say "farewell" to the Servant Songs, as some would have us do.[29]

27. H. W. Wolff, *Jesaja 53 im Urchristentum*, with a new introduction by P. Stuhlmacher (1984 = reprint of the 3rd ed., 1952), 108.

28. Unless otherwise noted, the Greek text of *1 Clement* — and of other writings of the Apostolic Fathers yet to be considered (i.e., *Barnabas; Martyrdom of Polycarp*) — is that of K. Bihlmeyer, *Die Apostolischen Väter: Neubearbeitung der Funckschen Ausgabe* (1924), 35-70. This text is reprinted in *Die Apostolischen Väter: Griechisch-deutsche Parallelausgabe*, trans. M. Dibelius and D.-A. Koch, rev. A. Lindemann und H. Paulsen (1992), 80-150. Our English translation is based upon that of M. W. Holmes, *The Apostolic Fathers: Greek Texts and Translations*, updated ed. (1999), 28-126, with occasional modifications as suggested by BDAG, the translation of Lake, or the commentaries of Lindemann and Lona. (The new edition of the LCL, *The Apostolic Fathers*, by B. D. Ehrman [2003] appeared too late to be used systematically in the English version of this essay, though see below, n. 50.) See K. Lake, *The Apostolic Fathers*, 2 vols., LCL (1912), 1:8-120; A. Lindemann, *Die Clemensbriefe*, HNT 17 / Die Apostolischen Väter 1 (1992); H. E. Lona, *Der erste Clemensbrief*, Kommentar zu den Apostolischen Vätern 2 (1998). See also the editions of J. B. Lightfoot, *The Apostolic Fathers*, 5 vols. in 2 parts, vols. 1/1 and 1/2: *S. Clement of Rome: A Revised Text, with Introductions, Notes, Dissertations, and Translations* (1890), 1/2:5-188; Annie Jaubert, *Épître aux Corinthiens: Clément de Rome*, SC 167 (1971), 98-204.

On Clement and his epistle see L. L. Welborn, "Clement, First Epistle of," *ABD* 1:1055-60; P. F. Beatrice, "Clement of Rome," *EECh* 1:181; D. Powell, "Clemens vom Rom," *TRE* 8 (1981): 113-20; A. Stuiber, "Clemens Romanus I," *RAC* 3 (1957): 188-97. In his farewell to members of his church history seminar in 1929, Adolf von Harnack spoke tellingly of "three-color printing" to describe *1 Clement*: "Our letter is no two-tone but a three-color print: Old Testament religion as understood in late Judaism, Hellenistic moral idealism, and the fact of the appearance of Christ (together with the kerygma and the new rules for life that this appearance has given as imperatives and released as powers)" — so Harnack, *Einführung in die Alte Kirchengeschichte: Das Schreiben der römischen Kirche an die Korinthische aus der Zeit Domitians (I. Klemensbrief) übersetzt und den Studierenden erklärt* (1929), 85-86. This corrects Harnack's own earlier evaluation of the letter in 1909 as a "two-tone print," in "Der erste Klemensbrief," *SPAW.PH* (1909): 38-63, here 56; reprinted in *Kleine Schriften zur Alten Kirche*, 2:59.

29. Cf. T. N. D. Mettinger, *A Farewell to the Servant Songs* (1978). Contrast Wolff: "The fact the chapter is cited to the end is most easily explained by the assumption that it was already in circulation as a unit and that Clement was no longer free to cite such a unit selectively" (*Jesaja 53 im Urchristentum*, 108-9).

The *context* of the letter is important for understanding its citation of Isaiah 53. By means of this letter, "the church of God which sojourns in Rome" (ἡ ἐκκλησία τοῦ θεοῦ ἡ παροικοῦσα Ῥώμην [salutation]) calls upon the divided Corinthian church (47.6-7) to keep the peace.[30] The representatives of the Roman church attack "a few reckless and arrogant persons" (ὀλίγα πρόσωπα προπετῆ καὶ αὐθάδη, 1.1) who had disturbed or even destroyed the earlier peaceful state of the church, a state which depends upon ταπεινοφροσύνη or "humility" (cf. 2.1),[31] by which "every faction and every schism" can be avoided (πᾶσα στάσις καὶ πᾶν σχίσμα, 2.6). But the author claims that instead of humility, each member of the dissenting group[32] "lives according to the lusts of his evil heart, inasmuch as they have taken up (an attitude of) unrighteousness and ungodly jealousy" (βαδίζειν κατὰ τὰς ἐπιθυμίας τῆς καρδίας αὐτοῦ τῆς πονηρᾶς, ζῆλον ἄδικον καὶ ἀσεβῆ ἀνειληφότας, 3.4). The letter is permeated by the demand for these people once again "to bow the neck and adopt the attitude of obedience" (63.1). It is in the context of this same admonition to

30. On the concept of εἰρήνη or "peace" see also E. Dinkler, "Eirene," *SHAW.PH* (1/1973). However, Dinkler does not consider *1 Clement*, which is surprising since he devotes twenty-five pages to the connection between "peace" and "the blood of Christ" (cf. Eph. 2:13) — a connection that *1 Clement* also recognizes.

31. 〚(Tr.) Terms from the "humility" or ταπεινο- word group are attested twenty-eight times in *1 Clement* (or twenty-nine times if the variant reading in 59.4 is counted [see below]). The term in *1 Clem.* 2.1 is not the noun ταπεινοφροσύνη but the verb ταπεινοφρονέω. In *1 Clement* this verb predominates over this noun by eleven occurrences to six — ταπεινοφρονέω in *1 Clem.* 2.1; 13.1, 3; 16.1, 2, 17; 17.2; 30.3; 38.2; 48.6; 62.2; ταπεινοφροσύνη in 21.8; 30.8; 31.4; 44.3; 56.1; 58.2. See also ταπεινόω (18.17, 18; 59.3 twice), ταπείνωσις (16.7 [= Isa. 53:8]; 53.2; 55.6), and the common adjective ταπεινός (30.3; 55.6; 59.3 and perhaps in 59.4). (Ταπεινός occurs in 59.4 only if the variant reading there of Codex Hierosolymitanus, 1056 c.e., is accepted: τοὺς ἐν θλίψει ἡμῶν σῶσον plus τοὺς ταπεινοὺς ἐλέησον, "have mercy on the humble." The last three Greek words are rejected by Bihlmeyer and Jaubert; accepted by Lightfoot and Holmes.) Finally, the rarer adjective ταπεινόφρων, -ον (occurring only once in the LXX, in Prov. 29:23, against sixty-seven LXX occurrences of ταπεινός) occurs in the substantival expression ὁ ταπεινόφρων at 38.2 in Codex Hierosolymitanus. Yet all the text editions in n. 28 above reject this reading in favor of the substantival participle ὁ ταπεινοφρονῶν in Codex Alexandrinus. Textually more certain, though not uncontested, is the occurrence of this adjective in 19.1 in the neuter substantival expression τὸ ταπεινόφρον, "humility" (contrast Codex A ταπεινοφρονον and Lightfoot's emendation to the participle ταπεινοφρονοῦν).〛

32. On the various interpretations of the dissenting group see Stuiber, *RAC* 3:190-91; H. von Campenhausen, *Kirchliches Amt und geistliche Vollmacht in den ersten drei Jahrhunderten*, BHT 14 (1953), 92-105. Harnack, *Einführung in die Alte Kirchengeschichte*, 92, says that because few dogmatic or moral principles were at stake in the Church unrest, it was ultimately little more than a "full-blown clique squabble" (*ausgewachsenen Cliquenzank*) fueled by a "personal clique system" (*persönliche Cliquenwirtschaft*).

ταπεινοφροσύνη[33] that the citation of Isaiah 53 belongs.[34] The pattern of the united spirit and humility is Christ,[35] called "the majestic scepter of God" (τὸ σκῆπτρον τῆς μεγαλωσύνης τοῦ θεοῦ), who "did not come with the pomp of arrogance or pride," but "in humility" (ταπεινοφρονῶν), just as the Holy Spirit previously spoke concerning him in Isaiah 53 (*1 Clem.* 16.2). The text is therefore read as a scriptural proof text for the Lord's *humility* and is used to call the Corinthians to become μιμηταί or "imitators" of this Lord:

> You see, dear friends, the kind of pattern (ὑπογραμμός) that has been given to us; for if the Lord so humbled himself (ἐταπεινοφρόνησεν), what should we do, who through him have come under the yoke of his grace? (*1 Clement* 16.17)[36]

While this orientation toward *ethical paraenesis* in the first instance naturally fits the problem in Corinth, it also suits the fundamental theological orientation of this writing — a fact that Adolf von Harnack pointed out, not least because he recognized in this orientation a close parallel to his own theology.[37]

33. Harnack places the exhortation to humility ("Klemensbrief," 47-48, esp. 47 n. 4 = *Kleine Schriften* 2:50) at the center of his interpretation of the letter as a call for "simple morality illuminated by the presence and power of God" (43 = 46). For a different accent see W. Grundmann, "ταπεινός κτλ.," *TDNT* 8:1-26, esp. 23-26 on *1 Clement* and other Apostolic Fathers; and Dihle, "Demut," *RAC* 3:735-78, esp. 752-54; cf. also Gelio, "Isaia 52,13–53,12," 125 n. 19.

34. The significance of Isaiah 53 corresponds to the significance of other Old Testament texts in the letter. This has been shown above all by W. Wrede in his *Untersuchungen zum Ersten Clemensbriefe* (1891), which he wrote at the encouragement of his "esteemed teacher, Herr Professor Dr. Harnack in Berlin."

35. This argument is similar to Paul's introduction to the Philippian hymn in Phil. 2:2-3: "Make my joy complete: be of the same mind, having the same love, being in full accord and of one mind. Do nothing from selfish ambition (ἐριθεία) or conceit (κενοδοξία), but in *humility* (ταπεινοφροσύνη) regard others as better than yourselves." Jaubert, *Épître aux Corinthiens*, 56 n. 3, also calls attention to the close points of contact between *1 Clement* and 1 Peter, particularly Peter's use of Isaiah 53 in 1 Pet. 2:21-25. See also O. Knoch, *Eigenart und Bedeutung der Eschatologie im theologischen Aufriß des ersten Clemensbriefes: Eine auslegungsgeschichtliche Untersuchung*, Theophaneia 17 (1964), 97-98.

36. *1 Clem.* 16.17: ὁρᾶτε, ἄνδρες ἀγαπητοί, τίς ὁ ὑπογραμμὸς ὁ δεδομένος ἡμῖν· εἰ γὰρ ὁ κύριος οὕτως ἐταπεινοφρόνησεν, τί ποιήσωμεν ἡμεῖς οἱ ὑπὸ τὸν ζυγὸν τῆς χάριτος αὐτοῦ ἐλθόντες; On the relationship of humility and faith see Knoch, *Eigenart und Bedeutung*, 229-30.

37. However, compare Harnack's comments on the soteriological function of the blood of Christ in *1 Clem.* 7.4 ("Klemensbrief," 51 = *Kleine Schriften* 2:54). See now E. W. Fisher, "'Let us look upon the Blood-of-Christ' (1 Clement 7:4)," *VC* 34 (1980): 218-36. Naturally, over against Harnack, one will also need to take account of the Old Testament prehistory of the ταπεινοφροσύνη word group. [(Tr.) Although the term ταπεινοφροσύνη is unattested in the LXX, its cognates ταπεινόω, ταπεινός, ταπεινότης, ταπεινόφρων, ταπεινόω, ταπεινοφρονέω, and

Because the writer is concerned with humility, his citation of the Servant text naturally does not begin with the divine oracle about the Servant's exaltation in Isaiah 52:13,[38] but with 53:1. The citation comprises Isaiah 53:1-12 in a version that is heavily dependent on the LXX (see the appendix at the end of this essay). R. Knopf has already noted that "the long citation was obviously not reproduced from memory, but was looked up and written down."[39] Without wishing to enter the complicated discussion about the underlying form of the text,[40] we may simply observe its closeness to the Alexandrian text-type of the LXX.[41]

The departures of the *1 Clement* text of Isaiah 53 from the Alexandrine text are minimal (see the appendix for details). But one interesting departure, too little

---

ταπείνωσις occur a total of 278 times. (See also above n. 31.) Furthermore, in the Old Testament Pseudepigrapha the ταπεινο- word group is represented forty times; cf. A.-M. Denis, *Concordance grecque des pseudépigraphes d'Ancien Testament* (1987), 728.]] On this word group in the LXX see Grundmann, "ταπεινός, κτλ.," *TDNT* 8:6-12. On the change in the picture of Christ, whereby he becomes a moral example of humility in *1 Clement,* see also Knoch, *Eigenart und Bedeutung der Eschatologie im theologischen Aufriß des ersten Clemensbriefes,* 280-81.

38. Isa. 53:12: ὁ παῖς μου . . . ὑψωθήσεται καὶ δοξασθήσεται σφόδρα, also pointed out by Wolff, *Jesaja 53 im Urchristentum,* 108.

39. R. Knopf, in W. Bauer, R. Knopf, M. Dibelius, and H. Windisch, *Die Apostolischen Väter,* HNT Ergänzungsband (1923), 69. Cf. Lightfoot's judgment: "Of the Septuagint Version his knowledge is very thorough and intimate" (J. B. Lightfoot, *S. Clement of Rome: An Appendix Containing the Newly Recovered Portions* [1877], 264, cited by W. Wrede, *Untersuchungen zum ersten Klemensbrief* [1891], 67). See the analysis of Clement's citations of Isaiah and their relationship to the Septuagint version in D. A. Hagner, *The Use of the Old and New Testaments in Clement of Rome,* NovTSup 34 (1973), 49-51.

40. Powell notes that in *1 Clement,* "there is no thoroughgoing agreement with any one of the main recensions of the LXX, which suggests that the Greek translations were not yet used in one accepted standard form" ("Clemens von Rom," *TRE* 8:113). On this problem see also A. Jaubert, who even here assumes that Clement's combined citation of Isa. 53:1-12 and Ps. 21:7-9 LXX (22:7-9 MT; 22:6-8 NRSV) in *1 Clem.* 16.2-14 and 15-16 proves that his *Vorlage* was a testimony source: "This way of combining two (or more) citations into one appears to be characteristic of *testimonia*" (*Épître aux Corinthiens,* 43-44, here 44); cf. also Knoch, *Eigenart,* 52, with n. 13.

41. See the manuscript grouping of J. Ziegler, *Isaias,* 3rd ed. (1983), 21-95, vol. 14 in the series *Septuaginta: Vetus Testamentum Graecum Auctoritate Academiae Scientarum Gottingensis editum.* On Codex Alexandrinus see also M. Harl, G. Dorival, and O. Munnich, *La Bible Grecque des Septante: Du Judaïsme Hellénistique au Christianisme Ancien* (1988), 134. [[(Tr.) According to Ziegler, the Alexandrine text-type is represented in Greek Isaiah by the famous uncials Alexandrinus and Sinaiticus (though S is mixed in Isaiah) and by related uncials (esp. Marchalianus [Q]), minuscules, and versions. The alternatives to the Alexandrine text in Isaiah include the Hexaplaric recension, represented for example by Vaticanus (B), and the recension of Lucian.]]

noticed, is the change from the dative of a term for sin in Isaiah 53:6, καὶ κύριος παρέδωκεν αὐτὸν ταῖς ἁμαρτίαις ἡμῶν, "And the Lord delivered him up *to our sins*" (Isa. 53:6), to the ὑπέρ construction with the genitive: καὶ κύριος παρέδωκεν αὐτὸν ὑπὲρ τῶν ἁμαρτιῶν ἡμῶν, "And the Lord delivered him up *for our sins*" (1 Clem. 16.7). This naturally recalls the New Testament ὑπέρ formulas, particularly the one in 1 Corinthians 15:3, Χριστὸς ἀπέθανεν ὑπὲρ τῶν ἁμαρτιῶν ἡμῶν, "Christ died *for our sins*."[42] One may follow the general thesis of Joachim Jeremias[43] and Harald Riesenfeld by supposing that Clement may consciously have changed the Septuagint's dative to ὑπέρ plus genitive in the light of his knowledge of Eucharistic sayings involving ὑπέρ, since these sayings themselves depart from the Septuagint of Isaiah 53, which lacks this preposition (cf. Mark 14:24: τὸ αἷμά μου τῆς διαθήκης τὸ ἐκχυννόμενον ὑπὲρ πολλῶν; Luke 22:19, 20: τὸ σῶμά μου τὸ ὑπὲρ ὑμῶν διδόμενον and τὸ αἷμα μου τὸ ὑπὲρ ὑμῶν ἐκχυννόμενον). Alternatively, one may envision a more simple process of change that is nevertheless liturgically motivated.[44] Either way, the fact of the change deserves attention.[45] See also Polycarp, *Philippians* 1.2, who

---

42. On the pre-Pauline formula Χριστὸς ἀπέθανεν ὑπὲρ τῶν ἁμαρτιῶν ἡμῶν κατὰ τὰς γραφάς (1 Cor. 15:3), see P. Stuhlmacher, *Das paulinische Evangelium*, I: *Vorgeschichte*, FRLANT 95 (1968), 269-74; H. Riesenfeld (and J. Jeremias), "ὑπέρ," *TWNT* 8:511-15, esp. 512 n. 12 = *TDNT* 8:508-52, esp. 509 n. 12.

43. Cf. J. Jeremias, *Die Abendmahlsworte Jesu*, 3rd ed. (1960) or 4th ed. (1967), 171 = *The Eucharistic Words of Jesus* (ET 1966), 179, item 14, on ὑπέρ in Mark 14:24; idem, "ὑπέρ," *TWNT* 8:514-15 with 514 n. 21 = *TDNT* 8:510-12 with 511 n. 21. [[(Tr.) In his *Eucharistic Words*, 179, Jeremias claims that the ὑπέρ in Mark 14:24 "can be recognized already as a rendering of a Semitic equivalent by the fact that ὑπέρ with the genitive is lacking in the LXX of Isa. 53 (where διά with the accusative and περί with the genitive stand)."]]

44. Jaubert says that Clement's direct application of Isaiah 53 to Christ's passion is "doubtless a mark of liturgical influence" (*Épître aux Corinthiens*, 70; so also 125 n. 3, on 1 Clem. 16.2: "caused by the liturgical usage of this pericope").

45. [[Expanded by translator]] Clement's departure in 1 Clem. 16.7 from the Old Greek or "Septuagint" of Isa. 53:6 says that the Lord delivers up the Servant "*for our sins*," ὑπὲρ τῶν ἁμαρτιῶν ἡμῶν, instead of the Septuagint's "*to our sins*," ταῖς ἁμαρτίαις ἡμῶν. This type of reading soon became an established part of the pre-Vulgate or Old Latin version(s). The Vulgate reads: *et Dominus posuit in eo* (= בּוֹ) *iniquitatem omnium nostrum*, just as our modern translations of the Hebrew: "and the Lord has laid on him (= בּוֹ) the iniquity of us all" (NRSV). But instead of making "him" the object of a preposition — cf. בּוֹ, "*in eo*," "on him" — Clement's version makes "him" the object of the verb and applies a preposition to the term for sin: καὶ κύριος παρέδωκεν αὐτὸν ὑπὲρ τῶν ἁμαρτιῶν ἡμῶν. This is exactly what several of the Old Latin versions have done; they regularly use the preposition *pro*, corresponding to the Greek ὑπέρ, in expressions such as "*pro delictis nostris*" and "*pro peccatis nostris*." See *Vetus Latina: Die Reste der Altlateinischen Bibel*, ed. by the Benediktinerkloster Beuron, Germany; *Esaias*, 2 vols., ed. R. Gryson, VL 12/1 (1987-93) and 12/2 (1993-97), esp. 12/2:1300-1302 at Isa. 53:6. The Old Latin recension X reads, *et dominus eum tradidit pro delictis nostris*, which is attested, for example, by Tertullian, *adv. Prax.* 30.3 (Tertullian, *Opera*, CCSL 2 [1954], "Adversus Praxean," ed. E. Kroymann and E. Evans, 1159-1205, here 1204 ll. 12-13). Using the same preposi-

speaks of our Lord Jesus Christ, "who endured *for* our sins, facing even death" (ὃς ὑπέμεινεν *ὑπὲρ* τῶν ἁμαρτιῶν ἡμῶν ἕως θανάτου καταντῆσαι).

For Clement, the Christian interpretation of Isaiah 53 is as self-evident as the inspiration of the prophets and the understanding of their texts as prophecies of Christ. Hence he introduces the citation unapologetically by saying, "The Holy Spirit spoke concerning him (sc. our Lord Jesus Christ)," τὸ πνεῦμα τὸ ἅγιον περὶ αὐτοῦ ἐλάλησεν (16.2).[46] If we furthermore consider Harnack's opinion that "*1 Clement* was considered a classic Christian document in the oldest Gentile church, and the church found itself with its ideals and strengths reflected in the letter,"[47] then we will not underestimate the influence of *1 Clement* upon the "victory parade" of Isaiah 52:13–53:12 in patristic argumentation.

Otherwise references to Isaiah 53 in the collection known as the "Apostolic Fathers"[48] are lacking, with the single exception of the *Epistle of Barnabas* 5.1-2. Here Isaiah 53 is interpreted in a soteriological direction (particularly in terms of baptism) that is already familiar from the New Testament:[49]

---

tion *pro* but a different term for sin is Cyprian, *Laps.* 17, *quem Deus tradidit pro peccatis nostris* (*Sancti Cypriani Episcopi Opera*, CCSL 3 [1972], "De Lapsis," ed. M. Bévenot, 221-42, here 230 l. 340). The essential elements of this reading, *tradidit pro peccatis nostris*, are found in three of the Old Latin recensions: K: *et deus tradidit illum pro peccatis nostris*; A: *et dominus tradidit illum pro peccatis nostris*; and E: *et deus tradidit eum pro peccatis nostris*. In addition to Tertullian and Cyprian, Ziegler, *Isaias*, 322, lists Tyconius, Augustine, and Irenaeus as witnesses to the *pro delictis/pro peccatis* reading: "Tert. III 287 *(pro delictis)* Cypr. Ir.[lat] Tyc. Aug." But of these the evidence of Irenaeus is difficult to confirm: Irenaeus is not cited for Isa. 53:6 in VL 12/2:1300-1302, whereas Cyprian and Tertullian both appear. Moreover, the editions of Irenaeus do not indicate that he quoted Isa. 53:6; the only references given are Isa. 53:2, 3, 4, 7, 8 in both of the following: W. W. Harvey, *Libros quinque adversus haereses*, 2 vols. (1857); A. Rousseau and L. Doutreleau, *Contre les hérésies: Irénée de Lyon*, 5 vols. in 10 (each 2 parts), SC 100/1-100/2, 152-53, 210-11, 263-64, 293-94.

46. Cf. Wrede's presentation of Clement's citation formulas (*Untersuchungen*, 74-75) and use of the Old Testament (75-78); more detail in Hagner, *Use of the Old and New Testaments*, 26-33.

47. Harnack, "Klemensbrief," 40.

48. J. A. Fischer, "Die ältesten Ausgaben der Patres Apostolici: Ein Beitrag zu Begriff und Begrenzung der Apostolischen Väter," *Historisches Jahrbuch* 94 (1974): 157-90 and 95 (1975): 88-119.

49. However, elsewhere in Barnabas, as Haag notes, "The sparceness of the use [of Isaiah 53] must come as a surprise in a document that so massively 'Christianizes' the Old Testament" (Haag, "Gottesknecht," 346). Cf. also R. A. Kraft, "Barnabas' Isaiah Text and the 'Testimony Book' Hypothesis," *JBL* 79 (1960): 349-50; idem, "Barnabas' Isaiah Text and Melito's Paschal Homily," *JBL* 80 (1961): 371-73; and P. Prigent, *L'Épitre de Barnabé I–XVI et ses sources*, EBib (1964), 157-68. On the following verse, *Barn.* 5.3, about the Lord's gift to Christians of knowledge of things past, present, and future, see K. Wengst, *Tradition und Theologie des Barnabasbriefes*, AKG 42 (1971), 15-16.

Εἰς τοῦτο γὰρ ὑπέρμεινεν ὁ κύριος παραδοῦναι τὴν σάρκα εἰς καταφθοράν, ἵνα τῇ ἀφέσει τῶν ἁμαρτιῶν ἁγνισθῶμεν, ὅ ἐστιν *ἐν τῷ αἵματος τοῦ ῥαντίσματος αὐτοῦ* [so Codex S; variant: *ἐν τῷ ῥαντίσματι αὐτοῦ τοῦ αἵματος,* Codex Hierosolymitanus and the Latin version].[50] (2) γέγραπται γὰρ περὶ αὐτοῦ ἃ μὲν πρὸς τὸν Ἰσραήλ, ἃ δὲ πρὸς ἡμᾶς. λέγει δὲ οὕτως· *ἐτραυματίσθη διὰ τὰς ἀνομίας ἡμῶν καὶ μεμαλάκισται διὰ τὰς ἁμαρτίας ἡμῶν· τῷ μώλωπι αὐτοῦ ἡμεῖς ἰάθημεν* [Isa. 53:5]· *ὡς πρόβατον ἐπὶ σφαγὴν ἤχθη καὶ ὡς ἀμνὸς ἐναντίον τοῦ κείροντος αὐτόν* [Isa. 53:7]. (*Epistle of Barnabas* 5.1-2)

For it was for this reason that the Lord endured the deliverance of his flesh to corruption, that we might be cleansed by the forgiveness of sins, that is, by his sprinkled blood [lit., "by the blood of his sprinkling"; other mss: "by the sprinkling of his blood"; see n. 50]. (2) For the Scripture concerning him relates partly to Israel and partly to us, and speaks as follows: "He was

---

50. [[(Tr.) The two readings of *Barn.* 5.1 are: (a) Codex Sinaiticus: ἐν τῷ αἵματος τοῦ ῥαντίσματος αὐτοῦ = "by his sprinkled blood"; and (b) Codex Hierosolymitanus and the Latin version: ἐν τῷ ῥαντίσματι αὐτοῦ τοῦ αἵματος = "by the sprinkling of his blood." Holmes, *Apostolic Fathers,* follows Lightfoot in favoring Sinaiticus in his text and translation (282, 283). He also includes the reading of Hierosolymitanus and the Latin version in his corresponding notes (282 n. 24; 283 n. 24). The Sinaiticus text is also read by Lake, LCL *Apostolic Fathers,* 1:354, and C.-H. Hunzinger, "ῥαντίζω κτλ.," *TDNT* 6:976-84, esp. 984 n. 45. The critical editions of Bihlmeyer, *Die Apostolischen Väter,* and R. A. Kraft, *Épître de Barnab,* SC 172 (1971) read with Hierosolymitanus, as does the new edition of the LCL, *The Apostolic Fathers,* by B. D. Ehrman, vol. 2 (2003), 24-26 with 26 n. 20. Nevertheless, the reading of Sinaiticus can be defended on the ground that it includes a "Hebrew" genitive, ἐν τῷ αἵματος τοῦ ῥαντίσματος αὐτοῦ, literally, "by the blood of his sprinkling." This Semitic type of construction is prevalent in biblical and Jewish Greek and therefore possibly original; it could easily have been changed in transmission before the late date of Codex Hierosolymitanus (1056 C.E.), especially since it is the more difficult reading (so Lake: the alternative represents "a natural correction of the more difficult phrase" in Sinaiticus [1:354 n. 1]). It might also translate poorly into Latin, as the Vulgate of Heb. 12:24 shows: αἵματι ῥαντισμοῦ, "blood of sprinkling," becomes the normal *sanguinis sparsionem,* "sprinkling of blood," thus reducing the value of the Latin evidence for Greek textual criticism. In any case both "sprinkled blood" and "sprinkling of blood" are biblical expressions, so that each manuscript tradition of *Barn.* 5.1 finds an echo in the New Testament, Sinaiticus echoing Heb. 12:24, and Hierosolymitanus echoing 1 Pet. 1:2: (a) Heb. 12:22-24: "But you have come . . . to the sprinkled blood [sc. of Christ]" (ἀλλὰ προσεληλύθατε . . . αἵματι ῥαντισμοῦ); (b) 1 Pet. 1:2: God's elect are chosen "for obedience and sprinkling of the blood of Jesus Christ" (εἰς ὑπακοὴν καὶ ῥαντισμὸν αἵματος Ἰησοῦ Χριστοῦ). Barnabas's term is not the biblical term ῥαντισμός used in these New Testament examples, but the rare term ῥάντισμα, found only here in the Apostolic Fathers and never in the NT or LXX. Nevertheless, Barnabas's term is clearly a synonym, and its underlying verbal idea, ῥαντίζω, "to sprinkle," has connotations of salvation and holiness in the LXX; see LXX Lev. 6:20 (NRSV 6:27); LXX Ps. 50:9 (MT 51:9) (NRSV 51:7); and Hunzinger, "ῥαντίζω."]]

wounded because of our transgressions, and has been afflicted because of our sins; by his wounds we were healed" (Isa. 53:5). "Like a sheep he was led to slaughter, and like a lamb [sc. he was silent] before his shearer" (Isa. 53:7). (*Epistle of Barnabas* 5.1-2)

Nevertheless, the exemplary significance of Christ's humility as the *paradigmatic humble person* before God remains an important part of the background even here in Barnabas. This background orientation will also guide us in understanding the use of Isaiah 53 in the acts of the martyrs.

2. The Acts of the Martyrs

Although it does not contain an explicit allusion to Isaiah 53, the *Martyrdom of Polycarp* provides an excellent example of how the few Pauline passages in which the apostle and the members of the Church are designated as μιμηταί or "imitators" of Christ[51] were expanded into a proper theory of meritorious "mimetic conformity," which then provides a bridge to Isaiah 53 in subsequent martyr accounts. It is the merit of the martyrs in the *Martyrdom of Polycarp* (2.3) that as "imitators of the Lord,"[52] they gain the forgiveness of sins.[53]

In contrast to Hans Freiherr von Campenhausen, I do not think that these particular features of the *Martyrdom of Polycarp* are to be ascribed to a later "Gospel redactor."[54] There are two reasons for this. First, Campenhausen's supposed

51. 1 Thess. 1:6; 2:14; 1 Cor. 4:16; cf. 1 Cor. 11:2.

52. *Mart. Pol.* 17.3; cf. 1.2.

53. Cf. *Mart. Pol.* 2.3: διὰ μιᾶς ὥρας τὴν αἰώνιον ζωὴν ἐξαγοραζόμενοι, "in one hour buying themselves eternal *life*" (so m = the Moscow MS; text in Bihlmeyer, *Die Apostolischen Väter*, 121 l. 23). For a similar use of ἐξαγοράζω as a term for redemption see Gal. 3:13; cf. F. Büchsel, "ἀγοράζω, ἐξαγοράζω," *TDNT* 1:124-28, esp. 126-28. To supplement Büchsel's somewhat weak treatment of the term's secular background see S. Lyonnet, "L'emploi paulinien de ἐξαγοράζειν au sens de 'redimere' est-il attesté dans littérature grecque?" *Bib* 42 (1961): 85-89; A. Deissmann, *Licht vom Osten* (1923), 271-87 = *Light from the Ancient East* (ET 1927), 319-30, esp. 324 n. 1; further literature in *TWNT* 10/2, *Literaturnachträge*, 956. [[(Tr.) *Mart. Pol.* 2.3 also contains a textual variant, κόλασιν, "fire" or "punishment," instead of Bihlmeyer's ζωήν (followed also by Lake, LCL *Apostolic Fathers* 2:314 with n. 2). Hence: διὰ μιᾶς ὥρας τὴν αἰώνιον κόλασιν ἐξαγοραζόμενοι = "[Fixing their eyes on the favour of Christ, they despised the tortures of this world], in one hour buying themselves an exemption from the eternal *fire*" (trans. Musurillo). So Greek MSS b, p, s, v, c, a; text in Holmes, *Apostolic Fathers*, 228 with n. 5, and in H. Musurillo, *The Acts of the Christian Martyrs: Introduction, Texts and Translations*, OECT (1972), 4 l. 2 with textual note.]]

54. H. von Campenhausen, "Bearbeitungen und Interpolationen des Polykarpmartyriums," *SHAW.PH* (3/1957) = idem, *Aus der Frühzeit des Christentums* (1963), 253-301. I can

"Gospel" redactor bears clear *Pauline* traits as well, but we may hardly date these too late, because they involve fundamental elements of the whole martyr theology. Second, Campenhausen concentrates on the supposedly surplus theological elements in the *Martyrdom of Polycarp* not included in the shorter version of this document in Eusebius (*Hist. eccl.* 4.15) in order to present these elements of the *Martyrdom* as secondary. But in so doing he pays much too little attention to the context of the fourth book of Eusebius's church history: Why should Eusebius, in writing about the historical dimension of the martyrs, have cited the *theological* framework *in extenso,* apart from his free citation style?[55]

The "example" theology of the *Martyrdom of Polycarp* is then taken up, so to speak, along the lines of *1 Clement* 16 in a letter about the "Martyrs of Lyons" in 177-178 C.E., where it is clearly connected to Isaiah 52:13–53:12.[56] The letter is written by the churches in Lyons and Vienne in Gaul to the churches in Asia and Phrygia and is quoted by Eusebius (*Hist. eccl.* 5.1.3–5.2.7). In it the churches in Gaul report the terrible tortures inflicted by "an infuriated populace" and a cruel governor upon their members (*Hist. eccl.* 5.1.7-9). But they immediately interpret this as a conflict between the mighty adversary, who by his attacks "anticipates his final coming which is sure to come" (5.1.5),[57] and their own small powers of resistance apart from the helping grace of God. After some of the Christians' pagan slaves falsely accuse the Christians of "Thyestean feasts

---

only hint here at my argument against von Campenhausen, which I hope to explain in more detail elsewhere. In the meantime see the critical objections of L. W. Barnard, "In Defence of Pseudo-Pionius' Account of Saint Polycarp's Martyrdom," in P. Granfield and J. A. Jungmann, eds., *Kyriakon: Festschrift für Johannes Quasten,* vol. 1, 2nd ed. (1973), 192-204, esp. 196-97.

55. B. Dehandschutter, *Martyrium Polycarpi: Een literair-kritische studie,* BETL 52 (1979), 140-55.

56. So already Wolff, *Jesaja 53 im Urchristentum,* 116. Substantial portions from this letter about the Martyrs of Lyons are quoted by Eusebius, our sole source of the text, in *Hist. eccl.* 5.1.3–5.2.7 (*Eusebius Werke,* Band 2: *Die Kirchengeschichte* [GCS 9], ed. E. Schwartz, 3 parts, vol. 2/1 [1903], 402 l. 11-430 l. 21). Schwartz's Greek text and an English translation are available in Lake, *Eusebius,* 406-41, and in Musurillo, *Acts of the Christian Martyrs,* xx-xxii (introduction), 62-85 (text and translation). The text is also available in G. Krüger and G. Ruhbach, *Ausgewählte Märtyrerakten,* SQS.NF 3, 4th ed. (1965), 18-28 on "Die Lugdunensischen Märtyrer." Recently W. A. Löhr has produced theses about the literary criticism of this letter, "Der Brief der Gemeinden von Lyon und Vienne (Eusebius, h.e. V,1-2(4))," in D. Papandreou, W. A. Bienert, and K. Schäferdiek, eds., *Oecumenica et Patristica,* Festschrift für W. Schneemelcher (1989), 135-49.

57. Eusebius, *Hist. eccl.* 5.1.5: παντὶ γὰρ σθένει ἐνέσκηψεν ὁ ἀντικείμενος, προοιμιαζόμενος ἤδη τὴν ἀδῶς μέλλουσιν ἔσεσθαι παρουσίαν αὐτοῦ (GCS *Eusebius* 2/1:402 ll. 20-21, ed. Schwartz), "The Adversary swooped down with full force, in this way anticipating his final coming which is sure to come" (trans. Musurillo, *Acts of the Christian Martyrs,* 63).

and Oedipodean intercourse,[58] and other things which it is not right for us either to speak of or to think of or even to believe that such things could ever happen among men" (5.1.14),[59] the persecutions begin to intensify.[60] In this context there is a report about the martyrdom of Sanctus, who again and again answered his accusers in Latin only with the formulaic *Christianus sum*, "I am a Christian," giving no other answer to questions concerning his name, home town, and origin.[61] When finally his torturers "fastened plates of heated brass to the tenderest parts of his body" (5.1.21), Sanctus demonstrated once again his firm and unbending faith. Immediately after this the letter says:

> His body was a witness to his treatment; it was all one *wound* (τραῦμα, cf. ἐτραυματίσθη, Isa. 53:5) and *bruise* (μώλωψ, so also Isa. 53:5), *wrenched and torn out of human shape* (συνεσπασμένον καὶ ἀποβεβληκὸς τὴν ἀνθρώπειον ἔξωθεν μορφήν, cf. Isa. 52:14, 53:2), but Christ suffering in him manifested great glory, overthrowing the adversary and showing for the example of the others how there is nothing fearful where there is the love of the father nor painful where there is the glory of Christ. (*Historia ecclesiastica* 5.1.23, LCL)[62]

58. ⟦(Tr.) "According to Greek mythology Thyestes had unconsciously eaten his children and Oedipus had married his mother" (Lake, *Eusebius*, LCL 1:413 n. 1).⟧

59. This final phrase constitutes an interesting commentary: ἀλλὰ μηδὲ πιστεύειν εἴ τι τοιοῦτο πώποτε παρὰ ἀνθρώποις ἐγένετο (GCS *Eusebius* 2/1:406 ll. 26-27, ed. Schwartz). When one reads the second-century C.E. Greek novel *Phoinikika* of Lollianus (P. Colon. inv. 3328; A. Henrichs, *Die Phoinikika des Lollianus: Fragmente eines neuen griechischen Romans*, Papyrologische Texte und Abhandlungen 14 [1972]), with its horrible descriptions of a slaughtered boy whose heart is halved and roasted with barley flour and oil (p. 114), making one of the participants nauseous because it is still tough and not tender (p. 119), then one can only underscore this comment of the Christians of Lyons and Vienne about the rarity of such extreme tortures. It not without a good historical reason that one finds attestation for such pagan feasts in ancient novels and the writings of the credulous Church Father Epiphanius of Salamis.

60. Eusebius, *Hist. eccl.* 5.1.14 (GCS *Eusebius* 2/1:406 ll. 20-26, ed. Schwartz). Naturally the motif of satanic activity also reappears here (H. Freiherr von Campenhausen, *Die Idee des Martyriums in der Alten Kirche* [1964], 156 with n. 6).

61. *Hist. eccl.* 5.1.20 (GCS *Eusebius* 2/1:410 ll. 2-6, ed. Schwartz). On Sanctus see G. Thomas, "La Condition sociale de l'Église de Lyon en 177," in J. Rougé and R. Turcan, eds., *Les Martyrs de Lyon (177), Lyon, 20-23 Septembre 1977*, Colloques internationaux du Centre National de la Recherche Scientifique no. 575 (1978), 102.

62. *Hist. eccl.* 5.1.23 (GCS *Eusebius* 2/1:410 ll. 13-19, ed. Schwartz): τὸ δὲ σωμάτιον μάρτυς ἦν τῶν συμβεβηκότων, ὅλων τραῦμα καὶ μώλωψ καὶ συνεσπασμένον καὶ ἀποβεβληκὸς τὴν ἀνθρώπειον ἔξωθεν μορφήν, ἐν ᾧ πάσχων Χριστὸς μεγάλας ἐπετέλει δόξας, καταργῶν τὸν ἀντικείμενον καὶ εἰς τὴν τῶν λοιπῶν ὑποτύπωσιν ὑποδεικνύων ὅτι μηδὲνφοβερὸν ὅπου πατρὸς ἀγάπη, μηδὲ ἀλεινόν ὅπου Χριστοῦ δόξα. On the martyrdom of Sanctus see also V. Saxer, *Bible et Hagiographie: Textes et thèmes bibliques dans les Actes des martyrs authentiques des premiers siècles* (1986), 45.

This text is linguistically connected to Isaiah 52:13–53:12 in several ways. First there are the obvious keywords for "wounding," τραῦμα (Eusebius) = ἐτραυματίσθη (Isa. 53:5) and a "bruise," μώλωψ (Eusebius) = τῷ μώλωπι αὐτοῦ ἡμεῖς ἰάθημεν (Isa. 53:5). Next come the attributive perfect participles (cf. συσπάω, ἀποβάλλω) about Sanctus's body being "*wrenched* and *torn* out of human shape," συνεσπασμένον καὶ ἀποβεβληκὸς τὴν ἀνθρώπειον ἔξωθεν μορφήν (Eusebius). This recalls both Isaiah 52:14, οὕτως ἀδοξήσει ἀπὸ ἀνθρώπων τὸ εἶδός σου, "so deglorified from among men will be your appearance," and Isaiah 53:3, ἀλλὰ τὸ εἶδος αὐτοῦ ἄτιμον ἐκλεῖπον παρὰ πάντας ἀνθρώπους, "But his appearance was dishonored, failing among all men" (cf. 53:2: οὐκ ἔστιν εἶδος αὐτῷ οὐδὲ δόξα . . . οὐκ εἶχεν εἶδος οὐδὲ κάλλος). Finally, the manifestation of "glory" in Sanctus's bitter suffering ties this martyr text to the glorification of the Servant in Isaiah 52:13 (δοξασθήσεται) and 53:10-11 (e.g., βούλεται κύριος . . . δεῖξαι αὐτῷ φῶς, "The Lord desires . . . to show him light").

Interestingly, however, Christ here is not simply a pattern to be imitated. Rather, in the martyrs it is Christ himself who suffers, supporting them in their battle against the devil.[63] Here the exemplary model is once again corrected in the direction of the Christological model: the wonderful reversal of fortunes in Isaiah 52:13–53:12 cannot be achieved through exemplarily patient or humble people, for the turning point in Sanctus's suffering is reached by *Christ* before God. Our passage therefore exhibits the limits of "martyr theology"; Isaiah 53 can be claimed in support of it only with difficulty.[64]

Accordingly, this Bible passage mostly fades into the background in the remaining acts of the martyrs, as the indexes to the text editions show.[65] The exemplary model of interpretation hardly had any future,[66] and the reason is not

---

63. Further references in Campenhausen, *Die Idee des Martyriums*, 89.

64. According to N. Brox, Isaiah 53 also had no historical significance for the origin of the ancient Church's martyr theology (criticizing O. Michel; Brox, *Zeuge und Märtyrer: Untersuchungen zur frühchristlichen Zeugnis-Terminologie*, SANT 5 [1961], 153).

65. Krüger and Ruhbach, *Ausgewählte Märtyrerakten*, index pp. 145-48, lists no references to Isaiah 53 outside of the Martyrs of Lyons. However, Saxer, *Bible et Hagiographie*, 148, points further to the martyrdom of the bishop *Phileas* of Thmuis in 306 C.E. (Eusebius, *Hist. eccl.* 8.10.2-10 = GCS Eusebius 2/2:760 l. 1-764 l. 9, ed. Schwartz). Moreover, in his work on the Martyrs of Palestine, Eusebius compares the martyr Apphianus of Caesarea with a "truly innocent lamb," ὡς ἀληθῶς ἀμνοῦ ἀκάκου μάρτυρος, Ἀπφιανόν, which could be interpreted as an allusion to Isa. 53:7. See *De martyribus Palaestinae* 4.2 (short recension), text in Schwartz, GCS Eusebius 2/2:912 l. 5, or in G. Bardy, *Histoire ecclésiastique: Eusèbe de Césarée*, vol. 3, SC 55 (1958), 128 l. 18; trans. H. J. Lawlor and J. E. L. Oulton, *The Ecclesiastical History and the Martyrs of Palestine*, vol. 1 (1927; reprinted 1954), 345: "that blessed martyr, that truly guileless lamb, I mean Apphianus."

66. Perhaps this impression would be relativized somewhat if one were to investigate the use of this passage in later homiletical texts: there is plenty of material for further work. Never-

hard to detect: Christians wished to avoid relativizing the exclusive claims of Christ evident in the Christological use of the passage. Therefore, the second model, to which we now turn, was apparently already dominant.

III. Christological Model I: Early Developments

1. Jewish-Christian Dialogue on Isaiah 53, I: Justin

The fourth Servant Song is cited by Justin, the "philosopher and martyr,"[67] both in his *First Apology*, addressed to the emperor Antoninus Pius and written around 150-155 C.E., and in the subsequent *Dialogue with Trypho*, ca. 155-160 C.E.[68] These documents are important, both as the earliest preserved witnesses of a dialogue with Jews about Isaiah 53 (the already mentioned dialogue of

---

theless, the exemplary model of interpretation is not used for example in the homily *In Sanctum Pascha*. Text in P. Nautin, *Homélies pascales*, vol. 1: *Une homélie inspirée du traité sur la Pâque d'Hippolyte*, SC 27 (1950), 117-91. See esp. *In Sanctum Pascha* §48 = Isa. 53:2-3 (SC 27:173 ll. 13-16, ed. Nautin); §18 = Isa. 53:7 (p. 149 ll. 12-14); §45.4 = Isa. 53:6 (p. 167 l. 14); §47.4 = 53:9 (p. 173 l. 8). [(Tr.) This work was earlier numbered as *CPG* 1, no. 1925 and ascribed to Hippolytus, as in Nautin's title, but it is now renumbered as *CPG* 2, no. 4611, "In sanctum pascha sermo 6," and included in *CPG* and *TLG* with the works of John Chrysostom; cf. L. Berkowitz and K. A. Squitier, *Thesaurus Linguae Graecae Canon of Greek Authors and Works*, 3rd ed. (1990), 228 no. 265.]

67. Tertullian, *Val.* 5.1; text in J.-C. Fredouille, *Contre les Valentiniens: Tertullien*, 2 vols. in 1, SC 280-81 (1980-81), 1:88 l. 8.

68. Generally on Justin see O. Skarsaune, "Justin der Märtyrer," *TRE* 17 (1988): 471-78 (lit.); R. M. Grant, "Justin Martyr," *ABD* 3 (1992), 1133-34; R. J. De Simone, "Justin," *EECh* 1 (1992), 463-64; S. Heid, "Iustinus Martyr I," *RAC* 19 (2000): 801-47. For the date of his writings see Harnack, *Geschichte der altchristlichen Literatur*, 2/1:275-81, and A. Wartelle, *Saint Justin: Apologies* (1987), 29-33. [(Tr.) Justin's Greek texts are from M. Marcovich, *Iustini Martyris Apologiae pro Christianis*, PTS 38 (1994); idem, *Iustini Martyris Dialogus cum Tryphone*, PTS 47 (1997). Texts from these editions are cited by chapter and paragraph number, with Marcovich's line numbers, which run continuously through a chapter. However, not all of Marcovich's conjectural emendations have been accepted (see below, nn. 111, 114, 122), and therefore it is useful to compare the unemended texts in E. J. Goodspeed, *Die ältesten Apologeten* (1914), 24-265. In English, the most comprehensive edition of Justin (though see also *ANF* 1:159-306), including both authentic and spurious works, is T. B. Falls, *Saint Justin Martyr: The First Apology, The Second Apology, Dialogue with Trypho, Exhortation to the Greeks, Discourse to the Greeks, The Monarchy or the Rule of God*, FC 6 (1948). Falls's translation of the *Dialogue* has recently been revised in the light of Marcovich's text: *Dialogue with Trypho*, trans. T. B. Falls, rev. T. P. Halton, ed. M. Slusser, FC Selections 3 (2003). For more literal renderings see A. Lukyn Williams, *Justin Martyr: The Dialogue with Trypho* (1930). The two Apologies are also newly retranslated: *The First and Second Apologies: St. Justin Martyr*, trans. L. W. Barnard, ACW 56 (1997). See also E. R. Hardy in C. C. Richardson, ed., *Early Christian Fathers*, LCC 1 (1953) 225-89; *ANF* 1:159-93.]

Aristo of Pella is now lost),[69] and as two of the most impressive examples of Christian interaction with this passage.

Once again at the beginning of our investigation we must make simple statistical observations. Among the seven longer citations of three or more verses of Isaiah 52:13–53:12 during the second century, up to and including Clement of Alexandria and Tertullian, five are to be found in Justin.[70] Moreover, of the 154 references to this passage in the first volume of the *Biblia Patristica*, 42 belong to Justin, almost a third of all references among the twenty authors. Finally, the index to M. Marcovich's editions of Justin's *1 Apology* and his *Dialogue* shows Isaiah to be, on the whole, Justin's favorite book of Scripture. Justin refers 34 times to Isaiah in his *1 Apology*, surpassed only by the 48 references to the Gospel of Matthew. But by far the greatest concentration of scriptural references is in the *Dialogue*, where Justin makes 233 references to Isaiah against 148 to Matthew. This gives totals of 267 references to Isaiah against 196 to Justin's next most popular biblical book, Matthew.[71]

Let us begin, then, with Justin's earlier work, the *1 Apology*, which naturally was directed to pagans, whereas the *Dialogue* was probably intended for Christians.[72] Justin cites from the book of Isaiah, including chapter 53, in the

---

69. For Aristo of Pella see above n. 22. However, the temporal priority of Aristo's *Dialogue* over Justin's is not entirely certain; cf. Voss, *Der Dialog*, 317.

70. See above n. 8.

71. See the "index locorum" in Marcovich, *Apologiae*, 171-73 (on Isaiah and Matthew); idem, *Dialogus*, 323-27. E. J. Goodspeed's edition, *Die ältesten Apologeten*, gives comparable figures but a lower overall number: *1 Apology*, 31 references to Isaiah, 50 to Matthew; *Dialogue*, 183 references to Isaiah, 93 to Matthew, totaling 214 references to Isaiah against 143 to Matthew. There are no references to Isaiah in Justin's *2 Apology*. For additional statistics and literature about Justin's Old Testament and New Testament citations see E. F. Osborn, *Justin Martyr*, BHT 47 (1973), 127-28 (Osborn credits Justin in his three writings with a total of forty-three citations of the LXX of Isaiah, of which twenty-five are "exact," twelve "slightly variant," and sixteen "variant"). On Justin's use of Isaiah 53 in exact citations, free citations, and mere allusions see also Wolff, *Jesaja 53 im Urchristentum*, 125-29. See now the corrected Scripture index of Marcovich's edition of the *Dialogue*, as summarized in the following essay by D. P. Bailey, "'Our Suffering and Crucified Messiah' (*Dial.* 111.2): Justin Martyr's Allusions to Isaiah 53 in His *Dialogue with Trypho* with Special Reference to the New Edition of M. Marcovich," below, pp. 344-45.

72. So C. H. Cosgrove, "Justin Martyr and the Emerging Christian Canon," *VC* 36 (1982): 209-32. [[(Tr.) See further T. Rajak, "Talking at Trypho: Christian Apologetic as Anti-Judaism in Justin's *Dialogue with Trypho the Jew*," in M. Edwards et al., eds., *Apologetics in the Roman Empire: Pagans, Jews, and Christians* (1999), 59-80. For another view (and criticisms of Cosgrove) see Marcovich, *Iustini Martyris Dialogus*, 64-65, for whom the primary (though not the only) audience will have been "Gentiles leaning towards Judaism" (p. 64).]] For the thesis of a mainly Christian audience see also M. Hengel, "Die Septuaginta als von den Christen beanspruchte

second main section of his apology (chs. 30–60),[73] in which he seeks to offer "proof" (ἀπόδειξις, *1 Apol.* 30.1),[74] by means of scriptural citations from the Old Testament,[75] that Christ was God's Son rather than a magician.[76] In a loose sequence that is only partly indebted to a chronological presentation of the life of Jesus or to the order of the Old Testament books, Justin mentions first references from "*Moses*, the first of the prophets" (*1 Apol.* 32.1),[77] followed by *Isaiah's* prophecy of the virgin birth in Isaiah 7:14 (ch. 33), *Micah's* prophecy about Bethlehem (ch. 34), various prophecies about Jesus' public ministry and death (chs. 35 and 48), his kingly reign (ch. 41), his ascension (ch. 45) and, as the crowning conclusion, the prophecies of Isaiah 53. These are intended to prove

---

Schriftensammlung bei Justin und den Vätern vor Origenes," in J. D. G. Dunn, ed., *Jews and Christians: The Parting of the Ways A.D. 70 to 135*, WUNT 1/66 (1992), 42 n. 17; cf. esp. the American reprint (Eerdmans, 1999) with new English translations, "The Septuagint as a Collection of Writings Claimed by Christians: Justin and the Church Fathers before Origen," in *Jews and Christians*, 42 n. 17 (translation modified): "The scholarly discussion [concerning the probable readership of the *Dialogue*] once revolved around whether the intended readers were Jews or Gentiles. But Justin could hardly have convinced Jews with his *Dialogue*, and Gentiles would have found the whole thing almost unreadable. The readers were more likely educated Christians positioned at the double front between Marcion (or the gnostics) on the one hand and 'hellenistic' Judaism (as strong as ever) on the other; or they were educated (Gentile or Jewish) sympathizers of the new faith. The *Dialogue's* ponderous argumentation made it ill-suited as a 'missionary writing.'" So also Voss, *Der Dialog*, 38-39.

73. On the literary structure of Justin's *1 Apology* see the remarks and literature in C. Markschies, "Platons König oder Vater Jesu Christi," in M. Hengel and A. M. Schwemer, eds., *Königsherrschaft Gottes und himmlischer Kult im Judentum, Urchristentum und in der hellenistischen Welt*, WUNT 55 (1991), 385-439, esp. 421 n. 192.

74. *1 Apol.* 30.1 l. 4 (ed. Marcovich): τὴν ἀπόδειξιν ἤδη ποιησόμεθα, "we will now offer proof" (trans. Barnard, ACW 56:43).

75. Justin classified only the *Old* Testament under the heading of "Scripture." See L. Abramowski, "Die 'Erinnerungen der Apostel' bei Justin," in P. Stuhlmacher, ed., *Das Evangelium und die Evangelien: Vorträge vom Tübinger Symposium 1982*, WUNT 28 (1983), 341-53, esp. 349 = ET, "The 'Memoirs of the Apostles' in Justin," in P. Stuhlmacher, ed., *The Gospel and the Gospels* (1991), 323-35, esp. 330; O. Skarsaune, *The Proof from Prophecy: A Study in Justin Martyr's Proof-Text Tradition: Text-Type, Provenance, Theological Profile*, NovTSup 56 (1987), 11-13. In this Justin resembles *1 Clement* (cf. Harnack, *Einführung in die Alte Kirchengeschichte*, 66-71, and B. M. Metzger, *The Canon of the New Testament* [1987], 40-49, esp. 43).

76. The major section in Justin's *1 Apology* 30-60 is divided into several parts: first a disposition (ch. 30), then the actual proof from the prophets (ch. 32-52; cf. Skarsaune, *Proof*, 139-40); from ch. 54 Justin deals with various challenges concerning the identity and uniqueness of Christ posed by Greek paganism, including mythic misappropriation of messianic prophecies (ch. 54) and Platonic philosophy (chs. 59-60).

77. On the following passages from the *1 Apology* see Skarsaune, *Proof*, 140-64.

Ὅτι δὲ καὶ ὑπὲρ ἡμῶν γενόμενος ἄνθρωπος παθεῖν καὶ ἀτιμασθῆναι ὑπέμεινε, καὶ πάλιν μετὰ δόξης παραγενήσεται. (*1 Apology* 50.1 lines 1-2, ed. Marcovich)

That, *for our sakes* [= hyperbaton][78] having become man, he endured suffering and dishonor, and will come again with glory. (ACW 56.57, trans. Barnard [modified])

Interestingly, the extensive citation of Isaiah 52:13–53:8a that follows in chapter 50 begins with the *concluding* verse of our passage, Isaiah 53:12, in *1 Apology* 50.2, followed immediately by Isaiah 52:13–53:8a in *1 Apology* 50.3-11. This order shows that Justin already understood the text as a unit. He relates this directly to "us" by promoting the soteriologically central concluding verse Isaiah 53:12 to the beginning of the quotation, and by placing the crucial ὑπὲρ ἡμῶν at the start (= hyperbaton) of his leading line in *1 Apology* 50.1 lines 1-2 (as above). He then begins his quotation in *1 Apology* 50.2 by citing Isaiah 53:12 in a non-Septuagint version:

Ἀνθ᾽ ὧν παρέδωκαν (LXX: παρεδόθη) εἰς θάνατον τὴν ψυχὴν (LXX: ἡ ψυχὴ) αὐτοῦ,[79] καὶ μετὰ τῶν ἀνόμων (LXX: ἐν τοῖς ἀνόμοις) ἐλογίσθη,[80] (LXX: καὶ) αὐτὸς ἁμαρτίας πολλῶν εἴληφε (LXX: ἀνήνεγκε) καὶ τοῖς ἀνόμοις ἐξιλάσεται (LXX: διὰ τὰς ἁμαρτίας αὐτῶν παρεδόθη). (*1 Apology* 50.2 lines 3-5, ed. Marcovich)[81]

---

78. On the translation of the pointedly fronted expression ὑπὲρ ἡμῶν as hyperbaton, cf. R. Kühner and B. Gerth, *Ausführliche Grammatik der Griechischen Sprache*, vol. 2/2, 3rd ed. (1904), 600 §607, and the note in Wartelle, *Saint Justin*, 280.

79. The original divine passive of the LXX at Isa. 53:12, παρεδόθη εἰς θάνατον ἡ ψυχὴ αὐτοῦ, "his soul *was delivered* to death," is here historicized and referred to the Jews: "*they* delivered his soul to death," παρέδωκαν εἰς θάνατον τὴν ψυχὴν αὐτοῦ (*1 Apol.* 50.2). However, since this reading is lacking in Ziegler's edition of *Isaias* in the Göttingen Septuagint, it appears not to have been very common.

80. Skarsaune, *Proof*, 63, notes that Justin's particular non-Septuagintal reading of Isa. 53:12, καὶ μετὰ τῶν ἀνόμων ἐλογίσθη ("and he was counted *with* the lawless"), is also attested in Luke 22:37.

81. *1 Apol.* 50.2, ed. Marcovich, 101 ll. 3-5. Regarding the interpretation of Justin's use of ἐξιλάσκομαι, it is interesting to note that in the LXX this verb usually translates the piel כִּפֶּר (cf. E. Hatch and H. A. Redpath, *A Concordance to the Septuagint and the Other Greek Versions of the Old Testament* [1897], 495-96, s.v. ἐξιλάσκεσθαι) and denotes the making of atonement (e.g., Lev. 4:20). Therefore I regard as misguided G. Rauschen's translation of *1 Apol.* 50.2 by "er wird sich mit den Übeltätern aussöhnen" = "he will reconcile himself with the lawless" (G. Rauschen, ed., *Frühchristliche Apologeten und Märtyrerakten, aus dem Griechischen und Lateinischen übersetzt*, Bibliothek der Kirchenväter, 2 vols. [1913], 1:62). The meaning is rather, "he will make atonement for the transgressors" (see also the next note). On the framing of the quotation of

Because *they delivered his soul* (LXX: *his soul was delivered*) to death, and he was counted *with* (LXX: *among*) the lawless, (LXX: *and*) he himself *has taken* (LXX: *bore*) the sins of many, and *he will make atonement for the lawless* (LXX: *he was delivered because of their sins*).

Several observations regarding the text suggest that Justin took his version of Isaiah 53:12 from a "testimony source" *(testimonium)* already specially compiled by Christians, and then used the verse as the heading for the whole section he cites.

The last line of Isaiah 53:12 in *1 Apology* 50.2 is considerably different from the LXX and resembles the later formulation of the *Targum of Isaiah.*[82] It is best explained as an attempt prior to Justin at the retranslation of the Masoretic Text.[83] However, Justin's remaining citation of Isaiah 52:13–53:12 corresponds almost exactly to the LXX version up to and including *1 Apology* 51.5, where the citation of Isaiah 53:12 follows the LXX except for one word (αὐτὸς παρεδόθη).[84]

Isa. 52:13–53:8a, 53:8b-12 by Isa. 53:12 see also Haag, "Gottesknecht," 348 with n. 19, and Wolff, *Jesaja 53 im Urchristentum,* 126. [[(Tr.) Similarly lacking the proper language of "atonement" for translating ἐξιλάσκομαι in *1 Apol.* 50.2 are ANF 1:179, which simply transposes the KJV of Isa. 53:12 into the future tense: "[he] shall make *intercession* for the transgressors," and T. B. Falls, *Saint Justin Martyr: The First Apology,* etc., FC 6:86: "[he] shall *pray* for the transgressors." Closer to the traditional English language of atonement is the translation shared by Hardy, *Early Christian Fathers,* 274, and Barnard, ACW 56:57, "[he] will make *propitiation* for the wicked." Nevertheless, (ἐξ)ιλάσκομαι in biblical and related writings is now usually rendered in the language of "atonement," e.g., Heb. 2:17, εἰς τὸ ἱλάσκεσθαι τὰς ἁμαρτίας τοῦ λαοῦ, "to make a sacrifice of *atonement* for the sins of the people" (NRSV).]]

82. To Justin's version of Isa. 53:12, "he will make atonement for the lawless" (*1 Apol.* 50.2), compare *Tg. Isa.* 53.12: "to the rebels it shall be forgiven for him" (trans. B. D. Chilton, *The Isaiah Targum,* ArBib 11 [1987], 105). Text in A. Sperber, *The Bible in Aramaic* 3 (1962), 108: וּלְמָרוֹדַיָּא יִשְׁתְּבֵיק בְּדִלֵיהּ; for the final word see Sperber's appendix s.v. "לֵיהּ."

83. Isa. 53:12 MT, וְלַפֹּשְׁעִים יַפְגִּיעַ, "and [he] made intercession for the transgressors" (NRSV). Skarsaune, *Proof,* 63, considers Justin's expression ἐξιλάσεται in *1 Apol.* 50.2 to be a "perfect rendering of MT יפגיע" (citing P. Katz, Skarsaune, *Proof,* 63 n. 96), adding that "ἐξιλάσκειν [*sic* — read ἐξιλάσκεσθαι, deponent] is a *hapax leg.* in Justin . . . and is thus hardly his own modification of the text" (63 n. 97). Skarsaune therefore concludes: "I suspect we have to do with a Christian version of Is 53:12 which Justin found in a testimony source" (63).

84. Justin's initial citation of Isa. 53:12 in *1 Apol.* 50.2 differs not only from the Septuagint but from his final citation of the verse in 51.5. We therefore need to compare three versions: (a) LXX; (b) *1 Apol.* 50.2; and (c) *1 Apol.* 51.5 (= LXX except for the addition of αὐτός in the last phrase):

LXX 53:12: ἀνθ' ὧν παρεδόθη   εἰς θάνατον   ἡ ψυχὴ   αὐτοῦ,
Apol. 50.2: ἀνθ' ὧν παρέδωκαν εἰς θάνατον   τὴν ψυχὴν αὐτοῦ,
Apol. 51.5: ἀνθ' ὧν παρεδόθη   εἰς θάνατον   ἡ ψυχὴ   αὐτοῦ,

Although Justin used a *testimonium,* his presentation of the text in this section is independent and intentionally theological. Therefore as far as this section is concerned, one will not be able to confirm H. W. Wolff's claim that "while Justin did not entirely miss the message of vicariousness in Isaiah 53, it nevertheless fades into the background compared with his discussions of the first and second coming of Christ."[85]

In Justin's citation of Isaiah 52:13–53:8a in the *1 Apology,* there are a few minor departures from the LXX in lexical form and word order, but basically the LXX text is followed.[86] After concluding this part of his citation with the apparent defeat of the Servant in Isaiah 53:8a, "in his humiliation, his judgment was taken away" (ἐν τῇ ταπεινώσει αὐτοῦ ἡ κρίσις αὐτοῦ ἤρθη, *1 Apol.* 50.11), Justin points out that "after He was crucified, even all His acquaintances deserted Him, having denied Him" (μετὰ οὖν τὸ σταυρωθῆναι αὐτὸν καὶ οἱ

LXX 53:12:	καὶ ἐν	τοῖς ἀνόμοις ἐλογίσθη·	
Apol. 50.2:	καὶ μετὰ	τῶν ἀνόμων ἐλογίσθη·	
Apol. 51.5:	καὶ ἐν	τοῖς ἀνόμοις ἐλογίσθη·	

LXX 53:12:	καὶ	αὐτὸς ἁμαρτίας πολλῶν ἀνήνεγκεν
Apol. 50.2:		αὐτὸς ἁμαρτίας πολλῶν εἴληφε
Apol. 51.5:	καὶ	αὐτὸς ἁμαρτίας πολλῶν ἀνήνεγκεν

LXX 53:12:	καὶ διὰ	τὰς ἁμαρτίας αὐτῶν	παρεδόθη.
Apol. 50.2:	καὶ	τοῖς ἀνόμοις	ἐξιλάσεται.
Apol. 51.5:	καὶ διὰ	τὰς ἀνομίας αὐτῶν αὐτὸς	παρεδόθη.

85. Wolff, *Jesaja 53 im Urchristentum,* 134; cf. also Haag, "Gottesknecht," 348-49. On the second coming of Christ see the section on *"The Second Coming* ἡ δευτέρα παρουσία" in Osborn, *Justin Martyr,* 187-92: "Justin is the first person to speak of Christ's *second* coming and to clearly distinguish it from his first coming" (187).

86. (For a more detailed account of the text of Isa. 52:10–54:6 as quoted in Justin's *Dialogue* 13, see below n. 107.) ⟦(Tr.) As an example of Justin's minor departures from the LXX of Isaiah 52–53 in the *1 Apology,* compare *1 Apol.* 50.4 (below). As he was later to do in the *Dialogue,* Justin has here inverted the word order of Isa. 52:14 into πολλοί ἐπὶ σέ (for LXX ἐπὶ σὲ πολλοί); but unlike his quotation in the *Dialogue,* Justin has dropped the phrase ἐπ' αὐτῷ from Isa. 52:15. Marcovich has restored it in brackets, ⟨ἐπ' αὐτῷ⟩, but only conjecturally, based not on the manuscripts of the *1 Apology* but on the LXX and the parallel in *Dial.* 13.3⟧:

LXX (Isa. 52:14-15): ὃν τρόπον ἐκστήσονται *ἐπὶ σὲ πολλοί* — οὕτως ἀδοξήσει ἀπὸ ἀνθρώπων τὸ εἶδός σου καὶ ἡ δόξα σου ἀπὸ τῶν ἀνθρώπων — οὕτως θαυμάσονται ἔθνη πολλὰ *ἐπ' αὐτῷ,* καὶ συνέξουσιν βασιλεῖς τὸ στόμα αὐτῶν· (Ziegler, *Isaias*).

Justin (*1 Apol.* 50.4): ὃν τρόπον ἐκστήσονται *πολλοί ἐπὶ σε* — οὕτως ἀδοξήσει ἀπὸ ἀνθρώπων τὸ εἶδός σου καὶ ἡ δόξα σου ἀπὸ τῶν ἀνθρώπων — οὕτως θαυμάσονται ἔθνη πολλὰ ⟨ἐπ' αὐτῷ⟩, καὶ συνέξουσι βασιλεῖς τὸ στόμα αὐτῶν· (*1 Apol.* 50.4 ll. 6-9, ed. Marcovich, italics modified).

γνώριμοι αὐτοῦ πάντες ἀπέστησαν, ἀρνησάμενοι αὐτόν, *1 Apol.* 50.12 [trans. Barnard]). But once Jesus had risen and appeared to them and had taught them to apply the Old Testament prophecies (including Isaiah 53) to himself, they watched him ascend into heaven, and they believed. Justin then concludes:

> [And after the disciples] received power[87] which He had sent from there [sc. from heaven], and went to every race of men and women, they taught these things and were called Apostles. (*1 Apology* 50.12, trans. Barnard, ACW 56.58)

The "things" which the apostles taught must have included the prophecies of Isaiah 53 according to *1 Apology* 50. Justin therefore connects the history of Christian proclamation very closely with the apostles' understanding of Isaiah 53. Following this in *1 Apology* 51 he cites the remainder of the passage, Isaiah 53:8b-12, in order to show "that He who suffers these things has an ineffable origin and reigns [Marcovich: *will reign*] over His enemies" (*1 Apol.* 51.1).[88] The complete citation of this text in chapters 50-51 of the *First Apology* makes clear its central place, at least for Justin. Because no other prophetic text is cited so fully in this document — and that in an apologetic writing intended for pagans — Justin apparently considers it to be the central proof text about the life and work of Christ for humanity.

In his *First Apology*, Justin quotes Isaiah 52:13–53:12 only once, but nevertheless completely and at a crucial point in his argument (*1 Apol.* 50-51). In his *Dialogue with Trypho*, to which we now turn, Justin quotes an even larger portion of text, Isaiah 52:10–54:6, near the beginning in *Dialogue* 13.2-9. But he also includes material from the fourth Servant Song in at least 27 subsequent paragraphs spread throughout 25 different chapters of this 142-chapter *Dialogue*. Moreover, there are additional allusions to Isaiah 53 by means of catchwords, particularly παθητός, "passible" or "susceptible to suffering," that have not usually been indexed but which bring the total number of passages involving Isaiah

---

87. Justin understands the Pentecostal Spirit as in Acts 1:8: "But you will receive power when the Holy Spirit has come upon you; and you will be my witnesses. . . ."

88. Trans. Barnard, ACW 56:58. For the idea of the Messiah's rule over his enemies cf. Ps. 110:1 (LXX 109:1). Text: *1 Apol.* 51.1 ll. 1-3 (ed. Marcovich, 103): Ἵνα δὲ μηνύσῃ ἡμῖν τὸ προφητικὸν πνεῦμα ὅτι ὁ ταῦτα πάσχων ἀνεκδιήγητον ἔχει τὸ γένος καὶ βασιλεύ<σ>ει τῶν ἐχθρῶν, ἔφη οὕτως· [plus Isa. 53:8b-12 full citation]. [[(Tr.) Marcovich corrects the reading βασιλεύει in l. 2 to the future βασιλεύ<σ>ει on the basis of the conjecture in Thirlby's 1722 edition (cf. Marcovich, x, 7-8) and the parallels in *1 Apol.* 41.2; *Dial.* 109.3; and Mic. 4:7 (see Marcovich's textual apparatus, p. 103). The phrase ἀνεκδιήγητον τὸ γένος ("ineffable origin") can be taken as a reference to the incarnation; so Lampe, *PGL*, 131 s.v. ἀνεκδιήγητος.]]

53 to about 36.[89] All this means that references and allusions to Isaiah 52:13–53:12 occur more frequently in this *Dialogue* than in any other work of early Christian literature.[90] Perhaps this is only to be expected in a disputation with an ed-

89. [(Tr.) The statistics above are based on D. P. Bailey's detailed study in the next essay (below, pp. 324-417) of the new edition by M. Marcovich, *Iustini Martyris Dialogus cum Tryphone*, PTS 47 (1997). The 28 passages containing material from Isaiah 53 (once Isa. 52:10–54:6) include the following, with direct Scripture quotations in boldface: *Dial.* **13.2-9**; 14.8; 17.1; 32.1 (Trypho); 32.2; 36.6; **42.2-3**; **43.3**; 49.2; 49.7; **63.2**; 68.4; **72.3**; **76.2**; 85.1; 88.8; 89.3; 90.1 (Trypho); 95.3; **97.2**; 100.2; **102.7**; 110.2; **111.3**; **114.2**; 118.4; 121.3; 137.1. (Because *Dial.* 114.2 contains distinct quotations of Isa. 53:7 and 53:1, it can be counted twice, yielding a total of 29 passages, which agrees with the figure of Osborn in the next note [n. 90].) A distinctive feature of Marcovich's edition is his italicizing of all but one of the 19 occurrences in 17 paragraphs of the term παθητός, "passible" or "susceptible to suffering." Marcovich understands this as an identifiable allusion to the "suffering" Messiah of Isaiah 53 in eight passages not already listed, as well as in *Dial.* 49.2; 100.2; 110.2 (as above): see *Dial.* 34.2; 36.1; 39.7; 68.9; 76.6; 89.2; 111.2; 126.1 (cf. Bailey §6.3, below, pp. 380-81). Adding these to the 28 brings to 36 the total number of *Dialogue* passages involving Isaiah 53.

As may be seen from Bailey's revised index of the *Dialogue* (below, pp. 344-45), the portion of Isaiah 53 most frequently alluded to is Isa. 53:2-3, about the "inglorious," "dishonorable," and "formless" Servant (cf. Justin's allusive terms ἄδοξος, ἄτιμος, ἀειδής). Although these verses are never directly quoted outside *Dialogue* 13, there are 11 allusions to Isa. 53:2-3 either alone (cf. *Dial.* 32.1; 36.6; 49.2; 49.7; 85.1; 88.8; 121.3) or in combination with other parts of Isaiah 53, including vv. 4, 5, 7, 8, 9, and 12 (cf. *Dial.* 14.8; 32.2; 89.3; 110.2). Next in frequency come the eight references to Isa. 53:8, excluding the passages that Marcovich refers to Isa. 53:8d only by reason of παθητός (but including once again the combinations in *Dial.* 14.8; 32.2; 89.3; 110.2), followed by the six references to Isa. 53:7 (including the combinations in *Dial.* 32.2 and 89.3). These are among the most frequently cited Old Testament verses in the *Dialogue*. However, Dan. 7:13-14, about the Son of Man coming on the clouds in glory, is referred to more often — 26 times according to Marcovich (sometimes in combination with Dan. 7:26 or 27), although this is still less than the 36 uses of various portions of Isaiah 53. Also more frequent than Isa. 53:2-3, 7, or 8 taken individually is Ps. 110[LXX 109]:4, about Melchizedek and his eternal priesthood, which is referred to about 19 times (including its combinations with Gen. 14:18; Dan. 7:14, 27). Other frequently cited Old Testament passages include Exod. 3:2, about the angel of the Lord that appeared to Moses in the burning bush and his identity with Christ (10 references, confined to *Dial.* 56, 59-60, 127-28); Exod. 17:9-13, about Moses' outstretched arms in the shape of a cross at the battle of Amalek as a type of the crucifixion (6 references); Num. 13:16, about the name-change of the son of Nun from Hoshea to Joshua = Jesus (8 references); Num. 21:6-9, about Moses' bronze snake in the wilderness (5 references); Deut. 21:23 (cf. Gal. 3:13), about the curse upon anyone hanged on a tree, i.e., crucified (9 references); Isa. 7:14, about the virgin birth (7 references); Isa. 24:5 and 55:3, about the eternal covenant (or law) (6 references); Jer. 4:22, about God's people as foolish children without faith (10 references), etc.]

90. "But the chief source of proof for the suffering of the Messiah is found in Isaiah lii-liii, which chapters are quoted at length and in part twenty-nine times. It is remarkable that nowhere in previous Christian literature is such citation used, except for one reference in 1 Clement" (Osborn, *Justin Martyr*, 103).

ucated Jewish dialogue partner; but historically it has also served *"to wrest the translation of the Seventy away from the Jews and turn it into a Christian Scripture"* (M. Hengel).[91]

We need not enter here into the controversial question of the identity of Justin's dialogue partner and the related question of the historicity of the dialogue.[92] I shall also pass over the much discussed question of the *testimonia* and the sources, especially the problem of Justin's lost *Syntagma*.[93] Because the literary situation at the time of the narrative depicted in the *Dialogue* — in Ephesus[94] toward the end of the Bar-Kochba Revolt in 135 C.E. (cf. *Dial.* 1.3) — is not identical with the situation at the time of the writing of the *Dialogue* some twenty to twenty-five years later in 155-160 C.E., the experiences of the "philosopher" Justin,[95] living in Rome at this time, in his conversations with a contemporary Roman Jewish community with close ties to Palestine will also have been incorporated into the *Dialogue*.[96] Eric F. Osborn helpfully summarizes recent research on this point:

91. Hengel, "The Septuagint as a Collection of Writings Claimed by Christians," 66 (translation modified; italics original).

92. Cf. N. Hyldahl, "Tryphon und Tarphon," *ST* 10 (1956): 77-90. [[(Tr.) On the historicity of Trypho and of certain parts of the *Dialogue* see now T. J. Horner, *Listening to Trypho: Justin Martyr's Dialogue Reconsidered*, CBET 28 (2001), and the interaction with this work by D. P. Bailey, below, pp. 325, 399-409.]]

93. I have already expressed some of my views about Justin's now-lost work, σύνταγμα κατὰ πασῶν τῶν γεγενημένων αἱρέσεων, *"Treatise against all the heresies that have arisen,"* which Justin mentions in *1 Apol.* 26.8 l. 33 (ed. Marcovich, 71). See Markschies, *Valentinus Gnosticus? Untersuchungen zur valentinianischen Gnosis mit einem Kommentar zu den Fragmenten Valentins*, WUNT 1/65 (1992), 380-82 (cf. also Skarsaune, *Proof*, 4-5). On the *testimonia* see P. Prigent, *Justin et l'Ancien Testament*, EBib (1964); Skarsaune, *Proof*, 4-9; and now M. C. Albl, *"And Scripture Cannot Be Broken": The Form and Function of the Early Christian Testimonia Collections*, NovTSup 96 (1999), 101-6.

94. So Eusebius, *Hist. eccl.* 4.18 (GCS *Eusebius* 2/1:364 ll. 24-25, ed. Schwartz).

95. See my *Valentinus Gnosticus*, 388-92; U. Neymeyr, *Die christlichen Lehrer im zweiten Jahrhundert: Ihre Lehrtätigkeit, ihr Selbstverständnis und ihre Geschichte*, Supplements to Vigiliae Christianae 4 (1989), 16-35. Hengel, "The Septuagint as a Collection of Writings Claimed by Christians," 50, points out that in his *Dialogue,* Justin "is dealing in a carefully considered fashion with the 'prophetic writings.' If we are genuinely to do justice to him, however, we must admittedly not limit our own search merely to pre-Justinian sources from which he may have drawn, and must consider instead that in the Dialogue he is already drawing on two or three decades as a Christian teacher himself, decades in which in both Ephesus and Rome he had ample opportunity to accumulate experience in discussions with Jewish teachers."

96. On the presence of Jewish teachers in Rome, cf. Str-B 3:23-24 (on Rom. 1:7); W. Bacher, *Die Aggada der Tannaiten*, 1, 2nd ed. (1903), 380-85; H. J. Leon, *The Jews of Ancient Rome* (1960).

There is no doubt that Justin was well acquainted with the Jewish exegesis of his day. . . . Trypho is a representative of neither Philonic nor Palestinian Judaism. He represents a more balanced and catholic position.[97]

After an introductory conversation about philosophy,[98] the dialogue begins with Trypho's direct devaluation of Christians: "But you [Christians] have believed this foolish rumor, and you have invented for yourselves a Christ for whom you blindly give up your lives" (*Dial.* 8.4).[99] He also makes concrete demands of them: "First, be circumcised, then (as is commanded in the Law) keep the Sabbath and the Feasts and God's New Moons, and, in short, do all the things that are written in the Law, and then perchance you will find mercy from God" (*Dial.* 8.4).[100] According to Trypho, until Elijah comes and anoints[101] the Christ or Messiah and manifests him to all, there is no Messiah, certainly not a suffering one; he therefore issues the challenge to Justin: "But when you have forsaken God and placed your hope on a man, what kind of salvation yet remains for you?" (*Dial.* 8.3).[102]

As Justin's response to this clearly shows, the ensuing controversy centers on the proper understanding of the Scriptures we call the Old Testament. Justin accuses Trypho of obeying teachers "who do not understand the Scriptures" (οἱ

97. Osborn, *Justin Martyr*, 95, with reference to W. A. Shotwell, *The Biblical Exegesis of Justin Martyr* (1965) (however, Shotwell hardly deals with Isaiah 53; cf. pp. 26, 36, 64); L. W. Barnard, "The Old Testament and Judaism in the Writings of Justin Martyr," *VT* 14 (1964): 395-406.

98. N. Hyldahl, *Philosophie und Christentum: Eine Interpretation der Einleitung zum Dialog Justins*, Acta theologica Danica 9 (1966).

99. Trans. Falls and Halton, *Dialogue with Trypho*, 16 (at 8.3). Text *Dial.* 8.4 ll. 27-28 (ed. Marcovich, 85): ὑμεῖς δέ, ματαίαν ἀκοὴν παραδεξάμενοι, Χριστὸν ἑαυτοῖς τινα ἀναπλάσσετε καὶ αὐτοῦ χάριν τὰ νῦν ἀσκόπως ἀπόλλυσθε.

100. Trans. Williams, *Dialogue*, 17. Text, *Dial.* 8.4 ll. 21-24 (ed. Marcovich, 85): πρῶτον μὲν περιτεμοῦ, εἶτα φύλαξον, ὡς νενόμισται, τὸ σάββατον καὶ τὰς ἑορτὰς καὶ τὰς νουμηνίας τοῦ θεοῦ, καὶ ἁπλῶς τὰ ἐν τῷ νόμῳ γεγραμμένα πάντα ποίει, καὶ τότε σοι ἴσως ἔλεος ἔσται παρὰ θεοῦ.

101. See *Dial.* 8.4; 49.1; and P. Pilhofer, "Wer salbt den Messias? Zum Streit um die Christologie im ersten Jahrhundert des jüdisch-christlichen Dialoges," in D.-A. Koch and H. Lichtenberger, eds., *Begegnungen zwischen Christentum und Judentum in Antike und Mittelalter: Festschrift für H. Schreckenberg zum 60. Geburtstag* (1993), 335-45. A. H. Goldfahn, "Justinus Martyr und die Agada," *Monatsschrift für Geschichte und Wissenschaft des Judenthums* 22 (1873): 194, claimed that the idea of the anointing of the Messiah that Justin attributes to Trypho is really Justin's own hypothesis; Pilhofer tries to prove the contrary.

102. Trans. Williams, *Dialogue*, 17. Text, *Dial.* 8.3 ll. 19-20 (ed. Marcovich, 85): καταλιπόντι δὲ τὸν θεὸν καὶ εἰς ἄνθρωπον ἐλπίσαντι ποία ἔτι περιλείπεται σωτηρία; See also *Dial.* 10.3 ll. 18-19 (ed. Marcovich, 87): ἐπ' ἄνθρωπον σταυρωθέντα τὰς ἐλπίδας ποιούμενοι, "you set your hopes on a man that was crucified" (Williams, *Dialogue,* 21).

οὐ συνίασι τὰς γραφάς, *Dial.* 9.1). That Jews and Christians both believe in one God, the God of Abraham, Isaac, and Jacob, is quickly agreed upon by our ancient discussion partners, as it is in discussions today (*Dial.* 11.1). But the parties are divided by the Christian notion that, as a replacement of the old covenant, there are to be "both a final law and a covenant that is superior to all others" (*Dial.* 11.2) — a law and covenant shortly thereafter identified with Christ himself: "As an eternal and final law was Christ given to us, and this covenant is sure" (11.2); "he is the new law and the new covenant" (11.4).[103] For Justin this leads to the theory of the *substitution of the Church for Israel* that is so sharply criticized today for its fatal historical consequences (*Dial.* 11.5):

> Ἰσραηλιτικὸν γὰρ τὸ ἀληθινόν, πνευματικόν, καὶ Ἰούδα γένος καὶ Ἰακὼβ καὶ Ἰσαὰκ καὶ Ἀβραάμ . . . ἡμεῖς ἐσμεν, οἱ διὰ τούτου τοῦ σταυρωθέντος Χριστοῦ τῷ θεῷ προσαχθέντες, ὡς καὶ προκοπτόντων ἡμῖν τῶν λόγων ἀποδειχθήσεται. (*Dialogue* 11.5 lines 32-37, ed. Marcovich)

> For we are the true and spiritual Israelite nation, and the race of Judah and of Jacob and Isaac and Abraham . . . — we, I say, are all this, who were brought near to God by him who was crucified, even Christ, as will be demonstrated in the course of our discussion. (*Dialogue* 11.5, trans. Williams [modified])[104]

Justin then proceeds to explain what constitutes the "new covenant" and the "new law" by including an extensive citation of Isaiah 52:10–54:6 = *Dialogue* 13.2-9. Recalling Isaiah's language of a bath — "wash yourselves, be clean!" (λούσασθε, καθαροὶ γένεσθε, Isa. 1:16) — Justin suggests that it was not to an ordinary "bath," βαλανεῖον (a nonbiblical word), that Isaiah sent the people to wash away their sins, but to the "laver of salvation" (τὸ σωτήριον λουτρόν).[105] Justin's explanation of this symbolism leads directly to his long citation of Isaiah 52:10–54:6. According to *Dialogue* 13.1-2 the laver is intended

> for those who repent and no longer cleanse themselves with the blood-shedding of goats and sheep, or the ashes of an heifer and offerings of meal, but by faith, through the blood of Christ and His death (cf. Heb 9:13-14).

---

103. *Dial.* 11.2 ll. 13-14 (ed. Marcovich, 88): Αἰώνιός τε ἡμῖν *νόμος* καὶ τελευταῖος ὁ Χριστὸς ἐδόθη καὶ ἡ *διαθήκη πιστή* (with αἰώνιός . . . *νόμος* alluding to Isa. 24:5; 55:3; and πιστή to Isa. 55:3 τὰ πιστά [Marcovich]); *Dial.* 11.4 ll. 30-31 (p. 89): οὗτός ἐστιν ὁ καινὸς νόμος καὶ *ἡ καινὴ διαθήκη*.

104. Cf. Osborn, *Justin Martyr*, 175-78.

105. "Laver of salvation," *Dial.* 13.1, trans. Williams. [[(Tr.) The normal biblical Greek word for the bronze tabernacle or temple artifact called the "laver" (RSV consistently; NRSV only in 2 Kings 16:17) or "basin" (NRSV) is not Justin's λουτρόν but rather λουτήρ, e.g., Exod. 30:18.]]

Who died for this cause, as Isaiah himself said, speaking thus: "The Lord shall uncover His holy arm before all the nations . . . [+ Isa. 52:10–54:6]." (*Dialogue* 13.1-2, trans. Williams)[106]

Justin's citation of Isaiah 52:10–54:6 in chapter 13.2-9, one of the longest connected citations in his *Dialogue*,[107] therefore serves to show that Christ died

---

106. *Dial.* 13.1-2 ll. 4-9 (ed. Marcovich, 90): τοῖς μεταγινώσκουσι καὶ μηκέτι αἵμασι τράγων καὶ προβάτων ἢ σποδῷ δαμάλεως ἢ σεμιδάλεως προσφοραῖς καθαριζομένοις, ἀλλὰ πίστει διὰ τοῦ αἵματος τοῦ Χριστοῦ καὶ τοῦ θανάτου αὐτοῦ, ὃς διὰ τοῦτο ἀπέθανεν, ὡς αὐτὸς Ἡσαίας ἔφη, οὕτως λέγων· Ἀποκαλύψει κύριος τὸν βραχίονα αὐτοῦ τὸν ἅγιον ἐνώπιον πάντων τῶν ἐθνῶν, κτλ. On this text see Prigent, *Justin et l'Ancien Testament*, 246-47 and Skarsaune, *Proof*, 179-80.

107. The *Dialogue*'s text of Isa. 52:10–54:6 (= *Dial.* 13.2-9) generally follows that of the critical LXX, though with certain minor departures as indicated in the translator's note below. Presumably it is cited more or less exactly because it is the basis of discussion for both interlocutors; their controversy concerns not least *this* text and its interpretation (cf. also Prigent, *Justin* [see n. 93], 248-49).

[(Tr.) The *Dialogue*'s text of Isa. 52:10–54:6 exhibits some 25 departures from the critical LXX text of J. Ziegler, *Isaias*. This appears to be a large number until we realize that only 12 of the textual variants are unique to Justin's *Dialogue* — i.e., not shared by any other copyist, manuscript, or recension. These Justinian readings are set in **boldface** below. Justin's unique readings are not very consequential, consisting of a shortening of the text in Isa. 52:12, 14; 54:5, 6; a lengthening in Isa. 52:11; 53:10; and a few simple replacements, i.e., εἰς for ἐπί (53:7), καὶ οὐχ for οὐδέ (53:9), and ἡμῶν for αὐτῶν (53:11). The rest of Justin's departures from Ziegler's text are all paralleled in Ziegler's apparatus. While no attempt has been made to reproduce this fully, exemplary evidence has been included below that agrees with Justin's readings, almost all of it earlier than the main manuscript of the *Dialogue*, codex *Parisinus graecus* 540, dated 1363 C.E. Codices B and V are both Origenic in Isaiah and therefore always included under the siglum for the full Origenic (Hexaplaric) recension, *O'*, which also includes 88 and Syh. The full Lucianic recension is represented by Ziegler's *Lᵐ*, including, e.g., Codices 22 and 93 (for the manuscripts that fall outside this group for a given reading, see Ziegler) and the catena group by C (also with subgroups). Codices A, Q, 26, 86, and 106 are considered Alexandrian in text-type, while Codex S is mixed, as are 449 and 770. Among the Church Fathers, the most important for present purposes is the earliest full citation of Isaiah 53 in *1 Clem.* 16.3-14; cf. below at Isa. 53:5 (transposition), 7 (omit αὐτόν), 8 (ἥκει). (See also the appendix of this essay for a full analysis of Clement's text.)

From the above survey of the main features of the manuscript tradition it will be easy to see that most of Justin's non-LXX readings are well supported by other manuscripts across the different text families. (The "etc." appended to almost every reading below serves as a cross-reference to the fuller evidence in Ziegler; it is lacking only for the two readings supported only by S* or S [cf. Isa. 52:10, 12].) The textual variations are indicated below as follows: (1) Only Justin's variant wordings over the critical LXX are italicized; (2) his alternatives or replacements to the LXX follow the slash or virgule: / ; (3) his additions over against the LXX are in italics within brackets, preceded by a plus: + [*addition*]; (4) his omissions over against the LXX are within brackets, preceded by a minus: - [omission]. Compare Isa. 52:10 ὄψονται πάντα +[*τὰ ἔθνη* (so S*) *καὶ*] τὰ ἄκρα τῆς γῆς · 52:11 ἀπόστητε, ἀπόστητε +[*ἀπόστητε*] · ἐξέλθατε/*ἐξέλθετε* (twice)

so that repentant sinners could cleanse themselves by faith through his blood. It includes more than just Isaiah 52:13–53:12 because 52:10 speaks of the revelation of the Lord's arm "before all the nations" and because 52:11 once again brings up the motif of purity, "touch no unclean thing."[108] This is precisely the new revelatory situation to which Justin has already referred in his polemic against the obsolete Horeb covenant (*Dial.* 11.1-2). The citation of Isaiah 54:1-6 at the end is naturally bound up with the theme of the new Israel. The extensive and comprehensive citation therefore represents the central proof text for the whole first main section of the *Dialogue*. The prophetic words which have just been cited speak mainly, as Justin repeatedly says in his summaries, of Christ's "first coming" (*Dial.* 14.8). But Justin's idea of the "second coming" of Christ "in glory" (ἐν δόξῃ, 14.8) or "with glory" (μετὰ δόξης, 110.2),[109] in addition to al-

---

(so 26, V, Qᶜ, etc.) (so B, V, 88, *C*, etc.) • μὴ ἅπτεσθε/μὴ ἅψησθε (so B, V, 88, *C*, etc.) • 52:12 ὅτι οὐ μετὰ ταραχῆς -[**ἐξελεύσεσθε οὐδὲ φυγῇ**] πορεύσεσθε/*πορεύεσθε* (so Qᶜ, 22, 93, *C*, etc.) • πορεύσεται γὰρ πρότερος/*πρὸ προσώπου* (so S) ὑμῶν κύριος • 52:14 ἐκστήσονται ἐπὶ σὲ πολλοί/ *πολλοὶ ἐπὶ σέ* (word order) (so *Lᵐ*, 449, 770, etc.) • ἀδοξήσει ἀπὸ ἀνθρώπων τὸ εἶδός -[**σου**] καὶ ἡ δόξα σου -[**ἀπὸ τῶν ἀνθρώπων**] • 53:3 ἐκλεῖπον παρὰ πάντας ἀνθρώπους/*παρὰ τοὺς υἱοὺς τῶν ἀνθρώπων* (so 106, *O′*, Qᵐᵍ, *Lᵐ*, etc.) • 53:5 αὐτὸς δὲ ἐτραυματίσθη διὰ τὰς ἀνομίας/*ἁμαρτίας* ἡμῶν καὶ μεμαλάκισται διὰ τὰς ἁμαρτίας/*ἀνομίας* ἡμῶν (transposed: ἁμαρτίας . . . ἀνομίας, so 86, *O′*, *C*, *1 Clem.*, etc.) • 53:7 οὐκ ἀνοίγει τὸ στόμα +[*αὐτοῦ*] (so 26, 106, 88-Syh, *Lᵐ*, *C*, etc.) • ὡς πρόβατον ἐπὶ/*εἰς* σφαγὴν ἤχθη • ὡς ἀμνὸς ἐναντίον τοῦ κείροντος -[αὐτὸν] (so S*, B, *C*, *1 Clem.*, etc.) ἄφωνος • 53:8 ἐν τῇ ταπεινώσει +[*αὐτοῦ*] (so 106, *Lᵐ*, 764, etc.) ἡ κρίσις αὐτοῦ ἤρθη • ἀπὸ τῶν ἀνομιῶν τοῦ λαοῦ μου ἤχθη/*ἤκει* (so Qᵐᵍ, *II′*, 449, 770, *1 Clem.*, etc.) εἰς θάνατον • 53:9 οὐδὲ/*καὶ οὐχ* εὑρέθη δόλος • 53:10 ἐὰν δῶτε περὶ +[*τῆς*] ἁμαρτίας • 53:11 καὶ τὰς ἁμαρτίας αὐτῶν/*ἡμῶν* αὐτὸς ἀνοίσει • 53:12 καὶ διὰ τὰς ἁμαρτίας/*ἀνομίας* (so S, Qᵐᵍ, *Lᵐ*, *C*, etc.) αὐτῶν παρεδόθη • 54:4 καὶ ὄνειδος τῆς χηρείας σου οὐ -[**μὴ**] (so S, V, 88, *Lᵐ*, *C*, etc.) μνησθήσῃ • 54:5 LXX: ὅτι κύριος -[ὁ] ποιῶν -[σε κύριος σαβαωθ] ὄνομα αὐτῷ = *Dialogue*: ὅτι κύριος *ἐποίησεν* ὄνομα *ἑαυτῷ* • 54:6 -[**οὐχ**] ὡς γυναῖκα καταλελειμμένην καὶ ὀλιγόψυχον κέκληκέν σε κύριος, -[**οὐδ′**] ὡς γυναῖκα ἐκ νεότητος μεμισημένην.]

108. Isa. 52:11: ἀκαθάρτου μὴ ἅπτεσθε.

109. Justin explains each of Christ's two comings to Trypho by allusions to Scripture first in *Dial.* 14.8 ll. 42-47 and then repeatedly throughout the *Dialogue* (ed. Marcovich, p. 94):

> Now of these and such-like words spoken by the prophets, Trypho, I said, some have been spoken with reference to the first coming of Christ, in which He has been proclaimed as about to appear both *without honour* (ἄτιμος) and *without form* (ἀειδής) and *mortal* (θνητὸς), but others have been spoken with reference to his second coming *in glory* (ἐν δόξῃ) and *upon the clouds* (ἐπάνω τῶν νεφελῶν), and your people *will see* (ὄψεται) and will recognize *Him whom they pierced* (ὃν ἐξεκέντησαν), as Hosea [read: Zechariah (12:10)], one of the Twelve Prophets, and Daniel foretold. (*Dialogue* 14.8, trans. Williams, 30)

[Expanded by translator] The references to Isaiah 53 are made by the individual keywords ἄτιμος, ἀειδής, and θνητός (later παθητός), only the first of which occurs in the text (τὸ εἶδος αὐτοῦ ἄτιμον, Isa. 53:3). Nevertheless, these are sufficient to create allusions respec-

luding to Daniel 7:14, may also be an echo of Isaiah 52:13, with its language of the Servant's "prosperity" and "exaltation" and especially of his "glorification" (δοξασθήσεται σφόδρα, Isa. 52:13), as Wolff has already suggested.[110]

Nevertheless, the "first coming" seems to me to be only one motif in Justin's interpretation of our text. What dominates is Justin's application of the text to the passion event, particularly to Christ's *suffering*.[111] The Messiah's suf-

---

tively to Isa. 53:2-3 (ἄτιμος, ἀειδής) and 8 (θηντός). Regarding Christ's second coming, other key phrases, ἐν δόξῃ and ἐπάνω τῶν νεφελῶν, create allusions respectively to Dan. 7:14 (LXX πᾶσα δόξα αὐτῷ λατρεύουσα; not in Theodotion-Daniel) and Dan. 7:13, while ὄψεται . . . εἰς ὃν ἐξεκέντησαν clearly alludes to Zech. 12:10 (cf. John 19:37). This special vocabulary that Justin creates right at the start in *Dial.* 14.8 continues to be useful for referring to Isaiah 53 throughout the *Dialogue*, and hence for distinguishing the two advents of Christ, since Isaiah 53 is Justin's main proof for the suffering Messiah of the first advent. Cf. *Dial.* 49.2; 110.2; and especially 32.2. Here the first advent is again characterized by allusions to Isa. 53:2, 8, 9, 5, 7 (*Dial.* 32.2 ll. 8-10). The second advent is identified once again as an occasion when, as Justin says directly to Trypho and the Jews, *"you will recognize the one whom you pierced,"* ἐπιγνώσεσθε εἰς ὃν ἐξεκεντήσατε (*Dial.* 32.2 ll. 11-12), alluding to Zech. 12:10. For Justin's use of Zech. 12:10 see Prigent, *Justin et l'Ancien Testament*, 80-81, and Skarsaune, *Proof*, 76-78, with a criticism of Prigent, 78 n. 126. For more details about the development of Justin's allusive vocabulary, see the following essay by D. P. Bailey, "'Our Suffering and Crucified Messiah.'"

110. Wolff, *Jesaja 53 im Urchristentum*, 133 with n. 605. [[(Tr.) For a different view of Wolff's thesis about Justin's use (or non-use) of the exaltation motif of Isa. 52:13, 15; 53:10b-12 in his *Dialogue*, see the discussion below by D. P. Bailey, pp. 360-62.]] For the role of Isaiah 53 in the context of the two Parousias see also Hippolytus, *Antichr.* 44.1, with a citation of Isa. 53:2-3. The text of the *Antichrist* is available in several places: GCS Hippolytus 1 (1897), 2 vols. in 1, ed. G. N. Bonwetsch (1/1) and H. Achelis, 1/2: *Hippolyt's kleinere exegetische und homiletische Schriften*, 1-47, esp. 28 ll. 2-8; E. Norelli, *Ippolito, L'Anticristo: De Antichristo*, Biblioteca patristica 10 (1987), 114-16, and G. Garitte, *Traités d'Hippolyte sur David et Goliath, sur le Cantique des Cantiques et sur l'Antéchrist: Version géorgienne*, 2 vols., CSCO 263-64 (1965), 2:72 ll. 23-28 (Latin translation; Georgian original in 1:97). For further references to Hippolytus's use of Isaiah 53 see Norelli, *Ippolito, L'Anticristo*, 222-23, and Gelio, "Isaia 52,13–53,12," 132-33.

111. [Expanded by translator] See for example *Dial.* 17.1: The Jews crucified a "spotless" and "righteous" man, "by means of whose stripes there is healing (cf. Isa. 53:5) for them who come unto the Father by Him" (trans. Williams). But it is especially the thoughts of Isa. 53:2-3 and also of 53:8, expressed by Justin's summary terms ἄτιμος, ἀειδής, ἄδοξος, and especially θνητός/παθητός, that become synonymous with Christ's passion: cf. *Dial.* 14.8; 32.1; 36.6; 49.2; 85.1; 100.2; 110.2, above n. 109, and the following essay by D. P. Bailey, esp. pp. 344-78. However, in *Dial.* 88.8 Justin can use one of these terms relating to Isa. 53:2-3, the adjective ἀειδής (genitive ἀειδοῦς), to talk not about the passion, but about Jesus' profession as a carpenter: "having *no comeliness* (ἀειδοῦς), as the Scriptures affirmed, he was thought to be a carpenter" (trans. Falls and Halton, *Dialogue with Trypho*, 138). Isa. 53:7 also contributes to the picture. This is quoted together with language borrowed from Jer. 11:19 in *Dial.* 72.3 ll. 17-19: καὶ αὐτὸς μνηεύεται, ὡς καὶ διὰ τοῦ Ἠσαίου προεφητεύθη, *ὡς πρόβατον ἐπὶ σφαγὴν ἀγόμενος*, καὶ ἐνθάδε *ὡς ἀρνίον ἄκακον* δηλοῦται (Marcovich, 195, conjectural emendations deleted; cf. Goodspeed, *Die ältesten*

fering is actually one of Trypho's arguments and a problem for Justin, and we hear a prelude here to the discussion between Rudolf Bultmann and his Göttingen colleague Joachim Jeremias about the antiquity of the concept of the suffering Messiah:[112]

> When I ceased Trypho said: "Sir, these and suchlike passages of scripture compel us to await One who is great and *glorious,* and takes over 'the everlasting kingdom' from 'the Ancient of days' as 'Son of man' [cf. Dan. 7:13-14, already cited by Justin in *Dial.* 31.3]. But this your so-called Christ is *without honour* and *glory* (cf. Isa. 53:2-3), so that He has even fallen into the uttermost 'curse that is in the law' of God (Deut. 21:23; cf. Gal. 3:13), for He was crucified." (*Dial.* 32.1, trans. Williams [modified])[113]

Apologeten) = "He Himself is also shown (as was prophesied too by Isaiah) *as led like a sheep to the slaughter,* and in accordance with this passage [actually Jer. 11:19], He is marked as *'an innocent lamb'*" (trans. Williams, 152-53 [modified]). Here we have two key terms for a "lamb": ἀμνός from LXX Isa. 53:7, and ἀρνίον from Jer. 11:19 (ἀρνίον ἄκακον), which here is meant to *refer* to Isa. 53:7. However, these two terms are not much used elsewhere in the *Dialogue:* ἀρνίον occurs only here and in the preceding paragraph (*Dial.* 72.2), while ἀμνός occurs only in Justin's quotations of LXX Isa. 53:7 in *Dial.* 13.5 and *Dial.* 114.2. As has already been suggested, *Dial.* 72.3 alludes not only to Isa. 53:7 but also to Jer. 11:19, ἐγὼ δὲ ὡς ἀρνίον ἄκακον ἀγόμενον τοῦ θύεσθαι, "I was led as an *innocent lamb* to be slaughtered." This combination of Jer. 11:19 and Isa. 53:7 is also found in other patristic authors; see Prigent, *Justin,* 191, and Skarsaune, *Proof,* 178-79.

112. Compare R. Bultmann, *Theologie des Neuen Testaments,* ed. O. Merk, 9th ed. (1984 = 3rd ed., 1958), 32, or *Theology of the New Testament,* 2 vols. (1951-55), 1:31, with J. Jeremias, "παῖς θεοῦ," *TWNT* 5:697-98 = *TDNT* 5:699-700, the concluding summary of section C, "παῖς θεοῦ in Later Judaism in the Period after the LXX." Nevertheless, Bultmann's terse comment about H. W. Wolff's dissertation *Jesaja 53 im Urchristentum* — "The attempt is hardly successful" (*Theologie,* 32 n. 1 = *Theology,* 1:31 note *) — leads the church historian to suspect that such a dialogue between Bultmann and Jeremias would have been shorter than that between Trypho and Justin, which lasted two full days. Jeremias writes: "The Messianic interpretation of the passion sayings in Is. 53:1-12 . . . can be traced back, . . . with a high degree of probability, to the pre-Christian period. Without exception right up to the Talmudic period the suffering of the Messiah is herewith regarded as coming before the definitive establishment or enforcement of his rule" (*TDNT* 5:699-700). Contrast Bultmann: "[T]he idea of a suffering, dying, rising Messiah or Son of Man was unknown to Judaism."

113. *Dial.* 32.1 ll. 1-6 (ed. Marcovich, 121): Καὶ ὁ Τρύφων παυσαμένου μου εἶπεν· Ὦ ἄνθρωπε, αὗται ἡμᾶς αἱ γραφαὶ καὶ τοιαῦται ἔνδοξον καὶ μέγαν ἀναμένειν τὸν παρὰ τοῦ παλαιοῦ τῶν ἡμερῶν ὡς υἱὸν ἀνθρώπου παραλαμβάνοντα τὴν αἰώνιον βασιλείαν ἀναγκάζουσιν· οὗτος δὲ ὁ ὑμέτερος λεγόμενος Χριστὸς ἄτιμος καὶ ἄδοξος γέγονεν, ὧν καὶ τῇ ἐσχάτῃ κατάρα τῇ ἐν τῷ νόμῳ τοῦ θεοῦ περιπεσεῖν· ἐσταυρώθη γάρ. On the significance of the curse of crucifixion for Justin see M. Hengel, *Crucifixion in the Ancient World and the Folly of the Message of the Cross,* trans. John Bowden (1977), reprinted in Hengel, *The Cross of the Son of God* (1986), 93-185, esp. 93-94, 109-10, 124 n. 27.

Justin admits that he would only be making "obscure and impossible statements" (ἀσαφῆ καὶ ἄπορα), *if* the Scripture had *not* spoken — and everything depends on this εἰ μή — as in fact it *has* spoken in the long passage Isaiah 52:10–54:6 already quoted in *Dialogue* 13.2-9. But as it is, Justin can reply clearly with a contrary-to-fact conditional sentence, *Dialogue* 32.2:

> If, Gentlemen, it had not been said by the scriptures (Εἰ μέν . . . μὴ ἀπὸ τῶν γραφῶν . . . ἐλέγετο [see n. 114]) which I have already related that *His form* would be *without glory* (cf. Isa. 53:2-3) and *His generation not to be described* (cf. 53:8), and that *for His death the rich should suffer death* (cf. 53:9), and that *by His stripes we were healed* (53:5), and that *He would be led as a sheep* (53:7); and I had not expounded (ἐξηγησάμην) that two Advents of His would take place, one in which He was pierced by you, and a second when you will recognize Him whom you pierced (cf. Zech. 12:10; John 19:37) . . . , [then] I should seem to be making obscure and impossible statements. (*Dialogue* 32.2, trans. Williams [modified])[114]

This Bible passage on its own justifies the discussion of the suffering Messiah; Justin's εἰ μή clause states the condition that makes possible a discourse about a suffering Messiah in the Old Testament. Whoever does not interpret the

---

114. *Dial.* 32.2 ll. 7-14 (ed. Marcovich, 121-22): Εἰ μέν, ὦ ἄνδρες, μὴ ἀπὸ τῶν γραφῶν, ὧν προανιστόρησα, ⟨ἀπέδειξα⟩ τὸ εἶδος αὐτοῦ ἄδοξον ⟨ὂν⟩ καὶ τὸ γένος αὐτοῦ ἀδιήγητον, καὶ ἀντὶ τοῦ θανάτου αὐτοῦ τοὺς πλουσίους θανατωθήσεσθαι, καὶ ⟨ὅτι⟩ τῷ μώλωπι αὐτοῦ ἡμεῖς ἰάθημεν, καὶ ὡς πρόβατον ἀχθήσεσθαι ἐλέγετο, καὶ δύο παρουσίας αὐτοῦ γενήσεσθαι ἐξηγησάμην, μίαν μὲν ἐν ᾗ ἐξεκεντήθη ὑφ' ὑμῶν, δευτέραν δὲ ὅτε ἐπιγνώσεσθε εἰς ὃν ἐξεκεντήσατε . . . , ἀσαφῆ καὶ ἄπορα ἐδόκουν ⟨ἂν⟩ λέγειν. For the conditional use of εἰ μή see Kühner and Gerth, *Ausführliche Grammatik* 2/2, 184, §510 4.b. [(Tr.) Significantly, however, Marcovich's attempt to improve Justin's text by conjecturally adding the ⟨ἀπέδειξα⟩, "I have proved," changes the reference of the εἰ μή condition discussed above, and therefore we must explain why we have not followed his emendation. Marcovich's text with the added ⟨ἀπέδειξα⟩ translates as: "If *I* had not *proved* (ἀπέδειξα) from the Scriptures which I have already related that *it was said* (ἐλέγετο) [presumably in the same Scriptures] that 'his form would be without glory,'" etc. This condition asks whether Justin has *proved* his case or not, whereas Justin's original condition asks whether it has been *said* by the Scriptures or not — certainly the more important question in this context. Marcovich presumably adds ἀπέδειξα in order to parallel the later ἐξηγησάμην, and because he apparently regards ἀποδεικνύειν ἀπὸ τῶν γραφῶν, "to prove *from* the Scriptures," to be the proper collocation. But Justin's original collocation λέγεσθαι ἀπὸ τῶν γραφῶν, "to be said *by* the Scriptures," is no less appropriate. For ἀπό can have the sense "by" as long as the Scriptures can be conceived as "the originator of the action denoted by the verb," here λέγειν (cf. BDAG 106 s.v. ἀπό, 5.d; cf. also LSJ 192 s.v. ἀπό III). This condition is met as long as it can be said that the Scripture λέγει (also λέγουσα), as it certainly does: cf. 4 Macc. 18:14; John 19:24, 37; Rom. 4:3; 9:17; 10:11; 11:2; Gal. 4:30; 1 Tim. 5:18; James 2:23; 4:5. For these reasons we have found it unnecessary to accept Marcovich's conjectural emendation of ἀπέδειξα.]]

passage in this way does not understand the Scripture properly, as Justin says later,[115] or rather does not understand it as the Holy Spirit, who speaks through Isaiah, would have it understood.[116] Accordingly Justin has his dialogue partner make a concession about the Scriptures four chapters later in *Dialogue* 36.1:

> And he [Trypho] answered: "Granting that even all this that you say is true, and that a Messiah who is *subject to suffering* (παθητός) was prophesied as destined to come [lit., to be] . . . — yet prove that this person [sc. Jesus] is the one about whom all this was prophesied."[117]

Here Trypho concedes Justin's point about a suffering Messiah prophesied in the Scriptures, only to demand of him proof that Jesus of Nazareth is this Messiah; the request is repeated in 39.7: "What we want you to prove is that Jesus is the Christ spoken of in the Scriptures." Justin delays answering several times (36.2; 39.8; cf. also 57.4) and then responds to Trypho only indirectly by demonstrating Jesus' preexistence and divine nature and personhood, and his miraculous conception and birth from a virgin according to Isaiah 7:14 (see *Dial.* 43; 48; 54-62).[118] It is a wide-ranging answer, but one that ultimately satisfies Trypho, who confesses: "My friend, you have proved your point with much force and copious arguments" (*Dial.* 63.1). But not until 75.1-2 does Justin provide an Old Testament text that is supposed to prove that *Jesus* is this Messiah, as Trypho had requested.[119]

---

115. On the Jews' lack of scriptural "understanding" see *Dial.* 34.1 and E. J. Goodspeed, *Index Apologeticus* (1912), 262 s.v. συνιέναι.

116. *Dial.* 114.2. On inspiration by the Logos or the Holy Spirit according to Justin see Osborn, *Justin Martyr*, 88.

117. *Dial.* 36.1 ll. 1-2, 5-6 (ed. Marcovich, 130): Κἀκεῖνος ἀπεκρίνατο· Ἔστω καὶ ταῦτα οὕτως ἔχοντα ὡς λέγεις, καὶ ὅτι *παθητὸς* Χριστὸς προεφητεύθη μέλλειν εἶναι . . . , εἰ οὗτος δέ ἐστι περὶ οὗ ταῦτα προεφητεύθη, ἀπόδειξον. [(Tr.) In his apparatus of parallels, Marcovich treat's Trypho's use of παθητός in *Dial.* 36.1 as an allusion to Isa. 53:8 ἤχθη εἰς θάνατον, but he does not index it as such. Trypho is credited with an *indexed* allusion to our passage only in *Dial.* 90.1, which is an indirect quotation of Isa. 53:7. See further Bailey, "'Our Suffering and Crucified Messiah,'" below, pp. 345, 365, 374-75, 393.]

118. On Isa. 7:14 LXX see Hengel, "The Septuagint as a Collection of Writings Claimed by Christians," 50-55, esp. 51 n. 51 on the significance of the virgin birth for Justin; cf. also Skarsaune, *Proof,* 200-201, 273.

119. In *Dial.* 75.1-2, Justin locates Jesus in the Old Testament by identifying him with *Joshua* (since their names are identical in Greek), who led the people into the Promised Land. From Exod. 23:21, "for my name is in him," which originally referred to the angel of the Exodus, Justin concludes that the name of God himself was Jesus: Ἐν δὲ τῷ βιβλίῳ τῆς Ἐξόδου, ὅτι αὐτοῦ τὸ ὄνομα τοῦ θεοῦ καὶ Ἰησοῦς ἦν . . . , διὰ Μωυσέως ἐν μυστηρίῳ ὁμοίως ἐξηγγέλθη [+ quotation of Exod. 23:20-21].

However, shortly before this in *Dialogue* 74.3, there is an apparent end of the first day of discussion according to Justin's literary arrangement, and the thread of the discussion was perhaps picked up on the second day with this unanswered question. It is difficult to know for sure, since the amount of material lost in the apparent mutilation of an early manuscript between *Dialogue* 74.3 and 74.4 is impossible to determine.[120]

However, Isaiah 52:13–53:12 is not used in the *Dialogue* only to provide attestation for the coming of a suffering Messiah or to describe the humble appearance of Jesus at his first coming. Justin also presents additional interpretations that show that the passage, especially Isaiah 53:8, was applied as a prophecy to *all* phases of the life of Jesus — including his birth, his resurrection and ascension, and the career of the apostles after him.

(1) *Jesus' divine origin and birth*. Isaiah 53:8b LXX might at first seem to be a prediction that, since "his life is taken from the earth" (αἴρεται ἀπὸ τῆς γῆς ἡ ζωὴ αὐτοῦ) and "he was led to death" (ἤχθη εἰς θάνατον), the Suffering Servant is destined to have no future descendants or "generation" (γενεά). This prompts Isaiah's rhetorical question, τὴν γενεὰν αὐτοῦ τίς διηγήσεται; "Who will declare (or describe) his generation?" However, Justin applies this phrase not to the Servant's *future* but to his *origin;* not to his *descendants* but to his own *descent*. While the one "generation" is made uncertain by the Servant's death and therefore cannot be "declared," the original "generation" or "begetting" of the Son himself by the Father before the beginning of time is certain: it simply cannot be "described" by mortals. This shift in meaning is made possible not only by the play on words between the Septuagint's verb διηγέομαι and Justin's adjective ἀνεκδιήγητος, -ον, but also by the similarity between the Septuagint's term γενεά that Justin cites, which usually denotes a "generation" of people, and Justin's own terms γένεσις and γένος, which here have more to do with an individual's *origin*. Hence Isaiah's prophecy of the Servant's *death* can also become a prophecy of Christ's *birth*, as in *Dialogue* 43.3:

> I turn to speak about the mystery of His *birth* (γένεσις), for this now claims our attention. Isaiah spoke thus about the *descent* (γένος) of Christ Himself, as has

---

120. The loss of text in chapter 74 occurred *before* the production of our main source for the *Dialogue*, the medieval Codex Parisinus gr. 450, written in 1363. But it was evidently not noticed by the scribe who wrote this manuscript, since it does not call attention to itself in the manuscript. It is therefore possible that the record of Day Two (Λόγος β'; Marcovich, 199) of the dialogue began in what is now the lacuna in chapter 74; cf. John of Damascus, ἐκ τοῦ πρὸς Τρύφωνα β' λόγου, ed. K. Holl, *Fragmente vornicänischer Kirchenväter aus den Sacra parallela,* TU 20/2 (1899), 34, as well as the Catena in Ps. 2:3 in Marcovich, *Iustini Martyris Dialogus cum Tryphone,* 315-16. For more detail see Skarsaune, *Proof,* 213-15; Marcovich, *Iustini Martyris Dialogus cum Tryphone,* 5-6.

already been written, in proof that it is indescribable (ἀνεκδιήγητον) by men: "Who shall describe (διηγήσεται) His *generation* (γενεά)? (Isa. 53:8b). For His life is taken from the earth, from the transgressions of my people was He led unto death (53:8c-d)." The prophetic spirit used these words to express the *indescribable* (ἀνεκδιήγητον) character of the *descent* (γένος) of this Man who was about to die, that we sinful men might be "healed by His stripes" (cf. Isa. 53:5). (*Dialogue* 43.3, trans. Williams [modified])[121]

(2) *Jesus' resurrection and ascension.* In *Dialogue* 63.2 Justin continues his exposition of Isaiah 53:8. Once again Isaiah 53:8b, "Who will declare his generation?" is cited, together with the next phrase from Isaiah 53:8c, "for his life is taken from the earth" (ὅτι αἴρεται ἀπὸ τῆς γῆς ἡ ζωὴ αὐτοῦ). As in *Dialogue* 43.3, Justin emphasizes not the human life taken from the earth but the "descent" or "origin" of the prophesied figure, in order to show Trypho that Christ had a divine origin (*Dial.* 63.2):

> Does it not seem to you [Trypho] to have been said [in Isa. 53:8b-c, just cited] that he did not have his *origin* (γένος) from humans — this one who was said by God "to have been delivered to death on account of the lawless deeds of the people"? (cf. Isa. 53:8d). (*Dialogue* 63.2)[122]

The last phrase about Christ having been "delivered to death on account of the lawless deeds of the people" is actually a conflation of Isaiah 53:8d, about someone being "led" (ἄγω) to death because of the lawless deeds of the people, and Isa-

---

121. *Dial.* 43.3 ll. 13-19 (ed. Marcovich, 140): περὶ δὲ τοῦ τῆς γενέσεως αὐτοῦ μυστηρίου ἤδη λέγειν κατεπείγοντος λέγω. Ἡσαΐας οὖν περὶ τοῦ γένους αὐτοῦ τοῦ Χριστοῦ, ὅτι ἀνεκδιήγητόν ἐστιν ἀνθρώποις, οὕτως ἔφη ὡς καὶ προγέγραπται· *Τὴν γενεὰν αὐτοῦ τίς διηγήσεται; Ὅτι αἴρεται ἀπὸ τῆς γῆς ἡ ζωὴ αὐτοῦ, ἀπὸ τῶν ἀνομιῶν τοῦ λαοῦ μου ἤχθη εἰς θάνατον.* Ὡς ἀνεκδιηγήτου οὖν ὄντος τοῦ γένους τούτου, ἀποθνήσκειν μέλλοντος, ἵνα τῷ μώλωπι αὐτοῦ ἰαθῶμεν οἱ ἁμαρτωλοὶ ἄνθρωποι, τὸ προφητικὸν πνεῦμα ταῦτα εἶπεν. On Justin's use of Isa. 53:8 see also De Durand, "Sa génération," 639-40; Gelio, "Isaia 52,13–53,12," 130-31. Wolff, *Jesaja 53 im Urchristentum*, 125, considers the fact that Justin chose to break his complete citation of Isa. 52:13–53:12 in *1 Apology* 50.3-51.5 precisely between Isa. 53:8a and 8b to be one indication of the importance of this verse for Justin.

122. *Dial.* 63.2 ll. 10-12 (ed. Marcovich, 178): οὐ δοκεῖ σοι λελέχθαι ὡς οὐκ ἐξ ἀνθρώπων ἔχοντος τὸ γένος τοῦ διὰ τὰς ἀνομίας τοῦ λαοῦ εἰς θάνατον παραδεδόσθαι εἰρημένου ὑπὸ τοῦ θεοῦ; On Jesus' "generation" or origin see Osborn, *Justin Martyr*, 28-29. A similar argument based on Isa. 53:8 is found in *Dial.* 68.4 (cf. also 76.2). Here Justin thinks that the question "Who shall declare his generation (γενεά)?" should prompt Trypho to agree that the Messiah is not "the seed of human parentage" (γένους ἀνθρώπου σπέρμα; Marcovich emends: ἀνθρωπ<εί>ου). However, Justin also gets frustrated when Trypho and his companions seem now to think differently about points they supposedly had already admitted; cf. *Dial.* 68.4: "I must ask this question in order to know whether you hold a different opinion from that which you already admitted" (trans. Falls and Halton, *Dialogue with Trypho*, 105).

iah 53:12, about being "delivered up" (παραδίδωμι) for the same reason. In addition to favoring the verb παραδίδωμι from Isaiah 53:12 (cf. παραδεδόσθαι), Justin also uses the same preposition διά (plus the accusative). But from Isaiah 53:8 he takes the ideas of "lawless deeds" and "death":

ἀπὸ τῶν	ἀνομιῶν	τοῦ λαοῦ	μου	ἤχθη	εἰς θάνατον		(Isaiah 53:8)
διὰ τὰς	ἀνομίας	τοῦ λαοῦ	—	—	εἰς θάνατον	παραδεδόσθαι	(*Dialogue* 63.2)
διὰ τὰς	ἁμαρτίας	αὐτῶν	—	—	— —	παρεδόθη	(Isaiah 53:12)

Justin has not yet exhausted Isaiah 53:8, for the phrase "his life was taken from the earth" is also a potential proof of Christ's *ascension*. Justin has included it here in response to Trypho's request that he also "prove that he [sc. Christ] afterwards rose and ascended into heaven," ὅτι μετὰ ταῦτα ἀναστὰς ἀνελήλυθεν εἰς τὸν οὐρανόν, ἀπόδειξον (*Dial.* 63.1 ll. 4-5). Later in *Dialogue* 97.2, the prophecy of Jesus' *resurrection* is more explicitly proved by a combination of Isaiah 57:2 and 53:9:

> Καὶ ὅτι ἔμελλεν ἀνίστασθαι, αὐτὸς Ἠσαΐας ἔφη· Ἡ ταφὴ αὐτοῦ ἦρται ἐκ τοῦ μέσου, καὶ Δώσω τοὺς πλουσίους ἀντὶ τοῦ θανάτου αὐτοῦ. (*Dialogue* 97.2 lines 10-12, ed. Marcovich)

> And that He was to rise, Isaiah himself has said: "His burial has been taken out of the midst (Isa. 57:2), and I will give the rich in place of his death (Isa. 53:9)." (*Dialogue* 97.2, trans. Williams)

(3) *The apostolic preaching.* Justin applies the Servant Song in yet another way in *Dialogue* 42.2. He has Isaiah impersonate the *future apostles:* Isaiah speaks "as though in the person of the apostles" (ὡς ἀπὸ προσώπου τῶν ἀποστόλων, *Dial.* 42.2 ll. 6-7). In the words, "Lord, who believed our report?" (Isa. 53:1), which Justin cites here, the apostles, through their representative Isaiah, are "saying (i.e., admitting) to Christ that <people> believe not by their report but by the power of him who sent them" (λεγόντων τῷ Χριστῷ ὅτι οὐχὶ τῇ ἀκοῇ αὐτῶν πιστεύουσιν <ἄνθρωποι> ἀλλὰ τῇ αὐτοῦ τοῦ πέμψαντος αὐτοὺς δυνάμει, *Dial.* 42.2 ll. 7-8, ed. Marcovich).[123]

123. However, we do not know for sure how much of the text of Isaiah 53 Justin originally included at this point. Our surviving text of the *Dialogue* quotes Isa. 53:1 and 53:2a as far as the words ὡς ῥίζα ἐν γῇ διψώσῃ, followed by a summary reference to the rest of the prophecy: "*We announced before Him as a child, as a root in a thirsty land,* and the rest of the prophecy as already stated," καὶ τὰ ἑξῆς τῆς προφητείας προλελεγμένα (*Dial.* 42.2 l. 11, ed. Marcovich). This could be the original wording, in which case it would be Justin's way of referring back to the text of Isa. 53:2b–54:6 already cited in *Dial.* 13.4-9 so that he would not need to repeat it here. But it could also be a later scribal abbreviation, an "et cetera" to avoid the need to copy the longer citation that Justin may have included. The text of Eusebius's Isaiah commentary shows that such abbreviated citations of well-known Bible passages were common; see GCS *Eusebius Werke,* vol. 9: *Der Jesajakommentar,* ed. J. Ziegler, 2nd ed. (1975), xli-xlii.

Further uses of the prophecy of Isaiah 53 are skillfully woven into Justin's unfolding argument. In *Dialogue* 89.1 Justin has Trypho admit that all the Scriptures Justin has cited refer to the Messiah, that the Messiah was to have the same name Ἰησοῦς as did Joshua son of Nun, and that the Messiah was to suffer. But that the Messiah should suffer a death *by crucifixion* that is cursed by the law in Deuteronomy 21:23 is harder to accept, and therefore Trypho demands proof that this fate was also prophesied by God. Naturally verses from the fourth Servant Song — verses 8d, 3, 4, 12, 7, 8b — are pressed into service. Justin uses his earlier counter-factual condition with εἰ μή (cf. *Dial.* 32.2) again here in 89.3:

> "If indeed Christ was not (εἰ μὲν μή) destined to suffer," said I to him, "and if the prophets did not foretell that 'because of the iniquities of the people He should be led to death' (Isa. 53:8d), and 'be dishonoured' (cf. ἠτιμάσθη, 53:3), and 'be scourged' (53:4?), and 'be reckoned among the ungodly' (53:12), and 'be led as a sheep to the slaughter' (53:7), whose 'birth,' says the prophet, 'no one can describe' (53:8b), it were well to be astonished (θαυμάζειν). But if this is the proper mark that distinguishes Him, and points Him out to all, how can we ourselves fail to be confident, now that we have believed in Him? Indeed all who have considered the words of the prophets will say that this person [Jesus] is the one referred to and no other, as soon as ever they hear that He was crucified." (*Dialogue* 89.3, trans. Williams [modified])[124]

Again there is only one passage, Isaiah 53, that keeps people from being totally "astonished" at the message of a dying Messiah who does away with the sins of others. This passage also enables people to believe this message. Trypho already knows that the Messiah was to be "led as a sheep to the slaughter," as Isaiah 53:7 says, but he does not yet think that this proves that he was to be crucified (cf. *Dial.* 90.1). Justin must therefore provide a whole series of typological references to the cross from the Scriptures, which do not particularly interest us here (cf. *Dial.* 90-111).[125] But it comes as no surprise when, after referring to the

---

124. *Dial.* 89.3 ll. 10-18 (ed. Marcovich, 225): Εἰ μὲν μὴ ἔμελλε πάσχειν ὁ Χριστός, φημὶ αὐτῷ ἐγώ, μηδὲ προεῖπον οἱ προφῆται ὅτι ἀπὸ τῶν ἀνομιῶν τοῦ λαοῦ ἀχθήσεται [LXX: ἤχθη] εἰς θάνατον καὶ ἀτιμωθήσεται [LXX: ἠτιμάσθη] καὶ μαστιχθήσεται καὶ ἐν τοῖς ἀνόμοις λογισθήσεται [LXX: ἐλογίσθη] καὶ ὡς πρόβατον ἐπὶ σφαγὴν ἀχθήσεται [LXX: ἤχθη], οὗ τὸ γένος ἐξηγήσασθαι ἔχειν οὐδένα, <ὥς> φησιν ὁ προφήτης, καλῶς εἶχε θαυμάζειν. Εἰ δὲ τοῦτό ἐστι τὸ χαρακτηρίζον αὐτὸν καὶ πᾶσι μηνύον, πῶς οὐχὶ καὶ ἡμεῖς θαρροῦντες πεπιστεύκαμεν εἰς αὐτόν; Καὶ ὅσοι νενοήκασι τὰ τῶν προφητῶν, τοῦτον φήσουσιν, οὐκ ἄλλον, εἰ μόνον ἀκούσειαν ὅτι οὗτος <ἐστιν ὁ> ἐσταυρωμένος.

125. However, *Dial.* 95.3 does head off a potential false conclusion: Even if the Father is the ultimate cause of the suffering that the Son bears for the world, those who delivered him up

Passover at the end of his summary of the types of the cross, Justin interprets it in the light of Isaiah 53:7:

> The Passover, indeed, was Christ, who was later sacrificed, as Isaiah foretold when he said, *He was led as a sheep to the slaughter* (Isa. 53:7). . . . Now, just as *the blood of the Passover* saved those who were in Egypt, so also the blood of Christ shall rescue from death all those who have believed in him. (*Dialogue* 111.3)[126]

As we have repeatedly seen, the fourth Servant Song plays an exceedingly important role for Justin, as is evident even from his linguistic usage and composition. He who alone is without sin — and this is indeed a necessary condition for his own salvation (cf. *Dial.* 102.7)[127] — bears the sins of the many. Yet Justin's frequent insistence upon the Messiah's second coming in glory does not detract from the atoning work of the Messiah in his shameful death. Here Justin also takes up a key saying which he originally scripted for Trypho at the beginning of the disputation, when he had Trypho describe him as εἰς ἄνθρωπον ἐλπίσας, as one who has "set [his] hope on a human being" (*Dial.* 8.3).[128] Justin

---

are not innocent. Hence Justin warns, "Let none of you say: If the Father wished Him to suffer these things, in order that by his stripes the human race should be healed (cf. Isa. 53:5), we did no wrong" (trans. Williams). Those who inflicted the wounds are not justified. See Skarsaune, *Proof,* 393-400.

126. Trans. Falls and Halton, *Dialogue with Trypho,* 320. Text *Dial.* 111.3 ll. 18-19, 21-22 (ed. Marcovich): Ἦν γὰρ τὸ πάσχα ὁ Χριστός, ὁ τυθεὶς ὕστερον, ὡς καὶ Ἡσαΐας ἔφη· Αὐτὸς ὡς πρόβατον ἐπὶ σφαγὴν ἤχθη. . . . Ὡς δὲ τοὺς ἐν Αἰγύπτῳ ἔσωσε τὸ αἷμα τοῦ πάσχα, οὕτως καὶ τοὺς πιστεύσαντας ῥύσεται ἐκ θανάτου τὸ αἷμα τοῦ Χριστοῦ.

127. [[(Tr.) Justin in *Dial.* 102.7 seems to regard the sinlessness of the Messiah as a necessary but not a sufficient condition for his salvation, for he says that even the sinless one cannot be saved without God. This sets up an *a fortiori* argument: since the sinless Messiah cannot be saved without God, it is all the more true that Trypho and his people cannot be saved without Christian hope: cf. *Dial.* 102.7 (with reference to Isa. 53:9), as well as the fuller explanation in the text above]]:

> For, if the Son of God clearly states that it is not because he is the Son, nor because he is powerful or wise, but that, even though he be sinless (for Isaiah said that he did not sin even by word, *for he has done no iniquity, neither was there deceit in his mouth* [Isa. 53:9]), he cannot be saved without God (ἄνευ τοῦ θεοῦ), how can you or others who expect to be saved without this hope (ἄνευ τῆς ἐλπίδος ταύτης), fail to realize that you are deceiving yourselves? (*Dial.* 102.7, trans. Falls and Halton, *Dialogue with Trypho,* 155).

128. [[(Tr.) Trypho initially thinks in *Dial.* 8.3 that Justin should be in doubt of his salvation: see above n. 102. There is a word-play on καταλείπω/περιλείπομαι: καταλιπόντι δὲ τὸν θεὸν καὶ εἰς ἄνθρωπον ἐλπίσαντι ποία ἔτι περιλείπεται σωτηρία; = "For having *left* God and hoped in a man, what salvation is still *left* [for you]?"]]

eventually turns this back upon Trypho in *Dialogue* 102.7. Would it not be self-deception, Justin asks, for Trypho and his friends to expect salvation "without this [sc. Christian] hope" (ἄνευ τῆς ἐλπίδος ταύτης) — especially since even the Messiah himself could not be saved "without God" (ἄνευ τοῦ θεοῦ) and likewise "hoped in the Lord" (ἤλπισεν ἐπὶ κύριον) according to the preceding citation of Psalm 22:9 (LXX 21:9) in *Dialogue* 98.3 and 101.3?[129]

This brings a certain closure to Justin's argument and therefore also to my presentation of him. What especially impresses me about this type of exposition is that, because Justin still stands relatively early in the history of interpretation, he feels no need either to problematize or to resolve the phenomenon of the Messiah's "shameful" death and his life "without appearance or beauty." His interpretation of the fourth Servant Song is still totally determined by the demands of the Jewish-Christian dialogue; no "Hellenization" of the kerygma has yet taken place on this point, no matter what one might say positively or negatively about the Hellenization of Justin's Christianity at other points.[130]

Shall we then follow Hans Walter Wolff in accusing Justin — in the light of his interpretation of Isaiah 53:8b (about the Messiah's "indescribable generation") or other passages — of "atomistic use of the Scripture" or of "arbitrary choice and length of citations," even though this may be explained by what Wolff calls Justin's "carefree joy in the Holy Scripture"?[131] I, for one, find Justin

---

129. [(Tr.) On the *a fortiori* argumentation here see n. 127 with its translation of *Dial.* 102.7. For the reference to Ps. 22:9 see Williams, *Dialogue*, 214 n. 3, and its cross-reference to 196 n. 3 on *Dial.* 92.6, "that you may be saved with Christ" (as Christ is "saved" in 102.7).]

130. See most recently D. Wyrwa, "Über die Begegnung des biblischen Glaubens mit dem griechischen Geist," *ZTK* 88 (1991): 29-67. Gelio summarizes: "Ecco allora che Is 53,2-3 è citato in contesti in cui si fa parola dell' aspetto dimesso di tutta la vita umana di Cristo, oppure, più propriamente descritta, della passione e morte" ("Isaia 52,13–53,12," 132).

131. Wolff, *Jesaja 53 im Urchristentum*, 132, 139 accuses Justin of the "atomistic use of Scripture." Presumably the origin of Wolff's dissertation, in a time of persecution of the confessing German Church (1942 in Halle), may help us understand why for him, the ultimate verification of Justin's exegesis of Isaiah 53 is the fact that he sealed his testimony with his own blood, as recorded in *The Acts of Justin*. [(Tr.) Significantly, Wolff interprets Justin's use of the title παῖς θεοῦ in his public testimony (as reported in his *Acts*) before his execution as "one final, purposeful reference to Isaiah 53" (Wolff, 141-42, here 142). See text and translation of the *Acts of Justin and Companions* 2.5, in H. Musurillo, ed., *The Acts of the Christian Martyrs*, OECT (1972), Recension B, 46-53, esp. ll. 11-16: Ὅπερ εὐσεβοῦμεν εἰς τὸν τῶν Χριστιανῶν θεόν . . . , καὶ κύριον Ἰησοῦν Χριστὸν παῖδα θεοῦ, ὃς καὶ προκεκήρυκται ὑπὸ τῶν προφητῶν μέλλων παραγίνεσθαι τῷ γένει τῶν ἀνθρώπων σωτηρίας κῆρυξ καὶ διδάσκαλος καλῶν μαθημάτων = "[The belief (δόγμα)] that we piously hold regarding the God of the Christians . . . , also regarding the Lord Jesus Christ, the παῖς [Musurillo: *child;* Wolff: *Servant*] of God, who was also foretold by the prophets as one who was to come down to mankind as a herald of salvation and a teacher of good doctrines."] Nevertheless, this single mention of the title παῖς θεοῦ in the *Acts of*

to have a very consistent interpretation, which works through almost all the verses of our passage exegetically and excludes none of them. The citations follow a clear line of thought and do not produce an arbitrary effect. The whole text is introduced right at the beginning (cf. Isa. 52:10–54:6 in *Dial.* 13.2-9); later only important portions are cited at the appropriate place. But "speculative interpretation" or "atomistic exegesis" is not yet to be found here.

2. Jewish-Christian Dialogue on Isaiah 53, II: Aphrahat the Persian Sage

Comparable with Justin's *Dialogue* is one of the Demonstrations (Syriac: *taḥw*ᵉ*yātā*ᶜ) of Aphrahat, "the Persian Sage,"[132] *Demonstration* 17, written in 343-344 C.E.: "On the Messiah, That He Is the Son of God."[133] The author lived among Christians friendly to Rome[134] in the Sasanian empire of Persia,

---

Justin 2.5 does not bear the weight Wolff has placed on it. On the *Acts* see R. Freudenberger, "Die Acta Justini als historisches Dokument," in K. Beyschlag, G. Maron, E. Wölfel, eds., *Humanitas-Christianitas: Walther von Loewenich zum 65. Geburtstag* (1968), 24-31.

132. On Aphrahat and his work (= Aphraates, the Persian sage, fl. 337-345 [Library of Congress]) see briefly "Aphrahat," *ODCC*, 3rd ed. (1997), 82; P. Bruns, "Afrahat," *RGG*, 4th ed. (1998), 138-39; R. Lavenant, "Aphraates," *EECh* 1 (1992), 54; more fully A. Vööbus, "Aphrahat" (originally published in 1960), *RAC Supplement* 1 (2001), 497-506 (bibliography); G. G. Blum, "Afraha," *TRE* 1 (1977), 625-35 (bibliography). See especially P. Bruns, *Das Christusbild Aphrahats des Persischen Weisen,* Hereditas 4 (1990), 69-81; the introduction to Bruns's German translation, Aphrahat, *Unterweisungen,* 2 vols., Fontes Christiani 5/1-2 (1991), 1:35-73; and the introduction to the English translation, Aphrahat, *Demonstrations,* vol. 1 (*Dem.* 1-10 only), trans. Kuriakose Valavanolickal, Catholic Theological Studies of India 3; HIRS India Series 28 (1999), 1:1-17.

133. Aphrahat, *Dem.* 15, title: *taḥwītā*ʾ *d*ᶜ*al m*ᵉ*šīḥā*ʾ *dabreh hū dalāhā*ʾ. (The transliteration of Syriac in this essay follows the guidelines in Beate Siewert-Mayer et al., eds., *Tübinger Atlas des Vorderen Orients: Register zu den Karten/General Index,* 3 vols., vol. 1: *Einleitung/Introduction, A-G* [1994], xxvii §6.) Syriac text in J. Parisot, "Aphraatis Sapientis Persae Demonstrationes," in *Patrologia Syriaca,* ed. R. Graffin, part I, vol. 1 (1894), 785, hereafter: PS 1/ 1:785, ed. Parisot. English translation of *Dem.* 17 in J. Neusner, *Aphrahat and Judaism: The Christian-Jewish Argument in Fourth-Century Iran,* StPB 19 (1971), 68-75 (cf. the older English translation of *Dem.* 17 by J. Gwynn in *NPNF,* 2nd series, 13:387-92). On *Dem.* 17 see esp. Bruns, *Das Christusbild Aphrahats,* 122-28, with further literature.

134. Cf. Aphrahat, *Dem.* 5, titled *taḥwītā*ʾ *daqrābē*ʾ, "Demonstration on Wars" (text in PS 1/1:184-238, ed. Parisot; trans. in *NPNF,* 2nd series, 13:352-62, or Valavanolickal, *Demonstrations,* 81-101, with summary, pp. 81-82). See A. Demandt, *Die Spätantike: Römische Geschichte von Diocletian bis Justinian, 284-565 n. Chr.,* Handbuch der Altertumswissenschaft 3/6 (1989), 78 n. 88; S. P. Brock, "Christians in the Sasanian Empire: A Case of Divided Loyalties," in S. Mews, ed., *Religion and National Identity,* SCH 18 (1982), 120.

whose king Sapor (Shapur) II (309-379) was interested in extending his empire at the expense of the Armenian empire and the Roman frontier provinces.[135] The text is written for a friend of Aphrahat to help him "reply to the Jews."[136] It is therefore a kind of "sample dialogue" and in this sense comparable to Justin.

This text too reports that the Jews (Babylonian Judaism)[137] reject a *crucified Messiah*. Aphrahat has his Jews say to the Christians, "Although God has no son, you say concerning this crucified Jesus that he is the son of God" (*Dem.* 17.1).[138] These Jews seek to disprove this by citing Deuteronomy 32:39 and Exodus 34:14. Against this, the Persian Sage seeks to show that God himself made Moses to be like God to Pharaoh (Exod. 7:1 = *Dem.* 17.3),[139] and that Israel is also called God's "firstborn son" (Exod. 4:22-23 = *Dem.* 17.4). Therefore Jesus is called "son" only in the same way as Israel is by God.[140] The prophets also called him "the son of God," as Aphrahat shows from Psalm 2:7 and Isaiah 9:6-7 (*Dem.* 17.9). The Jewish hope that when the Messiah comes, "Israel will be gathered together from all regions, and Jerusalem will be rebuilt and inhabited" is refuted

135. Demandt, *Die Spätantike*, 86, 105-6. Cf. the salutation in a letter from Sapor to the Roman Emperor Constantius II: *Rex regum Sapor, particeps siderum, frater Solis et Lunae, Constantio Caesari fratri meo salutem plurimam dico*, "I Sapor, King of Kings, partner with the Stars, brother of the Sun and Moon, to my brother Constantius Caesar offer most ample greeting" (Ammianus Marcellinus, 17.5.3, trans. J. C. Rolfe, LCL 1:332-33).

136. *Dem.* 17.12 (PS 1/1:816 ll. 1-5, ed. Parisot; trans. Neusner, *Aphrahat and Judaism*, 75).

137. On Aphrahat's relationships with Judaism see Bruns, trans., *Unterweisungen*, 1:54-56; K. Deppe, "Die Rolle des Alten Testamentes im Streit zwischen Christen und Juden nach dem Zeugnis Afrahats," in G. Wiessner, ed., *Erkenntnisse und Meinungen*, Göttinger Orientforschungen, series I, Syriaca, vol. 3 (1973), 83-107; Neusner, *Aphrahat and Judaism*.

138. *Dem.* 17.1: *wekad lat bᵉrāʾ lalāhāʾ ʾāmrīn ᵉ(n)tūn ʿelau(hi) dᵉhānāʾ yēšūʿ zᵉqīpāʾ bᵉrāʾ lam dalāhāʾ* (PS 1/1:785 ll. 6-8, ed. Parisot; trans. Neusner, *Aphrahat and Judaism*, 68).

139. Cf. the excursus, "Die 'Gottheit des Mose' (Ex 4,16/7,1) in syrischer und jüdischer Deutung" (= "The 'Divinity of Moses' [Exod. 4:16/7:1] in Syrian and Jewish Interpretation"), in Bruns, *Das Christusbild Aphrahats*, 128-33. Bruns claims that in the view of Aphrahat's Syrian Christian contemporary Ephraem Syrus, "The prophet Moses, in his fear of God, is simply a 'hollow and empty form' for God; he participates in God's almighty power and therefore is superior to his fellow creatures" (130). Regarding the Christological thought of Aphrahat, Bruns says: "The designation of a person as 'God' within the Jewish horizon of thought is thoroughly possible and is not necessarily associated with a softening of monotheism. . . . In this respect the apologetic efforts of the Persian Sage are not far removed from the interpretive tradition of his Jewish opponents" (133).

140. *Dem.* 17.4: *wᵉāp ḥᵉnan qᵉrayᵉnā(hi) lᵉhānāʾ mᵉšīhāʾ bᵉrēh dalāhāʾ dᵉbēh yīdanā(hi) lalāhāʾ, a(i)k daqrā(hi) līsrael bēri būkri*, "So we call this Messiah the son of God, for by him we know God, just as he called Israel 'my son, my first born'" (PS 1/1:789 ll. 19-22, ed. Parisot; trans. Neusner, *Aphrahat and Judaism*, 69).

with a citation of Daniel 9:26-27 (*Dem.* 17.10).[141] This states that the Anointed One or Messiah (מָשִׁיחַ) will be killed and that there will be war to the end, and mentions the appearance of the "abomination of desolation" on the temple mount of the *aelia capitolina*.

To support his idea of a *suffering Messiah*, Aphrahat cites central verses from Isaiah 52:13–53:12.[142] There follows an interesting passage in which potential applications of the fourth Servant Song to persons other than Jesus Christ are excluded (*Dem.* 17.10):

> By what wounds [then] were men healed? David was not killed, for he died in good old age, and was buried in Bethlehem (cf. 1 Kings 2:10).[143]

Similarly excluded is the possibility that the prophecies of Psalm 22:17-19 and Isaiah 52–53 might refer to Saul. Aphrahat grants to his Jewish interlocutors in *Dem.* 17.10 that the Philistines "*pierced* [Saul's] hands and his feet when they hung up his body on the wall of Bethshean," which would seem to fulfill Psalm 22:17 in Aphrahat's Syriac version, "they have *pierced* my hands and feet" (RSV [22:16], following the Greek, Syriac, and Jerome; contrast MT/NJPS: "*like lions* [singular כָּאֲרִי] they maul my hands and feet"). But Aphrahat counters that when this happened to Saul, he was already dead and could no longer suffer the agonies of Psalm 22, adding that Saul could also not fulfill Psalm 22:23, "in the midst of the church I shall praise you" (ed. Parisot, 808 ll. 17-18; trans. Neusner, 74). Aphrahat claims that these passages apply only to the crucified Messiah, Jesus Christ. He concludes in *Demonstration* 17.10 with citations of Isaiah 53:10 and 53:5: Christ is the prophesied Messiah of Israel[144] and the world; all his names appear already in the Old Testament[145] and mean nothing new when applied to Christ — certainly not blasphemy.

Nevertheless, Aphrahat's Christological tradition fits very poorly into our

---

141. *Dem.* 17.10 (PS 1/1:805 ll. 21-24, ed. Parisot; trans. Neusner, *Aphrahat and Judaism,* 73).

142. *Dem.* 17.10: *wᵉᶜal ḥašēh damšīḥāʾ dawīd ʾēmar,* "Concerning the passion of the Messiah, David said . . ." (followed by a citation of Ps. 22:17-19). *wᵉʾēšaᶜya ʾēmar,* "Isaiah said . . ." (followed by citations of Isa. 52:13-14, 15; 53:2, 5, with minor deviations from the Peshitta text). Text PS 1/1:805 l. 27-808 l. 1; 808 l. 5, ed. Parisot; trans. Neusner, *Aphrahat and Judaism,* 73-74.

143. *Dem.* 17.10, trans. Neusner, *Aphrahat and Judaism,* 74. Text: *b'aylē(i)n šūmātāʾ ētasīw bᵉnaynāsā? dawīd lā ētkᵉṭēl. mēṭal dᵉemīt bᵉsaikūtāʾ ṭābtāʾ wᵉʾetkᵉbar bē(i)t lᵉhēm* (PS 1/1:808 ll. 17-20, ed. Parisot).

144. On this see Bruns, *Das Christusbild Aphrahats,* 161-66.

145. *Dem.* 17.11: "We call him God like Moses, first born and son like Israel, Jesus like Jesus the son of Nun, priest like Aaron, king like David, great prophet like all of the prophets, shepherd like the shepherds who watched and tended Israel" (PS 1/1:813 ll. 8-14, ed. Parisot; trans. Neusner, *Aphrahat and Judaism,* 75).

Western dogma of Christ as *vere deus* and metaphysical Son of God as defined by the Councils of Nicea and Chalcedon, and this must not be concealed or watered down.[146] Peter Bruns writes:

> Aphrahat is at pains to establish the continuity between Judaism and Christianity by showing that without leaving the Jewish-Semitic way of thinking, a Jew can designate the Messiah as "God" or the "Son of God."[147]

The fourth Servant Song helps Aphrahat present even a suffering Messiah as a plausible figure against a "Jewish" — first and foremost *biblical* — background. From his argument we see that our text is still being used in a particular context *adversus Judaeos,* even 200 years after its nearest analogy in Justin.

3. Jewish-Christian Dialogue on Isaiah 53, III: Later Adversus Judaeos Texts and Dialogues

Here we may examine our first Latin text, the late *Altercatio legis inter Simonem Iudaeum et Theophilum Christianum* of Evagrius Gallicus (about 430 C.E.),[148] as representative of a large number of *Adversus Judaeos* texts.[149] There has been some doubt as to whether this is really an original Latin dialogue, but Harnack's attempt to identify it as a Latin translation of the lost Greek dialogue between

---

146. Moreover, as Bruns, *Das Christusbild Aphrahats,* 123, points out, the expression *bᵉrā' dalāhā'* ("son of God"; cf. Neusner, *Aphrahat and Judaism,* 68-69, 73, 75, passim), "does not necessarily designate a physical-genealogical sonship, but generally expresses an affiliation."

147. Bruns, *Das Christusbild Aphrahats,* 123-24.

148. To distinguish him from others of the same name, the author is identified in online library catalogs as Evagrius [Monachus], fl. 430; his work, the *Altercatio,* is *CPL,* 3rd ed., no. 482. See briefly A. Hamman, "Evagrius, monk," *EECh* 1:305. Text editions: E. Bratke, ed., *Scriptores ecclesiastici minores saecvlorvm IV. V. VI., fascicvlvs I. Evagrii Altercatio legis inter Simonem Ivdaevm et Theophilvm Christianvm,* CSEL 45 (1904) or more recently R. Demeulenaere, ed., "Altercatio legis inter Simonem Ivdaevm et Theophilvm Christianvm," in *Foebadius. Victricius. Leporius. Vincentius Lerinensis. Evagrius. Ruricius,* CCSL 64 (1985), 255-302.

149. A. von Harnack, "Die Altercatio Simonis Iudaei et Theophili Christiani, nebst Untersuchungen über die antijüdische Polemik in der alten Kirche," TU 1/3 (1883), 1-136 esp. 74-91. (There is also a 1999 reprint of TU 1 which, however, has misapplied the part title page for TU 1/1-2 to the whole volume, TU 1/1-4: *Die Überlieferung der griechischen Apologeten des zweiten Jahrhunderts in der alten Kirche und im Mittelalter,* by Adolf Harnack.) See also A. Lukyn Williams, *Adversus Judaeos: A Bird's-Eye View of Christian Apology until the Renaissance* (1935), 298-311; H. Schreckenberg, *Die christlichen Adversus-Judaeos-Texte und ihr literarisches und historisches Umfeld (1.-11. Jh.),* Europäische Hochschulschriften, Reihe 23, Theologie, Bd. 172, 4th ed. (1999).

Jason and Papiscus (see above n. 22)[150] fails to account for its rich use of later Western *Adversus Judaeos* literature.[151] Isaiah 52:13–53:12 is indeed one of the most often cited Bible passages in this document, with three explicit citations (all within the long section *Altercatio* §2.4 CSEL = §6 CCSL).[152] But since the modern editions of the text run to fifty pages, one should be careful about assuming too much based on so few citations.

Interestingly enough, here too the Christian quotation of Isaiah 53 is elicited by the Jewish interlocutor's question about the suffering of the Messiah, particularly whether death on a cross is not in fact a cursed death according to Deuteronomy 21:23. Simon the Jew says:

> But if Christ endured the yoke of this death and hung on a cross, why did we not receive this very tradition from the fathers and why did we not find that he suffered (this) in our Scriptures, so that we might rejoice if he were an enemy to our people? You will have something to blush about, Theophilus, if you do not at least prove that this was said. For it is written in Deuteronomy, "Cursed is everyone who hangs on a tree" (Deut. 21:23).[153]

Against this the Christian Theophilus argues from the context of Deuteronomy 21:23: Moses says this only about the sinner who has committed a mortal sin: "Sed hoc pro peccatore dixit, qui mortale peccatum admiserit" (p. 26 l. 10 CSEL = 278 ll. 19-20 CCSL). But Christ had no sin, "as all the prophets tes-

---

150. Cf. Harnack, "Altercatio," 115-30.

151. J. Quasten, *Patrology,* Italian edition by A. di Berardino, *Patrologia,* vol. 3: *Dal Concilio di Nicea (325) al Concilio di Calcedonia (451)* (1978), 483-84 = Quasten, *Patrology,* vol. 4: *The Golden Age of Latin Patristic Literature: From the Council of Nicea to the Council of Chalcedon,* ed. A. di Berardino, intro. J. Quasten, trans. P. Solari (1986), 509-10. On the question of a possible use of *testimonia* in this instance see Prigent, *Justin et l'Ancien Testament,* 178.

152. The citations include first a conflation of Isa. 53:9, 6 near the beginning of *Altercatio* §2.4 (CSEL, ed. Bratke) = §6 (CCSL, ed. Demeulenaere; see n. 148 for editions); then a citation of part of Isa. 53:12 two lines later in *Altercatio* 2.4 = 6; and finally a long conflated citation of Isa. 53:1-4, 7-9, 6, 12 near the end of *Altercatio* 2.4 = 6. The citations do not always follow the Vulgate (see below n. 155). They are found in the text editions as follows: Isa. 53:9, 6 in CSEL 45:27 ll. 1-3, ed. Bratke = CCSL 64:278 ll. 22-24, ed. Demeulenaere; Isa. 53:12 in CSEL 45:27 ll. 5-6 = CCSL 64:278 l. 26; Isa. 53:1-4, 7-9, 6, 12 in CSEL 45:32 l. 6-33 l. 9 = CCSL 64:283 ll. 91-104.

153. *Altercatio* 2.4 (CSEL 45:25 l. 13–26 l. 6, Bratke) = *Altercatio* 6 (CCSL 64:277 ll. 9-14, Demeulenaere): "Christus autem si patibulum mortis huius sustinuit et in cruce pependit, cur non hoc ipsum a patribus accepimus nec passum in scripturis nostris inuenimus, ut, si inimicus genti nostrae esset, gauderemus? Erubescere poteris, Theophile, si hoc dictum minime conprobaueris. Nam scriptum est in Deuteronomio [Deut. 21:23]: *maledictus omnis, qui pendet in ligno.*"

tify."[154] Theophilus claims that it was necessary for Christ to suffer so that the Scriptures would be fulfilled, citing Isaiah 53:9; 53:6; and 53:12 (together with Jer. 6:10) in a pre-Vulgate version:

> Dicit enim Esaias: "Quia peccatum non fecit nec dolus inuentus est in ore eius [Isa. 53:9], sed dominus tradidit illum pro peccatis nostris [Isa. 53:6]." Nam et alibi dixisse prophetam ostendimus: "Ecce verbum domini factum est illis in maledictum, et nolerunt illud [Jer. 6:10]." Et iterum dicit: "Inter maledictos deputatus est [Isa. 53:12]." (*Altercatio* 2.4 = 6)[155]

> For instance, Isaiah says: "Because he committed no sin, nor was any deceit found in his mouth [Isa. 53:9], but the Lord gave him up for our sins [Isa. 53:6]." For a prophet has also spoken in another place, saying, "Behold, the word of the Lord has been made into a curse to them, and they do not want it [Jer. 6:10]." And again he [Isaiah] says, "he was counted among the cursed [Isa. 53:12]."

After this comes an excerpt from Psalm 22 (vv. 17-23; Vulgate Psalm 21), which the Church Fathers especially liked to cite in this connection,[156] followed by a whole series of additional Scripture quotations. For proof of Jesus' humanity, more particularly of his "humility" *(humilitas)* in his first advent, there is once again a long citation from Isaiah 53, including verses 1-4, 7-9, 6, 12.[157] Simi-

---

154. *Altercatio* 2.4 (CSEL 45:26 ll. 11-12) = *Altercatio* 6 (CCSL 64:278 ll. 20-21): *Christus autem peccatum non habuit, sicut omnes prophetae testantur.*

155. *Altercatio* 2.4 (CSEL 45:27 ll. 1-5) = *Altercatio* 6 (CCSL 64:278 ll. 22-26). The Vulgate version reads: "Quod iniquitatem non fecerit neque dolus fuerit in ore eius" (Isa. 53:9). "Et Dominus posuit in eo iniquitatem omnium nostrum" (Isa. 53:6). "Ecce verbum Domini factum est eis in obprobrium et non suscipient illud" (Jer. 6:10). "Et Dominus posuit in eo iniquitatem omnium nostrum und cum sceleratis reputatus est" (Isa. 53:12). [(Tr.) Unlike the Vulgate version, where Jer. 6:10 and Isa. 53:12 are verbally unrelated (cf. *obprobrium, sceleratis*), the *Altercatio* version of Jer. 6:10 and Isa. 53:12 contains two related "curse" words formed from the participial adjective *maledictus* (cf. neuter substantive, *maledictum*) linking the two passages: "verbum domini factum est illis in *maledictum*" and "inter *maledictos* deputatus est." This language ultimately goes back to the curse of Deut. 21:23, about which the *Altercatio*'s disputants have debated only a few lines earlier: *"maledictus omnis, qui pendet in ligno"* (see above n. 153).]

156. *Altercatio* 2.4 (CSEL 45:27 ll. 12-28 l. 6) = *Altercatio* 6 (CCSL 64:278-79 ll. 31-38). See Prigent, *Justin et l'Ancien Testament,* 191; M. Mees, "Ps 22(21) und Is 53 in frühchristlicher Sicht," *Augustinianum* 22 (1982): 313-35.

157. "Revertaumur nunc ad humilitatem primi adventus Christi, de qua agebamus. Audi Esaiam prophetam . . . [followed by the citation of 53:1-4, 7-9, 6, 12]," *Altercatio* 2.4 (CSEL 45:32 ll. 4-5) = *Altercatio* 6 (CCSL 64:282 ll. 89-90). For a similar use of Justin's formula about Christ's

lar arguments are found in the spurious writing of Tertullian,[158] *Adversos Iudaeos.*[159]

In sum, within the genre *Adversos Judaeos*, one can recognize a continuity in handling the Bible passage Isaiah 52–53, even among authors as theologically different as Justin, Aphrahat, and Evagrius. Because of its plausible, and at that time completely natural, Christological interpretation, it remained a central proof text for a suffering Messiah and for the prophetic prediction of his death on the cross.

4. Apologetic Argumentation in the Early Christological Model: Melito of Sardis and Irenaeus

Melito, who died around 190, was bishop of the city of Sardis in the province of Lydia, Asia Minor. In a letter preserved by Eusebius, Melito's colleague Polycrates, bishop of Ephesus, refers to him as one of the departed "great luminaries" (μεγάλα στοιχεῖα) of Asia.[160] Melito refers to our Isaiah passage especially in two places: once in his Christological interpretation of the sacrifice of Isaac,[161] which has survived in three fragments of a catena (*Fragments* 9-11),[162]

"first advent" (above, n. 109), see the heading of Cyprian's citation of Isa. 53:1-7 in his *Ad Quirinum* (*Testimoniorum* 1.3), 2.13: *Quod humilis in primo adventus suo veniret* (*Sancti Cypriani episcopi opera,* CCSL 3:45 l. 1, ed. R. Weber).

158. Pseudo-Tertullian, *Adversus Iudaios,* designated as *CPL,* 3rd ed., no. 33; or Frede, *Kirchenschriftsteller,* VL 1/1 766, under siglum TE Jud.

159. Pseudo-Tertullian, *Adversus Iudaios* 10.15: "Nam mortem eius et passionem et sepulturam una uoce Esaiae uolo ostendere . . . [followed by a citation of Isa. 53:8-10]." Text: E. Kroyman, ed., "Adversus Iudaios," in Tertullian, *Opera,* 2 vols., CCSL 1-2 (1954), 2:1379 ll. 118-23; cf. also *Adv. Iud.* 10.16 (p. 1379 ll. 127-30 = Isa. 53:12).

160. Eusebius, *Hist. eccl.* 5.24 §2 ("luminaries") and §5 (including Melito). Text in *Eusebius Kirchengeschichte,* GCS *Eusebius* 2/1:490 l. 13 and 492 l. 3, ed. E. Schwartz; text and translation in Eusebius, *The Ecclesiastical History,* trans. Lake, LCL 1:504-7.

161. See P. R. Davies, "Martyrdom and Redemption: On the Development of Isaac Typology in the Early Church," in E. A. Livingstone, ed., *Studia Patristica* 17/2 (1982), 652-58; D. Lerch, *Isaaks Opferung christlich gedeutet: Eine auslegungsgeschichtliche Untersuchung,* BHT 12 (1950), 27-43; F. Nikolasch, *Das Lamm als Christussymbol in den Schriften der Väter* (1963), 24-60; O. Perler, "Typologie der Leiden des Herrn in Melitons Peri Pascha," in Granfield and Jungmann, *Kyriakon,* 1:256-65; R. L. Wilken, "Melito, the Jewish Community at Sardis, and the Sacrifice of Isaac," *TS* 37 (1976): 53-69.

162. The fragments are identified as coming from an uncertain work of Melito as *CPG* no. 1093, *Fragmenta,* nos. 9-11: *Ex opere incerto.* (Fragment 12, *Fragmentum in Gen. 22:13,* formerly attributed to Melito and sometimes mentioned in this connection, has been deleted from his corpus and is now attributed to Eusebius of Emesa: see *CPG* 1, no. 1093, item [12]; *CPG* 2, no.

and again in his paschal homily, *On Pascha*. In his interpretation of the Isaac story Melito writes (*Frag.* 9 ll. 1-12, 17-18):

Τοῦ μακαρίου Μελίτωνος Σάρδεων·
2 Ὡς γὰρ κριὸς ἐδέθη
    φησὶ περὶ τοῦ κυρίου ἡμῶν Ἰησοῦ Χριστοῦ
4   καὶ ὡς ἀμνὸς ἐκάρη
    καὶ ὡς πρόβατον εἰς σφαγὴν ἤχθη
6   καὶ ὡς ἀμνὸς ἐσταυρώθη·
    καὶ ἀβάστασε τὸ ξύλον ἐπὶ τοῖς ὤμοις αὐτοῦ
8   ἀναγόμανος σφαγῆναι ὡς Ἰσαὰκ ὑπὸ τοῦ πατρὸς αὐτοῦ.
    ἀλλὰ Χριστὸς ἔπαθεν, Ἰσαὰκ δὲ οὐκ ἔπαθεν·
10   τύπος γὰρ ἦν τοῦ μέλλοντος πάσχειν Χριστοῦ.
    ἀλλὰ καὶ ὁ τύπος Χριστὸς γενόμενος
12   ἔκπληξιν καὶ φόβον παρεῖχεν τοῖς ἀνθρώποις. . . .
17 ὁ δὲ Ἰσαὰκ σιγᾷ πεπεδημένος ὡς κριός,
    οὐκ ἀνοίγων τὸ στόμα οὐδὲ φθεγγόμενος φωνῇ.

Of blessed Melito of Sardis:
For as a ram he was bound
(he says concerning our Lord Jesus Christ)
   and *as a lamb* he was shorn
   and as a sheep he was led to slaughter,
   and as a lamb he was crucified;
and he carried the wood on his shoulders
   as he was led up to be slain like Isaac by his Father.
But Christ suffered, whereas Isaac did not suffer;
   for he was a model ("type") of the Christ who was going to suffer.
But by being merely the model of Christ
   he caused astonishment and fear among men. . . .
But Isaac was silent, bound like a ram,
   not opening his mouth nor uttering a word.[163]

3532; and S. G. Hall, ed., *On Pascha and Fragments: Melito of Sardis*, OECT [1979], xxxiii-xxxiv.) The text of Melito's authentic fragments on the sacrifice of Isaac is available in several places: J. B. Pitra, ed., *Spicilegium solesmense*, vol. 2 (1855), lxiv; J. C. T. von Otto, ed., *Corpus apologetarum Christianorum saeculi secundi*, 9 vols. in 5, vol. 9 (1872), 416-18; E. J. Goodspeed, *Die ältesten Apologeten* (1914), 312-13; O. Perler, ed., *Sur la Pâque et fragments: Méliton de Sardes*, SC 123 (1966), 134-37; Hall, *On Pascha and Fragments*, 74-76. See esp. Hall, pp. xxxii-xxxiv, xlix on the text and content of fragments 9-11.

163. Text and translation from Hall, *On Pascha and Fragments*, 74 ll. 1-12, 17-18 (text); p. 75 (translation).

Here a whole series of allusions to the fourth Servant Song may be detected. Like Isaac, who served as the antecedent "model" or "type" (τύπος), Christ too was "shorn" like a lamb and "led to slaughter" like a sheep (ll. 4-5), clearly echoing Isaiah 53:7.[164] Isaac — and therefore Christ — was also silent like a ram (κριός, l. 17).[165] The figure of Christ is so imposing that Isaac, by being merely his *type*, "caused astonishment and fear among men" (l. 12), alluding to Isaiah 52:14-15.[166] Melito, bishop of a city with a large and important Jewish community,[167] shows by his connection of Genesis 22 and Isaiah 53 how thoroughly he interprets the whole Old Testament as a Christian and how deeply his Christianity has been formed in debate with Judaism.[168]

In Melito's sermon *On Pascha* there is once again a whole series of allusions to our Isaiah text (including Isa. 52:14; 53:3, 4, 7, 8) according to the edition

164. ⟦(Tr.) The verbal parallelism between Melito, *Fragment* 9 ll. 4-5 (ed. Hall, 74) and Isa. 53:7 LXX is set out below. Melito's verbal parallel is slightly stronger than suggested by the italics in Hall's above-cited translation, where "shorn" is not in italics. In addition to his virtually exact parallel concerning the sheep in l. 5, ὡς πρόβατον εἰς (LXX: ἐπὶ) σφαγὴν ἤχθη, Melito also uses the same verb κείρω (aorist passive ἐκάρη) that the LXX uses for the lamb's "shearer," τοῦ κείροντος αὐτόν (present participle)⟧:

Melito				
Frag. 9 l. 4:	καὶ	ὡς ἀμνὸς		ἐκάρη
Isa. 53:7 LXX:	καὶ	ὡς ἀμνὸς ἐναντίον τοῦ		κείροντος αὐτὸν
Frag. 9 l. 5:	καὶ	ὡς πρόβατον	εἰς σφαγὴν	ἤχθη
Isa. 53:7 LXX:		ὡς πρόβατον	ἐπὶ σφαγὴν	ἤχθη

165. Again we may compare the precise wording of Melito, *Fragment* 9 ll. 17-18 (ed. Hall, 74) with that of Isa. 53:7 LXX:

Melito, l. 17:	ὁ δὲ	Ἰσαὰκ σιγᾷ πεπεδημένος	**ὡς κριός,**	
Melito, l. 18:		οὐκ ἀνοίγων τὸ στόμα	οὐδὲ φθεγγόμενος	*φωνῇ.*
Isa. 53:7 LXX:			**ὡς ἀμνὸς** . . .	*ἄφωνος*
	οὕτως	οὐκ ἀνοίγει τὸ στόμα		
		αὐτοῦ		

166. The allusion to Isa. 52:14-15 is verbally less exact than the one to Isa. 53:7 (see nn. 164-65). Compare Melito, *Fragment* 9 l. 12 (ed. Hall, 74): ἔκπληξιν καὶ φόβον παρεῖχεν τοῖς ἀνθρώποις, "he caused astonishment and fear among men," with Isa. 52:14, ὃν τρόπον ἐκστήσονται ἐπὶ σὲ πολλοί, "As many shall be astonished at you," and Isa. 52:15: οὕτως θαυμάσονται ἔθνη πολλὰ ἐπ' αὐτῷ, "So many nations will be amazed at him" (translations of LXX Isa. 52:14-15 from E. R. Ekblad, *Isaiah's Servant Poems According to the Septuagint*, CBET 23 [1999], 175).

167. Cf. Wilken, "Melito," 54-55. On the synagogue in Sardis see now H. Botermann, "Die Synagoge von Sardes: Eine Synagoge aus dem 4. Jahrhundert?" *ZNW* 81 (1990): 103-21.

168. This interpretation is supported by Wilken, "Melito," 58-64; for criticism, see Davies, "Martyrdom," 655-57.

of O. Perler,[169] whereas the more recent edition of S. G. Hall notes only the four actual quotations of Isaiah 53:7 (or 7-8) in *On Pascha*, plus the two in *Fragments* 9 (cf. Hall's index, p. 98). In either case this makes our text one of the most cited in this sermon. At the beginning of his sermon (§4), the bishop probes the *type* (Hall: "model") and the *truth* (Hall: "reality") of the mystery, differentiating picture from substance (*On Pascha*, 4 ll. 27-32):

> εἰ καὶ γὰρ   ὡς πρόβατον εἰς σφαγὴν ἤχθη,
>   ἀλλ' οὐκ ἦν   πρόβατον·
> εἰ καὶ   ὡς ἀμνὸς ἄφωνος,
>   ἀλλ' οὐδὲ   ἀμνὸς ἦν.
> ὁ μὲν γὰρ τύπος ἐγένετο,
>   ἡ δὲ ἀλήθεια ηὑρίσκετο.

> For although *as a sheep he was led to slaughter,*
>   yet he was not a sheep;
> although *as a lamb speechless,*
>   yet neither was he a lamb.
> For the model (τύπος) indeed existed,
>   but then the reality (ἀλήθεια) appeared.[170]

As the crowning conclusion of a whole series of prophetic citations which includes Jeremiah 11:19 (*On Pascha* 61-63),[171] Melito cites Isaiah 53:7, 8b in full (§§64-65), following the LXX except for a few poetic transpositions,[172] adding that all this and more was proclaimed by the prophets "about the mystery of the Pascha, which is Christ" (εἰς τὸ τοῦ πάσχα μυστήριον, ὅ ἐστιν Χριστός).

For the ongoing discussion of Isaiah 52–53 — to which I shall return briefly in conclusion (§V below) — I think it would be interesting to look at Melito's theopaschite ideas.[173] Anastasius the Sinaite (died ca. 700) was a mo-

---

169. Perler, *Sur la Pâque et fragments*, index, 251.

170. Trans. Hall, 5. Text, *On Pascha*, 4 (ed. Hall, 4 ll. 27-32; ed. Perler, 62 ll. 29-34). On the poetic structure of these lines see Markschies, *Valentinus Gnosticus?* 124-27.

171. Cf. Prigent, *Justin et l'Ancien Testament*, 191, and Perler's notes to *On Pascha* 61-65 in his edition, 168-70.

172. *On Pascha* 64-65 (ed. Hall, 34 ll. 443-46, citing Isa. 53:7, 8aβ; cf. ll. 448-49 for the above statement about the mystery of the Pascha = ed. Perler, 94). Isa. 53:7 is alluded to once again in the series of predications about Christ that begins in *On Pascha* 66; see esp. §70 ll. 495, 498 (ed. Hall, 38; cf. Perler, 98 l. 511 [*not* l. 512 as in his index], l. 515): Οὗτός ἐστιν ὁ ἀμνὸς ὁ ἄφωνος (495) . . . καὶ εἰς σφαγὴν συρεὶς (498): "He is the lamb that is speechless . . . and *dragged* [σύρω for LXX ἄγω] to slaughter."

173. On the πάθη of Christ in Melito see H. Frohnhofen, *APATHEIA TOU THEOU: Über die Affektlosigkeit Gottes in der griechischen Antike und bei den griechischsprachigen Kirchen-*

nastic and an opponent of Monophysitism.[174] In §12 of his own work titled the Ὁδηγός or "Guide" (PG 89:197 ll. 1-3), Anastasius attributes to a work by Melito that he calls *On the Passion* (ὁ λόγος ὁ εἰς τὸ πάθος) the following literally "theopaschite" (cf. πάσχω) as well as anti-Israelite sentence; the same sentence is reprinted in modern editions of Melito's works as *Fragment 7* (ed. Hall, 70; ed. Perler, 226):

> Ὁ θεὸς πέπονθεν ὑπὸ δεξιᾶς Ἰσραηλίτιδος.
> God has **suffered** *by an Israelite right hand.*

Hall in his introduction (p. xxxi) says that "*Fragment 7* is a slight misquotation by Anastasius of two phrases from *PP* [*Peri Pascha*] 96." This seems to be a sound judgment. It would appear that Anastasius the Sinaite, if he was indeed quoting the two lines 715-716 of *On Pascha* 96 as we have them below, has essentially started with the beginning of the one (i.e., "God") and finished with the end of the other (i.e., "*by an Israelite right hand*"), leaving out the middle ("the King of Israel") and changing the perfect passive of φονεύω (πεφόνευται, "he has been murdered") into the perfect active of πάσχω (πέπονθεν, "he has suffered"). The authentic version of Melito therefore runs (ed. Hall, 70):

> ὁ θεὸς πεφόνευται·
> ὁ βασιλεὺς τοῦ Ἰσραὴλ ἀνήρεται ὑπὸ δεξιᾶς Ἰσραηλίτιδος.

> the God has been **murdered**;
> the King of Israel has been **put to death** *by an Israelite right hand.*

We obviously have three different verbs here in these three lines, including the version of Anastasius: πάσχω, φονεύω, and ἀναίρω. (The form ἀνήρεται is found only here in *TLG* Greek literature. It is apparently an irregular spelling of the perfect ἀνήρται, with the present ending -εται substituting for the perfect -ται.) However, even if it is suggested (with Hall) that Melito did not actually predicate the verb πάσκω of God as Anastasius the Sinaite says he did, the authentic statements of Melito above are certainly no less theopaschite than Anastasius's version. Therefore the statement "God has *suffered* by an Israelite right hand" is *theologically,* if not necessarily literarily, authentic to Melito.[175]

---

vätern bis zu Georgios Thaumaturgos, Europäische Hochschulschriften, Reihe 23, Theologie, Bd. 318 (1987), 152-56.

174. Cf. A. De Nicola, "Anastasius the Sinaite," *EECh* 1:37; "Anastasius Sinaita," *ODCC*, 3rd ed., 57-58.

175. On Melito's theopaschite statements see further Hall, *On Pascha,* xliii-xliv. Grillmeier, *Christ in Christian Tradition,* 1:95 with n. 200 = *Jesus der Christus,* 1:209 with n. 200

In spite of this — or perhaps because of it — Melito's writings lack any attempt to tone down the crass statements of suffering that the Isaiah passage predicates of Jesus. For the qualifying lines cited above to the effect that Jesus was "*as* a sheep (ὡς πρόβατον) . . . yet not a sheep" (cf. *On Pascha* 4) concern only the animal imagery applied to Jesus, not the sufferings attributed to him. Melito is still on the same course of interpretation concerning Jesus' death and Isaiah 53 that Justin's *Dialogue* already marked out.

While the writings of Irenaeus of Lyons cannot be examined in detail here, we may refer to a few sections of his work *The Demonstration of the Apostolic Preaching,* originally written in Greek but preserved fully only in an Armenian version discovered in modern times.[176] In the second main part of this work, about the proof of revelation through the fulfillment of prophecy (§§42b-97), the bishop of Lyons comes to speak about Isaiah 52–53. Interestingly, although the Septuagint version of Isaiah 53:4 is written in the present tense — οὗτος τὰς ἁμαρτίας ἡμῶν φέρει καὶ περὶ ἡμῶν ὀδυνᾶται, "he *bears* our sins and *suffers pain* for us" — and although Irenaeus's non-Septuagintal Greek version, which is closer to the Hebrew (and borrowed from Matt. 8:17), contained an aorist tense, Irenaeus interprets it in a *future* sense:

> At this point let us speak of His healings. Isaiah says thus: *He took our infirmities and bare our sicknesses:* that is to say, He shall take, and shall bear. For there are passages in which the Spirit of God through the prophets recounts things that are to be as having taken place. (*Demonstration* 67)[177]

points out that the *praedicatio idiomatum* or exchange of Christological and theological attributes between Christ and God was widespread already during Mileto's time in the second century. This would make it theologically understandable how Melito *could* have written both about the *murder* of God (as in Melito, *On Pascha* §97 l. 915, ed. Hall) and about the *suffering* of God (as in Melito, *Frag.* 7 = Athanasius the Sinaite, Ὁδηγός §12, PG 89:197 ll. 1-3). [[(Tr.) Ironically, however, Grillmeier's somewhat misleadingly abbreviated linguistic presentation of Melito, *On Pascha* 96 differs little from that of Anastasius the Sinaite: Grillmeier writes out only the Greek of line 715 but follows with a translation that also includes the end of line 716, while skipping its beginning and leaving no indication of an ellipsis: "ὁ θεὸς πεφόνευται, "Gott selbst ist *durch die Hand Israels* [= line 716b, Hall] getötet worden (§96)" (Grillmeier, *Jesus der Christus,* 209). Melito did not say this in so many words: it is the "King of Israel" who has been put to death "by the hand of Israel."]]

176. Title: չււչք arakelakan karujuwṭeann (PO 12/5:659, ed. K. Ter-Mekerttschian and S. G. Wilson). Transliteration of the Armenian follows the *Tübingen Atlas des Vorderen Orients: General Index* (see above, n. 133), vol. 1, p. xxxii, §9.

177. Trans. J. A. Robinson, *St. Irenaeus: The Demonstration of the Apostolic Preaching* (1920), 128; Armenian text in PO 12/5:710. The application of Isa. 53:4 to Jesus' healings is found already in Matt. 8:17. According to W. R. Schoedel, *Ignatius of Antioch: A Commentary on the Letters of Ignatius of Antioch,* Hermeneia (1985), Matthew's non-Septuagintal wording καὶ τὰς

Irenaeus comes to this view in part because at the end of the preceding section (§66), he had just declared that the birth, growth, miraculous healings, rejection, crucifixion, suffering, and death of Christ were all predicted by the prophets.[178] He wants to prove this for Isaiah as well. In the next three sections (§§68-70) Isaiah 52:13–53:12 is once again cited at length and commented upon; the idiosyncrasies of the Greek show through even in the Armenian translation.[179]

In the early period of the ancient Church the Christological model remained — to use a Hegelian turn of phrase — in "antithesis." Isaiah 52:13–53:12

νόσους [ἡμῶν] ἐβάστασεν, "and bore our diseases" (LXX: καὶ περὶ ἡμῶν ὀδυνᾶται, "and suffers pain for us") has exerted a direct verbal influence on Ignatius, *Pol.* 1:3, πάντων τὰς νόσους βάσταζε ὡς τέλειος ἀθλητής, "*bear the diseases* of all as a perfect athlete." Moreover, we find the same words τὰς νόσους ἐβάστασε later in the Greek fragments of Irenaeus. Schoedel therefore traces a line of development from Matthew's version of Isa. 53:4 through Ignatius to Irenaeus, *Demonstration* 67-68 (as above) and *Haer.* 4.33.11-12. [[(Tr.) The Latin version of Irenaeus's originally Greek document, *Haer.* 4.33.11, once again has him presenting the verb tenses in Isa. 53:4 as future: *Ipse infirmitates nostras accipiet et langores portabit*, "He Himself 'shall take [upon Him] our weaknesses, and bear our sorrows'" (*Contre les hérésies: Irénée de Lyon. Livre IV*, 2 vols. in 1, SC 100, ed. A. Rousseau and L. Doutreleau [1965], 832 ll. 244-45; trans. *ANF* 1:510). However, as indicated above, the Greek fragment of *Against Heresies* at this point gives Isa. 53:4 in Matthew's version, where the verbs are aorist: αὐτὸς τὰς ἀσθενείας ἡμῶν ἔλαβε καὶ τὰς νόσους ἐβάστασε, *Haer.* 4.33.11 (SC 100:833 ll. 237-38). On Irenaeus's treatment of Christ's sufferings in *Dem.* 67-73, see now I. M. MacKenzie, *Irenaeus's Demonstration of the Apostolic Preaching: A Theological Commentary and Translation* (2002), 197-206, esp. 197 on Isa. 53:4.]]

178. Irenaeus, *Demonstration of the Apostolic Preaching*, trans. Robinson, 127-28; Armenian text in PO 12/5:709. On the question of the sources of *Dem.* 67 see Prigent, *Justin et l'Ancien Testament*, 168, and, for another point of view, Skarsaune, *Proof*, 448.

179. So, for example, S. Weber in his German translation of *Dem.* 68 notes that the Armenian for Isa. 53:2, *patmeçaḳ dēm zandiman nora jibr manouk, jibr armat i carawowt erki*, which Weber translates, "Wir haben erzählt ihm gegenüber gleichwie ein Kind, wie ein Wurzelschoß in dürrem Land" (similarly Robinson: "We declared before him as a child as a root in a dry ground," *Demonstration*, 129), corresponds exactly to the wording of Isa. 53:2 LXX. See S. Weber, "Des heiligen Irenäus Schrift zum Erweis der Apostolischen Verkündigung," in *Des heiligen Irenäus ausgewählte Schriften ins Deutsche uebersetzt*, 2 vols., Bibliothek der Kirchenväter 3-4 (1912), 2:631 with n. 1. [[(Tr.) This Armenian evidence is relevant to a well-known textual and exegetical problem. The first word of the Septuagint of Isa. 53:2, ἀνηγγείλαμεν ἐναντίον αὐτοῦ ὡς παιδίον ὡς ῥίζα ἐν γῇ διψώσῃ, "We announced before him like a little servant, like a root in thirsty ground" (trans. Ekblad, *Isaiah's Servant Poems*, 175), departs radically from the Hebrew and presents a sense that modern interpreters have found difficult — so difficult that Ziegler in his Göttingen edition emended ἀνηγγείλαμεν, "*we announced* before him," to ἀνέτειλε μέν, "for *he sprang up* before him," without any manuscript or patristic evidence whatsoever. See Ziegler, *Isaias*, 320 text; 99 discussion; against him Ekblad, 199-200, who solves the problem exegetically.]]

was held out as an important *testimonium* in apologetic contexts (above all to the Jews) and as a witness to the earthly life of Jesus. But more intensive "scientific" and theological work on the text began only later.

IV. Christological Model II: Later Developments: Commentaries and Councils

With the introduction of "scientific" exegesis[180] into Christian theology and the empire-wide standardization of the faith, our Bible passage was increasingly interpreted in the context of general problems in the philosophical doctrine of God, particularly in the controversy over the axiom of divine impassibility and its relative ranking among the divine principles. This also substantially changed the interpretation of the passage. The "simpler" Christological model, developed in the New Testament and applied in discussions with the Jews, became "Hellenized" in the second of the two senses described above (p. 231).

In this part of our investigation we also turn our attention to a completely different genre that ancient Church theologians used to study the text: the Bible commentary.[181] Too little remains of the first Bible commentaries by the likes of Papias[182] and Heracleon[183] to determine whether the fourth Servant Song played any role in them. Apart from Hippolytus, commenting on Scripture on a grand scale (and by this I also mean to a voluminous extent) did not begin until Origen, although he was certainly supported by a sponsor and professional

---

180. From the plethora of literature on the subject we may refer especially to B. Neuschäfer, *Origenes als Philologe*, 2 vols., Schweizerische Beiträge zur Altertumswissenschaft 18/1-2 (1987); J. van Oort and U. Wickert, eds., *Christliche Exegese zwischen Nicäa und Chalcedon* (1992).

181. G. Bardy, "Commentaires patristiques de la Bible," *DBSup* 2:73-103.

182. Papias's work bore the title, ΛΟΓΙΩΝ ΚΥΡΙΑΚΩΝ ΕΞΗΓΗΣΕΩΣ ΣΥΓΓΡΑΜ-ΜΑΤΑ ΠΕΝΤΕ. See among others U. H. J. Körtner, *Papias von Hierapolis*, FRLANT 133 (1983); J. Kürzinger, *Papias von Hierapolis und die Evangelien des Neuen Testaments: Gesammelte Aufsätze. Neuausgabe und Übersetzung der Fragmente. Kommentierte Bibliographie*, Eichstätter Materialien 4 (1983); F. Siegert, "Unbeachtete Papiaszitate bei armenischen Schriftstellern," *NTS* 27 (1981): 605-14 (modified in Kürzinger, 128-37). Cf. the review of Kürzinger and Körtner by B. Dehandschutter, *VC* 42 (1988): 401-6.

183. B. Aland, "Erwählungstheologie und Menschenklassenlehre: Die Theologie des Herakleon als Schlüssel zum Verständnis der christlichen Gnosis?" in *Gnosis and Gnosticism: Papers Read at the Eighth International Conference on Patristic Studies (Oxford, September 3-8, 1979)*, ed. M. Krause, Nag Hammadi Studies 17 (1977), 148-84; J.-M. Poffet, *La Méthode Exégétique d'Héracléon et d'Origène. Commentateurs de Jn 4: Jésus, la Samaritaine et les Samaritains*, Paradosis 28 (1985).

scribes. Here too we encounter the first well-known Christian "scientific" commentary on Isaiah. Unfortunately only an infinitesimally small remainder has survived of Origen's thirty-volume commentary.[184] But we do possess a very much less extensive two-volume commentary by Eusebius († 339; the work is *CPG* 2 no. 3468), Origen's academic grandson, who based his work partly on that of his esteemed teacher. We also have the Isaiah commentary of Jerome († 419/420)[185] and his Latin translation of Origen's nine homilies on Isaiah's visions (after 392),[186] as well as the interpretation of Theodoret († 466).[187] All these writers refer in one way or another to the "grand master" of scientific exegesis and philology.

184. *CPG* no. 1435, Origen, *In Isaiam libri xxx (fragmenta)*. The Isaiah commentary is dated about 235 c.e. by H. J. Vogt, *Der Kommentar zum Evangelium nach Mattäus: Origenes*, 3 vols., Bibliothek der griechischen Literatur, Abteilung Patristik, 18, 30, 38 (1983-93), 3:314, while the year 244 is favored by P. Nautin, *Origène: Sa vie et son oeuvre*, Christianisme Antique 1 (1977), 247-48, 411; cf. also Ziegler, GCS *Eusebius Werke*, 9:ix, xxxi-xxxiv. Interestingly, the Isaiah commentary was Origen's most extensive Old Testament commentary; cf. M. Simonetti, "L'interpretatione patristica del VT," *Augustinianum* 22 (1982): 7-33, esp. 25.

185. *CPL*, 3rd ed., no. 584, Jerome, *Commentarii in Esaiam* (formerly *Commentariorum in Isaiam libri XVIII*), ca. 408-410. Text in PL 24:17-964; Jerome, *Opera*, 14 vols., vol. 2: *Commentariorum in Esaiam libri I–XI*; vol. 2A: *Commentariorum in Esaiam libri XII-XVIII, in Esaia parvula adbreviatio*, ed. M. Adriaen, CCSL 73-73A (1963) (for criticism see R. Gryson, *Esaias*, VL 12 [1987], 12-13); and now *Commentaires de Jerome sur le prophète Isaie*, 5 vols., ed. R. Gryson, P.-A. Deproost, J. Coulie, et al., Vetus Latina: Aus der Geschichte der lateinischen Bibel, 23, 27, 30, 35, 36 (1993-99). Cf. F.-M. Abel, "Le commentaire de Sainte Jérôme sur Isaïe," *RB* 13 (1916): 200-225; S. M. Gozzo, "De S. Hieronymi Commentario in Isaiae Librum," *Antonianum* 35 (1960): 49-80, 169-214. J. N. D. Kelly calls Jerome's Isaiah commentary "the most successful and instructive example of his eclectic exegetical method" (*Jerome: His Life, Writings and Controversies* [1975], 301).

186. *CPG* no. 1437, Origen, *In Isaiam homiliae xxxii (fragmenta)*. Text of Jerome's Latin version, Origenis, "Homiliae in visiones Isaiae," in PG 13:219-54; GCS *Origenes*, vol. 8, ed. W. A. Baehrens (1925), 242-89. There is a French translation by J. Millet in a somewhat rare volume (only 6 cataloged copies in the United States) whose author is identified in online catalogs simply as Origen (even though it includes works by "Origène, Bernard de Clairvaux, Eusèbe le Gallican, Saint Augustin, Rupert de Deutz") and whose official title is simply *Isaïe* (cover title: *Isaïe expliqué par les Pères*), series: Collection Les Pères dans la foi 25 (1983), 21-87. Finally see two of Jerome's smaller works: CPL no. 585, *In Esaia parvula adbreviatio*, CCSL 73A:801-9 and his translation of a piece of polemic against Origen's interpretation of Isaiah by the Alexandrian patriarch Theophilus (†412), *CPG* no. 2683, *Tractatus contra Origenem de uisione Isaiae (fragmentum)*, translated about 402 (so Frede, *Kirchenschriftsteller*, VL 1/1 523, siglum HI Is tr 2).

187. *CPG* no. 6204, Theodoret, Bishop of Cyrrhus, *Interpretatio in Isaïam*. Text: *Kommentar zu Jesaia: Theodoret von Kyros*, ed. A. Möhle, MSU 5 (1932); *Commentaire sur Isaïe: Théodoret de Cyr*, 3 vols., ed. J.-N. Guinot, SC 276, 295, 315 (1980-84). Cf. K. Jüssen, "Die Christologie des Theodoret von Cyrus nach seinem neuveröffentlichten Isaiaskommentar," *TGl* 27 (1935): 438-52.

Besides the commentaries of Origen, his academic descendants Eusebius and Jerome, and Theodoret, the following surviving ancient Christian commentaries on Isaiah (including *Questions* and *Homilies*)[188] may be mentioned. First, among the works in Greek: (Pseudo) Basil of Caesarea († 379), *Commentarius in Is. 1–16;*[189] Cyril of Alexandria († 444), *Commentarius in Is.;*[190] John Chrysostom († 407), *Interpretatio in Is. 1–8;*[191] *Homiliae 1-6 in Is. 6:1;*[192] *Homilia in Is. 45:7;*[193] Hesychius of Jerusalem († after 450), *Epitome Isaiae Prophetae;*[194] Theodore of Heraclea († ca. 355), *Ex Interpretatione in Isaiam;*[195] Procopius of Gaza († ca. 538), *In Isaiam Prophetam Commentationum Variarum Epitome.*[196] There are significantly fewer works in Latin: outside Jerome we have for this period only Potamius of Lisbon († after 357), *De martyrio Esaiae prophetae.*[197] But we must not fail to mention the Syriac commentaries of (Pseudo) Ephraem († 373)[198] and Isho'dad of Merv (ninth century),[199] as well as the Syriac scholia of the Nestorian Theodore bar Koni

---

188. Cf. M. Simonetti, "Commentaries, Biblical," *EECh* 1:187. For texts and secondary studies on the history of interpretation of Isaiah, see W. Werbeck, "Jesajabuch," *RGG*, 3rd ed., 3:611.

189. *CPG* no. 2911, Basil of Caesarea (pseudonymous), *Enarratio in prophetam Isaiam.* Text PG 30:117-668; *Commento al profeta Isaia: San Basilio,* 2 vols., ed. P. Trevisan, Corona patrum Salesiana, Series graeca 4-5 (1939). Cf. Frede, *Kirchenschriftsteller,* VL 1/1 314, siglum PS-BAS Is.

190. *CPG* no. 5203, Cyrill of Alexandria, *Commentarius in Isaiam prophetam.* Text PG 70:9-1450.

191. *CPG* no. 4416, John Chrysostom, *In Isaiam (1–8, 10).* Text PG 56:11-94. There is also an Armenian version of the commentary on Isaiah 8–64, Venice 1880-87, but on this see Guinot, *Commentaire sur Isaïe: Théodoret de Cyr,* SC 276:19-20 n. 5 (lit.).

192. *CPG* no. 4417, John Chrysostom, *Vidi dominum (Isa. 6:1), homiliae 1-6.* Text PG 56:97-142 (the Latin translation of the first five homilies is by Erasmus).

193. *CPG* no. 4418, John Chrysostom, *Ego Dominus Deus feci lumen (Isa. 45:7).* Text PG 56:141-52.

194. *CPG* no. 6559, Hesychius of Jerusalem, *Interpretatio Isaiae.* Text *Hesychii Hierosolymitani interpretatio Isaiae prophetae,* ed. M. Faulhaber (1900); cf. PG 93:1339-86.

195. *CPG* no. 3561, Theodore of Heraclea, *Fragmenta in Isaiam in catenis.* Text PG 18:1307-78. Cf. M. Simonetti, "Theodore of Heraclea," *EECh* 2:824.

196. *CPG* no. 7434, Procopius of Gaza, *Catena in Isaiam.* Text PG 87/2:1817-2718.

197. *CPL,* 3rd ed., no. 543, Potamius, Bishop of Lisbon, *De martyrio Esaiae prophetae.* Text PL 8:1409-18 or A. C. Vega, *Opuscula omnia Potamii Olisiponensis* (1934), 35-36. Cf. M. Simonetti, "Potamius," *EECh* 2:706.

198. On Isaiah 43–66. Text in T. J. Lamy, ed., *Sancti Ephraem Syri Hymni et Sermones,* 4 vols. (1886), 2:103-214. Cf. D. D. Bundy, "The Peshitta of Isaiah 53:9 and the Syrian Commentators," *OrChr* 67 (1983): 32-45, esp. 33-34, and idem, "Isaiah 53 in East and West," 55-57.

199. Text: *Commentaire d'Išo'dad de Merv sur l'Ancien Testament,* ed. J.-M. Vosté and C. van den Eynde, part IV: *Isaïe et les Douze,* ed. C. van den Eynde, CSCO 303-4, *Scriptores Syri* tomes 128-29 (Syriac text with French trans.) (1969). Cf. R. Peters, "Iso'dad(h) von Merw," in F. W. Bautz, ed., *Biographisch-Bibliographisches Kirchenlexikon,* 22 vols. (1990), 2:1364-65 (bibliog.). We may pass over here the commentary of Dionysius bar Salībī († 1171; cf. Bundy,

(eighth century).[200] Lost works include the commentaries of Theodore of Mopsuestia († 428) and Didymus the Blind of Alexandria († 398).[201]

In sum, we have more scriptural commentary, but not many more interpretations of the fourth Servant Song in the period that Johannes Quasten called "The Golden Age of Patristic Literature."

1. Origen († 253-254) on Isaiah 52:13–53:12

The way from Justin to Origen[202] is not as far as one might think. Like Justin, the Alexandrian theologian also used Isaiah 53 in apologetic situations. In his tractate *Against Celsus* (244-249 C.E.),[203] Origen writes: "I remember that once in a discussion with some whom the Jews regarded as learned I used these prophecies" (*c. Cels.* 1.55, GCS 1:106 ll. 3-4).[204] The reference is to the "prophe-

---

"Peshitta of Isaiah 53:9," 41 with n. 53; idem, "Isaiah 53 in East and West," 57-59) and the scholia of Gregory Abū-l-Farağ (Barhebraeus; † 1171; cf. U. F. Tullberg, *Gregorii bar Hebraei in Jesaiam Scholia* [1842]; Bundy, "Peshitta of Isaiah 53:9," 42-43; idem, "Isaiah 53 in East and West," 60-61). For details see the German, *Der leidende Gottesknecht*, 228 n. 199.

200. Theodore bar Koni = bar Konai (Library of Congress). For criticism of the older text edition in CSCO 55, *Scriptores Syri* 19 and CSCO 69, *Scriptores Syri* 26, see the summary in Bundy, "Peshitta of Isaiah 53:9," 35 n. 18. [(Tr.) There is now a new edition: *Livre des scolies (recension d'Urmiah): Les collections annexées par Sylvain de Qardu: Théodore bar Kôni*, 2 vols., ed. and trans. R. Hespel, CSCO 464-65, *Scriptores Syri* tomes 197-98 (1984). Cf. J.-M. Sauget, "Theodore bar Koni," *EECh* 2:823; W. Schwaigert, "Theodorus bar Koni," in F. W. Bautz, ed., *Biographisch-Bibliographisches Kirchenlexikon* (1996), 11:967-68 (bibliography); L. Brade, *Untersuchungen zum Scholienbuch des Theodoros bar Koni*, Göttinger Orientforschungen, I. Reihe: Syriaca 8 (1975); S. H. Griffith, "Theodore Bar Koni's Scholia: A Nestorian *Summa Contra Gentiles* from the First Abbasid Century," in N. Garsoïan, T. Mathews, and R. Thompson, eds., *East of Byzantium: Syria and Armenia in the Formative Period* (1982), 53-72.]

201. See Guinot, *Commentaire sur Isaïe: Théodoret de Cyr*, SC 276:19-22.

202. Cf. Haag, "Gottesknecht," 352-55.

203. For this date see Vogt, *Kommentar zum Evangelium nach Mattäus*, 318; a date of 249 is suggested by Nautin, *Origène*, 375-76.

204. [Expanded by translator] Origen's texts are cited from the GCS series (details below); the text for *c. Cels.* is that of P. Koetschau, upon which H. Chadwick based his translation, quoted above, *Contra Celsum* (1st ed., 1953; 2nd ed., 1965), here p. 50. A new edition of the Greek text has become available since the German version of this essay, Origenes: *Contra Celsum libri VIII*, ed. M. Marcovich, VCSup 54 (2001). Readings from this text are occasionally given in the notes when they differ from Koetschau's (see, e.g., here and below, nn. 223, 229), but Chadwick's translation remains unchanged. Cf. here *c. Cels.* 1.55: Μέμνημαι δέ ποτε ἔν τινι πρὸς λεγομένους παρὰ Ἰουδαίοις σοφοὺς [ἐν]ζητήσει ταῖς προφητείας ταύταις χρησάμενος (GSC *Origenes* 1:106 ll. 3-4, ed. P. Koetschau; cf. Marcovich: συζητήσει). On Origen's arguments

cies" of Isaiah 52:13-15 and 53:1-8, which Origen had just quoted in full (*c. Cels.* 1.54),[205] as part of his effort to refute the defamatory pamphlet of the long deceased pagan philosopher Celsus. As is well known, in the first part of his invective, excepts of which are quoted by Origen, Celsus presents his own arguments against Christianity in the figure of an imaginary Jew (*c. Cels.* 1.28–2.79).[206] We may indeed wonder whether Origin's scriptural proof that Christ's suffering was already prophesied would have convinced Celsus's "Jew" or rather Celsus himself, for whom the main problem will have been Christianity's implications for the doctrine of divine impassibility.[207] In any case, as part of his argument, Origen gives a full report of a historical disputation he once had with some Jews about Isaiah 52–53, either during his first stay in Caesarea in 215-217 or later, after 230-231.[208] He begins with the Jewish response:

> At this the Jew said that these prophecies referred to the whole people as though of a single individual, since they were scattered in the dispersion and smitten, that as a result of the scattering of the Jews among the other nations many might become proselytes. In this way he explained the text: "Thy form shall be inglorious among men" (Isa. 52:14); and "those to whom he was not proclaimed shall see him" (52:15); and "being a man in calamity" (53:3). (*Contra Celsum* 1.55, GCS 1:106 ll. 4-10).[209]

---

with the Jews see N. R. M. De Lange, *Origen and the Jews: Studies in Jewish-Christian Relations in Third-Century Palestine*, University of Cambridge Oriental Publications 25 (1976), 20-21, and generally 98-102. We shall cite the following texts of Origen from the GCS edition: GCS *Origenes Werke*, vol. 1: *Die Schrift vom Martyrium. Buch I-IV Gegen Celsus*; vol. 2: *Buch V-VII Gegen Celsus. Die Schrift vom Gebet*, ed. P. Koetschau (1899); vol. 3: *Jeremiahomilien* (etc.), ed. E. Klostermann, rev. by P. Nautin, 2nd ed. (1983); vol. 6: *Homilien zum Hexateuch in Rufins Übersetzung*, ed. W. A. Baehrens (1920); vol. 10: *Origenes Matthäuserklärung*, 1: *Die griechisch erhaltenen Tomoi*, ed. E. Klostermann (1935); vol. 11: *Origenes Matthäuserklärung*, 2: *Die lateinische Übersetzung der Commentariorum Series*, ed. E. Klostermann, rev. by U. Treu (2nd ed., 1968; 1st ed., 1933).

205. *c. Cels.* 1.54 (GCS 1:105 l. 11-106 l. 2, ed. Koetschau).

206. On Celsus's knowledge of Judaism see P. Merlan, "Celsus," *RAC* 2:957-58, and De Lange, *Origen and the Jews*, 66-73, esp. 68-69.

207. On the axiom of divine impassibility in Middle Platonism see Frohnhofen, *APATHEIA TOU THEOU*, 87; W. Maas, *Unveränderlichkeit Gottes: Zum Verhältnis von griechisch-philosophischer und christlicher Gotteslehre*, Paderborner theologische Studien 1 (1974).

208. De Lange, *Origen and the Jews*, 20-28.

209. Trans. Chadwick, *Contra Celsum*, 50, biblical references added both in the translations and in the Greek texts (so throughout this essay). Text *c. Cels.* 1.55 (GCS 1:106 ll. 4-10, ed. Koetschau): ἐφ' οἷς ἔλεγεν ὁ Ἰουδαῖος ταῦτα πεπροφητεῦσθαι ὡς περὶ ἑνὸς τοῦ ὅλου λαοῦ, καὶ γενομένου ἐν τῇ προφάσει τοῦ ἐπεσπάρθαι Ἰουδαίους τοῖς λοιποῖς ἔθνεσι. καὶ οὕτω διηγεῖτο τὸ

Following this Origen says that he presented his interlocutor with "many arguments . . . which proved that there is no good reason for referring these prophecies about one individual to the whole people" (*c. Cels.* 1.55, GCS 1:106 ll. 10-12).[210] But in reality Origin at first cites only those expressions from Isaiah 53:4-5 that involve the "he"/"we" distinction and therefore virtually exclude a collective interpretation (*c. Cels.* 1.55, GCS 1:106 ll. 13-16). He discusses particularly Isaiah 53:8:

> But we seemed to put him [the Jewish interlocutor] in the greatest difficulty with the words "because of the iniquities of my people he was led to death" (Isa. 53:8). If according to them the people are the subject of the prophecy, why is this man said to have been "led to death because of the iniquities" of the people of God, if he is not different from the people of God? Who is this if not Jesus Christ, "by whose stripe" we who believe in him "were healed" (Isa. 53:5), when he put off the "principalities and powers" among us, and made a show of them "openly" on the cross (cf. Col. 2.15)? However, it is appropriate to a different occasion to explain each point in the prophecy and to study each detail. (*Contra Celsum* 1.55, GCS 1:106 ll. 20-29)[211]

While the above reflects Origen's arguments with the Jews he has met, in other chapters of *Against Celsus* he must answer the additional arguments of Celsus or Celsus's "Jew." Celsus frequently attempts to turn Christian claims,

---

"ἀδοξήσει ἀπὸ ἀνθρώπων τὸ εἶδός σου" [Isa. 52:14] καὶ τὸ "οἷς οὐκ ἀνηγγέλη περὶ αὐτοῦ ὄψονται" [52:15] καὶ τὸ "ἄνθρωπος ἐν πληγῇ ὤν" [53:3].

210. Trans. Chadwick, *Contra Celsum*, 50. Text *c. Cels.* 1.55 (GCS 1:106 ll. 10-12, ed. Koetschau): Πολλὰ μὲν οὖν τότ' ἐν τῇ ζητήσει λέλεκται τὰ ἐλέγχοντα ὅτι περί τινος ἑνὸς ταῦτα προφητευόμενα οὐκ εὐλόγως ἐκεῖνοι ἀνάγουσιν ἐπὶ ὅλον τὸν λαόν. In his homilies on Jeremiah from the year 242, Origen unquestionably assumes that Isaiah was referring to Christ in Isa. 53:7: ἐκεῖ μὲν οὖν περὶ αὐτοῦ (sc. Christ) Ἡσαΐας λέγει (*Homily* 10.1 on Jer. 11:18–12:19, GCS *Origenes* 3:71 l. 26, ed. Klostermann and Nautin). On the date of 242 for these homilies see *Die griechisch erhaltenen Jeremiahomilien: Origenes,* ed. and trans. E. Schadel, Bibliothek der griechischen Literatur, Abteilung Patristik, 10 (1980), 5-6.

211. Trans. Chadwick, *Contra Celsum*, 51, with references and quotation marks added according to the Greek, *c. Cels.* 2.55 (GCS 1:106 ll. 20-29, ed. Koetschau): μάλιστα δ' ἐδόξαμεν θλίβειν ἀπὸ τῆς φασκούσης λέξεως τό· "ἀπὸ τῶν ἀνομιῶν τοῦ λαοῦ μου ἤχθη εἰς θάνατον" [Isa. 53:8]. εἰ γὰρ ὁ λαὸς κατ' ἐκείνους εἰσὶν οἱ προφητευόμενοι, πῶς "ἀπὸ τῶν ἀνομιῶν τοῦ λαοῦ" τοῦ θεοῦ; λέγεται ἦχθαι "εἰς θάνατον" οὗτος, εἰ μὴ ἕτερος ὢν παρὰ τὸν λαὸν τοῦ θεοῦ τίς δ' οὗτος, εἰ μὴ Ἰησοῦς Χριστός, οὗ "τῷ μώλωπι" "ἰάθημεν" [Isa. 53:5] οἱ εἰς αὐτὸν πιστεύοντες, ἀπεκδυσαμένου "τὰς" ἐν ἡμῖν "ἀρχὰς καὶ ἐξουσίας" καὶ "παρρησίᾳ" [Col. 2:15] δειγματίσαντος αὐτὰς ἐν τῷ ξύλῳ; ἕκαστον δὲ τῶν ἐν προφητείᾳ σαφηνίσαι καὶ μηδὲν ἀβασάνιστον αὐτῶν παραλιπεῖν ἄλλου καιροῦ ἐστι.

including ones about Christ's deity, on their head, as in the following excerpt (*c. Cels.* 6.75):

ἐπειδὴ θεῖον πνεῦμα ἦν ἐν σώματι, πάντως τι παραλλάττειν αὐτὸ τῶν λοιπῶν ἐχρῆν ἢ κατὰ μέγεθος ἢ κάλλος ἢ ἀλκὴν ἢ φωνὴν ἢ κατάπληξιν ἢ πειθώ. Ἀμήχανον γὰρ ὅτῳ θεῖόν τι πλέον τῶν ἄλλων προσῆν μηδὲν ἄλλου διαφέρειν· (GCS 2:144 ll. 16-20)

If [as Christians claim] a divine spirit was in a body [sc. the body of Jesus], it must certainly have differed from other bodies in size or *beauty* [see below] or strength or voice or striking appearance or powers of persuasion. For it is impossible that a body which had something more divine than the rest should be no different from any other. (trans. Chadwick, 388 [italics added])

Celsus refutes the Christian claim using language that Christians themselves may have derived from Isaiah 53 (though Celsus does not quote Isaiah 53 literally). Christ cannot be divine by Celsus's reasoning and by Christians' own admission because, as he says (*c. Cels.* 6.75):

τοῦτο δὲ οὐδὲν ἄλλου διέφερεν, ἀλλ' ὥς φασι, μικρὸν καὶ δυσειδὲς καὶ ἀγεννὲς ἦν. (GCS 2:144 ll. 20-22)

Jesus' body was no different from any other, but, as they [sc. the Christians] say, was little and ugly and undistinguished. (trans. Chadwick, 388-89)

Origen responds by accusing Celsus of having invalidated his own argument by accepting that Isaiah's prophecy applies to Jesus: οὐκ εἶχεν εἶδος οὐδὲ κάλλος, "he had not form or beauty" (Isa. 53:2). For since the Gospels do not say that Jesus lacked form or beauty, Origen reasons in *Contra Celsum* 6.76 (GCS 2:145-46, esp. 146 ll. 5-13) that Celsus must have used Isaiah 53 for his claim that Jesus needed (but lacked) certain qualities that would have made him divine: μέγεθος, κάλλος, ἀλκή, φωνή, κατάπληξις, and πειθώ (GCS 2:144 ll. 16-19). Yet since κάλλος or "beauty" is the only item from this list that also occurs in Isaiah 53, Origen can be accused of picking and choosing Celsus's words, and it is not necessarily true that Celsus opportunistically "quotes things from [the Scriptures]" of Isaiah 53 (λέγει τὰ ἀπ' αὐτῶν), as Origen says.[212]

---

212. *c. Cels.* 6.75 (GCS 2:144 ll. 23-24, ed. Koetschau). Nevertheless, it is clear that Celsus did in fact know simple Christian Christological positions, such as the one Origen cites from Celsus's work twice in *c. Cels.* 6.69: "Since God is great and hard to perceive, he thrust his own Spirit into a body like ours, and sent him down here, that we might be able to hear and learn from him" (trans. Chadwick, 383; text GCS 2:139 ll. 1-4, 21-23, ed. Koetschau).

Celsus has a second argument relevant to ancient Christian uses of Isaiah 53. Not only Jesus' unimpressive body but also his manner of death speaks against his divinity. In a mocking allusion to the blood of Christ, Celsus says that the fluid that flowed on the cross was not even the mythic "juice" (ἰχώρ) that flows in the veins of the gods according to Homer (*c. Cels.* 1.66; 2.36).[213] Rather, Celsus sees Jesus' fate as the death of a mere human: "a man who was arrested most disgracefully and crucified" (*c. Cels.* 2.31).[214] To deal with this sort of thinking Origen repeatedly cites Isaiah 53:2 in *Contra Celsum* 6.75-76: "he had not form or beauty."[215] Nevertheless, in using this verse Origen avoids the crass harmonization of his predecessor Clement of Alexandria, who about thirty years before[216] had written about Isaiah 53:2:

> He displayed not the beauty of the flesh, which is only outward appearance, but the true beauty of body and soul: for the soul, the beauty of good deeds; for the body, that of immortality. (Clement, *Paedagogus* 3.3.3)[217]

Continuing his response to Celsus's dictum, "If a divine spirit was in a body, it must certainly have differed from other bodies," Origen follows up his citations of Isaiah 53:2 in *Contra Celsum* 6.75-76 (including a full quotation of Isa. 53:1-3 in *c. Cels.* 6.75) with an allegorical interpretation of the Transfiguration in *Contra Celsum* 6.77.[218] He says that only those who have received power

---

213. Homer, *Iliad* 5.340: ἰχών, οἷος πέρ τε ῥέει μακάρεσσι θεοῖσιν, "the ichor, such as flows in the blessed gods" (LCL, trans. Murray; rev. Wyatt, 2nd ed., 1999).

214. *c. Cels.* 2.31: ἄνθρωπον ἀτιμότατα ἀπαχθέντα καὶ ἀποτυμπανισθέντα (GCS 1:158 ll. 24-25, ed. Koetschau). For the use of ἀποτυμπανίζω with reference to crucifixion, see LSJ s.v.

215. Cf. esp. *c. Cels.* 6.75 (GCS 2:175 ll. 1-15, ed. Koetschau; ll. 5-10 contain a citation of Isa. 53:1-3). Cf. M. Eichinger, *Die Verklärung Christi bei Origenes: Die Bedeutung des Menschen Jesus in seiner Christologie,* Wiener Beiträge zur Theologie 23 (1969), 74-78.

216. I follow the dating of Clement's *Paedagogus* suggested by Harnack, *Geschichte der altchristlichen Literatur,* 2/1:11.

217. Clement of Alexandria, *Paedagogus* 3.3.3, trans. S. P. Wood, *Christ the Educator,* FC 23 (1954), 201. (Older trans. in *ANF* 3:272.) Text: ἀλλ' οὐ τὸ κάλλος τῆς σαρκὸς τὸ φαντασιαστικόν, τὸ δὲ ἀληθινόν καὶ τῆς ψυχῆς καὶ τὸ σώματος ἐνδείξατο κάλλος, τῆς μὲν τὸ εὐεργετικόν, τὸ δὲ ἀθάνατον τῆς σαρκός (GCS *Clemens Alexandrinus,* vol. 1: *Protrepticus und Paedagogus,* ed. O. Stählin, 2nd ed. [1936], 237 ll. 21-24; the same text in the new edition by M. Marcovich, *Clementis Alexandrini Paedagogus,* VCSup 61 [2002], 149 ll. 19-21). On the ugly appearance of Jesus see A. Grillmeier, "Die Herrlichkeit Gottes auf dem Antlitz Jesu Christi," in idem, *Mit ihm und in ihm: Christologische Forschungen und Perspektiven* (1978), 19-75, esp. 45-48, and Haag, "Gottesknecht," 352-53.

218. Cf. Eichinger, *Die Verklärung Christi bei Origenes.* A very similar interpretation of Isa. 53:2 is found in Origen's *Commentary on Matthew* 12.32 (GCS *Origenes* 10:140 l. 5-141 l. 3, ed. Klostermann). However, on the citation of Isa. 53:2 in *Comm. Matt.* 14.1 (GCS 10:274 ll. 4-5 [Latin]), see Vogt, *Kommentar zum Evangelium nach Mattäus,* 69 n. 7.

to follow Jesus up the mountain — by which he means the Gnostics within the Church — will be able to see that Christ had "a more divine form" (θειοτέραν μορφήν, GCS 2:147 l. 17) than his earthly form. Those who see in him no "form or beauty" fail to advance from the apparent "foolishness of preaching" (cf. 1 Cor. 1:21) to the true meaning of Jesus as "the immortal divine word."[219] But precisely this change from the miserable earthly form to the transfigured glorious form accessible only to those who ascend the mountain refutes the position of Celsus: Jesus' ability to appear in different "forms" to various people distinguishes him from normal human nature and must therefore be attributed to "the nature of the divine Logos" (ἡ τοῦ θείου λόγου φύσις).[220] In his *Commentary on Matthew*, which originated about the same time as *Against Celsus*,[221] Origen explains Matthew 16:27 ("The Son of Man is *to come in glory*," ἔρχεσθαι ἐν τῇ δόξῃ) by saying:

> It was necessary for this man to come in order that he might "bear our sins" and suffer pain "for us" (Isa. 53:4). Indeed, it was not appropriate for the one [who comes] in glory to bear "our sins and" to suffer pain "for us." But he comes in glory only after preparing the disciples through his epiphany, which did not have "form or beauty" (Isa. 53:2).[222]

To summarize: By using the arguments of his fictitious Jewish interlocutor, Celsus holds to the collective interpretation of the fourth Servant Song. In his refutation Origen proceeds in two steps: he first shows that the prophecy refers to Christ, and then tries to show that Celsus assumes the same thing and therefore contradicts himself. For the Christian from Alexandria the passage

---

219. [(Tr.) Although this summary is based on *c. Cels.* 6.77, the last phrase ὁ ἀθάνατος θεὸς λόγος, "the immortal divine word" (trans. Chadwick) is taken from *c. Cels.* 4.15 (GCS 1:285 l. 15, ed. Koetschau), and Origen presents a similar argument to *c. Cels.* 6.77 in *c. Cels.* 4.16 (GCS 1:285 l. 23-286 l. 7).]

220. *c. Cels.* 6.77 (GCS 2:146 l. 19-147 l. 6, ed. Koetschau). As Origen summarizes: ἔχει δέ τι καὶ μυστικώτερον ὁ λόγος, ἀπαγγέλλων τὰς τοῦ Ἰησοῦ διαφόρους μορφὰς ἀναφέρεσθαι ἐπὶ τὴν τοῦ θείου λόγου φύσιν (GCS 2:147 ll. 2-4): "The doctrine has an even more mysterious meaning since it proclaims that the different forms of Jesus are to be applied to the nature of the divine Logos" (trans. Chadwick, 390).

221. For the dates compare Nautin, *Origène*, 412 with 249; Vogt, *Kommentar zum Evangelium nach Mattäus*, 314 with 244-49.

222. Origen, *Comm. Matt.* 12.29 (GCS *Origenes* 10:132 l. 30-133 l. 4, ed. Klostermann): καὶ ἔδει αὐτὸν τοιοῦτον ἐληλυθέναι, ἵνα "τὰς ἁμαρτίας ἡμῶν φέρῃ καὶ περὶ ἡμῶν" ὀδυνηθῇ· οὐδὲ γὰρ ἔπρεπε τὸν ἐν δόξῃ φέρειν "τὰς ἁμαρτίας ἡμῶν καὶ" ὀδυνηθῆναι "περὶ ἡμῶν." ἀλλὰ καὶ ἔρχεται ἐν δόξῃ πορευτρεπίσας τοὺς μαθητὰς διὰ τῆς μὴ ἐχούσης "εἶδος μηδὲ κάλλος" ἐπιφανείας αὐτοῦ.

proves that Christ, as God's Logos, was not weak. To support this Origen takes the Gospel reports as his key: Christ suffered of his own free will. Although Celsus objects to Jesus' passivity, saying that "while he was alive he did *not* (οὐκ [see n. 223]) help himself," ζῶν μὲν οὐκ ἐπήρκεσεν ἑαυτῷ (*c. Cels.* 2.59),[223] Origen counters that such a denial of the Son of God's sovereignty could not find support in a verse such as Isaiah 53:7 (although Celsus does not actually quote this verse), ὡς πρόβατον ἐπὶ σφαγὴν ἤχθη, "like a sheep led to slaughter." For as Origen says (*c. Cels.* 2.59):

> εἰ δὲ τὸ "<οὐκ> ἐπήρκεσεν" ἀπὸ τῶν μέσων καὶ σωματικῶν λαμβάνει, φαμὲν ὅτι ἀπεδείξαμεν ἐκ τῶν εὐαγγελίων ὅτι ἑκὼν ἐπὶ ταῦτ' ἐλήλυθεν. (GCS 1:182 ll. 17-19)[224]

But if he [Celsus] takes his phrase *he did <not> help* [*sc. himself*] to refer to things indifferent and corporeal, we reply that we proved from the Gospels that of his own free will he underwent this. (trans. Chadwick, 112 [modified])

Even if Christ was helpless, it was only in indifferent and corporeal matters; but Origen believes he was not in fact helpless but in control of his destiny.[225] However, Origen's interpretation of Isaiah 52:13–53:12 is not based on the

---

223. [[Expanded by translator]] Trans. Chadwick, 112; text *c. Cels.* 2.59 (GCS 1:182 ll. 9-10, ed. Koetschau): ζῶν μὲν οὐκ ἐπήρκεσεν ἑαυτῷ. Here in this first reference to this idea on p. 182 line 9 of Koetschau's GCS edition, this statement "he did *not* help himself" is printed so as to include the negative particle οὐκ, since it is quoting Celsus's own work. But when Origen challenges this statement in lines 12 and 17 on the same page, he refers back to it merely as τὸ ἐπήρκεσεν ἑαυτῷ or simply τὸ ἐπήρκεσεν, without the οὐκ. Koetschau in his subsequent German translation of *Contra Celsum* rightly (though conjecturally) restores the οὐκ in these subsequent lines as well (see also the next note [n. 224]): P. Koetschau, trans., *Des Origenes ausgewählte Schriften*, 3 vols., including: *Des Origenes Acht Bücher gegen Celsus*, 2 vols., Bibliothek der Kirchenväter 52-53 (1926-27), 1:178 n. 1. Koetschau's conjecture is followed in the translation by Chadwick, *Contra Celsum*, 112, but not in the more recent text editions by M. Borret, *Contre Celse: Origène*, vol. 1, SC 132 (1967), at *c. Cels.* 2.59 l. 8 (p. 422), or M. Marcovich, Origenes: *Contra Celsum libri VIII*, 131 ll. 8-9, 13.

224. *c. Cels.* 2.59, GCS 1:182 ll. 17-19, ed. Koetschau, with the <οὐκ> restored as explained in the preceding note (n. 223).

225. Cf. also Origen, *Comm. Matt.* 27 on Matt. 23:29-36. Text in GCS *Origenes*, 11/2:45 ll. 19-27. (Cf. also the cross-reference mentioned in the apparatus on p. 45 to Origen, *Homily* 1.1 on Leviticus, text in GCS *Origenes* 6:280 ll. 5-10, ed. Baehrens.) In *Comm. Matt.* 27, the view of Christ's weak earthly existence that is open to all is set off less sharply from the spiritual understanding of those who consider his works of virtue (*opera virtutum eius*, GCS 11/2:45 l. 22) and thereby recognize Jesus as God.

New Testament witness to Christ alone, but also on a two-part hermeneutic divided into a pneumatic and a somatic understanding, in which the philosophical picture of God, above all the axiom of impassibility,[226] plays a central role.[227]

Nevertheless, Origen does reject the truly absurd corollaries of this picture of God and the heroes. For example, in *Contra Celsum* 7.53, pointing to other distinguished men who remained calm and spoke memorable sayings while dying the "noble death," Celsus, thinking that some such saying should also form the foundation of Christianity, asks, "What comparable saying did your God utter while he was being punished?"[228] In response Origen cites Isaiah 53:7, "he did not open his mouth" (οὐκ ἀνοίγει τὸ στόμα αὐτοῦ), adding that such silence required great "courage" (καρτερία) and "patience" (ὑπομονή) of Jesus: "He manifested a courage and patience superior to that of any of the Greeks who spoke while enduring torture."[229] Origen thus confirms Christ's virtues and incorporates them into his argument. Overly harsh invectives from Celsus, for example, "Anyone with similar shamelessness could say even of a robber and murderer who had been punished that he, forsooth, was not a robber but a god" (*c. Cels.* 2.44),[230] are refuted with a reference to the prophetic text: the innocent one was "numbered with the transgressors" (Isa. 53:12; cf. Luke 22:37).[231]

---

226. For the impassibility of the Logos see also *c. Cels.* 4.15 (GCS 1:285 ll. 17-18, ed. Koetschau).

227. So already P. Koetschau, GCS Origenes 1:xliii-xliv. For further literature on the question of the influence of Hellenistic philosophy on Origen see, e.g., Grillmeier, *Jesus der Christus*, 266-67 n. 115 = ET, *Christ in Christian Tradition*, 138 n. 115. I myself have attempted to use an example from Origen, *De oratione* 27.8 to illustrate Origen's way of interacting with pagan philosophical premises; see C. Markschies, "Was bedeutet οὐσία? Zwei Antworten bei Origenes und Ambrosius und deren Bedeutung für ihre Bibelerklärung und Theologie," in W. Geerlings and H. König, eds., *Origenes, Vir ecclesiasticus*, Hereditas 9 (1995), 59-82.

228. Trans. Chadwick, 440; cf. 441. For *c. Cels.* 7.53 see GCS 2:203 ll. 8-30, esp. ll. 23-24: τί τοιοῦτον ὁ ὑμέτερος θεὸς κολαζόμενος ἐφθέγξατο; Origen repeats this line of Celsus at the start of *c. Cels.* 7.55 (GCS 2:205 l. 5, ed. Koetschau).

229. *c. Cels.* 7.55: εἴποιμεν ἂν πρὸς αὐτὸν ὅτι ⟨τῇ⟩ παρὰ ταῖς μάστιξι καὶ ταῖς πολλαῖς αἰκίαις αὐτοῦ σιωπῇ παντὸς τοῦ ἐν Ἕλλησιν ἐν περιστάσεσι τυγχάνοντος φθεγξαμένου μᾶλλον ἐνέφηνε καρτερίαν καὶ ὑπομονήν (GCS 2:204 l. 30-205 l. 2, ed. Koetschau, corrected by the addition of ⟨τῇ⟩, as in Chadwick, *Contra Celsum*, 441 n. 6; M. Borret, ed., *Contre Celse*, vol. 4, SC 150 [1969], at 7.55 l. 3 [p. 142]; and Marcovich, *Contra Celsum*, 506 l. 23).

230. *c. Cels.* 2.44: φησὶν ὅτι δύναιτο ἂν τις ὁμοίως ἀναισχυντῶν καὶ περὶ λῃστοῦ καὶ ἀνδροφόνου κολασθέντος εἰπεῖν ὅτι οὗτός γε οὐχὶ λῃστὴς ἀλλὰ θεὸς ἦν (GCS 1:166 ll. 24-26, ed. Koetschau).

231. *c. Cels.* 2.44 (GCS 1:166 l. 30-167 l. 5, ed. Koetschau). For Origen's allusion to Isa. 53:12, see GCS 1:166 ll. 31-32: μετὰ ἀνόμων ἐλογίσθη; cf. LXX: ἐν τοῖς ἀνόμοις ἐλογίσθη and Luke 22:37: μετὰ ἀνόμων ἐλογίσθη.

As a result of the impassibility axiom, the absolute God-forsakenness and weakness of Christ in Gethsemane are explained away as an event of the body insignificant for the divine Logos, even though Origen adds that this body was sinless (with Isa. 53:9), despite all temptations (*c. Cels.* 1.69).[232] Nevertheless, as Alois Grillmeier says, "Although Origen's symbolism of his doctrine of the ascent seems to make the incarnation (and the corporeality) of Christ relative, it still has true saving significance and truly brings about salvation and thus also has true historicity."[233]

2. Eusebius of Caesarea, Isaiah Commentary (325-328 C.E.)

While of the thirty-volume Isaiah commentary by Origen only an infinitesimally small amount remains,[234] we possess the two-volume Isaiah commentary of his academic grandson Eusebius, thanks to Joseph Ziegler's fine edition.[235]

232. Responding to the charge of Celsus's Jew, addressed directly to Jesus, "a god would not have had a body such as yours," Origen replies with reference to Heb. 4:15; Isa. 53:9; and 2 Cor. 5:21 (*c. Cels.* 1.69): "But we say to this that at his advent into this life, as he was born of a woman, he assumed a body which was human and capable of dying a human death. For this reason, in addition to other things, we say that he was also a great wrestler, because his human body was 'tempted in all points' like all other men, and yet was no longer like sinful men in that it was entirely 'without sin' (Heb. 4:15). For it appears to us that 'he did no sin, neither was guile found in his mouth' (Isa. 53:9), and God delivered him up, 'who knew no sin,' as a pure offering for all those who had sinned (2 Cor. 5:21)" (trans. Chadwick, *Contra Celsum*, 64). Text *c. Cels.* 1.69 (GCS 1:123 ll. 10, 11-19, ed. Koetschau). Cf. also Eichinger, *Die Verklärung Christi bei Origenes*, 72-94.

233. Grillmeier, *Christ in Christian Tradition*, 1:145. The present treatment has passed over the use of Isaiah 54 in Origen's commentary on John; for this see Gelio, "Isaia 52,13–53,12," 121-22, and Haag, "Gottesknecht," 354-55.

234. See above n. 184.

235. GCS *Eusebius Werke*, vol. 9, ed. Ziegler; both of Eusebius's two books are presented in this single volume (pp. 1-203; 203-411). See also J.-M. van Cangh, "Nouveaux Fragments Hexaplaires: Commentaire sur Isaïe d'Eusèbe de Césarée," *RB* 71 (1978): 384-90; A. Möhle, "Ein neuer Fund zahlreicher Stücke aus den Jesaiaübersetzungen des Akylas, Symmachos und Theodotion: Probe eines neuen Field," *ZAW* 72 (1934): 176-84; idem, "Der Jesajakommentar des Eusebios von Kaisereia fast vollständig wieder aufgefunden," *ZNW* 33 (1934): 87-89. [[(Tr.) Prior to Ziegler's edition, which is based especially on the nearly complete text of the commentary rediscovered by A. Möhle in the 1930s in the margin of a Florentine biblical codex (Ziegler's siglum F), scholars had to depend on the version that Bernard de Montfaucon had assembled from medieval catenae in 1706: "Eusebii Pamphili Commentaria in Hesaiam," in *Collectio nova Patrum et Scriptorum Graecorum*, 2 vols. (1706), vol. 2; reprinted in Migne, PG 24 (1857), 77-526. While there is still no complete modern-language translation of Ziegler's or Montfaucon's edi-

This makes it possible for us to become better acquainted from a fresh perspective with the "father of the Church history" and Origenistic theologian,[236] who has received both praise and criticism depending upon the theological position of the beholder.[237] In his Bible commentaries Eusebius shows himself to be one of the most important Christian scholars of his time.[238] At the same time he has also been described as a philosopher in the "Theological Twilight," as Alois Grillmeier has titled his presentation.[239]

How limited our usual perception of Eusebius is may already be seen from a review of the bishop's bibliography: the philological and exegetical side of his work

---

tion (Montfaucon provided a translation into Latin), an important study has appeared since the German version of this essay: M. J. Hollerich, *Eusebius of Caesarea's Commentary on Isaiah: Christian Exegesis in the Age of Constantine*, Oxford Early Christian Studies (1999). See esp. Hollerich's section on "The New Edition of the *Commentary on Isaiah*" (pp. 15-18) for the pre-history and significance of Ziegler's edition. For initial interaction with elements of Hollerich's thesis see below nn. 255, 259.]]

236. Grillmeier, *Christ in Christian Tradition*, 167-68 with n. 1 (bibliography). Cf. H. G. Opitz, "Eusebius von Cäsarea als Theologe," *ZNW* 34 (1935): 1-20; F. Ricken, "Die Logoslehre bei Eusebius v. Cäsarea," *ThPh* 42 (1967): 341-58.

237. [[Expanded by translator]] Some of these criticisms have been made in response to Eusebius's *Life of Constantine*. As is well known, J. Burckhardt characterized Eusebius as "the first thoroughly dishonest historian of antiquity," although he also admits that "Eusebius is no fanatic; he understands Constantine's secular spirit and his cold and terrible lust for power well enough" (*Die Zeit Constantins des Großen* [2nd ed., 1880; 1st ed., 1853], reprinted in *Jacob Burckhardt — Gesamtausgabe*, 14 vols., vol. 2: *Die Zeit Constantins des Großen*, ed. F. Stähelin [1929], 276 = ET, *The Age of Constantine the Great*, trans. M. Hadas [1949; reprinted 1983], 283). B. Altaner similarly describes Eusebius as "the prototype of character-deficient state bishops." Against this see H. Lietzmann who, responding to Burckhardt's characterization, says: "No greater wrong could be done to this honourable man." He adds his own evaluation of Eusebius's *Life of Constantine*: "[Eusebius] dutifully presented his records in the literary form of an appreciation [of Constantine], but in doing so never forgot that he was a scientific historian" — so Lietzmann, *Geschichte der Alten Kirche*, 4 vols., vol. 3: *Die Reichskirche bis zum Tode Julius* (1938), 154 = ET, *From Constantine to Julian: A History of the Early Church, Volume III*, trans. B. L. Woolf (1950), 163; reprinted: *A History of the Early Church*, 4 vols. in 2, with foreword by W. H. C. Frend (1993), 2:735. Similarly F. Winkelmann: "One cannot truly call him a 'court bishop'" (*Euseb von Kaisareia: Der Vater der Kirchengeschichte* [1991], 146). Cf. also D. S. Balanos, "Zum Charakterbild des Kirchenhistorikers Eusebius," *TQ* 116 (1935): 309-22; M. J. Hollerich, "Religion and Politics in the Writings of Eusebius: Reassessing the First 'Court Theologian,'" *CH* 59 (1990): 309-25.

238. E. Schwartz, "Eusebios," *Paulys Realencyclopädie der classischen Altertumswissenschaft* 6/1 (1907), 1370-1439, esp. 1373 = idem, *Griechische Geschichtsschreiber* (1957), 495-598, esp. 499 (hereafter: 1373 = 499, etc.).

239. Grillmeier, *Christ in Christian Tradition*, 167.

constitutes nearly a third of his literary oeuvre.[240] Despite all the criticism of him from the personal and dogmatic sides, Photius, Patriarch of Constantinople († 891), still acknowledges: πολυμαθὴς δέ ἐστιν ὁ ἀνήρ, "the man is a polymath."[241] Hans Lietzmann describes Eusebius — Lietzmann's "predecessor" in terms of scholarly temperament — as "heir of the tradition of solid learning" embodied in Origen and his student Pamphilus, Eusebius's spiritual father.[242]

Turning our attention to the Isaiah commentary, which probably originated right after the Council of Nicaea,[243] it is noticeable first that in the whole rest of the document, apart from the six and a quarter pages of commentary on Isaiah 52:13–53:12 (GCS 9:332-39, ed. Ziegler), there are no further allusions to this text in the two volumes. Eusebius obviously did not regard the text as particularly central for the Old Testament book of Isaiah itself.[244] The text has a substantially higher value

240. Cf. the convenient survey of Eusebius's works in C. Curti, "Eusebius of Caesarea," *EECh* 1:299-301, who divides them into five categories: historical, apologetic, biblical and exegetical, and dogmatic. The biblical and exegetical works include the so-called Eusebian canons or *Canon Tables*, CPG no. 3465, text in E. Nestle and K. Aland, *Novum Testamentum Graece*, 27th ed. (1993), 84*-89*; *Onomasticon*, CPG no. 3466, text in GCS *Eusebius* 3/1, ed. E. Klostermann; *Evangelical Problems and Solutions*, CPG no. 3470, text in PG 22:880-1016 (also in part in H. Merkel, *Die Pluralität der Evangelien als theologisches und exegetisches Problem in der Alten Kirche*, Traditio christiana 3 [1978], 66-91); *Commentary on the Psalms*, CPG no. 3467; further *catena fragments*, CPG no. 3469; a lost work on the polygamy of the patriarchs (mentioned in Eusebius, *Dem. ev.* 1.9.20, text in GCS *Eusebius* 6:42 ll. 33-36, ed. Heikel, with a citation in Basil of Caesarea, *Spir.* 29.72, text in *Sur le Saint-Esprit: Basile de Césarée*, SC 17 bis, 2nd ed. [1968], 506 ll. 32-37, ed. B. Pruche); *On Easter*, CPG no. 3479, text in PG 24:693-706. On Eusebius's commentaries in general see E. Schwartz, "Eusebios," 1435 = 591 and now Winkelmann, *Euseb von Kaisareia*, 34-51. The new English edition of Jerome's *On Illustrious Men* also lists the modern editions and secondary studies of the works by Eusebius that Jerome cites: see *On Illustrious Men: Saint Jerome*, trans. T. P. Halton, FC 100 (1999), 113-15.

241. Nevertheless, Photius immediately thereafter charges Eusebius with lacking τὴν ἀγχίνοιαν καὶ τὸ σταθηρὸν τοῦ ἤθους, "wit and stability of character" (Photius, *Bibliothèque*, vol. 1, ed. R. Henry [1958], 11 ll. 2-4).

242. Lietzmann, *Geschichte der Alten Kirche*, 3:155 = *From Constantine to Julian: A History of the Early Church* (1950), 3:164 = *A History of the Early Church*, 4 vols. in 2 (1993), 2:736.

243. Hollerich suggests a date of 325-328 after a detailed discussion; see *Eusebius of Caesarea's Commentary on Isaiah*, 19-26. In his earlier treatment E. Schwartz pointed out that Eusebius's depiction of the distinguished imperial officials taking part in the worship services points to a time after 323 ("Eusebios," 1435 = 594). He refers to the passage in *Comm. Isa.* 1.62 on Isa. 11:6: εἰ δὲ καὶ βασιλικούς ποτε ἄνδρας ἀξιώμασι . . . θεάσοιο ἐν τῇ ἐκκλησίᾳ τοῦ θεοῦ (GCS *Eusebius* 9:84 ll. 8-9, ed. Ziegler).

244. [(Tr.) As was noted in the German version of this essay, it would appear at first glance that certain terms central to the fourth Servant Song, including the term παῖς itself (Isa. 52:13), are also not prominent throughout the rest of Eusebius's Isaiah commentary; Ziegler's index of Greek

in Eusebius's earlier *Demonstratio evangelica,*[245] written after 314 (thus a good while before the Council of Nicaea, so problematic for Eusebius). But both documents are closely related: in many passages one gets the distinct impression that when Eusebius commented on the whole book of Isaiah at least a good decade, if not more, after his *Demonstratio evangelica,* he was literally dependent on his earlier work.[246] This may also be due to his increasing workload; perhaps during the first years after taking over the office of bishop in 313, Eusebius had more time for scholarly work than when he was in the midst of sharp theological controversies and Church-political tasks, in which he was involved especially after 325.

In Eusebius's slightly more than six pages of commentary on Isaiah 52:13–53:12,[247] there is a noticeable absence of a set of features that were still characteristic of Origen's interpretation: there are no explicit explanations of words, and one misses any argumentation from the Hebrew text.[248] Similarly, no philologically justified decision is made between the different Greek translations; Eusebius simply shows the *particula veri* of each of the quoted translations, by Aquila, Symmachus, Theodotion, and of course the Septuagint. In fact, he quotes so freely from other biblical texts that it is difficult to avoid the impression of an interpretation purely by means of a mosaic of quotations: it is not without good reason that Jerome in his catalog of Church authors praises Eusebius's Bible knowledge: *in Scripturis divinis studiosissimus,* "extremely industrious in the study of the Sacred Scriptures."[249] A detailed prologue is missing in the Isaiah commentary; the basic hermeneutical de-

---

words lists only *three* references for παῖς (GCS 9:467 s.v.). But this index is hardly a concordance, and the reality is more complicated: there are in fact *eighty-seven occurrences* of the term παῖς (in all eight of its inflectional forms) in the Isaiah commentary — a figure easily determined from the electronic version of Ziegler's text in the *TLG* database. Further examination of these uses is necessary to see if any of these occurrences outside the commentary on Isaiah 53 refer to the Suffering Servant of Isaiah 53, rather than to other biblical "servants" of God or of the kings, etc.]

245. See also below nn. 275, 293, 294. The Scripture index of I. A. Heikel's edition of the *Demonstratio evangelica* (GCS *Eusebius* 6 [1913], 521) lists over fifty references to Isa. 52:13–53:12. By comparison LXX Ps. 109:1 (110:1) is cited about ten times (index, p. 517); Gen. 49:10 over twenty-five times (p. 513); and Isa. 7:14 similarly almost twenty-five times (p. 519). There are also a number of nested citations.

246. For the Isaiah commentary's literal borrowings from the *Demonstratio evangelica* see below nn. 276, 277, 290, and 308.

247. Eusebius, *Comm. Isa.* 2.42 (GCS 9:332 l. 34-339 l. 4, ed. Ziegler).

248. However, on Eusebius's use of Hebrew elsewhere in his exegetical work, see for example B. de Montfaucon, "Praeliminaria in Eusebii Commentaria in Psalmos," PG 23:22 B-C; regarding the Isaiah commentary see Montfaucon's "Praefatio," PG 24:88 C.

249. Jerome, *Vir. ill.* 81.1 (*Gli uomini illustri: De viris illustribus: Gerolamo,* ed. A. Ceresa-Gastaldo, Biblioteca patristica 12 [1988], 188; ET: *On Illustrious Men: Saint Jerome,* trans. T. P. Halton, FC 100 [1999], 113).

cisions regarding the literal and allegorical sense of Scripture are recalled at the beginning of the commentary in a mere seventeen lines and hardly differ from those of Origen.[250] However, since Eusebius says that the last volume of Origen's commentary concluded with the exegesis of Isaiah 30:5,[251] one cannot attribute Eusebius's exegesis of Isaiah 52–53 directly to that of his esteemed master.

Eusebius apparently understood our fourth Servant Song, Isaiah 52:13–53:12, as a unit in its own right, because he dedicated a whole chapter of his commentary to it (chapter 42 of book 2). Since Eusebius elsewhere frequently begins a new chapter of his commentary with each new chapter of Isaiah (though he can also have more than one chapter of commentary on a single chapter of Isaiah; e.g., Isaiah 49 = *Comm. Isa.* 2.35-36), his chapter divisions are not as telling for the delimitation of the first and second Servant Songs, which begin where the biblical chapters do in Isaiah 42 and 49; his chapter covering Isaiah 50:4-9, the third Servant Song, begins with Isaiah 50:1.[252] In any case prior to Bernhard Duhm, we would not expect any explicit indication of the connection between these passages as "Servant Songs."

It is hardly remarkable that the bishop of Caesarea interprets our text in terms of central Christological themes: ἡ εἰς ἀνθρώπους αὐτοῦ γένεσις καὶ ὁ μετὰ ταῦτα βίος, ὅ τε θάνατος καὶ ἡ τοῦ θανάτου αἰτία, "[Christ's] birth among men and his subsequent life, his death and the cause of his death."[253] Similarly, after quoting Philippians 2:8-9 and the first verse of the Servant Song, Isaiah 52:13, Eusebius says: δι' ὧν τὴν μετὰ τὸν θάνατον ἀνάστασιν αὐτοῦ καὶ τὴν εἰς οὐρανοὺς ἀνάληψίν τε καὶ ὕψωσιν σημαίνει, "through which he [sc. Isaiah] signifies his resurrection after death, his being taking up into heaven and his exaltation."[254] How-

---

250. Eusebius, *Comm. Isa.* 1 (GCS 9:3 ll. 1-17, ed. Ziegler). Cf. C. Curti, "Eusebius of Caesarea," *EECh* 1:299-301, esp. 300.

251. *Comm. Isa.* 98 on Isa. 30:1-5 (GCS 9:195 ll. 20-21, ed. Ziegler).

252. The first Servant Song, Isa. 42:1-9, is treated by Eusebius in *Comm. Isa.* 2.22 (GCS 9:268 l. 1-272 l. 7, ed. Ziegler); the second Servant Song, Isa. 49:1-9c, in *Comm. Isa.* 2.35 (GCS 9:308 l. 10-312 l. 22); and the third Servant Song, Isa. 50:4-9, in *Comm. Isa.* 2.37 (GCS 9:318 l. 26-320 l. 12). Theodoret treats the fourth Servant Song similarly to Eusebius, beginning section 17 of his commentary at Isa. 52:13 (Guinot, *Commentaire sur Isaïe*, 3:144). Nevertheless, there is no break in Theodoret's treatment at Isa. 42:1; 49:1; or 50:4.

253. *Comm. Isa.* 2.43 (on Isaiah 54, here on 54:1), summarizing the previous chapter, *Comm. Isa.* 2.42 on Isa. 52:13–53:12 (GCS 9:339 ll. 11-12, ed. Ziegler). Translations of Eusebius's Isaiah commentary are by Daniel P. Bailey, with the help of the German renderings in the original version of this essay.

254. *Comm. Isa.* 2.42 on Isa. 52:13 (GCS 9:333 ll. 6-7, ed. Ziegler). In *Dem. ev.* 3.2.69, Isaiah 53 (particularly 53:12) is once again connected with Phil. 2:8. Text in GCS *Eusebius Werke*, vol. 6: *Die Demonstratio Evangelica*, ed. I. A. Heikel (1913), 107 ll. 1-5; trans. W. J. Ferrar, *The Proof of the Gospel* (1920; reprinted 1981), 115, where, however, the allusion to Phil. 2:8 is not explicitly recognized: "He was obedient to the Father even unto death" (l. 3 from bottom).

ever, the surprising thing for me in Eusebius's interpretation of the fourth Servant Song is that he interprets it so consistently in the context of his own (subordinationist) Christological assumptions, even if it has been claimed that the expression of these assumptions was toned down between the time of the *Demonstratio evangelica* and the post-Nicene Isaiah commentary (M. J. Hollerich). From the start of his commentary on the fourth Servant Song in Isaiah 52:13, Eusebius's specific form of the Logos theology — the subordinated Logos of God took on flesh — enters into his exposition.[255] At the same time he tries to justify the translation of Aquila and his term δοῦλος, as distinct from the Septuagint's παῖς. Quoting both the Septuagint and Aquila's version (LXX: "Behold, my *servant* will understand," ἰδοὺ συνήσει ὁ παῖς μου; Aquila: "Behold, my *slave* will be made to understand," ἰδοὺ ἐπιστημονισθήσεται ὁ δοῦλός μου [GCS 9:333 ll. 18-19]), Eusebius interprets the verse as a prophecy about the Logos, which dwells in the flesh in place of the human soul, thus transcending the usual or normal human nature:[256]

> But this servant (παῖς) of God and slave (δοῦλος) was filled with all wisdom (cf. Luke 2:40) and knowledge, because he contained God the Logos in himself. Therefore it is said: "Behold, he will be made to understand, but he will also be exalted and glorified and raised high" (Isa. 52:13). But all these things were fulfilled with reference to the man, our Savior, because of his union with God the Logos.[257]

255. ⟦(Tr.) Hollerich, *Eusebius of Caesarea's Commentary on Isaiah*, 24-26, proposes the theory that Eusebius's commentary actually exhibits a "careful avoidance of subordinationist theological terminology" (p. 24), at least of the sort seen earlier in his *Demonstratio evangelica*, precisely because the commentary was written immediately after the Council of Nicaea (perhaps between the first and second sessions, 325-327 C.E.), at a time when Eusebius's Christological views were suspect. Nevertheless, Hollerich *confirms* the above observation concerning Eusebius's Logos theology: even in the Isaiah commentary, there is "an apparent adoption of the Logos-sarx framework, that is, the assumption that the Logos was substituted for a human soul in Christ" (p. 64). Hollerich finds this Christology in Eusebius, *Comm. Isa.* 2.51 on Isa. 61:1-3 (GCS 9:378 l. 36-379 l. 1, ed. Ziegler) as well as in phrases like τὸ δι' ἀνθρώπους ἀναληφθέν μοι ὄργανον σωματικόν, "the fleshly instrument assumed by me for the sake of men" (9:318 l. 27), and τὸν ἐμαυτοῦ σωματικὸν ἄνθρωπον, "my corporeal humanity" (9:319 l. 20) (see Hollerich, 64 with n. 210). See below n. 259 and especially n. 275 for the conclusion that there is little difference in Christology between the pre- and post-Nicene Eusebius.⟧

256. So Grillmeier, *Jesus der Christus*, 319 = *Christ in Christian Tradition*, 183.

257. *Comm. Isa.* 2.42 on Isa. 52:13: ἀλλ' οὗτος ὁ παῖς τοῦ θεοῦ καὶ ὁ δοῦλος πάσης "ἐπληροῦτο σοφίας" [cf. Luke 2:40] καὶ ἐπιστήμης τὸν θεὸν λόγον εἰς ἑαυτὸν χωρήσας. διὸ λέλεκται· "ἰδοὺ ἐπιστημονισθήσεται ἀλλὰ καὶ ὑψωθήσεται καὶ δοξασθήσεται καὶ μετεθρισθήσεται," ταῦτα δὲ πάντα ἐπληροῦτο περὶ τὸν ἄνθρωπον τοῦ σωτῆρος ἡμῶν διὰ τὴν πρὸς τὸν θεὸν λόγον ἕνωσιν (GCS 9:333 ll. 22-26, ed. Ziegler).

The assumed human being is unified with God the Logos. Eusebius leaves no doubt about the divinity of the Logos, about the divinity of Christ, but he understands it (as is well known) as a subordinated divinity, a divinity of second rank. This is shown clearly by a central Christological passage of Eusebius's Isaiah commentary, to which Bernard de Montfaucon drew attention already in 1706.[258] Commenting on Isaiah 43:11: ἐγὼ ὁ θεός, καὶ οὐκ ἔστιν πάρεξ ἐμοῦ σῴζων, "I am God, and beside me there is no savior," Eusebius formulates the following contrary-to-fact condition (for the translation of θεολογία as "divinity" rather than "theology," cf. *PGL* 628, θεολογία, G.2.a; *Hist. eccl.* 3.24.13):

μιᾶς γὰρ οὔσης ἀρχῆς μία εἴη ἂν θεότης, ᾗ συνπαραλαμβάνεται καὶ ἡ τοῦ μονογενοῦς αὐτοῦ θεολογία.[259]

For if there were one beginning, there would be one deity, into which also the divinity of his Only Begotten would be taken as an adjunct.

258. Namely in Montfaucon's Latin preface to his 1706 edition of Eusebius's Isaiah commentary (see n. 235), reprinted in PG 24:77-90, esp. 84 C-D. Montfaucon is referring to Eusebius's statement μιᾶς γὰρ οὔσης ἀρχῆς μία εἴη ἂν θεότης, etc. (see the next note [n. 259] with its text), which in Montfaucon's edition comes as a comment on Isa. 43:11, ἐγὼ ὁ θεός, etc., printed at the end of the paragraph on Isa. 43:12: see PG 24:397 D, last three lines of paragraph (= ll. 46-48 of col. 397). On the relationship between commentary and theology in Eusebius see also Haag, "Gottesknecht," 357. [[(Tr.) Since Eusebius's statement μιᾶς γὰρ οὔσης ἀρχῆς etc. — see the next note with its text — is located at very different positions in the two editions of the Isaiah commentary by Montfaucon and Ziegler, a potential cause of confusion may be cleared up here. In Montfaucon's edition (PG 24:397 ll. 46-48) the statement comes immediately *after* Isa. 43:11, ἐγὼ ὁ θεός, καὶ οὐκ ἔστιν πάρεξ ἐμοῦ σῴζων, "I am God, and beside me there is no savior," and is clearly a response to it. Montfaucon naturally relates it to 43:11 in his own preface, PG 24:84 C-D. However, in Ziegler's edition this is not immediately clear: μιᾶς γὰρ οὔσης ἀρχῆς etc. comes *between* Isa. 43:10 and 43:11 and concludes the paragraph to which 43:10 belongs (see GCS 9:279 l. 14). It must therefore refer at least to 43:10. Nevertheless, Eusebius's comment also refers forward to 43:11, as the introductory phrase of his next paragraph makes clear (GCS 9:279 ll. 15-16): ἐπιμένων δὲ ὁ λόγος τῇ αὐτῇ διδασκαλίᾳ ἐπιφέρει· "ἐγὼ θεός, καὶ οὐκ ἔστι πάρεξ ἐμοῦ σῴζων" = "Continuing on this topic, the [following] saying contributes to the same teaching: 'I am God, and beside me there is no other savior' (Isa. 43:11)." Here "the same teaching," ἡ αὐτὴ διδασκαλία, refers to the μιᾶς γὰρ οὔσης ἀρχῆς etc. in the preceding line, which just happens to form the end of the preceding paragraph.]]

259. *Comm. Isa.* 2.24 on Isa. 43:10-11 (GCS 9:279 ll. 13-14, ed. Ziegler). For the full context of this statement see the translator's comment in the preceding note. On the doctrine of Christ's divinity in Eusebius see Schwartz, "Eusebios," 1430 = 583. [[(Tr.) Hollerich in his brief analysis of the Christology of Eusebius's Isaiah commentary (*Eusebius of Caesarea's Commentary on Isaiah*, 64 with n. 212) considers GCS 9:279 ll. 4-9 but apparently does not consider the above-cited ll. 13-14. His comments about the Isaiah commentary's supposed "avoidance of subordinationist theological terminology" (p. 24; cf. above n. 255) may therefore need modification.]]

Eusebius's belief in the independent "divinity of the Only Begotten" who is not absorbed into the one deity protects him from Sabellianism (the belief in one deity that appears in different "modes" but does not subsist as distinct divine persons) by means of a strict subordination of the Only Begotten. As Eusebius says in another work *(De ecclesiastica theologia)*, Christ is "the living and subsisting only-begotten Son of God,"[260] who is incarnated in place of a soul in human flesh.

With a theologian who related the political history of his time to theology as strongly (and therefore also as problematically) as Eusebius did, it is no surprise that he goes on to interpret Isaiah 52:15b (καὶ συνέξουσιν βασιλεῖς τὸ στόμα αὐτῶν, "and kings will shut their mouths") in terms of recent history:

> And indeed the "kings," when they had uttered many blasphemous, godless, and profane words against him and persecuted his church, but ultimately had been unable to achieve anything after these vain efforts, "shut their mouths" and made way for his teaching; they were defeated in a later time and another way according to the opportunities and periods, because they were driven into a corner by God-sent blows.[261]

In his *Life of Constantine*,[262] his report about *The Martyrs of Palestine*,[263] and naturally also in his *Ecclesiastical History*, Eusebius describes these persecu-

---

260. *Eccl. theol.* 1.20.46: ὁ ζῶν καὶ ὑφεστὼς μονογενὴς υἱὸς τοῦ θεοῦ (GCS *Eusebius Werke* 4:88 ll. 18-19, eds. Klostermann and Hansen). For this use of ὑφίστημι as "to subsist" see Lampe, *PGL* 1467, def. B.2.

261. *Comm. Isa* 2.42 on Isa. 52:14-15 (GCS 9:333 l. 36-334 l. 4, ed. Ziegler): καὶ "βασιλεῖς" δὲ πολλὰ κατ᾽ αὐτοῦ βλάσφημα καὶ ἄθεα καὶ ἀσεβῆ ῥήματα φθεγξάμενοι καὶ τὴν ἐκκλησίαν αὐτοῦ διώξαντες, κᾆπειτα μηδὲν δυνηθέντες τέλος μετὰ τοὺς ματαίους πόνους "συνέσχον τὸ ἑαυτῶν στόμα" καὶ παρεχώρουν αὐτοῦ τῇ διδασκαλίᾳ ἡττώμενοι ἄλλοτε ἄλλως κατὰ καιροὺς καὶ χρόνους διὰ τὸ θεηλάτοις μάστιξι περιελαύνεσθαι.

262. *Vit. Const.* 1.15, ἤλαυνον μὲν γὰρ ἀπανταχοῦ γῆς τοὺς θεοσεβεῖς ἐξ ἐπιτάγματος τῶν κρατούντων οἱ κατ᾽ ἔθνος ἄρχοντες, "Provincial governors were throughout the world persecuting the godly by the decree of those in power" (GCS *Eusebius Werke*, vol. 1/1: *Über das Leben des Kaisers Konstantin*, ed. F. Winkelmann [1975], 23 ll. 15-17 = trans. A. Cameron and S. G. Hall, *Life of Constantine: Eusebius*, Clarendon Ancient History Series [1999], 75). See also *Vit. Const.* 1.23 (GCS 1/1:27 ll. 21-22) and 1.27.2 (p. 29 ll. 4-7): "As to the others who used the methods of war to persecute the churches of God, I have decided that it is not proper to report the way their lives ended" (1.23; Cameron and Hall, 78); "those [rulers] who had attached their personal hopes to many gods . . . had first been deceived by favourable predictions . . . but then met an unwelcome end" (1.27.2; Cameron and Hall, 80).

263. *Mart. Pal.* (short recension), preface 1-2 (GCS *Eusebius* 2/2:907 ll. 3-14, ed. Schwartz). Translation in H. J. Lawlor and J. E. L. Oulton, *The Ecclesiastical History and the Martyrs of Palestine*, vol. 1 (1927; reprinted 1954), 329-31.

tions and the futile efforts of the persecutors. Even more specific than his reference above to the defeated "kings" of Rome is Eusebius's immediately following allusion in the Isaiah commentary to Diocletian's persecution of the recent past, when Christians saw "the houses of prayer cast down to their foundations from top to bottom":[264]

> Some of them [sc. the pagan kings] "shut their mouths," but others issued a recantation, commanding the people by laws and edicts to build the prayer houses again and to bring to an end the usual (persecutions) of his church.[265]

The reader clearly recognizes an allusion to Diocletian's imperial edict of 24 February 303[266] enjoining the demolition of churches, and to the corresponding recantation signed by Constantine and Licinius on 30 April 311,[267] allowing them to be rebuilt. In his report about *The Martyrs of Palestine,* Eusebius likewise speaks of the παλινῳδία or "recantation" of the rulers.[268] The God-sent

---

264. *Hist. eccl.* 8.2.1 (trans. Lake, LCL 2:257; text GCS 2/2:740 ll. 16-18, ed. Schwartz). For the report of the re-consecrations of the newly built houses of prayer see *Hist. eccl.* 10.3.1 (Schwartz, 2/2:860 ll. 16-19; Lake, 2:395). Eusebius alludes to Isa. 53:4-5 in his address at the consecration of the church in Tyre in *Hist. eccl.* 10.4.12 (Schwartz, 2/2:866 ll. 14-16; Lake, 2:405).

265. *Comm. Isa.* 2.42 (GCS 9:334 ll. 5-8, ed. Ziegler): ἀλλ' οἱ μὲν αὐτῶν συνέσχον τὸ ἑαυτῶν στόμα, οἱ δὲ καὶ παλινῳδίαν ᾖδον νόμοις καὶ διατάγμασι τοὺς εὐκτηρίους οἴκους ἐγείρειν καὶ τὰ συνήθη πράττειν τὴν ἐκκλησίαν αὐτοῦ ἐγκελευόμενοι. On Constantine's avoidance of the crime of persecuting the Church see *Vit. Const.* 1.13.2 (GCS *Eusebius* 1:14 ll. 3-8, ed. Heikel; trans. Cameron and Hall, *Life of Constantine,* 74, or *NPNF,* 2nd series, 1:485).

266. H. G. Thümmel, *Die Kirche des Ostens im 3. und 4. Jahrhundert,* Kirchengeschichte in Einzeldarstellungen 1/4 (1988), 38-39.

267. See Lactantius, *Mort. Pers.* 34 (*L. Caeli Firmiani Lactanti Opera omnia,* CSEL 27/2:212 l. 10-213 l. 22, ed. S. Brandt and G. Laubmann), or Eusebius, *Hist. eccl.* 8.17.3-10 (GCS 2/2:790 l. 221-794 l. 22, ed. Schwartz; trans. Lake, LCL 2:316-21).

268. *Mart. Pal.* 13.14, the conclusion of the short recension: "But when the divine and heavenly grace manifested for us too its kindly and gracious visitation, then verily even the rulers of our day, those very persons by whose means hostile measures had long been prosecuted in our time, changed their minds in a most marvellous fashion and gave utterance to a recantation. Thus by kindly edicts and humane ordinances on our behalf they quenched the fires of persecution against us. The recantation also must be placed on record" (trans. Lawlor and Oulton, *The Ecclesiastical History and the Martyrs of Palestine,* 1:400). Text: ἀλλὰ γὰρ ὅτε καὶ τὴν καθ' ἡμᾶς ἐπισκοπὴν εὐμενῆ καὶ ἵλεω ἡ θεία καὶ οὐράνιος χάρις ἐνεδείκνυτο, τότε δῆτα καὶ οἱ καθ' ἡμᾶς ἄρχοντες, αὐτοὶ δὴ ἐκεῖονι δι' ὧν πάλαι τὰ τῶν καθ' ἡμᾶς ἐνηργεῖτο πολέμων, παραδοξότατα γνώμῃ μεταβαλλόμενοι παλινῳδίαν ᾖδον, χρηστοῖς περὶ ἡμῶν προγράμμασιν καὶ ἡμέροις διατάγμασιν τὴν καθ' ἡμῶν πυρκαϊὰν ἀποσβεννύτες· ἀναγραπτέα δὴ καὶ ἡ παλινῳδία (GCS 2/2:950 ll. 5-7, ed. Schwartz). The Syriac version includes a more extensive doxological conclusion; cf. also *Hist. eccl.* 8.16.1.

"blows" that Eusebius mentions in the context of Isaiah's "kings" may then be connected with several more specific reports in the *Ecclesiastical History,* including one about the end of Diocletian's life: he "fell a victim to a prolonged and most painful infirmity of the body."[269] One could think also of Maximinus, who less than a year after the persecution published the Christian-friendly ordinance recorded by Eusebius,[270] yet nevertheless died a cruel death which Eusebius relates in detail, not without a touch of satisfaction: "all at once he was smitten by a stroke of God over his whole body."[271] Finally, Eusebius says that after all the troubles of the Christians, God "made it manifest to all that God Himself had been watching over our affairs continually."[272] In the Isaiah commentary the kings are said to have been moved by the rapid spread of the gospel;[273] already in his *Ecclesiastical History* Eusebius says that "the saving word began to flood the whole world with light like the rays of the sun."[274]

We have here — positively speaking — nothing less than an attempt at "contextualization," the theological interpretation of the Bible in view of the challenges of the time and the situation of the Christians and the churches.

The beginning of Isaiah 53 is interpreted as a prophetic prediction of the birth of Jesus, because Eusebius frequently understood Isaiah 53:1b, ὁ βραχίων κυρίου, "the arm of the Lord" as a statement about the μονογενής and his birth:[275]

269. *Hist. eccl.,* Appendix to Book 8 (found in three manuscripts), §3 (trans. Lake, LCL 2:323; text GCS 2/2:796 ll. 14-15, ed. Schwartz).

270. *Hist. eccl.* 10.10.7-11 (trans. Lake, LCL 2:375-79; text GCS 2/2:842 ll. 5-844 l. 21, ed. Schwartz).

271. *Hist. eccl.* 9.10.14 (trans. Lake, LCL 2:381; text GCS 2/2:846 l. 18, ed. Schwartz; cf. 846 ll. 9-848 l. 8). Cf. also *Vit. Const.* 1.57-59 (GCS *Eusebius* 1/1:71 l. 8-72 l. 7, ed. Winkelmann; trans. Cameron and Hall, *Life of Constantine,* 93-94).

272. *Hist. eccl.* 10.8.15 (trans. Lake, LCL 2:357; text GCS 2/2:826 ll. 15-16, ed. Schwartz).

273. *Comm. Isa.* 2.42 on Isa. 52:13-14 (GCS 9:334 ll. 10-11, ed. Ziegler): τοῦτο γὰρ ἦν τὸ κινῆσαν τοὺς βασιλεῖς, λέγω δὲ τὸ διαδραμεῖν αὐτοῦ τὸν εὐαγγελικὸν λόγον καὶ ἐπὶ τὰ πορρωτάτω ἔθνη, "For it was this that moved the kings, I mean the spread of his evangelical word even to the most distant nations."

274. *Hist. eccl.* 2.3.1 (trans. Lake, LCL 1:115; text GCS 2/1:112 ll. 14-15, ed. Schwartz).

275. This identification is found for example in a collection of Scripture passages (see passage 27) in Eusebius's *De ecclesiastica theologia* 1.20, directed against Marcellus (GCS *Eusebius* 4, *Gegen Marcell: Über die kirchliche Theologie: Die Fragmente Marcells,* ed. E. Klostermann, rev. by G. C. Hansen, 2nd ed. [1972], 95 ll. 27-28). In his *Demonstratio evangelica* 2.48, Eusebius says that the miracle of Christ's conception (τῆς γενέσεως αὐτοῦ τὸ θαῦμα) is best explained by Isa. 53:1-2a. This text is cited according to the LXX (GCS *Eusebius* 6:103 ll. 28-32, ed. Heikel), followed by the versions of Aquila and Theodotion. Eusebius then declares: διὰ γὰρ τούτων μνημονεύσας ὁ προφήτης τοῦ βραχίονος τοῦ κυρίου, ὃς ἦν ὁ τοῦ θεοῦ λόγος, "For in this passage, the prophet having mentioned 'the Arm of the Lord,' which was the Word of God,

We have often shown that his "only begotten Son" is called the "arm" of God, who has been made known by means of the corresponding prophetic words to all the peoples who have believed in him. But the prophets of God, having marveled in their narratives at these things, further foretell the appearance among men of the predicted "servant" (παῖς) or the "slave" (δοῦλος) of God, saying (Isa. 53:2a): "We announced before him like a 'little servant' (παιδίον), like a root in thirsty ground," but according to Aquila, "and he will spring up," he says, "like a 'nursing infant' (τιθιζόμενον) before him, and like a root from untrodden ground."[276] (GCS 9:334-35)

When this statement is combined with the immediately following explanation in the Isaiah commentary, a special feature of its author's Christology again becomes clearly visible. Eusebius once again very sharply distinguishes the Logos of God or the "arm" of God (see above), as the person who acts in redemption, from the "tool" or "vessel" or "organ" of redemption — here called the "nursing infant" and "the one born of the virgin" — so that the Logos can also exist independently of this "tool" (cf. also τὸ ἀνθρώπειον σκεῦος, "the human vessel," Eusebius, *Dem. ev.* 4.13 [GCS 6:172 l. 13, Heikel]). Hence Eusebius continues on Isaiah 53:2:

> For "before him," he says — and I refer "him" to the above mentioned "arm" — "he will spring up like a nursing infant" (Isa. 53:2, Aquila). But this was the one who had been born of the virgin, [the infant] about whom it has been said through the earlier words, "Behold, the virgin shall be with

---

says . . ." (GCS 6:104 ll. 2-4, trans. Ferrar, *Proof of the Gospel,* 112). If we regard the *Demonstratio evangelica* as in any case pre-Nicene (with Quasten, *Patrology,* 3:332) and perhaps date it shortly after 314, then it shows that there was no great difference between the pre- and post-Nicene Eusebius. Cf. also van Cangh, "Nouveaux Fragments Hexaplaires," 389-90.

276. ⟦(Tr.) For the above translation of παιδίον in Isa. 53:2 LXX as "little servant" (rather than "child") see Ekblad, *Isaiah's Servant Poems According to the Septuagint,* 175, 198, 201-2, esp. 202 n. 116, and LSJ 1287, s.v. παιδίον II, "young slave." On the translation of τιθιζόμενον, see the next note [n. 277].⟧ Text: *Comm. Isa.* 2.42 on Isa. 53:1-4 (GCS 9:334 l. 35-335 l. 5, ed. Ziegler): "βραχίονα" δὲ τοῦ θεοῦ λέγεσθαι τὸν "μονογενῆ υἱὸν" αὐτοῦ πολλάκις ἀπεδείξαμεν, ὃς πᾶσι τοῖς εἰς αὐτὸν πεπιστευκόσιν ἔθνεσιν ἐγνώσθη ταῖς προφητικαῖς ἀκολούθως φωναῖς, ἀλλὰ γὰρ ταῦτα ἀποθαυμάσαντες οἱ τοῦ θεοῦ προφῆται διηγηματικῶς λοιπὸν τὴν τῆς εἰς ἀνθρώπους πάροδον τοῦ προλεχθέντος "παιδὸς" ἢ τοῦ "δούλου" τοῦ θεοῦ θεσπίζουσι λέγοντες· "ἀνηγγείλαμεν ὡς παιδίον ἐναντίον αὐτοῦ, ὡς ῥίζα ἐν γῇ διψώσῃ," κατὰ δὲ τὸν Ἀκύλαν· "καὶ ἀναβήσεταί" φησιν "ὡς τιθιζόμενον εἰς πρόσωπον αὐτοῦ καὶ ὡς ῥίζα ἀπὸ γῆς ἀβάτου." As we have already seen in part (see n. 275), Eusebius had already developed a very similar interpretation in *Dem. ev.* 3.2.48-51 (GCS 6:103 ll. 28-104 l. 13, ed. Heikel). There too the βραχίων or "arm" is identified with the Monogenes or rather the Word of God (6:104 l. 3); the "untrodden ground" is identified with the Virgin Mary, and Isa. 7:14 is cited. See also the text associated with the next note.

child, and shall bear a Son, and you shall call his name Immanuel" (Isa. 7:14). This was "the nursing infant" that sprang up "before the arm of God," as the word makes clear, saying, "as a root from untrodden ground"; speaking in riddles, he calls the virgin whom no one had mounted "untrodden ground."[277]

It is striking how Eusebius strives to hold both to the suffering of the redeemer[278] described in Isaiah 53:5-6 (as his ἰδιοποίησις or appropriation of our suffering) and to his redeeming death. This also holds true for other writings of Eusebius. According to Eusebius's *Theophania* or *Divine Manifestation*,[279] on the cross the Logos proved the mortality of his body or "mortal vessel," but also demonstrated that the eternal life he proclaimed was superior to death. As the end of the following excerpt shows, this demonstration of the power of life over death was the first of three reasons or causes for Christ's death, the second being to show that the divine power resided in the human body.[280] While the following portions of the *Theophania* are preserved only in

---

277. *Comm. Isa.* 2.42 on Isa. 53:1-4 (GCS 9:335 ll. 4-10, ed. Ziegler): εἰς πρόσωπον γὰρ αὐτοῦ φησι, λέγω δὲ τοῦ προλεχθέντος βραχίονος, "ἀναβήσεται ὡς τιθιζόμενον." τοῦτο δὲ ἦν τὸ ἐκ τῆς παρθένου γεγεννημένον, περὶ οὗ λέλεκται διὰ τῶν ἔμπροσθεν· "ἰδοὺ ἡ παρθένος ἐν γαστρὶ λήψεται [read also by other Church Fathers; LXX and Matt. 1:23 read ἕξει] καὶ τέξεται υἱόν, καὶ καλέσεις τὸ ὄνομα αὐτοῦ Ἐμμανουήλ," τοῦτ' ἦν "τὸ τιθιζόμενον" τὸ εἰς πρόσωπον "τοῦ βραχίονος τοῦ θεοῦ" ἀναβὰν ἑξῆς ὁ λόγος διασαφεῖ λέγων· "ὡς ῥίζα ἀπὸ γῆς ἀβάτου," "γῆν" μὲν "ἄβατον" αἰνιττόμενος τὴν παρθένον, ἧς οὐδεὶς ἐπιβεβήκει. A similar presentation may also be found (outside the parallel in *Dem. ev.* 3.2.50 = GCS 6:104 ll. 7-10, already discussed in the preceding note) in Theodoret, *Comm. Isa.* 17 on Isa. 53:2 (Guinot, *Commentaire sur Isaïe*, 3:43-45). ⟦(Tr.) Aquila's unusual form τιθιζόμενον in Isa. 53:2, here translated "nursing infant," is found in Greek literature only in Eusebius, with a total of seven occurrences, including four occurrences in *Dem. ev.* 3.2.49-50 = GCS 6:103 l. 33 and 6:104 ll. 4, 6, 9 (see above n. 276); and three occurrences in *Comm. Isa.* 2.42 = GCS 9:335 l. 3 (see the preceding note [n. 276]) and GCS 9:335 ll. 5, 7 (as above). Τιθιζόμενον is translated by Ferrar, *Proof of the Gospel*, 112 l. 14 = *Dem. ev.* 3.2.49 (= PG 22:180 B, §97) as: "And he shall be proclaimed as a *suckling* before his face" (καὶ ἀναρρηθήσεται ὡς τιθιζόμενον εἰς πρόσωπον αὐτου, GCS 6:103 ll. 32-33). However, Ferrar also gives Theodotion's term θηλάζον the same translation: "And he shall go up as a *suckling* before him" (καὶ ἀναβήσεται ὡς θηλάζον ἐνώπιον αὐτοῦ, GCS 6:104 ll. 1-2). For lexical analysis of τιθιζόμενον as a defective writing of τιτθιζόμενον, see n. 200 in the essay in this volume by Martin Hengel, with Daniel P. Bailey, "The Effective History of Isaiah 53 in the Pre-Christian Period."⟧

278. See also *Dem. ev.* 10.1.23 (GCS *Eusebius* 6:450 ll. 24-28, ed. Heikel) with a citation of Isa. 53:5b, 6b.

279. On the controversial dating of Eusebius's *Theophania* see Grillmeier, *Christ in Christian Tradition*, 168 n. 1 (lit.).

280. For the three reasons for Christ's death see Eusebius, *Theoph.* 3.57-59 (trans. Samuel Lee, *Eusebius, Bishop of Caesarea: On the Theophania or Divine Manifestation of Our Lord and*

Syriac, we also have some Greek fragments of the *Theophania* as well as parallels in Eusebius's *Praise of Constantine* (see the notes):

> And, just as one wishing to shew that some vessel was incombustible and its nature superior to fire, could in no other way establish this astonishing fact, except by placing the one which he held in his hand in the fire, and then taking it out of the fire, safe and sound; so also THE WORD OF GOD, the life-giver of all, willing to make it known that the mortal Vessel, of which He had availed himself for the redemption of man, was superior to death, and, to shew that He made it to participate in His own life, conducted the matter both well and virtuously as it was most convenient. He left the body for a short time, and consigned mortality to death for the rebuking of its (sinful) nature; and again, He soon raised up the same from death, for the purpose of proving that the Divine power, which was by Him, — that eternal life, (I say) which was preached by Him, — was superior to every kind of death. (§58) This therefore was the first cause. The second was, to shew that the Divine power resided in the human body. (*Theophania* 3.57-58)[281]

Saviour Jesus Christ [1843], 192-93). There is a parallel about the reasons for Christ's death in Eusebius's Tricentennial Oration "On Christ's Sepulchre," delivered before Constantine in Jerusalem, *De laudibus Constantini* = *Laud. Const.* 15.9-11: "(9) This, then, is the first and greatest reason for our Savior's struggle with death — to show His disciples that the death feared by all amounts to nothing, and to give proof of the life He promised through a manifest sight before their own eyes by making Himself the prototype of that immortality and life with God that is our common hope. (10) Another reason for the Resurrection would be to make manifest the divine power which dwelt within His body." "I may offer you even a third reason to account for the salutary death. (11) He was a sacrifice offered up to the All-Ruling God of the Universe on behalf of the entire human race." English translation by H. A. Drake, *In Praise of Constantine: A Historical Study and New Translation of Eusebius' Tricentennial Orations* (1976), 118-19. Greek text in GCS *Eusebius Werke*, vol. 1: *Über das Leben Constantins: Constantins Rede und die heilige Versammlung: Tricennastsrede an Constantin*, ed. I. A. Heikel (1902), 247 ll. 8-16, 25-27. On this oration see also Quasten, *Patrology*, 3:327-28.

281. *Theoph.* 3.57-58 (Syriac), trans. Lee, *Eusebius, Bishop of Caesarea*, 193, on the basis of Lee's edition of the Syriac: *Eusebius: On the Theophania, or, Divine Manifestation of Our Lord and Savior Jesus Christ: A Syriac Version* (1842). (This edition of the Syriac is also taken as the basis for the German translation by H. Gressmann, rev. by A. Laminski, GCS *Eusebius Werke*, vol. 3/2: *Die Theophanie* [2nd ed., 1992; 1st ed., 1904]). There is an almost exact Greek parallel to *Theoph.* 3.57 in Eusebius, *Laud. Const.* 15.6 (GCS *Eusebius* 1:246 ll. 4-16, ed. Heikel): ὥσπερ δὲ εἴ τις ἄκαυστον ἡμῖν καὶ πυρὸς κρεῖττον σκεῦός τι δεῖξαι ἠθέλησεν, οὐκ ἂν ἄλλως τὸ θαῦμα παρεστήσατο ἢ τῷ πυρὶ παραδοὺς τὸ μετὰ χεῖρας κἄπειτα αὐτὸ σῶον καὶ ἀδιάφθορον τοῦ πυρὸς ἐξελών, κατὰ ταῦτα δὴ καὶ ὁ τῶν ὅλων ζωοποιὸς τοῦ θεοῦ λόγος τὸ θνητὸν ὄργανον, ᾧ πρὸς ἀνθρώπων κέχρητο σωτηρίαν, κρεῖττον θανάτου δεῖξαι βουληθεὶς κοινωνόν τε ἀποφῆναι τῆς οἰκείας ζωῆς τε καὶ ἀθανασίας, εὖ μάλα χρησίμην ὑπῆει τὴν οἰκονομίαν, τὸ [μὲν] σῶμα πρὸς βραχὺ καταλιπὼν καὶ τὸ θνητὸν τῷ θανάτῳ παραδιδοὺς εἰς ἔλεγχον τῆς οἰκείας φύσεως, εἶτ' οὐκ

Divine power is superior to death and also dwells in the human body. Eusebius goes on to give a third reason for Christ's death:

> The third cause of (His) death was, the redemption that is (taught) in hidden (mystical) terms,[282] which are these in effect: He was the sacrifice which was consigned to death, for the souls of the whole race (of man): the sacrifice (I say) which was slain for the whole flock of mankind. . . . The sacrifice therefore, — the great offering, and that which was superior to all (other) sacrifices, — was the Body of our Saviour which was sacrificed as a Lamb. (*Theophania* 3.59)[283]

εἰς μακρὸν αὐτὸ τοῦ θανάτου πάλιν ὑφαιρούμενος, εἰς παράστασιν τῆς ἐνθέου δυνάμεως, δι' ἧς παντὸς θανάτου κρείττονα τὴν πρὸς αὐτοῦ καταγγελθεῖσαν ζωὴν ἀΐδιον ἔφαινεν = "Now if someone wished to prove to us that a given *vessel* (σκεῦος) was scorchproof and stronger than fire, he could not demonstrate the remarkable fact other than by delivering the one at hand to the fire and then taking it out of the fire safe and unscathed. In this same way, the Universal Life-giving Logos of God, wishing to prove that the mortal instrument (τὸ θνητὸν ὄργανον) which He had used for the salvation of mankind was stronger than death, and to reveal it as a participant in His own life and immortality, undertook a most useful arrangement. Abandoning His body for a brief time and surrendering His mortal form to death in proof of its own nature, not long after He raised it back from the dead as proof of His divine power. So doing, He proved that the eternal life promised by Him was stronger than any form of death" (trans. Drake, *In Praise of Constantine*, 118). On the role of Christ's body in his work of salvation see also *Dem. ev.* 3.4.27-29 (GCS *Eusebius* 6:114 l. 29-115 l. 9, ed. Heikel; trans. Ferrar, *Proof of the Gospel*, 125). On Christ's body as an ὄργανον or "instrument" see Eusebius's (perhaps spurious?) commentary on LXX Ps. 92:1 (MT 93:1), "The Lord reigns; he has clothed himself with majesty," in PG 23:1184 C-D, esp. ll. 37-40: Εἰκότως οὖν ὁ προὼν τοῦ Θεοῦ Λόγος, αὐτὸς ὢν ἡ ζωή, ἐπὶ καθαιρέσει τοῦ θανάτου θνητὸν ὄργανον τὸ σῶμα τὸ ἀνθρώπειον ἀναλαβών, καὶ τοῦτο τῷ θανάτῳ παραδούς· "Therefore naturally the preexistent Word of God, being himself the life, for the overthrow of death took up a mortal instrument, the human body, and delivered it to death" (trans. D. P. Bailey).

282. This particular reference to redemption taught "in hidden (mystical) terms" (Lee) or contained in the "secret Words (of Scripture)" (= "die geheimen Worte [der Schrift]," trans. Gressmann, GCS *Eusebius* 3/2:154 l. 15) is without a direct parallel in Eusebius's *Laud. Const.*, but there is a partial parallel for rest of the passage (see the next note).

283. Trans. Lee, *Theophania*, 193-94. Cf. Eusebius, *Laud. Const.* 15.11 (GCS 1:247 l. 27-248 l. 2, ed. Heikel): ἱερεῖον ἦν ὑπὲρ τοῦ κοινοῦ γένους ἀναπεμπόμενον τῷ παμβασιλεῖ θεῷ [τῶν ὅλων], ἱερεῖον ὑπὲρ τῆς τῶν ἀνθρώπων ἀγέλης καθιερούμενον, ἱερεῖον δαιμονικῆς πλάνης ἀποτρόπαιον. ἱερείου δῆτα ἑνὸς καὶ μεγάλου θύματος, τοῦ πανιέρου σώματος τοῦ σωτῆρος ἡμῶν, ὑπὲρ τοῦ τῶν ἀνθρώπων γένους σφαγιασθέντος καὶ πάντων ἐθνῶν τῶν πρὶν ἀσεβείᾳ δαιμονικῆς πλάνης ἐνεσχημένων ἀντίψυχον ἀνενεχθέντος, πᾶσα λοιπὸν ἡ τῶν ἀνάγνων καὶ ἀνιέρων δαιμόνων δύναμις καθῄρητο, ἐλέλυτό τε καὶ παρεῖτο αὐτίκα δυνάμει κρείττονι πᾶσα γεώδης καὶ ἀπατηλὸς πλάνη = "He was a sacrifice offered up to the All-Ruling God of the Universe on behalf of the entire human race, a sacrificial victim for averting demonic error. And in

After citing John 1:29; Isaiah 53:7, and Isaiah 53:4-6, Eusebius continues:

This bodily vessel therefore of the Word of God, was, for these reasons, sacrificed. But He, the great High Priest who officiates as Priest to God, the King of all, and Lord of all, is another distinct from the sacrifice, (viz.) THE WORD OF GOD, THE POWER OF GOD, and THE WISDOM OF GOD: He also, after no long time, raised the mortal [body] from death, making *it* [Lee: making *him*] the beginning of the redemption of us all and a participant in that immortal life which is with God. He vested *it* with the mark of victory over death and the demons' deeds [of slaughter], making *it* the apotropaic [sacrifice] against those human sacrifices which had been delivered down from ancient times, for the sake of all mankind. Hence also was the name of Messiah given to Him; which, among the Hebrews, attached in like manner to the chief priest. He therefore received the two names: the name of Jesus, implying the sacrifice of salvation; and that of the High Priest, the WORD OF GOD, who officiates as Priest for us all: — the custom of the Hebrews intimating this of the Messiah. (*Theophania* 3.59)[284]

fact, once this one great sacrificial victim, the All-Holy body of Our Savior, had been slaughtered on behalf of the human race and atonement offered for all races formerly ensnared in the impiety of demonic error, thereafter all the power of the impure and unholy demons was destroyed, and all the earthbound and guileful error immediately yielded to a stronger power and was done away with" (trans. Drake, *In Praise of Constantine*, 119). On Christ's "apotropaic" (ἀποτρόπαιον) or evil-averting sacrifice see also the next note.

284. [[(Tr.) The above is a modification of Lee's English translation (*Theophania*, 194-95) of the Syriac *Theoph*. 3.59, in the direction of Gressmann's German translation (GCS *Eusebius* 3/2:155 ll. 13-26). Gressmann refers the above italicized neuter pronoun "it" *(es)* to the mortal human body, *das Sterbliche* [*sc. Leib*], whereas Lee takes it as masculine and refers it to the Savior himself. The phrase "apotropaic [sacrifice]" translates Gressmann's "Abwehr(opfer)" which, while offered as a translation of the Syriac, also agrees with the Greek term ἀποτρόπαιον in Gressmann's Frag. 3 below.]] The Syriac of *Theoph*. 3.59 corresponds closely to the Greek of the same passage in Eusebius's *Theophania*, Greek Fragment 3, below; this in turn is verbally almost identical with *Laud. Const.* 15.13. *Italics* indicate the verbal differences between *Theophania* and *Laud. Const.* (not accounting for word order). *Theophania*, Frag. 3 (GCS 3/2:10 l. 19-11 l. 4, ed. Gressmann): τὸ μὲν οὖν *σωματικὸν* τοῦ θείου λόγου ὄργανον διὰ ταύτας καθιεροῦτο τὰς αἰτίας, ὁ δὲ μέγας ἀρχιερεὺς <ὁ τῷ πανηγεμόνι καὶ παμβασιλεῖ θεῷ ἱερώμενος>, ἕτερος ὢν παρὰ τὸ ἱερεῖον, θεοῦ λόγος *καὶ* "<θεοῦ> δύναμις καὶ <θεοῦ> σοφία" [1 Cor. 1:24], οὐκ εἰς μακρὰν τὸ θνητὸν ἀνεκαλεῖτο τοῦ θανάτου καὶ τοῦτο τῆς κοινῆς ἡμῶν σωτηρίας τὴν ἀπαρχὴν *ζωῆς ἐνθέου καὶ ἀθανασίας μέτοχον* παρίστη, τρόπαιον ἐπινίκιον κατὰ τοῦ θανάτου καὶ *κατὰ* τῆς δαιμονικῆς παρατάξεως τῶν τε πάλαι <συντελουμένων ἀνθρωπο>θυσιῶν ἀποτρόπαιον τοῦτο ὑπὲρ *ἁπάντων* ἀνθρώπων ἀνεγείρας. Compare *Laud. Const.* 15.13 (GCS *Eusebius* 1:248 ll. 15-23, ed. Heikel): τὸ μὲν οὖν ὄργανον *τὸ ἀνθρώπειον* τοῦ θείου λόγου διὰ ταύτας καθιεροῦτο τὰς αἰτίας, *οὗτος* δὲ ὁ μέγας ἀρχιερεὺς ὁ τῷ πανηγεμόνι καὶ παμβασιλεῖ θεῷ ἱερωμένος, ἕτερος ὢν παρὰ τὸ ἱερεῖον, θεοῦ λόγος, θεοῦ δύναμις καὶ θεοῦ σοφία, τὸ θνητὸν οὐκ εἰς μακρὸν ἀνεκαλεῖτο τοῦ θανάτου,

Returning to Eusebius's Isaiah commentary, we see that he refers Isaiah 53:5 to the Gospel passion narratives and combines it with the Pauline *theologoumenon* of the cursed death (cf. *Dem. ev.* 10.1.20 for the curse of Gal. 3:13 = Deut. 21:23). Perhaps this was triggered by the keyword ἀνομίαι, "lawless deeds," shared by both the Septuagint and Aquila's version of Isaiah 53:5:[285]

> "By his wounds," he says, "we were healed" (Isa. 53:5), since it was also fit-ting for him to bear wounds on his body, and to be struck with blows, and to be "flogged" (cf. John 19:1), and to be "slapped" in the face (cf. Matt. 26:67), and to be "struck on the head with a reed" (Matt. 27:30). Neverthe-less, these "wounds" were our savior: "For by his wounds we were healed."[286]

Making use once again of a post-Septuagintal Greek version (this time by Symmachus), Eusebius naturally interprets the language of the sheep not open-ing its mouth in Isaiah 53:7 in terms of Jesus' silence before Pilate:

> Then, instead of [the Septuagint reading], "And because of his oppression he does not open his mouth," Symmachus says, "He was brought, and he obeyed [sc. and he did not open his mouth: see below]" (Isa. 53:7a-[b]). But to whom was he "brought," except "to Pilate"? And "while being accused" (cf. Matt. 27:12a), "he was silent" (Matt. 26:63), and while being testified

---

καὶ τοῦτο τῷ *πατρὶ* τῆς κοινῆς ἡμῶν σωτηρίας τὴν ἀπαρχὴν παρίστῃ, τρόπαιον ἐπινίκιον κατὰ τοῦ θανάτου καὶ τῆς δαιμονικῆς παρατάξεως τῶν τε πάλαι συντελουμένων ἀνθρωποθυσιῶν ἀποτρόπαιον τοῦτο ὑπὲρ *πάντων* ἀνθρώπων ἀνεγείρας = "Thus the physical instrument of the divine Logos was sacrificed for these reasons. But He who is the Great High Priest dedicated to the All-Ruling and Almighty God, who is distinguished from the sacrificial victim as the Logos of God, the Power of God, and the Wisdom of God, not long after recalled His mortal body from the dead and presented it to the Father as the prototype of our common salvation, having raised it on behalf of mankind as a trophy of victory over death and the demonic host, and a safeguard [ἀποτρόπαιον] against the human sacrifices that formerly were performed" (trans. Drake, *In Praise of Constantine*, 119; cf. 178 n. 6 for comments on ἀποτρόπαιον and the τρόπαιον-ἀποτρόπαιον wordplay). On the motif of Christ as high priest in Eusebius see Grillmeier, *Christ in Christian Tradition*, 180 with n. 51 (bibliography).

285. Aquila's version of Isa. 53:5 according to Eusebius reads (GCS 9:336 ll. 6-7, ed. Ziegler): καὶ αὐτός φησι βεβηλωμένος ἀπὸ ἀθωσμιῶν ἡμῶν, συντετριμμένος ἀπὸ τῶν ἀνομιῶν ἡμῶν.

286. *Comm. Isa.* 2.42 on Isa. 53:5-6 (GCS 9:336 ll. 13-16, ed. Ziegler): καὶ "τῷ μώλωπι αὐτοῦ" φησιν "ἰάθημεν," ἐπεὶ καὶ μώλωπας εἰκὸς ἦν αὐτὸν φέρειν κατὰ τοῦ σώματος καὶ τραύματα τυπτόμενον καὶ "μαστιγούμενον" καὶ τὰς ὄψεις "ῥαπιζόμενον" "τήν τε κεφαλὴν καλάμῳ παιόμενον". πλὴν οἱ "μώλωπες" οὗτοι σωτῆρες ἦσαν ἡμῶν· "τῷ γὰρ μώλωπι αὐτοῦ ἡμεῖς ἰάθημεν."

against falsely, "he did not answer" (Matt. 27:12b). For this reason it is said according to Symmachus, "and he did not open his mouth" (Isa. 53:7b).[287]

Accordingly Eusebius in his interpretation of Isaiah 53:6 can also use key expressions from the biblical and early Christian sacrificial vocabulary, such as the two terms for a "ransom," ἀντίψυχον[288] and ἀντίλυτρον,[289] which he links to his interpretation of John 1:29:

> For "the Lord himself delivered him over to our sins" (LXX Isa. 53:6), so that he might become our exchange (ἀντίψυχον) and "ransom" (ἀντίλυτρον, 1 Tim. 2:6). In this way he has also become the "lamb of God," who "takes away" and purges "the sin of the world" (John 1:29). Therefore according to Symmachus it is said, "But the Lord has caused to fall upon him the iniquity of us all" (Isa. 53:6).[290]

287. *Comm. Isa.* 2.42 on Isa. 53:7 (GCS 9:336 ll. 25-29, ed. Ziegler): Εἶτ' ἀντὶ τοῦ· "καὶ αὐτὸς διὰ τὸ κεκακῶσθαι οὐκ ἀνοίγει τὸ στόμα," ὁ Σύμμαχος "προσηνέχθη" φησὶ "καὶ αὐτὸς ὑπήκουσε." τίνι δὲ "προσηνέχθη" ἀλλ' ἢ "τῷ Πιλάτῳ"; "καὶ ἐπειδὴ κατηγορούμενος" "ἐσιώπα" καὶ ψευδομαρτυρούμενος "οὐδὲν ἀπεκρίνατο," τούτου χάριν κατὰ τὸν Σύμμαχον εἴρηται· "καὶ οὐκ ἤνοιξε τὸ στόμα αὐτοῦ."

288. For this term see the writings of Ignatius (cf. also 4 Macc. 6:29; 17:21), where, however, the ἀντίψυχον is Ignatius himself rather than Jesus: *Eph.* 21:1: ἀντίψυχον ὑμῶν ἐγώ, "I am your expiation" (trans. Schoedel, *Ignatius of Antioch*, 95; contrast Lake, LCL *Apostolic Fathers*, 1:195, "May my soul be given for yours"); *Smyrn.* 10:2: ἀντίψυχον ὑμῶν τὸ πνεῦμά μου καὶ τὰ δεσμά μου, "My spirit and my bonds are your expiation" (Schoedel, 247; cf. Lake, 1:263, "May my spirit be for your life, and my bonds"); *Pol.* 2:3: κατὰ πάντα σου ἀντίψυχον ἐγὼ καὶ τὰ δεσμά μου, "In every way I am your expiation, as are my bonds" (Schoedel, 262; cf. Lake, 1:271: "In all things I am devoted to you, — I and my bonds"); *Pol.* 6:1: ἀντίψυχον ἐγὼ τῶν ὑποτασσομένων τῷ ἐπισκόπῳ, "I am an expiation of those subject to the bishop" (Schoedel, 274; cf. Lake, 1:273: "I am devoted to those who are subject to the bishop").

289. For ἀντίλυτρον see 1 Tim. 2:6 (its sole occurrence in biblical Greek); cf. F. Büchsel, "λύω κτλ.," *TDNT* 4:349, s.v. ἀντίλυτρον. The same two terms ἀντίψυχον and ἀντίλυτρον are juxtaposed in Eusebius, *Dem. ev.* 10.8.35, once again in an exposition of the fourth Servant Song, particularly Isa. 53:4-7: "Yea more — to wash away our sins He was crucified, suffering what we who were sinful should have suffered, as our *sacrifice* and *ransom* (ἀντίψυχον ἡμῶν καὶ ἀντίλυτρον γενόμενος), so that we may well say with the prophet, 'He bears our sins and is pained for us' (v. 4), and 'he was wounded for our sins, and bruised for our iniquities' (v. 5), so that 'by His stripes' we might be healed (v. 5); for 'the Lord hath given Him for our sins' (v. 6). So, as delivered up by the Father, as bruised, as bearing 'our sins,' 'He was led as a sheep to the slaughter' (v. 7)" (GCS 6:477 ll. 13-22, ed. Heikel; trans. Ferrar, *Proof of the Gospel*, 221 [modified]).

290. *Comm. Isa.* 2.42 on Isa. 53:5-6 (GCS 9:336 ll. 20-24, ed. Ziegler): αὐτὸς γὰρ "αὐτὸν παρεδίδου ὁ κύριος ταῖς ἁμαρτίαις ἡμῶν," ἵνα γένηται ἀντίψυχον καὶ "ἀντίλυτρον" ἡμῶν. οὕτω γὰρ καὶ "ἀμνὸς τοῦ θεοῦ" γέγονεν, "αἴρων" καὶ περικαθαίρων "τὴν ἁμαρτίαν τοῦ κόσμου." διὸ

Upon arriving at Isaiah 53:8, Eusebius alerts his readers to a partial change of theme from Christ's sufferings to his "birth" (γένεσις) or "generation" (γενεά), once again emphasizing the tension between the lowliness of this earthly existence and the exaltation of the Logos who was incarnated. Readers who ponder this will be caught up in wonder:

> Next, having gone through [Christ's] sufferings, [Isaiah] turns the minds of the listeners to the appearance of his birth, saying: "who will declare his generation?" (Isa. 53:8). For all the more will someone be caught up in wonder at his obedience in such things, when he comes to ponder who and what he is, and that the one who was "born of God," the "only begotten Son," endured all these things.[291]

After quoting Aquila, Symmachus, and Theodotion about Christ having his life taken away from the earth and being cut off from the land of the living, Eusebius presents his conclusion — already seen above in Origen's argument against the collective interpretation — with which readers who have followed him to this point may be expected to agree:

> It is clear that the prophet in these words prophesied these things neither about himself nor about the people, and as if suspicious of this, he adds the following, saying, "Because of the lawless deeds of my people he was led to death" (Isa. 53:8).[292]

κατὰ τὸν Σύμμαχον εἴρηται· "κύριος δὲ καταντῆσαι ἐποίησεν εἰς αὐτὸν τὴν ἀνομίαν πάντων ἡμῶν." Compare very similarly *Dem. ev.* 10.1.19-20, where in addition to Isa. 53:4, 6; John 1:29; and 1 Timothy (substituting ἀντίψυχον for ἀντίλυτρον), there are allusions to other soteriological verses including Gal. 3:13; 2 Cor. 5:21; and Rom. 8:3 (GCS 6:449 l. 30-450 l. 3, ed. Heikel; cf. trans. Ferrar, *Proof of the Gospel*, 195): διὸ λέλεκται· "καὶ κύριος παρέδωκεν αὐτὸν ταῖς ἁμαρτίαις ἡμῶν" [Isa. 53:6], καὶ "αὐτὸς τὰς ἁμαρτίας ἡμῶν φέρει" [Isa. 53:4]. γέγονε γοῦν "ὑπὲρ ἡμῶν κατάρα" [Gal. 3:13] "ὁ ἀμνὸς τοῦ θεοῦ ὁ αἴρων τὴν ἁμαρτίαν τοῦ κόσμου" [John 1:29], ὃν καὶ "μὴ γνόντα ἁμαρτίαν ὁ θεὸς ὑπὲρ ἡμῶν ἁμαρτίαν ἐποίησεν" [2 Cor. 5:21a], ἀντίψυχον ὑπὲρ πάντων ἡμῶν [cf. 1 Tim. 2:6] προέμενος αὐτόν, "ἵνα ἡμεῖς γενώμεθα δικαιοσύνη θεοῦ ἐν αὐτῷ" [2 Cor. 5:21b]. ἀλλ' ἐπεὶ καὶ "ἐν ὁμοιώματι σαρκὸς ἁμαρτίας" γενόμενος "κατέκρινεν τὴν ἁμαρτίαν ἐν τῇ σαρκί" [Rom. 8:3], εἰκότως προφέρεται τὰ ἐκκείμενα.

291. *Comm. Isa.* 2.42 on Isa. 53:8 (GCS 9:336 l. 30-337 l. 1, ed. Ziegler): Εἶτα διελθὼν αὐτοῦ τὰ πάθη ἀναπέμπει τὴν τῶν ἀκουόντων διάνοιαν ἐπὶ τὴν τῆς γενέσεως αὐτοῦ φαντασίαν ἐπιλέγων· "τὴν γενεὰν αὐτοῦ τίς διηγήσεται;" τότε γὰρ μάλιστα μεῖζόν τις λήψεται θαῦμα τῆς τῶν τοσούτων ὑπομονῆς, ὅταν εἰς ἔννοιαν ἔλθῃ τίς ὢν καὶ ὁποῖος καὶ "ἐκ θεοῦ γεγεννημένος" "μονογενὴς υἱὸς" ταῦτα πάντα ὑπέστη.

292. *Comm. Isa.* 2.42 on Isa. 53:8 (GCS 9:337 ll. 8-10, ed. Ziegler): σαφῶς δὲ ὁ προφήτης ἐν τούτοις ὅτι μήτε περὶ ἑαυτοῦ ταῦτ' ἐθέσπιζε μήτε περὶ τοῦ λαοῦ ὡς ἂν οἰηθείη παρέστησεν εἰπών· "ἀπὸ τῶν ἀνομιῶν τοῦ λαοῦ μου ἤχθη εἰς θάνατον."

How little remains here of the second-century controversy between Jews and Christians about the interpretation of this text may also be seen in certain passages from the *Demonstration of the Gospel*: Isaiah 53:8 is applied without scruple to the general doctrine of the unknowability of God or to the exclusive knowledge that the Son has of him (cf. Matt. 11:27).[293] Moreover, the phrase "Who shall declare his generation?" (Isa. 53:8) suggests human inability to understand "the generation of the Only-begotten of God," which is "beyond our conception, unexplained and unnamed, inconceivable and unimaginable." It therefore justifies the use of the necessary but potentially problematic metaphors "fragrance" (εὐωδία) and "ray of light" (φωτὸς αὐγή) for the generation of the Logos from the Father.[294]

In his comments on the Septuagint version of Isaiah 53:9a-b, "And I will give the wicked in place of his grave, and the rich in place of his death,"[295] Eusebius takes advantage of a change in the Hebrew grammatical number found in all the Greek versions (singular עָשִׁיר, "a rich man," becomes plural, καὶ τοὺς πλουσίους), and resorts once again to the special wording of Symmachus for a change of person from "*I* will give" to "*he* will give." This allows him to present the text as a prophecy of judgment by the exalted Lord: the "judge of the universe," the exalted Logos,[296] has already delivered Jesus' accusers to their enemies. This must be understood as a historical-theological interpretation of the catastrophe of 70 C.E.[297]

---

293. *Dem. ev.* 4.3.13 (GCS *Eusebius* 6:154 ll. 21-23, ed. Heikel; trans. Ferrar, *Proof of the Gospel*, 168). So also later in Theodoret, although in the fifth century he could speak more precisely of the "divine nature": Ἀπερινόητος γὰρ ἡ θεία φύσις, "the divine nature is incomprehensible" (*Comm. Isa.* 17, in Guinot, *Commentaire sur Isaïe*, 3:154 ll. 120-21).

294. *Dem. ev.* 5.1.18 (GCS 6:213 ll. 4-13, ed. Heikel; trans. Ferrar, *Proof of the Gospel*, 233). This passage is also translated and commented upon by Grillmeier, *Christ in Christian Tradition*, 174.

295. Isa. 53:9: καὶ δώσω τοὺς πονηροὺς ἀντὶ τῆς ταφῆς αὐτοῦ καὶ τοὺς πλουσίους ἀντὶ τοῦ θανάτου αὐτοῦ·

296. That the judge of the universe is Christ is clear in Eusebius, *Comm. Isa.* 1.65 on Isa. 13:4-5 (GCS 9:97 ll. 3-9, ed. Ziegler), where the expression ὁ τῶν ὅλων κριτής appears in the context of citations of Matt. 25:31, 34, 41; cf. also Ziegler's Greek word index s.v. κριτής (p. 463).

297. This interpretation is confirmed by *Dem. ev.* 3.2.59 (GCS 6:105 ll. 16-21, ed. Heikel): "ἀπὸ τῶν ἀνομιῶν τοῦ λαοῦ μου ἤχθη εἰς θάνατον" [Isa. 53:8]. εἶτ᾽ ἐπεὶ παραχρῆμα καὶ οὐκ εἰς μακρὸν μετὰ τὴν κατὰ τοῦ Χριστοῦ τόλμαν ὁ παντελὴς αὐτοὺς μετῆλθεν ὄλεθρος πολιορκηθέντας ὑπὸ Ῥωμαίων, οὐδὲ τοῦτο παριδὼν ἐπιλέγει· "καὶ δώσω τοὺς πονηροὺς ἀντὶ τῆς ταφῆς αὐτοῦ καὶ τοὺς πλουσίους ἀντὶ τοῦ θανάτου αὐτοῦ" [Isa. 53:9] = "'For the transgressions of my people he was led to death' (Isa. 53:8). And then because total destruction overtook them [sc. the Jews] immediately, and not a long time after their evil deed to Christ, when they were besieged by the Romans, he [Isaiah] does not pass this over either, but adds: 'And I will give the wicked for his tomb, and the rich for his death' (Isa. 53:9)" (Ferrar, *Proof of the Gospel*, 114).

Instead of: "And *I will give* (δώσω) the wicked in place of his grave [sc. and the rich (plural) in place of his death]" (LXX Isa. 53:9a-[b]), Symmachus says, "And *he will give* (δώσει) the ungodly in place of his grave." Who is he who "will give" but the judge of the universe? And whom [does he give] but those who did the things that were said, whom he delivered over immediately and not a long time afterwards to enemies and military opponents and takers of cities? And "the rich" of long ago, including those who were greedy for advantage, he will deliver over, he says, "in place of his death" (53:9b). The same then also immediately came to pass, that "from humanity was blotted the memory" of those who long ago counted much with the Jews — Pharisees and scribes and Sadducees, but in addition to them priests and chief priests and those honored with them with royal dignity. For these were the ones here called "the rich," whom "the wrath of God visited immediately" (cf. Eph. 5:6; Col. 3:6), because they subjected the Christ of God to such punishment, even though he was sinless.[298]

The historicizing interpretation of the passage as a reference to Jesus' passion is most clearly seen in Eusebius's commentary on Isaiah 53:12b:

And how "he was numbered among the transgressors" (Isa. 53:12b), the Gospel teaches: At the time when "the thieves" "were crucified together" with him on both sides, it says, so that the prophecy might be fulfilled — it is said namely in Mark (15:27): "And they crucified two thieves with him, one on his right and one on his left. (28) And the Scripture was fulfilled which says, 'And he was numbered with the transgressors.'"[299]

Theodoret and Chrysostom also adopted this interpretation: see Theodoret, *Commentaire sur Isaïe*, SC 315:156 ll. 129-135; Chrysostom, *In Isaiam prophetam interpretatio Sancti Joannis Chrysostomi archiepiscopi Constantinopolitani: Nunc primum ex Armenio in Latinum sermonem a Patribus Mekitharistis translata* (1887), 395 §§9-12.

298. *Comm. Isa.* 2.42 on Isa. 53:9-10 (GCS 9:337 ll. 11-22, ed. Ziegler): Ἀντὶ δὲ τοῦ· "καὶ δώσω τοὺς πονηροὺς ἀντὶ τῆς ταφῆς αὐτοῦ," ὁ Σύμμαχος· "καὶ δώσει" φησὶ "τοὺς ἀσεβεῖς ἀντὶ τῆς ταφῆς αὐτοῦ." τίς δὲ "δώσει" ἢ ὁ τῶν ὅλων κριτής; καὶ τίνας ἢ τοὺς τὰ εἰρημένα δεδρακότας, οὓς καὶ παρέδωκεν αὐτίκα καὶ οὐκ εἰς μακρὸν ἐχθροῖς καὶ πολεμίοις καὶ πολιορκηταῖς; καὶ τοὺς πάλαι δὲ πλουσίους, ἐν οἷς ἐπλεονέκτουν προτερήμασι, παραδώσειν φησὶν ἀντὶ τοῦ θανάτου αὐτοῦ. ὃ δὴ καὶ αὐτὸ παραχρῆμα συνέβη ὡς "ἐξ ἀνθρώπων ἀφανισθῆναι τὸ μνημόσυνον" τῶν πάλαι παρὰ Ἰουδαίοις πολλὰ δεδυνημένων, Φαρισαίων καὶ γραμματέων καὶ Σαδδουκαίων· καὶ ἔτι πρὸς τούτοις, ἱερέων τε καὶ ἀρχιερέων καὶ τῶν παρ' αὐτοῖς βασιλικῇ ἀξίᾳ τετιμημένων. οὗτοι γὰρ ἦσαν οἱ ἐνταῦθα λεγόμενοι πλούσιοι, οὓς "μετῆλθεν οὐκ εἰς μακρὰν ἡ ὀργὴ τοῦ θεοῦ," διότι ἀναμάρτητον ὄντα τὸν Χριστὸν τοῦ θεοῦ τοιαύτῃ κολάσει ὑποβεβλήκασι.

299. *Comm. Isa.* 2.42 on Isa. 53:11-12 (GCS 9:339 ll. 4-9, ed. Ziegler): πῶς δὲ "ἐν ἀνόμοις ἐλογίσθη," διδάσκει τὸ Εὐαγγέλιον, καθ' ὃν καιρὸν "συνεσταυροῦντο" αὐτῷ παρ' ἑκάτερα "οἱ λῃσταί," πεπληρῶσθαι λέγον τὴν προφητείαν· εἴρηται δ' οὖν παρὰ τῷ Μάρκῳ "καὶ σὺν αὐτῷ

Nevertheless, remarkably, the statement about the Servant's atoning death is at the same time taken very seriously; its effects are extended even to those who brought Jesus to his death. In this way Eusebius explains the puzzling second person plural in the Greek versions of Isaiah 53:10, which speaks of a potential plurality of people, rather than just a single person, making a sin offering: ἐὰν δῶτε περὶ ἁμαρτίας, ἡ ψυφὴ ὑμῶν ὄψεται σπέρμα μακρόβιον, "if you (plural) would give a sin offering, your soul will see a long-lived seed":

> According to all that has been said before, if anyone of those who have sinned against him would be willing to offer a sacrifice for his own sins, that is, to show confession and repentance for the sins committed, he will not lose his good hope.[300]

As we learn from his *Demonstration of the Gospel*, for Eusebius Christ's long-lived "seed" of Isaiah 53:10 can be either his eternal life or his eternal word, which can be "seen" only by those who confess and offer a sin offering.[301] The

---

ἐσταύρωσαν [Mark present: σταυροῦσιν] δύο λῃστάς, ἕνα ἐκ δεξιῶν καὶ ἕνα ἐξ εὐωνύμων. καὶ ἐπληρώθη ἡ γραφὴ ἡ λέγουσα· καὶ μετὰ τῶν ἀνόμων ἐλογίσθη." [[(Tr.) This quotation of Isa. 53:12 belongs to the original text of Luke 22:37 but is clearly secondary in Mark; numbered Mark 15:28, it is contained in the Majority Text and hence in the KJV, ASV, and NASB (in brackets). Eusebius appears to be the earliest Greek witness for its presence in Mark, though it also finds support in part of the Old Latin tradition as well as the Vulgate — see the apparatus for Mark 15:28 in the 27th edition of Nestle/Aland, where the testimony of Eusebius is newly included over against the 26th edition: E. Nestle and K. Aland et al., eds., *Novum Testamentum Graece*, 27th ed. (1993).]]

300. *Comm. Isa.* 2.42 on Isa. 53:9-10 (GCS 9:337 ll. 33-35, ed. Ziegler): μετὰ τὰ προλεχθέντα πάντα, εἴ τις τῶν εἰς αὐτὸν ἠσεβηκότων βουληθείη θυσίαν ἀνενεγκεῖν ὑπὲρ τῆς αὐτοῦ ἁμαρτίας, τοῦτ' ἔστιν ἐξομολόγησιν καὶ μετάνοιαν τῶν ἡμαρτημένων ἐνδείξασθαι, οὐκ ἀποτεύξεται τῆς εἰς αὐτὸν ἀγαθῆς ἐλπίδος. [[(Tr.) The English versions also have trouble with the second person *singular* verb in Isa. 53:10: אִם־תָּשִׂים אָשָׁם נַפְשׁוֹ, rendering it either literally, "When *you make* his life an offering for sin" (NRSV), or in the third person, "When *he makes* himself an offering for sin" (RSV; cf. NJB; NJPS).]]

301. *Dem. ev.* 3.2.61-62 (GCS 6:105 l. 31-106 l. 2, ed. Heikel): καὶ πῶς ἔσται; "ἐὰν δῶτε," φησίν, "περὶ ἁμαρτίας, ἡ ψυχὴ ὑμῶν ὄψεται σπέρμα μακρόβιον." οὐ πᾶσι γὰρ ἐφεῖται τὸ μακρόβιον τοῦ Χριστοῦ σπέρμα συνιδεῖν ἢ μόνοις τοῖς ἐξομολογησαμένοις καὶ τὰ δῶρα τὰ ὑπὲρ ἁμαρτιῶν προσάγουσι τῷ θεῷ. μόνων γὰρ τούτων "ἡ ψυχὴ ὄψεται σπέρμα μακρόβιον" τὸ τοῦ Χριστοῦ, ἤτοι τὴν αἰώνιον ζωὴν αὐτοῦ τὴν μετὰ τὸν θάνατον, ἢ τὸν καθ' ὅλης τῆς οἰκουμένης ἐπισπαρέντα αὐτοῦ λόγον μακρόβιον ἐσόμενον καὶ εἰς τὸ ἀεὶ διαρκέσοντα = "'If ye offer,' he says, 'for sin, your soul shall see a seed that prolongs its days.' For it is not allowed to all to see the seed of Christ that prolongs its days, but to those only who confess and bring the offerings for sins to God. For the soul of these only shall see the seed of Christ prolong its days, be it His eternal life after death, or the word sown by Him through the whole world, which will prolong its days and endure for ever" (Ferrar, *Proof of the Gospel*, 114).

Isaiah commentary focuses on the seed as the word and proceeds similarly, adding an allusion to the Parables of the Sower (Matt. 13:1-23) and of the Weeds among the Wheat (Matt. 13:24-30):

> "If you give" — you who undertook such things — the gift "which is for sin," you will get forgiveness and "your soul" will be saved; and not only will it be saved, but it will also "see the long-lived seed." And this was the seed that was sown by him to men, about which he taught "in parables" when he said, "the sower went out to sow," and again, "the kingdom of heaven is like a man who sowed good seed in his own field." Therefore if "you give a sin offering," "your soul will see" this spiritual and heavenly "seed."[302]

The last sentence about "this spiritual and heavenly seed" (τοῦτο τὸ λογικὸν καὶ οὐράνιον σπέρμα), which Eusebius elsewhere says is sown by the apostles,[303] is characteristic of his attempt to synthesize biblical and Middle Platonic ideas of the Logos. Finally, commenting on the phrase "and he will divide the spoils of the strong" (Isa. 53:12), Eusebius interprets "the strong ones" as the demons and says that Christ snatches prisoners from the demons and makes them his own spoils.[304]

Just as some elements of the text are historicized, others are interpreted in terms of Christological dogma and its technical vocabulary, including the idea of Christ's sinlessness in the commentary on Isaiah 53:9:

302. *Comm. Isa.* 2.42 on Isa. 53:9-10 (GCS 9:338 ll. 1-8, ed. Ziegler): "ἐὰν δῶτε" ὑμεῖς οἱ τὰ τοιαῦτα τολμήσαντες "τὸ ὑπὲρ ἁμαρτίας" δῶρον, τεύξεσθε ἀφέσεως καὶ "ἡ ψυχὴ ὑμῶν" σωθήσεται, καὶ οὐχ ἁπλῶς σωθήσεται, ἀλλὰ καὶ "ὄψεται τὸ μακρόβιον σπέρμα." τοῦτο δὲ ἦν τὸ ὑπ' αὐτοῦ καταβληθὲν εἰς ἀνθρώπους, περὶ οὗ "ἐν παραβολαῖς" διδάσκων ἔλεγεν· "ἐξῆλθεν ὁ σπείρων τοῦ σπεῖραι," καὶ πάλιν· "ὁμοία ἐστὶν ἡ βασιλεία τῶν οὐρανῶν ἀνθρώπῳ σπείραντι καλὸν σπέρμα ἐν τῷ ἰδίῳ ἀγρῷ." ἐὰν οὖν "δῶτε περὶ ἁμαρτίας," τοῦτο τὸ λογικὸν καὶ οὐράνιον "σπέρμα ὄψεται ἡ ψυχὴ ὑμῶν."

303. *Comm. Isa.* 1.32 on Isa. 4:2-3 (GCS 9:26 l. 28): it is the apostles who sow τὰ λογικὰ καὶ ἐπουράνια σπέρματα.

304. *Comm. Isa.* 2.42 on Isa. 53:11-12 (GCS 9:338 ll. 29-31, ed. Ziegler): καὶ "τῶν ἰσχυρῶν" δὲ "ἐμέρισε [LXX: μεριεῖ] σκῦλα" [Isa. 53:12], τῶν ἀντικειμένων δηλαδὴ δυνάμεων, τῶν τε πονηρῶν δαιμόνων, ὧν ἐξαρπάσας τὰς αἰχμαλώτους ὑπ' αὐτοῖς γενομένας ψυχάς, "σκῦλα" ἑαυτῷ ἐποιήσατο = "And 'he divided [LXX: will divide] the spoils of the strong,' clearly [means] of the hostile powers and of the evil demons, from whom he snatched the souls held captive under their power and made them 'spoils' for himself." Theodoret expresses the same idea more succinctly: Καὶ τῶν ἰσχυρῶν μεριεῖ σκῦλα [Isa. 53:12]. Ἰσχυροὺς καλεῖ τοὺς δαίμονας, σκῦλα δὲ τοὺς ἀνθρώπους, "He [Isaiah] calls the demons 'the strong,' and people 'the spoils'" (*Commentaire sur Isaïe*, SC 315:160 ll. 175-76, ed. Guinot).

[The leaders of Judaism] subjected the Christ of God to such punishment, even though he was sinless. Therefore he adds: "For he did not commit a sin [LXX: a lawless deed], nor was deceit found in his mouth" (Isa. 53:9). And this was the strangely marvelous thing[305] about our Savior's most divine virtue, I mean that throughout his life on earth he remained sinless and blameless in word and deed: "For no one has been pure from uncleanness, not even if his life was one day, or he was alone" (Job 14:4-5).[306]

Jesus' sinlessness is naturally guaranteed by the fact that the Logos lives in him — something Eusebius learned from Origen.[307] Because the Logos is active in Jesus but also effective in the world, Eusebius can connect the effect of individual forgiveness and salvation to the individual's confession. At the end of this interpretation stands a somewhat spectacular summary based on Isaiah 53:12a:

"For this reason he himself will inherit many" (Isa. 53:12a). For this reason namely, that he took upon himself the sins of the many, therefore he has also been able to make the many his inheritance.[308]

In conclusion, it must be admitted that there is little that is exciting in Eusebius's interpretation, which in many ways follows an old, well-marked

---

305. Greek τὸ ξένον; cf. Lampe, *PGL* 932 def. C.1.

306. *Comm. Isa.* 2.42 on Isa. 53:9-10 (GCS 9:337 ll. 21-26, ed. Ziegler): ἀναμάρτητον ὄντα τὸν Χριστὸν τοῦ θεοῦ τοιαύτῃ κολάσει ὑποβεβλήκασι. διὸ ἐπιλέγει· "ὅτι ἁμαρτίαν [LXX: ἀνομίαν] οὐκ ἐποίησεν, οὐδὲ εὑρέθη δόλος ἐν τῷ στόματι αὐτοῦ." καὶ τοῦτ' ἦν τὸ ξένον τῆς τοῦ σωτῆρος ἡμῶν θειοτέρας ἀρετῆς, λέγω δὲ τὸ δι' ὅλης τῆς τοῦ βίου ζωῆς ἀναμάρτητον καὶ ἀνεπίληπτον ἐν λόγῳ καὶ ἔργῳ. "οὐδεὶς γοῦν καθαρὸς γέγονεν ἀπὸ ῥύπου, οὐδ' εἰ μία ἡμέρα ἦν ἡ ζωὴ αὐτοῦ ἢ μόνος αὐτός." Eusebius's quotation from Job 14:4-5 departs from the LXX version: τίς γὰρ καθαρὸς ἔσται ἀπὸ ῥύπου; ἀλλ' οὐθείς. (5) ἐὰν καὶ μία ἡμέρα ὁ βίος αὐτοῦ ἐπὶ τῆς γῆς, ἀριθμητοὶ δὲ μῆνες αὐτοῦ παρὰ σοί, "For who shall be pure from uncleanness? No one. Even if his life should be one day upon the earth, his months are numbered before you."

307. Grillmeier, *Christ in Christian Tradition*, 146.

308. *Comm. Isa.* 2.42 on Isa. 53:11-12 (GCS 9:338 ll. 20-22, ed. Ziegler): "διὰ τοῦτο αὐτὸς κληρονομήσει πολλούς" [Isa. 53:12a]. διὰ τοῦτο γὰρ ἐπειδὴ εἰς ἑαυτὸν τὰς τῶν πολλῶν ἀνέλαβεν ἁμαρτίας, τούτου χάριν καὶ δεδύνηται κλῆρον ἑαυτῷ ποιήσασθαι τοὺς πάντας. A periphrastic interpretation of the last four verses of the fourth Servant Song is found in *Dem. ev.* 3.2.69-70 (GCS 6:107 ll. 2-14, ed. Heikel; trans. Ferrar, *Proof of the Gospel*, 116 [modified]): "For therefore He is said 'to inherit the many, and to share the spoils of the strong.' And I consider that it is beyond doubt that in these words the resurrection from the dead of the subject of the prophecy is shown. For how else can we regard Him as led as a sheep to the slaughter (Isa. 53:7), and delivered to death for the sins of the Jewish people (v. 8), numbered with transgressors (v. 12), and delivered to burial (v. 9), then cleansed by the Lord (v. 10), and seeing light with Him (v. 11), and inheriting many, and dividing the spoils with His friends (v. 12)?"

trail. If we knew the commentary of the slightly later figure Didymus the Blind of Alexandria, who was also influenced by Origen, lines of influence could perhaps be traced more precisely. Eusebius's original contribution remains very small, consisting for the most part of his theological application of the passage to the present, which he accomplishes with help of the statement about the kings in Isaiah 52:15b. But is it first and foremost originality that we expect from a commentary today? Or is it not rather solid scientific information, so that the old message can be preached in new, original words? Eusebius's commentary basically consists of the literal reproduction of the tetraplaric recensions for almost every verse of the biblical text — Aquila, Symmachus, Theodotion, and the Septuagint — and their explanation. Even if these explanations come out differently from the way we would organize a synoptic commentary on the ancient versions today,[309] in comparison to Theodoret's more random commentary, Eusebius still uses a consistent scientific procedure.

As is well known, increasingly precise formulation of the Christological dogma made Christ's suffering more and more of a problem — mention of the "axiom of divine impassibility" suffices to illustrate the point.[310] In the later fourth century and the fifth century, the theological topoi used to interpret Isaiah 52–53 generally followed the course of Origen's and Eusebius's thinking. Over against these Alexandrians, perhaps the Antiochians with their decided orientation to the biblical wording formed a certain exception. Theodoret of Cyrrhus, who must suffice here as an example, tried in his Isaiah commentary (ca. 447)[311] to maintain the reality of the suffering of *both* natures of Christ, as Isaiah 53 says:

> Next he teaches the appearance of the dishonor and disgrace: "Being a man in a plague" (Isa. 53:2). He showed the nature that received the passion: for the body was nailed to the cross, but the divine nature was making the passion its own.[312]

309. For this see H. Hegermann, *Jesaja 53 in Hexapla, Targum und Peschitta*, BFCT 2/56 (1954), including especially the synoptic presentation of the texts in the appendix. For commentary on Isaiah 53 after Eusebius, which cannot be covered here, see the overview in Haag, "Gottesknecht," 358-77, including Athanasius, Cyrill (pp. 358-61), John Chrysostom, Theodoret (pp. 361-64), and Procopius of Gaza (pp. 364-65).

310. Cf. Frohnhofen, *APATHEIA TOU THEOU*; W. Elert, "Die theopaschitische Formel," *TLZ* 75 (1950): 195-206; idem, "Der leidende Christus: Bild und Dogma," in *Der Ausgang der altkirchlichen Christologie: Eine Untersuchung über Theodor von Pharan und seine Zeit als Einführung in die alte Dogmengeschichte* (1957), 71-132.

311. Theodoret's editor and translator, Jean-Noel Guinot, dates the commentary around 447 (*Commentaire sur Isaïe*, 1:18-19).

312. Theodoret, *Comm. Isa.* 17 (Guinot, *Commentaire sur Isaïe*, 3:148 ll. 55-57): Εἶτα διδάσκει τῆς ἀτιμίας καὶ ἀδοξίας τὰ εἴδη· "Ἄνθρωπος ἐν πληγῇ ὤν" [Isa. 53:2]. Ἔδειξε [τὴν]

Whereas the body's being nailed (προσηλόω) to the cross was a passive event, Christ's divine nature *actively* appropriated the suffering. It is not automatically affected in a passive sense, but first makes itself into an affected nature,[313] thus preserving divine sovereignty.

3. Hilary of Poitiers, De Trinitate (355-356)[314]

Precisely against this background of Theodoret, the solution to the impassibility problem proposed by Hilary, bishop of Poitiers and untiring champion of Nicene orthodoxy,[315] looks very modest. In order to refute the Arian opponents who saw the suffering one as a God of inferior rank, Hilary lets himself be drawn into doubting the reality of Jesus' suffering at all, and justifies this with reference to Isaiah 52–53:

> Hence, the only-begotten God endured all the weaknesses of our sufferings that pressed upon Him, but He endured them by the power of His own nature. . . . Hence, He endured the weakness of our body in His own body in such a way as to take upon Himself the sufferings of our body by the power of His own body. Prophetic utterance also bears witness to this faith of ours when it declares: "He bears our sins and suffers for us. And we considered *him* to be in sorrows, in blows, and in torture. But he was wounded on account of our iniquities, and he was made weak on account of our sins" (Isa. 53:4-5). The judgment of human reasoning is therefore deceived if it concludes that He experiences pain because He suffers. (*De Trinitate* 10.47)[316]

φύσιν τὴν δεξαμένην τὸ πάθος· τὸ σῶμα γὰρ τῷ σταυρῷ προσηλώθη, ἡ δὲ θεότης ᾠκειοῦτο τὸ πάθος. On the sense of the verb οἰκειόω here and in the next note, see Lampe, *PGL* 938, def. B.4.

313. On the historical dogmatic situation presupposed here see Guinot, *Commentaire sur Isaïe*, 1:149-51 n. 3, who points to Cyrill of Alexandria, *Epistle* 3 to Nestorius, §6 (text: *Acta conciliorum oecumenicorum*, tome 1, vol. 1, part 1: *Concilium universale Ephesenum*, ed. E. Schwartz [1927], 33-42, esp. 37 ll. 9-12; numbered *Ep.* 17 in Lampe, *PGL* xx). [[(Tr.) Cyril says that the Son, who is begotten of the Father and therefore God the only begotten, is impassible (ἀπαθής) according to his own nature, but has nevertheless suffered in the flesh for us according to the Scriptures and was crucified in the body (on the divine nature of Christ as ἀπαθής see *PGL* 171, def. 4).]] Cyril then adds that when he was crucified, τὰ τῆς ἰδίας σαρκὸς ἀπαθῶς οἰκειούμενος πάθη, "he impassibly made his own the passions of his own flesh" (p. 37 ll. 11-12).

314. On the date of *De Trinitate* see, e.g., Quasten, *Patrology*, 4:40.

315. H. C. Brennecke, *Hilarius von Poitiers und die Bischofsopposition gegen Konstantius II: Untersuchungen zur dritten Phase des Arianischen Streites (337-361)*, PTS 26 (1984).

316. Hilary, *Trin.* 10.47, trans. S. McKenna, *The Trinity*, FC 25 (1954), 434-35 (modified). Text: *Passus igitur unigenitus Deus est omnes incurrentes in se passionum nostrarum infirmitates.*

At the end of this exposition of Isaiah 52–53 stands the claim that people would be wrong to speak of Jesus' suffering, because it is written, *et nos aestimauimus eum* (so Hilary; Vulgate: *et nos putavimus eum*) *in doloribus esse,* etc. — we merely *thought* of him as experiencing suffering; in reality he did not. For as Hilary says:

> *Et pro nobis dolet, non et doloris nostri dolet sensu, qui et "habitu ut homo repertus"* (Phil. 2:7);[317] *habens in se doloris corpus, sed non habens naturam dolendi.* (*De Trinitate* 10.47, CCSL 62A:501 ll. 20-22)

And He endures pain for us, but He does not endure pain with the feeling of our pain, because He who was also "found in appearance as man" (Phil. 2:7), while He has in Himself a body subject to pain, does not have a nature that feels pain. (FC 25:435, trans. McKenna [modified])

When Hilary says that Christ was "found in appearance *(habitus)* as man," one is tempted to say that this concerns only the outward *habitus*. The reader wonders how this can be; there is an explanation in an earlier chapter (*Trin.* 10.23):

> Jesus Christ . . . has assumed a true manhood according to the likeness of our manhood without sacrificing His divinity. Although a blow struck Him, or a wound pierced Him, or ropes bound Him, or a suspension raised Him, the things indeed wrought the vehemence of the passion, but did not bring Him the pain of the passion, just as any weapon that passes through water, penetrates fire, or wounds the air inflicts, it is true, all these pains which are proper to its *nature (natura)* so that it penetrates, it pierces, it wounds, but the pains that are directed against these objects do not linger in their nature, since it is contrary to nature for water to be penetrated, for

---

Sed passus uirtute naturae suae. . . . Secundum quod ita ex infirmitate corporis nostri passus in corpore est, ut passiones corporis nostri corporis sui uirtute susciperet. Et huius fidei nostrae etiam sermo propheticus testis est, cum ait: "Hic peccata nostra portat et pro nobis dolet. Et nos aestimauimus eum in doloribus esse et in plaga et in uexatione. Ipse autem uulneratus est propter iniquitates nostras, et infirmatus est propter peccata nostra." Fallitur ergo humanae aestimationis opinio, putans hunc dolere quod patitur (*Sancti Hilarii Pictaviensis Episcopi Opera: De Trinitate,* 2 vols., ed. P. Smulders, CCSL 62, 62A [1979-80], here CCSL 62A:500 l. 8-501 l. 17). Smulders's Latin text is now reprinted with French translation in *La Trinité: Hilaire de Poitiers,* ed. P. Smulders et al., 3 vols., SC 443, 448, 462 (1999-2001).

317. Hilary's quotation of Phil. 2:7 *habitu ut homo repertus* = σχήματι εὑρεθεὶς ὡς ἄνθρωπος follows a non-Vulgate version (cf. Vg.: *habitu inventus ut homo*). For Hilary's version see *Epistulae ad Philippenses et ad Colossenses,* ed. H. J. Frede, VL 24/2 (1966-71), 120, where it appears as a subset of text-type I.

fire to be pierced, or for the air to be wounded, although it is characteristic of the nature of a weapon to wound, to penetrate, and to pierce.[318]

Just as a weapon or missile penetrates through the air and so acts according to its nature, so also in Jesus' passion people and things act according to their nature: they strike, flog, nail, break bones. By the same token, just as the nature of the air cannot be changed when it is pierced through, so also the Son of God suffers no pain on the cross — his nature does not allow it. But does this "half-God" still possess full humanity on earth? At this point and with this author, the Christian interpretation of the text has run into a dead end. The dogmatic premises of the doctrine of God have completely superimposed their own framework onto the text that ought to be speaking here. This total suppression of the literal sense cannot be justified by the aim of anti-Arian polemic alone; this can only make it a little more understandable.[319] There were other no less anti-Arian solutions.

Hilary's complete dissolution and leveling of suffering in his interpretation of Isaiah 52–53 is especially conspicuous when we recall the theopaschite formulas of Melito[320] and the attempts of the two Alexandrians, Clement and Origen, to retain the literal sense of the ugliness of Christ despite all allegorizing (see above, pp. 287-91). In the Jewish-Christian dialogue of the second century people still seriously argued about the problem of Jesus' suffering; to doubt its reality or indeed to deny it, as Hilary did, would hardly have occurred to anyone in the Church, only to various "docetic" types at the margin or outside the mainstream Church.[321] Hilary's (basically

318. Trans. McKenna, FC 25:414-15. Hilary, *Trin.* 10.23 (CCSL 62A:477 ll. 2-13, ed. Smulders): *Christus Iesus . . . hominem uerum secundum similitudinem nostri hominis, non deficiens a se Deo, sumpsit. In quo, quamuis aut ictus incideret, aut uulnus descenderet, aut nodi concurrent, aut suspensio eleuarent, adferrent quidem haec inpetum passionis, non tamen dolorem passionis inferrent: ut telum aliquod aut aquam perforans aut ignem conpungnens aut aera uulnerans, omnes quidem has passiones naturae suae infert, ut foret, ut conpungat, ut uulneret, sed naturam suam in haec passio inlata non retinet, dum in natura non est, uel aquam forari, uel pungi ignem, uel aerem uulnerari, quamuis naturae teli sit et uulnerare et conpungere et forare.*

319. Further examples from the works of Hilary are provided by R. P. Hanson, *The Search for the Christian Doctrine of God: The Arian Controversy 318-381* (1988), 496-501. Although the relevance of such hermeneutical issues, including the interpretation of Isaiah 52–53, to the Arian controversy cannot be covered here, see De Durand, "Sa génération," 644-47, as well as B. Studer's detailed review in *Augustinianum* 22 (1982): 611-14 of P. C. Burns, *The Christology in Hilary of Poitiers' Commentary on Matthew*, SEAug 16 (1981).

320. Recall Melito of Sardis, *Fragment 7* (ed. Hall, *On Pascha*, 70): Ὁ θεὸς πέπονθεν ὑπὸ δεξιᾶς Ἰσραηλίτιδος, "God has suffered by an Israelite right hand" (see above n. 175).

321. Cf. N. Brox, "'Doketismus' — Eine Problemanzeige," *ZKG* 95 (1984): 301-14; P. Weigandt, "Der Doketismus im Urchristentum und in der theologischen Entwicklung des zweiten Jahrhunderts," Ph.D. dissertation, Heidelberg, 1961.

docetic)[322] dissolution of Christ's suffering shows how problematic Jesus' real suffering and bitter death — and therefore also Isaiah 52:13–53:12 — had become for the highly educated theologians of the fourth century. In this Hilary can be compared to Eusebius with his fundamental distinction between the crucified one and the Logos, and also with his idea that the Logos left the body for a short time while it was being crucified (see Eusebius, *Theoph.* 3.57, above p. 304). At this point the Christological development had distanced itself from the text, and one gets the impression that despite all the positive achievements of ancient Church Christology — which would be foolish to deny — it also had its deficits.

V. Conclusion

If exegetes today either allow Jesus' self-consciousness to be strongly stamped by Isaiah 52–53 according to the theses of Joachim Jeremias, or claim that the Christological understanding of this text is the only "true" one, then naturally the ancient Church and its Scripture interpretation will be relieved of the charge of having unreflectively adopted an already more or less problematic usurpation of a Jewish text by the individual New Testament authors. The exegesis of the ancient Church would thereby lose some of its characteristic strangeness for us, with its unbroken Christological interpretation of the prophetic text.

However one thinks here, the development of the exegesis of this text in the ancient Church does pose a problem. In essential points it leads very far away, not only from the passage's original Old Testament sense, but also from its original Christian sense. Of course the false trails of ancient Church exegesis need not in and of themselves cause sleepless nights for a Protestant theologian, since these traditions are not theologically normative in our church. Nevertheless, the development can serve today as a warning: In Eusebius's historical-theological interpretation and in Hilary's docetic interpretation — as well as in other problematic trends in the Christian exegesis of this text during the first centuries — one can see that a true interpretation, even *the* true interpretation, of a text does not protect against bitter errors in individual details. (And the docetic error is one of the most bitter errors of Christian theology.)

Nevertheless, the question about *the* true interpretation of a text has been raised; within a Christian theology one will hardly be able to say:

322. Hilary is judged similarly by Hanson, *The Search for the Christian Doctrine of God*, 501: "And yet Docetic he certainly was, albeit in a sophisticated way."

In vain; the genuine ring was not
Demonstrable; — almost as little as
Today the genuine faith.[323]

But one will also be at least as concerned to ensure that the entire Jewish interpretation of a text will not be declared untrue from the start, lest the access to the Father opened to all through the Servant again be obstructed by humans. Should we draw such lessons from our study of the history of Christian engagement with the fourth Servant Song, we will have used the inheritance entrusted to us wrongly. We inherit it rightly only when we adopt and keep both Jewish and patristic interpretations as conversation partners in our efforts at responsible interpretation today, without repeating them — or their errors.

---

323. Gotthold Ephraim Lessing, *Nathan der Weise*, Act 3, Scene 7, ll. 446-48: "Umsonst; der rechte Ring war nicht Erweislich; — Fast so unerweislich, als Uns jetzt — der rechte Glaube" (Lessing, *Werke und Briefe in zwölf Bänden*, ed. W. Barner et al., vol. 9 [1993], 557). English: "Nathan the Wise," trans. B. Q. Morgan, in *Nathan the Wise, Minna von Barnhelm, and Other Plays and Writings*, ed. P. Demetz (1991), 173-275, esp. 233.

APPENDIX:

Isaiah 53 in the Codex A
Text of 1 Clement 16:3-14

Daniel P. Bailey

As mentioned above (p. 237), Clement of Rome's text of Isa. 53:1-12 in *1 Clem.* 16:3-14 exhibits only minimal departures from the LXX. The following presentation illustrates this. The letter of *1 Clement* is attested most famously in the biblical manuscript Codex Alexandrinus (A),[1] but the A text of Isaiah 53 in *1 Clem.* 16:3-14 is independent and is not completely assimilated to the A text of the book of Isaiah. Admittedly, *1 Clement* sometimes agrees with the Alexandrine text type of Codex A in Isaiah 53 against the Origenic text of Vaticanus (B) or the mixed text of Sinaiticus (S) (see below, nn. 3, 14). But at other times *1 Clement* agrees with B and the Origenic recension that B represents, over against A (see nn. 6, 9). Since all the main Septuagint manuscripts are in reasonable agreement in Isaiah 53, the correct observation above that the text-type of *1 Clement* is basically Alexandrine is almost equivalent to saying that it resembles the Septuagint version of Isaiah 53 as a whole.

The Codex A text of *1 Clem.* 16:3-14 is reproduced below for comparison. The manuscript does not set off Isaiah 53 in any special way. *1 Clement* is also preserved in one other Greek manuscript, Codex Hierosolymitanus (H), as well as in Latin (L), Syriac (S), and Coptic (C, C¹) versions, whose evidence is included below. The *1 Clement* textual tradition of Isaiah 53 is also correlated against that of the Septuagint and its variants as represented in the editions of J. Ziegler (*Isaias*, vol. 14, Göttingen LXX [1939]) and A. Rahlfs (*Septuaginta* [1935]). For *1 Clement* we have used the editions of A. Jaubert (*Clément de Rome, Épître aux Corinthiens*, SC 167 [1971]) and K. Bihlmeyer (*Die apostolischen Väter* [1924]).

Boldface type below highlights portions of the Codex A text of *1 Clement* 16:3-14 that differ either from the critical LXX text of Ziegler or from the other

---

1. Cf. F. G. Kenyon, et al., eds., *The Codex Alexandrinus (Royal ms. 1 D v-viii) in Reduced Photographic Facsimile*, vol. 5: *New Testament and Clementine Epistles* (London: British Museum, 1909), fol. 161ʳ-161ᵛ, or E. M. Thompson, *Facsimile of the Codex Alexandrinus* (London: British Museum, 1879-83).

manuscripts or versions of *1 Clement,* in which case the A text of *1 Clement* may agree (nn. 2, 10) or disagree (nn. 6, 13) with the critical LXX. Several of the distinctive readings of *1 Clement* over against the critical LXX are also attested by other church fathers or various Septuagint manuscripts (see nn. 5, 6, 8, 9, 11, 12). This strengthens the impression that the *1 Clement* text of Isaiah 53 stands within the main Septuagint manuscript tradition; it is not a proto-recension of some other Greek version. The textual variants may involve word order (Isa. 53:3, 5, 10; see nn. 2, 6, 12), added words in *1 Clement* (Isa. 53:3; see n. 5), or the omission from *1 Clement* Codex A (or *1 Clem.* mss as a whole) of words preserved in other manuscripts (Isa. 53:3, 7, 8, 12: see nn. 3, 9, 10, 13). Clement's verb tense differs from that of the critical LXX text in Isa. 53:7 (κείραντος: see n. 8), and a different verb appears in Isa. 53:8 (ἥκει: see n. 11). The distinctive Clementine reading of Isa. 53:3 (see n. 4) repeats the term εἶδος, "form": ἀλλὰ τὸ εἶδος αὐτοῦ ἄτιμον, ἐκλεῖπον παρὰ *τὸ εἶδος* τῶν ἀνθρώπων, "but his form was dishonorable, inferior to *the form of* (other) men." But this is not substantially different from the LXX, ἐκλεῖπον παρὰ πάντας ἀνθρώπους, "inferior to all men." The most important and theologically interesting Clementine reading, καὶ κύριος παρέδωκεν αὐτὸν *ὑπὲρ* τῶν ἁμαρτιῶν ἡμῶν, "and the Lord delivered him *for* our sins [LXX: *to* our sins]" (Isa. 53:6; see n. 7), has already been discussed above (p. 238).

Verse numbers of *1 Clement* are in parentheses and boldfaced; verse numbers of Isaiah 53 are in plain type (cf. Jaubert, SC 167:124-28; Bihlmeyer, 43-44):

1 Clem. **16:(3)** Isa. 53:1 Κύριε, τίς ἐπίστευσεν τῇ ἀκοῇ ἡμῶν; καὶ ὁ βραχίων κυρίου τίνι ἀπεκαλύφθη; 2 Ἀνηγγείλαμεν ἐναντίον αὐτοῦ, ὡς παιδίον, ὡς ῥίζα ἐν γῇ διψώσῃ· 3 οὐκ ἔστιν **εἶδος αὐτῷ**[2] οὐδὲ δόξα, καὶ εἴδομεν αὐτόν, καὶ οὐκ εἶχεν εἶδος οὐδὲ κάλλος, ἀλλὰ τὸ εἶδος αὐτοῦ ἄτιμον, (omit καὶ[3]) ἐκλεῖπον παρὰ **τὸ εἶδος τῶν** ἀνθρώπων·[4] ἄνθρωπος ἐν πληγῇ ὢν **καὶ πόνῳ**[5] καὶ εἰδὼς φέρειν μαλακίαν, ὅτι ἀπέστραπται τὸ πρόσωπον αὐτοῦ, ἠτιμάσθη καὶ οὐκ ἐλογίσθη. **(4)** 4 Οὗτος τὰς ἁμαρτίας ἡμῶν φέρει καὶ περὶ ἡμῶν ὀδυνᾶται, καὶ ἡμεῖς ἐλογισάμεθα αὐτὸν εἶναι ἐν πόνῳ καὶ ἐν πληγῇ καὶ ἐν κακώσει.

---

2. Word order: εἶδος αὐτῷ *1 Clem.* ms A (= LXX text); transposed: αὐτῷ εἶδος *1 Clem.* ms H, Latin (LXX ms Q).

3. Inner-LXX variant: ἐκλεῖπον is preceded by καί (cf. MT) in S, the Origenic recension (including B), parts of the catena group, Justin Martyr, *1 Apol.* 50.6, etc. (details in Ziegler). The καί is absent from *1 Clem.* (also Justin *Dial.* 13.3) and from Codex A of Isaiah = LXX text (Rahlfs, Ziegler).

4. Cf. LXX text as attested by A, Q (cf. Rahlfs): ἐκλεῖπον παρὰ πάντας ἀνθρώπους.

5. *1 Clement's* καὶ πόνῳ in Isa. 53:3 is an addition over against the critical LXX text but is attested by two LXX mss (565, 958) and by Origen (cf. Ziegler). It is apparently an assimilation to the LXX's ἐν πόνῳ in Isa. 53:4.

(5) 5 Αὐτὸς δὲ ἐτραυματίσθη διὰ τὰς **ἁμαρτίας**[6] ἡμῶν καὶ μεμαλάκισται διὰ τὰς **ἀνομίας**[6] ἡμῶν· παιδεία εἰρήνης ἡμῶν ἐπ' αὐτόν, τῷ μώλωπι αὐτοῦ ἡμεῖς ἰάθημεν. (6) 6 Πάντες ὡς πρόβατα ἐπλανήθημεν, ἄνθρωπος τῇ ὁδῷ αὐτοῦ ἐπλανήθη. (7) Καὶ κύριος παρέδωκεν αὐτὸν **ὑπὲρ τῶν ἁμαρτιῶν**[7] ἡμῶν, 7 καὶ αὐτὸς διὰ τὸ κεκακῶσθαι οὐκ ἀνοίγει τὸ στόμα. Ὡς πρόβατον ἐπὶ σφαγὴν ἤχθη, καὶ ὡς ἀμνὸς ἐναντίον τοῦ **κείραντος**[8] (omit αὐτὸν[9]) ἄφωνος, οὕτως οὐκ ἀνοίγει τὸ στόμα αὐτοῦ. 8 Ἐν τῇ ταπεινώσει (omit αὐτοῦ[10]) ἡ κρίσις αὐτοῦ ἤρθη. (8) Τὴν γενεὰν αὐτοῦ τίς διηγήσεται; ὅτι αἴρεται ἀπὸ τῆς γῆς ἡ ζωὴ αὐτοῦ. (9) Ἀπὸ τῶν ἀνομιῶν τοῦ λαοῦ μου **ἥκει**[11] εἰς θάνατον. (10) 9 Καὶ δώσω τοὺς πονηροὺς ἀντὶ τῆς ταφῆς αὐτοῦ καὶ τοὺς πλουσίους ἀντὶ τοῦ θανάτου αὐτοῦ· ὅτι ἀνομίαν οὐκ ἐποίησεν, οὐδὲ εὑρέθη δόλος ἐν τῷ στόματι αὐτοῦ. 10 Καὶ κύριος βούλεται καθαρίσαι αὐτὸν τῆς πληγῆς. (11) Ἐὰν δῶτε περὶ ἁμαρτίας, ἡ ψυχὴ ὑμῶν ὄψεται σπέρμα μακρόβιον. (12) Καὶ **κύριος βούλεται**[12] ἀφελεῖν ἀπὸ τοῦ πόνου τῆς ψυχῆς αὐτοῦ, 11 δεῖξαι αὐτῷ φῶς καὶ πλάσαι τῇ συνέσει, δικαιῶσαι δίκαιον εὖ δουλεύοντα πολλοῖς· καὶ τὰς ἁμαρτίας αὐτῶν αὐτὸς ἀνοίσει. (13) 12 Διὰ τοῦτο αὐτὸς κληρονομήσει πολλοὺς καὶ τῶν ἰσχυρῶν μεριεῖ σκῦλα, ἀνθ' ὧν παρεδόθη εἰς θάνατον ἡ ψυχὴ αὐτοῦ, καὶ (omit ἐν[13]) τοῖς ἀνόμοις ἐλογίσθη· (14) καὶ αὐτὸς ἁμαρτίας πολλῶν ἀνήνεγκεν καὶ διὰ τὰς ἁμαρτίας[14] αὐτῶν παρεδόθη.

6. Word order: ἁμαρτίας . . . ἀνομίας *1 Clem.* ms A, Latin; LXX mss 86, B (with Origenic recension); catena group, Bohairic, Eusebius, etc. Transposed: ἀνομίας . . . ἁμαρτίας *1 Clem.* ms H, Syriac, Coptic (C, C¹); LXX text as attested by S, A.

7. Preposition + genitive or straight dative: ὑπὲρ τῶν ἁμαρτιῶν *1 Clem.*; ταῖς ἁμαρτίαις LXX text (Rahlfs, Ziegler).

8. Tense: aor. ptc. κείραντος *1 Clem.*, LXX mss Sᶜ A (+106) V etc.; Barnabas. Pres. ptc. κείροντος LXX text (cf. Acts 8:32).

9. LXX text (Rahlfs, Ziegler) reads αὐτόν with LXX Codex A. This is lacking in *1 Clement* and in LXX B (representing part of the Origenic recension), S, the catena group, Eusebius, etc.

10. In agreement with the LXX text, the Greek mss A and H of *1 Clement* lack the αὐτοῦ following ταπεινώσει in Isa. 53:8a. However, this word is included in the Latin, Syriac, and Coptic versions of *1 Clement* as well as in several LXX mss (106, Lucianic recension, etc.) and in most mss of Acts 8:33.

11. Word choice: ἥκει *1 Clem.*, LXX ms Qᵐᵍ, other LXX mss, Justin Martyr *Dial.* 13.8; *1 Apol.* 51.1, Theodoret. Read: ἤχθη LXX text.

12. Word order: κύριος βούλεται (second occurrence) *1 Clem.*, Sinaiticus, Eusebius; transposed: βούλεται κύριος LXX text.

13. Inclusion/exclusion of preposition ἐν: Omit, as in καὶ τοῖς ἀνόμοις, *1 Clem.* ms A; include: καὶ ἐν τοῖς ἀνόμοις LXX text, so also following mss and versions of *1 Clement*: H (cf. Luke 22:37), Latin *cum*, Syriac, Coptic¹.

14. Inner-LXX variant: text ἁμαρτίας LXX mss A, Q, followed by *1 Clem.* mss A, H. Variant ἀνομίας LXX mss S, B, Qᵐᵍ, 88-Syh, parts of the Lucianic and catena traditions, Justin Martyr *Dial.* 13.12; *1 Apol.* 51.5, Eusebius, Theodoret, etc.

"Our Suffering and Crucified Messiah" (Dial. *111.2*)

Justin Martyr's Allusions to Isaiah 53 in His Dialogue with Trypho *with Special Reference to the New Edition of M. Marcovich*

Daniel P. Bailey

Summary

Justin Martyr's *Dialogue with Trypho* makes the greatest use of Isaiah 53 of any Christian work of the first two centuries. Twelve passages quote material from Isaiah 53, but the number of additional passages that allude to Isaiah 53 is disputed. While the index of the older edition by E. J. Goodspeed (1914) lists a total of 25 passages, the citation apparatus — not the (faulty) index — of the new edition by M. Marcovich refers to Isaiah 53 in 36 passages (*Iustini Martyris Dialogus cum Tryphone*, PTS 47 [1997]). While Marcovich's figure of 36 is accurate, its accuracy is not immediately apparent, since Marcovich's apparatus includes allusions made by a term with no lexical contact to Isaiah 53. The term is παθητός, which describes the Messiah as "passible" or "susceptible to suffering." This occurs 19 times in 17 paragraphs. Marcovich italicizes 18 of the 19 occurrences and refers 11 of the 17 paragraphs to Isa 53:8d ("he was led to death"). By contrast, Goodspeed italicized only two of these occurrences, in *Dial.* 110.2 and 126.1, the latter being the only place where Justin explicitly attributes the idea of a "passible" Messiah to Isaiah. Is Marcovich then guilty of over-interpretation in the other instances? Or is there implicit in Justin's writing a literary structure and network of vocabulary that marks the term παθητός as Isaianic almost every time it is used? This study supports Marcovich's interpretation and explores the means that Justin uses to mark παθητός as Isaianic, such as the contrast of Isaiah 53 and Daniel 7 within the two Parousias scheme. Theologically, Trypho and Justin agree that the Messiah is to be παθητός according to Isaiah 53, but disagree whether a παθητὸς Χριστός has yet arrived, and over the force of the Torah's curse upon crucifixion in Deut 21:23. Against Trypho's notion of a Messiah who may suffer but not be cursed, i.e. crucified, Justin asserts, "Our suffering and crucified Messiah was not cursed by the law" (*Dial.* 111.2), and suggests that it is largely "Gentiles who believe in the suffering Messiah" (*Dial.* 52.1). This may reflect the historical reality both of an actual dialogue with an individual Trypho (T. J. Horner) and of the formative role that Isaiah 53 played in Justin's Christian community (D. J. Bingham).

1. Introduction: Editing and Interpretation

As A. Harnack has pointed out, Justin Martyr's *Dialogue with Trypho*[1] is the longest surviving Christian text prior to the works of Irenaeus and Tertullian.[2] It may originally have been almost as long as the four Gospels put together,[3] depending on the length of the lost section between the passages currently num-

---

1. The following texts and translations of Justin's *Dialogue with Trypho* have been consulted. Texts are taken from Marcovich (cited by his name alone), both with and without his conjectural emendations <. . .>, as indicated (see e.g. n. 22). See also the reservations about Marcovich's textual criticism by T. P. Halton (below n. 33). The *Dialogue* is cited by the standard paragraph numbers, followed by Marcovich's line numbers (*ll.*) where necessary. See M. Marcovich, *Iustini Martyris Dialogus cum Tryphone*, PTS 47 (1997); E. J. Goodspeed, *Die ältesten Apologeten* (1914), 90-265; G. Archambault, *Dialogue avec Tryphon*, 2 vols. (1909); Johann Karl Theodor (J. C. T.) von Otto, *Corpus apologetarum Christianorum saeculi secundi,* 9 vols. in 5: Vol. 1, *Iustini philosophi et martyris opera quae feruntur omnia,* 2 parts (Jena, ³1876-1877), part 2, pp. 1-499. (See the review of these editions in Marcovich, 6-7.) Translations: St. Justin Martyr, *Dialogue with Trypho,* trans. T. B. Falls, rev. T. P. Halton, ed. M. Slusser, FC Selections 3 (2003) (cited as Falls and Halton); original edition: *The First Apology, The Second Apology, Dialogue with Trypho* (etc.), trans. T. B. Falls, FC 6 (1948); *The Dialogue with Trypho,* trans. A. Lukyn Williams (1930). Translations of the *Dialogue* in this essay have usually kept an eye on Williams or Falls and Halton, yet modifications [= mod.] and original translations have also been introduced. Translation and commentary on Isa 52:13–53:12 LXX may be found in by E. R. Ekblad, *Isaiah's Servant Poems According to the Septuagint,* CBET 23 (1999) 167-266.

2. Cf. A. Harnack, "Judentum und Judenchristentum in Justins Dialog mit Trypho nebst einer Collation der Pariser Handschrift Nr. 450," TU 39/1 (1913) 47-98, esp. 47. Cf. T. J. Horner, *Listening to Trypho: Justin Martyr's* Dialogue *Reconsidered,* CBET 28 (2001) 7: "The *Dialogue* is a long and rambling text. It is far and away the longest Christian document we have from the second century." Apparently Horner means not the longest second-century Christian document absolutely (Irenaeus's *Against Heresies* is much longer), but the longest one relevant to "the study of early Jewish/Christian relations" (p. 6).

3. Cf. Harnack (see n. 2), 47, also cited by A. Rudolph, *"Denn wir sind jenes Volk . . .": Die neue Gottesverehrung in Justins Dialog mit dem Juden Tryphon in historisch-theologischer Sicht,* Hereditas 15 (1999) 2 with n. 6.

bered *Dial.* 74.3 and 74.4.[4] Justin's *Dialogue* also presents the greatest amount of material and the most sustained argument from Isaiah 53 of any work of the first two centuries. There is no complete modern commentary on this material,[5] perhaps because of its great extent and a certain amount of repetition in Justin's allusions and argument. But precisely because of this, it is important in a volume such as the present one, which aims, as the editors say, to provide a "workbook" for further research, to have an accurate count of references and allusions to Isaiah 53 in the *Dialogue*.

In his preceding essay in this volume on Isaiah 53 in the patristic literature, C. Markschies has included an appreciative treatment of Justin's accomplishment both in his *Dialogue* and in his *1 Apology* (where he also quotes Isaiah 53; cf. *1 Apol.* 50-51). He calls them "two of the most impressive examples of Christian interaction with this passage" (p. 246) and defends Justin against the charge of "atomistic" exegesis by one of his modern interpreters, H. W. Wolff (p. 267). In this study I wish to confirm Markschies's appreciation of the *Dialogue* — I presuppose his treatment and bibliography (pp. 245-68) — and to focus on material that was not the focus of his study, nor of any study to my knowledge,[6] perhaps in part because it is highlighted only in the new text edition by Miroslav Marcovich. This appeared a year after the German of the present volume: *Iustini Martyris Dialogus cum Tryphone*, PTS 47 (1997).

After reviewing Marcovich's edition and supplementing its index under Isaiah 53 (which has significant omissions), I have provided a mini-commentary on most of the passages where Marcovich has used italics to indicate the influence on Justin by Isaiah 53 or Daniel 7, not only for biblical quotations and identifiable phrases, but also for single terms that presumably allude to these texts without being literally present in them. These include ἄτιμος,

---

4. On the lacuna between *Dial.* 74.3 and 74.4 see Marcovich, 5-6, 199 (apparatus); O. Skarsaune, *The Proof from Prophecy: A Study in Justin Martyr's Proof-Text Tradition: Text-Type, Provenance, Theological Profile*, NovTSup 56 (1987) 213-215; Rudolph, *"Denn wir sind jenes Volk,"* 22-23.

5. I understand that Herder's new series *Kommentar zu frühchristlichen Apologeten* (including e.g. *An Diognet* by H. E. Lona [2001]) is to include a volume on Justin's *Dialogue*.

6. In particular there is no passage-by-passage commentary on the *Dialogue*'s 17 passages containing the key term παθητός to determine how many of these occurrences allude to Isaiah 53, such as I have provided below in §6.2. Previous studies have mentioned that Justin uses the term "very often" and have referred readers to E. J. Goodspeed, *Index Apologeticus, sive clavis Iustini Marturis operum* (1912) 209 s.v., who gives an accurate list (see below, n. 25). See e.g. W. C. van Unnik, "Der Fluch der Gekreuzigten: Deuteronomium 21,23 in der Deutung Justinus des Märtyrers," in C. Andresen and G. Klein, eds., *Theologia Crucis — Signum Crucis. Festschrift für Erich Dinkler zum 70. Geburtstag* (1979), 483-499, esp. 488 n. 26; Rudolph, *"Denn wir sind jenes Volk"* (see n. 3), 183 n. 356.

ἀειδής, ἄδοξος, "without honor," "without form," "without glory," which Marcovich and others recognize as an allusion to Isa 53:2-3 (only ἄτιμος literally occurs there, v. 3); the contrasting term "glorious," ἔνδοξος, alluding to Dan 7:14 LXX, and especially παθητός. This last term occurs 19 times in 17 passages of the *Dialogue* and deserves special attention.

Marcovich refers παθητός, which Justin uses to identify the Messiah as "passible" or "susceptible to suffering," to Isa 53:8d, "he was led to death." Despite the fact that the language "suffering," παθητός or πάσχειν, is not literally in the text of Isaiah 53, Marcovich's identification of παθητός with Isa 53:8 is uncontroversial in the sense that Justin's "passible" Messiah is clearly a "mortal" one (cf. θνητός, *Dial.* 14.8). But it is not clear whether the *Dialogue's* language of a "suffering Messiah" necessarily alludes to Isaiah 53 in every instance. Marcovich himself seems to think that the strength of the allusion varies. Once his oversight regarding *Dial.* 39.2 is corrected, it appears that Marcovich provides 11 of the 17 paragraphs containing παθητός with a reference to Isa 53:8, leaving six of the paragraphs unsupported.[7] On the other hand, Marcovich italicizes all but one (cf. *Dial.* 99.2) of these occurrences of παθητός and lists all of them in two places: at the first occurrence of παθητός in *Dial.* 34.2, and at the only occurrence of its synonym θνητός in *Dial.* 14.8.

Marcovich's edition thus immediately suggests an interpretation or an approach to the "suffering Messiah" — one which I, at least, would not have taken had I not been led in this direction by this particular edition. Unfortunately, Marcovich is no longer with us to answer questions about the assumptions underlying his invaluable new edition.[8] Without necessarily setting out to do so, this essay, which began as an attempt to understand Marcovich's editing, has become in the end a justification of it, though criticisms will also be noted. In the most detailed section (see §6), I have measured the differing strengths of the allusion to Isaiah 53 made by παθητός and have concluded that I would draw the line exactly where Marcovich has: there is an identifiable allusion to Isaiah 53 in 11 of the 17 paragraphs where the term occurs (see §6.3).

Examining the data associated with παθητός and other allusions to Isaiah 53 leads me to support some recent trends in research. D. J. Bingham has suggested that Isaiah 53 may have played a formative role in the self-understanding of Justin's community, which I would see mirrored in the phrase with which I have titled this essay: "Our suffering and crucified Messiah" (*Dial.* 111.2). I also support T. J. Horner's thesis about a more authentic, individual voice behind

---

7. For references see below nn. 25, 27.

8. Marcovich died on June 14, 2001. Halton in Falls and Halton, xi, calls the edition "invaluable" and refers to tribute to Marcovich by D. Sansone in *Gnomon* 73 (2001) 746-48.

the figure of Trypho, and see this reflected, as Horner does, in the *Dialogue's* discussion of Deut 21:23. On the other hand, it becomes clear over against H. W. Wolff that unlike Justin's *1 Apology,* the *Dialogue* does not take full advantage of the potential for an exalted Servant according to Isa 52:13.

I begin with an overview of the biblical images of a suffering savior in the *Dialogue* (§2), followed by a statement of the questions that will guide this investigation (§3). This leads to an overview of Marcovich's edition (§4), including a new index (§4.2), which forms the basis for studies of Justin's allusive vocabulary and associated themes (§§5-6). These include the network of ἄτιμος, ἀειδής, and ἄδοξος (§5.2), of which the most important is ἄτιμος (§5.3), the theme of the two Parousias (§5.4), and H. W. Wolff's thesis about an exalted Servant in the *Dialogue* (§5.5). The focal term παθητός is included where relevant in these sections (cf. §5.1), but it also receives its own extended treatment (§6). At the end of the study (§7), I address the kinds of literary and historical issues that interest specialists in Justin Martyr and in the history of Christian-Jewish relations in the second century. My aim throughout is to think about the science and art of identifying biblical allusions in a patristic text, and to appreciate the role this language might play both inside and outside the *Dialogue.*

2. The Suffering Messiah in the *Dialogue*

Isaiah 53 provides the most important figure of a suffering savior in the *Dialogue,* followed by Psalm 22 (LXX 21). Nevertheless, these two passages play very different roles in the *Dialogue* as a whole, because Psalm 22 is confined to a single, originally independent section, in which Trypho's voice is not heard (*Dial.* 97-106), whereas references to Isaiah 53 occur throughout the *Dialogue* and in some of the most important exchanges between Justin and Trypho (cf. esp. *Dial.* 89.2–90.1). Furthermore, the *Dialogue* contains many other biblical images of salvation through suffering or sacrifice not tied to Isaiah 53 or Psalm 22. It must also be determined whether Isaiah 53 is used for suffering alone, or for suffering plus the exaltation theme in Isa 52:13.

2.1 Isaiah 53 and Other Proofs of a Suffering Messiah

The Messiah of Isaiah 53 is almost exclusively a *suffering* Messiah as far as Justin Martyr's *Dialogue with Trypho* is concerned. Justin certainly knows of the "exalted" and "greatly glorified" Servant-Messiah of Isa 52:13 LXX (cf. ὑψωθήσεται, δοξασθήσεται σφόδρα), but he takes advantage of this only in his

1 Apology. Here his long quotation — introduced by a non-LXX version of Isa 53:12b-d,[9] followed by Isa 52:13–53:8a in *1 Apol.* 50.2-11, then after a short break by Isa 53:8b-12 in *1 Apol.* 51.1-5 — relocates the final half-verse about suffering (53:12b-d) to the head of Isaiah's opening statement about exaltation (52:13), thus giving equal emphasis to each: Christ "endured suffering and dishonor, and will come again with glory," παθεῖν καὶ ἀτιμασθῆναι ὑπέμεινε, καὶ πάλιν μετὰ δόξης παραγενήσεται (*1 Apol.* 50.1). By contrast, in his *Dialogue,* outside the initial long quotation of Isa 52:10–54:6 in *Dial.* 13.2-9, Justin does not cite or clearly allude to the exaltation motif at the beginning of the fourth Servant Song in 52:13 (*contra* H. W. Wolff).[10] Instead, he looks elsewhere for this motif, above all to Dan 7:13-14 for its language of the Son of Man "coming on the clouds" or "with glory," which he frequently combines with contrasting allusions to Isaiah 53.

There are several other potential proofs for an exalted Servant in Isaiah 53 that Justin does not take advantage of in his *Dialogue.* Corresponding to 52:13 at the beginning is 53:12a near the end of the Servant Song, about the Servant dividing the spoils of the strong. Yet the only phrase that Justin takes directly from Isa 53:12 is from v. 12c and involves suffering or dishonor: "and he was counted among the lawless" (cf. *Dial.* 89.3; see below §4.1). By the same token, when M. Marcovich in his edition provides a reference to Isa 53:12 at *Dial.* 110.2, it supports the idea not of an exalted Christ who "divides the spoils," but of a *crucified* Christ: σταυρούμενος.

Isaiah 52:15a, "Kings will shut their mouth," could be taken as a prediction of the triumph of the Servant and the subjection of the foreign, pagan kings to his judgment.[11] It begins Justin's scriptural quotation in *Dial.* 118.4. Nevertheless, Justin's point is not Isaiah's original point — that the exalted Servant will stun earthly kings into a guilty silence. Already in the LXX this point is beginning to weaken: instead of the Servant "startling" the nations, the nations are

---

9. *1 Apol.* 50.2, text: M. Marcovich, *Iustini Martyris Apologiae pro Christianis,* PTS 38 (1994) 50 *ll.* 3-5: Ἀνθ' ὧν παρέδωκαν εἰς θάνατον τὴν ψυχὴν αὐτοῦ, καὶ μετὰ τῶν ἀνόμων ἐλογίσθη, αὐτὸς ἁμαρτίας πολλῶν εἴληφε καὶ τοῖς ἀνόμοις ἐξιλάσεται, "Because they delivered His soul to death, and he was counted with the wicked, He has borne the sins of many, and will make propitiation [atonement] for the wicked" (trans. L. W. Barnard, *St. Justin Martyr, The First and Second Apologies,* ACW 56 [1997] 57).

10. See below, §5.5. Cf. H. W. Wolff, *Jesaja 53 im Urchristentum* (³1952), 133-134. In the next few pages I discuss Wolff's passages, including Justin's uses of Isa 52:15–53:1 in *Dial.* 118.4 and of Isa 53:9 in *Dial.* 32.2; 97.2.

11. See M. Hengel, "Zur Wirkungsgeschichte von Jes 53 in vorchristlicher Zeit," in Janowski and Stuhlmacher, eds., *Der leidende Gottesknecht,* 77 = ET above, p. 122. The German edition is cited favorably by E. R. Ekblad, *Isaiah's Servant Poems* (see n. 1), 188 with n. 59.

"amazed" or "astonished" at the Servant (Isa 52:15a, θαυμάσονται ἔθνη πολλὰ ἐπ᾿ αὐτῷ).[12] Although Justin's clearest reference to the understandable human astonishment at the Servant's sufferings comes earlier, in *Dial.* 89.3, and Isaiah's phrase about astonishment is not quoted here in *Dial.* 118.4, Justin does seem to identify himself and his fellow Christian believers with these Gentile nations, as those who "move past astonishment to faith."[13] He sees this prophesied in Isa 52:15b–53:1, with which he concludes his quotation:

> For they to whom it was not told of him, shall see; and they that heard not, shall understand. Lord, who has believed our report? And to whom has the arm of the Lord been revealed? (*Dial.* 118.4)

It is Gentile believers like Justin — those not previously "told" — who have become the "seeing" and "understanding" audience of God's revelation instead of currently unbelieving Jews like Trypho. Justin speaks here for the benefit of Trypho's companions, who appear to include Gentiles leaning towards becoming "proselytes," not to Christianity, but to Judaism (cf. also *Dial.* 23.3).[14]

The potential for a triumphant reading of Isa 53:9 LXX that would emphasize the Lord (perhaps even the Servant)[15] as the future judge is also not fully exploited by Justin. According to E. R. Ekblad, the Septuagint of Isa 53:9 "offers a completely different interpretation from that of the MT, which describes the innocent servant's identification with and humble burial . . . among criminals and a rich man." By contrast, the LXX represents a "distinct interpre-

---

12. Cf. Ekblad, *Isaiah's Servant Poems*, 187-189.

13. D. J. Bingham, "Justin and Isaiah 53," *VC* 53 (2000) 248-261, esp. 252. I return to the point at the end of 7.1.

14. According to Marcovich, Justin's *Dialogue* "seems to be addressed primarily to a group of Gentiles at Rome leaning towards Judaism (and represented by Trypho's companions; cf. *Dial.* 23.3)" (p. vii; cf. 64-65). In *Dial.* 23.3, Justin addresses both Trypho "and those who want to become proselytes" (καὶ τοῖς βουλομένοις προσηλύτοις γενέσθαι). Marcovich comments: "At *Dial.* 23.3, the term *proselytes* must have its usual meaning of 'proselytes to the Jewish faith,' as in *Dial.* 80.1 and in chapters 122-123. It cannot mean 'proselytes (to the true faith),' i.e., Christianity" (64). On the target readership of the *Dialogue* see further C. Markschies, above, p. 246 n. 72.

15. Ekblad responds critically to the suggestion made in the German version of M. Hengel's essay that Isa 53:9 LXX may understand the Servant himself as the future judge. See Hengel, "Zur Wirkungsgeschichte," in *Der leidende Gottesknecht,* 78 with n. 125 = ET above, p. 123 with n. 176. Ekblad writes: "Hengel goes too far in linking this text [sc. Isa 53:9 LXX] back to 52:14-15 to strengthen his argument that the servant is here depicted as the judge of the wicked and the rich. While he is correct in pointing to Jewish traditions that interpret this in terms of the final judgment (see note 125 [= p. 123 n. 177 above]), the Lord is clearly the subject of δώσω and there is no desired αὐτῷ following δώσω to support his hypothesis" (*Isaiah's Servant Poems,* 237 n. 281).

tation that the Lord speaks here of his future retribution against the wicked and the rich."[16] Ekblad translates:

καὶ δώσω τοὺς πονηροὺς ἀντὶ τῆς ταφῆς αὐτοῦ καὶ τοὺς πλουσίους ἀντὶ τοῦ θανάτου αὐτοῦ.

And I [the Lord] will give the wicked in place of (ἀντί) his burial and the rich in place of (ἀντί) his death. (Isa 53:9a)

In the light of the ἀντί, Ekblad explains: "the Lord will eventually exercise divine justice, burying the wicked in place of the innocent servant."[17]

Justin initially seems to take Isa 53:9a even further in this direction. To him the text says that "in place of his [the Servant's] death the rich will be *put to death*," ἀντὶ τοῦ θανάτου αὐτοῦ τοὺς πλουσίους θανατωθήσεσθαι (*Dial.* 32.1). Yet Justin does not think of this judgment on the rich as already having taken place, and he still focuses on the Servant's death and lack of glory at his first coming. More positive is Justin's later use of Isa 53:9a in *Dial.* 97.2. Here he interprets Isa 57:2, "His burial has been taken out of the midst," together with Isa 53:9a, "I will give the rich in place of his death," as prophecies of Christ's resurrection that have already been fulfilled.

There are many other Old Testament passages besides Isaiah 53 to which Justin refers for a suffering Messiah in his *Dialogue*. Most of these proofs also appear in the New Testament. They include:

1. Zechariah's *Pierced One* (Zech 12:10; John 19:37; Rev 1:7; cf. *Dial.* 32.2; 64.7; *1 Apol.* 52.12), also referred to as a "crucified" one (*Dial.* 14.8; 118.1)[18] and falsely attributed to Hosea (*Dial.* 14.8);

2. Zechariah's *Stricken One:* "strike the shepherd" (Zech 13:7; Matt 26:31; Mark 14:27; cf. *Dial.* 53.5);

3. Deuteronomy's oft-cited *Cursed One*, hanging on a tree (Deut 21:23; cf. Gal 3:13) — a problem naturally raised by Trypho and frequently alluded to by both dialogue partners;[19]

16. Ekblad, *Isaiah's Servant Poems*, 237.

17. Ekblad, *Isaiah's Servant Poems*, 238.

18. The allusion to Zech 12:10 in *Dial.* 118.1 *ll.* 2-3 is not indexed as such by Marcovich (who indexes these lines under Zech 12:12), but is recognized in his citation apparatus at this point (lines 2-3: "cf. Zch 12:10 et 12 + Apc 1:7; Jo 19:37"). In general readers must rely on Marcovich's apparatus and not on his (incomplete) index.

19. Cf. *Dial.* 32.1 (Trypho); 89.2 (Trypho); 90.1; 93.4; 94.5; 95.2; 96.1; 111.2; 131.2. Marcovich italicizes the "curse" language (κατάρα, ἐπικατάρατος, κεκατηραμένος, etc.) in every instance except for *Dial.* 93.4 and 111.2, yet still provides an apparatus reference to Deut 21:23 and Gal 3:13 for these two passages. The final passage, *Dial.* 131.2, is indexed under Deut 21:23 even though it

4. Isaiah's perishing *Righteous One* of Isa 57:1-4 (*Dial.* 16.4; 110.6), though the main application here is to Christians;[20]

5. Isaiah's *Righteous One who is "taken away,"* according to Justin's text of Isa 3:10, ἄρωμεν τὸν δίκαιον, "let us *take away* the righteous one" (*Dial.* 137.3);[21]

6. The *paschal lamb* of the book of Exodus, including the application of its blood, as a type of Christ and indirectly of Christians (cf. *Dial.* 40.1-3; Exod 12:7, 11, 21; 1 Cor 5:7; also *Dial.* 72.1; 111.3 with Isa 53:7);

7. The *two goats* of the Levitical *Day of Atonement* — scapegoat and sacrificial goat — as a type of Christ and his two comings (Lev 16; *Dial.* 40.4; cf. 111.1);

---

lacks the explicit "curse" language; it speaks of Christians as those "who have been called by God by means of the mystery of the *despised* and *dishonorable* cross," οἵτινες διὰ τοῦ ἐξουθενημένου καὶ ὀνείδους μεστοῦ μυστηρίου τοῦ σταυροῦ κληθέντες ὑπὸ τοῦ θεοῦ. Justin stops short of calling the cross "cursed," against which he defends it in *Dial.* 111.2 (cf. 90.3).

20. It becomes clear in *Dial.* 110.6 that Justin applies Isa 57:1-4 to both Christ and Christians and that the main application is positive. Justin says that he and other Christians "are assured by God that we are to be *taken from the earth,* together with the most righteous and only immaculate and sinless Christ," followed by a quotation of Isa 57:1b that includes the plural "and *righteous men* are taken away." Nevertheless, in *Dial.* 16.4 the scriptural usage is more subtle; Justin links the righteous Jesus, *including his sufferings,* to some extent with the "righteous one" of Isa 57:1-4. He begins *Dial.* 16.4 with a different scriptural allusion: "For you (Jews) have murdered the Righteous One, and his prophets before him" (ἀπεκτείνατε γὰρ τὸν δίκαιον καὶ πρὸ αὐτοῦ τοὺς προφήτας αὐτοῦ). This draws most directly on Acts 7:52 and 1 Thess 2:15. Justin concludes *Dial.* 16.4 by apparently linking Jesus, as the murdered Righteous One, with the perishing righteous one that is the initial subject of his quotation of Isa 57:1-4: "See how the righteous has perished," ἴδετε ὡς ὁ δίκαιος ἀπώλετο (Isa 57:1a). Thus far, Justin's application of Isa 57:1 in *Dial.* 16.4 would seem to be negative. However, between these two points Justin has introduced another theme, that of the persecution of Christians, and therefore he also finds a plural and more positive application of the same passage. As indicated, the LXX actually includes a plural phrase in Isa 57:1b, καὶ ἄνδρες δίκαιοι αἴρονται, "and *righteous men* are taken away." But Justin omits this in *Dial.* 16.4 (he includes it in *Dial.* 110.6, above), continuing with the singular in Isa 57:1c, ἀπὸ γὰρ προσώπου ἀδικίας ἦρται ὁ δίκαιος, "the righteous one has been taken away from before the face of injustice." As hinted here, and as the rest of Justin's quotation shows, the righteous one has actually experienced something positive: "his burial shall be in peace, he is taken away from among us" (Isa 57:2 in *Dial.* 14.6, trans. Falls and Halton, punctuating with Rahlfs and Ziegler, ἔσται ἐν εἰρήνῃ ἡ ταφὴ αὐτοῦ, ἦρται ἐκ τοῦ μέσου, against Marcovich, who places the comma after εἰρήνῃ). This peace and removal from suffering is what Justin hopes for on behalf of persecuted Christians.

21. In *Dial.* 137.3 Justin attributes his reading ἄρωμεν in Isa 3:10 to the LXX (cf. Isa 57:1c in preceding note: ἦρται ὁ δίκαιος). However, the LXX of Isa 3:10 actually reads δήσωμεν, "*let us bind* the righteous one." For Justin's ἄρωμεν Marcovich refers to other Christian writers including Hegesippius (quoted in Eusebius), Clement of Alexandria, and Tertullian. Halton (p. 206 n. 6) refers to Prov 1:12b, ἄρωμεν αὐτοῦ τὴν μνήμην ἐκ γῆς, "let us remove his memory from the earth."

8. The "innocent lamb" (ἀρνίον ἄκακον) facing slaughter in Jer 11:19 LXX, representing the prophet Jeremiah and prefiguring Christ as the "sheep led to the slaughter" of Isa 53:7 (*Dial.* 72.2-3);

9. The bloody *sacrificial victim* more generally, which is the heading under which Justin introduces his long quotation of Isa 52:10–54:6 in *Dial.* 13.2-9. The properly repentant include those

> who are no longer *made pure by the blood of goats* and sheep, . . . but by faith through *the blood of Christ* and his death [cf. Heb 9:13-14], who died for this precise purpose, as Isaiah himself says in these words: . . . (follows Isa 52:10–54:6) (*Dial.* 13.1; cf. 13.2-9)

10. The *bronze serpent* of Num 21:6-9 (*Dial.* 91.4; 94.1-5; 112.1; 131.4; cf. *1 Apol.* 60; *Barn.* 12.6-7), though Justin is considerably more cautious about this image than is John 3:14;[22]

---

22. See esp. *Dial.* 91.4. Apparently fearing some misunderstanding or misuse by Christian members of his audience, Justin is displeased with the idea that Christian faith might be likened to belief in a serpent, even by an Old Testament typology approved by the New Testament. The Old Testament itself has reservations about Moses' bronze serpent, which was later set up as an idol called Nehustan and had to be destroyed by King Hezekiah (2 Kings 18:4). Rather than presenting the bronze serpent typology as a purely salvific image of the cross, as in John 3:14, in *Dial.* 91.4 Justin wants his readers to understand that the cross defeats the ancient serpent, their enemy. Justin refuses to read the story of the bronze serpent in Num 21:8-9 apart from the cursing of the crafty serpent in Gen 3:14. This I take to be the point of the somewhat tangled sentences below. Marcovich has attempted to untangle the syntax by moving the participle ἐσταυρωμένον, "crucified," forward from its position below (p. 228 line 31 in his edition) to the end of the first sentence <. . .>, *Dial.* 91.4: ἡ ἀνάθεσις φαίνεται γεγενημένη ἐπὶ σωτηρίᾳ τῶν πιστευόντων <ἐπὶ τὸν ἐσταυρωμένον>. ὅτι διὰ τοῦ σταυροῦσθαι μέλλοντος θάνατος γενήσεσθαι ἔκτοτε προεκηρύσσετο τῷ ὄφει, σωτηρία δὲ τοῖς καταδακνομένοις ὑπ' αὐτοῦ, "The erecting (of the bronze serpent) was clearly intended for the salvation of those who believe <in the crucified one>. For through the one destined to be crucified, death was proclaimed in advance to the serpent (cf. Gen 3:14-15), but salvation to those who were bitten by it." Halton leaves ἐσταυρωμένον in its traditional place in the following translation (modified at ἐσταυρωμένον, where for "crucified Son," Halton renders "sent his Son into the world *to be crucified*"):

> Likewise, the figure [type] and sign [= bronze serpent, not named, Num 21:8-9], erected to counteract the effects of the *serpents* that bit Israel, was clearly intended for the salvation of those who believe that this sign was to show that through the crucified one death was to come to *the serpent* (cf. Gen 3:15), but salvation to those who had been bitten by it [= all humanity? See *Dial.* 94.2] and who had sought protection of him who sent his *crucified* [ἐσταυρωμένον, deleted by Marcovich] Son into the world. *For the prophetic Spirit did not instruct us through Moses to believe in a serpent,* since he announced that it was *cursed* by God from the beginning (Gen 3:14), and through Isaiah he informs us that it

11. Moses' *cross-shaped outstretched arms* at the battle against Amalek (cf. Exod 17:8-13), which, while not an image of suffering or sacrifice *per se,* is Justin's favorite physical picture of the cross (cf. *Dial.* 91.3; 93.5; 97.1; 111.1; 112.2; 131.4);

12. David's statement, "The Lord has reigned *from the tree*" (Ps 96 [LXX 95]:10), including the textually uncertain words "from the tree" (cf. *Dial.* 73.1, 4 [Otto]). This phrase, which Justin thinks Jewish scholars deleted from the original Septuagint, seems to have predicted Christ's death on the cross;[23]

13. David's *God-forsaken One* of Psalm 22 (LXX 21) — crucial for Justin (cf. *Dial.* 97-106) as well as for the Gospels; cf. the "cry of dereliction" (Matt 27:46; Mark 15:34).

2.2 *Statistics on the Use of Isaiah 53 in the Dialogue*

Of these biblical passages about suffering and sacrifice, Psalm 22 receives the longest connected treatment in the *Dialogue,* chaps. 97-106, while Isaiah 53 is the most widely distributed among the different parts. It appears in 21 different passages of the *Dialogue* according to the index of the recent edition by M. Marcovich. Yet this figure is too low, owing to several unexplainable omissions in Marcovich's index. A better overview is provided by the older edition of E. J. Goodspeed (*Die ältesten Apologeten* [1914]). Here one finds 26 references to the *Dialogue* indexed under verses or combinations of verses between Isa 52:15 and 53:12, and once under Isa 52:10–54:6 = *Dial.* 13.2-9. According to Goodspeed, there are actually not 26 but 25 different passages of the *Dialogue* reflecting uses of Isaiah 53 — one chapter (*Dial.* 13.2-9) and 24 paragraphs, within a total of 142 chapters. The figure of 26 entries in the index arises only because one of these paragraphs, *Dial.* 114.2, is correctly indexed twice; it contains two distinct quotations of Isa 53:7 and Isa 53:1.

Although Marcovich's index is faulty, his edition reopens the question of statistics. By using the generous information provided by his citation apparatus and his italicizing of key terms in the text, one can extend the list of quotations and of potential allusions to Isaiah 53 from 25 to 42 different passages of the *Di-*

---

will be *slain* as an enemy *by the great sword,* which is Christ (Isa 27:1). (*Dial.* 91.4; cf. Falls and Halton, 142, italics, parenthetical material, and pronouns added: "it" = the serpent)

By referring to the bronze serpent only obliquely as a "type and sign," Justin avoids calling it a "serpent" in the singular so that he can reserve this for the cursed *serpent* in the Garden (Gen 3:14); in the wilderness we have only "serpents," not "the serpent."

23. See briefly Falls and Halton, 113 nn. 7-8 at *Dial.* 73.1, 4, with literature.

alogue. My studies confirm 36 of these 42 passages as either quotations or identifiable echoes (see esp. §6).

2.3 The παθητὸς Χριστός in Marcovich's Edition of the Dialogue

Marcovich in his review of previous editions of the *Dialogue* complains about Goodspeed that "his scripture references are a mess" (p. 7). Nevertheless, Marcovich's index is inferior to Goodspeed's in that it excludes four passages that Goodspeed includes: *Dial.* 14.8; 95.3; 100.2 and 110.2 (though Goodspeed misses another: *Dial.* 121.3).[24] These are all places where Marcovich has important identifications of Isaiah 53 in his citation apparatus.

I have therefore expanded and corrected Marcovich's index to include as many as 42 passages of the *Dialogue* potentially involving Isaiah 53. (For the index see below, §4.2.) The major expansion comes by including all the passages in which Marcovich italicizes the crucial term παθητός, "passible," "capable of suffering" — or in case of Jesus Christ actually "suffering," i.e., *suffering* unto *death:* εἰς θάνατον (Isa 53:8; cf. v. 12). This term does not occur in Isaiah 53 or the Greek Old Testament (cf. Acts 26:23), but as already indicated, it occurs 19 times in the *Dialogue* in 17 different paragraphs. As if to highlight its importance, Marcovich lists all 17 paragraphs at the first occurrence of παθητός in *Dial.* 34.2, as well as at the occurrence of its synonym θνητός in *Dial.* 14.8.[25] Yet he indexes only one of these paragraphs under Isaiah 53, *Dial.* 49.2, and even then not because it contains παθητός.[26] When Marcovich gives an apparatus reference for παθητός, as he does in 10 of its 17 passages (or 11 of 17 with the addition of *Dial.* 39.7, which was apparently overlooked), he refers it specifically to Isa 53:8, often quoting the words from the last phrase (v. 8d), ἤχθη εἰς θάνατον, "he was led to death."[27] If παθητός alludes to Isaiah 53, as this edition

---

24. *Dial.* 121.3 is a significant omission because it is the final allusion to Isa 53:3 in the *Dialogue* by the important term ἄτιμος. Its absence from both Goodspeed's and Marcovich's index probably explains why it is also lacking in Bingham's list of Justin's references to Isa 53:2-3 ("Justin and Isaiah 53" [see n. 13], 251 n. 12). For full coverage see my Table 1 in §5.2.

25. See the 19 uses of παθητός in *Dial.* 34.2; 36.1 twice; 39.7; 41.1; 49.2; 52.1 twice; 68.9; 70.4; 74.1; 76.6; 85.2; 89.2; 99.2; 100.2; 110.2; 111.2; 126.1. In Marcovich's edition see pp. 125, 130, 136, 138, 150, 155, 189, 192, 197, 202, 216, 225, 240, 241, 258, 260, 287.

26. *Dial.* 49.2 is entered in the index only under Isa 53:2-3, not under Isa 53:8, where Marcovich locates the idea of the παθητὸς Χριστός.

27. The phrase "παθητός [or παθητόν, etc.]: cf. Is 53:8 ἤχθη εἰς θάνατον" is noted at five passages in Marcovich's edition, representing six occurrences of παθητός: *Dial.* 34.2; 36.1 (2x);

suggests, then it is Justin's single most frequent term for doing so, followed by ἄτιμος, "without honor" (cf. Isa 53:3), with nine occurrences.

Both Justin and Trypho use παθητός.[28] The term keeps the discussion moving — or expresses Trypho's pardonable impatience and Justin's repeated promise to return to the point — precisely by appearing where other quotations of or allusions to Isaiah 53 do not. Because there is so little overlap, adding the παθητός passages greatly increases the total number of *Dialogue* passages where one might look for a reference or allusion to Isaiah 53.

Of the 25 passages previously indexed by Goodspeed between Isa 52:10 and 54:6, παθητός occurs in only three, *Dial.* 49.2; 100.2 and 110.2. This means that 14 of the 17 παθητός passages are new to our list. I add to this *Dial.* 32.1 and 121.3 based on Marcovich's apparatus (references to Isa 53:2-3 at *Dial.* 32.1 *l.* 4 and 121.3 *l.* 18) and *Dial.* 49.7 based on his use of italics (ἄδοξος in 49.7 *l.* 54), bringing the total to 42.

The 42 passages that clearly or potentially use Isaiah 53 are listed below. (For my conclusions about those usages, see §6.3 below.) Those containing παθητός are italicized. The equals sign (=) shows the three παθητός passages where there was already an existing reference in Goodspeed, and boldface is used to indicate direct quotations. In two places there are adjacent paragraphs: *Dial.* 32.1 and 32.2; *Dial.* 89.2 and 89.3. However, since there are a change of speaker from Trypho to Justin in each pair and different allusions in each paragraph, they are indexed separately. The sole unitalicized use of παθητός in *Dial.* 99.2 is included for completeness, even though it turns out not to contain an allusion to Isaiah 53:

> **13.2-9**; 14.8; 17.1; 32.1; 32.2; *34.2*; *36.1*; 36.6; *39.7*; 41.1; **42.2-3**; **43.3**; 49.2 = 49.2;
> *49.7*; *52.1*; **63.2**; **68.4**; 68.9; 70.4; *72.3*; 74.1; **76.2**; 76.6; 85.1; *85.2*; 88.8; 89.2; 89.3;
> 90.1; 95.3; **97.2**; 99.2; 100.2 = 100.2; **102.7**; 110.2 = 110.2; *111.2*; **111.3**; **114.2**; **118.4**;
> 121.3; *126.1*; 137.1

68.9; 76.6; 126.1 (in *Dial.* 36.1 the note is given only for the first of the two uses of παθητός in line 2, but presumably also applies to the occurrence in line 4). In five other passages the reference to Isa 53:8 is given without the Greek phrase: *Dial.* 49.2; 89.2; 100.2; 110.2; 111.2. One additional passage that Marcovich did not refer to Isa 53:8 because of an oversight should be included, because it meets the criteria: *Dial.* 39.7 (see passage 3 in §6.2). This gives a total of 12 allusive uses of παθητός in 11 passages. The remaining six passages, representing seven occurrences of παθητός, are not supported by comments in Marcovich's apparatus: *Dial.* 41.1; 52.1 (2x); 70.4; 74.1; 85.2; 99.2. Hence 11 of 17, or two thirds of the παθητός passages, are counted as allusions to the idea of suffering unto death in Isa 53:8.

28. For Trypho's uses of παθητός see *Dial.* 36.1; 39.7; 74.1; 89.2.

3. Leading Questions

In the remaining sections of this essay, questions must be raised to make this statistical information useful. Why is παθητός regularly explained by a reference to Isa 53:8 in Marcovich's apparatus, when neither παθητός nor πάσχειν occurs here or elsewhere in the fourth Servant Song? How does its association with Justin's allusive terms for Isa 53:2-3, such as ἄτιμος, ἀειδής, and ἄδοξος — "without honor," "without form," "without glory" — give παθητός its Isaianic profile? What role is played in these contexts by the use of Isaianic language for Christ's first coming and of Danielic language for his second coming on the clouds in glory (cf. Dan 7:13-14)? Since some of these questions have already been addressed in this volume by C. Markschies, especially from a historical and theological angle, I will concentrate on Justin's allusive vocabulary.

I return near the end of the essay to the question of how the language of Justin's *Dialogue* may shed light on second-century discussions between Jews and Christians about Isaiah 53 and Deut 21:23 (see §7.2) or between Justin and Gnostics about the reality of Christ's passion (§7.4). However, my primary question in this essay is not a historian's question, but a reader's one. Marcovich has edited the *Dialogue* with *modern* readers in view. We must therefore ask ourselves, Do *we* see in this document what he sees? Can we reasonably be expected to discover from a close reading of the text that certain terms — including especially παθητός, but also ἄτιμος, ἀειδής, and ἄδοξος — almost always echo a particular Old Testament text, Isaiah 53? And does the antonym of ἄδοξος, namely ἔνδοξος, "glorious," always allude to Dan 7:14? Do we agree with the italics that Marcovich typically applies to these "allusive" terms, almost always apart from explicit quotations of Scripture?

Because of a coincidence in the manuscript transmission of the *Dialogue,* Marcovich happens to mention the term παθητός in his introduction. Παθητός forms the key term in the title given the *Dialogue* by the scribe of a *Catena in Ps* 2 that preserves some authentic material now lost in the main manuscript of the *Dialogue, Parisinus graecus* 450 (siglum *A*). The Greek heading of the fragment, which originally belonged in Day II of the *Dialogue*,[29] gives Justin's whole work the title Περὶ τοῦ εἰ παθητὸς ὁ Χριστός, "On Whether the Messiah Is Due To Suffer."[30]

---

29. Λόγος β'. This Day II originally began somewhere between the texts numbered *Dial.* 74.3 and *Dial.* 74.4 in our modern editions of the *Dialogue* (Marcovich, pp. 198-199). The division into two Λόγοι was intended to separate the first and second days of the discussion. See Marcovich, 4-6, 199 (apparatus).

30. Τοῦ ἁγίου Ἰουστίνου φιλοσόφου καὶ μάρτυρος ἐκ τοῦ β' Λόγου Περὶ τοῦ εἰ παθητὸς ὁ Χριστός. The fragment bearing this title is reprinted in Marcovich's Appendix (pp.

Marcovich agrees with the title and uses it to confirm the authenticity of the fragment because, as he says, in the *Dialogue*,

> the theme, "Is the Messiah due to suffer?," makes one of the key issues (deriving from Isaiah 53:8 ἀπὸ τῶν ἀνομιῶν τοῦ λαοῦ μου ἤχθη εἰς θάνατον). (Marcovich, 4)

Here we have a mention of Marcovich's identification of παθητός with Isa 53:8, without an explanation.[31] We shall therefore look to the text itself for that explanation, which I believe is, for the most part, forthcoming (cf. esp. *Dial.* 89.2-3).

Marcovich has edited Justin's *Dialogue* differently from his earlier edition of Justin's two *Apologies* in the same series.[32] The difference can be seen precisely in Marcovich's treatment of παθητός. The *Apologies* volume has different typesetting: direct scriptural quotations are set within quotation marks, but there are no italics for scriptural allusions, as in the *Dialogue*. Hence in *1 Apol.* 52.3, where the term παθητός occurs with another allusive term ἄτιμος and a contrasting allusion to Dan 7:13-14 ("he will come from heaven with glory"), there is a clearly identifiable allusion to Isaiah 53, particularly as that text has just been cited in full in *1 Apol.* 50-51. Both παθητός and ἄτιμος would have been italicized according to the editing standards of the *Dialogue*. But they are not marked in Marcovich's text of the *1 Apology*, and the marginal reference to Isa 53:2-3 is intended to cover both terms, without adding Isa 53:8 for παθητός, as Marcovich would do in the *Dialogue*.

315-316). That the title is intended to characterize the whole *Dialogue* and not just the fragment is confirmed by the fact that the fragment does not actually contain the term παθητός, though in keeping with the *Dialogue* it does refer to the suffering of crucifixion. Justin refers to the occasion when the Jews "bound together the hands and feet of the crucified Christ," ὅτε συνέδησαν χεῖρας καὶ πόδας τοῦ σταυρουμένου Χριστοῦ (Marcovich, 316 *ll.* 13-14).

31. See n. 1 for other editions of the *Dialogue*. The identification of the *Dialogue's* uses of παθητός with Isa 53:8 was previously made by Goodspeed, but only in *Dial.* 110.2, where παθητός, ἄδοξος, ἄτιμος, and σταυρούμενος are all underlined, with reference to Isa 53:2-3, 8 (Marcovich adds v. 12, apparently for σταυρούμενος). Archambault (p. 162) refers the second of the *Dialogue's* uses of παθητός, in *Dial.* 36.1, to *Dial.* 13.4 = Isa 53:2-4. He also provides a cross-reference to Irenaeus, *Demonstration* 71 (also noted by Williams, 66 n. 5), where the surviving Armenian translation is based on a now lost Greek text that evidently included the term παθητός: "Scripture tells us that Christ . . . was to become a man *subject to suffering*" (*Proof of the Apostolic Preaching*, trans. J. P. Smith, ACW 16 [1952] 93, italics added). Otto also notices παθητός in *Dial.* 36.1 (123 n. 1), but he does not connect it with Isaiah 53, noting only Acts 26:2-3.

32. M. Marcovich, *Iustini Martyris Apologiae pro Christianis*, PTS 38 (1994).

The following limited review[33] of Marcovich's treatment of Isaiah 53 in the *Dialogue* will enable us to create a better index as a basis for further work.

4. Overview of Marcovich's Edition of the *Dialogue*

Although it is impossible here to comment in detail on all of the *Dialogue*'s uses of Isaiah 53, it will be helpful to survey these uses, beginning with the problems of indexing (§4.1) and leading to a new index (§4.2).

4.1 Marcovich's Identification of Scriptural Quotations and Allusions

There are some important omissions in Marcovich's index of biblical quotations and allusions involving Isaiah 53. In *Dial.* 95.3 Justin, with a view to the subject of Jewish responsibility for the death of Jesus, puts a hypothetical quotation of Isaiah 53 into the mouth of Trypho and his compatriots: "And let none of you say, 'If the Father willed him to suffer these things, in order that *by his wounds healing might come* to the human race, then we did nothing wrong.'"[34] This is a clear

33. A full review of Marcovich's edition would include his *textual criticism*: "The *Dialogue* is preserved virtually in a single manuscript — the invaluable *Parisinus gr* 450" (p. 1). Marcovich's textual criticism necessarily involves the frequent conjectural emendation of this manuscript. As T. P. Halton comments: "Not all of his emendations, however, have been adopted, if only because, to steal a colleague's joke, his Greek is so much better than Justin's!" (Falls and Halton [see n. 1], xi). Marcovich's textual emendation of *Dial.* 80.1 is questioned by Horner, *Listening to Trypho* (see n. 2) 205, n. 267. While I have examined a few of Marcovich's emendations in my Translator's notes in C. Markschies's essay above (see nn. 68, 111, 114, 122), a full evaluation is beyond the scope of this essay. I merely comment on Marcovich's emendations as they come up. See above, n. 22 and below, pp. 375-76 on *Dial.* 100.2 (with reference to Thirlby).

34. *Dial.* 95.3 (Marcovich, 234): καὶ μή τις ὑμῶν λεγέτω· Εἰ ὁ πατὴρ αὐτὸν ἠθέλησε ταῦτα παθεῖν, ἵνα τῷ μώλωπι αὐτοῦ ἴασις γένηται τῷ γένει τῶν ἀνθρώπων, ἡμεῖς οὐδὲν ἠδικήσαμεν. For the context compare *Dial.* 95.2; for a similarly-worded allusion to Isa 53:5 see *Dial.* 17.1, Justin: δι' οὗ τῶν μωλώπων ἴασις γίνεται (indexed by Marcovich); for a similar argument about the divine necessity of the crucifixion not mitigating human (Jewish) responsibility, cf. *Dial.* 141.1. The "we" language that Justin attributes to Trypho and his Jewish compatriots here in *Dial.* 95.3 presupposes group solidarity of second-century Jews with their first-century counterparts. It is of course unlikely that Justin's actual interlocutors would play into his hands by trying to quote his favorite Scripture, Isaiah 53, in their defense. The theological formulation here is Christian, resembling Acts 2:23: the existence of an immutable divine plan does not eliminate human responsibility. As Peter tells the "men of Israel" in his Pentecost sermon, "This man, handed over

allusion to Isa 53:5 and the only allusion in its paragraph (though see Matt 23:31 par. in the preceding *Dial.* 95.2). It is missing in Marcovich's index.

More serious is the absence of any index entry for Isa 53:12. Since we know that Justin did not necessarily amass all his Old Testament proofs from independent study of the Old Testament, but also used many proofs already contained in the New Testament or current in Justin's contemporary Christian apologetics or testimony sources (cf. O. Skarsaune), modern readers will want to know whether he has taken advantage of the only undisputed quotation from Isaiah 53 in any of the Gospel passion narratives. The passage is Luke 22:37, where Jesus says:

> For I tell you, this scripture must be fulfilled in me, "And he was counted among the lawless" (καὶ μετὰ ἀνόμων ἐλογίσθη, for LXX καὶ ἐν τοῖς ἀνόμοις ἐλογίσθη [read by Justin in the *Dialogue*]); and indeed what is written about me is being fulfilled.

The Old Testament passage is obviously Isa 53:12 (v. 12c). And it is just as obviously alluded to in *Dial.* 89.3. Goodspeed indexes *Dial.* 89.3 in a single entry under Isa 53:2, 4, 7, 8, 12 because of its combined allusion (see below). Yet there is no hint in Marcovich's index that Justin has made any use of Isa 53:12. Marcovich supplies the necessary reference in his citation apparatus at *Dial.* 89.3 (lines 11-13). But to say that the needed information may therefore be found on the 157th page (p. 225) of a Greek text covering 248 pages (pp. 69-316) is to defeat the purpose of an index.

One might initially wonder whether Justin's reference to Isa 53:12 at *Dial.* 89.3 was left unindexed by Marcovich because it is an indirect quotation introduced by ὅτι, rather than a direct quotation.[35] Nevertheless, the difference between indirect and direct discourse does not account for Marcovich's indexing. Almost all the scripturally allusive verbs in *Dial.* 89.3, where Isa 53:12 is indi-

---

to you according to the definite plan and foreknowledge of God, you crucified and killed by the hands of those outside the law" (NRSV).

35. Justin understands that the prophets were looking forward to Christ and would have thought of his sufferings as future. He therefore retains the original (future) tense of the speaker when reporting the speaker's ideas, where English does not. Justin is explicit about this prophetic perspective in another place. The prophets were so certain about their vision of the future that they could express it in the language of the past, *Dial.* 114.2: "When the Holy Spirit says through Isaiah, *He was led as a sheep to the slaughter, and as a lamb before the shearer* (Isa 53:7), he speaks as though the passion (τὸ πάθος) had already taken place. And again, when he says, *I have stretched out my hands to a disobedient and contradicting people* (Isa 65:2) and, *Lord, who has believed our report* (Isa 53:1), he likewise speaks of events as though they had already happened" (trans. Falls and Halton).

rectly quoted, are the future of indirect discourse — hence the repeated "would be" instead of "will be" in the translation below. Marcovich has simply indexed some of these allusions to the exclusion of others without discernable criteria:[36]

προεῖπον οἱ προφῆται ὅτι *ἀπὸ τῶν ἀνομιῶν τοῦ λαοῦ ἀχθήσεται* [LXX: ἤχθη] *εἰς θάνατον* καὶ *ἀτιμωθήσεται* [LXX: ἠτιμάσθη] καὶ *μαστιχθήσεται* [not in LXX] καὶ *ἐν τοῖς ἀνόμοις λογισθήσεται* [LXX: ἐλογίσθη] καὶ *ὡς πρόβατον ἐπὶ σφαγὴν ἀχθήσεται* [LXX: ἤχθη], *οὗ τὸ γένος ἐξηγήσασθαι ἔχειν οὐδένα*, <ὥς> φησιν ὁ προφήτης. (text: Marcovich, 225, lines 10-14)

The prophets predicted that (ὅτι) *because of the iniquities of the people he would be led to death* (Isa 53:8d), and *would be dishonored* (53:3), and *would be scourged* (53:4), and *would be counted among the lawless* (53:12c), and *would be led as a sheep to the slaughter* (53:7), *whose birth no one can describe* (53:8b), as the prophet (sc. Isaiah) says. (*Dial.* 89.3)

In his apparatus at *Dial.* 89.3 Marcovich correctly records a combined allusion to Isa 53:8 [d] + 3 + 4 + 12 [c] + 8 [b]. But he breaks up this combination in his index, apparently intending to provide a separate entry for each verse. Unfortunately, he successfully indexes only Isa 53:8, while crediting it with the line numbers (*Dial.* 89.3 lines 11-13) that cover the whole set of allusions; one wonders whether this has been influenced by the *inclusio* beginning and ending with v. 8. Marcovich also tries to index the allusion to Isa 53:4 that he rightly finds in *Dial.* 89.3 line 12, μαστιχθήσεται, but he mistakenly gives the reference as line 19, which does not exist.

The origin or precedent for Justin's use of μαστιχθήσεται in *Dial.* 89.3 and the reasoning behind Marcovich's identification of this language with Isa 53:4 (so also Goodspeed) are not initially obvious, because the language of "scourging" or "beating" (μαστιγόω) is not found in LXX Isa 53:4. Marcovich suggestively notes Theodotion's translation of this portion of Isa 53:4 by the perfect passive participle μεμαστιγωμένον, as in the phrase "we considered him *scourged*." Marcovich has presumably taken this from Ziegler's edition *(Isaias)*, where the Greek evidence for Theodotion is provided by the margin of the otherwise Alexandrian LXX MS 86.[37] Marcovich also provides the Latin evidence *flagellatum*. But his vague presentation could lead readers to assume that this is an independent Latin translation that just happens to be in agreement with Theodotion's Greek reading: "μεμαστιγωμένον

---

36. Although some of the indexing of the volume may have been done by Marcovich's assistant Walter Spencer (p. ix), I shall continue to speak of Marcovich as both editor and indexer.

37. See Ziegler, *Isaias*, 321, lower "Hexapla" apparatus, plus his comments on MS 88 on pp. 21-22, 78, 109, 113-14.

Theodotion, *flagellatum* Hilarius (cf. Is 50:6)."[38] In fact the latter is the Latin testimony to Theodotion's Greek, and Marcovich has misidentified the Latin source as Hilary, whereas Ziegler's abbreviation "Hi." actually stands for "Hi[eronymus]" = *Jerome*.[39] If the *Dialogue* is dated ca. 155-160 C.E. with Justin's death ca. 165, and the translating and editing work of the "historical" Theodotion ca. 180-190,[40] then it is not clear that the latter is directly relevant.[41] Nor does there appear to be any evidence of the influence of an earlier "Ur-Theodotion" recension on Justin's text or interpretation of Isaiah 53.[42]

There might be a simpler explanation of Justin's language for alluding to Isa 53:4. The Septuagint expresses the Servant's plight in terms of nouns: καὶ ἡμεῖς ἐλογισάμεθα αὐτὸν εἶναι ἐν πόνῳ καὶ ἐν πληγῇ καὶ ἐν κακώσει, "we considered him to be in *pain* and in a *plague* and in *oppression*" (Isa 53:4b).[43] The term πληγή also occurs in 53:3, "being a man in a plague." But the underlying Hebrew terms are par-

---

38. Isa 50:6 reads: "I gave my back to whips (μάστιγας), and my cheeks to blows (ῥαπίσματα)."

39. Jerome's expression *flagellatum*, rendering Theodotion's μεμαστιγωμένον, may be found in his *Commentariorum in Isaiam prophetam*, book 14, PL 25:525 C: "Et non putavimus eum esse immundum, sive *in dolore* [LXX: ἐν πληγῇ], ut Septuaginta transtulerunt, pro quo Aquila et Symmachus posuerunt *leprosum*, Theodotio, *flagellatum*."

40. For the date of Justin's *Dialogue* see O. Skarsaune, "Justin der Märtyrer," *TRE* 17 (1988) 471-478, esp. 472; R. J. De Simone, "Justin," *EECh* 1 (1992) 463-464; Rudolph, *"Denn wir sind jenes Volk"* (see n. 3), 23. For Theodotion see G. Ladocsi, "Theodotion," *EECh* 2:829, and L. J. Greenspoon, "Theodotion, Theodotion's Version," *ABD* 6:447-448.

41. The comparison of any textual tendencies in Greek Isaiah with the so-called "Theodotion" version of Daniel would probably be inappropriate, since the translator of Daniel is commonly thought not to be the Theodotion of the θ′ materials in other parts of the Greek Old Testament (cf. e.g. J. Ziegler, *Susanna. Daniel. Bel et Draco*, Göttingen LXX [1954] 28-29 n. 1). Nevertheless, in the one large passage where it can be checked, Marcovich (p. 118, apparatus) notes that Justin's text of Dan 7:9-28 in *Dial.* 31.2-7 differs both from the LXX and from so-called "Theodotion" Daniel: "Iustini textus ab LXX et versione Theodotionis (= θ′) differt," citing Prigent (sc. *Justin et l'Ancien Testament* [1964]), 78-79. But at the most important point in Dan 7:13-14 = *Dial.* 31.3-4 *ll.* 15-20 (Marcovich, 119), Justin's text is *not* like the Daniel of "Theodotion." Justin's subsequent use of Daniel depends on the fact that his text of Dan 7:14 resembles the LXX by including the term δόξα, which "Theodotion" lacks. Both Justin and the LXX conclude Dan 7:14 with καὶ πᾶσα δόξα λατρεύουσα, the LXX adding αὐτῷ.

42. I have collated Justin's text of Isa 52:10–54:6 in *Dial.* 13.2-9 against Ziegler's edition of the LXX and presented the results on p. 256 n. 107 of C. Markschies's essay above. While I find 25 departures from Ziegler in point of detail, almost all are minor, and most agree with known variants of the LXX. Justin's text of Isaiah 53 in the *Dialogue* is still basically the LXX and not a known Jewish recension or Christian testimony source. As mentioned above (see n. 9), there is an interesting non-LXX text of Isa 53:12d in *1 Apol.* 50.2, καὶ τοῖς ἀνόμοις ἐξιλάσεται, "and he will *make atonement* for the lawless." But this is hardly Theodotionic — Theodotion reads *et impios torquebit*, "and he will *torture* the impious."

43. Trans. Ekblad, *Isaiah's Servant Poems* (see n. 1), 211; cf. 216-217.

ticiples. Prior to Justin, Aquila had begun the process of conforming the Greek to the Hebrew and naturally chose participles: ἡμεῖς δὲ ἐλογισάμεθα αὐτὸν τετραυματισμένον πεπληγότα ὑπὸ θεοῦ καὶ τεταπεινωμένον.[44] The participle πεπληγότα, "stricken," is Aquila's alternative to LXX's πληγή. Justin may have similarly thought of this passage in terms of verbs rather than nouns. Since πληγή can also mean the "blow" or "stripe" suffered in a beating or scourging (cf. Falls and Halton: "under the stroke," Isa 53:4 = *Dial.* 13.4), it would be a short step to μαστιγόω. The connection is given in the well-known passage from Deuteronomy about the forty stripes or lashes: "If the unrighteous man is worthy of stripes (πληγῶν) . . . , [the judges] shall scourge (μαστιγώσουσιν) him with forty. But they shall not add; for if they add, to scourge (μαστιγῶσαι) him more than these stripes (ὑπὲρ ταύτας τὰς πληγὰς πλείους), then your brother will be degraded in your eyes" (Deut 25:2-3). But even apart from this reference, the connection that Justin could have made on his own between LXX πληγή and his use of μαστιγόω would be fairly obvious.

4.2 A New Index of Marcovich's Edition

Dial. 89.3 represents just one example of the problems of identifying and indexing allusions, not all of which can be solved here. We can, however, hope to improve on Marcovich's index, at least by incorporating as much of the useful material from his citation apparatus as possible. What is needed is an index that both lists every paragraph in which an allusion to Isaiah 53 can be found, and gives an impression of what can be found there in terms of specific verses, yet without too much duplication. For this the format of Goodspeed is useful, which keeps each series of connected allusions together, thus counting *Dial.* 89.3 and *Dial.* 32.2 for example as single occasions of alluding to Isaiah 53.

Goodspeed does not distinguish quotations from allusions, nor does Marcovich's index. But in Marcovich's citation apparatus the direct quotations are usually given their Scripture references directly, while the allusions are given a reference only after a preceding "cf."[45] These judgments should also be reflected in the index.

For completeness we index here all 19 occurrences of παθητός, even

---

44. Aquila as preserved by Eusebius, *Commentarius in Isaiam*, 2.42; text in J. Ziegler, ed., GCS *Eusebius Werke*, vol. 9: *Der Jesajakommentar* (1975) 335 *l.* 38-336 *l.* 2. See also Ziegler, *Isaias*.

45. The convention of Marcovich's "cf." for allusions is nowhere stated but is generally reliable. However, if this is the convention, then it is misapplied in the apparatus at *Dial.* 102.7 *ll.* 49-50. Here the reference "cf. Is 53:9" is given for what is almost an exact quotation of the LXX, which Justin attributes directly to Isaiah: ὡς Ἠσαίας φησίν . . . , ἀνομίαν γὰρ οὐκ ἐποίησεν οὐδὲ δόλον τῷ στόματι, for LXX ὅτι ἀνομίαν οὐκ ἐποίησεν, οὐδὲ εὑρέθη δόλος ἐν τῷ στόματι αὐτοῦ.

though Marcovich leaves one of them unitalicized (*Dial.* 99.2) and leaves seven of them (in six paragraphs) without an apparatus reference to Isa 53:8. Because the πάσχειν language is not found in Isa 53:8 or elsewhere in the fourth Servant Song, Marcovich's links between this passage and παθητός are not particularly strong. Justin makes more recognizable use of another part of Isa 53:8 — verse b. We may therefore subdivide:

(Isa 53:8a) ἐν τῇ ταπεινώσει ἡ κρίσις αὐτοῦ ἤρθη· (8b) τὴν γενεὰν αὐτοῦ τίς διηγήσεται; (8c) ὅτι αἴρεται ἀπὸ τῆς γῆς ἡ ζωὴ αὐτοῦ, (8d) ἀπὸ τῶν ἀνομιῶν τοῦ λαοῦ μου ἤχθη εἰς θάνατον.

The division of Isa 53:9a and b will be obvious. We may also distinguish:

(Isa 53:12b) ἀνθ᾽ ὧν παρεδόθη εἰς θάνατον ἡ ψυχὴ αὐτοῦ, (12c) καὶ ἐν τοῖς ἀνόμοις ἐλογίσθη, (12d) καὶ αὐτὸς ἁμαρτίας πολλῶν ἀνήνεγκεν καὶ διὰ τὰς ἁμαρτίας αὐτῶν παρεδόθη.

The index below uses boldface for direct quotations. Not counting the entry under Isa 53:8d παθητός, each paragraph of the *Dialogue* is entered if possible only once, though *Dial.* 114.2 appears under both Isa 53:1-2 and 53:7, as in Goodspeed (and Marcovich). Within the entry on 53:8d παθητός, the three passages that intersect with the rest of the index, *Dial.* 49.2; 100.2; 110.2, have been underlined. Otherwise the index contains 28 passages, including the 25 from Goodspeed, plus *Dial.* 32.1 (Isa 53:2-3), *Dial.* 49.7 (Isa 53:2), and *Dial.* 121.3 (Isa 53:2-3), yielding a total of 42, once the 14 non-underlined passages under Isa 53:8d παθητός are included.

The line numbers *(ll.)* are from Marcovich. Parenthetical information is given about the named source of quotations and allusions — "Isaiah," "the Word," "the prophets," or "the Scriptures" — and about the speaker in those few places where the *Dialogue* allows Isaiah 53 to be quoted or alluded to by Trypho. Outside the entries under Isa 53:8d παθητός, all of the Scripture identifications below are supported by Marcovich's apparatus except one, which is suggested by his italics (cf. *Dial.* 49.7 under Isa 53:2). The seven paragraphs which found no entry in Marcovich's original index, *Dial.* 14.8; 32.1; 49.7; 95.3; 100.2; 110.2; 121.3, have been restored; see under Isa 53:2; vv. 2-3; vv. 2-3, 8d; vv. 2-3, 8d, 12; and Isa 53:5:

Isaiah	Dialogue
52:10–54:6	**13.2-9** *ll.* **8-58** ("Isaiah")
52:15–53:1	**118.4** *ll.* **25-28** ("Isaiah")
53:1	**114.2** *ll.* **10-11** ("Isaiah")
53:1-2	**42.2-3** *ll.* **9-13** ("Isaiah")
53:2	49.7 (not in apparatus; cf. text: ἄδοξος ἐφάνη, line 54)
53:2-3	32.1 *l.* 4: Trypho, "the Scriptures"; 36.6 *ll.* 35-36; 49.2 *ll.* 14-15 ("the Word"); 85.1 *ll.* 6-7 ("Isaiah"); 88.8 *ll.* 39-40 ("the Scriptures"); 121.3 *l.* 18
53:2-3, 5, 7, 8b, 9a	32.2 *ll.* 8-10 ("the Scriptures")
53:2-3, 8d	14.8 *l.* 43 ("the prophets"); 100.2 *ll.* 13-14 ("the Scriptures")
53:2-3, 8d, 12	110.2 *ll.* 9-10
53:3, 4, 7, 8b, 8d, 12c	89.3 *ll.* 11-13 ("the prophets . . . the prophet");
53:5	17.1 *ll.* 4-5; 32.2 *l.* 10; 43.3 *l.* 18; 95.3 *l.* 19: Trypho (only hypothetically, according to Justin); 137.1 *ll.* 2-3
53:7	**72.3** *ll.* **18-19** ("Isaiah"); 90.1 *l.* 2: Trypho, "the Scriptures"; **111.3** *l.* **19** ("Isaiah"); **114.2** *ll.* **7-8** ("Isaiah")
53:8b	68.4 *l.* 32 ("the Word"); **76.2** *l.* **8** ("Isaiah");
53:8b-d	**43.3** *ll.* **15-18** ("Isaiah"); **63.2** *ll.* **9-10**, 11-12 ("Isaiah")
53:8d (παθητός)	34.2 *l.* 14 (cf. Isa 53:8); 36.1 twice *ll.* 2 and 3: Trypho, "the prophets" (cf. Isa 53:8); 39.7 *l.* 35: Trypho, "the Scriptures" (no ref.); 41.1 *l.* 9 (no ref.); 49.2 *l.* 14 (cf. Isa 53:8); 52.1 twice *ll.* 2 and 4 (no ref.); 68.9 *l.* 61 (cf. Isa 53:8); 70.4 *l.* 25 (no ref.); 74.1 *l.* 5: Trypho (no ref.); 76.6 *l.* 34 (cf. Isa 53:8); 85.2 *l.* 13 (no ref.); 89.2 *l.* 7: Trypho, "the Scriptures" (cf. Isa 53:8); 99.2 *l.* 14 (no italics; no ref.); 100.2 *l.* 14 (cf. Isa 53:8); 110.2 *l.* 9 (cf. Isa 53:8); 111.2 *l.* 13 (cf. Isa 53:8); 126.1 *l.* 5 (cf. Isa 53:8) ("Isaiah")
53:9a	**97.2** *l.* **12** ("Isaiah")
53:9b	**102.7** *ll.* **49-50** ("Isaiah")

5. Justin's Allusive Vocabulary

Much can be learned about the *Dialogue's* internal argument and perhaps even about its external religious and social settings by examining not just Justin's quotations but especially his allusions to Isaiah 53. The above index shows that slightly under half of the passages (12 of 28) outside the entry on Isa 53:8d παθητός involve the direct quotation of material from Isaiah 53. But some of the most important passages for the *Dialogue's* purposes are alluded to rather than quoted. This is always the case for the inglorious, dishonored, formless Messiah of Isa 53:2-3. Echoes of Isa 53:2-3 occur in the combined allusions in *Dial.* 14.8; 32.2 (cf. Trypho in 32.1); 89.3; 110.2, as well as in isolation from other allusions to Isaiah 53 in *Dial.* 36.6; 49.2; 49.7; 85.1; 88.8 and 121.3.

In this section we survey the usage of the terms ἄτιμος, ἀειδής, ἄδοξος, θνητός, and παθητός (see §5.2), as well as of the key term on the other side, ἔνδοξος (opposite of ἄδοξος), referring to the Messiah's "glorious" apprearance at his second advent (cf. Dan 7:14 LXX). The fomer terms either allude to Isaiah 53 or to no specific Scripture passage at all. The adjective ἄτιμος is a particularly dedicated term which always alludes to Isaiah 53 (being taken directly from 53:3). It can be shown that when necessary, Justin uses other cognate terms for being "dishonored" (ἀτιμάζω) or dying "dishonorably" (ἀτίμως) in interpreting passages other than Isaiah 53 (see §5.3).

Consideration of both sets of terms allows us to see how they cooperate in the expression of the two Parousias theme (§5.4; cf. also Table 1 in §5.2). Understanding this theme also explains why in the *Dialogue* Justin has used Isaiah 53 more schematically for the suffering theme alone and not for both suffering and glorification, as in the *1 Apology* and in the mixed presentation of the *1 Apology* and the *Dialogue* by H. W. Wolff (see §5.5). Following all this in 6 is a more specific investigation into the use of παθητός, which also begins our discussion here.

5.1 The παθητὸς Χριστός: A Distinctly Isaianic Allusion?

As our updated index of Marcovich's edition shows, παθητός tends to occur in paragraphs that were not indexed under Isaiah 53 in the otherwise reliable index of Goodspeed. There is overlap only in *Dial.* 49.2; 100.2 and 110.2. Nevertheless παθητός, with its 19 occurrences in 17 paragraphs, is clearly an important term. This is evident especially in its first and last occurrences in the *Dialogue*. When it first appears in *Dial.* 34.2, παθητός forms the climax of the sequence about Christ's life prior to his ascension. Justin says that in the Scriptures,

Christ is spoken of as a *King*, and a *Priest*, and *God*, and *Lord*, and *an Angel*, and *a Man*, and *a Leader*, and *a Stone*, and *a Begotten Son*, and as one *who at first endured suffering* [i.e. became παθητός], then ascended into heaven, and as *returning* to earth *with glory* and *having the eternal kingdom*. (*Dial.* 34.2, trans. Falls and Halton)

The obvious question is, If παθητός usually occurs apart from other references to Isaiah 53 (as here), how do we know that it is Isaianic? The short answer comes in the final occurrence of παθητός in *Dial.* 126.1. It is undisputable that παθητός is marked as Isaianic in this instance; Justin pulls out all the stops and gives the prophetic attributions of all his favorite predicates of Christ:

"But Trypho," I continued, "if you had known who he is who at one time is called *angel of great counsel*, and *Man* by Ezekiel, and the *Son of Man* by Daniel, and a *child* (παιδίον [not παῖς]) by Isaiah, and *Christ* and *God* [and] *who is to be adored* by David, and *Christ* and *Stone* by many prophets, and *Wisdom* by Solomon and Joseph and Judah, and a *Star* by Moses, and *Dawn* by Zechariah, and the *Suffering One* (παθητός) and *Jacob* and *Israel* again by Isaiah, and a *Rod* and *Flower* and *Cornerstone* and *Son of God* you would not have blasphemed him who has come, and assumed human nature, and suffered, and ascended into heaven. And he shall return again, and *then your twelve tribes will weep*" (*Dial.* 126.1, trans. Falls and Halton)

As impressive as this is, in itself it does not prove that Isa 53:8 is specifically in view with the "Isaianic" term παθητός, nor that Justin's readers should have recognized all along what becomes explicit only here at the end, nor that παθητός is necessarily pregnant Bible language that should be italicized every time (save once) that it is used, as in Marcovich. On the other hand, if παθητός is largely Isaianic throughout the *Dialogue*, then it joins the Danielic "Son of Man" as one of the two most important predicates of Christ listed above.

We must ask how many of the other uses of παθητός outside its final occurrence in *Dial.* 126.1 were linked with Isaiah 53 in the thinking of Justin or his interlocutors. Goodspeed in his edition recognizes by italics only two places where παθητός represents scripturally allusive language, here in *Dial.* 126.1 and in 110.2. He offers no reference to Isaiah 53 in *Dial.* 126.1, presumably because Isaiah is already mentioned in the text, and because the places where Isaiah will have identified Christ the Servant with "Jacob" and "Israel" will also be obvious to modern readers[46] — though this may also show Justin thinking more in

---

46. Cf. *Dial.* 123.8; 135.2 for Isa 42:1 LXX, *not* MT, which lacks the names "Jacob" and "Israel"; cf. also Isa 41:8; 44:1, 21. Cf. Skarsaune, *The Proof of Prophecy* (see n. 4), 60-61.

terms of connected "Servant Songs" than many modern interpreters are inclined to do. In *Dial.* 110.2 Goodspeed italicizes the crucial terms παθητὸς καὶ ἄδοξος καὶ ἄτιμος καὶ σταυρούμενος, giving a reference to Isa 53:2, 3, 8 (Marcovich adds v. 12). But where παθητός occurs in a similar matrix of terms (ἄτιμος and ἀειδής) in *Dial.* 49.2 and 100.2, Goodspeed does not italicize it, leaving the criteria unclear.

The language of suffering in general is not always associated with Isaiah 53. When Justin alludes to the suffering Messiah by means of the δεῖ παθεῖν formula of the Gospel passion predictions, he can attribute the idea either to the prophets generally (*Dial.* 106.1) or to Zechariah, for his expression, "Strike the shepherd, and his sheep will be scattered" (Zech 13:7; cf. *Dial.* 53.5). On the other hand, Justin presents Jesus as defining his own passion in terms of Isaiah 53 in *Dial.* 76.6-7 (cf. παθητός in *Dial.* 76.6 with Mark 8:31 par. in 76.7) and 100.2-3 (cf. ἀειδής, ἄτιμος, παθητός in *Dial.* 100.2 with Mark 8:31 par. in 100.3). Justin's Jesus is aware of the prophecy of Isaiah 53 and its role in his first advent and teaches his apostles accordingly (cf. esp. *Dial.* 76.6), even though many modern interpreters think that the historical Jesus did not.

Regarding παθητός and Isaiah 53, even though it is clear that the term means "suffering" in the sense of its synonym θνητός, "mortal" or "dying," which Justin uses in *Dial.* 14.8 (see below), it is not immediately clear that Justin must have been thinking specifically of ἤχθη εἰς θάνατον, "he was led to death," as in Isa 53:8d (Marcovich). As far as statements of death in Isaiah 53 are concerned, Justin could equally well have had in mind παρεδόθη εἰς θάνατον ἡ ψυχὴ αὐτοῦ, "his soul was delivered to death," from Isa 53:12b. However, since Isa 53:12b is not quoted outside the full citation of Isa 52:10–54:6 in *Dial.* 13.2-9 (here 13.7), the language from Isa 53:8d — including the direct quotation ἤχθη εἰς θάνατον in *Dial.* 43.3 (cf. 13.6 ἤκει) and the indirect quotation ἀχθήσεται εἰς θάνατον in *Dial.* 89.3 — is slightly more accessible.[47]

Dial. 89.2-3 turns out to be the key passage supporting Marcovich's editing; he effectively applies its specificity to other passages. In *Dial.* 89.2 Trypho uses παθητός to admit that the prophesied Messiah must suffer, although he continues to doubt whether he can legitimately be crucified (cf. Deut 21:23). Justin confirms in *Dial.* 89.3 that the Messiah who is to be παθητός was prophesied in Isa 53:8d. As we have seen (§4.1), he quotes this indirectly as ἀπὸ τῶν ἀνομιῶν τοῦ λαοῦ μου ἀχθήσεται (LXX ἤχθη) εἰς θάνατον. This is the closest the *Dialogue* comes to linking παθητός and Isa 53:8d.

---

47. The phrase διὰ τὰς ἀνομίας τοῦ λαοῦ εἰς θάνατον παραδεδόσθαι in *Dial.* 63.2 also alludes primarily to Isa 53:8d (LXX: ἀπὸ τῶν ἀνομιῶν), but replaces Isaiah's ἤχθη with the divine passive παραδεδόσθαι borrowed from Isa 53:12d (παρεδόθη).

5.2 Παθητός *in the Network of* ἄτιμος, ἀειδής, *and* ἄδοξος

The preceding section has shown that only a few occurrences of παθητός are clearly marked as Isaianic, the strongest cases being in *Dial.* 89.2 and 126.1. We must therefore examine παθητός in the context of other terms that give it meaning and define it as Isaianic long before Justin finally says that Christ is called "*Suffering One* (παθητός) and *Jacob* and *Israel* by Isaiah" (*Dial.* 126.1).

As noted above, because the Messiah's suffering involves suffering *death*, Justin can understand παθητός, "passible," as a synonym for θνητός, "mortal," which Justin uses once, very early in the *Dialogue* in 14.8, shortly after his long quotation of Isa 52:10–54:6 in *Dial.* 13. Both terms are anchored to Isaiah 53 by appearing together not with explicit quotations of Isaiah 53, but with other terms that allude to this passage. Justin's allusive terms include especially the adjectives ἄτιμος, "without honor," ἀειδής, "without appearance" or "without form" (cf. τὸ εἶδος), ἄδοξος, "without glory," and θνητός, "mortal" — all terms that obviously apply to the Servant of Isaiah 53. Yet only ἄτιμος is actually taken from Isaiah 53 — see v. 3: τὸ εἶδος αὐτοῦ ἄτιμον, "his form was *without honor/dishonorable.*" This adjective also resonates with the verb ἠτιμάσθη at the end of v. 3: "he was *dishonored,*" which Justin uses in the indirect quotation in *Dial.* 89.3 (ἀτιμωθήσεται). While both θνητός and παθητός are interpreted by Marcovich as alluding to Isa 53:8d, the negative terms ἀειδής and ἄδοξος allude more definitely to the repeated denial to the Servant of the qualities of εἶδος and δόξα in Isa 53:2-3. *Honor, form, and glory* are the repeated concepts of Isaiah that Justin picks up. Isaiah says:

οὐκ ἔστιν *εἶδος* αὐτῷ οὐδὲ *δόξα·* καὶ εἴδομεν αὐτόν, καὶ οὐκ εἶχεν *εἶδος* οὐδὲ κάλλος· (3) ἀλλὰ τὸ *εἶδος* αὐτοῦ *ἄτιμον* ἐκλεῖπον παρὰ πάντας ἀνθρώπους. . . . *ἠτιμάσθη* καὶ οὐκ ἐλογίσθη.

There is neither *form* to him nor *glory*. And we saw him, and he had neither *form* nor beauty. (3) But his *form* was *without honor,* inferior to that of all men. . . . He was *dishonored* and not regarded. (Isa 53:2-3)

Justin echoes Isa 53:2-3 in some 11 passages (see below), once including all three terms ἄτιμος, ἀειδής, and ἄδοξος, together with Isaiah's term εἶδος, in *Dial.* 36.6:

οἱ ἐν οὐρανῷ ἄρχοντες ἑώρων *ἀειδῆ* καὶ *ἄτιμον* τὸ *εἶδος* καὶ *ἄδοξον* ἔχοντα αὐτόν. . . .

The rulers in heaven saw him being *with respect to his appearance* (τὸ εἶδος) *without form,* and *without honor,* and *without glory.* . . .

Ἄδοξος here in combination with εἶδος could secondarily allude to Isa 52:14, οὕτως *ἀδοξήσει ἀπὸ ἀνθρώπων τὸ εἶδός σου καὶ ἡ δόξα σου ἀπὸ τῶν ἀνθρώπων*.

The four terms ἄτιμος, ἀειδής, ἄδοξος, and θνητός occur a total of 23 times in 12 passages in Justin's *Dialogue*. But since the first passage, *Dial.* 13.4, is simply the quotation of Isa 53:3 (ἄτιμος) within the long quotation of Isa 52:10–53:14, we may reckon with 11 passages of Justin's own writing. These are presented in Table 1 on p. 351.

The table is complete for the first four terms, ἄτιμος, ἀειδής, ἄδοξος, and θνητός. However, there are 16 occurrences of παθητός not represented in the table, and six relevant occurrences of ἔνδοξος (cf. Dan 7:14). The P stands for a mention of the first or second Parousia.

All these terms or expressions make allusion to Scripture in all these passages: ἄτιμος, ἀειδής, ἄδοξος to Isa 53:2-3 (see above), θνητός and παθητός to Isa 53:8 (Marcovich), and ἔνδοξος, ἐν δόξῃ, or μετὰ δόξης to Dan 7:14 (Marcovich). Marcovich italicizes all these terms in all these passages, with the exception of the second of the two occurrences of ἄδοξος in *Dial.* 49.7, and the occurrence of ἔνδοξος in 36.6, where it refers to Solomon (≠). Marcovich also provides apparatus references to Isa 53:2-3, 8 and Dan 7:13-14 for the respective terms in all these places (again except for *Dial.* 49.7).

Unfortunately, these allusions to Isaiah 53 are not well served by Marcovich's index. It is futile to try to discover the criteria for inclusion and exclusion.[48] The boldface ● in Table 1 shows how few of these terms have caused a reference to their associated verses — only vv. 2-3 in case of Isaiah 53 — to be entered into Marcovich's index. Marcovich treats the language alluding to Daniel 7, ἔνδοξος and related expressions, better than he treats the language alluding to Isaiah 53. This seems strange, since the linguistic claim of this term on its biblical text is no stronger: clearly both ἄδοξος and ἔνδοξος make the same claim on the biblical term δόξα, whether it occurs negatively in Isa 53:2-3, or positively in Dan 7:14 LXX.

---

48. Of the 11 passages of Justin's writing in Table 1, only three are properly indexed: *Dial.* 36.6; 85.1; 88.8. Of the remaining 8 passages, two are not indexed by Marcovich under either Isaiah 53 or Dan 7:13-14: cf. *Dial.* 49.7-8 and 100.2. An additional four are not indexed under Isaiah 53, but only under Dan 7:13-14, even though both Isaiah and Daniel contribute equally to the two advents and the movement from dishonor to glory (cf. ἔνδοξος): Dial 14.8; 32.1; 110.1-2, 121.3. *Dial.* 32.2 is indexed under Isaiah 53, but not for its allusion to Isa 53:2-3 by means of ἄδοξος, which was missed; it contains a combined allusion to Isa 53:2-3 + 8b + 9 + 5 + 7 (see above). Similarly, *Dial.* 49.2 is indexed for its allusion to Isa 53:2-3 by ἄτιμος and ἀειδής and to Dan 7:14 by ἔνδοξος, but not for the allusion to Isa 53:8 by παθητός that Marcovich notes in his apparatus.

Table 1. Justin's Allusive Vocabulary for Isaiah 53

Dialogue:	13.4	14.8	32.1*	32.2	36.6*	49.2	49.7-8	85.1	88.8	100.2	110.1-2	121.3
ἄτιμος (9x)	●	○	○		●	●		●!		○	○	○
ἀειδής (7x)		○			●	●		●!	●	○	○	○
ἄδοξος (6x)		○	○	○	●		2x				○	
θνητός (1x)		○										
παθητός (19x)						○				○	○	
1st/2d Parousia		P		P		P	P				P	P
ἔνδοξος (11x)			●		≠	●	○				●	●
[ἐν δόξῃ] or [μετὰ δόξης] (cf. Dan 7:14)		[●]									[●]	

● = in Marcovich's index
○ = in Marcovich's apparatus, not indexed
P = Parousia
* = spoken by Trypho
! = attributed to Isaiah and David (85.1)

The Danielic language of ἔνδοξος ("glorious") is included because Daniel 7 is Justin's proof for the exaltation of the Messiah, just as Isaiah 53 is for his suffering; the two work in tandem. Six of the passages above explain that the Messiah lacks glory and honor, and suffers, only during the first of his two advents or Parousias (P).[49] This is typically matched by a statement of his exaltation ἐν τῇ *ἐνδόξῳ* αὐτοῦ παρουσίᾳ, "at his *glorious* Parousia" (or similar), which is contrasted with Christ's "Isaianic" first Parousia in *Dial.* 49.2; 49.7-8; 110.1-2; 121.3, and other passages not in the table (see below §5.4).

The near equivalence of παθητός and θνητός for Justin results in part from the fact that θνητός appears only once, within a network of vocabulary that undeniably alludes to Isaiah 53 (vv. 2-3), and then is later replaced in this network by παθητός. Justin says that Christ's first advent or Parousia is the one

> in which he is proclaimed as appearing *without honor* (ἄτιμος) and *without form* (ἀειδής) and *mortal* (θνητός). (*Dial.* 14.8)

Later the same sequence of ἄτιμος and ἀειδής is followed, but the third element is moved to the front, with παθητός substituting for θνητός. Hence the first Parousia is the one

> in which he will appear *liable to suffering* (παθητός) and *without honor* (ἄτιμος) and *without form* (ἀειδής). (*Dial.* 49.2)

The equivalence within this structure of παθητός and θνητός is clear. *Dial.* 100.2 repeats the same three terms as 49.2. It fronts ἀειδής and adds a reference to a "man," possibly alluding, at least secondarily, to the traditional "man of sorrows, and acquainted with grief" (Isa 53:3). By becoming incarnate by a virgin, Christ condescended to become

> a man *without form* (ἀειδής) and *without honor* (ἄδοξος) and *liable to suffering* (παθητός). (*Dial.* 100.2)

Finally the two advents theme is used once again to explain παθητός. Again this is placed at the front of the sequence, and it is furthermore joined, together with the terms ἄτιμος and ἄδοξος, by a reference to crucifixion, σταυρούμενος. The first Parousia is the one

---

49. For a helpful table of the *Dialogue's* references to the two comings of Christ, including the six "P" passages in our table above, plus *Dial.* 31.1; 34.2; 36.1; 52.1, 4; 120.4, see Skarsaune, *The Proof from Prophecy* (see n. 4), 155 (cf. 156).

in which [Christ] is proclaimed as *liable to suffering* (παθητός) and *without glory* (ἄδοξος) and *without honor* (ἄτιμος) and *crucified* (σταυρούμενος). (*Dial.* 110.2)

All this proves that structurally speaking, the two terms παθητός and θνητός occupy exactly the same semantic space in the *Dialogue*. Stylistically speaking, however, it is perhaps not surprising that Jesus is referred to only once as a "mortal" Messiah but 19 times as a "suffering" or "passible" one. In the Gospels, too, the language of suffering (παθεῖν) is given prominence, both as the leading term of the first passion prediction, δεῖ τὸν υἱὸν τοῦ ἀνθρώπου πολλὰ παθεῖν, etc. (Mark 8:31 = Luke 9:22; cf. Matt 16:21),[50] which Justin quotes three times (*Dial.* 51.2; 76.7; 100.3), and as the key prophetic term about the Messiah's fate to which Jesus returns in instructing the disciples on the road to Emmaus in Luke 24:26 (ταῦτα ἔδει παθεῖν τὸν χριστόν) and in his appearance soon thereafter to the eleven in Jerusalem in Luke 24:46 (οὕτως γέγραπται παθεῖν τὸν χριστόν), to which Justin also alludes (*Dial.* 53.5; 106.1).

5.3 Dedicated Uses of ἄτιμος

With its nine occurrences, ἄτιμος, "without honor" or "dishonorable," is the *Dialogue*'s second most frequent term for alluding to the Servant of Isaiah 53, after παθητός, "passible."[51] It is the only one of Justin's allusive terms taken directly from the text of Isaiah 53 — see the quotation of Isa 53:3 in *Dial.* 13.4 — and it is present from the beginning to the end of Justin's allusions to Isaiah 53: see *Dial.* 14.8; 32.1; 36.6; 49.2; 85.1; 100.2; 110.2; 121.3. Only the final use of παθητός occurs after this, in *Dial.* 126.1. Unlike παθητός, ἄτιμος never appears apart from other allusive terms for Isaiah 53. This is graphically presented in Table 1.

As may be seen from the table, ἄτιμος is most frequently accompanied by ἀειδής, with seven occurrences, referring to the Servant's lack of "form" (εἶδος) at his first coming. Apart from *Dial.* 88.8, ἀειδής never appears without ἄτιμος. The two are paired as closely in the *Dialogue* as they are in the Scripture: ἀλλὰ τὸ εἶδος αὐτοῦ ἄτιμον (Isa 53:3). Where ἀειδής is lacking, ἄδοξος fills in to accompany ἄτιμος (*Dial.* 32.1; 110.2). Finally, παθητός and θνητός combine either with ἄτιμος and ἀειδής (*Dial.* 14.8; 49.2; 100.2) or with ἄτιμος and ἄδοξος (*Dial.* 110.2).

---

50. In quoting the first passion prediction in *Dial.* 51.2; 76.7; 100.3, Justin always replaces Jesus' own language of the Son of Man being "killed" (ἀποκτανθῆναι) with the more specific language of his being "crucified" (σταυρωθῆναι) found later in the two angels' summary of Jesus' passion prediction in Luke 24:7.

51. See ἄτιμος in *Dial.* 13.4; 14.8; 32.1; 36.6; 49.2; 85.1; 100.2; 110.2; 121.3.

Since the present study is devoted to the possibility of weighing the allusive force of individual terms, it is relevant to note that ἄτιμος is a "pure" term, never "diluted" by application to other passages than Isaiah 53. In other words, when Justin needs to talk about the Messiah being *dishonored,* if his scriptural proof is not Isaiah 53, he will not use the adjective ἄτιμος, but a cognate term from the same root.

Hence in his excursus on Psalm 22, when Justin interprets Ps 22 (LXX 21):7, "I am a worm, and not a man; the reproach of men, and the outcast of the people," he uses ἀτιμάζω rather than ἄτιμος to describe how Christ was "dishonored" by the people of his own nation: "He is *the outcast of the people,* for he was cast out and *dishonored* by your [plural] people," ἐξουθένημα δὲ τοῦ λαοῦ, ὅτι ὑπὸ τοῦ λαοῦ ὑμῶν ἐξουδενωθεὶς [Otto: ἐξουθενηθεὶς] καὶ ἀτιμωθείς (*Dial.* 101.2).

Similarly, when explaining how Christ, having been made the scapegoat (ἀποπομπαῖος) by the Jewish leaders at his first coming, will be recognized at his second coming as also having been the goat chosen as the sacrificial victim (εἰς προσφοράν), Justin says: "You shall recognize him who was *treated dishonorably* by you and who was a sacrificial offering for all sinners," ἐπιγνωσθήσεσθε αὐτόν, τὸν ἀτιμωθέντα ὑφ' ὑμῶν, καὶ προσφορὰ ἦν ὑπὲρ πάντων τῶν . . . ἁμαρτωλῶν (*Dial.* 40.4).

Again, when the *Dialogue* has Trypho object to Jesus' Messiahship based on Deuteronomy's "cursed by God is anyone who is hanged on a tree" (Deut 21:23), here understood as anyone who is "crucified," the term used is not ἄτιμος but the adverb ἀτίμως. Trypho says: "We doubt whether the Messiah should be so *dishonorably* crucified," εἰ δὲ καὶ ἀτίμως οὕτως σταυρωθῆναι τὸν Χριστόν, ἀπορεῖμεν (*Dial.* 89.2).[52]

Two paragraphs later Trypho, in the only quotation given to him from

---

52. These lexical details are not always appreciated. Bingham misses the difference between ἄτιμος and ἀτίμως here in *Dial.* 89.2 and misprints Justin's Greek as the adjective, while correctly translating as an adverb: "Trypho doubts 'whether Christ should be so *shamefully* (ἄτιμος) crucified' (*Dial.* 89.2; M, 224-25)" ("Justin and Isaiah 53" [see n. 13], 251, italics added, citing but misprinting Marcovich's text, ἀτίμως [M]). In treating Trypho's related statement in *Dial.* 90.1 (see the next note), Bingham repeats the same confusion of ἄτιμος with Justin's ἀτίμως and adds the confusion of αἰσχρός and αἰσχρῶς, this time translating both as adjectives: Trypho doubts whether the Christ should "die so *disgraceful* (αἰσχρός) and *shameful* (ἄτιμος) a death" (p. 251, italics added). The translation "so disgraceful and shameful a death" resembles that of T. B. Falls in FC 6 (see n. 1), 291. Bingham has in effect — certainly not intentionally — adjusted the printing of the Greek to fit the periphrastic translation of Falls. The adverbs here admittedly derive from the cited adjectives, but it is not standard practice to eliminate the difference in their citation forms.

Isaiah 53 (though it is an indirect quotation with the future ἀχθήσεσθαι instead
of the LXX's aorist ἤχθη), goes so far as to suggest that for the Messiah to be a
human *sacrificial victim*, a "sheep led to the slaughter" (Isa 53:7) — which bears
some analogy to the precepts of the law (though human, especially child sacrifice is of course forbidden) — would be noble or at least more comprehensible
than his dying "dishonorably" by crucifixion according to Deut 21:23:

> We are indeed aware that he [sc. the Messiah] was to *suffer* and to be *led as a
> sheep* [*sc. to the slaughter*]. But prove to us that he was to be crucified and
> thus to die *disgracefully* (αἰσχρῶς) and *dishonorably* (ἀτίμως) by the death
> cursed in the law. (*Dial.* 90.1)[53]

These passages underscore that the adjective ἄτιμος is the only term of
Justin's allusive vocabulary taken directly from Isaiah 53 (cf. v. 3), and he keeps
it that way. At most we find two passages in which the Isaianic reference of
ἄτιμος is joined by a reference to David's God-forsaken One of Psalm 22, once
by verbal allusion and once by direct mention. In *Dial.* 121.3 Marcovich rightly
sees a reference to Isa 53:2-3 by the first two terms and to Ps 22 (LXX 21):7 by the
participle: ἐν τῇ ἀτίμῳ καὶ ἀειδεῖ καὶ ἐξουθενημένῃ πρώτῃ παρουσίᾳ αὐτοῦ, "at
his *dishonorable* and *formless* and *despised* first coming" (*Dial.* 121.3).[54] The direct mention of David together with Isaiah as the two prophets of the suffering
Messiah comes in *Dial.* 85.1. Here, however, the language of suffering — once
again ἄτιμος and ἀειδής — is that of the star witness, Isaiah, and David is added
only as a corroborating witness:

> Then, too, some of you dare to explain the following words, *Lift up your
> gates, O you princes, and be you lifted up, O eternal gates, that the King of*

53. Text in Marcovich, p. 225 (italics modified above): παθεῖν μὲν γὰρ καὶ ὡς πρόβατον
ἀχθήσεσθαι οἴδαμεν· εἰ δὲ καὶ σταυρωθῆναι καὶ οὕτως αἰσχρῶς καὶ ἀτίμως ἀποθανεῖν διὰ τοῦ
κεκατηραμένου ἐν τῷ νόμῳ θανάτου, ἀπόδειξον ἡμῖν (*Dial.* 90.1). While παθεῖν is italicized here, it
is given no explanation in Marcovich's citation apparatus, though in the context one would naturally assume that Marcovich sees παθεῖν, like παθητός, as a pregnant summary of Isaiah 53.

54. For ἐξουθενημένη (ἐξουθενέω) here in *Dial.* 121.3, compare the participle from a synonymous verb, ἐξουδενωθείς (ἐξουδενόω), used in Justin's explanation of Ps 22:7 in *Dial.* 101.2,
discussed above. Cf. LSJ 598: ἐξουθενέω = ἐξουδενόω. This slight difference becomes a point of
textual criticism in the editions. Hence at *Dial.* 101.2 line 15 Marcovich (p. 243) reads
ἐξουδενωθείς with codex *Parisinus gr* 450 (= A), but notes that Otto corrects to ἐξουθενηθείς to
match the participle with the noun ἐξουθένημα in Justin's text of Ps 22 (LXX 21):7 in the same
line. Justin has the same term in his full quotation of the psalm in *Dial.* 98.3 line 13, though as
Marcovich rightly notes (p. 238), the variant ἐξουθένημα/ἐξουδένημα is also found in LXX
manuscripts; see S, A, R as against B and U. Justin also once reads ἐξουδένωμα for Ps 22:7 in
Dial. 101.1; the term is also found in Ps 90 (LXX 89):5.

Glory may enter (Ps 24 [LXX 23]:7), as if they referred to Hezekiah, while others of you apply them to Solomon. We can prove, to the contrary, that they were spoken neither of the one, nor of the other, nor quite simply of any of your kings, but solely of this Christ of ours, who appeared *without form* and *without honor* (τὸν ἀειδῆ καὶ ἄτιμον φανέντα), as Isaiah, David, and all the Scriptures testify, who is *Lord of hosts* (cf. Ps 24 [LXX 23]:10) by the will of the Father, who bestowed that honor upon him. (*Dial.* 85.1 trans. Falls and Halton [mod.])

If David, in addition to Isaiah, testifies anywhere to Christ enduring the disgrace of being *without form* and *without honor,* then it must be in Psalm 22 (LXX 21), though Justin begins to expound this only in *Dial.* 97. However, no doubt part of the reason for including David in *Dial.* 85.1 is that he is the author of the opening quotation from Psalm 24 (LXX 23):7. See similarly *Dial.* 36.6:

Now, when these heavenly princes saw that he was in appearance *without form,* and *without honor,* and *without glory (ἀειδῆ* καὶ *ἄτιμον τὸ εἶδος* καὶ *ἄδοξον)* and (therefore) failed to recognize him (sc. as divine), they asked, *Who is this King of Glory?* (Ps 24 [LXX 23]:8). And the Holy Spirit, either in his own name or in the Father's, answered, *The Lord of Hosts. He is the King of Glory* (v. 10).

Despite its association with material from Psalms 22 and 24, the distinctly Isaianic reference of ἄτιμος (and ἀειδής and ἄδοξος) has not been compromised in any of these cases. The priority of Isaiah remains clear.

5.4 Isaiah and Daniel: The Two Parousias

The Isaianic reference of παθητός is established not only by its occurrence with the allusive terms for Isa 53:2-3, ἄτιμος, ἀειδής, and ἄδοξος in *Dial.* 49.2; 100.2; and 110.2, but also by its contrast with Dan 7:13-14 within the scheme of the two advents or Parousias.[55] This phenomenon makes an appearance in Table 1 in §5.2. Whereas that table is complete for the occurrences of ἄτιμος, ἀειδής, ἄδοξος, and θνητός, it only hints at the larger structure that Justin has set up to make Christ's first coming primarily "Isaianic" and his second "Danielic." The latter is associated especially with the term ἔνδοξος as the antonym of ἄδοξος; the two occur together in *Dial.* 32.1; 49.7-8; 110.1-2. On the other hand, not every use of the term παρουσία is clearly associated with the language of Daniel 7 or

---

55. On the two Parousias see also Rudolph, *"Denn wir sind jenes Volk"* (see n. 3), 193-196.

Isaiah 53, and there are ways of speaking of Christ's "coming again" without using the term παρουσία.

We may summarize the *Dialogue's* usage of παρουσία and of the broader theme of the two advents as follows. The term παρουσία occurs 27 times in 23 paragraphs, with two occurrences in four of these paragraphs: *Dial.* 14:8; 49.2; 49.7; 121.3 (marked with 2*x* below). *Dial.* 49.7 continues into 49.8, with another occurrence, so counting *Dial.* 49.7-8 as one passage yields a total of 22 passages. Of these, six overlap with the vocabulary network for Isaiah 53 or Daniel 7 already identified in Table 1 above; these are printed in **boldface** below. The list can be extended to include references to Christ's coming, or coming again, *without* the term παρουσία, as in the four passages *Dial.* 34.2 (see below §6.2, item 1); 64.7; 76.6 (see below §6.2, item 10); 120.4. These non-Parousia references are underlined. Finally, παθητός is also found in six of the passages; these references are *italicized:*

> *Dial.* **14.8** (*παρουσία* 2*x*); 31.1; **32.2**; 34.2; 35.8; *36.1;* 40.4; 45.5; **49.2** (2*x*); **49.7** (2*x*)-**49.8** (1*x*); 51.2; *52.1;* 52.4; 53.1; 54.1; 64.7; 69.7; 76.6; 88.2; **110.2**; 110.5; 111.1; 118.2; 120.3; 120.4; **121.3** (2*x*)

It can be seen from the bold endpoints *Dial.* 14.8 and 121.3 that the two Parousias language basically enters and exits the *Dialogue* at the same place as do allusions to Isaiah 53 (except for the use of παθητός in *Dial.* 126.1 and the near-quotation of Isa 53:5 in *Dial.* 137.1).

In the network of ἄτιμος, ἀειδής, and ἄδοξος, Justin's allusions to Isaiah are usually subtle; to name him as the source in every instance would ruin the effect. Isaiah is not named in most of the paragraphs listed in Table 1. However, the first time this network appears, in *Dial.* 14:8, is also the first occurrence of the two advents theme. Here Justin tells Trypho — and more importantly his readers — how he expects his two major Scripture passages, Isaiah 53 and Daniel 7, to work together to accomplish his purposes:

> Τῶν τε λόγων τούτων καὶ τοιούτων εἰρημένων ὑπὸ τῶν προφητῶν, ἔλεγον, ὦ Τρύφων, οἱ μὲν εἴρηνται εἰς τὴν πρώτην παρουσίαν τοῦ Χριστοῦ, ἐν ᾗ καὶ *ἄτιμος* καὶ *ἀειδής* καὶ *θνητὸς* φανήσεσθαι κεκηρυγμένος ἐστίν, οἱ δὲ εἰς τὴν δευτέραν αὐτοῦ παρουσίαν, ὅτε *ἐν δόξῃ* καὶ *ἐπάνω τῶν νεφελῶν παρέσται,* καὶ *ὄψεται ὁ λαὸς ὑμῶν καὶ γνωριεῖ εἰς ὃν ἐξεκέντησαν,* ὡς Ὡσηέ, εἷς τῶν δώδεκα προφητῶν, καὶ Δανιὴλ προεῖπον, εἰρημένοι εἰσί. (*Dial.* 14.8; Marcovich, 94)

"Now of these and similar words spoken by the Prophets, Trypho," I said, "some have been spoken with reference to the first coming of Christ, in which he is proclaimed as appearing (sc. in the future [φανήσεσθαι]) *without honor (ἄτιμος)* and *without form (ἀειδής)* and *mortal (θνητός)*. But others have been spoken with reference to his second coming *in glory (ἐν δόξῃ)* and *upon the clouds (ἐπάνω τῶν νεφελῶν)*, and your people *will see* and will recognize *him whom they pierced (ὃν ἐξεκέντησαν)*, as Hosea, one of the Twelve Prophets, and Daniel foretold. (*Dial.* 14.8)

The member of the Twelve Prophets to be identified here is obviously not "Hosea" but Zechariah (cf. Zech 12:10). The Daniel reference is also easily recognized. While Justin's text of Dan 7:14, presented later in *Dial.* 31.4, does not literally say that the Son of Man will come "in glory" (ἐν δόξῃ) or "with glory" (μετὰ δόξης, cf. 34.2; 110.2),[56] it agrees with the LXX in recording that when the Son of Man came on the clouds during Daniel's night vision, "all glory" was there "serving" him, καὶ πᾶσα δόξα λατρεύουσα (sc. αὐτῷ). Justin will subsequently shorten his adverbial prepositional phrase ἐν δόξῃ to the adjective ἔνδοξος and use it to describe this second coming as "glorious" (first used in this sense in *Dial.* 31.1).

The unstated reference here in *Dial.* 14.8 to *Isaiah* as the principal prophet of the Messiah's passion at his first advent is no less certain than the stated reference to Daniel. It is not just that the allusive vocabulary for Isaiah 53, *without honor (ἄτιμος)* and *without form (ἀειδής)* and *mortal (θνητός)*, is used. Rather, when Justin refers to "these and similar words spoken by the Prophets," he refers "these words" about Christ's first coming to the two long passages he has just quoted from Isaiah, while any "similar words" that might be spoken by other prophets have not yet been mentioned; it is Isaiah who is taken as both representative and preeminent. Justin has just finished writing out Isa 52:10–54:6 and Isa 55:3-13 between the beginning of chapter 13 and here in *Dial.* 14.8. The identification is therefore not in question.

Justin thus defines the first Parousia as Isaianic and the second as Danielic from the very start. When he next mentions the theme, he reinforces it with a long quotation from Dan 7:9-28 in *Dial.* 31.2-7 to parallel his long quotation of Isaiah 52:10–54:6 in *Dial.* 13.2-9. In introducing this Justin says,

If such power is shown to have accompanied, and even now accompanies, the economy of his Passion (τῇ τοῦ πάθους αὐτοῦ οἰκονομίᾳ), just think how great shall be his power at his *glorious* coming (ἡ ἐν τῇ ἐνδόξῳ γινομένῃ αὐτοῦ παρουσίᾳ [sc. δύναμις])! For, as Daniel foretold, *He shall come on the*

---

56. The language of the Son of Man coming "in" or "with" glory is found in Matt 16:27; 24:30; 25:31 and has understandably influenced the way Justin presents Daniel's prophecy.

clouds as the Son of Man, accompanied by his angels. (*Dial.* 31.1, trans. Falls and Halton)

Marcovich here italicizes ἔνδοξος and refers it to Dan 7:13-14; it is the first occurrence of the term in this sense,[57] and it essentially takes over the role of ἐν δόξῃ in *Dial.* 14.8 (Marcovich links the two occurrences in his apparatus). Subsequently Marcovich will always italicize ἔνδοξος, since it never fails to carry an allusion to Dan 7:14, as it does here in 31.1,[58] in its remaining 10 relevant occurrences.[59] In other words, he treats ἔνδοξος as he does its antonym ἄδοξος and the other terms alluding to Isaiah 53, ἄτιμος, ἀειδής, θνητός, and παθητός. Interestingly, the Daniel language never "outruns" the Isaiah language: ἄτιμος, ἀειδής, and ἔνδοξος all have their final occurrence in *Dial.* 121.3.

Of the eleven relevant occurrences of ἔνδοξος, five occur in the network of ἄτιμος, ἀειδής, and ἔνδοξος and therefore are firmly fixed within the two advents scheme defined by Isaiah 53 and Daniel 7 (see Table 1, on p. 351 above). The final allusion to both of the "two advents" Scripture passages in *Dial.* 121.3 is hardly in doubt, even though the two attributed quotations belong to Zechariah, and the opening allusion is to Psalm 72 (LXX 71):

> [121.2] Thus the Word said, His name shall arise above the sun (cf. Ps 72:17). And Zechariah affirms, *The Dawn is his name* (Zech 6:12). [121.3] And again, *They shall mourn tribe by tribe* (Zech 12:12; cf. *Dial.* 32.2). But, if he was so brilliant and powerful at his first coming, which was *without honor* and *without form* and *scorned* (ἐν τῇ ἀτίμῳ καὶ ἀειδεῖ καὶ ἐξουθενημένῃ πρώτῃ παρουσίᾳ αὐτοῦ), that he is known in every nation, and some men of every nationality have repented of their former wicked manner of life; and even the devils were subject to his name and all the powers and kingdoms fear his name more than they fear all the dead, shall he not at his *glorious* coming (ἐν τῇ ἐνδόξῳ αὐτοῦ παρουσίᾳ) completely destroy all who hated him

---

57. There have been three irrelevant occurrences of ἔνδοξος before *Dial.* 31.1, and there will be two after. Twice the expression τὰ ἔνδοξα, "glorious things," occurs in a quotation of Isa 64:3, 11 in *Dial.* 25.4 *l.* 17 and 25.5 *l.* 31. In *Dial.* 2.2 the ἔνδοξοι are "illustrious men," such as the early philosophers. *Dial.* 36.6 speaks of Solomon as a "glorious king." The term's final occurrence is in the phrase "magnificent chariots" (*Dial.* 131.3).

58. Somewhat puzzlingly, Marcovich refers ἔνδοξος in *Dial.* 31.1 line 2 (cf. ἐν τῇ ἐνδόξῳ . . . αὐτοῦ παρουσίᾳ) not, as expected, to πᾶσα δόξα λατρεύουσα in line 19 but to ἐξουσία in line 18 of *Dial.* 31 (= Dan 7:14).

59. Cf. ἔνδοξος in *Dial.* 31.1; 32.1; 35.8; 36.1; 36.6; 49.2; 49.8; 83.4; 86.1; 110.1; 121.3. As with the other terms, Marcovich gives (almost) all the references for ἔνδοξος at its first relevant occurrence in *Dial.* 31.1, including the related expressions ἐν δόξῃ (*Dial.* 14.8) and μετὰ δόξης (*Dial.* 34.2; 110.2).

and maliciously turned their backs on him, while bestowing upon his faithful followers rest and every other blessing they expected? (*Dial.* 121.2-3, trans. Falls and Halton [mod.])

This is the last mention of the two advents theme (unfortunately unindexed under Isaiah 53, an essential part of this theme, in both Marcovich and Goodspeed). It recalls the *a fortiori* argument about the surprising power of the first *inglorious* coming and the necessarily greater power of the second *glorious* coming that Justin used at his second mention of the two advents theme — his first relevant use of ἔνδοξος — in *Dial.* 31.1. As indicated in §5.3, Marcovich recognizes the allusions here in *Dial.* 121.3 to Isa 53:2-3 (ἄτιμος, ἀειδής) and Dan 7:14 (ἔνδοξος). The remaining italicized term in *Dial.* 121.3, the participle ἐξουθενημένη, alludes to Psalm 22 (LXX 21):7, ἐξουθένημα. Language from Justin's second most important scriptural proof of the suffering Messiah, Psalm 22 (cf. *Dial.* 97-106), thus joins the language of his most important proof, Isaiah 53.

5.5 H. W. Wolff on the Exaltation Motif in Isaiah 52:13

Knowledge of Justin's two advents theme can help to differentiate his uses of Isaiah 53 in the *Dialogue* from those in his *1 Apology*. I believe that these differences were not sufficiently taken into account in the classic work by H. W. Wolff, *Jesaja 53 im Urchristentum*.

I disagree with W. H. Wolff to the extent that he allows the *1 Apology* to influence his reading of the *Dialogue*'s distinct approach to — read: non-use of — the exaltation motif of the Servant in Isa 52:13. He writes:

> In five passages [sc. of Justin's writings, including the *1 Apology* and the *Dialogue*], the mention of the first Parousia which was without form and without honor is followed by the mention of a second Parousia "with glory." It makes sense to see here as well an allusion to our prophecy, especially to Isa 52:13.[60]

The five passages according to Wolff (133 n. 605) are *1 Apol.* 50.1 and *Dial.* 110.2: μετὰ δόξης; *Dial.* 49.2, 8 and 121.3: ἔνδοξος. He refers all five to Isa 52:13, δοξασθήσεται σφόδρα.

Wolff wishes to use Isa 52:13–53:12 as a source for both the first and second Parousias. I have argued by contrast that according to the *Dialogue*, the first Parousia was prophesied by Isaiah and the second by Daniel. What Wolff fails to

---

60. Wolff, *Jesaja 53 im Urchristentum* (³1952), 133, followed by C. Markschies, above p. 258 with n. 110.

mention here is that in the *Dialogue* the first, "Isaianic" Parousia — in addition to being *without form* (ἀειδής) and *without honor* (ἄτιμος) — is also *inglorious,* ἄδοξος (cf. *Dial.* 110.2, which Wolff mentions, and *Dial.* 32.2 and 49.7, which he does not). This language *contrasts* the inglorious Servant of Isaiah 53 with the glorious Son of Man of Daniel 7, so that in these contexts at least, Isaiah 53 cannot sustain the "glory" motif that Wolff attributes to it.

Wolff mentions ἔνδοξος in *Dial.* 49.8 and refers this to Isa 52:13. However, if Isaiah 53 is reflected in this context, it is more likely in *Dial.* 49.7, line 54: "Christ appeared *without glory/inglorious* at his first advent," ὁ Χριστὸς τῇ πρώτῃ παρουσίᾳ ἄδοξος ἐφάνη (italicized by Marcovich, without a reference to Isa 53:2-3). This directly contrasts with the ἔνδοξος that Wolff mentions in *Dial.* 49.8, ἐν τῇ ἐνδόξῳ παρουσίᾳ τοῦ Χριστοῦ, "at the *glorious* (second) advent of Christ." Given what the two Parousias theme expresses elsewhere, it would require special pleading to refer ἔνδοξος to Isa 52:13, as Wolff does, rather than to Dan 7:14 (this happens to be the only place where Marcovich fails to refer the language of Christ's ἔνδοξος παρουσία to Dan 7:14, but I count it as an identifiable allusion). One would have to argue for example that there is no carry-over into *Dial.* 49.7-8 of similar language in *Dial.* 49.2, where the Messiah first appears as παθητὸς καὶ ἄτιμος καὶ ἀειδής (cf. Isa 53:2-3, 8) and then comes again as ἔνδοξος and as κριτὴς ἁπάντων (cf. Dan 7:14, 26).

Along the same lines, Wolff refers to Isa 52:13 in order to explain the statement in *Dial.* 110.2 line 10 about Christ's coming *from the heavens* "with glory" (μετὰ δόξης), when this clearly belongs to Daniel in Justin's two Parousias scheme. What is left for Isaiah in lines 9-10 is the oft-repeated language of Christ being proclaimed as παθητὸς καὶ ἄδοξος καὶ ἄτιμος καὶ σταυρούμενος, as *"passible* and *without glory* and *without honor* and *crucified"* at his first advent — a reference to Isa 53:8 (παθητός), vv. 2-3 (without honor, glory), and presumably Deut 21:23 (crucified). A few lines before this in line 5 (*Dial.* 110.1), Justin claims that he understands the Jewish teaching that the Messiah either has not arrived, or is here among us but not yet *"manifest and glorious,"* ἐμφανὴς καὶ ἔνδοξος, again with reference to Dan 7:14 (Marcovich). The contrast between Isaiah's figure as ἄδοξος and Daniel's as ἔνδοξος could hardly be more plain.

In *Dial.* 121.3 (Marcovich, p. 279, *ll.* 17-26), where Wolff once again interprets ἔνδοξος in terms of Isaiah's exalted Servant in Isa 53:12, we do not have the contrast of ἄδοξος and ἔνδοξος found in *Dial.* 49.7-8 and 110.1-2. But we do find essentially the same contrast of the Parousias as predicted by Isaiah and Daniel — the one *"without honor* and *without form* and *scorned"* (*Dial.* 121.3 *l.* 18; cf. Isa 53:2-3; Ps 22 [LXX 21]:7), the other *"glorious"* (*Dial.* 121.3 *l.* 23; cf. Dan 7:14 = *Dial.* 31.4 *l.* 19).

The problem Wolff has encountered is that of distinguishing an author from his book. That Justin *the author* knew both an exalted Isaianic Servant and an exalted Danielic Son of Man and could have merged them in his *Dialogue* is not in doubt in the light of *1 Apol.* 50.1. Nevertheless, this is not what Justin's *written* document, the *Dialogue,* is doing. It is much more schematic: Christ's *inglorious* (ἄδοξος) first Parousia was prophesied by Isaiah and his *glorious* (ἔνδοξος) second

Parousia by Daniel. Justin began to lay out this scheme in one passage in his *1 Apology* (52.3). But since this work lacks the long quotation of Dan 7:9-28 in *Dial.* 31.2-7 that gives Daniel and Isaiah equal weight in the *Dialogue*, it is understandable that Wolff has placed the emphasis on Isaiah, even for the exaltation motif. The prophecies of the two comings in *1 Apol.* 52.3 are not attributed respectively to Isaiah and Daniel as they are in *Dial.* 14.8. Rather, Justin writes:

> For the prophets have proclaimed two comings of His: one, which has already happened, as that of a dishonored and suffering man (ὡς ἀτίμου καὶ παθητοῦ ἀνθρώπου); and the second, when, as has been proclaimed, He will come from heaven with glory (μετὰ δόξης) with His angelic host. (*1 Apol.* 52.3; trans. Barnard)

In the hindsight of the *Dialogue*, the contrast between Isaianic and Danielic language becomes clear, and even in the context of the *1 Apology*, the allusions to Isaiah 53 and Daniel 7 should not be missed. But they have not been fully developed.

6. Catalogue of the *Dialogue's* Uses of παθητός

Our remaining task is to assess the differing strength or level of the allusion to Isaiah 53 (if any) in the 17 paragraphs containing παθητός. This will help us to evaluate — if necessary, to criticize — Marcovich's application of "allusive" italics to παθητός in all but one of these instances (cf. *Dial.* 99.2). In the process of determining the strength of the allusions to Isaiah 53, we will also note the different grammatical uses of παθητός in the predicate or attributive positions.

6.1 Levels of Allusion of παθητός

In the final occurrence of the term in *Dial.* 126.1, Justin explicitly names *Isaiah* as the prophet who predicted that the Messiah would be called παθητός. We can safely assume that Justin had in mind Isaiah chapter 53, if not Isa 53:8 (Marcovich). Let us therefore assign the reference to Isaiah 53 made by παθητός in *Dial.* 126.1 the highest level of allusive force: *Level 5*.

Next in the level of allusion come those three places where παθητός participates in the Isaianic vocabulary network of ἄτιμος, ἀειδής, ἄδοξος, and θνητός discussed in Table 1, even though Isaiah is not named in these instances (though cf. *Dial.* 14.8). See *Dial.* 49.2; 100.2; 110.2. These, too, are not in doubt. The contrast of the two Parousias and of παθητός with ἔνδοξος in *Dial.* 49.2 and 110.2 furthermore confirms that we are dealing with the language of Isaiah, contrasted with that of Daniel. Let us therefore assign an "Isaianic" *Level 4* to these two passages, with *Level 3.5* for *Dial.* 100.2.

The theme of the two Parousias, including the Danielic language of ἔνδοξος, intersects with the vocabulary network for Isaiah 53 in *Dial.* 49.2 and 110.2. Yet it also goes beyond this network. Where it does, we will assign an Isaianic allusion to those uses of παθητός that are not supported by other language recalling Isaiah 53, but that are nevertheless defined over against the "glory" of Daniel 7. Often these passages contrast the two Parousias, yet the term παρουσία need not be used to get the point across. This is yet another level of allusion, the largest category of the uses of παθητός: *Level 3*.

At levels less than Level 3, we will sort out the παθητός passages individually.

6.2 Commentary on the Dialogue's Uses of παθητός

Marcovich is the source of the italics in the Greek and the parenthetical biblical references inserted into the translations of the 17 παθητός passages presented below. The translations take as starting-point the version of Falls and Halton (cf. also Williams), but introduce changes to highlight lexical and grammatical points of interest.

Terms in a predicate position, including παθητός and others, are underlined. Boldface is used for the driving verb. The predications can be created either by passive verbs, e.g. κηρύσσεται, προεφητεύθη, κέκληται, or by intransitive verbs, e.g. ἔσται, φανήσεται, γίνεσθαι. The few attributive and substantival uses of παθητός are not underlined but are identified in the comments. The rare use of the object-complement, e.g. *God made him* (object) *passible* (complement), is marked by double underlining of the complement (cf. *Dial.* 68.9; 89.2). The strength of allusion to Isaiah 53 is indicated by the different "Levels" defined above.

1. Dial. 34.2

ὁ γὰρ Χριστὸς <u>*βασιλεὺς*</u> καὶ <u>*ἱερεὺς*</u> καὶ <u>*θεὸς*</u> καὶ <u>*κύριος*</u> καὶ <u>*ἄγγελος*</u> καὶ <u>*ἄνθρωπος*</u> καὶ <u>*ἀρχιστράτηγος*</u> καὶ <u>*λίθος*</u> καὶ <u>*παιδίον γεννώμενον*</u> καὶ <u>*παθητὸς* γενόμενος</u> <u>πρῶτον</u>, εἶτα <u>εἰς οὐρανὸν ἀνερχόμενος</u> καὶ <u>πάλιν</u> <u>*παραγινόμενος μετὰ δόξης*</u> καὶ <u>*αἰώνιον τὴν βασιλείαν ἔχων*</u> **κεκήρυκται**, ὡς ἀπὸ πασῶν τῶν γραφῶν ἀποδείκνυμι.

Justin: For Christ **is proclaimed** as <u>*King,*</u> and <u>*Priest,*</u> and <u>*God,*</u> and <u>*Lord,*</u> and <u>*Angel,*</u> and <u>*Man,*</u> and <u>*Chief Captain,*</u> and <u>*Stone,*</u> and <u>*Child Born,*</u> and as having been at first *subject to suffering* (Isa 53:8), then as ascended into heaven, and *returning* [to earth] *with glory* (Dan 7:14), and *having the eternal kingdom* (Dan 7:27), as I prove from all the Scriptures.

Marcovich (apparatus [abbreviated]): βασιλεύς: Luke 1:33; 1 Cor 15:25; Dan 7:14; Isa 9:7 [= throne of David]; *Mart. Polyc.* 21 et al. ǀ ἄγγελος: cf. Exod 3:2 et al.; Isa 9:6; *Constit. apos.* 2.30.2 ǀ ἀρχιστράτηγος: cf. Josh 5:14-15 ǀ λίθος: cf. Dan 2:34, 45; Isa 28:16 (Eph 2:20; 1 Pet 2:6) ǀ παιδίον γεννώμενον; cf. Isa 9:6 (Ziegler/NRSV; cf. MT/Rahlfs 9:5) παιδίον ἐγεννήθη ὑμῖν et 53:2.

Allusion Level 3 (παθητός Isa 53:8 + μετὰ δόξης Dan 7:14 + αἰώνιον βασιλείαν Dan 7:27). This is the first use of παθητός in the *Dialogue*. It functions as an adjective in the predicate position, with the meaning ὁ Χριστὸς . . . κεκήρυκται . . . παθητὸς γενόμενος πρῶτον, "Christ . . . is proclaimed as . . . having become at first subject to suffering" (technically, the participle γενόμενος is the predicate of κεκήρυκται, and παθητός is the predicate of γενόμενος). Here and elsewhere the predicates of Christ usually precede the verb. Because all of the other predicates preceding παθητός are nouns, it would be appropriate to translate παθητός substantivally as well: "as one *who at first endured suffering*" (Falls and Halton).

The term παρουσία, which is often the mark of a Level 3 allusion to Isaiah 53, does not occur here. Nevertheless, the contrast of πρῶτον and εἶτα, *at first* subject to suffering, but *then* returning with glory, is a material if not formal reference to the two Parousias, which in turn strengthens the allusion made by παθητός to Isaiah, Justin's prophet of the first Parousia. This is backed up by the allusions to Dan 7:14 and 7:27, as noted by Marcovich, although in the LXX of the latter the "eternal kingdom"[61] is given not to the Son of Man but to "the people of the Most High," whom he represents.

This passage is typical of Marcovich's editing over against Goodspeed's, where no italics or marginal references are given for this passage. The phrase παθητός γενόμενος is preceded by nine other predicates of Christ: βασιλεύς, ἱερεύς, θεός, κύριος, ἄγγελος, ἄνθρωπος, ἀρχιστράτηγος, λίθος, παιδίον γεννώμενον. Four are provided with references in Marcovich's apparatus (as above); space constraints may have prevented references for the others (cf.

---

61. In *Dial.* 34.2, αἰώνιον in the expression αἰώνιον τὴν βασιλείαν ἔχων could be the adverbial use of the neuter adjective, "having the kingdom *eternally*" (cf. Williams [see n. 1], 66, "for ever"). But I have translated it as an adjective (with Falls and Halton) in the light of Justin's text of Dan 7:27 (= LXX), βασιλεῦσαι βασιλείαν αἰώνιον, "to rule an *eternal* kingdom" (*Dial.* 31.7). See also *Dial.* 39.7.

Marcovich, preface, viii-ix). Although Isa 53:2 is provided as a secondary reference for παιδίον γεννώμενον, clearly Isa 9:5 (Ziegler 9:6) is the primary reference; παθητός still basically stands as the sole term alluding to Isaiah 53.

2. *Dial.* 36.1

Κἀκεῖνος ἀπεκρίνατο· Ἔστω καὶ ταῦτα οὕτως ἔχοντα ὡς λέγεις, καὶ ὅτι <u>παθητὸς</u> Χριστὸς **προεφητεύθη** <u>μέλλειν εἶναι</u>, καὶ *λίθος* κέκληται, καὶ *ἔνδοξος* μετὰ τὴν πρώτην αὐτοῦ παρουσίαν, ἐν ᾗ <u>παθητὸς</u> φαίνεσθαι κεκήρυκτο, *ἐλευσόμενος* καὶ *κριτὴς πάντων* λοιπὸν καὶ *αἰώνιος βασιλεὺς* καὶ *ἱερεὺς* γενησόμενος· εἰ οὗτος δέ ἐστι περὶ οὗ ταῦτα προεφητεύθη, ἀπόδειξον.

Trypho: Let it be [granted] that these things are as you say, and that Christ (the Messiah) was **prophesied** as <u>destined to be *subject to suffering*</u> (Isa 53:8), and that he is called a *Stone,* and that he will *come glorious* (Dan 7:13-14)[62] after his first Parousia (in which he is proclaimed as appearing *subject to suffering*), and thereafter will be *Judge of all* (Dan 7:14, 26) and *Eternal King* (Dan 7:14, 27) and *Priest* (Ps 110 [LXX 109]:4). But prove that he [sc. Jesus Christ, *Dial.* 35.8] is the one about whom these things were prophesied.

Allusion Level 3 (παθητός Isa 53:8 + ἔνδοξος ἐλευσόμενος Dan 7:13-14 + Dan 7:26, 27 + Parousia). All the elements and limitations of the paradigmatic Level 3 allusion are here: the Messiah is παθητός at his "Isaianic" first Parousia and ἔνδοξος at his "Danielic" second Parousia, yet the Isaianic allusion is formally supported only by παθητός without other allusive terms such as ἄτιμος. The connection with Daniel is strengthened by the language of the "judge of all" (cf. Dan 7:14 = *Dial.* 31.4, καὶ ἐδόθη αὐτῷ ἐξουσία; Dan 7:26 = *Dial.* 31.7, ἡ κρίσις ἐκάθισε) and the "eternal king" (cf. Dan 7:14 = *Dial.* 31.4, ἡ βασιλεία αὐτοῦ οὐ μὴ φθαρῇ; Dan 7:27 = *Dial.* 31.7, βασιλεῦσαι βασιλείαν αἰώνιον). Trypho is presented as agreeing with Justin that the Messiah is destined to suffer according to Isaiah 53 and to return triumphant according to Daniel 7. Trypho only wants proof that Jesus meets these criteria. But he is met with one of Justin's typical delays, after having become inquisitive in response to Justin's prayer in the preceding paragraph (*Dial.* 35.8) that he and his companions

---

62. I translate ἔνδοξος ἐλευσόμενος here and in *Dial.* 49.2 (ἐλεύσεται) not entirely elegantly with a predicate adjective, "come *glorious*" (cf. more naturally Williams, 71, "come *in glory*"), on the analogy of "arrive late" or "come sick," and to differentiate it from the adverbial prepositional phrases in "to come *in glory*" (ἐν δόξῃ) or "*with glory*" (μετὰ δόξης); cf. *Dial.* 14.8; 34.2; 110.2.

might become believers in Jesus Christ, who will thus be saved at his glorious (ἔνδοξος) second coming.

3. *Dial.* 39.7

Καὶ ὁ Τρύφων· Ἤδη οὖν τὸν λόγον ἀπόδος ἡμῖν, ὅτι οὗτος, ὃν φῄς ἐσταυρῶσθαι καὶ ἀνεληλυθέναι εἰς τὸν οὐρανόν, ἐστὶν ὁ Χριστὸς τοῦ θεοῦ. ὅτι γὰρ καὶ <u>παθητὸς</u> ὁ Χριστὸς διὰ τῶν γραφῶν **κηρύσσεται**, καὶ *μετὰ δόξης πάλιν παραγίνεσθαι, καὶ αἰώνιον τὴν βασιλείαν πάντων τῶν ἐθνῶν λήψεσθαι, πάσης βασιλείας αὐτῷ ὑποτασσομένης,* ἱκανῶς διὰ τῶν προανιστορημένων ὑπὸ σοῦ γραφῶν ἀποδέδεικται· ὅτι δὲ οὗτός ἐστιν, ἀπόδειξον ἡμῖν.

Trypho: Please give us finally the reason why this man, whom you say was cruci-fied and ascended into heaven, is the Christ of God. For the fact that the Christ (Messiah) is **proclaimed** by the Scriptures as *subject to suffering*, and as to come again *with glory* (Dan 7:14) and *to receive the eternal kingdom over all the nations with every kingdom subject to him* (Dan 7:27), has been sufficiently proved by your previously-quoted Scriptures. But prove to us that this man [Jesus] is he [the Messiah].

Allusion Level 3 (παθητός [Isa 53:8 — no ref. in Marcovich] + μετὰ δόξης Dan 7:14 + Dan 7:27). The formal elements of the allusion are very similar to those in the preceding passage, *Dial.* 36.1. This is the only place where Marcovich has failed to refer παθητός to Isa 53:8 when it contrasts with the "glory" language of Dan 7:14, and therefore it appears to be an oversight. Ac-cordingly, I have revised the statistics throughout this essay, as if Marcovich had provided a reference to Isa 53:8 here, as elsewhere.

The allusion to Dan 7:14 is made here by μετὰ δόξης rather than ἔνδοξος, and the verbal expression πάλιν παραγίνεσθαι, "to come again," substitutes for the explicit language of the Parousia. The rhetorical situation is also similar to *Dial.* 36.1. Here Trypho's willing use of language summarizing Daniel 7 and Isa-iah 53 is prompted again by Justin's mention of Christ's second coming, de-scribed as the occasion when "he comes again (ἕως πάλιν παρῇ) and destroys all" of those who persecuted his followers (*Dial.* 39.6). Given the allusive lan-guage, the "previously-quoted Scriptures" Trypho refers to must include espe-cially Isa 52:10–54:6 (*Dial.* 13.2-9) and Dan 7:9-28 (*Dial.* 31.2-7), confirming once again that παθητός is the *Dialogue's* principal summary term for Isaiah 53. Trypho's understandable impatience for an answer is expressed by the ἤδη. Once again he is offered little more than a promise of detailed proof at a later time, coupled with Justin's claim that he has already proved the point and that

Trypho has admitted it (*Dial.* 39.8). What Trypho has admitted includes the centrality of both Isaiah 53 and Daniel 7 for describing the Messiah's destiny, independent of the question of whether Jesus is this Messiah.

4. *Dial.* 41.1

Justin: Jesus Christ our Lord ordered us to *do this* [sc. partake of the bread of the Eucharist] *in remembrance* (Luke 22:19) of the suffering which he suffered on behalf of those who are being purged in soul from all iniquity, in order that we should at the same time give thanks to God . . . for having set us free from the evil in which we had (hitherto) been, and for *having destroyed the powers and the authorities* (Col 2:15) with a complete destruction by means of **him who became** *liable to suffering* according to his will (cf. Williams, 81-82) = . . . ἵνα ἅμα τε εὐχαριστῶμεν τῷ θεῷ . . . ὑπὲρ τοῦ ἀπὸ τῆς κακίας, ἐν ᾗ γεγόναμεν, ἠλευθερωκέναι ἡμᾶς, καὶ τὰς ἀρχὰς καὶ τὰς ἐξουσίας καταλελυκέναι τελείαν κατάλυσιν διὰ **τοῦ** *παθητοῦ* **γενομένου** κατὰ τὴν βουλὴν αὐτοῦ.

Allusion Level 1. This is the first place where Marcovich has intentionally not provided παθητός with a reference to Isa 53:8 (in *Dial.* 39.7 the omission of Isa 53:8 appears to have been an oversight). None of the supports from other allusive language for Isaiah 53 or the Isaiah–Daniel contrast are here; the Scripture quotation is from Col 2:15. Nevertheless, παθητός is still printed in italics, presumably to show that it has a definite scriptural basis in the *Dialogue* as a whole. Παθητός is the predicate of the substantival participle ὁ γενόμενος.

5. *Dial.* 49.2

Ἐὰν οὖν ὁ λόγος ἀναγκάζῃ ὁμολογεῖν ὅτι δύο παρουσίαι τοῦ Χριστοῦ προεφητεύοντο γενησόμεναι, μία μέν, ἐν ᾗ *παθητὸς καὶ ἄτιμος καὶ ἀειδὴς* **φανήσεται**, ἡ δὲ ἑτέρα, ἐν ᾗ καὶ *ἔνδοξος καὶ κριτὴς ἁπάντων* **ἐλεύσεται**, ὡς καὶ ἐν πολλοῖς τοῖς προλελεγμένοις ἀποδέδεικται, οὐχὶ τῆς φοβερᾶς καὶ μεγάλης ἡμέρας τοῦτ' ἔστι τῆς δευτέρας παρουσίας αὐτοῦ, πρόοδον γενήσεσθαι τὸν Ἠλίαν νοήσομεν τὸν λόγον τοῦ θεοῦ κεκηρυχέναι;

Justin: If, therefore, Scripture forces you to admit that it was predicted that there would be two advents of the Messiah — one in which **he will appear** *subject to suffering* (Isa 53:8) and *without honor* and *without form* (Isa 53:2-3) and the second in which **he will come** *glorious* (Dan 7:14) and *as judge of all* (Dan 7:26), as has been proved by the many previously quoted [Scriptures] — must we not [also] conclude that the word of God has foretold that Elijah will be the forerunner of *the great and terrible day* (Mal 3:23; LXX 3:22 Rahlfs), namely, of his second advent? (trans. Falls and Halton, 74 [mod.])

Allusion Level 4 (παθητός Isa 53:8 + ἄτιμος καὶ ἀειδής Isa 53:2-3 + ἔνδοξος Dan 7:14 + κριτὴς ἁπάντων Dan 7:26 + Parousia). This is the classic Level 4 allusion, where in addition to the contrast of Isaiah and Daniel and the two Parousias, παθητός gets help from other language alluding to Isaiah 53, i.e. ἄτιμος and ἀειδής. This language, which also includes ἄδοξος and θνητός and has an independent connection to the two Parousias theme, has already been established long before this: cf. *Dial.* 14.8; 32.1; 32.2; 36.6 and above Table 1 (p. 351). Two networks of language alluding to Isaiah 53 here combine for the first time to strengthen the echo of Scripture.

That the *Dialogue* has firmly established this way of alluding to Isaiah 53 is confirmed by the unobtrusive way in which the language can be used here, not to highlight Isaiah 53 and Daniel 7, but to bring in an additional point on which Trypho has wanted clarification from the beginning (cf. *Dial.* 8.4, renewed here in 49.1), namely that the scriptural prophecies about Elijah in Mal 3:23 (LXX 3:22; NRSV 4:5) also support the idea of the Messiah's second coming. In connection with his first coming, Justin argues that Elijah's spirit has already appeared in the person of John the Baptist, without the glory of the great and terrible day of the Lord, in keeping with the inglorious first coming of the Messiah (cf. *Dial.* 49.3-8, esp. 49.7). This is intended to provide Trypho with the necessary proof that Elijah has already come to anoint the Messiah.

6. *Dial.* 52.1

Καὶ διὰ Ἰακὼβ δὲ τοῦ πατριάρχου προεφητεύθη ὅτι δύο τοῦ Χριστοῦ παρουσίαι ἔσονται, καὶ ὅτι ἐν τῇ πρώτῃ *παθητὸς* ἔσται, καὶ ὅτι μετὰ τὸ αὐτὸν ἐλθεῖν οὔτε προφήτης οὔτε βασιλεὺς ἐν τῷ γένει ὑμῶν, ἐπήνεγκα, καὶ ὅτι τὰ ἔθνη, πιστεύοντα ἐπὶ τὸν *παθητὸν* Χριστόν, πάλιν παραγενησόμενον προσδοκήσει. (Marcovich, 155, text-critical additions removed)

Justin: It was also prophesied by the patriarch Jacob that there would be two Parousias of Christ, and that in the first he **would be** *subject to suffering* (predicate), and that after this coming your people would have neither prophet nor king, and that the Gentiles who believe in the *suffering* Christ (attributive) would look forward to his second coming. (cf. Falls and Halton, 78 [mod.])

Allusion Level 2 (παθητός + Parousia). Marcovich italicizes but does not annotate these two occurrences of παθητός. Their stated connection with the

Parousias relates them to a structure which elsewhere defines παθητός as Isaianic in contrast to that which is Danielic. Yet the "glory" language of Daniel that might have made this a Level 3 allusion to Isaiah 53 is not present. Instead it is Jacob who, in his blessing of Judah in Gen 49:8-12, quoted immediately after this in *Dial.* 52.2, is said to have prophesied the two Parousias, including the idea that at first the Messiah would be subject to suffering.

Nevertheless, this does not make Jacob the prophet of the suffering Messiah. Jacob's blessing of Judah in Gen 49:8-12 is cited in the present context not for the suffering theme, which it lacks, but for the phrase "he shall be the expectation of nations" (Gen 49:10 = *Dial.* 52.2 *ll.* 12-13). Justin has a point of contact with a social reality that goes beyond the literary world of the *Dialogue,* since he himself is part of the community of "Gentiles who believe in the suffering Christ [and] look forward to his second coming." In this community the question is no longer εἰ παθητὸς ὁ Χριστός, "Is the Messiah due to suffer?" All the *Dialogue's* uses of παθητός until now have been in the predicate position, as in this question. This indicates the way the topic has been debated between Trypho and Justin. Accordingly when Trypho agrees with the prophecy of Isaiah 53 using this language, it is not with the idea of an already existent παθητὸς Χριστός, but with the idea that the Scriptures predict a Χριστός who will become παθητός. Trypho and his Jewish teachers do not in fact believe that this — or any other — Messiah has yet come, in part because Elijah has not yet come to anoint him (cf. *Dial.* 8.3; 49.1).

By contrast, the attributive phrase "suffering Messiah," which appears only here and in *Dial.* 111.2, is more settled, Christian usage. This raises the question of what this language means outside the text of the *Dialogue.* Using literary criteria I have determined that in the present text, *Dial.* 52.1, παθητός does not make a definite allusion to the suffering Christ of Isaiah 53 because it does not have support from other allusions to Isaiah 53 or from a contrast with Daniel 7. But what about the readers outside the text? Do the "Gentiles who believe in the suffering Christ" know him as the Christ whose sufferings were predicted above all by Isaiah 53? If D. J. Bingham is correct to suggest that Isaiah 53 was used for Christian orientation and identity formation in Justin's community (see the end of §7.1 below), then in that community the phrase "suffering Christ" may have had a greater Isaianic resonance — much like our modern language of the "suffering Servant" — than it has in its literary setting here in *Dial.* 52.1. This is especially true if these Gentiles are among the "well-instructed Christians" that Justin mentions (cf. *Dial.* 93.5). Nevertheless, I agree with Marcovich's assessment of the literary setting and with his decision not to refer παθητός to Isa 53:8. I have therefore rated the allusion as Level 2 — just below the clearly identifiable allusions, which start at Level 2.5 (see the summary below, §6.3).

7. *Dial.* 68.9

Ἃς δ' ἂν λέγωμεν αὐτοῖς γραφάς, αἳ διαρρήδην τὸν Χριστὸν <u>καὶ *παθητὸν*</u> [complement in accusative; cf. also *Dial.* 89.2] <u>*καὶ προσκυνητὸν καὶ θεὸν*</u> ἀπο-δεικνύουσιν, ἃς καὶ προανιστόρησα ὑμῖν, ταύτας εἰς Χριστὸν μὲν εἰρῆσθαι ἀναγκαζόμενοι συντίθενται, τοῦτον δὲ μὴ εἶναι τὸν Χριστὸν τολμῶσι λέγειν, ἐλεύσεσθαι δὲ <ἄλλον> καὶ παθεῖν καὶ βασιλεῦσαι καὶ προσκυνητὸν γενέσθαι <καὶ> θεὸν ὁμολογοῦσιν·

Justin: Under pressure, they [sc. some of the Jewish teachers] are forced to agree that some of the Scriptures we cited — passages already quoted to you which clearly prove Christ to be *subject to suffering* (Isa 53:8), and *worshipped* (Ps 45 [LXX 44]:13) *and God* — were indeed spoken of Christ. They dare to deny that he whom we worship is the Christ, yet they confess that <another> will come and suffer and rule (cf. Dan 7:27) and be worshipped <and> be God. (trans. Falls and Halton, 107 [mod.])

Allusion Level 2.5 (Isa 53:8 + possible allusion to Dan 7:27 + backward reference to previously-cited Scriptures). Marcovich's text-critical insertions are accepted here and enclosed in angle brackets: <. . .>. Halton translates "another," <ἄλλον>, but accidentally drops the final noun θεόν, which is textually not in doubt: "be worshipped <and> be *God*" (Falls included it). The predicates παθητόν and προσκυνητόν are in the accusative (only here and in *Dial.* 89.2) as the complement of the direct object τὸν Χριστόν. Of the several "Scriptures" already cited to prove that the Christ is "subject to suffering," Isaiah 53 must be the principal one, since at this point we have not yet had Justin's exposition of Psalm 22 (*Dial.* 97-106). Justin presents the Jewish teachers as claiming to have their own alternative Messiah who will fulfill the same prophecies, yet be someone other than Jesus. That their Messiah will both "suffer" and "rule" (cf. Dan 7:27 βασιλεῦσαι βασιλείαν αἰώνιον) fits the Isaiah–Daniel pattern that the *Dialogue* has already established.

8. *Dial.* 70.4

Justin: It is quite evident that this prophecy [Isa 33:13-19] also alludes to the bread which our Christ gave us to offer in remembrance of the Body which he assumed for the sake of those who believe in him, for whom he also *suffered* [δι' οὓς καὶ *παθητὸς* **γέγονε**], and also to the cup which he taught us to offer in the Eucharist, in commemoration of his Blood. (trans. Falls and Halton, 110)

Allusion Level 1. Marcovich italicizes παθητός but provides it with no reference to Isaiah 53. The phrase is not literally "those for whom he suffered" but "for whom he *became passible.*" There might be a slight reminder of Isaiah 53, simply because this adjective is most often associated with that passage.

9. *Dial.* 74.1

Justin [*Dial.* 73.1]: Furthermore, from a verse of the Ninety-fifth Psalm of David [MT Ps 96] they [sc. some of Trypho's Jewish teachers] have left out the short phrase, *from the tree.* For they have changed the verse, *Say you to the Gentiles: The Lord has reigned from the tree,* to *Say you to the Gentiles: The Lord has reigned* [LXX Ps 95:10]. [73.2] Now, no one of your people was ever said to have reigned as God and king over the Gentiles, except the crucified one.

Trypho [*Dial.* 74.1, after Justin's quotation of LXX Ps 95:1-13]: We are aware that it is at our request that you have quoted those passages for us. But the psalm of David which you just cited (LXX Ps 95) seems to me to have been spoken of nobody other than the Father, who created the heavens and the earth. You, however, claim that it refers to *him who suffered,* and who you are anxious to prove is the Christ (σὺ δ᾽ αὐτὸν φῇς εἰς τὸν παθητὸν τοῦτον, ὃν καὶ Χριστὸν εἶναι σπουδάζεις ἀποδεικνύναι, εἰρῆσθαι). (trans. Falls and Halton, 113-14)

Allusion Level 0.5. Grammatically, this is the only place in the *Dialogue* where ὁ παθητός occurs as a clearly substantival expression (though see the anarthrous use in *Dial.* 121.6). Marcovich italicizes it, but provides no Scripture reference. Trypho understands that Justin came to LXX Psalm 95 with a ready-made idea of the Suffering One, whom he wanted to find attested in this additional Scripture passage. The idea that *Justin* brings to Psalm 95 is formed by Isaiah 53. This can be counted as a weak allusion. Significantly, Trypho considers ὁ παθητός with reference to the Messiah to be a *Christian* rather than a Jewish expression. See below §7.1.

10. *Dial.* 76.6

Justin: [76.6] Now, if Christ was cryptically **proclaimed** by the prophets as about to become *subject to suffering* (Isa 53:8) and after that *to rule over all* (Dan 7:27) (Εἰ γὰρ διὰ τῶν προφητῶν παρακεκαλυμμένως **κεκήρυκτο** *παθητὸς γενησόμενος* ὁ Χριστὸς καὶ μετὰ ταῦτα *πάντων κυριεύσων*), it was still practically impossible for anyone to grasp the full meaning of such prophecies, until Christ himself convinced his apostles that such things were explicitly proclaimed in the Scriptures. [76.7] For (γάρ) before his crucifixion he exclaimed, *The Son of Man must suffer many things, and be rejected by the Scribes and Pharisees, and be crucified, and rise again on the third day.* (Mark 8:31 par.; cf. Falls and Halton, 119 [mod.])

Allusion Level 3 (παθητός Isa 53:8 + πάντων κυριεύσων Dan 7:27 + implied two Parousias theme). Because we have both the suffering and the exaltation theme, there are at least two of "the prophets" in view here, Isaiah and Daniel. To the extent that the rest of the prophets are included, they are represented as speaking the language of Isaiah — who by now "owns" the term παθητός — and Daniel. Jesus is moreover depicted as understanding his destiny from Isaiah 53 and Daniel 7. See also *Dial.* 100.2-3.

11. *Dial.* 85.2

Justin:
κατὰ γὰρ τοῦ ὀνόματος αὐτοῦ τούτου τοῦ υἱοῦ τοῦ θεοῦ
   καὶ *πρωτοτόκου πάσης κτίσεως,*
καὶ διὰ παρθένου γεννηθέντος
   καὶ *παθητοῦ* γενομένου ἀνθρώπου,
καὶ σταυρωθέντος ἐπὶ Ποντίου Πιλάτου ὑπὸ τοῦ λαοῦ ὑμῶν
   καὶ ἀποθανόντος,
καὶ ἀναστάντος ἐκ νεκρῶν
   καὶ ἀναβάντος εἰς τὸν οὐρανόν,
πᾶν δαιμόνιον ἐξορκιζόμενον
   νικᾶται καὶ ὑποτάσσεται.

In the name of this true Son of God
   and *first-born of all creation* (Col. 1:15),
who was born of a virgin
   and became a *passible* man,
and was crucified by your people under Pontius Pilate
   and died,
and rose from the dead
   and ascended into heaven,
every demon when exorcized
   is vanquished and subdued.

Allusion Level 0.5. Marcovich italicizes παθητός but provides no Scripture reference. There has just been a clear allusion to Isa 53:2-3 (ἀειδής καὶ ἄτιμος) and a mention of Isaiah (and David) in the preceding paragraph, *Dial.* 85.1. This may give παθητός a slight Isaianic resonance here, especially since it refers to the stage in Christ's career preeminently described by Isaiah 53. Nevertheless, the emphasis here is not so much on the Messiah's "Isaianic" suffering as on the virgin-born humanity that was its prerequisite (see below §7.4).

The adjective παθητοῦ in *Dial.* 85.2 should probably be taken as above, attributively with ἀνθρώπου, "a *possible* man" (cf. Williams, "a man liable to suffering"). So also *Dial.* 99.2. Alternatively, ἀνθρώπου could be the head of the whole phrase, modified by the two participles: "a man who was *born* of a virgin and *became* passible." The former makes for better parallelism by giving independent emphasis to γεννηθέντος and γενομένου. Justin fronts παθητοῦ to bring it as close as possible to γεννηθέντος, emphasizing that suffering follows from incarnation. Halton in his revision of Falls's translation eliminates any link between the Messiah's birth and his sufferings by accidentally erasing the phrase *and became a passible man:* "who was born of a virgin, who was crucified" (132). Falls does not omit the phrase, but against the parallelism he relates the suffering more closely with the crucifixion than with the incarnation: "who was the First-born of all creatures, who was born of a virgin, who suffered and was crucified" (283). While it would not be an unknown rhetorical figure (hendiadys), the coordination of "who suffered and was crucified" in the translation seems unnecessary if being "passible" already means being capable of suffering death. My understanding of the parallelism is suggested by Marcovich's punctuation (as above).

12. *Dial.* 89.2

Trypho: [89.1] You know very well that we Jews (τὸ γένος ἡμῶν) are all expecting the Messiah, and we admit that all your Scriptural quotations refer to him. I also admit that the name Jesus [Joshua], which was given to the son of Nun, has prompted me to incline to this opinion. [89.2] But whether he is to be so dishonorably crucified, we doubt; for it is said in the Law, *Cursed is he who is crucified* (ἐπικατάρατος γὰρ ὁ σταυρούμενος, cf. Deut 21:23). Consequently, on this point I will be very hard to persuade. That the Scriptures **proclaim** the Christ as *subject to suffering* is clear (παθητὸν μὲν τὸν Χριστὸν ὅτι αἱ γραφαὶ **κηρύσσουσι**, φανερόν ἐστιν). But we would like to learn whether it is by means of the suffering cursed in the law (διὰ τοῦ ἐν τῷ νόμῳ κεκατηραμένου πάθους), if you can prove this.

Justin: [89.3] If indeed Christ had not been destined to suffer (Εἰ μὲν μὴ ἔμελλε πάσχειν ὁ Χριστός), and had the prophets not predicted that *because of the iniq-*

uities of the people he would be led to death (Isa 53:8d), and *would be dishonored* (53:3), and *would be scourged* (53:4), and *would be counted among the lawless* (53:12c), and *would be led as a sheep to the slaughter* (53:7), *whose birth no one can describe* (53:8b), as the prophet (sc. Isaiah) says, then you would have had good reason to be astonished [sc. at Christ's crucifixion]. But if this is what characterizes him and reveals him to all, how can we do otherwise than confidently believe in him? And all who have grasped the meaning of the prophets' words, as soon as they hear that he was crucified, will affirm that he [Jesus] is the Christ and no other.

Allusion Level 4.5 (παθητός + quotation of Isa 53:8d + <ὥς> φησιν ὁ προφήτης [= Isaiah]). (For Greek text, cf. p. 341.) This is the strongest connection of the term παθητός with Isaiah 53 in the *Dialogue* outside the explicit statement in *Dial.* 126.1 that Christ was called παθητός by Isaiah. Indeed, the statement here is even stronger because the link is explicitly with phrases from Isaiah 53 (esp. 53:8), and the prophet Isaiah is virtually named by the narrowing from "the prophets" to "the prophet" (cf. <ὥς> φησιν ὁ προφήτης).

Justin's impressive combined citation of Isa 53:8d + 3 + 4 + 12c + 8b here has already been discussed above (§4.1) and in the essay by C. Markschies (p. 265 with n. 124). Here we focus on Trypho's question in *Dial.* 89.2 and its link to Justin's answer. This is Trypho's last and most successful use of παθητός, at least in terms of getting a response from Justin (though Trypho's voice disappears after *Dial.* 90.1 until *Dial.* 118.5). It is the point to which the *Dialogue* has been heading ever since Trypho first used the term in *Dial.* 36.1 (cf. also 39.7; 74.1).

Whatever else Trypho does here, he provides Marcovich with a justification for his editing. Justin answers Trypho's question about the type of the Messiah's suffering or πάθος, the sense in which he becomes παθητός, by a clear quotation (in indirect discourse) of Isa 53:8d, προεῖπον οἱ προφῆται ὅτι *ἀπὸ τῶν ἀνομιῶν τοῦ λαοῦ ἀχθήσεται* [LXX: ἤχθη] *εἰς θάνατον*. The Messiah's becoming "passible" is immediately connected with his being *led to death for the iniquities of the people*. It is the proximity of Trypho's use of παθητός and Justin's quotation of Isa 53:8d that makes the best case for Marcovich's identifying 11 (including *Dial.* 39.7) of the 17 passages containing παθητός with Isa 53:8, not just with Isaiah 53 generally.

Rhetorically, by agreeing that the Messiah is to be παθητός, Trypho is already agreeing that the Messiah is prefigured by Isaiah 53. What he wants is a defense of the crucifixion against the curse of Deut 21:23. But here Justin simply offers him more of Isaiah 53, on the assumption that anyone already prepared to accept such a suffering Messiah will not be too offended at a crucified one and will be able to fit this into the picture of Isaiah 53. Justin will not address the "apparent" curse of Christ's cross (cf. *Dial.* 90.3) until after Trypho's renewed request for an explanation in *Dial.* 90.1. Justin has also not yet discussed the more particular picture of the piercing of hands and feet in Ps 22 (LXX 21):17-19 (cf. *Dial.* 97.3; 98.4; 104.1). That Trypho does not accept Isaiah 53 as an answer to Deut 21:23 is stated plainly at the beginning of the next exchange:

> We are indeed aware that he (the Messiah) was to *suffer* and to be *led as a sheep* [*sc. to the slaughter*] (Isa 53:7). But prove to us that he was to be crucified and die disgracefully and dishonorably by the *death cursed* in the law (cf. Deut 21:23). (*Dial.* 90.1)

Trypho here forms a chain-style citation, picking up Justin's last relevant phrase, from Isa 53:7 (skipping over the nearest phrase, *whose birth no one can describe*, Isa 53:8b). For more on the rhetorical setting of *Dial.* 89.1-90.1, see below, §7.2.

13. *Dial.* 99.2

Justin: [Jesus] prayed thus: *Father, if it be possible, let this cup pass away from me;* but he ended his prayer by saying, *Still, let it be as you will, not as I,* thus making it clear that he had really become a man capable of suffering (δηλῶν διὰ τούτων ὅτι ἀληθῶς <u>παθητὸς ἄνθρωπος</u> **γεγένηται**). (trans. Falls and Halton, 150)

Allusion Level Zero (?). As in *Dial.* 85.2 and below in *Dial.* 100.2, παθητός is in an attributive position with ἄνθρωπος, "a *passible* man." This is the only one of the 19 occurrences of παθητός that Marcovich does not italicize. Presumably this means that no outside text of Scripture needs to be supplied by the reader of this passage to grasp its full force. Since this and the next occurrence of παθητός in *Dial.* 100.2 (which is italicized and referred to Isa 53:8) are both set in the context of Justin's exposition of Psalm 22 (LXX 21) in *Dial.* 97-106, and since *Dial.* 100.2 relates Christ's becoming "passible" to the virgin birth (cf. also above *Dial.* 85.2), Justin seems to have concerns here that go beyond Isaiah 53 or Deut 21:23 and in fact revolve around the problem of docetism (see below, §7.4).

14. *Dial.* 100.2

Justin: . . . <u>ἄνθρωπος</u> ἀειδής καὶ ἄτιμος καὶ παθητὸς ὑπέμεινε **γενέσθαι**, "he condescended to become a man *without form* and *without honor* (Isa 53:3) and *subject to suffering* (Isa 53:8)."

Allusion Level 3.5 (ἀειδής καὶ ἄτιμος Isa 53:3 + παθητός Isa 53:8). Grammatically, the noun ἄνθρωπος is a predicate nominative with γενέσθαι, and the following three adjectives modify it attributively. Unlike the other occurrences of παθητός in *Dial.* 49.2 and 110.2 (Level 4) that combine with other terms recalling Isaiah 53 (as here ἀειδής and ἄτιμος), this occurrence of the suffering motif is not contrasted with the glory motif (ἔνδοξος) of Dan 7:14, which I have defined as an essential part of the Level 4 allusion. Therefore it may be assigned to Level 3.5. Nevertheless, there is no doubt about its resonance with Isaiah 53. The only question is why ἄνθρωπος was not also italicized in the light of its use in Isa 53:3, the same verse from which ἄτιμος and (indirectly) ἀειδής are taken. Presumably Justin's starting point here is not a man who suffers, but a man who by means of conception by a virgin has been "made flesh," σαρκοποιηθείς. This is the prerequisite for true, not merely docetic, suffering (see §7.4).

15. *Dial.* 110.2

Justin: [110.1] Gentlemen, I am aware that your teachers admit that this whole pericope [Mic 4:1-7 = *Dial.* 109.2-3] refers to the Christ; I also know that they affirm that Christ has not yet come. But they say that even if he has come, it is not known who he is, until he shall become manifest and *glorious* (ἐμφανὴς καὶ ἔνδοξος); then, they say, he shall be known. [110.2] They further state, everything foretold in the above-quoted pericope is [still] to be verified, as if not a word of the prophecy had yet been fulfilled. What irrational beings! For they have missed the point of all the cited passages, namely, that two Parousias of Christ have been announced: the first, in which he is **proclaimed** to be *subject to suffering* and *without glory* and *without honor* and *crucified* (μία μέν, ἐν ᾗ *παθητὸς καὶ ἄδοξος καὶ ἄτιμος καὶ σταυρούμενος* **κεκήρυκται**); and the second, in which *he will come from the heavens with glory* (ἡ δὲ δευτέρα, ἐν ᾗ *μετὰ δόξης ἀπὸ τῶν οὐρανῶν παρέσται*), when *the man of apostasy* (2 Thess 2:3), *who* also *utters extraordinary things against the Most High* (Dan 7:25; 11:36), will boldly attempt to perpetrate unlawful deeds on earth against us Christians. For we Christians, who have gained knowledge of the true worship of God from the Law and from *the Word which went forth from Jerusalem* (Mic 4:2 = Isa 2:3) by way of the apostles of Jesus, have run for protection to the God of Jacob and the God of Israel. (cf. Falls and Halton, 164 [mod.])

Allusion Level 4 (Marcovich: παθητός Isa 53:8 + ἄδοξος καὶ ἄτιμος Isa 53:2-3 + σταυρούμενος Isa 53:12 with Isa 33:17 [so Marcovich; but cf. Deut 21:23] + μετὰ δόξης ἀπὸ τῶν οὐρανῶν παρέσται Dan 7:13-14 with Isa 33:17 [= βασιλέα μετὰ δόξης ὄψεσθε, "you will see a king with glory"] + Parousias). For the formal elements compare *Dial.* 49.2; 100.2. I have quoted the context at length to show that it is not really about Isaiah 53 and Dan 7:13-14, even though these comprise "all the cited passages" needed to understand Justin's language, unless we are to refer additionally to Deut 21:23 for σταυρούμενος (see below). At this late stage in the *Dialogue* Justin is simply trotting out his already established Isaianic and Danielic language of the two Parousias to make another point. He is dissatisfied with Jewish exegesis of Mic 4:1-7, which he has quoted immediately prior to this in *Dial.* 109.2-3. He is happy that Jewish interpreters refer the whole passage to the Messiah, but disappointed that the Jews, failing to take his own approach of the two Parousias, place the fulfillment exclusively in the future (or in an undisclosed Messiah in the present), thus preventing the text from being partly fulfilled in the present mission of the church. Instead, for Justin, *the Word which went forth from Jerusalem* refers to the event of the apostolic preaching (*Dial.* 110.2). The phrase *each one of us sitting under his vine* (Mic 4:4) is fulfilled in the current Christian practice of monogamy, living with one's own "vine" (*Dial.* 110.3).

Dial. 110.2 provides one of the few places in the citation apparatus where Marcovich's identification of scriptural parallels might require further thought. It is unclear what phrase from Isaiah 53 Marcovich has in mind for the participle σταυρούμενος, "crucified." In contrast to his treatment of the combined allusions in *Dial.* 32.2; 89.3, where the allusions are identified individually following the *Dialogue's* order, Marcovich's apparatus note at *Dial.* 110.2 gives the allusions only in Isaiah's order, "cf. Is 53:2, 3, 8 et 12," for παθητὸς καὶ ἄδοξος καὶ ἄτιμος καὶ σταυρούμενος. Since Isa 53:8 usually goes with παθητός, this leaves Isa 53:12 for σταυρούμενος. Presumably the intended phrase is Isa 53:12b, παρεδόθη εἰς θάνατον ἡ ψυχὴ αὐτοῦ, but this is not substantially different from v. 8d, ἤχθη εἰς θάνατον. Alternatively, since the crucifixion of Jesus actually placed him between two "lawless men," Marcovich could have in mind "he was numbered among the lawless" from Isa 53:12c. But it is not clear whether Justin would have made this connection, since only later manuscripts of Mark add Mark 15:28, which cites Isa 53:12c as an interpretation of Mark 15:27 about the thieves on the right and the left (cf. KJV).

At first glance, the participle in *Dial.* 110.2 would rather seem to recall ἐπικατάρατος ὁ σταυρούμενος in *Dial.* 89.2, with reference to Deut 21:23. Since each of the *Dialogue's* nine allusions to Deut 21:23 interprets it in terms of crucifixion (see n. 19), we would expect any Old Testament allusion created by σταυρούμενος in *Dial.* 110.2 to be focused primarily here. The only problem is that *Dial.* 110.2 is set within the framework of the two Parousias, which usually contrasts only Isaiah 53 with Daniel 7.

The solution probably lies in the observation that *Dial.* 110.2 comes late in the *Dialogue,* after the proofs about the cross in *Dial.* 90-96 and the Psalm 22 excursus in *Dial.* 97-106. Here Justin's neat divisions of language begin to break down. We observe this blurring of boundaries for example in *Dial.* 121.3: ἐν τῇ ἀτίμῳ καὶ ἀειδεῖ καὶ ἐξουθενημένῃ πρώτῃ παρουσίᾳ αὐτοῦ, "at his *dishonorable* and *formless* and *despised* first coming," with allusions to Isa 53:2-3 by the first two terms and to Ps 22 (LXX 21):7 ἐξουθένημα (read by Justin in *Dial.* 98.3) by the participle ἐξουθενημένη (see above n. 54). By the time we arrive here at *Dial.* 110.2, Justin will have already proved that Christ was only apparently cursed (cf. *Dial* 90.3) and that the cross is a sign of salvation in the Old Testament. Therefore in *Dial.* 110.2 we can regard Justin as combining allusions to Isaiah 53 and Deut 21:23 positively rather than defensively, especially after his Pauline-style argument that Christ *successfully* took upon himself the curses of the whole human race (cf. *Dial.* 95.1-2).

16. *Dial.* 111.2

ὁ οὖν *παθητὸς* ἡμῶν καὶ σταυρωθεὶς Χριστὸς οὐ κατηράθη ὑπὸ τοῦ νόμου, ἀλλὰ μόνος σώσειν τοὺς μὴ ἀφισταμένους τῆς πίστεως αὐτοῦ ἐδήλου.

Justin: Our *suffering* (Isa 53:8) and crucified Christ was not cursed by the Law (Deut 21:23), but showed that he alone would save those who hold firm to his faith.[63]

Allusion Level 2.5 (παθητός Isa 53:8 + Deut 21:23 + Isa 53:7 in *Dial.* 111.3). The striking expression ὁ παθητὸς ἡμῶν καὶ σταυρωθεὶς Χριστός, "Our suffering and crucified Christ," combined with the defense against the "curse" charge of Deut 21:23, is unique and therefore difficult to classify by the criteria we have been using. The attributive expression ὁ παθητὸς Χριστός has occurred once before, in *Dial.* 52.1, where Justin refers to "the Gentiles who believe in the suffering Christ." Here he includes himself in that community: "*Our* suffering Christ." The difference is that in *Dial.* 52.1, the suffering Christ did not need to be defended against the charge of being cursed by the law of Deut 21:23.

That παθητός here refers above all to *Isaiah's* suffering Christ — as Marcovich's reference to Isa 53:8 suggests — is made likely by two factors. First and most obviously, there is an attributed quotation of Isaiah, not of Isa 53:8 but of 53:7, in the next paragraph, *Dial.* 111.3. Here, *He was led as a sheep to the*

---

63. The phrase "his faith" (Falls and Halton) presumably means "faith in him," ἡ πίστις αὐτοῦ (objective genitive). Here in *Dial.* 111.2 it does not seem to refer to Jesus' personal faith in God, which would take "the faith *of* Jesus" as a subjective genitive. Nevertheless, the idea that even the sinless Christ needs to be saved by God, and does so through "hoping in him" according to Ps 22:9 (LXX 21:9), is present in *Dial.* 102.7. On this see C. Markschies, above p. 226, with the expanded Translator's note (n. 127).

slaughter is applied to Christ, who is said more particularly to have become the Passover sacrifice (τὸ πάσχα), as in 1 Cor 5:7.

The reference to the παθητὸς Χριστός in *Dial.* 111.2 is also informed by the role that the παθητός language has played in the defense against Deut 21:23 in *Dial.* 89.2-3. There Trypho agrees that the Scriptures state that the Messiah is to be παθητός (cf. also *Dial.* 36.1; 39.7), but he adds a request for Justin to show that this suffering should take the form cursed by the law, namely crucifixion. Justin does not provide a direct defense against Deut 21:23 in *Dial.* 89.3. Instead, he produces his most impressive combined quotation (in indirect discourse) of unmistakable phrases from Isa 53:8d + 3 + 4 + 12c + 8b, adding at the end that this was spoken by "the prophet" (sc. Isaiah), and not just by "the prophets" generally (as in the introduction of the quotation).

17. *Dial.* 126.1

Τίς δ' ἐστὶν οὗτος, ὃς . . . <u>παιδίον</u> διὰ 'Ησαίου . . . καὶ <u>παθητὸς καὶ Ἰακὼβ καὶ Ἰσραὴλ</u> πάλιν διὰ 'Ησαίου . . . **κέκληται** . . . , εἰ ἐγνώκειτε, ὦ Τρύφων, ἔφην, οὐκ ἂν ἐβλασφημεῖτε εἰς αὐτὸν ἤδη καὶ παραγενόμενον καὶ γεννηθέντα καὶ παθόντα καὶ ἀναβάντα εἰς τὸν οὐρανόν· ὃς καὶ πάλιν παρέσται, καὶ τότε *κόψονται* ὑμῶν αἱ δώδεκα φυλαί.

Justin: Who this is who is **called** . . . <u>a *child*</u> by Isaiah (9:5) . . . and the <u>*Suffering One* and *Jacob* and *Israel*</u> again by Isaiah (53:8; 42:1 [cf. 41:8; 44:1]) — if you had known this, Trypho, I said, then you would not have blasphemed him who has come, and assumed human nature, and suffered, and ascended into heaven. And he shall return again, and then your *twelve tribes will weep* (Zech 12:12) (cf. Falls and Halton, 126 [mod.])

Allusion Level 5 (παθητός Isa 53:8 + name of Isaiah). For a fuller presentation of this passage see above §5.1. In terms of English style it makes sense to translate παθητός here substantivally as the *Suffering One* (Falls and Halton), though its only certain substantival use is in *Dial.* 74.1 (cf. 34.2). The sequence γεννηθέντα καὶ παθόντα may again show the close connection between incarnation and real human suffering (see above on *Dial.* 85.2 and below, §7.4).

We know from this text that Justin associates παθητός preeminently with Isaiah. That he further focuses that term on Isa 53:8 (so Marcovich) is better proved by *Dial.* 89.2-3. In this final summary it is difficult to imagine that Justin has in mind primarily Isa 53:8 and not Isaiah 53 as a whole, for when Justin similarly says in *Dial.* 85.1 that both Isaiah and David prophesied a Messiah without form or honor, he surely has in mind Psalm 22 (LXX 21) as a whole and not just his favorite statement from it, "they have pierced my hands and feet" (v. 17; cf. *Dial.* 97.3, 4 [line 23: ὠρύγη]; 98.4; 104.1; *1 Apol.* 35.5; 38.4). On the other hand, where παθητός appears with the allusive terms ἄτιμος, ἀειδής, and ἄδοξος in *Dial.* 100.2 and 110.2, it is necessary for Marcovich to distinguish its allusion to Isa 53:8 from the allusion the other terms make to Isa 53:2-3. On the whole, there can be no great complaint about an over-specificity of Marcovich's apparatus notes regarding παθητός and Isa 53:8.

6.3 Summary of the Uses of *παθητός*

The above analysis of the 17 παθητός passages has uncovered rational criteria that confirm Marcovich's editing. There is a discernable dividing line between the occurrences of παθητός that he refers to Isa 53:8 in his apparatus and those that he does not. The threshold is Level 2.5 on my scale, below which Scripture references to Isa 53:8 are not given Marcovich's apparatus, though italics are still used in his text (except for *Dial.* 99.2; see §7.4). The results are as follows:

Level 5. παθητός (cf. Isa 53:8) + named reference to Isaiah: *Dial.* 126.1 (1)

Level 4.5. παθητός (cf. Isa 53:8) + quotation of Isa 53:8d + <ὥς> φησιν ὁ προφήτης (= Isaiah): *Dial.* 89.2-3 (1)

Level 4. παθητός (cf. Isa 53:8) + ἄτιμος, ἀειδής, or ἄδοξος (cf. Isa 53:2-3) + ἔνδοξος or μετὰ δόξης (cf. Dan 7:13-14) + two Parousias: *Dial.* 49.2 (includes κριτὴς ἁπάντων, cf. Dan 7:26); *Dial.* 110.2 (includes σταυρούμενος, cf. Deut 21:23) (2)

Level 3.5. παθητός (cf. Isa 53:8) + ἀειδής + ἄτιμος (cf. Isa 53:2-3), but without an allusion to Daniel 7: *Dial.* 100.2 (1)

Level 3. παθητός (cf. Isa 53:8) + allusions by ἔνδοξος, μετὰ δόξης, etc. to Dan 7:13-14, often including the two Parousias, and occasionally including allusions to judgment in Dan 7:26, or to ruling or having a kingdom in Dan 7.27: *Dial.* 34.2; 36.1 (παθητός 2x); 39.7 (without reference to Isa 53:8 in Marcovich); 76:6 (no Dan 7:14; cf. 7:27) (4)

Level 2.5. Two passages, for different reasons: *Dial.* 68.9 παθητός (cf. Isa 53:8) + possible allusion to Dan 7:27; *Dial.* 111.2 παθητός (cf. Isa 53:8) + defense against Deut 21:23 (2)

Level 2. Attributive παθητὸς Χριστός + two Parousias, but without language alluding to Dan 7:14: *Dial.* 52.1. Presumably the "Gentiles who believe in the *suffering* Christ" will know, if they have been "well instructed" (cf. *Dial.* 93.5), that this παθητὸς Χριστός is the Messiah predicted especially by Isaiah 53. But the phrase is not marked as Isaianic by the usual markers of the *Dialogue* and is not referred to Isa 53:8 by Marcovich (1)

Levels 0-2. No certain allusion to Isaiah 53, different possible levels of scriptural "echo." See above on *Dial.* 41.1; 52.1; 70.4; 74.1; 85.2; 99.2 (6)

In sum, of the 17 παθητός passages, 11 allude to Isaiah 53 and 6 do not (*Dial.* 41.1; 52.1; 70.4; 74.1; 85.2; 99.2). This is suggested by Marcovich's apparatus and by the independent categories above.

Grammatically, 11 of the 19 uses of παθητός are in a predicate nominative position. In two instances, *Dial.* 68.9 and 89.2, παθητός is the complement to the direct object and is therefore a predicate accusative. It is found attributively twice with Χριστός (*Dial.* 52.1 [2d occurrence]; 111.2), and thrice with ἄνθρωπος (85.2; 99.2; 100.2 [ἄνθρωπος . . . παθητός]). There is one articular substantival use, τὸν παθητόν (*Dial.* 74.1). The anarthrous uses in the first and last occurrences of παθητός in *Dial.* 34.2 and 126.1 are probably predicate adjectives in the nominative (included in the total of 11 above), but there can be little objection to translating them as substantival, given that the other predicates of Christ in these passages are nouns.

7. Historical Evaluation of Allusive Language

In interpreting the data collected and categorized above, we can now begin to include historical as well as linguistic and literary criteria.

7.1 Christian Setting: The παθητὸς Χριστός and Gentile Christianity

In the only New Testament use of παθητός in Acts 26:23, Paul says that Moses and the prophets predicted: εἰ παθητὸς ὁ χριστός, "that the Messiah must *suffer*" (NRSV).[64] In other words, the Messiah must become *"subject to suffering"* or "passible." The adjective is used in a predicate position. So also in the *Dialogue*. Most of the passages construe παθητός as a *predicate* of Christ, and the debate between Justin and Trypho centers on whether the Scriptures state or do not state that the Messiah will or can have this predicate. A typical construction from Justin's side runs: Christ has been proclaimed in the Scriptures as being, or being destined to become, *passible* at his first Parousia.

---

64. On this use of εἰ = "that," see BDAG 278 s.v. εἰ 2.

The predicate position of παθητός is a good index of the still thoroughly Jewish quality of the discussion of the Messiah throughout most of the *Dialogue*.[65] Attributive expressions such as "suffering Messiah" or παθητός Χριστός cannot be used until it has been settled *whether* the Messiah must become παθητός.

The importance that this sort of language will acquire in the *Dialogue* is hinted at right from the beginning. Trypho poses an objection to Justin and his fellow Christians by essentially saying to them: You claim to be pious but you do not keep the precepts of the Jewish law, such as circumcision and the Sabbath and festivals, to separate yourselves from the other Gentiles. Rather, "you set your hopes on a *crucified man*," ἐπ᾽ ἄνθρωπον σταυρωθέντα τὰς ἐλπίδας ποιούμενοι (*Dial.* 10.3; cf. 8.3: "you have placed your hope in a man"). Justin does not disown this "crucified man" but confesses him as the core of Christian faith. Significantly, however, Justin speaks in this instance not of a crucified *man,* but of a crucified *Messiah* — something Trypho will never say in their discussion. After claiming that Christians have good reason not to obey the Jewish law because God has superseded it with a new law and a new covenant, Justin presents one of his best defenses of the crucifixion, pointing to its fruits:

> διὰ τοῦ ὀνόματος αὐτοῦ τοῦ σταυρωθέντος Ἰησοῦ Χριστοῦ ⟨ἀνθρώπους⟩ ἀπὸ τῶν εἰδώλων καὶ τῆς ἄλλης ἀδικίας προσελθόντας τῷ θεῷ . . .
> (Marcovich, 89)

> Through the name of *the very one who was crucified,* Jesus Christ, ⟨people⟩ have drawn near to God from idols and all other iniquity, etc. (*Dial.* 11.4).[66]

---

65. Tellingly, the predicate position of παθητός that is the norm elsewhere disappears along with Trypho in Justin's excursus on Psalm 22 (*Dial.* 97-106), where the polemical context is no longer Judaism but Gnostic docetism. See below §7.4.

66. I take the participle σταυρωθέντος here in *Dial.* 11.4 as substantival, with Williams, "by the name of Him who was crucified, Jesus Christ" (p. 23). This leaves the name "Jesus Christ" to stand out clearly in apposition at the end of the phrase — something that is not as clear in the attributive construction of Falls and Halton, "through the name of the crucified Jesus Christ" (tautology). Against Williams, I have construed αὐτοῦ here in *Dial.* 11.4 with the following τοῦ σταυρωθέντος as an intensive pronoun, "the crucified one *himself*" or "the *very one* who was crucified." See the parallel in *Dial.* 71.2, οὗτος αὐτὸς ὁ σταυρωθείς, where Williams does translate as intensive: "this very One who was crucified" (p. 151). My intensive rendering of *Dial.* 11.4 provides a better response to Trypho's mention of the *crucified man* upon whom Christians have set their hopes in *Dial.* 10.3. The αὐτοῦ in 11.4 could also be taken as possessive after ὀνόματος, "the name *of him* who was crucified," with Williams. But then αὐτοῦ is not needed at all, and it would have been just as well to say, "the name of the crucified."

Justin immediately follows this expressed use of Jesus Christ as a name with the full titular sense of ὁ Χριστός as *the Messiah:*

ἡμεῖς ἐσμεν, οἱ διὰ τοῦ σταυρωθέντος Χριστοῦ τῷ θεῷ προσαχθέντες

We are those who have been brought to God through this *crucified Messiah.* (*Dial.* 11.5)[67]

Only with the wording "crucified Messiah" rather than the usual "crucified Christ" does the phrase encapsulate the tension that will unfold in the *Dialogue.*[68] To translate the earlier phrase in *Dial.* 11.4 attributively, "through the name of the crucified Jesus Christ" (Falls and Halton), results in a tautology: everybody knows that Jesus Christ was crucified, but the question is whether the *Messiah* could be crucified in the light of the curse on crucifixion in Deut 21:23. This becomes one of the most pressing questions in the *Dialogue.*

In the light of the unsettled debate between Justin and Trypho about the identity of the Messiah, it is ironic that in one of the rare places where the term "Messiah" appears in the translation of Falls and Halton, there is no supporting term in the Greek, *Dial.* 32.1. Here Trypho addresses Justin:

> Sir, your quotations from Scripture prove that we must look forward to that *glorious* and great Messiah who, *as the Son of Man, receives the everlasting kingdom from the Ancient of Days* (cf. Dan 7:13-14, 27). But, the one whom you call Christ was *without glory and honor* [the translation reversing ἄτιμος καὶ ἄδοξος, cf. Isa 53:2-3] to such an extent that he incurred the last *curse of God's law* (cf. Deut 21:23), namely, he was crucified. (*Dial.* 32.1, trans. Falls and Halton, 48-49, italics and references added)

Trypho begins by referring to the glorious Son of Man of Dan 7:13-14, 27 because Justin has just finished quoting Dan 7:9-28 in *Dial.* 31.2-7. Falls originally added the reference, which Halton retains, to Daniel's Son of Man as the

---

67. I agree with Williams in taking σταυρωθέντος as substantival in *Dial.* 11.4, but not here in *Dial.* 11.5, where he translates: "we . . . were brought nigh to God by *him who was crucified,* even Christ" (italics added), thus understanding Χριστοῦ as an appositive.

68. The NRSV translators correctly realize this when they begin the New Testament not with the traditional reference to "Jesus Christ" (KJV; RSV) but with "An account of the genealogy of Jesus *the Messiah,* the son of David, the son of Abraham" (Matt 1:1). The term "Messiah" rather than "Christ" predominates in the NRSV where the question of the identity of the Messiah against a Jewish background is in view, particularly in the Gospels and Acts, but also in Paul, e.g. Rom 9:5: "to them [the Israelites] belong the patriarchs, and from them, according to the flesh, comes the Messiah, who is over all, God blessed forever."

Messiah, presumably in the light of known Jewish interpretations of the Son of Man.[69] However, the term "Messiah" is not in the Greek, where Trypho admits only that Daniel 7 compels him and his compatriots to await a "glorious and great [one]," ἔνδοξον καὶ μέγαν.

Trypho's following reference to "this so-called Christ of yours," οὗτος ὁ ὑμέτερος λεγόμενος Χριστός (*Dial.* 32.1), involves a twofold sense: "the one whom you mistakenly regard as the (Jewish) Messiah [a title] and therefore call Christ [a proper name]." A similar consciousness of the difference between Jewish and Christian usage is found in Trypho's first use of Χριστός, where Trypho says to Justin and his fellow Christians: "you invent for yourselves *a certain* Christ," Χριστὸν ἑαυτοῖς τινα ἀναπλάσσετε (*Dial.* 8.4).[70] That Trypho in *Dial.* 32.1 means to accuse Christians of misappropriating a Jewish term and title is clear from his allusion to the curse of Deut 21:23: Christians have hopelessly separated the title from any possible biblical context. Justin insists that Christians have done no such thing, since the Scriptures themselves refer to the Messiah as without honor and glory in Isa 53:2-3. Since Trypho usually responds to Justin's Scripture quotations rather than initiating, it is disputed whether we should imagine him here taking the initiative in alluding to Isa 53:2-3 by the terms ἄτιμος and ἄδοξος (see below §7.3).

All this conditions the language of παθητός and its attributive and predicate positions. Even if Justin can persuade Trypho to agree in theory that the prophets predicted that the Messiah would be παθητός, as he begins to do here in *Dial.* 32.2 without yet using the term (cf. 14.8, θνητός), there is still the question of whether Jesus is this predicted suffering figure, which Trypho raises in his first use of παθητός in *Dial.* 36.1, after its introduction by Justin in *Dial.* 34.2. Justin delays answering; Trypho persists, again using παθητός (*Dial.* 39.7), followed by another delay, thus providing the formula for a long-drawn-out dialogue. Trypho's uses of παθητός are a good index of where we are in the argument, and they keep the theme of a suffering Messiah alive in the absence of satisfying answers from Justin or other allusions to Isaiah 53. In the climax of this aspect of the discussion in *Dial.* 89.1 Trypho agrees, as he had in *Dial.* 36.1 and 39.7, that the Scriptures proclaim the Messiah to be passible: παθητὸν μὲν τὸν Χριστὸν . . . αἱ γραφαὶ κηρύσσουσι. But he still does not believe that the Scriptures justify a form of suffering cursed by the law, namely crucifixion.

In the midst of this, however, there is another, more settled or "Christian"

---

69. Cf. the references at *Dial.* 32.1 to *1 Enoch* 37–71; *4 Ezra* 13 and rabbinic sources in Williams, 62 n. 2, and now Marcovich, p. 121 apparatus, lines 2-3.

70. Cf. C. Setzer, "'You invent a Christ': Christological Claims as Points of Jewish-Christian Dispute," *Union Seminary Quarterly Review* 44 (1991) 315-328.

use of the term παθητός. Tellingly, the *Dialogue's* only clear use of the substantival expression ὁ παθητός, "the one who suffered," involves Trypho repeating what he believes to be *Justin's* position (*Dial.* 74.1). Given the framework of the *Dialogue,* for Trypho himself to admit that *Jesus* is the one who suffered — as distinct from his admission that *the Messiah,* whoever he may be, might be one who suffers — would be to admit that he suffered *according to the Scriptures* (especially Isaiah 53) and is therefore the promised Messiah. It is not accidental that Trypho never uses this language.

To put it another way, for Justin, the suffering Messiah and the crucified Messiah are one and the same and therefore his expressions for them are equivalent (or co-referential). But for Trypho they are not, and therefore he cannot or will not use either of these expressions attributively, even though he is willing to discuss παθητός as a messianic predicate in theory. It is almost as if Trypho could accept Jesus' version of the passion prediction, the Son of Man must *suffer* (Luke 9:22), but not the angels' summary of it in Luke 24:7, the Son of Man must be *crucified* — a merely hypothetical illustration that is nevertheless not without a point of contact in the literary world of the *Dialogue,* where Trypho claims to have read certain things recorded in what he calls "the Gospel" (*Dial.* 10.2).[71]

Most striking is Justin's attributive phrase, ὁ παθητὸς ἡμῶν καὶ σταυρωθεὶς Χριστός, "our suffering and crucified Messiah," in the second last use of παθητός in *Dial.* 111.2. The figure is a hendiadys: "suffering" and "crucified" are two ways of referring to the same thing: the suffering *was* crucifixion. The attributive expression "crucified Messiah" also occurs in *Dial.* 96.1 and in the catena fragment preserving a lost section of the *Dialogue;*[72] see also "the crucified Jesus" (*Dial.* 34.8; 35.2). It must be part of Justin's purpose to move his readers to ownership of his and his community's suffering-crucified Messiah.[73] Nevertheless, Justin does not over-use such Christian language. In *Dial.* 110.1-3 he explains how certain prophecies from Mic 4:1-7 quoted in *Dial.* 109 were fulfilled in the Gentile believers (cf. *Dial.* 109.1), of which he is one. Justin says:

71. Although he does not mention this hypothetical illustration, Horner, *Listening to Trypho,* 59, assumes that the authentic historical figure of Trypho brought to the discussion certain facts from his reading of the Gospels (*Dial.* 10.2), such as his knowledge of Jesus' resurrection in *Dial.* 63.1, which Justin did not need to supply to the literary figure of Trypho in the *Dialogue.*

72. Marcovich, Appendix, p. 316, *ll.* 13-14; see above, n. 30.

73. Note, however, that Justin's invitation to Trypho to be "initiated" or become "perfect" by becoming a Christian in *Dial.* 8.2 (cf. Falls and Halton, 15 with n. 21) precedes Trypho's objection about the Christians' "crucified man" in *Dial.* 10.2.

We who delighted in war . . . have converted . . . our *swords into ploughshares* (cf. Mic 4:3 = *Dial.* 109.2), . . . and we cultivate piety, justice, brotherly charity, faith, and hope, which we derive from the Father himself *through the crucified one* (διὰ τοῦ σταυρωθέντος). (*Dial.* 110.3)

The Gentile connection is even more explicit in *Dial.* 52.1. Justin here speaks of τὰ ἔθνη πιστεύοντα ἐπὶ τὸν παθητὸν Χριστόν, "*the Gentiles* who believe in the suffering Messiah." Again, this is equivalent to the crucified Jesus. In *Dial.* 34.8, Justin speaks of "those from the Gentiles who know God, the creator of the universe, through the crucified Jesus" or "through Jesus the crucified" (διὰ Ἰησοῦ τοῦ σταυρωθέντος). That this is an issue differentiating Jew from Gentile means that we are still not entirely removed from Paul's time, when the preaching of "Christ crucified" was a stumbling block to Jews, even if it is no longer foolishness to all the Gentiles at the time of Justin (cf. 1 Cor 1:23).[74]

The *Dialogue*'s clear separation of Jewish and Christian ways of speaking about the potential of a suffering Messiah could be a literary artifice that tells us little about the actual contacts of Jews and Christians over this issue. However, it seems here that we can say more. At the conclusion of his treatment of Justin above, C. Markschies wrote:

> What especially impresses me about this type of exposition is that, because Justin still stands relatively early in the history of interpretation, he feels no need either to problematize or to resolve the phenomenon of the Messiah's "shameful" death and his life "without appearance or beauty." His interpretation of the fourth Servant Song is still totally determined by the demands of the Jewish-Christian dialogue; no "Hellenization" of the kerygma has yet taken place on this point. (p. 267)

Christian teaching has not yet become burdened by a Greek-type doctrine of divine impassibility applied to Christ, as would later be evidenced by

---

74. Many interpreters think that "Christ crucified" (Χριστὸν ἐσταυρωμένον) was a stumbling block to Jews at Paul's time precisely because some Jews had already understood the curse on crucifixion according to Deut 21:23, which clearly became the sticking point later for the literary figure of Trypho in the *Dialogue* (though whether the authentic Trypho held this view is debated: see §7.2 with reference to J. M. Lieu). W. C. van Unnik, "Der Fluch" (see n. 6), 483, mentions that the commentaries on 1 Corinthians by Lietzmann and Kümmel and by Conzelmann use Justin's *Dialogue* (esp. chap. 32) to illustrate the Jewish objection in 1 Cor 1:23, though van Unnik thinks it cannot be proved whether Paul has this objection in view in Gal 3:13, because he uses Deut 21:23 positively as proof of salvation from the curse, not in a polemical context with a known Jewish interlocutor, as in the *Dialogue*.

Hilary of Poitiers (cf. Markschies, pp. 316-19). But there is more: a predominately Gentile Christianity is still defined by an essentially Jewish tension about a suffering — indeed crucified — Messiah. It is not a theological problem long-since solved; it is still a cause of astonishment, but one in which the Gentiles have been able to move "past astonishment to faith," in the telling phrase of D. J. Bingham.[75] Gentile believers follow the "astonished" or "amazed" nations of Isa 52:15–53:1 who are their prototype: "So many nations will be astonished at him." (Justin does not actually quote this line of Isa 52:15a in *Dial.* 118.4, but see his similar use of θαυμάζειν in *Dial.* 89.3.) Yet despite this, they will "see," "understand," and "believe," as Justin implies when he quotes this passage in *Dial.* 118.4. That the Gentiles should also be depicted in the *Dialogue* as those who believe in a "suffering (and crucified) Messiah" informed by the teaching of Isaiah 53 (even if the crucifixion is not directly proved there) fits seamlessly with this.

Bingham in his article attempts to outline "a more comprehensive role for Isaiah 53 in Justin's community" than has been possible in previous scholarship. He concludes: "I could very easily see this prophetic passage [sc. Isa 52:10–54:6] in its connection to other biblical texts being taught in pre-baptismal instruction." According to Bingham, Justin's reading of Isaiah 53

> specifically gives the baptized and the baptismal candidate a perspective of the community's distinctiveness as the "believers" [cf. Isa 53:1, τίς ἐπίστευσεν, etc.], and the "repentant" [cf. *Dial.* 13.1]. . . . It orients the community to the essential features of its Christology: incarnation, of divine origin [cf. Isa 53:8 γενεά], the bloody death of crucifixion for the cleansing of sinners and the resurrection of the dead [cf. Isa 53:9 with 57:2 in *Dial.* 97.2].[76]

There are additional arguments that can strengthen Bingham's thesis about the formative influence of Servant passages, particularly in the Gentile Christian community. Justin quotes Isa 42:1-4 for the phrases "Jacob my servant," "Israel my elect," and "in his name shall the Gentiles hope," in order to show that the Gentiles hope in the Servant who is not the patriarch Jacob but Jesus (*Dial.* 135.2-3; cf. 123.8). Shortly before this in *Dial.* 134.4, Justin uses the language of "serving" in a possible allusion to Isa 53:11, δίκαιον εὖ δουλεύοντα πολλοῖς (seldom noted), combined with a clear allusion to Phil 2:8, μέχρι θανάτου, θανάτου δὲ σταυροῦ, to argue that the serving Christ is particularly

75. D. J. Bingham, "Justin and Isaiah 53," *VC* 53 (2000) 248-261, esp. 252.

76. Bingham, "Justin and Isaiah 53," 259, parenthetical references added from Bingham's preceding argument. For Isa 53:1 see p. 252; for 53:8 pp. 256-257; for 53:9 p. 257.

skilled — as Jacob was with Laban — in picking out a multi-national people for himself:[77]

> Jacob served Laban for the spotted and speckled sheep, and Christ served, even *to the servitude of the cross* (ἐδούλευσε καὶ τὴν μέχρι σταυροῦ δουλείαν), for men of different colors and features from every nationality, redeeming them by his blood and the mystery of the cross. (*Dial.* 134.4, trans. Falls and Halton)

Bingham may be right to suggest that Isaiah 53 "orients" Justin's community to the crucifixion. However, Justin himself makes it clear in *Dial.* 89.3 that crucifixion is something that needs to be *added* to the picture of Isaiah 53, on which he and Trypho otherwise agree, but he also suggests that this is something that people of faith add naturally. Justin believes that Trypho's problem is that he is still "astonished" by the crucifixion in the light of Deut 21:23 (cf. *Dial.* 89.2).[78] Justin agrees that Trypho would have good reason to be astonished — καλῶς εἶχε θαυμάζειν[79] — but only if he had not read or grasped the meaning of the prophet Isaiah's words (*Dial.* 89.3 l. 14). Justin does not differentiate Jews like Trypho from Gentile believers (like the majority of his community) on the basis that one group has the right to be astonished and therefore to reject the crucifixion (based on the law) while the other does not. Gentiles, too, are astonished, just like the nations of Isa 52:15, and there are additional motives for Gentile rejection of this kind of suffering in the Hellenistic docetism that Justin combats in his excursus on Psalm 22 (see below §7.4). For Justin the difference between the believer and the unbeliever is not based on nationality or the Jew–Gentile distinction:

> All who have grasped the meaning of the prophets' words will say that it [sc. the suffering savior of Isaiah 53] is he and no other, as soon as they hear that he was crucified [Marcovich: that <he is the> crucified one]. (*Dial.* 89.3)

The crucifixion is not in Isaiah 53 but is in the meaning of the prophets' words — here the plural "prophets," even though the allusions are from Isaiah

---

77. Cf. *Dial.* 52.4, where Christians are "made up of all nationalities" as distinct from the Jews. In the light of the interest of New Testament scholars in the issue of Jewish "national righteousness" and exclusive "boundary markers" at the time of Paul, it is intriguing to think that by Justin's time the internationality and inclusivity of the Christian community may have become the basis of another kind of "boasting."

78. This is in keeping with Bingham's argument, although the use of θαυμάζειν in *Dial.* 89.2 is not one of the pieces of evidence he has used.

79. Third person impersonal: "it were well to be astonished" (Williams).

53. Trypho is not to be outdone by appeals to the prophets' words; he approvingly takes up Justin's allusion to Isa 53:7 about the sheep led to the slaughter and then renews his request for an answer about the curse of crucifixion (*Dial.* 90.1). This will have to be pursued. Nevertheless, it would be unfair to suggest that Gentile belief in a suffering-crucified Messiah was necessarily an inconsequential matter because of Gentile freedom from the Jewish law.[80]

7.2 Jewish Setting: The παθητὸς Χριστός and Deut 21:23

Trypho can theoretically consider a Messiah who becomes παθητός or who is proclaimed in the Scriptures as παθητός, as long as παθητός is in the predicate position as a potentiality rather than a reality. However, I have shown above that the substantival construction ὁ παθητός (*Dial.* 74.1) and the attributive phrases ὁ παθητὸς Χριστός (*Dial.* 52.1) and ὁ παθητὸς ἡμῶν καὶ σταυρωθεὶς Χριστός (*Dial.* 111.2) are distinctly Christian in the setting of the *Dialogue* itself, and that both Justin and Trypho understand this. This could be a matter of Justin the author carefully controlling the language of his two literary characters, but even if this is merely good fiction, it will also reflect the way people actually spoke. This subtle grammatical difference mirrors the more acute and academically debated difference between the two interlocutors regarding Deut 21:23.[81] In the process of dealing with whether Christ is "cursed" because he was "hung on a tree" when crucified, Justin eventually transitions into his own charge that Jews are unjustly cursing and persecuting the Christians and will some day pay the consequences:

> But, if you curse him and those who believe in him, and, whenever it is in your power, put them to death, how will you prevent retribution from being demanded of you for having laid hands on him, as of unjust and sinful men who are completely devoid of feeling and wisdom? (*Dial.* 95.4, trans. Falls and Halton)

---

80. The cross was a scandal and an existential issue for all early Christians. A "curse" or anything associated with it was a terrible possibility in the eyes of ancient people, whether Jews, Christians, or pagans. Justin's theology that through the apparently cursed cross, Jesus took upon himself and nullified the curse upon all humanity (*Dial.* 95.1-2), is therefore highly relevant to his context. Cf. esp. van Unnik, "Der Fluch" (see n. 6), 496-499.

81. On Deut 21:23 in the *Dialogue* see esp. van Unnik, "Der Fluch," who offers additional analysis beyond my limited focus here. Cf. also Skarsaune, *Proof* (see n. 4), 216-220; Rudolph, *"Denn wir sind jenes Volk"* (see n. 3), 187-191; C. D. Allert, *Revelation, Truth, Canon and Interpretation: Studies in Justin Martyr's* Dialogue with Trypho, VCSup 64 (2002) 232-236, esp. 232.

Jews are accused of persecuting Christians, apparently as an extension of their charge that the Christ whom Christians worship is cursed by the law.[82] Modern scholars are interested in differentiating the rhetoric from the reality. It becomes a matter of historical interest to determine whether Jews actually applied the charge of Deut 21:23 to Christ and by extension to Christians. Some New Testament historians believe that Paul the Pharisee shared a contemporary Jewish view that Deut 21:23 placed a curse upon a crucified victim, and that he may even have used this as a basis for his persecution of the church.[83] It was because he was so familiar with the charge from this hostile angle that he was able, indeed obligated, after his apostolic call to understand how this curse was turned into blessing (cf. Gal 3:13-14).

82. For further references to "cursing" of Christians by Jews in the *Dialogue* see van Unnik, "Der Fluch," 497 with n. 59; J. M. Lieu, "Reading in Canon and Community: Deuteronomy 21.22-34, A Test Case for Dialogue," M. Daniel Carroll R., D. J. A. Clines, and P. R. Davies, eds., *The Bible in Human Society: Essays in Honour of John Rogerson,* JSOTSup 200 (1995) 317-334, esp. 328 with n. 41. Lieu summarizes: "Deut. 21.23 is thus integrated with Justin's repeated charges of extreme Jewish hostility against Christians, among which 'cursing' is but one, albeit significant, component."

83. Cf. Lieu, "Reading in Canon and Community," 331 with n. 52 (literature). For the background to Paul's use of Deut 21:23 in Gal 3:13 see M. Wilcox, "'Upon the Tree' — Deut 21:22-23 in the New Testament," *JBL* 96 (1977) 85-99, esp. 86-90. See further H.-W. Kuhn, "Jesus als Gekreuzigter in der frühchristlicher Verkündigung bis zur Mitte des 2. Jahrhunderts," *ZTK* 72 (1975) 1-46, esp. 33 (Jewish application of Deut 21:23 to crucifixion); P. Stuhlmacher, *Biblische Theologie des Neuen Testaments,* vol. 1 (1992) 156: "In all historical probability the proven application of Deut 21:22-23 to Jesus' crucifixion found in Paul (Gal 3:13) and the sermons in Acts (cf. Acts 5:30; 10:39; 13:29) is to be traced back to Jewish roots. Deuteronomy 21:23 says according to the Masoretic Text as well as the Septuagint [and Symmachus] that everyone who hangs on a 'tree,' that is, on a cross, is cursed by God. . . . As the Qumran Temple Scroll documents, this Scripture verse was applied already in pre-Christian Judaism to the crucifixion of Jews who had betrayed or done evil to their people; hanged on the cross they counted as 'those cursed by God and man' (cf. 11QTemple [11Q19] 64:6-13)" (see esp. line 12; *DSSSE* 1287). (As indicated by the bracketed "[and Symmachus]," Stuhlmacher's 1992 edition of his *Biblische Theologie,* vol. 1, grouped Symmachus's translation of Deut 21:23 together with the subjective-genitive understanding of a "curse of God" [קללת אלהים] as "cursed *by* God" found clearly in the LXX and probably in the MT. However, this reference has been removed from Stuhlmacher's forthcoming English edition.) For the intepretation of Symmachus see Kuhn, 35 n. 151; G. Jeremias, *Der Lehrer der Gerechtigkeit,* SUNT 2 [1963] 133 n. 6; M. J. Bernstein, "כי קללת אלהים תלוי [Deut. 21:23]: A Study in Early Jewish Exegesis," *JQR* 74 [1983-1984] 21-45, esp. 28.) The pre-Christian Paul shared this understanding of the curse upon the crucified (Stuhlmacher, 246-47). For Deuteronomy's "tree" as a reference to crucifixion see also 4QpNah (4Q169) frags. 3-4, col. i, 6-8, "who hanged living men [from the tree]"; "it is [hor]rible for the one hanged alive from the tree" (*DSSSE* 337); see further Kuhn, 33-34 with n. 144; G. Jeremias, 127-139, esp. 132-33. For the debate about 11QT 64:10-12 see Lieu, 330 n. 46, 333 n. 64; M. Hengel, *Crucifixion* (1977), 84 with n. 2.

Partly in response to this, Judith Lieu has written a stimulating essay about the different possible readings of Deut 21:23 in different communities, appropriately titled, "Reading in Canon and Community: Deuteronomy 21.22-34, A Test Case for Dialogue" (see n. 82). In the light of the potential diversity of interpretation, Lieu is convinced that we ought *not* to say what P. Stuhlmacher has said:

> Every Jew opposed to Jesus could — indeed had — to say with Deut. 21:22-23: This one who has been hung on the cross has suffered his just punishment; he died "cursed of God!"[84]

Lieu objects to Stuhlmacher's "had to say" on the grounds that it suggests more uniformity to Jewish interpretation than might actually have been the case, and projects a known Christian understanding of Deut 21:22-23 on to a less-well-known pre-Christian Judaism: "Here, the Christian reading of the text has become history [i.e. Jewish history], and the necessity of that 'had' excludes all other readings" (332). At the same time Lieu is not uninterested in history, and she admits that "Jewish interpretation of Deut. 21.23 *may* yet have light to throw on Jesus' crucifixion and burial" (331). But she does not take a definite position on whether the persecutor "Saul" used Deut 21:23 against the "blasphemous" Christian preaching of a Jewish Messiah, citing, apparently skeptically, only others who hold this opinion (331 n. 52). Yet her reference to "the" Christian reading of the text suggests that she thinks the pre-Christian Paul may not have held it. Lieu's position is that this is a contextualized reading in a Christian setting, and that "alternative readings may be no less contextualized than those which take place in a Christian setting" (334). Here she cites to good effect M. Hengel: the rabbis did not generally adopt a Christian-type interpretation of Deut 21.23 as applying to crucifixion (*m. Sanh.* 6:4 speaks only of the hanging up of the corpses of those executed by stoning), apparently because they did not wish to place a curse upon the thousands of other Jews besides Jesus who were crucified in the Roman period.[85]

Interestingly, Lieu has a more definite approach to the use or rather non-use of the curse charge of Deut 21:23 in Jewish interactions with Christians in

---

84. Lieu, "Reading in Canon and Community," 332-33, citing P. Stuhlmacher, *Jesus of Nazareth — Christ of Faith,* trans. S. Schatzmann (1993), 35. Original German: *Jesus von Nazareth — Christus des Glaubens* (1988), 36.

85. Lieu, 334 n. 69, with reference to M. Hengel, *Crucifixion in the Ancient World and the Folly of the Message of the Cross* (1977), 85; reprinted in idem, *The Cross of the Son of God* (1986), 93-185, esp. 177. It should also be noted that rabbinic interpretation does not generally interpret Deut 21:23 as involving a curse "from God" or "by God," as in the LXX (κεκατηραμένος ὑπὸ θεοῦ). See van Unnik, "Der Fluch" (see n. 6), 486 with n. 17; Bernstein, "Study" (see n. 83).

the second century. It was perhaps more important in inner-Christian controversies than in Jewish-Christian debate: "Irenaeus cites Deut. 21.23 in an inner-
Christian argument, Tertullian debates it with Marcion, as perhaps did Justin
before him."[86] While Lieu does not attempt to resolve the broader debate about
whether the Jews were in the habit of "cursing" Christians, as Justin says in various contexts, but simply notes the historical problem of the "benediction
against the heretics" or *Birkat ha-Minim* (328 n. 43), she takes a firmer stand
against the historicity of Trypho's allusions to Deut 21:23 in the *Dialogue*. In a
footnote she speaks tentatively of "Trypho's 'Jewish?' objection" (331 n. 53). In a
summary she cautions that "evidence for Jews interpreting Deut. 21.23 to show
that one crucified was cursed by God and could not be the Messiah . . . is provided only by Jews who speak through Christian mouths: Justin's Trypho, Jews
whose objections provoke Tertullian's alternative exegesis, those later demanded by Jerome's exegetical tradition and argument" (331). Her introduction
of the topic is more telling. After referring to Trypho's initial mention and repeated reintroduction of Deuteronomy's curse against crucifixion in *Dial.* 32.1;
89.2; and 90.1, Lieu writes:

> The touch of realism in Justin's hesitancy to take up the challenge tempts us
> to forget that he is pulling the strings, or wielding the pen; is this a genuine
> Jewish reading of the text? (p. 327)

Contrast this with the more recent reading of Trypho by T. J. Horner in
his *Listening to Trypho*. Horner interprets Justin's initial hesitancy to take up the
curse charge — combined with his confidence in having dealt with it later (cf.
Dial. 90-96) where critical modern readers see his defense as weak — as evidence of the historicity of Trypho's use of Deut 21:23. Perhaps there is more
than Lieu's "touch of realism" in this. The figure of Trypho is not fully under
the control of Justin who, while "wielding the pen," is not necessarily "pulling
the strings." Horner summarizes:

> Lifting Trypho out of the text reveals a consistent figure who does not ap-
> pear to be based on any Jewish stereotype or Christian invention. He is nei-
> ther Justin's puppet [cf. Lieu's "strings"] nor is he blindly obdurate. This ex-
> amination reveals an individual voice with its own sensibility, style, and
> agenda. It is a voice which defies fiction. His personality is unique, consis-
> tent, and idiosyncratic. Perhaps more surprisingly, his function in the text
> actually weakens Justin's argument in some places. These chapters [chs. 5-6

---

86. Lieu, 331 with n. 56, citing Irenaeus, *Adv. Haer.* 3.28.3; 4.20.2; 5.18.1; Tertullian, *Adv.
Marc.* 3.18.1; 5.3.10.

in Horner] attempt to show that the figure of Trypho is authentic and should not be defined as a literary invention or a conglomerate Jewish figure. Once this picture is presented, it is clear that the intricacies of Trypho's depiction could not be due entirely to Justin's literary skill. It is implausible and inappropriate to imagine Justin crafting his Jewish disputant in such a way as to erode some of the basic tenets of his Christian argument. (p. 12)

Horner's picture of Trypho's individuality and his lack of conformity to the *Dialogue*'s argumentative plan is based to a great extent on Trypho's use of Deut 21:23. Horner believes that Trypho's problematizing of the crucifixion of Jesus remains in Justin's text not because it is fictional, but "because Justin is convinced that he has refuted [it] successfully" (11).[87] Deut 21:23 is crucial to a study of Isaiah 53 in the *Dialogue*, because Justin and Trypho can agree on the latter but not on the former, though as Horner suggests, their agreement is more apparent than real: they are actually talking past each other.

In dealing with the occurrence of παθητός in *Dial.* 89.2 (above, §6.2, item 12), I analyzed the chain of allusions in *Dial.* 89.1–90.1. Trypho's use of παθητός leads into Justin's quotation "he was led to death," after which we are led out of Justin's quotation about "the sheep led to the slaughter" by Trypho's assertion that he knows all about this "sheep" but wants to know why Christ had to die shamefully and dishonorably by the cursed death of crucifixion.

Horner takes a similar view of the rhetorical situation that begins in *Dial.* 32.1 with Trypho's introduction of the curse of crucifixion and ends with Trypho's final request for an explanation in *Dial.* 90.1.[88] But he goes further by

---

87. Horner generally thinks that Justin does not answer Trypho's question about the curse on crucifixion very successfully, not even in the special section *Dial.* 91-97, which Horner thinks Justin wrote later to answer the questions remaining after his original exchange with Trypho (see Horner, 151, quoted below, pp. 394-95). However, Horner's bibliography does not list the essay by van Unnik, "Der Fluch" (see n. 6), who sees Justin's answers as theologically more compelling.

88. Cf. also van Unnik, "Der Fluch," 486-90. See esp. Horner, *Listening to Trypho*, 150-51: "Instead of addressing the issue [of the curse in *Dial.* 32.1], Justin tries to refute the charge by providing Scriptural support for a suffering messiah. He does not address the problem of the curse. Later in the *Dialogue*, however, it becomes apparent — to the reader at least — that for Trypho suffering is one thing, crucifixion quite another. Justin did not understand this at chapter 32 and continues the confusion at chapter 89 where the problem is raised again. . . . Even after [Trypho's] clear request for clarification [in *Dial.* 89.2], Justin speaks only of the prophetic necessity of the messiah's suffering, not of crucifixion [cf. 89.3]. Trypho reiterates his concern in the next chapter [*Dial.* 90.1]. . . . It is at this point that Justin launches into one of his more creative exegetical blocks on the symbolism of the cross in the Hebrew Scriptures [*Dial.* 91-97]." Cf. also p. 156: "Trypho's concession at chapter 36 [sc. about a Messiah who is παθητός, 36.1] is technically not a concession because Trypho has not raised an objection to a suffering messiah. His problem is with a crucified and therefore a cursed Messiah, not a suffering one."

positing a preliminary free-standing "Trypho Text" consisting almost exclusively of dialogue material which Justin will have written around 135 C.E. shortly after his actual conversations with Trypho, and then later expanded to the *Dialogue* as we know it.[89] Horner spends more time delimiting and defending this hypothetical document than explaining what purpose it served for Justin at the time it was written. We do know that Horner thinks that Justin later found it inadequate and supplemented it for publication: "The many additions of testimonia, repetition of arguments, Christian exegesis, and polemic were added to the document as an act of erudition and reflects [*sic*] Justin's accumulated experience as a Christian teacher" (p. 32).

Significantly in Horner's view, Trypho drops out of the picture precisely at the point where he last asks for clarification regarding crucifixion in *Dial.* 90.1; in *Dial.* 90.2 his voice only provides a transition to the next topic. Trypho's voice does not reappear again until *Dial.* 118.5. Justin's two sections following Trypho's question about crucifixion deal appropriately with saving images of the cross in the Old Testament (*Dial.* 90.3–97.2) and Psalm 22 (*Dial.* 97.3–106.4). But they are presented without any interruption from Trypho and thus take on the form of a monologue.[90] Horner therefore understands them as separate sections that were not originally part of Justin's conversations with Trypho. In fact, Justin may have added them later precisely because he was unable at the time to answer Trypho's objections; this scenario obviously presupposes the historicity of those objections. Since Horner's explanation involves crucial elements of his thesis, it is best to quote him at length. In response to Trypho's question about crucifixion in *Dial.* 90.1,

> Justin gives an extended Christian midrash (*Dial.* 91–97) on wood and the shape of the cross. This precedes the inserted homily on Psalm 22 (*Dial.* 98–106). . . . These two sets of chapters (*Dial.* 91–97 and 98–106) are not included in the reconstructed Trypho Text. This is a particularly telling interpolation since Justin, more than once, missed Trypho's point about the curse of the Law. After this confusion, he unleashes a stream of proof texts on the symbolism of the cross. This kind of exposition comes abruptly and the shift in tone, style, and form is striking. It is an unnatural shift from

89. On the hypothetical Trypho Text see Horner, *Listening to Trypho,* 9, 10, 32, 33-63, 199-206, 209-210.

90. Rudolph, *"Denn wir sind jenes Volk"* (see n. 3), 71-82, discusses various proposals for the structure of the *Dialogue.* She agrees (p. 79) that it takes on the form of a monologue after *Dial.* 96 or *Dial.* 108 (the end of the excursus on Psalm 22). But Horner is more radical in including the preceding section on the shape of the cross in *Dial.* 91-96 in the monologue and dating it after Justin's original exchange with Trypho.

confusion to clarity and uninterrupted explanation. If Justin knew so much about the significance of the cross and crucifixion at the time of the exchange, why does he appear to misunderstand Trypho's comment? Why allow Trypho to make him appear mistaken or caught in his own confusion? This kind of phenomenon forces us to look outside Justin's apologetic agenda for reasons why this exchange is in the text at all. These sections were probably later additions by Justin intended to address the questions raised by Trypho, but not adequately addressed in the Trypho Text. (p. 151)

While Horner's reconstruction of a "Trypho Text" representing the original discussions between our two interlocutors may need modification to make sufficient room for Isaiah 53 (see the next section), his observations about the flow of the discussion between Trypho and Justin on the topic of crucifixion ring true. Justin has frequently "hesitated," as even Lieu admits, and when he finally does give his "answers" to explain what he calls the "apparent" curse of the cross (*Dial.* 90.3), Trypho is no longer around to say whether he is satisfied by those answers. This to me would seem to indicate the presence of an authentic Jewish objection that Justin indeed found difficult. When Lieu suggests that "Justin's answer is tortuous" (327), he must have been driven to it by something. If it is not by his exchange with one or several authentic Jewish interlocutors, then we may have trouble suggesting another situation, since the docetic setting of the Psalm 22 excursus in *Dial.* 97–106 reflects very different concerns.

Although language alluding to Isaiah 53 has carried Justin's exposition of a suffering Messiah thus far, his defense of the cross draws upon different images and is less self-evident. While still interacting with Trypho, Justin suggested that Trypho should have been able to use the astonishing enough picture of Isaiah 53 to get over the only slightly more astonishing picture of Deut 21:23 (cf. *Dial.* 89.2-3), but this in reality is an answer that appears to have worked only for Gentile Christians. Justin's following answers in *Dial.* 90–96 are formally addressed to the Jews, although since Trypho is no longer responding, we can only seek to follow Justin's argument and not to assess its persuasive force.[91]

It is already established that *Scripture* — above all Isaiah 53 — states that the Messiah will be παθητός. This suffering, whatever form it takes, cannot then be invalidated by another part of Scripture, not even by the Law. Justin states this principle in another place: He says that he would rather admit that he does not know the meaning of a passage than admit that some passages of Scripture contradict others (*Dial.* 65.2). Against the charge of Deut 21:23, Justin begins in

---

91. On Justin's defense of the cross against Deut 21:23 see also Rudolph, *"Denn wir sind jenes Volk,"* 187-191.

Dial. 90.4-5 by using his favorite Old Testament image of salvation, the *victory against Amalek* made possible by the outstretched arms of Moses in the shape of a cross, supported by Aaron and Hur, with "Joshua" = "Jesus" leading as general in the battle (cf. Exod 17:8-13, and *Dial.* 91.3; 93.5; 97.1; 111.1; 112.2; 131.4). Since the sign of the cross was the only thing that ensured victory in this battle, and the victory was threatened when Moses's arms no longer made the shape of the cross, it cannot be a cursed thing. Justin therefore speaks only of "this *apparent* curse" of Christ and his cross, ταύτην τὴν δοκοῦσαν κατάραν (*Dial.* 90.3; cf. 95.2).[92] By showing the deeper meaning of the cross as a sign of salvation, Moses also showed the curse on it to be only apparent, untrue at the deeper symbolic or allegorical level of types and parables (*Dial.* 90.2), which can be understood only by those given the grace to understand (*Dial.* 92.1) that which is generally concealed from the multitude (*Dial.* 90.2).[93] Although the Jews were given the starting point to understand in the sign of Moses, they were not willing to do so (*Dial.* 93.5).

Next to the image of the battle with Amalek, other biblical pictures of the cross include the horn of the unicorn, found in Deut 33:17 LXX (*Dial.* 91.1-2) and in Ps 22 (LXX 21):22 (*Dial.* 98.5; 105.1-2), and the bronze serpent in the wilderness, which Justin uses with more caution.[94] Earlier Justin had suggested that the Passover lamb being roasted resembles the cross in that it is supported by two perpendicular spits (*Dial.* 40.3). Justin also interprets the Lord's statement in Isa 65:2, "I have stretched out my hands to an unbelieving and contradicting people," as a prediction of Jesus' hands being stretched out in crucifixion (*Dial.* 97.2). Not all the pictures are equally self-evident. Because the unicorn's horn does not look like a cross, Justin has to explain that it forms the upright post of the cross, and that "the ends of the crosspiece resemble horns joined to that one horn" (*Dial.* 91.2). Apparently he can take it for granted that the shape of a "serpent" is seldom straight and therefore in its curvature resembles a cross.

In his final combination of such images in *Dial.* 131.4-5, Justin reasserts that the Jews have already been given at least two saving experiences of the cross in their history, the serpent that saved those bitten by serpents, and the outstretched arms of Moses. They should have interpreted these as signs pointing forward to the crucified Jesus. In between in *Dial.* 111.2 we seem at first glance to encounter a mere assertion that the crucified Christ is not cursed: "our suffer-

---

92. On Justin's use of the cross-like images of the battle of Amalek, as well as the bronze serpent, in his section devoted to Deut 21:23, namely *Dial.* 89-106, see also Skarsaune, *Proof* (see n. 4), 216-220; Allert, *Revelation* (see n. 81), 235-36.

93. Cf. van Unnik, "Der Fluch," 489-91; Skarsaune, *Proof,* 218 with n. 77.

94. See above n. 22; *Dial.* 91.4; 94.1-5; 112.1; 131.4; *1 Apol.* 60; *Barn.* 12.6-7.

ing and crucified Christ was not cursed by the law." However, in this context, in addition to his quotation of Isa 53:7 about the sheep led to the slaughter and his connection of Christ's blood with the saving blood of the Passover (cf. *Dial.* 111.3; 1 Cor 5:7), Justin surrounds the idea of the suffering and crucified Christ who saves those who hold firm to "his faith" — here presumably meaning "faith in him" (ἡ πίστις αὐτοῦ, objective genitive)[95] — with other biblical examples of salvation. These include the two goats on the Day of Atonement symbolizing the two comings of Christ (*Dial.* 111.1 with 40.4), Jesus' blood represented in the red rope that saved Rahab (*Dial.* 111.4), and the Amalek image.

In his use of the Amalek image in *Dial.* 111.1-2, Justin argues that Jesus must be greater than Moses and "Joshua" = Ἰησοῦς (Jesus), because while two different men were needed to be "the type of the cross and the type of the name," mysteries which neither could have borne by himself, the one man Jesus has the power to unite both in himself. As one greater than Moses and Joshua, Jesus Christ cannot have been cursed:

> One [either Moses or Joshua = "Jesus"] of himself could not have borne both these mysteries, that is, the type of the cross and the type of the name. For this power is, and was, and shall be, the attribute of only one, at whose name every power shudders and suffers agonizing pain, because it is to be destroyed by him. Our suffering and crucified Christ was not cursed by the Law, but showed that he alone would save those who hold firm to his faith. (*Dial.* 111.2, trans. Falls and Halton, 166)

Justin asserts that a cross-based salvation both works — i.e. *saves* those who have faith — and has biblical precedent. Here Justin argues by analogy without defending Christ directly against the charge of Deut 21:23, which has no direct answer. He only accuses Jewish exegetes who would use such an argument of explaining Scripture so literally as to make even Moses a violator of the law for making the bronze serpent, an image that the law forbids (*Dial.* 112.1). The pragmatic argument about what the cross achieves in the lives of believers came up as early as *Dial.* 11.4 and is repeated in *Dial.* 94.5. Here Justin also seeks to get God involved in his argument based on the non-contradiction of biblical passages (cf. *Dial.* 94:1):

95. The use of "his faith" (trans. Falls and Halton) in *Dial.* 111.2 does not seem to refer to Jesus' personal faith in God (taking the faith *of* Jesus as a subjective genitive). Nevertheless, the related idea that even the sinless Christ needs to be saved by God and is saved through "hoping in him" according to Ps 22:9 (LXX 21:9) is present in *Dial.* 102.7. On this see C. Markschies, above p. 266, with the expanded Translator's note (n. 127).

As God ordered the sign [sc. of the cross] to be made by the brazen serpent
. . . and yet is not guilty, so in the Law a curse is placed upon men who are
crucified, but not upon the Christ of God, by whom all who have committed deeds deserving a curse are saved. (*Dial.* 94.5, trans. Falls and Halton)

As Moses cannot be guilty for making the serpent as ordered (cf. *Dial.*
94.1; 112.1), neither can God be guilty for ordering it, and therefore the formal
contradiction of the law against fashioning idols is not a material objection. In
the absence of Trypho's voice, one of the interlocutors who joins the discussion
on the second day is left to approve of Justin's argument and admit that there is
no legal defense of Moses' action, other than the fact that Scripture records it
without censure (*Dial.* 94.4).

The last sentence in the quotation above is developed in the following
paragraph: "For indeed, the entire human race is under a curse" (*Dial.* 95.1).
This includes Gentiles as well as Jews, as Justin argues from Deut 27:26, similarly to Paul in Gal 3:10 (although apparently Paul did not include the Gentiles
under the Torah's curse): "Cursed be everyone that abides not in the words of
the book of the Law so as to do them" (*Dial.* 95.1). Justin concludes that "the Father of the Universe willed that his Christ should shoulder the curses of the
whole human race" (*Dial.* 95.2). Justin has developed this idea of substitutionary atonement or transference of curse and punishment apart from explicit
quotations of or allusions to Isaiah 53. This may be because the MT's familiar
idea of transference, "The Lord has laid on him the iniquity of us all" (Isa 53:6),
has become in the Septuagint the milder, "and the Lord has delivered him to
our sins."[96] Therefore, while Isaiah 53 has provided the most important scriptural testimony to the suffering Messiah in the *Dialogue*, the difficult Deut 21:23
is still needed to provide an essential part of the theology, including discernible
"Pauline" features.[97]

---

96. On the theological changes in the LXX of Isaiah 53 over against the MT, see D. Sapp,
"The LXX, 1QIsa, and MT Versions of Isaiah 53 and the Christian Doctrine of Atonement," in
W. H. Bellinger and W. R. Farmer, eds., *Jesus and the Suffering Servant* (1998), 170-92.

97. Cf. van Unnik, "Der Fluch" (see n. 6), 498-99, including similarities and differences
between Justin and Paul. Skarsaune, *Proof* (see n. 4), speaks of "the Pauline argument of *Dial.* 95
concerning Deut 21:23" (218, 220) and contrasts this with "the non-Pauline argument that Deut
21:23 is not valid for Jesus" (220). Even though Justin's use of the brazen serpent as a defense
against the apparent curse of the cross is technically "non-Pauline material" (220), Skarsaune
contends that "broadly speaking, Justin has combined a Johannine motive [cf. John 3:14] with a
Pauline argument" (216). Skarsaune (219 n. 78) also criticizes van Unnik (498-99) for his thesis
that Justin was not "dependent" on Paul for the use of Deut 27:26 and 21:23, but that both used a
common tradition; Skarsaune thinks that Justin used conflicting traditions, one of which was
Pauline.

A similar universalistic note is sounded by the image of the bronze serpent. All humans have been bitten by the ancient serpent, yet God declares that he will deliver "all who believe in him who was to be put to death by this sign [foreshadowed by the bronze serpent], namely, the cross" (*Dial.* 94.2).

Finally, Deut 21:23 provides a prediction not only of Christ's manner of death but of the behavior of the Jews. This, Justin says, "strengthens our hope which is sustained by the crucified Christ, not becaue the crucified one is cursed by God, but because God predicted what would be done by all of you Jews" (*Dial.* 96.1). This includes not only Jewish complicity in the death of Jesus but their cursing of his followers in their synagogues (*Dial.* 96.2). And this in turn brings us back to our starting point concerning the still-unanswered question about the wider historical significance of the language of Deut 21:23, which goes beyond our scope here.

7.3 Isaiah 53 and the Composition of the Dialogue: A Reply to T. J. Horner

Theories about the composition of Justin's *Dialogue* can be extremely intricate, as O. Skarsaune's standard work *The Proof of Prophecy* testifies, and obviously such theories cannot be proposed apart from some degree of speculation. Nevertheless, allusions to Isaiah 53 run through various sections of the *Dialogue*, including some that are thought by some interpreters to have been originally independent units. My study of allusive language therefore has a bearing on issues of composition, particularly as understood by T. J. Horner in his *Listening to Trypho* (above, n. 2). This topic is relevant here because Horner understands the placement of the long quotation of Isa 52:10–54:6 in *Dial.* 13.2-9, which he dates as a later addition — *not* part of the independent and earlier hypothetical document that he calls the "Trypho Text" — to be one of the main inconsistencies in this otherwise consistent document.

As Horner is the first to admit, "extracting a hypothetical text [from a later document] is an inexact science" (p. 61). Nevertheless, one of his main objects is to engage in this science. Horner reconstructs from excerpts of the full *Dialogue* "a separate and earlier text (the Trypho Text)" that allows him to assign his two different textual layers two different dates: "one for the Trypho Text (circa 135 C.E.) and the other for the full *Dialogue* (circa 160 C.E.)" (p. 7).

Horner rightly understands the general consistency of the Trypho Text and of the "authentic" — not necessarily verbatim — voice of the historical Trypho that emerges from it to be the result of his objective (and relatively simple) criteria rather than his presuppositions. A mere presumption of consistency would surely have been tempted to eliminate the complications that result from the Trypho Text's failure to include a long quotation of Isaiah 53. Instead, Horner judges the long quotation of Isa. 52:10–54:6 in *Dial.* 13.2-9 to be *outside* the Trypho Text, even though he knows that knowledge of this passage is necessary to understand the material *inside* the Trypho Text. He excludes *Dial.* 13 from the Trypho Text on the grounds that it "would require special pleading" (p. 60) to include such a long citation of Scripture with no dialogue — his primary criterion for Trypho material — and no exegetically significant departures from the LXX (cf. pp. 40-41; *Dial.* 13 is already eliminated [40 n. 82]). (On the text of Isa. 52:10–54:6 in *Dial.* 13 see my note in C. Markschies's essay above, p. 256 n. 107.) Because Justin's allusions to Isaiah 53 in *Dial.* 14.8 (cf. Isa 53:2-3, 8) and 17.1 (cf. Isa 53:5) occur only within Justin's "monologue," not surrounded by "words or sayings attributed directly to Trypho" (p. 9), these, too, are deemed to have been absent from the exchange between Justin and Trypho, or at least from Justin's *record* of that exchange, the Trypho Text.

Horner reconstructs a hypothetical text whose discussion of Isaiah 53 begins only in the chapter now numbered *Dial.* 32 — the same place where Justin and Trypho's actual *interaction* on this passage begins in the final document. The problem is how to understand this abrupt beginning when all its antecedents have been removed. In *Dial.* 32 first Trypho (32.1) and then Justin (32.2) allude to Isaiah 53 without its having been previously quoted or alluded to in the Trypho Text. This Horner reconstructs as *Dial.* 1-10; 18.2b-19; 25-39 (80 following 36); 44-47; 79; 87-90; 118; 123; 142 (p. 39).

Precisely what Horner is claiming about the introduction of allusions to Isaiah 53 into the Trypho Text is complicated. His presentation of *Dial.* 32.1 is marred — as Dr. Horner himself admits (letter of May 10, 2004) — by a substantial yet virtually undetectable typographical error. The order of the names below (to which boldface has been added) should be first *Trypho* and then *Justin,* but these have been accidentally interchanged:

> Chapter 32.1) **Justin:** Gives **Trypho** a synopsis quote from Isaiah which describes the form of the messiah as inglorious (from *Dial.* 13 [Is. 52.10–54.6] non-Trypho material . . .). (Horner, 57)

This unintended reversal of the names is problematic precisely because it is so plausible. All the quotations of or allusions to Isaiah 53 in the final document to this point (*Dial.* 13.2-9; 14.8; 17.1) have indeed come from Justin. Therefore, it is easy to imagine that even in the preliminary document, it is *Justin* — not Trypho (to whom the statement is formally attributed) — who introduces Isaiah 53 in *Dial.* 32.1, as Horner's misprint suggests. In the final document, Isaiah 53 (= *Dial.* 13) has the same foundational relationship to the first elaboration of the two Parousias in *Dial.* 14.8 as Daniel 7 (= *Dial.* 31) has to its second elaboration in *Dial.* 32.2 (see above, §5.4). Readers of Horner may therefore understand him to be saying that

"Justin [the author] gives Trypho [his literary figure] a synopsis quote from Isaiah," in order to contrast Isaiah 53 and Daniel 7 in *Dial.* 32.1 and thus to lay the groundwork for the two Parousias theme in the Trypho Text (or to resume it in the full *Dialogue,* from *Dial.* 14.8). In the Trypho Text the two Parousias theme is found first in Justin's material in *Dial.* 32.2 — although Daniel 7 is not actually present here (see *Dial.* 32.3-4 and Horner, 59) — and again within the same Trypho Block in *Dial.* 34.2; 36.1; 39.7, where the Isaiah–Daniel contrast is fundamental. (The Parousias theme also occurs outside the Trypho Text, e.g., in *Dial.* 14.8; 49.2; 76.6; 110.2.) Unfortunately for Horner, this presentation is equivalent to saying that Justin puts the "synopsis quote" of Isaiah 53 into Trypho's mouth: "your so-called Christ was *without honor* (ἄτιμος) and *without glory* (ἄδοξος)" (cf. Isa. 53:2-3). If fabricated, this piece of "dialogue" undercuts (but does not necessarily destroy) Horner's larger thesis about Trypho's authenticity and gives him the old reputation as a "straw man" (p. 8) from which Horner is trying to rehabilitate him. Horner intended to say the reverse. The name preceding the colon above should be *Trypho,* the speaker in *Dial.* 32.1. Horner meant to say that *Trypho* gives *Justin* a synopsis quote from Isaiah 53.

In his analysis of *Dial.* 32 on pp. 60-61 (where he lists four possibilities), Horner explains the difference between the Trypho Text and the final *Dialogue* by referring to a later-added "reference" to Isaiah 53. By this he means a *cross-reference* (see below) and not an *allusion.* Horner does not mean to say that the *allusions* to Isaiah 53 currently found in *Dial.* 32.1 (Trypho) and 32.2 (Justin) were once absent from the Trypho Text. We have already clarified Horner's position that the authentic Trypho presents Justin with an *allusion* to Isaiah 53 — Horner's "synopsis quote" (p. 57) — in *Dial.* 32.1. Horner does mention the possibility that *Dial.* 32.1-2 could be a later (wholesale?) expansion within the Trypho Text, but he does "not believe there are sufficient grounds" for eliminating this exchange entirely from the original document (p. 61). Horner in fact treats 32.1 and 32.2 as authentic elsewhere (e.g., pp. 35, 42, 45, 57, 148, 150, 156, 200, 211). Moreover, Justin's chain-style allusion to Isa 53:2-3 + 8b + 9 + 7 in *Dial.* 32.2 is essential to the coherence of Horner's Trypho Text. In the absence of the anchoring quotation of Isa. 52:10–54:6 in *Dial.* 13, the Trypho Text depends for its discussions of Isaiah 53 either on an exhaustive knowledge of this text by both interlocutors (which is nowhere stated but could be historically accurate), or on the written foundation of a few allusions in *Dial.* 32.2. Horner tries to show that *Dial.* 32.2 is sufficient for the internal coherence of the Trypho Text. He therefore makes this passage rather than *Dial.* 13 the point of contact for Trypho's backward references in *Dial.* 39.7 and 90.1 to Justin's proofs of a suffering Messiah (pp. 58-59).

Horner's analysis of the Trypho Text's version of *Dial.* 32.1-2 suggests no great difference between the scriptural allusions in the original and final documents. Instead, he believes that Justin added only a scriptural *cross-reference* in *Dial.* 32.2 back to the current chapter 13 when he added that chapter. He believes "that there might have been some expansion within the Trypho Text and that the [cross-]reference

[in *Dial.* 32.2] back to Isaiah [52:10–54:6 in *Dial.* 13] might have been added later"
(p. 61). Or again: "Justin may have added to chapters 32 and 66 and included
[cross]-references to scriptural passages that were included [only] in the expanded
text," i.e., Isa 52:10–54:6 in *Dial.* 13.2-9 and Isa 7:10-17; 8:4 in *Dial.* 43.5-6 (p. 61).
(However, only *Dial.* 13 and 32 concern us here.) These would then be the only two
instances of "visible editing of the Trypho Text" (p. 61).

I assume that Horner's proposed addition to the Trypho Text's version of
Dial. 32.2 concerns mainly Justin's cross-referencing phrase "from the Scriptures
that I have previously cited" (ἀπὸ τῶν γραφῶν, ὧν προανιστόρησα). Although the
plural "Scriptures" is used, this could refer primarily to the current citation in *Dial.*
13 of the single Scripture passage Isa 52:10–54:6, since this is the source of Justin's
first string of allusions in *Dial.* 32.2, lines 8-10 (Marcovich). However, I believe that
the phrase could also have in view Justin's immediately following address to Trypho
and the Jewish people based on Zechariah 12 in *Dial.* 32.2, lines 12-14: "you shall recognize the one whom you pierced (Zech 12:10), and your tribes shall mourn tribe by
tribe, the women apart and the men apart (Zech. 12:12)." This quotation could have
been present in the original Trypho Text but included under Justin's cross-reference
to previous "Scriptures" only in the redaction. The only prior mention of this Zechariah text in *Dial.* 14.8 (where it is falsely attributed to Hosea) was likewise added in
the final redaction according to Horner, where it is continuous with the preceding
quotations of Isa 52:10–54:6 in *Dial.* 13.2-9 and of Isa 55:3-13 in *Dial.* 14.4-7. Although Horner focuses on the addition of Isaiah 53 in *Dial.* 13, it would be consistent with his method to assume that Justin was also using his new gloss about previous "Scriptures" to cover his new allusion to Zech. 12:10 in *Dial.* 14.8.

With this summary and explanation of Horner's thesis, it remains to offer a
critique and suggestions for further research. Horner has expressed what he thinks
about Justin's original and added material in *Dial.* 32.2, but the real question concerns Trypho and his involvement with Isaiah 53 in *Dial.* 32.1. It is particularly important to ask how Trypho got involved in the discussion of Isaiah 53, both in the
Trypho Text and in the historical exchange. While Horner does not always strictly
differentiate these, certainly there are places where he does address the historicity of
the exchange in the light of some of the potentially surprising features of Justin's
record of it. For example, Horner says (pp. 58-59) that after his initial statements in
chapters 8 and 10, Trypho introduces only one new topic into the Trypho Text, the
resurrection of Jesus (*Dial.* 63.1). But he believes that Trypho's prior knowledge of
the resurrection, independent of any statements by Justin in the Trypho Text, could
be historically authentic, since Trypho claims to have read the Gospels on his own
(cf. *Dial.* 10.2). The same reasoning could also be applied to Trypho's prior knowledge of the crucifixion, although I have not found this argument in Horner (he may
have assumed it when he treated Trypho's use of Deut 21:23 as authentic). Trypho
introduces the crucifixion in *Dial.* 10.3, just after his claim about reading the Gospels, and then resumes it, adding an allusion to the curse of Deut 21:23, precisely in
our problem passage, *Dial.* 32.1. If the exchange is in any way historical, then it is

reasonable to assume that Trypho introduced both the crucifixion in *Dial.* 10.3 and the curse on it in *Dial.* 32.1.

But was Trypho the one to introduce Isaiah 53? Dr. Horner has suggested in correspondence that Trypho might also have had independent knowledge of Isaiah 53 as a text "which was often used against Christians." But he did not use this argument in his book to soften the abruptness that results when Trypho, rather than Justin, is the first to allude to Isaiah 53 in the Trypho Text, in *Dial.* 32.1. Horner's misprint on p. 57 says that the allusion to Isa 53:2-3 in *Dial.* 32.1 about the Christian Messiah as "without honor or glory" is actually Justin's material, falsely attributed to Trypho, whereas Horner meant to say that it is authentic to Trypho. But there may be a cost to this authenticity that Horner has not taken into account.

When we arrive at *Dial.* 32.1, Justin has just finished quoting Dan 7:9-28 in *Dial.* 31.2-7 — completely in the *Dialogue*, or partly in the Trypho Text (p. 45). Yet the contrast of Isaiah 53 and Daniel 7 that first appears in *Dial.* 32.1 according to the Trypho Text, and the two Parousias scheme that follows from it, are known to be Justin's construction, which runs through the entire *Dialogue*, including the non-Trypho portions. Horner runs the risk of making Trypho in 32.1 the introducer of this central Justinian theme.

To set the stage, in *Dial.* 31.1 Justin, after noting that Jesus had power over the demons before his passion, reasons that he must be destined to have even greater power "at his *glorious* (ἐνδόξῳ) Parousia." Justin's reference here to Dan 7:13 here is certain even if the Trypho Text contained only *Dial.* 31.1. For Justin continues: "For *He shall come on the clouds as the Son of Man,* as Daniel foretold (7:13), *accompanied by his angels* (Matt. 16:27)." In response Trypho will pick up Justin's word ἔνδοξος (see below) and perhaps other content from Justin's quotation of Daniel 7, depending on whether it was fully quoted in the original exchange. To paraphrase Trypho's response in *Dial.* 32.1:

> Indeed, my dear Justin, the Scriptures (sc. including Daniel 7, to which you have just alluded) teach us Jews to await "a *glorious* (ἔνδοξον) and great [sc. Messiah] who as Son of Man receives the eternal kingdom from the Ancient of Days" (cf. Dan. 7:13-14, 27). But you Christians believe in a different "Messiah," improperly so called — one who is not only "without honor and glory" (ἄτιμος καὶ ἄδοξος) (sc. according to Isaiah 53), but who has also fallen under "the ultimate curse (κατάρα) of God's law" (sc. as in Deut. 21:23), for he was crucified (ἐσταυρώθη γάρ). (cf. *Dial.* 32.1)

Justin's readers must supply the explicit references for the Scripture allusions to Daniel 7, Isaiah 53, and Deut 21:23, but they are unambiguous. Trypho first picks up Justin's Danielic keyword ἔνδοξος, "glorious." Since Justin also used the expression "Son of Man" in 31.1, this too belongs to Trypho's response rather than his initiative. Horner believes that Trypho may furthermore have known Daniel well enough to have introduced the phrase "Ancient of Days" to fill out Justin's Danielic allusion on his own (p. 41), even if Justin never quoted all of Dan 7:9-28 in the exchange. This full quotation is therefore unnecessary to the Trypho Text's coherence, as long as Justin alluded to Daniel 7 in *Dial.* 31.1 (p. 45). Horner likewise regards Trypho's mention of Jesus' crucifixion in *Dial.* 32.1 as authentic, because Trypho simply resumes what he said earlier in the Trypho Text in *Dial.* 10.3, where he is the introducer of this theme (p. 57).

Unfortunately, outside his misprint on p. 57, Horner does not comment in detail about the authenticity of Trypho's allusion to Isa 53:2-3 in *Dial.* 32.1. Most of Horner's subsequent discussions of *Dial.* 32.1 concern Trypho's allusion to the curse of Deut 21:23 (e.g., pp. 150, 156), which first appears in *Dial.* 32.1, both in the Trypho Text and in the full *Dialogue*. But of all the features that first appear in the Trypho Text in *Dial.* 31-32, including allusions to Daniel 7, Isaiah 53, Deut 21:23, and Zech. 12:10, the allusion to Isaiah 53 in the mouth of Trypho is the hardest to reconcile historically. To make Trypho the first to contrast Isaiah 53 and Daniel 7, as in Horner's Trypho Text, is tantamount to making him the inventor of the two Parousias scheme — hardly something Horner would wish to claim. The Trypho of *Dial.* 32.1 either "walks into Justin's trap" (from which Horner wants to rescue him, p. 8) or is too prescient of Justin's argument in 32.2, which will be the first explicit mention of *two* Parousias in the Trypho Text: *Dial.* 31.1 mentions only the "glorious (i.e., second) coming," and *Dial.* 14.8 is outside the Trypho Text.

Is it historically probable that Trypho would have been the first to bring up Isaiah 53? This is hardly likely, given that Isaiah 53 already had a history of Christological application in the New Testament and beyond (esp. *1 Clement* 16) and that it could be used messianically — not negatively, as Trypho does in *Dial.* 32.1 — even in pre-Christian Jewish sources and in the *Targum of Isaiah* (cf. M. Hengel and J. Ådna above). Trypho initially understands Isaiah 53 as a proof *against* the messiahship of Jesus by linking it negatively with the curse on crucifixion in Deut 21:23 and by contrasting it with the more properly Jewish teaching about the Messiah's or the Son of Man's glory and everlasting kingdom according to Daniel 7 (cf. vv. 13-14, 27). Yet as Horner acknowledges, Trypho will soon come to agree that the future Messiah could be described as a "suffering" (παθητός) figure according to Isaiah 53 (cf. *Dial.* 36.1; 39.7; 89.2; critically 74.1; of these, Horner traces only 39.7 back to the use of Isaiah 53 in *Dial.* 32 [p. 58]). But Trypho will never cease doubting, until his voice temporarily disappears (after *Dial.* 90.1), that Jesus could be this Messiah, since he was crucified — and therefore cursed. *Dial.* 32.1 therefore represents the brief moment when Isaiah 53 and Deut 21:23 are still closely linked in Trypho's mind.

I believe that making Trypho the first to contrast Isaiah 53 and Daniel 7, as Horner's Trypho Text does, makes him too "Christian" and comes at too great a cost to Horner's otherwise attractive thesis about Trypho's historicity. Something has to give if Horner is to avoid making Trypho the inventor or anticipator of the Christian idea of the two Parousias. I would suggest that at least one of Horner's following three claims needs to be modified: (1) the Trypho Text is a free-standing, autonomous document; (2) this hypothetical document's discussion of a suffering and gloriously returning Messiah began only in *Dial.* 31.1 and 32.1-2; (3) the Trypho Text's version of *Dial.* 32.1 already included Trypho's "synopsis quote" of Isaiah 53, which has been taken over unmodified into the full *Dialogue.* Abandoning or modifying any one of these theses would be better than the current version of Horner's book — assuming that I have understood it correctly (despite its misprints, gaps, and ambiguities).

It should be clear that I have no desire to see Horner's thesis fail in its entirety, since I have already used Horner positively to balance out the discussion with Judith Lieu about the authenticity or otherwise of Jewish uses of Deut 21:23 in the second century (above, §7.2). However, as Horner's theory of composition continues to be discussed, perhaps one or more of the following three modifications to his three claims may point a way forward:

(1) *Autonomy of the Trypho Text?* Horner understands his reconstructed Trypho Text to be "an autonomous document with its own internal logic, balance, and flow," to the extent that it is virtually "free-standing" (p. 33). But this begs the question: *free-standing for whom?* Horner has understandably been so busy "Listening to Trypho" that he has not (yet) clarified what role the hypothetical Trypho Text will have played in Justin's own life around 135 C.E. If the Trypho Text was merely a set of (private?) notes for Justin's memory with a view to a future work, as Horner implies but never develops (pp. 62, 195; cf. 19, with reference to Williams), then Justin could have begun his write-up at any point in the exchange without adding historical details that he knew he would never forget.

For example, let us assume that in Justin's notes, Trypho is indeed the first to mention Isaiah 53 and the Isaiah–Daniel contrast which grounds the two Parousias, as currently in Horner's Trypho Text (*Dial.* 32.1). Certainly Justin will remember that this was not actually so, regardless of when he rereads his notes. If in the final redaction he adds a long quotation of Isa. 52:10–54:6 in *Dial.* 13 and an Isaiah–Daniel contrast along with the two Parousias in *Dial.* 14.8, then, while not in the original notes and not in the exchange — not at least in the detail in which it now appears — this final presentation will be closer to the facts than the supposedly more pristine Trypho Text, which makes Trypho the initiator of these ideas.

The price of this modification is that the Trypho Text becomes something less than the "free-standing and autonomous" document that Horner understands it to be (p. 33). It is still dependent on its author and the unwritten information that he alone brings to it. But since the author was presumably the only reader of his own notes — and barring striking new discoveries it is doubtful whether we will ever be able to say more than this about the Trypho Text — this lack of autonomy seems no great defect.

(2) *An absence of allusions to Isaiah 53 prior to Dial. 32.1?* In Horner's theoretical reconstruction, *Dial.* 13 and other allusions to Isaiah 53 (cf. *Dial.* 14.8; 17.1) are formally and materially absent from the Trypho Text until *Dial.* 32.1-2, and Isaiah 53 is present

(together with Daniel 7) in *Dial.* 32.1. Making both these claims at once would seem to commit Horner to a Trypho Text that presents Trypho as the first of the two interlocutors to make the Isaiah–Daniel contrast literarily, even if he was not the first historically. This is an important consideration in the light of Horner's aim of learning something about the history from the literature. However, since abandoning either of these claims greatly eases the tensions, we should explore both options, which leads to solutions respectively inside and outside Horner's method.

In keeping with Horner's method, we could treat Isaiah 53 much as he has treated Daniel 7. The final version of *Dial.* 32.1 becomes asymmetrical when placed into Horner's limited Trypho Text. Trypho's allusions to the glorious Son of Man of Daniel 7 and to Deut 21:23 with reference to crucifixion are supported by prior material in the Trypho Text, but his allusion to Isaiah 53 is not. The simplest solution, assuming (with Horner) that the Trypho Text is both internally consistent and *complete* — i.e., "free-standing" and "autonomous" — is to hypothesize that there was once a prior allusion to Isaiah 53 in the mouth of Justin in the preliminary Trypho Text, but that this has fallen out or been consciously edited out (by Justin) in the final redaction. It was not needed in the light of *Dial.* 13 and 14.8.

Horner himself seems to say something like this in the second of his four options on p. 60, except that he appears to attribute the "editing" of the Trypho Text not to Justin but to later copyists of the full *Dialogue*. Although it is not his preferred solution, Horner suggests that the backward cross-reference in *Dial.* 32.2 that now refers *only* to the long quotation in *Dial.* 13, outside the Trypho Text, might have referred *additionally* to a similar — and therefore in the context of the final *Dialogue*, superfluous — quotation inside the Trypho Text that has since been "lost in transmission" by "later copyists." This would have the advantage of preserving *Dial.* 32.2 as unedited material from the Trypho document, including its now-suspicious cross-reference, which goes nowhere in the Trypho Text as it can currently be reconstructed from our manuscripts.

Yet this is a very odd solution. It appears to imply — although here, as elsewhere, Horner is frustratingly vague — that the full *Dialogue* once contained both *Dial.* 13 and a similar long quotation of Isaiah 53 located closer to the dialogue material and therefore within the free-standing Trypho Text. Although Justin ultimately cut this up and inserted it — clumsily (p. 96) — at various places in the Dialogue, he did not fail to reproduce its original quotation of Isaiah 53. The "later copyists" will then have been responsible for transmitting two potentially longer quotations of Isaiah 53, one in *Dial.* 13 and the other at an unknown location within the Trypho Text. Conveniently, they edited out only the latter. I find this unbelievable, and Horner can probably do better. He has already convincingly argued that the Trypho Text could get by on the issue of consistency merely with the brief allusion to Daniel 7 in *Dial.* 31.1, without the full quotation now in *Dial.* 31.2-7, which he attributes to the final redaction (p. 45; cf. 41). Why not argue something similar for Isaiah 53? Although I cannot propose a precise location within Horner's Trypho Text, an original allusion or summary quotation of Isaiah 53, similar to that for

Daniel 7 in *Dial.* 31.1, could very well have been present in this preliminary text, providing the same kind (if not necessarily the same extent) of support for *Dial.* 32.1-2 as the final *Dialogue* does. The summary quotation might have been located relatively early in the document, like the current *Dial.* 13. In fact, in the long quotation there could even be something that Justin "laid over" (cf. p. 41) an earlier summary that was part of his Trypho Text. (See also Horner's first option on p. 60: chapter 13 could be a "Trypho chapter"; Horner might find this easier to accept if it was originally shorter than the current chapter 13.)

(3) *A lack of editing of Dial. 32.1 between the Trypho Text and the full Dialogue?* Although it is not in keeping with Horner's method, we could also reconstruct a historically plausible statement by Trypho simply by removing the brief phrase ἄτιμος καὶ ἄδοξος from the Trypho Text's version of *Dial.* 32.1. This would remove the allusion to Isa 53:2-3 as well as the implausible invention of the contrast of Isaiah 53 and Daniel 7 by a Jewish interlocutor. The cost of this modification is that Justin as author or editor becomes the one to put the "Isaianic" words into Trypho's mouth in the redaction, thus setting him up for Justin's answer in *Dial.* 32.2. (This is essentially what is claimed by Horner's misprint about *Dial.* 32.1 on p. 57, which may make more sense than he realizes.) In the redaction, Trypho is no longer the first to quote Isaiah 53 or to contrast Isaiah 53 and Daniel 7 as he is in Horner's Trypho Text, because of the addition of Justin's statements in *Dial.* 13 and 14.8. A modified Trypho Text, lacking Isaiah 53 in *Dial.* 32.1, would read more like the final document and — although not necessarily for that reason — would have a greater chance of being historically authentic.

Evaluation. Horner may regard the cost of my third option above as too high for his theory of Trypho's authenticity, because he has been meticulous in marshalling evidence for his claim that there are only two instances of "visible editing of the Trypho Text" (p. 61). These merely involve Justin's added cross-references back to the extra Scripture quotations in the final redaction, including the cross-reference to *Dial.* 13 in Justin's own material in *Dial.* 32.2, which does not affect Trypho's material in 32.1. Yet in evaluating Horner's picture of Trypho we must really evaluate his picture of Justin. Essential to Horner's project is a Justin who borders on the schizophrenic. Justin the interlocutor, Justin the recorder of the original exchange, and Justin the author of the full *Dialogue* are potentially three — but more probably two — "people," metaphorically speaking, since the interlocutor and the recorder are virtually identical.

Justin the recorder is very conscientious in Horner's view. He rarely if ever puts words into Trypho's mouth. He also has some aesthetic sense, since his record hangs together and flows well (though he apparently loses this sense when he later destroys the coherence of the Trypho Text in the final document). Yet Justin cannot take the full credit, because it is really the historical Trypho who has enabled him to transcend himself and write this way. Axiomatic to Horner's theory of Trypho's authenticity is that Justin — speaking now of the other Justin, the author of the full *Dialogue* — could not have made him up. The Trypho of the original Trypho Text is less fabricated and contrived than Justin was literarily capable of. In fact Justin never realized the ways in which Trypho had outsmarted him; it is rather Horner (and other critics) who must do this after the fact. Horner can do so, he says, because Justin himself is (or became) a bad writer — digressive, repetitive, monotonous, verbose, harshly polemical, and so on according to a long-recognized (and probably fair) characterization. We can therefore see the seams between the original and the later material. Fortunately for Horner's historical investigation, the final *Dialogue* is a clumsy cut-and-paste job into which some original pieces were pasted intact with almost no editing; it is not a skillful piece of "weaving":

> It is not the non-Trypho material which has any kind of interconnectedness. The *Dialogue* appears to have been inflated by repeated arguments, exegetical forays, polemical tracts, typological expositions, and unnecessary passages of LXX. . . . This non-Trypho material does not exhibit any strong connections either to the Trypho blocks or within itself. In fact, the absence of any linking statements between this material and the Trypho material is part of the reason why the Trypho blocks could be detected at all. In contrast, the material in the Trypho blocks is internally coherent and does not need the non-Trypho material to make sense. Had Justin been more careful in weaving his own material into the Trypho blocks, the shifts would not have been so clear and the Trypho Text would not have been discernible. This kind of careless assemblage compromises the literary quality of the full *Dialogue,* but it greatly increases its transparency, reliability, and its value as a window into Jewish/Christian relations during the second century. (p. 196)

Perhaps, then, we should see Justin as a bad writer but a good character, because he has preserved for us a "valuable window." On the other hand, maybe he is not such a good character, because of the ways in which he can be overly polemical, at least by today's standards. My question is whether these two "characters" might ever come together in our analysis of Justin's final product. I have proposed in my third option above one way in which this could happen: Justin could have added the three brief words ἄτιμος καὶ ἄδοξος ("without honor and glory") to Trypho's voice in *Dial.* 32.1 at the same time as he added ἀπὸ τῶν γραφῶν, ὧν προανιστόρησα ("from the Scriptures that I have previously cited") to his own voice in *Dial.* 32.2. There is no doubt that this benefits Justin and sets up Trypho to play right into his hand. To that extent the additions could be called "polemical," though not as polemical as some other sections. But this is consistent with what we know about Justin as the writer of the full *Dialogue.* Perhaps a little less separation between Justin the faithful recorder and Justin the goal-oriented author might benefit future discussions of the possible shape of an original Trypho Text.

I do not believe that a Justin who inserts material into certain locations within the stream of Trypho's authentic words would necessarily be a bad character, nor would I wish to attribute such a value judgment to Horner. Certainly we ought not assume too much about the proper sequencing of the exchanges in Justin's *Dialogue* if we cannot safely assume the same for the Gospels or Acts. I have focused on *Dial.* 13-14 and 31-32 because these are important for Horner's theory of composition and for our own appreciation of Isaiah 53 in the *Dialogue*. But we must not lose sight of the big picture. It is not inauthentic for Trypho to be involved in the language of Isaiah 53. His involvement is rather required as early as his uses of παθητός in *Dial.* 36.1 and 39.7. These appear in response to Justin's (and the *Dialogue*'s) first use of παθητός in 34.2, which is also the first passage in the Trypho Text to contrast Isaiah 53 and Daniel 7, if this contrast was not introduced by Trypho in *Dial.* 32.1. Horner's Trypho Text is problematic only if Trypho is understood to introduce the Isaiah–Daniel contrast both in the text *and* in the historical exchange. The assumptions about history are therefore more important than those about the preliminary text. I have already reasoned in my first option above that if a Trypho Text existed at all, Justin himself will have been able to recognize any differences between the text and the history on this point, regardless of the shape of his preliminary notes.

Horner's most valuable contribution for our purposes has been to show that Justin and Trypho are talking past each other in their uses of Isaiah 53 and Deut 21:23 (see above, pp. 392-95). This strengthens the case for the substantial authenticity or historicity of both uses by both interlocutors, with Isaiah 53 introduced by Justin and Deut 21:23 by Trypho. This is certainly the most logical order of introduction and the one suggested by the final *Dialogue*, whatever the subsequent discussion may determine about possible earlier forms of the text.

7.4 Anti-Docetic Setting: The παθητὸς ἄνθρωπος and Real Suffering

Issues of composition arise in a different way in the material we are about to consider. In this section we will encounter traces of arguments that Justin appears to have had not with Trypho or other Jews, but with Gnostic-leaning Christians with a docetic Christology.[98] Much of this material falls within Justin's excursus on Psalm 22 (LXX 21), bounded approximately by *Dial.* 97.3-106.4 (or 107 or 108). According to Marcovich's index, quotations of Psalm 22

---

98. So also P. Haeuser, *Des heiligen Philosophen und Märtyrers Justinus Dialog mit dem Juden Tryphon,* Bibliothek der Kirchenväter 33 (1917) 170 n. 3; Rudoph, *"Denn wir sind jenes Volk"* (see n. 3), 183 with n. 357, and especially L. Abramowski, "Die 'Erinnerungen der Apostel' bei Justin," in P. Stuhlmacher, ed., *Das Evangelium und die Evangelien,* WUNT 28 (1983) 341-354, esp. 343-44, 348-49 = ET, "The 'Memoirs of the Apostles' in Justin," in *The Gospel and the Gospels* (1991) 323-335, esp. 325-26, 329-30. Abramowski points out that Justin's emphasis in his Psalm 22 excursus on the *written* Gospels or ἀπομνημονεύματα was especially appropriate to combating the Gnostics, who favored the *"viva vox"* (349 = ET 330).

are confined to this section, though prior to this in *Dial.* 85.1, Justin is probably alluding secondarily to Psalm 22 (primarily to Isaiah 53) when he claims that both Isaiah and David said that the Messiah would appear without form or honor. Marcovich also sees an allusion to Ps 22:7 ἐξουθένημα (cf. *Dial.* 98.3) in *Dial.* 121.3, ἐξουθενημένη.[99]

Experts on the composition of the *Dialogue* generally regard Justin's treatment of Psalm 22 as having once been an independent unit which Justin may have used on other occasions.[100] O. Skarsaune regards Justin's exposition of Psalm 22 to be his most "ambitious," "original," and "independent" work,[101] while N. Koltun-Fromm evaluates Justin's significance as the first known writer to produce a christological interpretation of the whole of Psalm 22.[102]

A significant marker of the Psalm 22 excursus as a once separate document may lie in the fact that references to the ἀπομνημονεύματα or *Memoirs* of the Apostles, namely the Gospels (probably in their canonical form), occur 13 times in this section but nowhere else in the *Dialogue*.[103] It is therefore intrigu-

---

99. Once again, it is important for readers of an edition of the *Dialogue* to know that there are allusions to Psalm 22 outside the excursus in *Dial.* 97-106. But unfortunately, while the allusion to Ps 22:7 in *Dial.* 121.3 is recorded in Marcovich's apparatus (p. 279, line 18), it is not indexed.

100. See Skarsaune, *The Proof of Prophecy* (see n. 4), 216, 220-227, including his summary and modification of Bousset in 221 nn. 81-82 (cf. W. Bousset, *Jüdisch-christlicher Schulbetrieb in Alexandria und Rom. Literarische Untersuchungen zu Philo und Clemens von Alexandria, Justin und Irenäus*, FRLANT 23 [1915]); Horner, *Listening to Trypho*, 38, 151; Rudolph, "Denn wir sind jenes Volk," 55-57, 79 with n. 447, 183; Abramowski, "'Erinnerungen,'" 342 = ET 324.

101. Skarsaune, *Proof*, 220, 227, cf. 470: "Justin seems most independent in his work with Ps 22," though technically Skarsaune is comparing here only Justin's treatment of other psalms. Cf. approvingly Rudolph, 79 n. 447.

102. N. Koltun-Fromm, "Psalm 22's Christological Interpretive Tradition in Light of Christian Anti-Jewish Polemic," *Journal of Early Christian Studies* 6 (1998) 37-57, esp. 46-48, 51-53, 57. Justin is also the first known writer to clearly interpret Ps 22 (LXX 21):17 in terms of the "piercing" of the nails of crucifixion. The earlier parallel in *Barn.* 5.13, καθήλωσόν μου τὰς σάρκας, "nail my flesh," is inexact and refers most nearly to Ps 119 (LXX 118):120, καθήλωσόν ἐκ τοῦ φόβου σου τὰς σάρκας μου, "penetrate/nail through my flesh by the fear of you." For the LXX translator's confusion about the original Hebrew of Ps 119, cf. LSJ 853, s.v. καθηλόω II, or J. Lust, E. Eynikel, and K. Hauspie, *A Greek-English Lexicon of the Septuagint* (1992-1996), s.v.

103. As argued by Bousset, *Jüdisch-christlicher Schulbetrieb*, 292-93, followed by Abramowski, "'Erinnerungen,'" 342 = ET 324. For the ἀπομνημονεύματα see *Dial.* 100.4; 101.3; 102.5; 103.6; 103.8; 104.1; 105.1; 105.5; 105.6; 106.1; 106.3; 106.4; 107.1. The last occurrence of ἀπομνημονεύματα in *Dial.* 107.1 offers reason for extending the section past the last reference to Psalm 22 in *Dial.* 106.2 into Justin's treatment of the resurrection or "The Sign of Jonah," which is made a separate chapter in Falls and Halton, *Dial.* 107-109. See Abramowski, "'Erinnerungen,'" 342 = ET 324.

ing to note that vocabulary alluding to Isaiah 53, including ἀειδής and ἄτιμος, also intersects with this section, thus tying it in with the rest of the *Dialogue* and increasing the strength of Isaiah 53 as a scarlet thread. Skarsaune believes that these ties were created after Justin's composition of the Psalm 22 excursus; the added materials, including *Dial.* 100.1-6 with its allusions to Isa 53:2-3, 8 in *Dial.* 100.3, "show clear inter-relations to each other and to other passages in the *Dialogue*."[104] Nevertheless, Justin's allusions to Isaiah 53 and his term παθητός also take on a new function within the Psalm 22 excursus, combining with concerns about the reality of Christ's sufferings. This shows the flexibility of the allusive language. It is not by accident that the only occurrence of παθητός that Marcovich does not italicize, in *Dial.* 99.2, falls in this section.

We may begin with one of the clear allusions to Isaiah 53 within Justin's exposition of Psalm 22. According to *Dial.* 100.2, Christ "condescended (ὑπέμεινε) to become a man *without form* and *without honor* and *subject to suffering*," ἄνθρωπος *ἀειδής* καὶ *ἄτιμος* καὶ *παθητός*. Parallel to the παθητὸς Χριστός or "suffering *Messiah*" discussed above in §7.1, here we have a παθητὸς ἄνθρωπος, a "suffering *man*." The issues are different, as we shall see. The language of the suffering man in *Dial.* 100.2 combined with language alluding to Isaiah 53 might recall for English speakers the famous "man of sorrows and acquainted with grief" of the King James Version and Handel's *Messiah* — accurately but less poetically rendered in a translation of the Greek as "being a man in a plague, and knowing (how) to bear sickness" (Isa 53:3; Ekblad [n. 1], 205). Since Marcovich italicizes *ἀειδής*, *ἄτιμος*, and *παθητός* in *Dial.* 100.2 as alluding to Isaiah 53 (vv. 2-3, 8), we might wonder why ἄνθρωπος was not also included as an allusion to Isa 53:3, especially since ἀειδής and ἄτιμος allude to an earlier phrase in the same verse: ἀλλὰ τὸ εἶδος αὐτοῦ ἄτιμον . . . ἄνθρωπος ἐν πληγῇ ὢν καὶ εἰδὼς φέρειν μαλακίαν.

There is no reason why the *Dialogue*'s ἄνθρωπος in 100.2 cannot be connected to Isaiah's ἄνθρωπος of Isa 53:3. Nevertheless, the reason why Justin uses ἄνθρωπος here is not primarily because it is in the text of Isa 53:3. Rather, it is needed to stress his idea of *incarnation*, which is also attested by Isa 53:8b, "Who shall declare his generation?," although Justin does not quote this in his Psalm 22 excursus. The full context of *Dial.* 100.2-3 illustrates the connection of the term ἄνθρωπος with the incarnation:

[Christ] revealed to us (cf. Matt 11:27 = *Dial.* 100.1) by his grace all that we know from the Scriptures, so that we know him as the *first-begotten* of God *before all creatures* (Col. 1:15, 17), and as Son of the patriarchs, since he be-

---

104. Skarsaune, *Proof,* 221 with n. 82.

came incarnate by a virgin (cf. Isa 7:14) of their race, and condescended to become a man *without comeliness* or *honor* and *subject to suffering*. [100.3] Hence, he alluded to his imminent passion in this way: *The Son of Man must suffer many things and be rejected by the Pharisees and Scribes, and be crucified and rise again on the third day* (Mark 8:31 par.). He called himself *Son of Man* either because of his birth by the Virgin who was, as I said, of the family of David and Jacob and Isaac and Abraham, or because Adam himself was the father of those above-named patriarchs, from whom Mary traces her descent. (*Dial.* 100.2-3, trans. Falls and Halton, italics modified)

As in *Dial.* 76.6, Justin here has Jesus defining his mission in terms of Isaiah 53. The phrase "became incarnate" is literally "having been made flesh," σαρκοποιηθείς.[105] The coordination of this by "and" with the idea of becoming passible is not given in the Greek, if we accept Marcovich's transposition of the καί from the beginning of the chain <u>καὶ</u> ἄνθρωπος ἀειδής, ἄτιμος καὶ παθητός in ms A to the position here occupied by the comma between ἀειδής and ἄτιμος (as first proposed by Thirlby in 1722). If we then read σαρκοποιηθείς as grammatically subordinate to the following main clause ὑπέμεινε, a stronger connection results between incarnation and passibility:

ἐπειδή, διὰ τῆς ἀπὸ γένους αὐτῶν παρθένου σαρκοποιηθείς, ἄνθρωπος ἀειδής καὶ ἄτιμος καὶ παθητὸς ὑπέμεινε γενέσθαι.

. . . since by being made flesh by a virgin of their race, he condescended to become a man *without form* and *without honor* and *passible*. (*Dial.* 100.2)

This does not deny the importance of Jesus' Jewish origin, which together with Mary's is followed up in *Dial.* 100.3, as indicated, but it puts it in perspective by showing its significance for the whole human race. Shortly after this in *Dial.* 100.4, Justin says: "he has become human through the Virgin (διὰ τῆς παρθένου ἄνθρωπος γεγονέναι), in order that the disobedience caused by the serpent might be destroyed in the same manner in which it had originated." Justin understands becoming human as the antidote to sin originating with humans.[106]

---

105. See the similarly anti-docetic use of σάρξ in 1 John 4:2; the true Christian spirit must confess "that Jesus Christ has come in the flesh."

106. Skarsaune, *Proof,* 223, refers to this sort of material as expressing a "recapitulation" theme and even talks of a "recapitulation" *source,* which he elsewhere calls the "anti-Hezekiah" source (cf. 220, 221 n. 82, 225, 226-27, 234-42 and Skarsaune's chapter on the recapitulation idea, 380-400, esp. 393-99 on types of the passion). Early Christian exegesis of the gospel "interpreted the Son of God concept in 'recapitulation' terms: Christ proves himself to be the Son of God by conquering where Adam was conquered" (223; cf. 220). Skarsaune adds: "The Eve/Mary typology in *Dial.* 100:5f is an additional motif in accord with the basic idea" (223).

The terms ἄνθρωπος and παθητός come together (without ἀειδής and ἄτιμος) earlier in *Dial*. 99.2. Here, however, the emphasis is not on Christ's becoming a man in the incarnation, as in *Dial*. 100.2, but on his confirming through his prayer "Thy will be done" in the Garden that he had indeed become a παθητὸς ἄνθρωπος, "a man capable of suffering."

Dial. 103.8 is similar. Christ's perspiring drops of blood during his Garden prayer was mentioned in the *Memoirs* of the apostles, the Gospels,

> so that we may understand that the Father wished his Son to endure *in reality* these severe sufferings for us (ἐν τοιούτοις πάθεσιν ἀληθῶς γεγονέναι δι' ἡμᾶς), and may not declare that, since he was the Son of God, he did not *feel* (οὐκ ἀντελαμβάνετο) what was done and inflicted upon him. (*Dial*. 103.8, trans. Falls and Halton, italics added)

Here we have a new theme: Who was it who suggested that because he was the Son of God, Jesus did not *feel* what was done to him, or more literally "did not *take part* in the things that were taking place or happening to him" (οὐκ ἀντελαμβάνετο τῶν γινομένων καὶ συμβαινόντων αὐτῷ)? Certainly neither of our discussion partners, for this concern is foreign to the *Dialogue* to this point, and the voice of Trypho is in any case absent from this excursus on Psalm 22. The language of *Dial*. 103.8 has an obvious "anti-docetic" ring to it. Justin has admitted that Christ might at first glance "seem" to be cursed according to the law, until the pictures of the cross in the Old Testament are properly understood (cf. *Dial*. 90.1, ταύτην τὴν δοκοῦσαν κατάραν), but here he denies that Jesus only "seemingly" suffered: his sufferings were real.

All three of the passages just mentioned share a common anti-docetic emphasis on the truth and bodily reality of Christ's sufferings. See ἀληθῶς παθητὸς ἄνθρωπος γεγένηται in *Dial*. 99.2, σαρκοποιηθείς in *Dial*. 100.2, and ἐν τοιούτοις πάθεσιν ἀληθῶς γεγονέναι in *Dial*. 103.8. (We may also compare Ignatius, *Trall*. 9.1, ἀληθῶς ἐσταυρώθη.) Shortly before all this in *Dial*. 98.1, when introducing his quotation of Psalm 22 (LXX 21):2-24, Justin gives his only concise definition of what it means to be a παθητὸς ἄνθρωπος: it means to be ἄνθρωπος ἀντιληπτικὸς παθῶν. This may be translated not simply as "a man who was capable of suffering" (Falls and Halton) but as "a man who had a share in sufferings," with Williams (205 n. 1), who considers this "stronger than the common 'liable to suffering,'" referring to the παθητὸς ἄνθρωπος of *Dial*. 99.2.

This language has a different flavor and concern from the earlier discussion, when Justin and Trypho were agreeing that the predicted Messiah would *suffer* according to Isaiah 53, but disagreeing over whether he could be *crucified* in the light of Deut 21:23. At the same time, since the final edition of the *Dia-*

logue shows signs that Justin attempted to unify his language, it is worth noting a few other places where incarnation and atonement seem to be related, some of them involving Isaiah 53.

In *Dial.* 63.1 Trypho asks for scriptural proof of the Christian idea that Christ "condescended to become man by a virgin (ἄνθρωπος γεννηθῆναι . . . ὑπέμεινεν, cf. *Dial.* 100.2), and to be crucified, and to die." Justin answers with a mixed direct and indirect quotation of Isa 53:8 that emphasizes that this divine origin (cf. "Who shall declare his generation?," v. 8b)[107] is predicated precisely of the one who was said to have been handed over by God because of the sins of the people (v. 8d). Similarly after the direct quotation of Isa 53:8b-d in *Dial.* 43.3, Justin's comments include an allusion to the "stripes" of Isa 53:5: "The prophetic Spirit thus declared that the birth of him who was to die in order to *heal us* sinners *by his stripes* was inexpressible." Both passages show Isaiah 53 to be a comprehensive proof for both incarnation and atonement. Although *Dial.* 67.6 lacks an allusion to Isaiah 53, it attests the same connection between becoming human and suffering found in *Dial.* 63.1 and 100.2. Here Justin says, "I confess that he condescended (ὑπομεῖναι αὐτόν) to *dying by crucifixion,* and becoming human, and suffering whatever those of your race inflicted on him" (67.6). By placing first what happened last, namely *death by crucifixion* (the order is rationalized in Falls and Halton: incarnation followed by crucifixion), Justin stresses that this was the real purpose of Christ's becoming human. Referring to Zech 12:10, Justin similarly shows that at Christ's second coming, people will naturally connect the incarnation and the atonement when they look upon the one "who became a man in the midst of men" as the "pierced one" (*Dial.* 64.7).

In *Dial.* 72.2 Justin complains that Trypho's Jewish teachers have removed certain passages from the Septuagint "by which this very One who was crucified is proclaimed to have been proved as God, and man, and crucified, and dying" (trans. Williams). Apparently the effect of the crucifixion is called into question if Jesus was not both "God and man." Finally, in the creedal-type sequence in *Dial.* 85.2 (see §6.2, item 11), incarnation and atonement are linked by the parallelism: "who was born of a virgin and [so] became a passible man" (καὶ διὰ παρθένου γεννηθέντος καὶ παθητοῦ γενομένου ἀνθρώπου). See also *Dial.* 126.1: γεννηθέντα καὶ παθόντα.

It is interesting to note that in combating docetism, Justin does not risk even mentioning Christ's divine impassibility, as Ignatius of Antioch does in similar contexts: "first passible and then impassible" (πρῶτον παθητὸς καὶ τότε

---

107. See my Translator's expansion of the excursus on Isa 53:8b, "Who shall declare his generation?," in the preceding essay by C. Markschies, above, pp. 262-64.

ἀπαθής, *Eph.* 7:2); "impassible, for our sakes passible" (τὸν ἀπαθῆ, τὸν δι' ὑμᾶς παθητόν, *Pol.* 3:2). W. R. Schoedel's comment that Ignatius's use of the concept of Christ's impassibility is "uncomplicated by later debates"[108] is therefore all the more true of Justin, who does not use the term. This highlights once again the great distance between a second-century apologist like Justin and the virtually docetic "high" Christology of a figure like Hilary of Poitiers, as pointed out at the end of C. Markschies's essay.

8. Conclusion

In this essay I have provided a comprehensive survey and categorization of the allusive language for Isaiah 53 in Justin's *Dialogue with Trypho* and have evaluated M. Marcovich's treatment of this language, supplementing his index to reflect more fully the rich information in his apparatus. After correcting the apparatus at *Dial.* 39.7 to include the reference to Isa 53:8 that Marcovich supplies in similar contexts, I have determined that there is an identifiable allusion to Isaiah 53 in 11 of the 17 paragraphs containing the term παθητός, "passible" or "susceptible to suffering." I have shown that Justin has various means of anchoring this term to Isaiah 53 (summarized in §6.3). These include a named reference to Isaiah (*Dial.* 126.1), an exchange between Trypho and Justin in which παθητός and Isa 53:8d are clearly linked (*Dial.* 89.2-3), passages where παθητός occurs with the other allusive terms ἄτιμος, ἀειδής, or ἄδοξος (*Dial.* 49.2; 100.2; 110.2) or where the allusion to Isaiah 53 by παθητός is complemented by one to Daniel 7 within the two Parousias scheme (*Dial.* 34.2; 36.1; 39.7; 76.6), and a couple other techniques (cf. *Dial.* 68.9; 111.2). The fact that Marcovich declines to italicize the one occurrence of παθητός where it makes sense not to do so — where it relates in the immediate context to Jesus' prayer in the Garden of Gethsemane as evidence of his becoming a παθητὸς ἄνθρωπος (*Dial.* 99.2), though this is not far removed from a clear allusion to Isaiah 53, also involving the παθητὸς ἄνθρωπος (cf. *Dial.* 100.2) — proves that his procedure is not arbitrary.

Justin's allusive language for Isaiah 53 must claim the attention of interpreters of the final form of the *Dialogue* because it ties together separate units that may have had independent composition histories. Prior to Justin's excursus on Psalm 22 in *Dial.* 97-106, the great majority of the quotations and allusions to Isaiah 53 occur within T. J. Horner's hypothetical "Trypho Text" in

---

108. W. R. Schoedel. *Ignatius of Antioch: A Commentary on the Letters of Ignatius of Antioch*, Hermeneia (1985) 61; cf. 59, 267 for the anti-docetic context.

which Justin presumably records his original exchange with Trypho.[109] Whether or not Justin actually wrote out the whole text of Isa 52:10–54:6 in his first draft of the Trypho document is an unprovable and relatively inconsequential point, but Horner's thesis about the authenticity of Trypho's voice does well to have Isaiah 53 fully part of the discussion between the two interlocutors. Allusions to Isaiah 53, while less frequent in the *Dialogue's* exegetical section on Psalm 22 (*Dial.* 97-106), are no less important. This illustrates the flexibility and unifying force of this language.

Justin's allusions to Isaiah 53 may also be a source of historical information. This language was probably important to Justin's largely Gentile Christian community (so already in 1 *Clem.* 16:1-14, though as a case-study in servant-like humility rather than Christology and atonement),[110] as D. J. Bingham has argued; Bingham based his case largely on the direct quotations, and I have simply sought to supplement it from the allusions. Gentiles as well as Jews have the right to be "astonished" (θαυμάζειν) at the message of a suffering savior (*Dial.* 89.3; cf. Isa 52:15; *Dial.* 118.4), but Justin thinks that all who accept the message of Isaiah 53 should be able to overcome this astonishment, even though he knows that at the moment, it is largely "Gentiles who believe in the suffering Messiah" (*Dial.* 52.1) and who find no scriptural contradiction in a "suffering and crucified Messiah" (*Dial.* 111.2). Yet genuine Jewish concerns also seem to be reflected. The different ways in which Justin and Trypho discuss Isaiah 53 and Deut 21:23 indicate either skillful fiction writing or (following Horner) an authentic dialogue in which two interlocutors very humanly combine disagreement with misunderstanding. Finally, Justin's desire to combat the docetic Christology that he appears to have encountered is seen when he stresses the incarnation as the prerequisite to the passion, and specifically spells out the meaning of his otherwise "Isaianic" term παθητός as ἄνθρωπος ἀντιληπτικὸς παθῶν (*Dial.* 98.1).

---

109. In the Trypho block *Dial.* 25-39, compare the uses of Isaiah 53 in *Dial.* 32.1; 32.2; 34.2; 36.1; 36.6; 39.7; in the next block in *Dial.* 44-77, see *Dial.* 49.2; 49.7; 52.1; 63.2; 68.4; 68.9; 70.4; 72.3; 74.1; 76.2; 76.6; and in the climactic *Dial.* 87-90, see *Dial.* 88.8; 89.2; 89.3; 90.1.

110. Because I have focused on the language of a "suffering" Messiah I have been unable to deal with other ways in which Isaiah 53 may have been formative for Justin's community. These include the community's ecclesiology. In *Dial.* 42.3 Justin uses the language from 1 Cor 12:12 about the many members but the one body: many people form one church. But he finds an Old Testament proof of the point in Isa 53:2. In a surprising interpretation of the phrase "We preached before him as a little child (παιδίον)," the singular "child" interprets not primarily Jesus as the Servant but the many "we" who become as one "child," that is, one church: the passage "proves that sinners shall obey him as servants (ὑπηρετῆσαι), and shall also become as one child in his sight" (Falls and Halton). Cf. Bingham, "Justin and Isaiah 53," *VC* 54 (2000) 252, and Skarsaune, *Proof,* 116.

The present study has added linguistic precision to some findings that are already well known in the study of Justin's *Dialogue* (e.g. the importance of both Isaiah 53 and Daniel 7 in the two Parousias), and has probed other areas of more recent interest. It is to be hoped that such groundwork will smooth the way for those seeking to comment more comprehensively on the literary and historical issues. It is hard to over-estimate the role of Isaiah 53 in this fascinating but difficult document.

Isaiah 53 in the Sefer Hizzuk Emunah ("Faith Strengthened") of Rabbi Isaac ben Abraham of Troki

For Hartmut Gese on his 65th birthday

Stefan Schreiner

Summary

The city of Troki, in present-day Lithuania, represents in microcosm the Polish-Lithuanian commonwealth of the sixteenth century. Here representatives of various religious communities — Protestants, Polish Roman Catholics, Russian Orthodox, Unitarians, and Jews of the Rabbanite and Karaite traditions — had the opportunity for serious religious dialogue. Rabbi Isaac ben Abraham (ca. 1525–ca. 1586), leader of the Karaite community in Troki, participated in these discussions and wrote his influential anti-Christian polemical work, the *Sefer Hizzuk Emunah,* as a result. While previous studies have praised this work's masterful summary of 1,500 years of Jewish-Christian debate, little attention has been devoted to its refutation of Christian proofs from Isaiah 53, which forms one of its longest chapters. Isaac's treatment is valuable because it goes beyond brief polemical theses to serious exegetical engagement with the text. He combines Karaite and Rabbanite exegetical traditions with his own insights, for example, concerning a theology of Israel's (continuing) exile, in order to counter Christian claims that he likewise knew very well. Isaac's "collective" understanding of the Suffering Servant as applying only to the people of Israel precludes individual messianic interpretations. The interpretations of Isaiah 53 that Jews and Christians discussed four hundred years ago are therefore much the same as those that occupy the Jewish-Christian dialogue today.

1. The Author and His Book

Hardly any passage of the Hebrew Bible is and has been of such fundamental importance in the history of Jewish-Christian debate, or has played such a central role in it, as has the fourth Servant Song of Second Isaiah. Nor has any other passage experienced such different and sometimes mutually exclusive interpretations as this one. It is not simply that its Jewish and Christian interpretations diverge from each another and often oppose each other. Rather, even within Jewish circles, opinions about the "correct interpretation" can differ just as much as the Christian interpretations do. The interpretations passed down to us from history reflect this diversity. It is therefore impossible to review them in a few pages, but fortunately this is also unnecessary, because it has already been done repeatedly and at length, both for the Jewish history of interpretation and for its Christian counterpart.[1] Instead, in this essay a single interpretation will be introduced, but one which deserves more attention than it has received, because of the identity of its author and the inherent interest of its contents. I have in mind the sixteenth-century Rabbi Isaac ben Abraham (ca. 1525–ca. 1586) of Troki, Lithuania, and his *Sefer Hizzuk Emunah* (also transliterated as Hizuk),[2] a work that has been given various titles in English, including

---

1. See the history of interpretation in H. Haag, *Der Gottesknecht bei Deuterojesaja*, EdF 233 (1985), esp. 55-58 on medieval Jewish interpreters, even though Isaac of Troki (see n. 2) is not mentioned. The Jewish history of interpretation of Isaiah 53 — including that of Isaac of Troki — is documented in A. Neubauer and S. R. Driver, *The Fifty-Third Chapter of Isaiah According to the Jewish Interpreters,* 2 vols. (1876-77), reprinted, ed. H. M. Orlinsky (1969), hereafter referred to as Neubauer and Driver. Other informative resumes of the history interpretation include H. A. Fischel, "Die Deuterojesajanischen Gottesknechtslieder in der juedischen Auslegung," *HUCA* 18 (1944): 53-76 — though once again Isaac of Troki is not mentioned by Fischel — and J. Rembaum, "The Development of a Jewish Exegetical Tradition Regarding Isaiah 53," *HTR* 75 (1982): 289-311. See also F. Varo, *Los canticos del Siervo en la exegesis hispano-hebrea* (1993), 15-41 (introduction) and 283-99 (conclusions).

2. Isaac of Troki, ספר חזוק אמונה = *Sefer Hizuk Emunah*. Principal edition: David Deutsch, ed. and trans., ספר חזוק אמונה: מר׳ יצחק בר׳ אברהם. German parallel title: *Befestigung im Glauben, von Rabbi Jitzchak, Sohn Abrahams . . . Zweite vielfach vermehrte Ausgabe* (Sohrau, Ober-Schlesien: Selbstverlag des Herausgebers; Breslau: Commissionsverlag von H. Skutsch, 2nd ed., 1873; 1st ed., Sohrau, 1865; all page references are to the second edition). Total pages ix plus 438. A more accessible edition of Deutsch's Hebrew text of Isaac's analysis of Isaiah 53 (i.e., *Sefer Hizuk Emunah,* part I, ch. 22) is available in Neubauer and Driver, Hebrew text 1:219-30; English translation, 2:243-57.

⟦(Tr.) This hard-to-find edition by D. Deutsch — of which there appear to be only about sixteen cataloged copies of the 1873 edition in the United States — can be located in online library catalogs in various ways: under the transliterated Hebrew title, *Sefer Hizuk Emunah* or *Hizuk Emunah;* under the German title, *Befestigung im Glauben* (some libraries give this as the

Faith Strengthened and *Bulwark of the Truth*.[3] This book attracted attention as soon as it became known,[4] although it first circulated only in handmade copies. But its real influence began in 1681 when J. C. Wagenseil incorporated it into his anthology *Tela ignea satanae* ("Satan's Fiery Arrows"),[5] presenting the Hebrew text with a Latin translation,[6] under the title *Rabbi Isaaci Liber Chissuk Emuna (Munium Fidei)*. However, this aspect of the book's history and influence cannot be traced here.[7]

---

primary title); under the author, Troki, Isaac ben Abraham, 1533-94; or under the editor-translator, Deutsch, David, 1810-73. The book is also available in microform: 1st ed. 1865 in the series Hebrew Books from the Harvard College Library (1991); 2nd ed. 1873 from Bay Microfilm (1988) or the History of Religions Preservation Project, Chicago, University of Chicago Library (1999). I have consulted the University of Chicago microfilm for the present translation.]]

3. *Faith Strengthened* is the title of the 1851 English translation by Moses Mocatta (see below n. 6); *Bulwark of the Truth* is the title given in Neubauer and Driver, 2:xiii, item 36.

4. Already in 1644 pastor Johann Müller of Hamburg wrote a polemic against Isaac under the title *Judaeismus und Judenthumb, das ist ausführlicher Bericht von des jüdischen Volcks Unglauben, Blindheit und Verstockung* (1644). On this see G. Müller, "Christlich-jüdisches Religionsgespräch im Zeitalter der protestantischen Orthodoxie: Die Auseinandersetzung Johann Müllers mit Isaak Trokis *Hizzuk Emuna*," in G. Müller and W. Zeller, eds., *Glaube, Geist, Geschichte*, Festschrift für Ernst Benz (1967), 513-24.

5. J. C. Wagenseil, *Tela ignea satanae*, 2 vols. (1681; reprinted 1970). Wagenseil's edition is the first printed edition of the *Sefer Hizzuk Emunah*, whereas the edition by Deutsch actually counts as the *editio princeps* from the Jewish side.

6. Wagenseil, *Tela ignea satanae*, 2/2, 480 pages (Hebrew text and Latin translation). However, over against the text of Deutsch's standard edition, Wagenseil's Hebrew text exhibits many departures that in part distort or reverse the sense. Cf. also J. C. Wolff, *Bibliotheca Hebraea*, vol. 4 (1733), 648-718. An English translation of Wagenseil's text was prepared by Moses Mocatta in 1851, although it could not be published until 1866 in London; see also the Ktav reprint: *Faith Strengthened*, translated by M. Mocatta, with a new introduction by T. Weiss-Rosmarin (1970).

7. Wagenseil's Latin translation of the work served among others the French Encyclopedists, especially Voltaire, as a source of abundant arguments for their own criticism of Christianity. [[(Tr.) Cf., e.g., J. Szechtman, "Voltaire on Isaac Troki's Hizzuk Emunah," *JQR* n.s. 48 (1957-58): 53-57.]] At the beginning of the twentieth century Rev. A. Luykin Williams felt it necessary to write a comprehensive refutation of this book under the title *A Manual of Christian Evidence for the Jewish People*, 2 vols. (1919-20). Referring to Deutsch's *editio princeps* of 1865, Franz Delitzsch in a lecture in Berlin on April 28, 1870 remarked that "it has now come so far that a Schlesian rabbi, sponsored by the Baron von Rothschild in Paris, has edited and translated into German one of the most spiteful controversial writings against Christianity, the *Hizzuk Emunah* by Isaac of Troki, recommending it with words of Voltaire's universal high regard" (F. Delitzsch, *Welche Anforderungen stellt die Gegenwart an die Missions-Arbeit unter den Juden?* [1870], 6). I owe this reference to Delitzsch's lecture to my colleague H. Lichtenberger. [[(Tr.) For Deutsch's quotation of Voltaire, which he cites as "most valid testimony," see Deutsch, *Befestigung im Glauben*, preface, pp. vi-vii.]]

Before we turn to the book itself and its interpretation of the fourth Servant Song, a few remarks are in order about the author and the book's origin, even though on the whole we know little about the author and his life.[8] The day of his birth is unknown, as is the day of his death. Not even the years of his birth and death are recorded. Presumably he was born in 1525 (or 1533) to a Karaite family in the Lithuanian city of Troki (Trakai). The Karaites were an inner-Jewish opposition movement from the ninth century who rejected rabbinic tradition and held to the Hebrew Bible as the sole norm.[9] Next to the Crim Peninsula, they had their spiritual and cultural center in Poland and Lithuania ever since the High Middle Ages.[10]

We first learn something about Rabbi Isaac in the year 1553, which has also been recorded as the year of his first public appearance. In 1553 the Karaites as well as the so-called Rabbanite Jews (who held to the rabbinic tradition) were granted autonomy, judicial recognition as a self-governing religious community with power to elect their own parliament or *waad*. Isaac was chosen as speaker of the Karaites and became one of the three *dayyanim* (judges) of the city. As such he had the task of representing the Karaites at both local and regional levels to the state and churches. During his term of office Troki developed into a citadel of Karaism, possessing its own spiritual center in its *Bet ha-Midrash* or House of Instruction founded in 1576, of which Isaac was rector. Isaac probably died in his hometown of Troki in 1586.

8. On this see I. Markon, "Troki 2," *Jüdisches Lexikon* 4/2 (1930), 1058-59; I. Newman, "Troki, Isaac ben Abraham," *EncJud* 15 (1971), 1403-4. See further A. Geiger, *Isaak Troki, ein Apologet des Judentums* (1853), reprinted in idem, *Nachgelassene Schriften*, vol. 3 (1885), 178-223; M. Balaban, *Historja i literatura żydowska, ze szczególnym uwzględnieniem historji Żydów w Polsce*, vol. 3 (1925; reprinted 1982), 254ff.; S. Dubnow, *Weltgeschichte des jüdischen Volkes*, trans. A. Steinberg, vol. 6 (1927), 379-85; M. Waysblum, "Isaac of Troki and Christian Controversy in the XVI Century," *JJS* 3 (1952): 62-77; E. L. Dietrich, "Das jüdisch-christliche Religionsgespräch am Ausgang des 16. Jahrhunderts nach dem Handbuch des R. Isaak Troki," *Jud* 14 (1958): 1-39, esp. 1-8 (and in dependence on Dietrich, H. J. Schoeps, *Jüdisch-christliches Religionsgespräch in neunzehn Jahrhunderten* [1961; reprinted ed. E. Brocke, 1984], 87-96); E. I. J. Rosenthal, "Jüdische Antwort," in K. H. Rengstorf and S. von Kortzfleisch, eds., *Kirche und Synagoge —Handbuch zur Geschichte von Christen und Juden*, vol. 1 (1968; reprinted 1988), 307-62, esp. 354-57; S. W. Baron, *A Social and Religious History of the Jews*, vol. 16 (1976), 75-76 with 351 n. 82; J. Maier, *Geschichte der jüdischen Religion*, 2nd ed. (1992), 506.

9. For an overview of the history and culture of the Karaites in the form of a self-presentation see S. Szyszman, *Das Karäertum — Lehre und Geschichte* (1983), with further literature. See also N. Schur, *History of the Karaites*, BEATAJ 29 (1992), with literature.

10. See A. Zajaczkowski, *Karaims in Poland: History, Language, Folklore, Science* (1961); Baron, *Social and Religious History*, 8-9 with 320 n. 7; Szyszman, *Das Karäertum*, 85ff., 111ff; N. Davies, *God's Playground — A History of Poland*, vol. 1, 4th ed. (1986), 191-92; Schur, *History of the Karaites*, 101-12.

Troki in Isaac ben Abraham's day was a city that offered refuge to many religious communities. It had a Polish-Lithuanian Roman Catholic church, a Russian Orthodox church, a Reformed church, a Unitarian church, a Tatar Muslim community, and not least a Rabbanite and a Karaite community. M. Waysblum has rightly called Troki "a microcosm of the mighty Polish-Lithuanian Commonwealth."[11] In the sixteenth century, which has not without reason been called the century of tolerance in the Polish-Lithuanian Commonwealth,[12] Troki was a center of inter-religious dialogue, despite the efforts of the Dominican monastery there to re-Catholicize the country after the Council of Trent.

Most notable were the religious dialogues that took place from 1567 to 1583 between Jewish scholars of the Rabbanite and Karaite traditions, on the one hand, and various dissident Christian groups, including Unitarians and the so-called "Judaizantes,"[13] on the other hand. These were not forced disputations as we know them especially from France and Spain during the High Middle Ages,[14] but were real dialogues that earn our respect even today for their intensity and openness.[15] One of the participants in these religious dialogues was Isaac ben Abraham, whose conversation partners included not only Unitarians, but also Russian Orthodox and Roman Catholic Christians.[16]

11. Waysblum, "Isaac of Troki," 6. Cf. also Baron, *Social and Religious History,* 61-74 with 343-51 nn. 67-81.

12. J. Tazbir, *Geschichte der polnischen Toleranz* (1973).

13. On the Polish *Judaizantes* see J. Juszczyk, "O badaniach nad judaizantyzmem," *Kwartalnik Historyczny* 76 (1969): 141-51.

14. See H. Maccoby, *Judaism on Trial: Jewish-Christian Disputation in the Middle Ages,* (1st ed., 1982; 2nd ed., 1984), esp. 19-94; S. Schreiner, "Von den theologischen Zwangsdisputationen des Mittelalters zum jüdisch-christlichen Dialog heute," *Jud* 42 (1986): 141-57; Maier, *Geschichte,* 424-36 (literature); B. Lewis and F. Niewöhner, eds., *Religionsgespräche im Mittelalter,* Wolfenbütteler Mittelalter-Studien 4 (1992). Within this essay collection see especially the contributions by M. Awerbuch, "Die Religionsgespräche in Salomo Ibn Vergas *Shevet Jehuda*" (43-59); R. Chazan, "The Barcelona Disputation of 1263: Goals, Tactics, and Achievements" (77-91); J. Cohen, "Towards a Functional Classification of Jewish Anti-Christian Polemic in the High Middle Ages" (93-114); and D. Berger, "Christians, Gentiles, and the Talmud: A Fourteenth-Century Jewish Response to the Attack on Rabbinic Judaism" (115-30).

15. See esp. H. H. Ben-Sasson, "Jews and Christian Sectarians: Existential Similarity and Dialectical Tensions in Sixteenth-Century Moravia and Poland-Lithuania," *Viator: Medieval and Renaissance Studies* 4 (1973): 369-85; Baron, *Social and Religious History,* 66ff. with 345ff.; J. Friedman, "The Reformation and Jewish Antichristian Polemics," *Bibliothèque d'Humanisme et Renaissance* 41 (1979): 83-97. See further J. Tazbir, "Dysputacje religijne w Polsce XVI w.," in idem, *Świat panów pasków* (1986), 161-76, 286f.; idem, "Stosunek protestantów do Żydów," in idem, *Świat panów pasków* (1986), 195-212, 289-92; and idem, "Żydzi w opinii staropolskiej," in idem, *Świat panów pasków* (1986), 213-41, 292-94.

16. Waysblum, "Isaac of Troki," 71-72.

One result of these dialogues was Isaac's book *Sefer Hizzuk Emunah.* In this compendium Isaac collects and then refutes the Christian objections to Judaism known to him from many conversations as well as exegetical proofs used in Christological interpretation of the Old Testament. According to his pupil Joseph ben Mordecai Malinowski of Cracow, who wrote a preface to his teacher's book and published it after his death, Isaac began the book around 1578-79 and worked on it until his death without completing it. It therefore remained to be completed by his pupil, who "published" the book (albeit in manuscript rather than printed form) in 1594.[17]

The immediate occasion for Isaac's compiling the book was the conversion of an apparently considerable number of Lithuanian Jews, above all business people and intellectuals, who chose for whatever reasons to live as members of Christian society.[18] In the light of this experience Isaac felt inwardly compelled to write his *Faith Strengthened,* as he says, "in order to *strengthen the hands that are weak* because of the lack of understanding of our faith and to *make firm the knees that are feeble* because of the long duration of our exile" (Deutsch, 8).[19] His leitmotif was Rabbi Eleazar's dictum from *m. 'Abot* 2.14: "Be alert to study the Law and know how to make answer to an unbeliever" (Deutsch, 7).[20]

Without wishing to survey the whole book,[21] it will be helpful here at least to convey its underlying scheme. (For the Hebrew pagination we refer to the edition by Deutsch [see n. 2]; followed by the English pagination of Mocatta [see n. 6].) As Isaac explains in his preface, the first part of fifty chapters (Deutsch, 29-282; Mocatta, 5-226) contains

> the objections that the Christians raise against us [and our biblical interpretation] and the proofs they cite [from the Hebrew Bible] for their faith, as well as my refutations, including some of the objections that I bring

17. See Joseph ben Mordecai in his "preface of the student of the author" (הקדמת תלמיד המחבר, *Haqdamat Talmid ha-Mehabber*), ed. Deutsch, 1-6.

18. Isaac reports about this in his "preface of the author" (הקדמת המחבר, *Haqdamat ha-Mehabber*), ed. Deutsch, 6-13.

19. The italicized citation is from Isa. 35:3. Joseph Kimchi (ca. 1105-ca. 1170) placed the same verse at the beginning of his own apologetic work; see *Sefer ha-Berit*, ed. F. Talmage (1974), 21.

20. This text appears repeatedly as the leitmotif in Jewish polemic-apologetic works; see Schreiner, "Zwangsdisputationen," 142.

21. A sufficient survey is provided by the detailed table of contents of the *Sefer Hizzuk Emunah*, compiled partly by the author himself and partly by his student. See ed. Deutsch, 14-28. (Unfortunately, this table of contents is not reproduced in Mocatta's English translation.) An instructive overview of the book's main themes is available in Dietrich, "Das jüdisch-christliche Religionsgespräch."

against them and their faith from their own words [i.e., in the New Testament]. (Deutsch, 12; Mocatta, iii)

The second part, although consisting of 100 chapters, is much shorter (Deutsch, 283-354; Mocatta, 227-95) and "contains refutations of the words of the author of their Gospel."[22] Therefore in the first part Isaac deals with the Christian or Christological interpretation of the Hebrew Bible, while in the second he engages the New Testament Scriptures.

Especially noteworthy is the learning that speaks from this book. Although Isaac ben Abraham was a Karaite, he was also familiar with the Rabbanite tradition, which he appeals to approvingly and sometimes cites literally, though he does not always give the name and title of the cited author and work.[23] Therefore in many passages Isaac's dependence upon Rabbanite sources can be discerned only on the basis of apparent similarities in argumentation. But it is not only the Jewish tradition with which Isaac was familiar. Although he himself knew neither Latin nor Greek, he did know the Christian Scriptures and their interpretation at first hand, including the Vulgate in the Roman Catholic translation into Polish by Jan von Lwów (Johannes Lemberg), that is, the so-called *Cracow Bible (Krakauer Bibel)*, as well as the Greek New Testament in the Protestant translation of 1563, the so-called *Brest Bible (Brester Bibel)*. But the most lasting influence upon Isaac was the literature of the Unitarians.[24] Pride of place goes to the 1572 edition of the Bible (the so-called *Nieswiez Bible*) with philological and historical commentary by Szymon (Simon) Budny (1530-93),[25] spiritual leader of that faction of Lithuanian Unitari-

---

22. Ed. Deutsch, 12; Mocatta, iii. This second part of the *Sefer Hizzuk Emunah* is only a torso that the student-editor presumably made out of his master's material. The thorough revision and reworking of the first part is clearly lacking in this second part.

23. A list of the scholars whom Isaac cites by name is provided in the edition by Deutsch, 395. Cf. Waysblum, "Isaac of Troki," 67-68.

24. Information about Isaac's Unitarian sources is provided by R. Dán, "Isaac Troky and his 'Antitrinitarian' Sources," in R. Dán, ed., *Occident and Orient — A Tribute to the Memory of Alexander Scheiber* (1988), 69-82. Cf. also J. M. Rosenthal, "Marcin Czechowic and Jacob of Belzyce: Arian-Jewish Encounters in 16th century Poland," *PAAJR* 34 (1966): 77-95; further idem, "R. Ya'aqov mi-Belżyce we-siphro ha-wikkuchi," *Gal-Ed* 1 (1973): 13-30.

25. On this see Waysblum, "Isaac of Troki," 73ff. The historical-critical biblical exegesis of Szymon Budny, one of the best Christian Hebraists of his time, anticipated modern biblical criticism in many respects. Cf. H. Merczyng, *Szymon Budny jako krytyk tekstów biblijnych* (1913). On Budny's person and work see S. Kot, "Szymon Budny — der größte Häretiker Litauens im 16. Jahrhundert," in *Wiener Archiv für Geschichte des Slaventums und Osteuropas*, vol. 2: *Studien zur älteren Geschichte Osteuropas* (1956), 63-118. Kot also edited Budny's main theological work of 1583, *O urzędzie miecza używającem* (1932).

ans known as the Non-Adorantes.[26] Also influential were works by Niccolà Paruta (153?-1581), Marcin Czechowic (1532-1615), and others. Similarly Isaac's historical knowledge was not gleaned only from Jewish sources, as was usual within the Jewish community in his day, but also from Polish sources such as Marcin Bielski's famous *Kronika swiata* (Cracow, 1553).

However, the special value and significance of the polemical apologetic handbook *Sefer Hizzuk Emunah* lies in the fact that its author did not confine himself to the usual polemics in thesis form. What distinguishes this handbook, next to its clear organization, is above all the exegetical acumen displayed in Isaac's refutation of Christian biblical interpretation. At the same time he was a master of summary. Therefore his book also draws a summary from 1,500 years of Jewish-Christian debate. As M. Waysblum tellingly puts it, "All the controversy, the subject of endless duels since the beginning of Christianity, is here — so to speak — put in a nutshell."[27] And what is true of Isaac's book as a whole is especially true of his debate with the Christian interpretation of the fourth Servant Song, which has previously received almost no attention.[28] The importance of this debate for Isaac himself is attested not least by the exhaustive detail with which he argues here. It is no accident that Isaac's chapter on Isaiah 53 (*Sefer Hizzuk Emunah,* part I, ch. 22) is one of the longest in the book (see Deutsch, 145-62; the Hebrew text is also in Neubauer and Driver, 1:219-30; English translation in Neubauer and Driver, 2:243-57).

2. The Interpretation of Isaiah 52:13–53:12 in the *Sefer Hizzuk Emunah*

Chapter 22 of the *Sefer Hizzuk Emunah,* which deals with Isaiah 53, is structured as follows. Isaac begins this chapter, as he does every chapter, with (I) a summary of the Christian interpretation of the pericope under discussion (Deutsch, 145; Neubauer and Driver, 2:243; hereafter 145/243) and (II) its accompanying refutation (146/243-44). There follows in III/A a summary presentation (פרוש הפרק בדרך כלל) of the author's counter-position (146-54/

---

26. The epithet "Non-Adorantes" derives from the title of a work by Adam Neuser (died 1576), *De non adorando et invocando Christo* (1562). Neuser was a Lutheran pastor in Heidelberg who converted to Islam and served in the bodyguard of the Turkish sultan in Constantinople. Cf. F. Hauss, "Neuser, Adam," *RGG,* 3rd ed., 4:1438-39 and now M. Wriedt in *RGG,* 4th ed., 6:251-52.

27. Waysblum, "Isaac of Troki," 73.

28. As already noted, Fischel, "Die Deuterojesajanischen Gottesknechtslieder in der juedischen Auslegung," does not mention Isaac at all.

244-49) and the detailed verse-by-verse justification that concludes the chapter (154-62/249-57). Since a similar scheme underlies the medieval Jewish commentaries of Ibn Ezra, Rashi, and David Kimchi, and since Isaac shares some of their views, we reprint their commentaries as an appendix to this essay and cite parallels to Isaac's interpretation in many of the following notes.[29]

Below we present the translation of Isaac of Troki from Neubauer and Driver (2:243-57 [see n. 1]), often modified to reflect the new German translation of Isaac's Hebrew text in the original version of this essay. Where Neubauer and Driver abbreviate Scripture quotations we have written them in full, as Isaac did. The running Scripture text is based on the NRSV, with slight modifications.

Sepher Hizzuk Emunah, chapter 22

I. Summary of the Christian Interpretation

"See, my servant shall prosper; he shall be exalted and lifted up, and shall be very high" (Isa. 52:13). From this verse, as also from the following verses from "Who has believed what we have heard?" (53:1) until "and he made intercession for the transgressors" (53:12), the Nazarenes [i.e., Christians] argue that Isaiah the prophet, peace be upon him, prophesied these verses about Jesus the Nazarene, for it is about him that he said, "he shall be exalted and lifted up, and shall be very high" (52:13b). For this saying applies to him and to him alone. In the same way Isaiah is supposed to have said about him, "Surely he has borne our infirmities and carried our diseases, etc." (53:4) and "But he was wounded for our transgressions, crushed for our iniquities, etc." (53:5). For he gave himself over to affliction for their sakes, to save their souls by his death from the hand of Satan, who ruled over them. (Neubauer and Driver, 2:243 [modified])

---

29. The following parallels to Isaac of Troki from the medieval Jewish commentators are cited from the text collection of Neubauer and Driver in the form: Hebrew pagination/English pagination. See Rashi (1040-1105) in Neubauer and Driver, 1:37-39/2:37-39; Abraham ibn Ezra (1093-1168) in Neubauer and Driver, 1:43-47/2:43-48; David Kimchi (1160-1235) in Neubauer and Driver, 1:48-54/2:49-56. An analysis of Ibn Ezra's interpretation of the Servant Songs (with a Spanish translation) is presented by Varo, *Los canticos del Siervo*, 67-102, esp. 89ff. on Isaiah 53.

II. Refutation of the Christian Interpretation

Against this Christian or rather Christological interpretation Isaac claims that this pericope cannot be applied to the Messiah in general, and certainly not to Jesus of Nazareth in particular.[30] Why this is impossible Isaac explains in his refutation of the Christian interpretation, which he owes to an exegesis of the pericope in terms of its "plain sense" or *peshat,* the only sense to which Isaac feels obligated.[31] He summarizes the result in the following six points (cf. Neubauer and Driver, 2:243-44 [modified]):

> Answer [to the Christian interpretation]: This argument of theirs is not valid.
>
> (a) For where the text says, "See, my servant shall prosper; he shall be exalted and lifted up, etc." (52:13), how can they apply this to Jesus of Nazareth, since they themselves, according to their own absurd tenets, assign to him deity, and how could God in any prophecy be called a *servant* (עבד)?[32] If now the objector maintains that he is termed a "servant" [only] with respect to his material nature (גופניות),[33] and "God" (אלוהים) with respect to his spiritual nature (רוחניות), we must reply that it has already been irrefutably demonstrated with full scriptural proofs in chapter 10[34] that even from the point of view of the Gospel, Jesus the Nazarene is not God, and still less so from his own standpoint: he never in any place speaks of himself as God, as will be further shown in the second part of this treatise by a detailed examination of the individual expressions used by the Evangelists.[35]

30. So also Ibn Ezra on Isa. 52:13 (Neubauer and Driver, 1:43/2:43). Cf. J. Sarachek, *The Doctrine of the Messiah in Medieval Jewish Literature,* 2nd ed. (1968), 116.

31. According to *b. Shabbat* 63a: אין מקרא יוצא מידי פשוטו, "A verse cannot depart from its plain meaning."

32. This objection already appears in the report of Rabbi Moses ben Nachman (Nachmanides) (1195-1270) about his disputation with the monk Pablo Christiani in Barcelona in 1263. See H.-G. von Mutius, *Die christlich-jüdische Zwangsdisputation zu Barcelona (1263): Nach dem hebräischen Protokoll des Moses Nachmanides,* Judentum und Umwelt 5 (1982), 107. From there Nachmanides incorporated this objection into his Isaiah commentary; cf. Varo, *Los canticos del Siervo,* 126f., as well as Sarachek, *Doctrine of the Messiah,* 181, 184-86, and Rosenthal, "Jüdische Antwort," 338-40.

33. According to Ibn Ezra on Isa. 52:13 (Neubauer and Driver, 1:43/2:43), it is the Christians who claim that the term "servant" refers only to the physical body of Jesus.

34. *Sefer Hizzuk Emunah,* part 1, ch. 10, ed. Deutsch, 79-86; trans. Mocatta, 46-50. As New Testament proofs that Jesus believed himself to be only a man and not God, Isaac cites Matt. 12:32; 20:18, 28; Mark 3:28-29; Luke 12:19; John 8:40; Rom. 5:15 (ed. Deutsch, 84ff.; Mocatta, 49-50).

35. However, Isaac has done this only very fragmentarily in part 2, chs. 12 (ed. Deutsch, 294-95) and 16 (ed. Deutsch, 297).

(b) It must in addition be remembered that the words "he shall be exalted and lifted up, and shall be very high" were not fulfilled in him, since he was condemned to death like any other common man among the people.

(c) Nor was the prediction "he shall see his seed [i.e., offspring]" (53:10b) ever fulfilled in him: he had no seed (זרע);[36] and it cannot be said that his disciples are here meant by his "seed," for we never find disciples termed "seed" but only "sons" (בנים), just as teachers are spoken of as "their fathers" (אבותם). The term "seed" is restricted to the descendants of a man, who come forth out of his loins.

(d) Similarly we do not find that "he shall prolong his days" (53:10b),[37] for he was put to death when thirty-three years old. And they [the Christians] cannot legitimately refer this expression to the Godhead, because the deity is not determined by *length of days* (אריכות ימים);[38] "he is the first and he is the last; and his years have no end."[39]

(e) Then, again, of whom will they interpret the verse, "Therefore I will allot him a portion with the many, and he shall divide the spoil with the mighty" (53:12a)?[40] Who are the many and the mighty that are made his equals, and with whom, as they imagine, is he to divide spoil?

36. The same argument is found in Ibn Ezra (Neubauer and Driver, 1:43/2:43).

37. The same argument once again in Ibn Ezra (Neubauer and Driver, 1:43/2:43).

38. This was already stated by Moses ben Maimon, also known as Maimonides or Rambam (1135-1204) (cf. Maier, *Geschichte*, 274-88 [literature]), in the fourth of his "Thirteen Fundamental Principles" *(ikkarim)* of Jewish faith, which are to be found within his commentary on the Mishnah in the introduction to his comments on *Sanhedrin* 10 (see A. Altmann, "Articles of Faith," *EncJud* 3:654-60, esp. 655-56). Maimonides says: "The fourth fundamental principle is the firstness [i.e., eternity] of God, that is to say that this unity whom we have described is the absolute first. Everything that exists other than Him is not first in relation to Him," cited according to *Maimonides' Commentary on the Mishnah: Tractate Sanhedrin,* trans. Fred Rosner (1981), 152; another translation in Moses Maimonides, *A Maimonides Reader,* ed. I. Twersky (1972), 418. The original Judeo-Arabic text with Hebrew translation is available in J. Holzer, *Zur Geschichte der Dogmenlehre in der jüdischen Religionsphilosophie des Mittelalters: Mose Maimûni's Einleitung zu Chelek* (1901), 22, and in Yosef Kafah, ed., משנה עם פירוש רבינו משה בן מימון, *Mishnah 'im perush Rabenu Mosheh ben Maimon,* vol. 4 (1964), 211-12.

39. Citation of Isa. 44:6 (cf. 48:12) and Ps. 102:27 (MT 102:28). Isaac apparently cannot share the interpretation put forward by the commentator and grammarian David Kimchi in his commentary on Ps. 21:5, according to which the biblical אורך ימים, "length of days," should be understood as חיי העולם הבא, "life in the world to come." (For Kimchi's text see A. Darom, ed., *Ha-Perush ha-Shalem 'al Tehillim,* 4th ed. [1979], 53.) In the case of Jesus this would mean that the יאריך ימים ("he shall lengthen his days") in Isa. 53:10b refers to his life after the resurrection, not to his (short) life on earth, as Isaac assumes.

40. This objection too is already found in Ibn Ezra (Neubauer and Driver, 1:43/2:43).

(f) And when it is said, "he made intercession (יַפְגִּיעַ)[41] for the transgressors" (53:12b), to whom did he intercede for them if, as their fond belief
will have it, he was God himself?

So much for Isaac's objections to the Christian interpretation of the
pericope. Remarkably, he does not go into the verses that stand at the center of
the Christian application of this passage to Jesus according to his own summary of the Christian teaching (above, point I), namely, Isaiah 53:4-5 (with vv.
3, 6b-9). He consciously goes around these verses for quite comprehensible reasons, since as a Karaite he neither can nor will refute the idea of vicarious suffering as such which these verses attest.[42] The idea of vicarious suffering is actually central for Isaac as well, as we shall see. Nevertheless, the *subject* of the
vicarious suffering is a different one for Isaac, and he understands vicarious
suffering in a different sense. Although Isaac does not reject the idea of vicarious suffering as such, he is unable to accept its reference to *Jesus*. Furthermore it
is important to Isaac, as it was to David Kimchi, to make a distinction regarding
the character of this vicarious suffering. For just as there is a difference between
the (innocent) suffering of a righteous person, which raises the question of
theodicy,[43] and the killing of an innocent person, which breaks an existing
law[44] — as rabbinic tradition clearly illustrates with reference to the story of
Achan's theft (Joshua 7) or the case of the Gibeonites (2 Samuel 21)[45] — so also

---

41. However, over the course of history, the classical Jewish Bible commentators have not
all agreed as to whether the verb פגע (hiphil הפגיע) actually means "to make intercession/en-
treaty" or "to besiege." Here Isaac follows Ibn Ezra (Neubauer and Driver, 1:47/2:48) and David
Kimchi (1:53/2:55): ולפושעים יפגיע in Isa. 53:12 means מתפלל בעבור הרשעים. These two commentators in turn follow Rashi: "הפגיע means *aspirer* in French and is an expression for תחנה
[*supplication, urgent plea*]" (cf. Neubauer and Driver, 1:47/2:38). [(Tr.) The translations of
Neubauer and Driver convey these and similar Hebrew grammatical arguments inadequately, if
at all; often the Hebrew words under discussion are not even mentioned. See the more precise
German translations, also consulted for the present English version of this essay, by Natan
Hutterer, *Die mittelalterlichen jüd. Kommentare zu den Ebed-JHWH-Liedern des Jesaja* (1938), 15-
17 on Rashi, 22-26 on Ibn Ezra, and 34-40 on Kimchi. While Hutterer's rare work is essentially
unavailable outside Germany, his translations are reprinted as an appendix to the original German version of this essay: S. Schreiner, "Jes 52:13–53:12 in der Auslegung des *Sepher Chizzuq
Emunah* von R. Isaak ben Avraham aus Troki," in B. Janowski and P. Stuhlmacher, eds., *Der
leidende Gottesknecht*, FAT 14 (1996), 159-95, esp. 184-95.]

42. Moreover, in accepting a certain kind of vicarious suffering (i.e., Israel for the nations: see below), Isaac appears to have adopted, once again without acknowledging his source,
the enlightening argument of David Kimchi on Isa. 53:4 (Neubauer and Driver, 1:50/2:51-52).

43. Cf. Gen. 18:25.

44. Cf. Deut. 24:16 (with 2 Kings 14:6; 2 Chron. 25:4); also Jer. 31:29f; Ezek. 18:20.

45. Cf. *b. Yebam.* 79a with Rashi's commentary on it.

in this case a line must be drawn between deserved and undeserved vicarious suffering.

III. Rabbi Isaac ben Abraham's Interpretation

Isaac's objections to the Christian interpretation form only the beginning of the chapter. After the refutation, his own interpretation follows, though much of this is not totally original. Rather, Isaac repeatedly has recourse to exegetical traditions, that is, Bible commentaries and philological studies, especially those of Abraham Ibn Ezra and David Kimchi.[46] Although he is a Karaite, he uses and often agrees with this Rabbanite tradition, although, as already observed, he does not always name the particular author or work.

III.1. The Identity of the Servant

As in all interpretations of Isaiah 53, the question about the identity of the Servant stands at the center also for Isaac. For him, despite the address in the singular, the passage need not deal with an individual at all. On the contrary, in keeping with Hillel's seventh exegetical rule, according to which each matter must be interpreted from its context,[47] only a collective interpretation of the Servant comes into consideration. Because in the remainder of the book of Deutero-Isaiah, which forms the context of the Servant Songs, it is always Jacob/Israel that is meant or addressed as the "servant," this must also be the case in the songs themselves.[48] Isaac

---

46. The influence of Ibn Ezra and David Kimchi as well as Rashi upon Isaac of Troki has already been shown in several of the preceding notes.

47. On this see H. L. Strack and G. Stemberger, *Introduction to the Talmud and Midrash,* trans. M. Bockmuehl (1991; reprinted 1992), 23.

48. Ibn Ezra makes it expressly clear that in Isa. 52:12 and 54:1, i.e., immediately before and after the fourth Servant Song, the people of Israel are spoken of. In order nevertheless to retain the singular "my Servant" he refers the expression *Servant* to "each individual belonging to Israel, and consequently God's servant, who is in exile" (Neubauer and Driver, 1:43/2:43), thus understanding *Servant* as a collective singular. Moreover, Ibn Ezra develops a thesis about the Servant as a *corporate personality* from the juxtaposition in Isa. 53:3 of אִישׁ ("a *man* of suffering") — which here means the *whole of Israel* (as in Exod. 15:3) — and its plural אִישִׁים ("He was despised and forsaken by *men*"), by which the *nations of the world* are to be understood. Hence "if עַבְדִּי be understood of the nation, then אִישׁ will be used to signify 'a being' in general" (Neubauer and Driver, 1:44 /2:45). So now also Varo, *Los canticos del Siervo,* 101f. with nn. 199-200, with reference to U. Simon, "Ibn Ezra between Medievalism and Modernism: The Case of Isaiah XL–LXVI," in J. A. Emerton, ed., *Congress Volume: Salamanca, 1983,* VTSup 36 (1985), 257-71, esp. 267-68.

of course does not stand alone with his collective interpretation of the fourth Song in terms of the "people of Israel" (אומ תישׂראל)[49] — an expression he uses remarkably often. Nevertheless, it is surprising that he has made this interpretation his own, since Karaite exegesis otherwise usually interprets the Servant as applying to the righteous Karaites, the prophets, and occasionally even to the Messiah.[50] Over against this Isaac says:

> The truth is, the whole *parashah* from "See, my servant shall prosper" (52:13)[51] with the following verses until "and he made intercession for the transgressors" (53:12) was spoken prophetically to Isaiah, peace be upon him, with reference to the people of Israel, who were enduring the yoke of exile, and who are called "my servant," in the singular, as frequently elsewhere [verses are cited]:[52] You see that in all these passages Scripture designates the Israelite nation as a "servant," or as "his servant," in the singular. And so when the Ten Commandments were given we observe that the Almighty, blessed be he, spoke to 600,000 men[53] in the singular number,[54] "I am the Lord, *thy* God," etc. (Neubauer and Driver, 2:244 [modified]).

For Isaac the Servant is thus not the people of Israel absolutely, *but the people of Israel suffering in exile.* This means first Israel in the Babylonian exile, then also every generation of Israel that suffers in exile,[55] because the Babylonian exile (גולה) is understood to prefigure all other exiles (גלות).[56] Although

49. On this see the overview in Fischel, "Gottesknechtslieder," 74-76; and Sarachek, *Doctrine of the Messiah*, passim. Also relevant is M. Awerbuch, *Christlich-jüdische Begegnung im Zeitalter der Frühscholastik*, Abhandlungen zum christlich-jüdischen Dialog 8 (1980), 121ff.

50. References in Fischel, "Gottesknechtslieder," 60 with n. 32; Sarachek, *Doctrine of the Messiah*, 37.

51. For the meaning of the verb ישׂכיל (שׂכל), Isaac refers to 1 Sam. 18:14 (Deutsch, 154/ Neubauer and Driver, 2:249). The same reference is found in David Kimchi's commentary on the passage (Neubauer and Driver, 1:48/2:49).

52. The verses cited include Isa. 41:8-9; 44:1-2, 21; 45:4; Jer. 30:10; 46:27-28; and Ps. 136:22. The first two references were already used in the same context by Moses ben Nachman: see Mutius, *Zwangsdisputation*, 92, and Varo, *Los canticos del Siervo*, 126-27.

53. Namely, the 600,000 men who according to Exod. 12:37 (cf. Exod. 38:26; Num. 1:46; 2:32; 11:21; 26:51) departed from Egypt and stood at the foot of Mount Sinai (Exod. 20:18, 21; Deut. 4:11).

54. Although this problem has occupied interpreters for ages, in our context it is insignificant.

55. See on this Fischel, "Gottesknechtslieder," 57ff.

56. We are still lacking a recent comprehensive investigation of the problem of *exile* in Jewish history. The fundamental preliminary works were produced decades ago by Y. Kaufmann, *Golah ve-Nekhar: Mehqar histori-sotsyologi bi-sche'elat goralo shel 'am Yisra'el mi-*

the idea that Isaiah 53 reflects the historical fate of the people of Israel in the exile is not in itself new[57] — already in antiquity it was presented by Jewish exegetes[58] — nevertheless it was extensively used and developed in the context of Jewish-Christian controversy only in the Middle Ages, first in 1170 by Jacob ben Reuben of southern France in his book *Milhamot ha-Shem* (ch. 55),[59] whose example others followed. For Isaac, Christian objections do not nullify this identification of the Servant with Israel in exile.[60] According to him, the Christians claim:

> It was never at any time either seen or heard of that the people of Israel bore sickness or pain, or received stripes for the iniquity of other nations. (Neubauer and Driver, 2:244)

That Israel suffered vicariously for the sins of the nations is indeed what Isaiah 53:4-5 would seem to say when the "he" is referred to the Servant Israel and the "we" or the first-person plural suffixes to the nations of the world. Therefore, according to Isaac, Christians reject the identification of "he" with Israel precisely by rejecting the notion that Israel's sufferings in exile were vicarious: "Even the calamities and chastisement which they [the people of Israel] did endure were for their own sins, and not for those of other people" (Neubauer and Driver, 2:244). For the Christians whom Isaac cites here, the suffering of Israel is therefore not an innocent suffering in the sense of the above-

---

yeme kedem ve-'ad ha-zeman ha-zeh, 2 vols. (1929-30), and Y. Baer, *Galut* (1936). A stimulating outline of such an investigation has now been presented by Y. H. Yerushalmi, "Exil und Vertreibung in der jüdischen Geschichte," in idem, *Ein Feld in Anatot: Versuche über jüdische Geschichte* (1993), 21-38.

57. David Kimchi begins his interpretation with the programmatic statement: "This *parashah* refers to the captivity (exile) of Israel" (Neubauer and Driver, 1:48/2:49).

58. The identification of the Servant with Israel in Jewish interpretation is reported, e.g., by Origen, *c. Celsum* 1.55. For the Servant of Isaiah 53 as Israel see Justin Martyr, *Dialogue,* ch. 22. For the Servant of Isa. 42:1ff. and 49:1ff. see Fischel, "Gottesknechtslieder," 59, and von Mutius, *Zwangsdisputation,* 93, 95.

59. Jacob ben Reuben, *Milhamot ha-shem,* ed. Judah Rosenthal (1963), 108. The text is also available in Neubauer and Driver, 1:55-58/2:57-60. For an analysis of the text see now Varo, *Los canticos del Siervo,* 105-15. Outside this writing nothing is known about the author; cf. Maier, *Geschichte,* 434, and Varo, *Los canticos del Siervo,* 103-4.

60. In the context of the usual Christian objection to the identification of the Servant with Israel, it is all the more remarkable that such a respected Bible commentator as Andrew of St. Victor followed the Jewish interpretation in his Isaiah commentary, referring to the Servant as the people of Israel suffering in the Babylonian exile. Cf. on this B. Smalley, *The Study of the Bible in the Middle Ages,* 3rd ed. (1983), 164ff., 391f.

mentioned problem of theodicy, but a deserved suffering in the sense of just punishment.[61]

Against this Isaac holds:

> It is a common custom in the mouth of the prophets to describe the miseries (צרות) and humiliation (שפלות) of the captivity under the image of sickness (חולי) or wounds (מכה),[62] [and vice-versa to describe redemption and deliverance] as medicine (ארוכה) and healing (מרפא).[63] [. . .] From all these passages it is plain that Scripture speaks of the exile, with its attendant misery and weariness, as a sickness (חולי), a wound (מכה), a breach (שבר), a stripe (חבורה); while redemption (גאולה), freedom (רווח), and deliverance (הצלה) are descried in the metaphor of healing (רפואה) or medicine (ארוכה). (Neubauer and Driver, 2:244-45 [modified])

Certainly Isaac with this reply has hardly weakened the objection of the Christians, because he has done no more than to show that it is lexicographically *possible* that Isaiah 53:4-5 refers to the exile or the suffering in the exile. This neither addresses nor answers the question of what reason and meaning the exile might have when interpreted this way, for example, whether Israel's sufferings in exile can be interpreted as vicarious. Nevertheless Isaac returns to this in another place (see below III.3).

In keeping with this explanation, according to which Isaiah 53 speaks not of the Servant absolutely but of the historically concrete Servant Israel suffering in exile,[64] Isaac then interprets or rather historicizes the statements of suffering

---

61. Specifically punishment for "the murder of the Messiah and of God" (Neubauer and Driver, 2:246). See below, pp. 438-39.

62. At this point several verses are quoted in full: Isa. 1:5-6; 30:26; Hos. 6:1; Lam. 2:13; Jer. 10:19, 20; 30:12, 17 (abbreviated in Neubauer and Driver, 2:244-45; more fully in ed. Deutsch, 147-48). The main reference for the topic discussed here is the juxtaposition of Jer. 30:17//30:18.

63. The Scriptures quoted here include Jer. 30:18-19; 33:6, 7-8 (for the full text see ed. Deutsch, 148). Significantly for Isaac, these verses (esp. Jer. 33:6) confirm that the image of healing refers to recovery from the exile.

64. Because of this concrete identification of the Servant as the nation, N. Hutterer in his translation of Rashi, Ibn Ezra, and Kimchi on Isaiah 53 (see n. 41) consistently writes the neuter third singular pronoun "it" (= the whole people, the Servant Israel) rather than the masculine "he" (= an individual Servant). [(Tr.) This device, adopted consistently by Hutterer, is also occasionally used by Neubauer and Driver for the collective interpretation of the Servant. Compare, for example, the respective renderings of Rashi on Isa. 53:2, where Rashi has the Gentile nations speaking: "'*Es* war (ursprünglich) ohne Gestalt und Schöne, daß wir *es* hätten ansehen mögen und ohne Aussehen, daß wir Gefallen an *ihm* hätten' [Jes 53,2]: da wir *es* anfangs ohne Aussehen sahen, wie konnten wir Gefallen an *ihm* finden?" (Hutterer, *Die mittelalterlichen jüd. Kommentare* 15, reprinted in Schreiner, "Sepher Chizzuq Emunah," 184, italics added). Similarly

in verses 7ff., in which he recognizes a presentation of actual events, as Ibn Ezra, David Kimchi, and others had already done before him. By the "we" who speak in 53:1-10, making their confession of guilt (to which we return in section III.2), Isaac understands the nations of the world in whose midst Israel lived and still lives in exile, among whom Israel suffered and still suffers. In this historicizing sense he then interprets 53:7-9, which is part of the confession of guilt by the nations of the world, as follows:

> *He was oppressed, and he was afflicted, yet he did not open his mouth; like a lamb that is led to the slaughter, and like a sheep that before its shearers is silent, so he did not open his mouth* (Isa. 53:7). [The Gentiles say of Israel]:
> "When he was under our power in exile,[65] he was increasingly 'oppressed'[66] and 'afflicted'; we 'oppressed' him for money, exacting from him 'tribute' (מנדה), 'poll-tax' (בלו),[67] and 'way-toll' (הלך)[68] (Ezra 4:13), and other [taxes],[69] and much money in addition by every description of fraudulent device.[70] We 'afflicted' his person with diverse

---

Neubauer and Driver: "From the first *it* [sc. this people] had no form and no comeliness, and when we saw *it* without any comeliness how could we desire *it!*" (2:37, italics modified).

65. For this reason the Jews also call the exile שעבוד מלכויות, "slavery under the rule of the nations," whereas Christians refer to it as *servitus Judaeorum*; see Yerushalmi, "Exil," 26-27.

66. Ibn Ezra explains the נגש in Isa. 53:7 as a niphal form (Neubauer and Driver, 1:45/ 2:46).

67. A "poll-tax" (Ezra 4:13 NJPS) in the amount of one Polish Gulden per person — Isaac here uses the Aramaic term בלו (cf. Heb. גלגולת, Polish *poglówne*) — was levied by the Polish treasury since 1549.

68. The "way-toll" (NRSV "toll"; NJPS "land-tax"; Aramaic הלך in Ezra 4:13; Polish *kozubalec*) was to be paid by Jews, for example, when they went past a Christian school or another public building.

69. On the many and diverse taxes upon the Jews in Poland and Lithuania, which were to be paid partly to the treasury, partly also to the institutions of Jewish self-government (especially to the *Kahal*, the executive committee of the community), see Balaban, *Historja i literatura żydowska*, 3:203-4; M. S. Lew, *The Jews in Poland: Their Political, Economic, Social, and Communal Life in the Sixteenth Century as Reflected in the Works of Rabbi Moses Isserles* (1944), 90-92; Baron, *Social and Religious History*, 288-90 with 452 nn. 88-89.

70. In his detailed comments on Isa. 53:9, "although he had done no violence, and there was no deceit in his mouth," including a reference to Ps. 44:22 (MT 44:23), "Because of you we are being killed all day long," Isaac is even more clear: "We were incessantly framing fraudulent devices against him to put him to death, just as the wicked are put to death for their crimes: similarly we were in the habit of murdering 'the rich' (Isa. 53:9) by various contrivances for the sake of his riches; and even the poor Israelite was invested by us with the reputation of being rich, and tortured cruelly for the purpose of forcing him to disclose where his money was secreted. And all this occurred 'although he had done no violence'; he was not put to death for any wickedness that he had committed, but simply in order that we might secure his wealth; and also be-

wounds:[71] yet, in spite of all this, 'he did not open his mouth' to cry out or complain of what we did to him, but endured everything 'like a lamb' that cries not while being 'led to the slaughter,'[72] and 'like a sheep which, while men are shearing it,[73] is silent and dumb,' and which does not even quiver like a ram by reason of its weakness (for in every species the female is weaker than the male).[74] In the same manner, Israel was weak and prostrate in captivity; and therefore 'he did not open his mouth,' because there was no one to deliver him out of our hands,[75] as the psalmist says, 'You give us as sheep to be eaten' (Ps. 44:12)."[76] (Neubauer and Driver, 2:252-53 [modified])

If the collective interpretation of the Servant *ipso facto* excludes an interpretation focusing on the person of the Messiah as an individual,[77] in Isaac's view it nevertheless does not exclude an interpretation focusing on the messianic age, the age of redemption for Israel. He therefore refers the pericope to this. In so doing he once again, without explicitly saying so, follows the example of David Kimchi, for whom the whole book of Deutero-Isaiah refers to the messianic age.[78]

---

cause he would not confess to our lying belief, nor by acknowledging it utter 'deceit in his mouth', at a time when a single word — though spoken in deceit, and though his heart might not be in accordance with the declaration of his lips — would have been sufficient to release him from any one of the varied forms of death to which we might have sentenced him" (ed. Deutsch, 159; Neubauer and Driver, 2:254).

71. Similarly David Kimchi explains his comments on Isa. 53:7, with reference to 2 Kings 23:35 and Deut. 15:15: "'He was pressed' for money (as in 2 Kings 23:35; Deut. 15:2) and 'he was afflicted' bodily, for his body was afflicted with wounds (stripes)" (Neubauer and Driver, 1:51/2:52 [modified]). Although an evaluation of these and similar statements from the perspective of social and legal history would be enlightening, it would far exceed the scope of this essay.

72. Here Isaac reads לשחוט instead of the MT's לטבח, "to the slaughter" (Isa. 53:7).

73. Here Isaac reads a finite verb for "shearing" instead of the MT's participle גזזיה, "shearers."

74. The same analogy is in David Kimchi on Isa. 53:7 (Neubauer and Driver, 1:51/2:53).

75. On this see Ibn Ezra on Isa. 53:7: "'He opened not his mouth.' There is no need to interpret these words, for every Jew in exile exemplifies their truth: in the hour of his affliction he never opens his mouth to speak, even though he alone is just amongst them all: for he has no care in this world except for the service of God; he knows no prince or dignitary who will stand before him in the breach when men rise up against him (cf. Ps. 106:23; 124:2)" (Neubauer and Driver, 1:45/2:46 [modified]).

76. After this follow citations of Ps. 44:23 and Jer. 50:17.

77. Despite the individual messianic interpretation of the Targum, which Isaac certainly knew.

78. See Kimchi's commentary on Isa. 40:1, a German translation of which is provided by Hutterer, *Die mittelalterlichen jüd. Kommentare,* 26 n. 2. [[(Tr.) Unfortunately, we are lacking a modern critical edition of Kimchi's Hebrew text, since Finkelstein's edition covers only Isaiah 1–

By directing his view into the future, the messianic age, Isaiah proclaims according to Isaac a word of comfort for Israel which is hard-pressed in every generation:

> The general design, then, of the prophecy contained in this *parashah* "See, my servant shall prosper, etc." is to confirm and encourage us in the assurance that although by our exiles we[79] are exceedingly depressed and brought down, even to the dust, there is still hope for us hereafter, that through the Lord's compassion on us we may again be "high and exalted," and that from the time of redemption onwards our position may rise until the nations of the world and even their kings, when they see the salvation of Israel and their elevation to the highest conceivable pitch of dignity and greatness, become astonished and awe-struck at the spectacle: for just as before "they were astonished" (Isa. 52:14)[80] at our depression in exile, when every nation on the face of the earth "looked down" upon us and "despised" us,[81] so they will then be astonished in like manner at our exaltation. (Neubauer and Driver, 2:245 [modified])

In his detailed exegesis of Isaiah 52:13-14 Isaac adds:

> יַשְׂכִּיל [in Isa. 52:13] signifies *to prosper* . . . the meaning being that Israel will prosper when he comes forth from the captivity of Edom and Ishmael,[82]

39: Louis Finkelstein, ed., *The Commentary of David Kimhi on Isaiah, Part I, Chapters 1–39*, Columbia University Oriental Studies 19 (1926).] Similarly Ibn Ezra thought that Isaiah 40 begins the message of comfort proclaiming future salvation from the present exile (German in Hutterer, *Die mittelalterlichen jüd. Kommentare*, 20); indeed, Ibn Ezra was the first to identify *Second Isaiah* as a book by a later prophet, distinct from the book of *First Isaiah*. It is therefore to him — and not to B. Duhm — that we owe the original discovery of the Servant Songs; cf. U. Simon, "Ibn Ezra between Medievalism and Modernism."

79. Because of his thoroughgoing identification of the Servant with Israel's suffering in the present exile, Isaac does not hesitate to change the "he" of the statements about suffering in Isa. 52:13–53:12 consistently into a "we" that includes him and his Jewish contemporaries.

80. For this expression "be astonished" (שָׁמֵם) in Isa. 52:14 Isaac refers to Ezek. 28:18 (Neubauer and Driver, 2:250), David Kimchi to Ezek. 3:15 (1:48/2:49). By contrast, Ibn Ezra connects שָׁמֵם with Lev. 26:32 (1:43/2:44).

81. Cf. Isa. 53:3.

82. The reference to Edom and Ishmael is also found in Ibn Ezra on Isa. 52:14 (Neubauer and Driver, 1:44/2:44) and David Kimchi on 52:14, who refers to Ibn Ezra (1:48/2:49). Neubauer and Driver identify Ishmael as a symbol for Muslims and Edom as a symbol for Christians (44 note *d*). On this popular typology see S. Zeitlin, "The Origin of the Term *Edom* for Rome and the Roman Church," *JQR* 60 (1969-70): 262-63. See further G. D. Cohen, "Esau as Symbol in Early Medieval Thought," in A. Altmann, ed., *Jewish Medieval and Renaissance Studies*, Studies and Texts 4 (1967), 19-48; B. Septimus, "'Better under Edom than under Ishmael': The History of a Saying" (Hebrew), *Zion* 47 (1982): 103-11; Maier, *Geschichte*, 140ff.

who are spoken of above as "the uncircumcised (ערל) and the unclean
(טמא)" (Isa. 52:1); from that time onward "he shall be exalted and lifted up,
and shall be very high." The idea of elevation is expressed in every form in
order to indicate that our future exaltation will be the highest possible or
imaginable even for the choicest of the human kind.[83] [. . .] "Just as many
were astonished at you" (52:14), because of your depression and the length of
your captivity, so that they said to one another, "For his countenance is
marred[84] beyond that of any other man, and his form more than the rest of
the children of men,". . . so will they then be astonished at the greatness of
our exaltation. (Neubauer and Driver, 2:249-50 [modified])

III.2. The Confession of the Nations

For Isaac the word of comfort to Israel, Isaiah 52:13–53:12, falls into two
parts: Whereas at the beginning (52:13-15) and the end (53:11-12) God speaks
about his Servant (Israel), so in the "we" of the intervening verses 1-10 the
many nations (גוים רבים) express themselves. The Servant Israel will let
them speak this way (cf. 52:15a) only when they experience the time of his
salvation and exaltation. Like David Kimchi before him,[85] so also Isaac,[86] in
contrast to Ibn Ezra,[87] explains the verb form יזה (hiphil of נזה) in Isaiah
52:15 with reference to Micah 2:6 as synonymous with יטיף (hiphil of נטף),
"let flow." This he understands as a metaphor for speech, a flow of words.
The subject of the causative יזה, "to make to speak," is the Servant. Isaac
therefore understands Isaiah 52:14-15 to mean: "Just as many were astonished

---

83. Isaac here says that the piling up of verbs in Isa. 52:13 has a superlative meaning (ed.
Deutsch, 154), as David Kimchi had already said (Neubauer and Driver, 1:48/2:49).

84. This term משחת (NRSV: "marred") in Isa. 53:14 is likewise taken as an adjective by
both Ibn Ezra (Neubauer and Driver, 1:44/2:44) and David Kimchi (1:48/2:49 bottom, though
mistakenly numbered as a comment on Isa. 53:15). [[(Tr.) On this hard-to-analyze form מָשְׁחַת
see *HALOT* 2:644.]]

85. See Kimchi's explanation of Isa. 52:15: "יזה has the sense of *speaking*, like הטיף, which
means both *to sprinkle* or *drop* (Judg. 5:4) and also *to speak* (Mic. 2:6)" (Neubauer and Driver,
1:48/2:50). Compare Isaac: "יזה has a causative force, and signifies *to make to speak*, from נטף,
Mic. 2:6" (Neubauer and Driver, 2:250).

86. Isaac once again follows David Kimchi without naming his source.

87. Ibn Ezra is very different, taking advantage of the possible translation of יזה in Isa.
52:13 as "*sprinkle* many nations" (cf. KJV; NASB; NIV): "As it was true that his countenance
was marred in the eyes of all who saw him, *so* [כן] will the time come for him to take vengeance of them and *sprinkle* [יזה] them, i.e., shed their blood" (Neubauer and Driver 1:44/
2:44).

at him,[88] . . . so will *he* now *cause* many nations *to speak* (יזה), and kings shall shut (יקפצו) their mouths because of him [in astonishment]."[89] In their astonishment at the great events of the messianic age, the time of Israel's redemption and restoration which the nations will witness, they will make a confession, specifically a confession of guilt, to the Servant Israel for what they have done to him. It is this confession of guilt that Isaac sees in 53:1-10.[90]

> [The nations] will speak of him [the Servant Israel] continually, saying to one another:
>
> "Lo, now we perceive clearly[91] that 'all we like the sheep[92] without a shepherd[93] have gone astray, we have turned each after his own way' (53:6), and 'Our fathers have inherited nothing but lies, worthless things in which there is no profit' (Jer. 16:19),[94] neither is there any divine law, or true religion, in any nation of the world except in Israel.[95] From this we see further

88. Isaac's text of Isa. 52:14 actually follows the MT reading עליך, "at you" (see Deutsch, 154 line 17; cf. line 20). However, his close linking of vv. 14 and 15 suggests that he understood the second person עליך of 52:14 in the light of the third person עליו (NRSV: "because of him") in the MT of 52:15 (cf. Deutsch, 1534 line 26), a form also attested in 52:14 by the Peshitta, Targum, and a few Hebrew manuscripts (cf. *BHS*) and mentioned already by Ibn Ezra (cf. Varo, *Los canticos del Siervo*, 93). According to Fischel, "Gottesknechtslieder," 68, the same change is found in the important Bible commentator R. Tanhum ben Yosef Ha-Yerushalmi (died 1291).

89. See the edition by Deutsch, 154 bottom (Neubauer and Driver 2:250 fail to reproduce Isaac's citation of Isa. 52:14-15). For the picture of mouths being shut Isaac refers to Job 5:16 and Mic. 7:16 (Neubauer and Driver mistakenly give the reference as Mic. 7:10). He thereby follows neither Ibn Ezra nor David Kimchi.

90. Once again this view is not without precedent. See Fischel, "Gottesknechtslieder," 69; R. Gradwohl, *Bibelauslegungen aus jüdischen Quellen*, vol. 4 (1989), 267ff.

91. So according to Rashi on Isa. 52:15: The MT reading התבוננו, "they will understand" (בִּין), means הסתכלו, "they will perceive clearly" or "observe" (cf. Neubauer and Driver, 1:37/2:38).

92. The fact that this expression "like *the* sheep" (כַּצֹאן) includes the definite article already drew the attention of David Kimchi: "Like *the* sheep, those viz. without a shepherd; he uses the article to point to the particular kind of sheep who would go astray, those viz. without a shepherd" (Neubauer and Driver, 1:51/2:52). However, Kimchi does not refer to Num. 27:17 as Isaac does (see the next note).

93. The inserted phrase "without a shepherd" is from Num. 27:17.

94. Jeremiah 16:19 is also cited at this point by Ibn Ezra (Neubauer and Driver, 1:45/2:46) and David Kimchi (Neubauer and Driver, 1:50/2:51).

95. This statement may also be traced back to *Sifre* 32 on Deut. 6:5 (trans. R. Hammer, *Sifre: A Tannaitic Commentary on the Book of Deuteronomy*, YJS 24 [1986], 59-62). According to Y. H. Yerushalmi ("Sephardisches Judentum zwischen Kreuz und Halbmond," in idem, *Ein Feld in Anatot*, 39-52, esp. 46), the "clear knowledge" or perception here attributed to the Gentiles is

that the chastisements and calamities borne by Israel during their captivity did not fall upon them for their own iniquity; it was we who for the multitude of our sins had rendered ourselves liable to endure them, but the sickness and the pain [cf. Isa. 53:4] which ought to have been ours came upon them, in order to make atonement (לכפר)[96] for our guilt in treating them as our slaves;[97] and, indeed, they were ever praying and interceding for our peace and the prosperity of our kingdoms (53:12); we however, on the contrary, thought that these troubles had fallen upon them because of the greatness of their iniquity, i.e., the murder of the Messiah and of God."

Thus far extend the words of the Gentiles. (Neubauer and Driver, 2:245-46 [modified])

What the Christians here "thought," according to Isaac, is naturally the idea which has been repeated ever since the time of Melito of Sardis (died 180)[98] that the κυριοκτονία or θεοκτονία, the "murder of the Messiah" or "murder of God," was the reason for the exile of the Jews. To be sure the Jewish tradition also knows the prayer מפני חטאינו גלינו מארצינו etc., "on account of our sins (plural) we were exiled from our land."[99] This found a place in the first comprehensive *siddur* (daily prayerbook)[100] by Gaon R. Saadia ben Joseph al-Fayumi (860-942),[101] in the Mussaf prayer for the three pilgrimage festivals. However, the hubris of the Christians is not only that they made of the plural *sins* the singular *sin*, but also that they pretend to know on account of *which particular sin* the exile occurred.[102]

---

also the scarlet thread that runs through all the apologetic literature since the Spanish Middle Ages. See also Varo, *Los canticos del Siervo*, 96 with nn. 152-53.

96. Isaac interprets this issue of atonement almost "Christologically" based on his understanding of Israel's election, according to which Israel is a collective priest (cf. Exod. 19:6) whose task includes making atonement for others' sins (see below, pp. 446-47). Similarly Rashi on Isa. 53:4: "The servant is punished ביסוריהן של ישראל = להיות כל האומות מתכפרות in order that by Israel's sufferings *atonement might be made* for all other nations" (Neubauer and Driver, 1:38/2:38 [modified]). See on this Joseph Albo (1380-1444), *Sefer ha-'Ikkarim* (Book of Principles) 4.13, Hebrew with English translation, ed. I. Husik (1946), 4/1:113ff.

97. See above, p. 434 with n. 65.

98. See on this H. Schreckenberg, *Die christlichen Adversus-Judaeos-Texte und ihr literarisches und historisches Umfeld,* 3 vols. (1st ed.: vol. 1, 1982; vol. 2, 1988; vol. 3, 1994 [2nd ed. of vol. 2, 1991; 4th ed. of vol. 1, 1999]), 1:201-4, passim; vol. 2, passim.

99. Text and translation in S. Singer, trans., *The Authorised Daily Prayer Book of the United Hebrew Congregations of the British Empire* (1st ed., 1890; 23rd ed., 1954), 234.

100. So Maier, *Geschichte,* 232.

101. סדור רב סעדיה גאון, *Siddur R. Saadja Gaon* (Hebrew and Judeo-Arabic), ed. I. Davidson, S. Assaf, and J. Joel, 5th ed. (1985), 151. On R. Saadia Gaon see Maier, *Geschichte,* 254-57 (literature); *EncJud* 14:543-55.

102. See on this Yerushalmi, "Exil," 26.

Nevertheless, it is a remarkable realization that Isaac has the nations express in their confession. It represents no less than the attempt to trace the meaning, or rather the mystery, of the history of Israel in exile.[103] Isaac develops the beginnings of a *theology of exile* which deserves attention. But before we examine this we should look at the individual exegetical comments that explain the "we" speech in more detail. For example, on Isaiah 53:1-3 Isaac writes:

> *Who has believed what we have heard? And to whom has the arm of the Lord been revealed?* (Isa. 53:1). The interpretation: When the Gentiles behold the prosperity of Israel they will say:
>
> "'Who among us believed the report which we heard' of him [the Servant Israel] from the prophets? Yet now we are seeing with our own eyes more than we then heard.[104] And even what we heard we did not believe, how, namely, 'the arm of the Lord' would be 'revealed' upon him, because he [the Servant Israel] seemed in our sight to be insignificant and despised."
>
> *For he grew up before him like a young plant, and like a root out of dry ground; he had no form or majesty that we should look at him, nothing in his appearance that we should desire him* (Isa. 53:2). The interpretation [of the Gentiles continues]:
>
> "But it is not to be wondered at, if we failed to believe: the ascent [of the Servant Israel] to the elevation he now holds was not accomplished by a natural process; but in a marvelous and miraculous manner, like the growth of a sucker out of 'a root in dry ground.'[105] While he was in captivity, there was no one who conceived the possibility of his ever emerging from it: to the eye of human intelligence it seemed impracticable, because 'he had no form or majesty' and no beauty of face, but was 'marred and disfigured beyond all other men' (cf. 52:14).[106] Therefore we had no desiring or

---

103. Cf. on this N. Berdjajev, *Der Sinn der Geschichte* (1925), ch. 5, "Das Geschick der Juden" (128-53), although some statements contain unfortunate expressions that are problematic from today's standpoint.

104. The same in Rashi (Neubauer and Driver, 1:38/2:37), Ibn Ezra (1:44/2:44), and David Kimchi (1:49/2:50).

105. Here too Isaac finds himself in agreement with Ibn Ezra (Neubauer and Driver, 1:44/2:44-45) and David Kimchi (1:49/2:50), for whom the end of the exile is nothing less than a miracle.

106. At another point, in his interpretation of Isa. 52:14b, Isaac points out that "it is a custom of the Gentiles, when they see a man very much disfigured, to say, אדם זה מכוער כיהודי, This man is as ugly as a Jew" (ed. Deutsch, 154; Neubauer and Driver, 2:250). Similar figures of speech are cited at this point by Ibn Ezra (Neubauer and Driver, 2:44) and David Kimchi (Neubauer and Driver, 2:49).

longing to 'look at him,' but 'despised him' (53:3) and held him in abhorrence."

He was despised and rejected by others; a man of suffering and acquainted
with infirmity; and as one from whom others hide their faces he was despised,
and we held him of no account (Isa. 53:3). The interpretation [of the Gentiles
continues]:

"How indeed could we have desired him, when he was the most despised
and insignificant of men? For it was his lot to be enduring continually every
mental suffering and every bodily wrong — such were the chastisements of
the captivity, here spoken of metaphorically as 'suffering' and 'infirmity.' In
his humiliation and depression we would not look at him, but spurned and
depreciated him, till we would esteem him for nought." (Neubauer and
Driver, 2:250-51 [modified])

Following this description of Israel's situation, which is informative despite its indefiniteness, comes the first insight that is distinguished by a remarkably self-critical tone. In his interpretation of Isaiah 53:3-4 Isaac writes:

The nations continue declaring their conviction:
"Since we now have it confirmed by ocular proof that the truth is with
Israel, and that 'all we like sheep have gone astray' (53:6), it follows that the
calamities in which the chastisements of exile consisted did not come upon
him for his own iniquity, but that the infirmities and diseases (under which
image they are here represented), which ought in justice to have fallen upon
us, fell instead upon him [cf. 'Surely he has borne our infirmities and carried our diseases,' 53:4a]. Although 'we accounted him stricken, struck
down, and afflicted by God' (53:4b)[107] for his [Israel's] unbounded spirit of
rebellion against God (להפלגת מריו באלוהים), it did not happen to Israel
thus. Rather, '[he was wounded][108] for our transgressions, crushed for our
iniquities,' not for his own iniquities and transgressions. Thus says the
Scripture: 'he was wounded for our transgressions, crushed for our iniquities, etc.' (53:5a)."

"And the meaning of the words מוסר שלומנו עליו ('the chastisement of
our peace was upon him,' 53:5b) is: The present world is a world of alteration and change, and its goodness is not perfect or complete; it has no

---

107. See above, p. 435.

108. Ibn Ezra (Neubauer and Driver, 1:45/2:45) identifies מחולל in Isa. 53:5 as the polal
participle of חלל (so also *HALOT* 1:320, s.v. חלל II, although in two manuscripts of Ibn Ezra's
commentary the form is derived from חיל; see on this Varo, *Los canticos del Siervo*, 95 n. 146). By
contrast Isaac (ed. Deutsch 156; Neubauer and Driver, 2:251) as well as David Kimchi (Neubauer
and Driver, 1:50/2:52) explain it as the polal participle (i.e., passive of the polel) of the root חיל.

peace that is free from suffering, no prosperity unruffled by vexations and strife, no joy untouched by sorrow and sighing; all its happiness and all its delights are commingled with misfortune and grief. So we, they say, saw that while the peace fell to our lot, the chastisement attending it fell upon him: he received bruises and stripes, i.e., the penalties of exile, and we received medicine and healing — in other words, prosperity and power." (Neubauer and Driver, 2:251-52 [modified])

Strikingly, Isaac passes over the question normally dealt with by the classical commentaries at this point of whether Israel's vicarious suffering occurred both *through* the sins of the nations and *for* these sins in the sense of Lamentations 5:7 ("Our fathers sinned; they are no more, and we bear their iniquities").[109]

---

109. That this question is not easy to answer is attested by David Kimchi: "What, then, is the meaning of *carrying our sicknesses* etc. [in Isa. 53:4]? What Jeremiah says in his Lamentations, 'Our fathers sinned and are not, and we bear their iniquities' (Lam. 5:7), is not parallel; this, firstly, resembles rather Exod. 20:5, *visiting the iniquity of the fathers upon the children*, i.e., when the children still continue to adhere to the works of their fathers, according to the addition *as regards them that hate me . . .* ; and, secondly, Jeremiah is speaking in the style of mourners, whose words, springing out of the midst of pain and distress, are not regulated by measure and weight. Here the phrases put into the mouth of the Gentiles, such as 'he hath carried our sickness' etc., are merely the expression of their own thoughts; it is not asserted that Israel actually bore the iniquity of the Gentiles, but the latter only imagine it to be the case when they see, at the time of Deliverance, that the faith which Israel adhered to was the true one, while that which they themselves had adhered to was the false; accordingly they say, 'Our fathers have inherited nothing but falsehood' (Jer. 16:19). Here, then, they ask, What can be the cause of the pains endured by Israel in captivity? They cannot be attributed to their own iniquity, for *they* adhered to the truth, whereas *we* who enjoyed peace and tranquillity, quietude and security, were adhering to falsehood; it follows, therefore, that the sickness and pain which ought to have fallen upon us has fallen upon them, and they are our ransom (כופר) and the price of our atonement (כפרה)" (Neubauer and Driver, 1:50/2:51-52).

Regarding the first argument, the early rabbinic interpretations of Exod. 20:5 frequently discussed how its assertion that God "visits the iniquity of the fathers on the children to the third and the fourth generations of those who hate me" could be brought into agreement with Deut. 24:16 (cf. similarly Jer. 31:30; Ezek. 18:20), which says that "Fathers shall not be put to death for their sons, nor shall sons be put to death for their fathers; everyone shall be put to death for his own sin." The results of these exegetical discussions are shown in the Palestinian Targumim *Neofiti 1, Onqelos,* and *Pseudo-Jonathan,* which add an insertion to show that Exod. 20:5 applies only *"when the so(n)s continue in sin after their fathers" (Tg. Neof.)* or "when the children follow their *fathers in sinning" (Tg. Onq.); Pseudo-Jonathan* lacks this insertion but agrees with the others in limiting vengeance to "the *rebellious* sons." See M. McNamara, *The Aramaic Bible: Targum Neofiti 1: Exodus,* trans. M. McNamara, notes R. Hayward, bound with *Targum Pseudo-Jonathan: Exodus,* trans. M. Maher, ArBib 2 (1994), 85 with n. 5 *(Tg. Neof.),* 218

The parallelism of מוּסַר שְׁלוֹמֵנוּ עָלָיו, "the chastisement of our peace was upon him," to וּבַחֲבֻרָתוֹ נִרְפָּא לָנוּ[110], "and by his bruises/stripes we are healed" (53:5b end), leads Isaac to different interpretive possibilities on account of the ambiguity of the consonantal text of וּבַחֲבֻרָתוֹ. This in turn leads to a further thought:

> The meaning of בחברתו [נרפא לנו] is to be derived from פצע וחבורה, "bruises and sores" (Isa. 1:6), expect that the former [חבורה] is a qal form, while the latter [חבורה, MT חַבּוּרָה] is a dagesh form.[111] It is possible, however, to derive [בחברתו] from חבר with the sense appertaining to the word in Hos. 4:17, חבור עצבים אפרים ("Ephraim is *joined* to idols"). חברתו will then be a substantive with a suffix of the third person, formed like גבורתו. And the meaning will be that by being in one *union* and fellowship (חבורה)[112] with us, he used to intercede with God for our adversities, and God used to hear his prayer and send forth healing for our wounds. (Neubauer and Driver, 2:252 [modified])

This raises the question of the Servant as mediator, which is referred to in greater detail in the last part of the confession of the nations. The mediatorial function of the Servant Israel is not at all exhausted by Israel's vicarious suffering. Next to the passive element of vicariousness in suffering enters an active element: the central message of the whole fourth Servant Song for Isaac depends on the connection of both elements. But first we must look at Isaac's interpretation of 53:6, which reminds him of the compensation[113] coming to the Servant

---

with n. 7 (*Tg. Ps.-J.*); *Targum Onqelos to Exodus*, trans. B. Grossfeld, ArBib 7 (1988), 54 with 55 n. 2. The discussion is summarized in *b. Ber.* 7a (see further Grossfeld). David Kimchi shares this view.

110. For the meaning of נרפא in Isa. 53:5 Isaac refers to Exod. 15:26 (Neubauer and Driver, 2:252).

111. The same in David Kimchi (Neubauer and Driver, 1:51/2:52).

112. Because the MT of Isa. 53:5b is written defectively, בחברתו, it would be possible instead of the MT's *ba-havurato* (בַחֲבֻרָתוֹ) to read *be-hevrato*. The latter would clearly be translated, "by (in) his fellowship." Perhaps the ambivalence that Isaac mentions was originally intended in the Bible text. If so, there would be an ambivalence here comparable to the ambivalence of the suffixed forms "*our* infirmities" and "*our* diseases" in v. 4, which includes both the infirmity etc. that we caused him and the infirmity we deserve.

113. This idea of compensation in the messianic age also belongs to the repertoire of the interpretations that found literary expression in the Targum to the Prophets and later references to it; see on this von Mutius, *Zwangsdisputation*, 98ff.; Sarachek, *Doctrine of the Messiah*, passim; G. Scholem, "Zum Verständnis der messianischen Idee im Judentum," in idem, *Judaica*, vol. 1, 2nd ed. (1968), 7-74, esp. 50ff. See also Baron, *Social and Religious History*, 5:138-208 with 353-87, esp. 184ff. with 375ff. nn. 46-53.

Israel in the messianic age and forms a transition to the second aspect of the Servant's mediatorial function. Regarding 53:6 Isaac says:

> In this verse the Gentiles all confess their iniquity, which is at last revealed before the sun, saying:
>
> "Now we are sure that the truth has been all along with Israel and not with us; for 'all we like sheep without a shepherd have gone astray, we have turned each after his own way,' i.e., each of our nations has turned to its own gods,[114] but now we know that these were no gods, as it is written, 'to you shall the nations come from the ends of the earth and say: Our fathers have inherited nothing but lies, worthless things in which there is no profit' (Jer. 16:19).[115] And immediately afterwards: 'Can man make gods for himself? Yet they are not gods!' (Jer. 16:20). For this we would have been liable to an infinite penalty, had not the Almighty 'caused the penalty of us all to meet upon him.' Accordingly until now he has performed our service for us, carried our yoke, and borne our pains; but henceforth it is we who, voluntarily and heartily, shall have to do work for him, as it is written, 'And strangers will stand and pasture your flocks' (Isa. 61:5)."[116] (Neubauer and Driver, 2:252 [modified])

III.3. The Reason and Meaning of Suffering

All this raises the difficult question of the reason and meaning of the history summarized and interpreted in the nations' confession, and therefore the question of the reason and meaning of suffering. Isaac does not shy away from attempting to answer this difficult question. On the contrary his answer, grounded in the medieval doctrine of general and special (individual) providence,[117] is unmistakable. Isaac begins his answer with an appeal to the doctrine of general providence, especially as developed by Judah ben Samuel ha-Levi (1075-1141)[118] in his *Sefer ha-Kuzari* 2.44.[119] Isaac writes:

---

114. Nevertheless, according to Mic. 4:5 (cf. Isa. 2:5) this would not be offensive.

115. The same in Ibn Ezra on Isa. 53:6 (Neubauer and Driver, 1:45/2:46).

116. Immediately after this Isaac quotes Isa. 49:23.

117. See on this I. Husik, *A History of Medieval Jewish Philosophy*, 3rd ed. (1969), 290ff., 346ff.; L. Jacobs, *Principles of Jewish Faith* (1964), 320ff.; Maier, *Geschichte*, 370-76.

118. On Judah ha-Levi's person and work see Maier, *Geschichte*, 270-73; EncJud 10:355-66.

119. On this see J. Guttmann, *Die Philosophie des Judentums* (1985), 146f.; C. Sirat, *A History of Jewish Philosophy in the Middle Ages*, 2nd ed. (1990), 116f.

To this it may be added that the nations of the world, being as insignificant in the eyes of the creator as animals, do not have their sins visited upon them from heaven by [special] providence, except when they either do harm to Israel while engaged in executing God's pleasure, or perpetrate some great enormity (חמס גדול), such as was committed by the generation of the flood[120] or by Sodom and Gomorrah: in such cases the Almighty visits their iniquity and consumes them utterly.[121] Israel, however, is treated differently: in his love for us, God demands the penalty for our offences in this life little by little, by means of exiles and partial punishments, without making a full end of us, as he assures us by the mouth of his prophets. . . .[122] (Neubauer and Driver, 2:246 [modified])

Judah ha-Levi wrote similarly in *Kuzari* 2.44 (trans. Hirschfeld):[123]

He forgives the sins of his people, causing the first of them to vanish first. He does not allow our sins to become overwhelming, or they would destroy us completely by their multitude. Thus he says: "For the iniquity of the Amorites is not yet full" (Gen. 15:16). He left them alone till the ailment of their sins had become fatal.[124]

---

120. Gen. 6:5ff.

121. Gen. 18:20-21; 19:23-29. Cf. Nah. 3:19 (also 2:12-13; 3:1); Jonah 1:2 (also 3:2; 4:8). On the biblical-theological implications of this topic see H. M. Orlinsky, "Nationalism-Universalism and Internationalism in Ancient Israel," in H. T. Frank and W. L. Reed, eds., *Translating and Understanding the Old Testament: Essays in Honor of Herbert Gordon May* (1970), 206-36.

122. Here follow quotations of Jer. 30:11; Amos 3:2; and Prov. 3:12. This idea of dialectical providence is also found in the work of Baḥya ben Asher ben Ḥlava, d. 1340 (Library of Congress), *Kad ha-Kemaḥ*, a critical edition of which is available in כתבי רבינו בחיי = *Kitve Rabenu Baḥya*, ed. C. B. Chavel (1st ed., 1969; 6th ed., 1991), 15-451; see s.v. השגחה, pp. 135-57, esp. 136ff. See also the English translation, Baḥya (or Bachya) ben Asher, *Encyclopedia of Torah Thoughts*, trans. C. B. Chavel (1980), 182-204, esp. 183ff. (for more on the author, see Chavel's preface, ix-xiv). Such narrow particularism is countered already by the book of Jonah; see S. Schreiner, "Das Buch Jona: Ein kritisches Resümee der Geschichte Israels," in *Theologische Versuche* 9, ed. J. Rogge and G. Schille (1977), 37-45.

123. Translation of the original Judeo-Arabic of *The Kuzari* 2.44 by Hartwig Hirschfeld, *Kitab al Khazari: The Kuzari: An Argument for the Faith of Israel* (1905; reprinted 1964), 110. An English translation of Judah ibn Tibon's Hebrew version of 1167 (written shortly after the Arabic version) is available in N. Daniel Korobkin, *The Kuzari: In Defense of the Despised Faith* (1998), 92. The Arabic and Hebrew texts are available in Judah ha-Levi, *Das Buch Al-Chazari*, ed. H. Hirschfeld (1887; reprinted 1970), 106-7.

124. This thought already occurs in 2 Macc. 6:13, 15; similarly R. Abahu in *b. Abodah Zarah* 4a, with reference to Amos 3:2. Cf. on this Rashi on Exod. 32:13 in *Torat Hayim: Sefer Shemot II*, ed. M. L. Katzenellenbogen (1988), 192, and Joseph Albo, *Sefer ha-'Ikkarim* 4.38, ed. I. Husik (see n.96) 4/2:377-78.

According to Isaac the saying "the Lord reproves the one he loves" (Prov. 3:12) applies to Israel, and Israel alone; it is laid upon Israel to suffer for its own sins and vicariously for the sins of the nations, as in Isa. 53:4. This results from Isaac's understanding of Israel's election[125] and from the place Israel occupies among the nations because of its election. But election as Isaac understands it includes this "reproof," as Judah ha-Levi had already formulated it in *Sefer ha-Kuzari* 2.44:

> Now we are burdened by them [sc. the infirmities and diseases of Isa. 53:4], whilst the whole world enjoys rest and prosperity. The trials which meet us are meant to prove our faith, to cleanse us completely, and to remove all taint from us. If we are good the Divine Influence is with us in this world. (trans. Hirschfeld)

But this is not the only view that Isaac shares with Judah ha-Levi; he seems also to have borrowed from ha-Levi (*Kuzari* 2.34-45)[126] both the pictorial language and the Scripture proofs[127] used to describe the place of Israel among the nations. Once again without disclosing his source, Isaac quotes Judah ha-Levi almost verbatim:

> The reason for this is that Israel is the choicest of human kind, just as the heart is the choicest organ in the body; when, therefore, they are in exile in the midst of the nations, like the heart in the midst of the other organs, they bear all the calamities which fall upon the Gentiles in whose midst they are, exactly as the heart bears the bitterness and anguish of all the body in the centre of which it resides. (Neubauer and Driver, 2:246)[128]

As the heart of humanity Israel must live in the midst of the world of the nations in exile, for only thus can it fulfill its mission to the world. And just as the heart's functions are not limited to bearing suffering but include the heart's effect upon the larger organism to make the organism survive, so in Isaac's view the exile is not only a passion story but a task, since election does not imply only patience or suffering for others but includes active service for others. Such is the thought that Isaac derives from Exodus 19:5-6 ("a kingdom of priests") and Isaiah 61:6 ("you shall be called priests of the Lord"):

125. With reference to Ps. 135:4; Deut. 32:9 (Neubauer and Driver, 2:248).

126. For texts and translations see n. 123: Arabic and Hebrew in Hirschfeld, *Das Buch Al-Chazari*, 102-7; English in Hirschfeld, *Kitab al Khazari*, 107-11, and in Korobkin, *The Kuzari*, 89-93.

127. Ps. 106:35-36; Amos 3:2; Prov. 14:10.

128. The Scripture proofs are Ps. 106:35-36 and Prov. 14:10.

Scripture thus addresses the whole Israelite nation by the title of "priests," in order to teach us that as the priests and Levites used to give the people instruction in the law and the commandments — as it is written, "They teach Jacob your ordinances, and Israel your law" (Deut. 33:10) — so Israel will teach and instruct the nations among whom they are dispersed in the words of the living God; as it is written, "Declare his glory among the nations, his marvelous works among all the peoples" (Ps. 96:3).[129] . . . And as the Levites and priests were supported by the offerings and tithes of the Israelites, so will the people of Israel be supported in the future by the gifts of the Gentiles, in recognition of the services done to them while in exile, and as a reward for their instructions.[130] (Neubauer and Driver, 2:247 [modified])

That Israel despite all its sufferings in the exile nevertheless has accepted and fulfilled its vicarious service for the nations is a fact that Isaac finds expressed symbolically in a liturgical act that he explains in his exposition of the verse "and he made intercession for the transgressors" (Isa. 53:12):

He [the Servant Israel] used to pray to God on behalf of the Gentile transgressors: although they caused him the greatest suffering, he nevertheless interceded and supplicated for their peace and the prosperity of their kingdoms, entreating the Almighty to give the rain of their land in its season, as the inspired prophet enjoins, "But seek the welfare of the city where I have sent you into exile, and pray to the Lord on its behalf" (Jer. 29:7); and our Rabbis, "Pray for the peace of the ruling power";[131] and as we Jews[132] repeat continually in our prayers,[133] "O our God, that art in heaven, give life and peace to the King our master; O our God, that art in heaven, give peace in the earth; O our God, that art in heaven, give peace in the kingdom; O our God, that art in heaven, give dew and rain for a blessing in due season upon the earth; O our God, that art in heaven, give seed to the sower and bread to

---

129. Ps. 105:1 is added as a further Scripture proof. Usually Isa. 42:6 and 49:6 supply the key for this understanding; according to David Kimchi, Israel is almost indispensable for the existence of the world (see on this Fischel, "Gottesknechtslieder," 69).

130. As Scripture proofs Isa. 61:6; Gen. 22:18; 28:14 are cited. Isaac discusses this in more detail in ch. 13 (ed. Deutsch, 97-99).

131. Rabbi Hanina in *m.* ʾ*Abot* 3:2 (trans. Danby, 450); cf. *b.* ʿ*Abodah Zarah* 4a.

132. The fact that Isaac as a Karaite here joins with the Rabbanite liturgical tradition deserves attention.

133. Cf. I. Elbogen, *Der jüdische Gottesdienst in seiner geschichtlichen Entwicklung*, 3rd ed. (1931; reprinted 1967), 222-23 = ET, *Jewish Liturgy: A Comprehensive History*, trans. R. P. Scheindlin (1993), 178-79; A. Millgram, *Jewish Worship* (1971), 189-91.

the eater," as it is laid down in the Order of Prayer according to both the Spanish (Sephardic), and many other uses.[134] (Neubauer and Driver, 2:256-57)

Israel is the teacher of the nations who goes before them and shows them the way (with reference to Zech. 8:23; Num. 10:32; Jer. 35:19; Isa. 66:22); it is therefore exposed to more dangers and threats than the other nations. Isaiah 53:5 (cf. "wounded," "bruises," etc.) says the same thing according to Isaac: "Various vexations and accidents of the road will befall the leaders traveling in the front, especially in a host marching to battle, when those in the vanguard are exposed to wounds and blows and bruises" (Neubauer and Driver, 2:248-49 [modified]). Nevertheless — and this is the sense of Isaiah 53:12 — "when they defeat their enemies and divide the spoil, then those who follow after them have a share in the booty without having suffered anything," albeit with the limitation that "as those who advance first to the battle receive more wounds than those who come after them, so they also obtain a larger amount of the spoil" (Neubauer and Driver, 2:249). Applied to the history of Israel, it appears that compensation for the injuries Israel suffered in this world will follow only in the messianic age. Isaac derives this from Isaiah 51:22; 52:1ff.; and 54:1ff., 9-10, and therefore from the *inclusio* of our pericope, which once again confirms for him the seventh exegetical rule of Hillel. He therefore concludes his overall interpretation of Isaiah 53 with a citation of Isaiah 54:9-10:

> This is like the days of Noah to me: Just as I swore that the waters of Noah would never again go over the earth, so I have sworn that I will not be angry with you and will not rebuke you. For the mountains may depart and the hills be removed, but my steadfast love shall not depart from you, and my covenant of peace shall not be removed, says the Lord, who has compassion on you. (Isa. 54:9-10 NRSV; cf. Neubauer and Driver, 2:249)

3. Conclusion

If we ask in conclusion what makes Isaac ben Abraham's interpretation of the fourth Servant Song in his *Sefer Hizzuk Emunah* important and interesting (as detailed in our introduction), then three observations must be made:

First and foremost we should appreciate the contribution Isaac's work makes to the history of interpretation of Isaiah 52:13–53:12. Although he was a

---

134. Hence in addition to the Sephardic tradition, the Ashkenazic tradition also knows of the Prayer for the Fatherland (cf. Singer, *Authorised Daily Prayer Book,* 153).

Karaite, he by no means lived in or knew only the Karaite tradition. On the contrary, his book shows, page after page, that he was obviously very familiar with and skilled in the use of the classical Rabbanite Bible commentaries, the *Mikraot Gedolot.* Over long stretches, his interpretation follows the classical Rabbanite exegesis seamlessly. Yet despite his dependence on other commentaries he also had his own thing to say and knew how to formulate it persuasively in individual exegetical comments. Of no less importance are his theological thoughts, his beginnings of a theology of the exile, developed in an effort to make sense of Jewish existence in exile, which would repay closer study. These theological thoughts are all the more remarkable because Isaac, a Karaite, was able to combine in them both Rabbanite and Karaite traditions.

Second, Isaac's book is of special worth because of the context from which it grew. Coming out of the immediate experience of and participation in Jewish-Christian religious dialogue, Isaac's interpretation documents at the same time the level of these discussions as carried out in the second half of the sixteenth century in Poland-Lithuania between representatives of very different Christian and Jewish faith traditions. What is presented here is not simply a polemical exchange; it is rather an intensive debate with the other tradition at a level that earns respect, especially on account of the impressive knowledge on which the discussion rests. As is mentioned in our introduction and as is evident throughout his book, Isaac also knew the Christian tradition and its exegesis very well and wrote from this knowledge. The questions and problems discussed at that time, 400 years ago, by Jews and Christians of the most diverse orientations have basically remained questions and problems until today — questions which now as then are on the agenda of Jewish-Christian or Christian-Jewish religious dialogue.

Finally, Isaac's book deserves attention as a historical document from the end of the post-Reformation period. It testifies at least indirectly to the tolerance and the intellectual liberality of his time, which despite all the social and legal discrimination against the Jews, about which Isaac was by no means silent, nevertheless facilitated religious discussions of the type in which Isaac himself participated.[135]

135. I would like to thank my research assistant Roland Deines for the various suggestions and critical remarks which he contributed to the German version of this essay.

APPENDIX:

Rashi, Ibn Ezra, and Kimchi on Isaiah 53

As mentioned above on p. 426, we reprint here the translations from Neubauer and Driver (*The Fifty-Third Chapter of Isaiah According to the Jewish Interpreters,* vol. 2) of the medieval Hebrew commentaries on Isaiah 53 by R. Solomon ben Isaac, better known as Rashi (1040-1105), R. Abraham ibn Ezra (1093-1168), and R. David Kimchi, also known as Radaq (1160-1235). (See respectively pp. 37-39, 43-48, 49-56 in Neubauer and Driver, vol. 2.) All three are frequently referred to in the notes. The translations are presented here in unmodified form, even though in the footnotes they have sometimes been modified to bring out the force of certain grammatical arguments (see also n. 41). The running pagination from Neubauer and Driver has been included below in square brackets.

1. Commentary of Rashi on Isaiah 53

LII. [p. 37] ¹³*Behold* in the latter days *my servant* Jacob, i.e. the righteous who are in him, *will prosper:* 14 *as many* peoples *were amazed* at you when they saw your depression, and said one to another, See how their form is dark and worn beyond that of other men, *so* marred, viz. as we see with our own eyes, 15 *so* now will his hand also be mighty, and Israel shall 'cast down the horns of the nations which have scattered them' (Zech. ii.4.), and *kings* shall *close their mouths* in amazement, for glory *which had not been told them* concerning any man will *they have seen in him and observed.*

LIII. ¹Had we, they will say to each other, had we heard from others what now we are beholding, *who would* ever *have believed it? upon whom has the arm of the Lord* ever *been revealed* as now in splendour and greatness? ²*Before* such greatness came upon it, this people was in deep depression, and sprang up out of itself like one of the suckers of a tree, or like a root out of the dry earth: from the first it had no form and no comeliness, *and* when *we saw it* without any comeliness *how could we desire it!* (נחמדהו as an exclamation.) ³*Most despised and forlornest of men.* This prophet speaks constantly of the whole people as one man, as xliv.1, 2, and above lii.13 (where ישכיל means *to prosper,* as

1 Sam. xviii.14). *And* as a result of their shame and depression they were *as* men *hiding* their *faces from us* — like a person stricken [with leprosy], who is afraid to look up, they had their faces bound up that we might not see them: [4]*but* — such is always the signification [p. 38] of אכז — *but* now we perceive that this was not merely a consequence of their own depression: Israel suffered in order that by his sufferings atonement might be made for all other nations: the sickness which ought to have fallen upon us was carried by him. *We* indeed *thought* that he had been hated of God: but it was not so; he was wounded for our transgressions, and bruised for our iniquities; [5]the *chastisement of the peace* that was for us fell *upon him;* he was chastised in order that the whole world might have peace. [6]*All we like sheep have gone astray:* it is now revealed how all the Gentiles have erred. *Yet the Lord* let himself be entreated by him (*asprier,* in French), and propitiated for the iniquity of us all, in that he refrained from destroying his world. [7]*He was oppressed* under oppressors and persecutors, *and answered,* viz. with words of treachery (*surparler,* in French): he endured, *but was silent,* like a sheep led to the slaughter which opens not its mouth, and like a lamb which before her shearers is dumb. The words ולא יפתח פיו belong to the 'sheep.' [8]The prophet here publishes the glad tidings of Israel's release, representing the Gentiles as announcing it in the latter days when they see him *taken from* the *confinement* in which he had been kept by their hands, and *from* the *judgment* or sentence which he had hitherto borne. *His generation,* i.e. the years of weariness and toil which had passed over him, *who could declare? for* from the first he had been *cut off* and exiled *from the land of the living,* i.e. the land of Israel; because *for the transgression of* his *people* the *stroke* of exile had fallen *upon* the just who were among *them.* [9]*He gave* himself over to whatever burial the wicked Gentiles might decree: for the Gentiles used to condemn the Israelites to be murdered and then buried like asses in the bellies of dogs. He agreed, then, to be buried according to the judgment of (את) the wicked, refusing to deny the living God; and according to the judgment of (את) the ruler he gave himself up to any form of death which had been decreed upon him, *because* he would not deny God by perpetrating violence and [p. 39] doing evil, like all the nations amongst whom he was a sojourner: *neither was there any deceit in his mouth,* sc. in consenting to the worship of idols as though they had been God. [10]*But the Holy One was pleased to bruise him,* and to lead him back into prosperity: so for this cause he *brought* him *into sickness.* He then says, I will see *whether his soul* is so consecrated and devoted to my holiness as to *return itself* as *a trespass-offering* for all his rebelliousness: if so I will then pay him his reward, and he shall *see seed,* etc. אשם, as in the history of the Philistines (1 Sam. vi.3), is the fine or satisfaction which a man gives to one against whom he has committed some offence (in Fr.

amende). [11]*Of the labour of his own soul* [i.e. of his own work] he ate and was satisfied: he did not plunder or rob other people: *by his knowledge my servant* ever meted out falthfull judgment to all that came to be tried before him, and, as happens with the righteous always (as it is said Num. xviii.1), *bare their iniquities.* [12]*Therefore,* i.e. because he did this, I will divide him an inheritance and a lot *among the great,* sc. with the early patriarchs, *because he poured out* (הערה as Gen. xxiv.20) *his soul to die, and was numbered with the transgressors,* i.e., endured punishment as though he had been a sinner or transgressor himself, *and* for the sake of others *bore the sin of many. And* in virtue of his sufferings — because through him the world received prosperity — he *interceded for the transgressors.*

2. Commentary of Abraham ibn Ezra on Isaiah 53

[p. 43] This Parashah is an extremely difficult one. Our opponents say that it refers to their God, supposing the *'servant'* to signify his body: this, however, is not possible, for the body cannot 'understand' even during a man's lifetime. Moreover, if their view be correct, what will be the meaning of 'seeing seed?' for he (their God) saw no son; or of 'prolonging days,' which is equally untrue of him; or of 'dividing spoil with the strong?' The proof of its proper meaning lies in the passages immediately before (lii.12, where 'you' signifies Israel), and immediately afterwards (liv.1, where 'the barren one' designates the congregation of Israel); similarly *my servant* means each individual belonging to Israel, and consequently God's servant, who is in exile. But many have explained it of the Messiah, because our Rabbis have said[1] that in the day when the Sanctuary was laid waste, the Messiah was born, and that he was bound in fetters (Jer. xl.1). Several of the verses, however, have then no meaning, for instance, 'despised and forlorn of men,' 'taken from prison and judgment,' 'made his grave with the wicked,' 'will see seed, and prolong days.' R. Saʿadyah interprets the whole Parashah of Jeremiah; and this interpretation is attractive. Jeremiah 'scattered[2] many nations' by the word of prophecy which was in his mouth (i.9f., cf. v. 14); he 'came up before him like a sucker,' for when he began to prophesy he was a youth (i.6); 'the Lord laid upon him the iniquity of us all,' and he 'carried the sin of many,' when he stood before God to speak good for them, and to turn away the wrath from them (xviii.20); he was 'led like a sheep to the slaughter,' as he says himself (xi.19); and he 'divided spoil with the

---

1. Midrash *Ekha,* i.16.
2. So Saʿadyah renders זוי: see Neubauer and Driver, 2:17.

mighty,' when the captain of the guard [p. 44] gave him 'victuals and a portion of meat' (xl.5). But in my judgment the Parashah is more intimately connected with the context, for what object can there be in mentioning Jeremiah when consolations addressed to Israel form the subject of the prophet's discourse both before and after? In fact, he is simply speaking of each one of God's servants who is in exile; or, which is more probable, 'my servant' may mean Israel as a whole, as in xli.8.

LII. [13]*My servant shall understand* that he will yet be high again. נשׂא is Nif'al. [14]שׁממו as Lev. xxvi.32: every one who sees the servant of God *will be astonished.* The word *many* alludes to the nations; and after כן the copula must be supplied — 'So marred *was* . . .' משׁחת is then an adjective; and in form תָּארוֹ[3] resembles רחבו. The phenomenon alluded to is well known: how many nations are there in the world who think that the features of the Jew are disfigured and unlike those of other men, and ask whether a Jew has a mouth or an eye! This is done, for example, in the countries of Ishma'el and 'Edom[4]. [15]כן יזה is the continuation of ירום ונשׂא: as it was true that his countenance was marred in the eyes of all who saw him, *so* will the time come for him to take vengeance of them and *sprinkle* them, i.e. shed their blood. And then *kings will shut their mouths* עליו, i.e. *because of him; for what had not been told them they will* then *have seen,* because it never entered into the heart of the nations to suppose that there could ever be deliverance for Israel.

LIII. [1]*Then they will say, Who* ever *believed* that things would happen in accordance with this report that we hear? *upon whom was the arm of the Lord ever revealed* as it has been revealed upon these? [2]*Each of God's servants belonging to Israel (or the whole of Israel) was *springing up before him like* [p. 45] *a sucker* (Hos. xiv.7), or *like a root out of the dry earth* which produces no fruit. *He had no form:* to be explained according to lii.14. In ונראהו ולא מראה the force of לא extends over the second word as well as that which immediately belongs to it — 'he had *no* form, and we did *not* desire him:' so Prov. xxi.14 יכפה must be understood in the second half of the verse. [3]*He was despised and ceasing from men,* i.e. ceased to be reckoned among men: *a man of pains,* sc. the servant of God; or if עבדי be understood of the nation, then אישׁ will be used to signify 'a being' in general, as Ex. xv.3[5]. The expressions *pains* and *sickness* allude to the distress occasioned by exile. *And it was as though one hid his face from him:* even

---

3. So our editions: but Ibn 'Ezra, as Friedländer suggests, may probably have read תָּארוֹ, which in fact occurs in a MS. of the Bodleian Library, assigned (see Neubauer, Catal. No. 69) to the 13th century.

4. I.e., among Mohammedans and Christians.

5. On this passage, compare Friedländer's note.

to this day there are non-Israelites who when they see a Jew, hide their faces from him; the phrase meaning that they will not look at him for the purpose of saving him. [4]The substance of the verse is as follows: — It was we who caused his sickness; yet he carried it, and bore all the pains wherewith we pained him. *We,* however, thought that he had been *stricken* with the stroke or plague of leprosy (Lev. xiii.5). מוכה is in *st. constr.:* it was God who smote him and afflicted him because the sicknesses ought to have come upon us, whose laws were altogether vanity, but they came upon Israel instead, whose law was a law of faithfulness. This is proved by the words, 'All we like sheep had gone astray.' [5]מחולל is ptcp. of חולל. *The chastisement of our peace* is that which perpetuates our peace; and this rested *upon him;* as is clear from the words 'and by his stripes we are healed.' By *our transgressions* are meant the sufferings inflicted on Israel by the nations, for which, as Joel says (iv.21), God will visit them; as to the meaning of *the chastisement of our peace,* it is well known that all the time that Israel is in the humiliation of exile the nations will have peace, for do you not find it written of the time of deliverance that it will be a 'time of distress' (Dan. xii.1); and again, when those who had been [p. 46] sent brought back word that the whole earth was 'sitting still and at rest,' that the angel answered and said, 'Until when wilt thou not have mercy on Jerusalem' (Zech. i.11f.)? which implies that Jerusalem will not receive mercy during the whole time that the nations are at rest. [6]*All we,* etc.: at last, then, they confess the truth, exactly as in Jer. xvi.19, 'nothing but lies have our fathers inherited.' The words bear reference to the false supposition of ver. 4. הפגיע is from פגע, Gen. xxviii.11; and עון is here used in the sense of *penalty* for sin, as 1 Sam. xxviii.10, Gen. xv.16, Lam. iv.6. Others render הפגיע *made to intercede,* cf. Jer. vii.16, understanding עון in its usual acceptation of iniquity; the sense of the whole will then be that Israel interceded with God, in order that there might be peace in the world, cf. Jer. xxix.7; but עון in this case agrees but harshly with הפניע בו. [7]נגש Nif'al. *He opened not his mouth:* there is no need to interpret these words, for every Jew in exile exemplifies their truth: in the hour of his affliction he never opens his mouth to speak, even though he alone is just amongst them all: for he has no care in this world except for the service of God; he knows no prince or dignitary who will stand before him in the breach when men rise up against him (Ps. cvi.23, cxxiv.2): he opens not his mouth at any time. [8]*From confinement,* etc.: God, however, will redeem Israel, i.e. the righteous of them. *He was taken:* God took him out of prison, where he was confined under a condemnation of vengeance. ישוחח like שיח Job xii.8: 'who announced to the men of his generation that it would be so?' *for he was* already *cut off from the land of life.* מפשע עמי: these are the words of each separate nation, 'the stroke that has fallen upon Israel is owing to our transgressions' (like מחולל מפשעינו ver. 5); or, as is more correct, 'for the

transgression of my people the stroke will come upon them[6],' — למש being
equivalent to להם *for* [p. 47] or *upon them*. [9]Some explain במותיו 'in his deaths'
of those who died in exile; but others derive it from בָּמוֹת Deut. xxxiii.29, i.e.,
the building erected over a grave: במותיו will then be parallel to קברו. עשור
ואת is parallel to את רשעים, and alludes to the nations who, as compared with
Israel, are wealthy. In my opinion the real meaning of the verse is this: it is intended to describe the distress of the Israelites in exile, which was so intense
that, like Samson (Judg. xvi.30), they desired to die with the nations amongst
whom they dwelt — the sense of *and he made* being *and he made* in his own
mind, i.e. *purposed to make,* cf. Josh. xxiv.9. And that this desire arose indeed
from their distress is shewn by what follows, *because he did no violence,* etc.; for
the Gentiles ill-treated Israel gratuitously, and not on account of any evil deed
or word of which they had been guilty — a view which will also accord equally
with either signification of ויתן[7]. If it be objected that in במות the *qameṣ* is un-
alterable (as in בָּמוֹתִימוֹ Deut. xxxiii.29), and that therefore בָּמוֹתָיו cannot be
derived from it, it may be replied that this word can assume two forms in *st.*
constr. like סרים, from which we find both סָרִיסֵי (Gen. xl.7) and also סְרִיסֵי
(Esth. ii.21 al.). [10]*To bruise him,* i.e. to chasten him in captivity: דכאו is Pi'el, like
דברו (Gen. xxxvii.4); and החלי is from חלה, but formed after the manner of
verbs ל"א, cf. תחלואיה Deut. xxix.21. *If his soul,* he continues, *puts* its *trespass*
before God, i.e. if he confesses his sin — or, in other words, if his soul puts before him the fear of the Lord — he will see sons and prolong his days, so that he
and they together will see the salvation of God. The prophet speaks here of the
generation which will return to the law of God when the end, the advent of the
Messiah, has taken place. *And the Lord's pleasure shall prosper in his hand,* alluding to the Law, when the nations are converted to the true religion. [11]*For the tra-*
vail of his soul, i.e. as a reward for what he has endured, *he will see* — either, that
is, his desire or prosperity [p. 48] generally — until he is satisfied, because *by his*
knowledge he will justify many, viz. the nations whom Israel will teach to fulfil
the law. And the meaning of his *bearing their iniquities* is that Israel, acting in a
different manner from that in which the Gentiles had acted towards them, will
share in the pain suffered by the latter for their sins. Or — and this is, I think,
preferable, as the next verse seems to shew — the meaning may be that Israel
will pray to God for the Gentiles: in this case, cf. Zech. xiv.17. [12]All the interpreters say that this verse alludes metaphorically to those who perished in defence
of the doctrine of the Divine Unity, רבים (as Esth. i.8), meaning *the great ones*

---

6. I.e., upon the various nations. Ibn 'Ezra considers that, had Israel alone been intended,
the singular *upon him* would have been employed.

7. Namely, either literally *and he made* or *and he purposed to make.*

(i.e., the prophets), and עצומיח denoting the patriarchs; the sense accordingly is that those who died in that cause will have a portion with the prophets. Although true in itself, however, such a sense does not agree with the rest of the Parashah, and in my opinion the meaning is rather this: 'I will give Israel a portion of spoil and plunder from many nations (את before עצומים signifying *from*, as Ex. ix.29), as a reward for his having poured out his soul to die.' Some, however, explain הערה in the sense of *uncover, expose openly*. I prefer the sense here given (cf. Gen. xxiv.20, although there the conjugation is different), which is also confirmed by Ps. cxli.8, where עָרָה evidently means *to pour out*. Thus Israel *was numbered with* those who had transgressed against God, *and carried the sin of many*, because through his pains the Gentiles had peace; and the sin which they ought to have carried was borne by him. He also *interceded for the transgressors*, i.e. the Gentiles; as it is said, Jer. xxix.7, 'And seek ye the peace of the city whither I have caused you to be carried away captives.' I have now explained for you the whole Parashah: in my opinion the expression *my servant* (lii.13, liii.11) denotes the same person who is the subject of xlii.1, xlix.3; cf. xlix.6; and the mystery is to be understood as I hinted in the middle of the book (ch. xl). Thus all these Parashahs are connected intimately together.

3. Commentary of David Kimchi on Isaiah 53

[p. 49] This Parashah refers to the captivity of Israel, who are here called 'my servant,' as in xli.8; the prophet says, 'Behold the time will come when my servant will prosper, and be high, and exalted exceedingly.' ישכיל means *to prosper*, as 1 Sam. xviii.14, and as the word is interpreted by Yonathan.[1] And because the exaltation of Israel is to be very great, the prophet uses a multiplicity of terms to express the idea: ירום ונשא וגבה.

I will now proceed to expound the Parashah as it is expounded by my father of blessed memory in the *Sepher hag-Galuy* and the *Sepher hab-B'rith*, composed by him in answer to the heretics.

[14] שמם means *to be astonished*, as Ezek. iii.15: 'as they were astonished at the extent of thy depression;' and it was natural that they should be thus astonished, for they saw that his countenance and form were marred beyond any man's. The prophet speaks at one moment in the second person, at another in the third, saying 'at *thee*,' but '*his* countenance,' '*his* form;' this is the custom of Scripture in countless passages, as we have elsewhere shewn. The learned Rabbi Abraham Ibn 'Ezra explains the words by pointing out how many nations there

---

1. In the Thargum: see Neubauer and Driver, 2:5.

are in the world who believe that the features of the Jew are disfigured and un-like those of other men, and remarking that some even go so far as to ask, — in the country of Ishmael or Edom, for example, — whether a Jew has a mouth or an eye. ¹⁵מ‎שחת‎ ⟦(Tr.) Actually verse 14; see above, n. 84.⟧ (with Ḥireq under the מ‎) is an adjective like מבדלות‎ (Josh. xvi.9), also with Ḥireq. And תארו‎ has Ḥolem, because [p. 50] of the א‎. [Verse 15] יזה‎ has the sense of *speaking*, like הטיף‎, which means both *to sprinkle* or *drop* (Judg. v.4) and also *to speak* (Mic. ii.6). The verb has a causative force, *fera parler* in French. The prophet means to say, As they were astonished at his depression, so will they now be astonished to see his greatness, and will be talking of it continually. *At him kings will shut their mouth* — even to kings, as it is said lxii.2, will his glory appear in its greatness. יקפצו‎ is either *to open*, as Cant. ii.8, where קפץ‎ signifies the opening out of the steps in leaping, or *to shut*, as Deut. xv.7. Either meaning is possible here: the kings may *open* their mouth to tell of his greatness, or *close* their mouth by placing their hand upon it in amazement. *For they will see then more of his greatness than* what had been told them, and perceive more of it than *they had heard of.*

LIII. ¹Then the Gentiles will say, *Who* was there that *believed the report* which we heard concerning him from the prophets' lips, or from those who spoke in their name? We never believed what we are now seeing with our own eyes. And *upon whom was the arm of the Lord ever revealed* as it is now revealed upon him? Or על מי‎ may be spoken contemptuously, meaning, Who was he that the arm of the Lord should be revealed upon him? ²כיונק‎ as Hos. xiv.7: Is-rael was like a sucker without beauty springing up out of a root in the dry soil. In my opinion, however, the allusion is rather to Israel's coming up out of exile, which was as surprising and wondrous as for a sucker to spring up out of the dry ground, or for a tree or herbage to flourish there. *Sucker* and *root* are paral-lel terms for the expression of the same idea; and the meaning of לפניו‎ is that Israel was continually before God, and so nearer to him than any other nation. Yet while in captivity *he had no form and no comeliness* — 'form' meaning of course a beautiful form: and *we looked at him, but* he had *no beauty* in his looks; his countenance was deformed and disfigured, unlike other men's. ונחמדהו‎; the preceding לא‎ stands in place of two: 'we did not desire him,' but rather loathed him. [p. 51] ³Not only did we not desire him, *he was* even *despised* in our eyes. חדל אישים‎; i.e. the *most insignificant* of men, or, perhaps, *forlorn* of men, be-cause they would not associate with him. The *pains* and *sickness* spoken of are the sufferings of exile; and ידוע‎ means that he was *taught* and accustomed to have the yoke of exile pass over him. *And we were* like men hiding their faces *from him;* we would not look at him because of the loathing we felt for him, and we accounted him for nought. ⁴The prophet Ezekiel (xviii.20) says the son shall not suffer for the iniquity of the father, nor the father for the iniquity of the son: *a fortiori,* therefore, one man cannot suffer for another man, or one people for another people; what, then, is the meaning of his *carrying our sicknesses* etc. What Jeremiah says in his Lamentations, 'Our fathers sinned and are not, and we bear their iniquities' (v. 7), is not parallel; this, firstly, resembles rather Ex. xx.5, *visiting the iniquity of the fathers upon the children,* i.e. when the children still continue to adhere to the works of their fathers, according to the addition *as regards them that hate me;* for it is a judgment from God when the son bears both his own iniquity and his father's as well: and, secondly, Jeremiah is speaking in the style of mourners, whose words, springing out of the midst of pain and distress, are not regulated by measure and weight. Here the phrases put into the mouth of the Gentiles, such as 'he hath carried our sicknesses' etc., are merely the expression of their own thoughts; it is not asserted that Israel actually bore the iniquity of the Gentiles, but the latter only imagine it to be the case when they see, at the time of Deliverance, that the faith which Israel adhered to was the true one, while that which they themselves had adhered to was the false; accordingly they say (Jer. xvi.19), 'Our fathers have inherited nothing but falsehood.' Here, then, they ask, What can be the cause of the pains endured by Israel in captivity? they cannot be attributed to their own iniquity, for *they* adhered to the truth, whereas *we* who enjoyed peace and tranquillity, quietude [p. 52] and security, were adhering to falsehood; it follows, therefore, that the sickness and pain which ought to have fallen upon us has fallen upon them, and they are our ransom and the price of our atonement. While they were in exile, however, *we thought* that they were *smitten* by the hand *of God* for their iniquity; but now we see that it was not for their iniquity but for ours, as it is said, 'He suffered pangs for our transgressions.' [5] מחולל is Po'lel, from the same root and with the same meaning as חיל (Ps. xlviii.7); for מדכא cf. Ps. cxliii.3. שלומינו is equivalent to כלנו *the whole of us,* cf. Jer. xiii.19 הגלת שלומים, i.e. it is carried away, an *entire* or *complete* captivity: 'the chastisements which were to have come upon us, have fallen, the whole of them, upon him.' Others explain שלומנו in its ordinary meaning: 'the chastisements which ought to have come upon us for our sins *while we were at peace* have fallen on him.' בחבורתו is from חדורה (Ex. xxi.25), only without the *Dagesh.* 'Stripe' like 'stroke,' ver. 8, is used metaphorically of the sufferings in exile. *We were healed,* as Ex. xv.26; or he may allude to the misfortunes which would fall upon the Gentiles, but prevail only for a time: the Gentiles would then be *healed,* while Israel would be left in calamity. [6]*Like the* sheep, those, viz. without a shepherd; he uses the article to point to the particular kind of sheep who would go astray, those, viz. without a shepherd. Each people *turned* after its own god: but now we see that *all we had gone astray,* while Israel had been in possession of the truth. הפגיע; it is the penalty which *lights upon* them, and it is God who causes it to do so when he sends misfortune upon them. עָוֹן means here the *penalty* of sin: so Gen. xv.16. [7]*He was pressed* (for money, as 2 Kings xxiii.35, Deut. xv.2) *and he was afflicted,* sc. bodily (for his body was afflicted with stripes): yet notwithstanding this, he opened not his mouth — was not permitted to cry out and complain at what we were doing to him, but was as a sheep led to slaughter, which does not open its mouth and cry; and as a lamb dumb before her shearers. The simile of the sheep is intended to express his [p. 53] bodily affliction and exhaustion; and that of the lamb to express the extortion he suffered, which is compared to *fleecing;* the prophet likens Israel to a רָחֵל (fem.) and not to a כֶּבֶשׂ (masc.), on account of his excessive weakness and prostration while in captivity, for with every animal the female is weaker than the male. נֶאֱלָמָה is *Mil'el,* being the perf. Nif'al. *Yet he opened not his mouth,* neither at his bodily sufferings, nor at the loss of his possessions. [8]*From* the *coercion* of exile, in which he was confined, *and from* the *judgment* of captivity when judgments were inflicted upon him, — from all this *he was taken* and redeemed. *And who* was there that *said* or suspected (cf. Gen. xxi.7) that his generation would attain to such greatness? יְשׂוֹחֵחַ means *to speak,* Po'lel from שׂוּחַ: so Ps. cxliii.5. *For he was cut off from the land of life,* viz. when he was in exile from his own country, which is called the *land of life,* as in Ps. cxvi.9. Or the phrase may be explained thus: In exile he was really considered to have been cut off from the land of the living, how then were we to think that such greatness as this would ever be his? *For the transgression of my people.* Each nation will make this confession, saying that in consequence of their own transgression, and not Israel's, had the *stroke* fallen *upon them.* [9]They were ever killing Israel while in exile, just as though he had done wrong, classing him with the wicked whom men put to death on account of their wickedness, although he had done no violence, and although there was no word of guile in his mouth. The meaning of וַיִּתֵּן is that he gave himself voluntarily to death: they were ready to release him if he would renounce his own law and transfer his allegiance to theirs; but rather than do this, he met a voluntary death, cf. Ps. xliv.23. And *with the rich* also, who are slain for the sake of their wealth: this, and not his wickedness, was the cause of his being murdered. The plural מוֹתָיו is employed because they used to be put to death in many ways: some were burnt, some were slain, and others were stoned — they gave themselves over to any form of death for the sake of [p. 54] the unity of the Godhead. [10]Still in his pains and sufferings while in captivity we trace nothing but the operations of the divine *pleasure:* Israel himself adhered to the Law, which is a law of faithfulness (cf. Ps. cxix.142), and suffered martyrdom on behalf of it; since his pains cannot imply that he was caught in his own iniquities, we must suppose that it was the divine pleasure thus *to bruise and sicken him:* we do not understand all the mysteries of God's purposes. (In הַחֲלִי the third radical א is wanting: although the verb is generally ל״ה, the word before us is formed and pronounced as though it were ל״א.) Only this do we see clearly, that he will receive a full reward for the misfortune he has endured; *if,* then, *his soul* gives itself in place of *a trespass-offering* (as he says above, 'with the wicked'), *he will see* much *seed,* as the prophet Zechariah says of them (x.8, 10), and Ezekiel (xxxvi.37); he will *lengthen days,* as is said at the end of the book (lxv.22), and by Zechariah (viii.4); and whereas during the exile it was the Lord's pleasure to bruise him, in return for this *the Lord's pleasure shall prosper in his hand,* for he will multiply him and do good to him exceedingly. — At this point the words of the Gentiles cease, and those of God begin. [11]*For the travail of his soul* which he bore in exile, his reward shall be that he will *see and be satisfied,* i.e. he will see prosperity so as to be satisfied therewith. 'My servant' here still means Israel, as we said at the beginning of the Parashah; and דַעְתּוֹ denotes his knowledge of the Lord, as xi.9, Jer. xxxi.33. *My servant* Israel, who will be *righteous* and know the Lord, *will, by his knowledge, make righteous* many nations, as it is written, Is. ii.3, 'He will teach us of his ways, and we will walk in his paths;' and by his righteousness will *bear the iniquities* of the Gentiles, for by it there will be peace and prosperity in the whole world, even for the Gentiles. [12]The *mighty* and the *strong* are here Gog and Magog, and the peoples who come with him to Jerusalem, as is described by Zechariah (xii.14). And this glorious fortune will be his *because he poured out* [p. 55] *his soul to die:* i.e. because in exile he resigned himself to death at the hands of the Gentiles: their wealth will be for his wealth which they had taken, and their soul for his soul, for, as Ezekiel writes (xxxix.4), 'All the host of Gog and Magog will die there.' הֶעֱרָה is *to pour out,* as Gen. xxiv.20, but in a different conjugation; and '*with* the transgressors' is like '*with* the wicked,' as we have explained the words in ver. 8. *And he carried the sin of many:* this may be supposed to refer to the time of the captivity; he means to say that Israel *bore* the consequences of *the sin of many,* i.e. of the Gentiles when they sinned against him, and he bore the sufferings which their sin occasioned; cf. Ex. v.16. Nevertheless, he continued *interceding* for the wicked who were *transgressing* against him, and sought blessings on their land from the Lord; cf. Jer. xxix.7. The Hif. of פגע is used with the same idea of supplication or prayer in lix.16, Jer. xxxvi.25. The reference may, however, be to the time of deliverance: the meaning will then be similar to that assigned to the words, 'He will bear their iniquities,' in the last verse.

I should like to ask the Nazarenes [Christians] who explain this Parashah of Jesus, how the prophet could have said, 'He shall be lifted up and lofty exceedingly?' If this alludes to the flesh, Jesus was not 'lifted up' except when he was suspended upon the cross; if it refers to the Godhead, then he was mighty and lifted up from the beginning [so that it could not be said, He *will* be lifted up]. Moreover, the prophet says *to them* (למו), ver. 8, but then he ought to have said *to him* (לו), for למו is plural, being equivalent to להם. Again he says, 'He shall see seed:' if this refers to his flesh, then he had no seed; if to his Godhead, as the literal sense is inappropriate, they explain the word *seed* as alluding to his disciples, although his disciples are nowhere spoken of as either *sons* or *seed*. He says, too, 'He shall lengthen days;' but in the flesh he did not lengthen days, and if he says of his Godhead that as a reward [for suffering] he will have long life, are not the days of God [p. 56] from everlasting to everlasting (cf. Ps. xc.2)? Lastly, he says, 'And he interceded for the transgressors;' but if he is God himself, to whom could he intercede? — Our Rabbis[2] explain it of Moses, supposing that he 'poured out his soul to die' when he resigned himself to death (Ex. xxxii.32), that he was 'numbered with the transgressors' because he was numbered with those who died in the wilderness, that he 'bore the sin of many' when he made atonement for the making of the golden calf, and that he 'interceded for the transgressors' when he sought for mercy on the transgressions of Israel[3].

---

2. See *b. Sotah* 14a as quoted in Neubauer and Driver, 2:8.

3. The MSS continue with the translation of Yonathan; see Neubauer and Driver, 2:5-6.

A Classified Bibliography on Isaiah 53

Wolfgang Hüllstrung and Gerlinde Feine

Updated by Daniel P. Bailey

A comprehensive bibliography on the Servant in Second Isaiah through 1985 may be found in H. Haag, *Der Gottesknecht bei Deuterojesaja*, EdF 233 (Darmstadt ²1993), XVII-XLIII. The present bibliography focuses on literature dealing explicitly with Isa 52:13–53:12 and seeks complete coverage at least for the Old Testament realm (see section 1) until spring 1996, updated through 2003. This does not generally include book reviews and bibliographies, and includes only a selection of studies on the history or present state of research. It passes over Old and New Testament introductions and the standard commentaries on Second Isaiah and New Testament books citing Isaiah 53, but includes works of Old and New Testament theology. Reference works and dictionaries have been consulted for philological entries and summaries of subjects such as the "Servant," "atonement," and "Second Isaiah." The bibliography is subdivided into four sections:

1. Old Testament
2. Ancient Judaism, Ancient Versions, Jewish Interpretation
3. New Testament and Early Christianity
4. Updated bibliography

There is some overlap between the first three sections and therefore individual works may be cited in two or all three of them. The first two were compiled by Wolfgang Hüllstrung and the third by Gerlinde Feine. Daniel P. Bailey corrected parts of the bibliography and provided an update for its 2004 printing.

1. Old Testament

Ackroyd, P. R. "Meaning and Exegesis." In *Words and Meanings: Essays Presented to David W. Thomas*, ed. by P. R. Ackroyd and B. Lindars, Cambridge 1968, 1-14, esp. 11ff.

Ahlström, G. W. "Notes to Isaiah 53:8f." *BZ* 13 (1969) 95-98.

Alexius, P. "De passione Servi Yahweh (iuxta Is. 52:13-15; 53:1-12)." *VD* 14 (1934) 342-352.

Allen, L. C. "Isaiah LIII 11 and Its Echoes." *VoxEv* 1 (1962) 24-28.

———. "Isaiah LIII, 2 Again." *VT* 21 (1971) 490.

Alonso, A. "The Problem of the Servant Songs." *Scripture* 18 (1966) 18-26.

———. "Anotaciones críticas a Isaías 53:8." *CDios* 181 (1968) 89-100.

———. "La suerte del Siervo: Isaías 53:9-10." *CDios* 181 (1968) 292-305.

Balla, E. "Das Problem des Leides in der israelitisch-jüdischen Religion." In *Eucharisterion. Studien zur Religion und Literatur des Alten und Neuen Testaments. Hermann Gunkel zum 60. Geburtstag, dem 23. Mai 1922 dargebracht. 1. Teil*, ed. by H. Schmidt, Göttingen 1923, 214-260, esp. 245-247.

Baltzer, K. "Zur formgeschichtlichen Bestimmung der Texte vom Gottes-Knecht im Deuterojesaja-Buch." In *Probleme biblischer Theologie. G. von Rad zum 70. Geburtstag*, ed. by H. W. Wolff, Munich 1971, 27-43, esp. 40-42.

———. *Die Biographie der Propheten*, Neukirchen-Vluyn 1975, esp. 171-177.

———. "Jes 52,13: Die 'Erhöhung' des 'Gottesknechtes.'" In *Religious Propaganda and Missionary Competition in the New Testament World*, ed. by L. Bormann et al., Leiden 1994, 45-56.

Baron, D. *The Servant of Jehovah: The Sufferings of the Messiah and the Glory That Should Follow. An Exposition of Isaiah LIII*, Grand Rapids ³1922.

Barstadt, H. M. "Tjenersangene hos Deuterojesaja. Et eksegetisk villspor." *NTT* 83 (1982) 235-244.

———. "The Future of the 'Servant Songs': Some Reflections on the Relationship of Biblical Scholarship to Its Own Tradition." In *Language, Theology, and the Bible: Essays in Honour of James Barr*, ed. by S. E. Balentine and J. Barton, Oxford 1994, 261-270.

Barth-Frommel, M.-C. "Le Serviteur du Seigneur dans Esaïe 40–55." *FoiVie* 70 (1971) 48-65.

Barthélemy, D. *Critique Textuelle de l'Ancien Testament*, vol. 2: *Isaïe, Jérémie, Lamentations* (OBO 50/2), Fribourg 1986, 385-407.

Bastiaens, J. C. *Interpretaties van Jesaja 53. Een intertextueel onderzoek naar de lijdende Knecht in Jes 53 (MT/LXX) en in Lk 22:14-38, Hand 3:12-26, Hand 4:23-31 en Hand 8:26-40* (TFT-Studies 22), Tilburg 1993, 29-93.

Battenfield, J. R. "Isaiah LIII 10: Taking an 'if' out of the sacrifice of the Servant." *VT* 32 (1982) 485.

Beauchamp, P. "Lecture et relecture du quatrième chant du Serviteur. D'Isaïe à Jean."

In *Le Deutéro- et le Trito-Isaïe (Is 40–66)*, ed. by J. Vermeylen (BETL 81), Louvain 1989, 325-355.

Beecher, W. J. "The Servant" (1903). In *Classical Evangelical Essays in Old Testament Interpretation*, ed. by W. C. Kaiser, Grand Rapids 1972, 187-204.

Beer, G. "Die Gedichte vom Knechte Jahwes in Jes 40–55. Ein textkritischer und metrischer Wiederherstellungsversuch." In *Abhandlungen zur semitischen Religionskunde und Sprachwissenschaft. W. W. Grafen von Baudissin zum 26. September 1917*, ed. by W. Frankenberg and F. Küchler (BZAW 33), Giessen 1918, 36-46.

Begg, C. "Zedekiah and the Servant." *ETL* 62 (1986) 393-398.

Begrich, J. *Studien zu Deuterojesaja*, Stuttgart 1938. Reprinted, ed. by W. Zimmerli, TB 20, Munich 1963, esp. 62-66.

Behler, G. M. *Serviteur et Roi. Les quatre chants sur le "Serviteur de Dieu" à la lumière de leur accomplissement dans le Christ*, Uzès 1976, 95-139.

Bentzen, A. *Messias — Moses redivivus — Menschensohn* (ATANT 17), Zürich 1948, 53-67 = *King and Messiah*, 2d ed., ed. by G. W. Anderson, Oxford ²1970, 54-67.

Bertholet, A. *Zu Jesaja 53. Ein Erklärungsversuch*, Freiburg 1899.

Blank, J. "Der leidende Gottesknecht (Jes 53)." In *Woran wir leiden*, ed. by P. Pawlowsky and E. Schuster, Innsbruck 1979, 28-67.

Blank, S. H. *Prophetic Faith in Isaiah*, London 1958, esp. 86-100.

Bleeker, L. H. K. "Jojachin, der Ebed-Jahwe." *ZAW* 40 (1922) 136.

Blenkinsopp, J. "A Jewish Sect of the Persian Period." *CBQ* 52 (1990) 5-20.

Blocher, H. *Songs of the Servant: Isaiah's Good News*, London 1975.

Blythin, I. "A Consideration of Difficulties in the Hebrew Text of Isaiah 53:11." *BT* 17 (1966) 27-31.

Boadt, L. "Intentional Alliteration in Second Isaiah." *CBQ* 45 (1983) 353-363.

Boer, P. A. H. de. *Second-Isaiah's Message*, Leiden 1956, esp. 102-117.

Breslauer, S. "Power, Compassion and the Servant of the Lord in Second Isaiah." *Encounter* 48 (1987) 163-178.

Brunot, A. "Le Poème du Serviteur et ses problèmes (Isaïe XL–LV)." *RThom* 61 (1961) 5-24.

Bruston, C. "Le Serviteur de l'Eternel dans l'avenir." In *Vom Alten Testament. Karl Marti zum siebzigsten Geburtstag*, ed. by K. Budde (BZAW 41), Giessen 1925, 37-44.

Buber, M. *Der Glaube der Propheten*, Heidelberg ²1984, esp. 246-281.

Budde, K. *Die sogenannten Ebed-Jahwe-Lieder und die Bedeutung des Knechtes Jahwes in Jes. 40–55. Ein Minoritätsvotum*, Giessen 1900.

Buri, F. *Vom Sinn des Leidens. Eine Auslegung des Liedes vom leidenden Gottesknecht Jesaja 53*, Basel 1963.

Burrows, E. N. B. "The Servant of Yahweh in Isaiah: An Interpretation." In *The Gospel of the Infancy and Other Biblical Essays*, ed. by E. F. Sutcliffe, London 1940, 59-80.

Cañellas, G. "La figura del Siervo de Yahve." *CuBi* 276 (1980) 19-36.

Caspari, W. *Lieder und Gottessprüche der Rückwanderer (Jesaja 40–55)* (BZAW 65), Giessen 1934.

Cazelles, H. "Les poèmes du Serviteur. Leur place, leur structure, leur théologie." *RevScRel* 43 (1955) 5-55.

———. "Le roi Yoyakin et le Serviteur du Seigneur." In *Proceedings of the Fifth World Congress of Jewish Studies, the Hebrew University, Mount Scopus-Givat Ram, Jerusalem, 3-11 August, 1969*, 5 vols.; vol. 1, ed. by P. Peli, Jerusalem 1972, 1:121-125.

Ceresco, A. R. "The Rhetorical Strategy of the Fourth Servant Song (Isaiah 52:13–53:12): Poetry and the Exodus–New Exodus." *CBQ* 56 (1994) 42-55.

Chavasse, C. "The Suffering Servant and Moses." *CQR* 165 (1964) 152-163.

Cheyne, T. K. *The Mines of Isaiah Re-Explored*, London 1912, 55-71.

Clifford, R. J. "Book of Isaiah. Second Isaiah." *ABD* III 490-501, esp. 499f.

Clines, D. J. A. *I, He, We, and They: A Literary Approach to Isaiah 53* (JSOTSup 1), Sheffield 1976.

Cobb, W. H. "The Servant of Jahveh." *JBL* 14 (1895) 95-113.

Collins, J. J. "The Suffering Servant: Scapegoat or Example?" *PIBA* 4 (1980) 59-67.

Condamin, A. "Le Serviteur de Iahvé. Un nouvel argument pour le sens individuel messianique." *RB* 17 (1908) 162-181, esp. 166-168.

Cook, S. A. "The Servant of the Lord." *ExpTim* 34 (1922-23) 440-442.

Coppens, J. "Nieuw licht over de Ebed-Jahweh-Liederen." In *Pro regno pro sanctuario. Een bundel studies en bijdragen van vrienden en vereerders bij de zestigste verjaardag van Prof. Dr. G. van der Leeuw*, ed. by W. J. Kooiman, Nijkerk 1950, 115-123.

———. "Les origines littéraires des Poèmes du Serviteur de Yahvé." *Bib* 40 (1959) 248-258.

———. "Le Serviteur de Yahvé. Vers la solution d'un énigme." In *Sacra pagina. Miscellanea biblica Congressus Internationalis Catholici de Re Biblica*, 2 vols., ed. by J. Coppens, A. Descamps, and E. Massaux (BETL 32-33), Paris and Gembloux 1959, 1:434-454.

———. "La finale du quatrième chant du Serviteur (Is. LIII,10-12). Un essai de solution." *ETL* 39 (1963) 114-121.

———. "Le messianisme israélite. La relève prophétique IV. Le Serviteur de Yahvé. Figure prophétique de l'avenir." *ETL* 48 (1972) 5-36, esp. 13ff.

———. "La mission du Serviteur et de Yahvé et son statut eschatologique." *ETL* 48 (1972) 343-371.

———. *Le Messianisme et sa Relève prophétique. Les anticipations vétérotestamentaires. Leur accomplissement en Jésus* (BETL 38), Louvain ²1989, 52-84, esp. 60ff.

———. "Le Serviteur de Yahvé. Personnification de Sion-Jérusalem en tant que centre cultuel des rapatriés." *ETL* 52 (1976) 344-346.

Cornill, C. H. "Jesaja 53,12." *ZAW* 36 (1916) 243-244.

Dahood, M. "Phoenician Elements in Isaiah 52:13–53:12." In *Near Eastern Studies in Honor of W. F. Albright*, ed. by H. Goedicke, Baltimore 1971, 63-73.

————. "Isaiah 53:8-12 and Massoretic Misconstructions." *Bib* 63 (1982) 566-570.

Dalton, W. J. "The Fourth Song of the Servant of Yahweh Is. 52:13–53:12, *Scripture* 9-10 (1958) 1-10.

Day, J. "*DA'AṮ* 'Humiliation' in Isaiah LIII 11 in the Light of Isaiah LIII 3 and Daniel XII 4, and the Oldest Known Interpretation of the Suffering Servant." *VT* 30 (1980) 97-103.

Deist, F. E. "Reflections on Reinterpretation in and of Isaiah 53." *OTEs* 3 (1985) 1-11.

Diebner, B. "'āšām (Jes 53,10) und *amnos* (Jes 53,7 LXX). Ein Nachtrag." *DBAT* 16 (1982) 49-67.

Dion, P. E. "Les chants du Serviteur de Yahweh et quelques passages apparentés d'Is 40–55. Un essai sur leurs limites précises et sur leurs origines respectives." *Bib* 51 (1970) 17-38.

————. "L'universalisme religieux dans les différentes couches rédactionelles d'Isaïe 40–55." *Bib* 51 (1970) 161-182.

Dip, G. "Plegaria y sufrimiento del siervo di Yavé." *EE* 41 (1965) 303-350.

Dix, G. H. "The Influence of Babylonian Ideas on Jewish Messianism." *JTS* 26 (1925) 241-256, esp. 251-255.

Driver, G. R. "Linguistic and Textual Problems: Isaiah XL–LXVI." *JTS* 36 (1935) 396-406, esp. 403-4.

————. "Isaiah 52:13–53:12: The Servant of the Lord." In *In Memoriam Paul Kahle*, ed. by M. Hack and G. Fohrer (BZAW 103), Berlin 1968, 90-105.

Dürr, L. *Ursprung und Ausbau der israelitisch-jüdischen Heilandserwartung. Ein Beitrag zur Theologie des Alten Testaments*, Berlin 1925, 125-152.

Duhm, B. *Die Theologie der Propheten als Grundlage für die innere Entwicklungs-geschichte der israelitischen Religion*, Bonn 1875, 287-301.

Dumbrell, W. J. "The Role of the Servant in Isaiah 40–55." *RTR* 48 (1989) 105-113.

Edelkoort, A. H. *De Christusverwachting in het Oude Testament*, Wageningen 1941, esp. 372-436.

Ehrlich, A. B. *Randglossen zur hebräischen Bibel. Textkritisches, Sprachliches und Sachliches*. Vol. 4: *Jesaia, Jeremia*, Leipzig 1912 (repr. 1968), 190-193.

Eissfeldt, O. *Der Gottesknecht bei Deuterojesaja (Jes. 40–55) im Lichte der israelitischen Anschauung von Gemeinschaft und Individuum* (BRGA 2), Halle 1933.

Elliger, K. *Deuterojesaja in seinem Verhältnis zu Tritojesaja* (BWANT 63), Stuttgart 1933, 6-27.

————. "Jes 53,10: Alte crux — neuer Vorschlag." *MIOF* 15 (1969) 228-233.

————. "Textkritisches zu Deuterojesaja." In *Near Eastern Studies in Honor of W. F. Albright*, ed. by H. Goedicke, Baltimore 1971, 13-119.

————. "Nochmals Textkritisches zu Jes 53." In *Wort, Lied und Gottesspruch. Festschrift für Joseph Ziegler*, ed. by J. Schreiner (FB 2), Würzburg 1972, 137-144.

Engnell, I. "Till frågan om Ebed Jahve-sångerna och den lidande Messias hos 'Deuterojesaja.'" *SEÅ* 10 (1945) 31-65, esp. 49-62.

————. "The 'Ebed Yahweh Songs and the Suffering Messiah in 'Deutero-Isaiah.'" *BJRL* 31 (1948) 54-93.

Eynikel, E. "De liederen van de lijdende dienaar van Jahwe." *Collationes* 22 (1992) 115-127.

Farley, F. A. "Jeremiah and 'The Suffering Servant of Jehovah' in Deutero-Isaiah." *ExpTim* 38 (1926-27) 521-524.

Feldmann, F. *Die Weissagungen über den Gottesknecht im Buche Jesaias* (Biblische Zeitfragen 2/10), Münster ³1913, esp. 13ff.

Feuillet, A. "Le messianisme du livre d'Isaïe. Ses rapports avec l'histoire et les traditions d'Israël." *RSR* 36 (1949) 182-228.

———. "Les poèmes du Serviteur." In idem, *Études d'exégèse et de théologie biblique. Ancien Testament,* Paris 1975, 119-179.

———. "La religion d'Israël, préparation de celle de Christ. Les poèmes du Serviteur de la seconde partie du livre d'Isaïe." *Div* 37 (1993) 215-224.

Findeisen, I. H. "Ueber Jesaja 53,9." *ZKWL* 8 (1987) 123-132.

Fischer, J. *Isaias 40–55 und die Perikopen vom Gottesknecht. Eine kritisch-exegetische Studie* (ATA VI/4-5), Münster 1916.

———. *Wer ist der Ebed in den Perikopen Js 42,1-7; 49,1-9a; 50,4-9; 52,13–53,12? Eine exegetische Studie* (ATA VIII/5), Münster 1922.

———. *In welcher Schrift lag das Buch Isaias den LXX vor? Eine textkritische Studie* (BZAW 56), Giessen 1930, 62.

Fischer, M. "Vom leidenden Gottesknecht nach Jesaja 53." In *Abraham unser Vater. Juden und Christen im Gespräch über die Bibel. Festschrift für Otto Michel,* ed. by O. Betz, M. Hengel, and P. Schmidt (AGSU 5), Leiden 1963, 116-128.

Fohrer, G. "Zehn Jahre Literatur zur alttestamentlichen Prophetie (1951-1960)." *TRu* 28 (1962) 1-75, 235-297, 301-374, esp. 235-249.

———. "Neue Literatur zur alttestamentlichen Prophetie (1961-1970)." *TRu* 45 (1980) 23-39, esp. 36-38.

———. "Stellvertretung und Schuldopfer in Jesaja 52,13–53,12 vor dem Hintergrund des Alten Testaments und des Alten Orients" (1969). Reprinted in idem, *Studien zu alttestamentlichen Texten und Themen (1966-1972)* (BZAW 155), Berlin 1981, 24-43.

———. "Das Alte Testament und das Thema 'Christologie.'" *EvT* 30 (1970) 281-298, esp. 286-291.

Franco, E. "La morte del Servo sofferente in Is. 53." In *Gesù e la sua morte: Atti della XXVII Settimana biblica,* by Associazione Biblica Italiana, G. Boggio, A. Bonora, S. Cipriani et al., Brescia 1984, 219-236.

Friedlaender, H. *Der Knecht Gottes: Schicksal, Aufgabe, Trost. Die Lieder vom Knecht Gottes aus Jirmejahu und Jeschajahu in der Buber-Rosenzweigschen Übersetzung, eingeleitet und erläutert von Henri Friedlaender.* 's-Gravenhage: L. J. C. Boucher, 1947.

Füglister, N. "Exilische Schrifttexte: Der Gottesknecht." In *Mysterium salutis. Grundriss heilsgeschichtlicher Dogmatik,* 5 vols. in 7, ed. by J. Feiner and M. Löhrer. Vol. 3: *Das Christusereignis,* 2 vols., ed. by J. Alfaro, Einsiedeln 1969-1970, 3/1:151-173.

————. "Kirche als Knecht Gottes und der Menschen. Israel bei Deuterojesaja." *BK* 3 (1984) 109-122.

Füllkrug, G. *Der Gottesknecht des Deuterojesaja. Eine kritisch-exegetische und biblisch-theologische Studie,* Göttingen 1899.

Gelston, A. "Isaiah LIII 11." *VT* 21 (1971) 524-527.

————. "Isaiah 52:13–53:12. An Eclectic Text and a Supplementary Note on the Hebrew Manuscript Kennicott 96." *JSS* 35 (1990) 187-211.

————. "Knowledge, Humiliation or Suffering: A Lexical, Textual and Exegetical Problem in Isaiah 53." In *Of Prophets' Visions and the Wisdom of Sages: Essays in Honour of R. Norman Whybray on His Seventieth Birthday,* ed. by H. A. McKay and D. J. A. Clines (JSOTSup 162), Sheffield 1993, 126-141.

Gerleman, G. "Der Gottesknecht bei Deuterojesaja." In idem, *Studien zur alttestamentlichen Theologie,* Franz Delitzsch Vorlesungen 1978, Heidelberg 1980, 38-60.

Giesebrecht, F. *Beiträge zur Jesajakritik,* Göttingen 1890, esp. 146-185.

————. *Der Knecht Jahves des Deuterojesaia,* Königsberg 1902.

Ginsberg, H. L. "The Arm of YHWH in Isaiah 51–63 and the Text of Isa 53:10-11." *JBL* 77 (1958) 152-156.

Gispen, W. H. "Jesaja 53,10 en het schuldoffer." *GTT* 71 (1971) 193-204.

Goldingay, J. *God's Prophet, God's Servant: A Study in Jeremiah and Isaiah 40–55,* Exeter 1984, 139-159.

Goossens, W. "Het plaatsvervangend en uitboetend lijden van den Messias in de profetieën van Jahveh's Knecht in het boek Isaias (XL–LV)." *CGan* 31 (1948) 10-29.

Gordon, R. P. "Isaiah LIII 2." *VT* 20 (1970) 491-492.

Gosker, R. "Jesaja 53 — ein Denklied, *TeKo* 7 (1980) 5-18.

Gosse, B. "Isaïe 52,13–53,12 et Isaïe 6." *RB* 98 (1991) 537-543.

Grelot, P. *Les poèmes du serviteur. De la lecture critique à l'herméneutique* (LD 103), Paris 1981, 138-189.

————. "Serviteur de YHWH." *DBSup* 12:958-1016.

Gressmann, H. *Der Ursprung der israelitisch-jüdischen Eschatologie,* Göttingen 1905, esp. 301-333.

————. "Die literarische Analyse Deuterojesajas." *ZAW* 34 (1914) 254-297, esp. 296-297.

————. *Der Messias* (FRLANT 26), Göttingen 1929, esp. 285-340.

Gross, H. "Ebed Jahwe. I. AT." *LTK* 3:622-624.

Günther, H. *Gottes Knecht und Gottes Recht. Zum Verständnis der Knecht-Gottes-Lieder* (Oberurseler Hefte 6), Oberursel 1976.

Guillaume, A. "The Servant Poems in the Deutero-Isaiah." *Theology* 12 (1926) 2-10, 63-72.

Gunkel, H. *Ein Vorläufer Jesu,* Bern 1921.

————. "Jesaja 53: eine prophetische Liturgie." *ZAW* 42 (1924) 177-208.

Haag, E. "Das Opfer des Gottesknechts (Jes 53,10)." *TTZ* 86 (1977) 81-98.

————. "Die Botschaft vom Gottesknecht — ein Weg zur Überwindung der Gewalt." In *Gewalt und Gewaltlosigkeit im Alten Testament* (QD 96), ed. by N. Lohfink, Freiburg 1983, 159-213.

————. "Stellvertretung und Sühne nach Jesaja 53." *TTZ* 105 (1996) 1-20.

Haag, H. "Das Lied vom leidenden Gottesknecht (Is 52,13–53,12)." *BK* 16 (1961) 3-5.

————. *Der Gottesknecht bei Deuterojesaja* (EdF 233), Darmstadt ²1993, esp. 173-184.

Halévy, J. "Le ʿèbèd jhwh d'Isaïe, LII,13–LIII,12." *RSEHA* 7 (1899) 193-213, 289-312.

Haupt, P. "Understandest thou what thou readest?" In *Vom Alten Testament. Karl Marti zum siebzigsten Geburtstag*, ed. by K. Budde (BZAW 41), Giessen 1925, 118-127.

Helberg, J. L. "Nahum — Jonah — Lamentations — Isaiah 51-53: A Possibility for Establishing a Connection." In *Biblical Essays 1969. Proceedings of the 12th meeting of Die Ou-Testamentiese Werkgemeenskap in Suid-Afrika*, ed. by A. H. von Zyl, Potchefstroom 1969, 46-55.

Heller, J. "Hiding of the Face: A Study of Is 53:3" (1958). Reprinted in idem, *An der Quelle des Lebens*, Frankfurt 1988, 45-48.

Henning-Hess, H. "Bemerkungen zum ASCHAM-Begriff in Jes 53,10." *ZAW* 109 (1997) 618-626.

Hermisson, H.-J. "Der Lohn des Knechts." In *Die Botschaft und die Boten. Festschrift für H. W. Wolff zum 70. Geburtstag*, ed. by J. Jeremias and L. Perlitt, Neukirchen-Vluyn 1981, 269-287, esp. 283-287.

————. "Israel und der Gottesknecht bei Deuterojesaja." *ZTK* 79 (1982) 1-24.

————. "Voreiliger Abschied von den Gottesknechtsliedern." *TRu* 49 (1984) 209-222.

————. "Deuterojesaja-Probleme. Ein kritischer Literaturbericht." *VF* 31 (1986) 53-84.

————. "Einheit und Komplexität Deuterojesajas: Probleme der Redaktionsgeschichte von Jes 40–55." In *Le Deutéro- et le Trito-Isaïe* (Is 40–66), ed. by J. Vermeylen (BETL 81), Louvain 1989, 287-312.

Hertzberg, H. W. "Die 'Abtrünnigen' und die 'Vielen'. Ein Beitrag zu Jesaja 53." In *Verbannung und Heimkehr. Beiträge zur Geschichte und Theologie Israels im 6. und 5. Jahrhundert v.Chr. Wilhelm Rudolph zum 70. Geburtstag*, ed. by A. Kuschke, Tübingen 1961, 97-108.

Hollenberg, D. E. "Nationalism and 'the Nations' in Isaiah XL-LV." *VT* 19 (1969) 23-36.

Hooke, S. H. "The Theory and Practice of Substitution." *VT* 2 (1951) 2-17.

Hoonacker, A. van. "'ébed Iahvé et la composition littéraire des chapîtres XL ss. d'Isaïe." *RB* 18 (1909) 497-528.

————. "Questions de critique littéraire et d'exégèse touchant les chapîtres XL ss. d'Isaïe." *RB* 19 (1910) 557-572, 565ff.

Hyatt, J. P. "The Sources of the Suffering Servant Idea." *JNES* 3 (1944) 79-86.

Jakovljević, R. "The Sense of Ebed Yahweh's Suffering." *CV* 30 (1987) 59-62.

Janowski, B. "Er trug unsere Sünden. Jes 53 und die Dramatik der Stellvertretung" (1993). Reprinted in idem, *Gottes Gegenwart in Israel. Beiträge zur Theologie des Alten Testaments*, Neukirchen-Vluyn 1993, 303-326. [Translated as pp. 48-74 of the present volume.]

————. "Sühne. 1. Altes Testament und Judentum." *EKL*[3] 4:552-555, esp. 553-554 = "Atonement. 1. OT and Judaism." *EC* 1:152-154.

Jeppesen, K. "Herrens lidende tjener i historien og traditions-historien." In *Tekster og Tolkninger: Ti studier i Det gamle Testamente*, ed. by K. Jeppesen and F. H. Cryer, Aarhus 1986, 113-126.

————. "Herrens tjener og Herrens tjenere. Om Jes 40–66." In *Studier i Jesajabogen*, ed. by B. Rosendal, Aarhus 1989, 68-93.

————. "From 'You, My Servant' to 'the Hand of the Lord Is with My Servant.'" *SJOT* 4 (1990) 113-129.

————. "Mother Zion, Father Servant: A Reading of Isaiah 49-55." In *Of Prophets' Visions and the Wisdom of Sages: Essays in Honour of R. Norman Whybray on His Seventieth Birthday*, ed. by H. A. McKay and D. J. A. Clines (JSOTSup 162), Sheffield 1993, 109-125.

Junker, H. "Der Sinn der sogenannten Ebed-Jahwe-Stücke." *TTZ* 79 (1970) 1-12.

Kaiser, O. *Der königliche Knecht. Eine traditionsgeschichtlich-exegetische Studie über die Ebed-Jahwe-Lieder bei Deuterojesaja* (FRLANT 70), Göttingen ²1962.

Kapelrud, A. S. *Et folk på hjemferd: Trøsteprofeten, den annen Jesaja, og hans budskap*, Oslo 1964, esp. 70-84.

————. "Second Isaiah and the Suffering Servant." In *Hommages à André Dupont-Sommer*, ed. by A. Caquot and M. Philonenko, Paris 1971, 297-303.

————. "The Identity of the Suffering Servant." In *Near Eastern Studies in Honor of W. F. Albright*, ed. by H. Goedicke, Baltimore 1971, 307-314.

————. "The Main Concern of Second Isaiah." *VT* 32 (1982) 50-58.

Kehnscherper, G. "Der 'Sklave Gottes' bei Deuterojesaja." *FF* 40 (1966) 279-282.

Kelley, P. H. "Doing It God's Way." *RevExp* 88 (1992) 81-94.

Kennett, R. H. *The Servant of the Lord*, London 1911.

Kida, K. "Second Isaiah and the Suffering Servant. A New Proposal for a Solution." *AJBI* 5 (1979) 45-66.

————. "The Prophet, the Servant and Cyrus in the Prophecies of Second Isaiah." *AJBI* 16 (1990) 3-29.

Kiesow, K. "Deuterojesaja — ein Neuanfang in der Glaubenskrise." *BiLi* 63 (1990) 33-36.

————. "Die Gottesknechtslieder — Israels Auftrag für die Menschheit." *BiLi* 63 (1990) 156-159.

Kittel, R. "Jesaja 53 und der leidende Messias im Alten Testament. Akademische Antrittsrede an der Universität Leipzig 5. November 1898." In idem, *Zur Theologie des Alten Testaments. Zwei akademische Vorlesungen*, Leipzig 1899, 15-31.

————. *Gestalten und Gedanken in Israel*, Leipzig 1925, 389-431.

————. *Geschichte des Volkes Israel.* 3 vols in 4. Vol. 3, part 1: *Die Zeit der Wegführung nach Babel und die Aufrichtung der neuen Gemeinde*, Stuttgart 1927, 222-257.

Kleinknecht, K. T. *Der leidende Gerechtfertigte. Die alttestamentlich-jüdische Tradition* vom "*leidenden Gerechten*" *und ihre Rezeption bei Paulus* (WUNT II/13), Tübingen ²1988, 42-56.

König, E. "Deuterojesajanisches." *NKZ* 9 (1898) 895-935, 937-997.

Koenig, J. *Oracles et liturgies de l'exil babylonien* (EHPhR 69), Paris 1988, 125-180.

Komlosh, Y. "The Countenance of the Servant of the Lord, Was It Marred?" *JQR* 65 (1974-75) 217-220.

Kraetzschmar, R. *Der leidende Gottesknecht (Jes 52,13–53,12)*, n.p. 1899.

Kratz, R. G. *Kyros im Deuterojesaja-Buch. Redaktionsgeschichtliche Untersuchungen zu Entstehung und Theologie von Jes 40–55* (FAT 1), Tübingen 1991, esp. 144-147.

Krupp, K. "Solidarität und Friede Gottes. Zu den Gedanken der Stellvertretung und des neuen Bundes in der Botschaft des Propheten Deuterojesaja." *Katechetische Blätter* 107 (1982) 736-742.

Kruse, C. G. "The Servant Songs. Interpretative Trends Since C. R. North." *Studia biblica et theologica* 8 (1978) 3-27.

Kruse, H. "Carmina Servi Jahve." *VD* 29 (1951) 286-295.

Kühn, R. "Leid als besondere Glaubenssituation des Menschen und Jahwes Zuspruch im Alten Testament." *WiWei* 45 (1982) 97-130.

Kutsch, E. "Sein Leiden und Tod — unser Heil. Eine Auslegung von Jesaja 52,13–53,12" (1967). Reprinted in idem, *Kleine Schriften zum Alten Testament. Zum 65. Geburtstag*, ed. by L. Schmidt and K. Eberlein (BZAW 168), Berlin 1986, 169-196.

Laato, A. "The Composition of Isaiah 40–55." *JBL* 109 (1990) 207-228.

———. *The Servant YHWH and Cyrus: A Reinterpretation of the Exilic Messianic Programme in Isaiah 40–55* (ConBOT 35), 1992, esp. 130-154.

Lack, R. *La symbolique du livre d'Isaïe. Essai sur l'image littéraire comme élément de structuration* (AnBib 59), Rome 1973, esp. 113-115.

Landy, F. "The Construction of the Subject and the Symbolic Order: A Reading of the Last Three Suffering Servant Songs." In *Among the Prophets: Language, Image and Structure of the Prophetic Writings*, ed. by P. R. Davies and D. J. A. Clines (JSOTSup 144), Sheffield 1993, 60-71.

Langdon, R. "The 'Ebed Yahweh and Jeremiah." Diss. Southern Baptist Theological Seminary, 1980.

Laue, L. *Die Ebed-Jahwe-Lieder im II. Teil des Jesaia exegetisch-kritisch und biblisch-theologisch untersucht*, Wittenberg 1898.

———. "Nochmals die Ebed-Jahwe-Lieder im Deuterojesaja." *TSK* 77 (1904) 319-379, esp. 343-362.

Leene, H. "Kan een fictionele gestalte onze plaats innemen? Overwegingen bij de uitleg van Jesaja 53." *GTT* 93 (1993) 232-253.

Leeuw, V. de. "De koninklijke verklaring van de Ebed-Jahweh-Zangen." *ETL* 28 (1952) 449-471.

———. "Le Serviteur de Jahvé: Figure royale ou prophétique?" In *L'attente du Messie*, ed. by L. Cerfaux, Brügge 1954, 51-56.

———. *De Ebed Jahweh-Profetieën. Historisch-Kritisch Underzoek naar hun Ontstaan en hun Betekenis*, Assen 1956, esp. 215-257.

Lennox, R. "The Servant of Yahweh in the Old Testament." *ThTo* 15 (1958) 315-320.

Lescow, T. *Das Stufenschema. Untersuchungen zur Struktur alttestamentlicher Texte* (BZAW 211), Berlin 1992, 216-227.

Leveen, J. "יזה" in Isaiah LII:15." *JJS* 7 (1956) 93-94.

Ley, J. "Die Bedeutung des 'Ebed-Jahwe' im zweiten Teil des Propheten Jesaia mit Berücksichtigung neuerer Forschungen." *TSK* 72 (1899) 163-206.

———. "Zur Erklärung der Bedeutung des Knechtes Jahwe in den sogenannten Ebed-Jahwe-Liedern." *TSK* 74 (1901) 659-669, esp. 662-664.

Liagre Böhl, F. M. T. de. *De "Knecht des Heeren" in Jezaja 53*, Haarlem 1923.

———. "Prophetentum und stellvertretendes Leiden in Assyrien und Israel." In idem, *Opera Minora. Studies en Bijdragen op Assyriologisch en Oudtestamentisch Terrein*, Groningen 1953, 63-80.

Lind, M. C. "Monotheism, Power, and Justice: A Study in Isaiah 40–55." *CBQ* 46 (1984) 432-446.

Lindblom, J. "Die Ebed Jahwe-Orakel in der neuentdeckten Jesajahandschrift DSIa." *ZAW* 63 (1951) 235-248.

———. *The Servant Songs in Deutero-Isaiah: A New Attempt to Solve an Old Problem*, Lund 1951.

Lindhagen, C. "The Servant Motif in the Old Testament: A Preliminary Study to the 'Ebed-Yahweh Problem' in Deutero-Isaiah." Diss. Uppsala 1950.

———. "Important Hypothesis Reconsidered 9: The Servant of the Lord." *ExpTim* 67 (1955-56) 279-283, 300-302.

Lindonk, W. J. van. "De Ebed Jahwe." *NedTT* 13 (1958-1959) 10-26, esp. 22ff.

Lindsey, F. D. "Isaiah's Songs of the Servant, Part 4: The Career of the Servant in Isaiah 52:13–53:12." *BSac* 139 (1982) 312-329.

———. "Isaiah's Songs of the Servant, Part 5: The Career of the Servant in Isaiah 52:13–53:12." *BSac* 140 (1983) 21-39.

———. *The Servant Songs: A Study in Isaiah*, Chicago 1985.

Ljund, I. *Tradition and Interpretation: A Study of the Use and Application of Formulaic Language in the So-Called Ebed YHWH-Psalms* (ConBOT 12), Lund 1978.

Lofthouse, W. F. "Some Reflections on the 'Servant Songs.'" *JTS* 48 (1947) 169-176.

MacRae, A. A. "The Servant of the Lord in Isaiah." *BSac* 121 (1964) 125-132, 218-227.

Maecklenburg, A. "Über die Auffassung des Berufsleidens des Ebed-Jahwe in Jes 52,13–53,12." *ZWT* 48 (1905) 483-517.

Mamorstein, A. "Zur Erklärung von Jes 53." *ZAW* 44 (1926) 260-265.

Martin-Achard, R. "Trois études sur Esaïe 53." *RTP* 114 (1982) 159-170.

———. *La mort en face selon la Bible hébraïque*, Geneva 1988, 113-125.

Matheus, F. *Singt dem Herrn ein neues Lied. Die Hymnen Deuterojesajas* (SBS 141), Stuttgart 1990, 104-132.

May, H. G. "The Righteous Servant in Second Isaiah's Songs." *ZAW* 66 (1954) 236-244.

Melugin, R. F. *The Formation of Isaiah 40–55* (BZAW 141), Berlin 1976, 73-76, 167-169.

Mennekes, F. *Verachtet und gepriesen. Die vier Gottesknechtslieder des Jesaja in der Gemeinde ausgelegt*, Stuttgart 1985, 91-111.

Merrill, E. "The Literary Character of Isaiah 40–55, Part 2: Literary Genres in Isaiah 40–55." *BSac* 144 (1987) 144-156.

Mesters, C. *Die Botschaft des leidenden Volkes,* Neukirchen-Vluyn 1982, 91-134.

Mettinger, T. N. D. "Die Ebed-Jahwe-Lieder. Ein fragwürdiges Axiom." *ASTI* 11 (1978) 68-76.

———. *A Farewell to the Servant Songs. A Critical Examination of an Exegetical Axiom* (SMHVL 1982-1983), Lund 1983.

Michel, D. "Deuterojesaja." *TRE* 8:510-530.

———. "Gottesknecht. (I) AT." In *Neues Bibel-Lexikon,* 3 vols., ed. by M. Görg and B. Lang, Zürich 1988, 1:932-934.

Millard, A. R. "Isaiah 53:2." *TynBul* 20 (1969) 127.

Miller, J. W. "Prophetic Conflict in Second Isaiah: The Servant Songs in the Light of Their Context." In *Wort — Gebot — Glaube. Beiträge zur Theologie des Alten Testaments. W. Eichrodt zum 80. Geburtstag,* ed. by H. J. Stoebe (ATANT 59), Zürich 1970, 77-85.

Minn, H. R. *The Servant Songs,* Christchurch (New Zealand) 1966.

Monteith, J. "A New View of Isaiah LIII." *ExpTim* 36 (1924-25) 498-502.

Morgenstern, J. "The Suffering Servant — A New Solution." *VT* 11 (1961) 292-320, 406-431.

———. "Two Additional Notes to 'The Suffering Servant — A New Solution.'" *VT* 13 (1963) 321-332.

Mowinckel, S. *Der Knecht Jahwäs,* Giessen 1921.

———. "Die Komposition des deuterojesajanischen Buches." *ZAW* 49 (1931) 87-112, 242-260, esp. 245ff.

———. *He That Cometh,* Nashville and New York 1956, 187-257.

Müller, H.-P. "Ein Vorschlag zu Jes 53,10f." *ZAW* 81 (1969) 377-380.

Murray, H. "An Approach to the Fourth Servant Song (Isa 52:13–53:12)." *Compass* 13 (1979) 43-46.

Nakazawa, K. *The Suffering Servant — Studies in Is. 53,* Tokyo ³1975.

———. "A New Proposal for the Emendation of the Text Isaiah 53:11." *AJBI* 2 (1976) 101-111.

———. "The Servant Songs — A Review after Three Decades." *Orient* 18 (1982) 65-82.

———. "Some Disputed Phrases in the Latter Half of Isaiah 53." *The Study of Bible Translating* 22 (1984) 32-39.

Nápole, G. M. "'Mi salvación por siempre será y mi justicia no caerá.' Salvación en Is 40–55." *RevBib* 50 (1988) 143-164.

North, C. R. "Who Was the Servant of the Lord in Isaiah LIII?" *ExpTim* 52 (1940-41) 181-184, 219-221.

———. "The Suffering Servant: Current Scandinavian Discussions." *SJT* 3 (1950) 363-379.

———. *The Suffering Servant in Deutero-Isaiah: An Historical and Critical Study,* London ²1956.

Nyberg, H. S. "Smärtornas man. En studie till Jes. 52,13–53,12." *SEÅ* 7 (1942) 5-82.

Oberholzer, J. P. "'Die Kneg van Jahwe' in Deuterojesaja." *Hervomde Teologiese Studies* 22 (1966) 11-37, esp. 23-31.

O'Donnell, R. E. "A Possible Source for the Suffering of the Servant in Isaiah 52:13–53:12." *DunR* 4 (1964) 29-42.

Olley, J. W. "'The Many': How Is Isa 53:12a to Be Understood?" *Bib* 68 (1987) 330-356.

Oorschot, J. van. *Von Babel zum Zion. Eine literarkritische und redaktionsgeschichtliche Untersuchung* (BZAW 206), Berlin 1993, esp. 178-196.

Orelli, C. von. *Der Knecht Jahve's im Jesajabuche,* Berlin 1908.

Orlinsky, H. M. *The So-Called "Suffering Servant" in Isaiah 53,* The Goldenson Lecture 1964, Cincinnati 1964.

———. "The So-Called 'Servant of the Lord' and 'Suffering Servant' in Second Isaiah." In *Studies on the Second Part of the Book of Isaiah,* by H. M. Orlinsky and N. H. Snaith (VTSup 14), Leiden 1967, 1-133.

Pákozdy, L. M. von. *Der Ebed Jahweh in der Theologie Deuterojesajas. Deuterojesajanische Studien II,* Debrecen 1942.

Palache, J. L. *The 'Ebed-Jahveh Enigma in Pseudo-Isaiah. A New Point of View,* Amsterdam 1934.

Paul, S. M. "Servant of the Lord." *EncJud* 14:1187.

Payne, D. F. "The Servant of the Lord: Language and Interpretation." *EvQ* 43 (1971) 131-143.

———. "Recent Trends in the Study of Isaiah 53." *IBS* 1 (1979) 3-18.

Peake, A. S. *The Problem of Suffering in the Old Testament,* London 1904, 30-72, 163-177.

———. *The Servant of Yahweh and Other Lectures,* Manchester 1931.

Phillips, A. "The Servant — Symbol of Divine Powerlessness." *ExpTim* 90 (1978-79) 370-374.

Pidoux, G. "Le serviteur souffrant d'Esaïe 53." *RTP* 6 (1956) 36-46.

Pipal, B. "The Lord's Ebed in the Exile." *CV* 13 (1970) 177-180.

Ploeg, J. van der. *Les chants du Serviteur de Jahvé dans la seconde partie du livre d'Isaïe (Chap. 40–55),* Paris 1936, esp. 51-63.

Praetorius, F. "Bemerkungen zu den Gedichten vom Knechte Jahwes." *ZAW* 36 (1916) 8-20.

———. *Die Gedichte des Deuterojesaja. Metrische und textkritische Bemerkungen,* Berlin 1922, 90-96.

———. *Nachträge und Verbesserungen zu Deutero-Jesaias,* Halle 1927, 41-48.

Preuss, H. D. *Deuterjesaja. Eine Einführung in seine Botschaft,* Neukirchen-Vluyn 1976, 92-106.

Press, R. "Der Gottesknecht im Alten Testament." *ZAW* 67 (1955) 67-99.

Raabe, P. R. "The Effect of Repetition in the Suffering Servant Songs." *JBL* 103 (1984) 77-81.

Rad, G. von. *Theologie des Alten Testaments,* Band 2: *Die Theologie der prophetischen Überlieferung,* Munich [10]1993, esp. 264-274 = *Old Testament Theology,* vol. 2: *The*

Theology of Israel's Prophetic Traditions, translated by D. M. G. Stalker, New York, 1965, esp. 250-262.

Reicke, B. "The Knowledge of the Suffering Servant." In *Das ferne und nahe Wort. Festschrift Leonhard Rost zur Vollendung seines 70. Lebensjahres am 30. November 1966 gewidmet,* ed. by F. Maass (BZAW 105), Berlin 1967, 186-192.

Reiterer, F. V. *Gerechtigkeit als Heil:* צדק *bei Deuterojesaja. Aussage und Vergleich mit der alttestamentlichen Tradition,* Graz 1976, esp. 106-114.

―――. "Stellvertretung — Leid — Jenseitshoffnung. Die Botschaft des vierten Gottesknechtsliedes (Jes 52,13–53,12)." *Heiliger Dienst* 36 (1982) 12-32.

Ricciardi, A. "Los cantos del siervo de Yavé." *Cuadernos de Teología* 4 (1975-77) 124-128.

Riesener, I. *Der Stamm* עבד *im Alten Testament* (BZAW 149), Berlin 1979, esp. 235-247.

Rignell, L. G. "Isa. LII 13-LIII 12." *VT* 3 (1953) 87-92.

―――. *A Study of Isaiah Ch. 40–55,* Lund 1956, 78-84.

Ringgren, H. "König und Messias." *ZAW* 64 (1952) 120-147, esp. 141-147.

―――. *The Messiah in the Old Testament* (SBT 18), London 1956, esp. 46-53.

―――. "Zur Komposition von Jesaja 49-55." In *Beiträge zur alttestamentlichen Theologie. Festschrift für Walther Zimmerli zum 70. Geburtstag,* ed. by H. Donner, R. Hanhart, and R. Smend, Göttingen 1977, 371-376.

Ringgren, H., U. Rüterswörden, and H. Simian-Yofre. "עָבַד" *TWAT* 5:982-1012 = *TDOT* 10:376-405.

Robinson, T. H. "Note on the Text and Interpretation of Isaiah 53:3, 11." *ExpTim* 71 (1959-60) 383.

Roodenburg, P. C. *Israel, de knecht en de knechten. Een onderzoek naar de betekenis en de functie van het nomen in Jesaja 40–66,* Meppel 1974.

Roth, W. M. W. "The Anonymity of the Suffering Servant." *JBL* 83 (1964) 171-179.

Rowley, H. H. "The Servant's Mission: The Servant Songs and Evangelism." *Interp* 8 (1954) 259-272.

―――. "The Servant of the Lord in the Light of Three Decades of Criticism." In idem, *The Servant of the Lord and Other Essays on the Old Testament,* Oxford ²1965, 3-60.

―――. "Knecht Jahwes." *RGG*³ 3:1680-1683.

Roy, H. *Israel und die Welt in Jesaja 40–55. Ein Beitrag zur Ebed-Jahwe-Frage,* Beigabe zum Beitrage des theologischen Seminariums der Brudergemeine in Gnadenfeld, Leipzig 1903.

Rubinstein, A. "Isaiah LII 14 מִשְׁחַת and the DSIa Variant." *Bib* 35 (1954) 475-479.

Rudolph, W. "Der exilische Messias. Ein Beitrag zur Ebed-Jahwe-Frage." *ZAW* 43 (1925) 90-114.

―――. "Die Ebed-Jahwe-Lieder als geschichtliche Wirklichkeit." *ZAW* 46 (1928) 156-166.

Ruppert, L. "Der leidende Gottesknecht." *Concilium: Internationale Zeitschrift für Theologie* 12 (1976) 571-575.

―――. "Schuld und Schuld-Lösen nach Jesaja 53." In *Schulderfahrung und Schuld-*

bewältigung. Christen im Umgang mit der Schuld, ed. by G. Kaufmann (SPK 21), Paderborn 1982, 17-34.

―――. "Der leidende Gerechte." in *Die Entstehung der jüdischen Martyrologie*, ed. by J. W. van Henten (StPB 38), Leiden 1989, 88-126.

―――. "Das Heil der Völker (Heilsuniversalismus) in Deutero- und 'Trito'-Jesaja." *MTZ* 45 (1994) 137-159.

―――. "Mein Knecht, der gerechte, macht die Vielen gerecht, und ihre Verschuldungen — er trägt sie (Jes 53,11)." *BZ* 40 (1996) 1-17.

Ruprecht, E. "Die Auslegungsgeschichte zu den sogenannten Gottesknechtsliedern im Buche Deuterojesaja unter methodischen Gesichtspunkten bis zu Bernhard Duhm." Diss. Universität Heidelberg, 1972.

―――. "Knecht Gottes." *EKL*[3] 2:1316-1317 = "Servant of the Lord." *EC* vol. 4, forthcoming.

Saebø, M. "Vom Individuellen zum Kollektiven. Zur Frage einer innerbiblischen Interpretation." In *Schöpfung und Befreiung. Festschrift für C. Westermann zum 80. Geburtstag*, ed. by R. Albertz, F. W. Golka, and J. Kegler, Stuttgart 1989, 116-125.

Salguero, J. "Vestigios de la doctrina de Is. 53 en el Antiguo Testamento." *CuBi* 22 (1965) 67-86.

Sauer, G. "Deuterojesaja und die Lieder vom Gottesknecht." In *Geschichtsmächtigkeit und Geduld. Festschrift der Evangelisch-Theologischen Fakultät der Universität Wien*, ed. by G. Fitzer, EvT Sonderheft, Munich 1972, 58-66.

Sawyer, J. F. A. "Daughter of Zion and Servant of the Lord in Isaiah: A Comparison." *JSOT* 44 (1989) 89-107.

Scharbert, J. "Stellvertretendes Sühneleiden in den Ebed-Jahwe-Liedern und in altorientalischen Ritualtexten." *BZ* 2 (1958) 190-213.

―――. *Heilsmittler im Alten Testament und im Alten Orient*, Freiburg 1964, esp. 178-212.

―――. *Deuterojesaja — der "Knecht" Jahwes?* Hamburg 1995.

Schelhaas, J. *De lijdende Knecht des Heeren*, Groningen 1933.

Schian, M. "Die Ebed-Jahwe-Lieder in Jes. 40–66." Diss. Universität Leipzig, 1894.

Schmidt, W. H. "Die Ohnmacht des Messias." *KD* 15 (1969) 18-34, esp. 30ff.

Schuermans, Y. "De Lijdende Dienaar van Yahweh volgens Isaias XL–LV." *CMech* 41 (1956) 561-578.

Schwager, R. *Brauchen wir einen Sündenbock? Gewalt und Erlösung in den biblischen Schriften*, Munich 1978, 134-142 = *Must There Be Scapegoats? Violence and Redemption in the Bible*, translated by M. L. Assad, San Francisco 1987.

Schwarz, G. "'. . . wie ein Reis vor ihm'?" *ZAW* 83 (1971) 255-256.

―――. "'. . . sieht er . . . wird er satt . . .'?" *ZAW* 84 (1972) 356-358.

Seitz, C. R. *Zion's Final Destiny: The Development of the Book of Isaiah*, Minneapolis 1991, 202ff.

Sekine, S. "Die Theodizee des Leidens im deuterojesajanischen Buch unter redaktionsgeschichtlichem Gesichtspunkt." *AJBI* 8 (1982) 50-112.

Sellin, E. *Serubbabel. Ein Beitrag zur Geschichte der messianischen Erwartung und der Entstehung des Judentums,* Leipzig 1898, 148-180.

―――. *Studien zur Entstehungsgeschichte der jüdischen Gemeinde nach dem babylonischen Exil. I. Der Knecht Gottes bei Deuterojesaja,* Leipzig 1901, esp. 108-115.

―――. *Das Rätsel des deuterojesajanischen Buches,* Leipzig 1908, esp. 37-52.

―――. *Mose und seine Bedeutung für die israelitisch-jüdische Religionsgeschichte,* Leipzig and Erlangen 1922, 94-101.

―――. "Tritojesaja, Deuterojesaja und das Gottesknechtsproblem." *NKZ* 41 (1930) 145-173.

―――. "Die Lösung des deuterojesajanischen Gottesknechtsrätsels." *ZAW* 55 (1937) 177-217.

Seybold, K. "Thesen zur Entstehung der Lieder vom Gottesknecht." *BN* 3 (1977) 33f.

Sicre, J. L. "La mediación de Ciro y la del Siervo de Dios en Deuteroisaias." *EE* 50 (1975) 179-210, esp. 192ff.

Smart, J. D. "A New Approach to the 'Ebed-Yahweh' Problem." *ExpTim* 45 (1933-34) 168-172.

Snaith, N. H. "The So-Called Servant Songs." *ExpTim* 56 (1944-45) 79-81.

―――. "The Servant of the Lord in Deutero-Isaiah." In *Studies in Old Testament Prophecy,* ed. by H. H. Rowley, Edinburgh 1950, 187-200.

―――. "Isaiah 40–66: A Study of the Teaching of the Second Isaiah and Its Consequences." In *Studies on the Second Part of the Book of Isaiah,* by H. M. Orlinsky and N. H. Snaith (VTSup 14), Leiden 1967, 135-264, esp. 166-176.

Soggin, J. A. "Tod und Auferstehung des leidenden Gottesknechtes Jesaja 53,8-10." *ZAW* 87 (1975) 346-355.

Sonne, I. "Isaiah 53:10-12." *JBL* 78 (1959) 335-342.

Sorg, T. "Stellvertretung (Jes 52,13–53,12)." *TBei* 16 (1985) 251-255.

Spykerboer, H. C. "The Structure and Composition of Deutero-Isaiah. With Special Reference to the Polemics against Idolatry." Diss. University of Groningen 1976, 174-178.

Staerk, W. "Bemerkungen zu den Ebed Jahwe-Liedern in Jes. 40ff." *ZWT* 51 (1909) 28-56, esp. 45ff.

―――. *Die Ebed Jahwe-Lieder in Jesaja 40ff. Ein Beitrag zur Deuterojesaja-Kritik,* Leipzig 1913, 103-142.

―――. "Zum Ebed Jahwe-Problem." *ZAW* 44 (1926) 242-260.

Stamm, J. J. *Das Leiden des Unschuldigen in Babylon und Israel* (ATANT 10), Zürich 1946, 68-75.

Steck, O. H. "Aspekte des Gottesknechts in Jes 52,13–53,12" (1985). Reprinted in idem, *Gottesknecht und Zion. Gesammelte Aufsätze zu Deuterojesaja* (FAT 4), Tübingen 1992, 22-43.

―――. "Gottesvolk und Gottesknecht in Jes 40–66." *JBTh* 7 (1992) 51-75.

―――. "Die Gottesknechts-Texte und ihre redaktionelle Rezeption im Zweiten

Jesaja." In idem, *Gottesknecht und Zion. Gesammelte Aufsätze zu Deuterojesaja* (FAT 4), Tübingen 1992, 149-172.

Steinmann, J. *Le livre de la consolation d'Israël et les prophètes du retour de l'exil* (LD 28), Paris 1960, esp. 169-175.

Stern, P. "The 'Blind Servant' Imagery of Deutero-Isaiah and Its Implications." *Bib* 75 (1994) 224-232.

Swartzentruber, A. O. "The Servant Songs in Relation to Their Context in Deutero-Isaiah: A Critique of Contemporary Methodologies." Diss. Princeton 1970.

Thomas, D. Winton. "A Consideration of Isaiah LIII in the Light of Recent Textual and Philological Study." *ETL* 44 (1968) 79-86.

Tournay, R. J. "Les chants du Serviteur dans la seconde partie d'Isaïe." *RB* 59 (1952) 481-512.

Treves, M. "Isaiah 53." *VT* 24 (1974) 98-108.

Vattioni, F. "Is 53,2a e i miti orientali." *RivB* 5 (1957) 288-298.

Vermeylen, J. "Isaïe 53 et le ralliement d'Éphraïm." In *"Wer ist wie du, Herr, unter den Göttern?" Studien zur Theologie und Religionsgeschichte Israels für Otto Kaiser zum 70. Geburtstag*, ed. by I. Kottsieper, J. van Oorschot, D. Römheld, and H. M. Wahl, Göttingen 1994, 342-354.

Vischer, W. "Der Gottesknecht." *Jahrbuch der Theologischen Schule Bethel* 1 (1930) 59-115.

Vogt, E. "Die Ebed-Jahwe-Lieder und ihre Ergänzungen." *EE* 34 (1960) 775-788.

Volck, W. "Jes. 52,13ff.–K. 53." *Theologisches Literaturblatt* 23 (1902) 1-2, 17-19, 25-30.

Volz, P. "Jesaja 53." In *Karl Budde zum siebzigsten Geburtstag am 13. April 1920*, ed. by K. Marti (BZAW 34), Giessen 1920, 180-190.

Vriezen, T. C. "The Term *Hizza*: Lustration and Consecration." *Oudtestamentische Studien* 7 (1950) 201-235.

Waldow, H. E. von. "Anlass und Hintergrund der Verkündigung des Deuterojesaja." Diss. Universität Bonn, 1953, 52-57.

―――. "The Servant of the Lord, Israel, the Jews and the People of God." In *Intergerini Parietis Septum (Eph. 2:14). Essays Presented to Markus Barth on His Sixty-Fifth Birthday*, ed. by D. Y. Hadidian (PTMS 33), Pittsburgh 1981, 355-369.

―――. "Der Gottesknecht bei Deuterojesaja. Israel, die Juden und die Kirche Jesu Christi." *TZ* 41 (1985) 201-219.

Ward, J. M. "The Servant's Knowledge in Isaiah 40–55." In *Israelite Wisdom: Theological and Literary Essays in Honour of S. Terrien*, ed. by J. G. Gammie, W. A. Brueggemann, L. Humphreys, and J. M. Ward, New York 1978, 121-136.

Waterman, L. "The Martyred Servant Motif of Is 53." *JBL* 56 (1937) 27-34.

Watts, R. E. "The Meaning of *'ālāw yiqpᵉṣu mᵉlākîm pîhem* in Isaiah LII 15." *VT* 40 (1990) 327-335.

―――. "Consolation or Confrontation? Isaiah 40–55 and the Delay of the New Exodus." *TynBul* 41 (1990) 31-59, esp. 49-58.

Weippert, M. "Die 'Konfessionen' Deuterojesajas." In *Schöpfung und Befreiung.*

Festschrift für C. Westermann zum 80. Geburtstag, ed. by R. Albertz, F. W. Golka, and J. Kegler, Stuttgart 1989, 104-115.

Welshman, H. "The Atonement Effected by the Servant: Is 52:13–53:12." *Biblical Theology* 23 (1973) 46-49.

Wénin, A. "Le poème dit du 'Serviteur souffrant' (Is 52:13–53:12). Proposition de lecture." *FoiTe* 24 (1994) 493-507.

Westermann, C. "עֶבֶד." *THAT* 2:182-200 = *TLOT* 2:819-832.

Whitley, C. F. "Textual Notes on Deutero-Isaiah." *VT* 11 (1961) 457-461, esp. 459ff.

Whybray, R. N. *Thanksgiving for a Liberated Prophet: An Interpretation of Isaiah Chapter 53* (JSOTSup 4), Sheffield 1978.

Wilcox, P., and D. Paton-Williams. "The Servant Songs in Deutero-Isaiah." *JSOT* 42 (1988) 79-102, esp. 94-98.

Williams, P. H. "The Poems about Incomparable Yahweh's Servant in Isaiah 40–55." *SJT* 11 (1968) 73-87, esp. 84-86.

Williamson, H. G. M. "*da'at* in Isaiah LIII 11." *VT* 28 (1978) 118-122.

———. *The Book Called Isaiah: Deutero-Isaiah's Role in Composition and Redaction,* Oxford 1994.

Wilshire, L. E. "The Servant-City: A New Interpretation of the 'Servant of the Lord' in the Servant Songs of Deutero-Isaiah." *JBL* 94 (1975) 356-367.

Wilson, A. *The Nations in Deutero-Isaiah: A Study on Composition and Structure* (ANETS 1), Lewiston, NY 1986.

Wocken, Ä. "Der Reiche im Alten Testament. Ein Beitrag zu Isaias 53,9." *TTZ* 62 (1953) 52-58.

Wolf, H. M. "The Relationship between Isaiah's Final Servant Song (52:13–53:12) and Chapters 1-6." In *A Tribute to Gleason Archer: Essays on the Old Testament,* ed. by W. C. Kaiser and R. F. Youngblood, Chicago 1986, 251-259.

Wolff, H. W. "Wer ist der Gottesknecht in Jesaja 53?" *EvT* 22 (1962) 338-342.

Workmar, G. C. *The Servant of Jehova, or The Passion-Scripture of Prophecy Analysed and Elucidated,* London and New York 1907.

Woude, A. S. van der. "De Liederen van de Knecht des Heren." *Homiletica et Biblica* 24 (1965) 1-6, 25-31, 49-51, esp. 30ff.

Wurtz, W. "Zu den Gottesknechtsliedern." In *Exeget zwischen Bibelkommission und Offenbarungskonstitution. Festschrift für A. Stöger,* ed. by F. Staudinger, St. Pölten 1990, 171-184.

Young, E. J. "The Origin of the Suffering Servant Idea." *WTJ* 13 (1950-51) 19-33.

———. *Isaiah Fifty-Three: A Devotional and Expository Study,* Grand Rapids 1952.

Zillessen, A. "Israel in Darstellung und Beurteilung Deuterojesajas (40–55)." *ZAW* 24 (1904) 251-295, esp. 273-292.

Zimmerli, W. "Zur Vorgeschichte von Jes 53" (1968). Reprinted in idem, *Studien zur alttestamentlichen Theologie und Prophetie* (TB 51), Munich 1974, 213-221.

Zimmerli, W. (and J. Jeremias). "παῖς θεοῦ." *TWNT* 5:653-713, esp. A.II.5, pp. 664-672 = *TDNT* 5:654-717, esp. A.II.5, pp. 666-673.

Zorell, F. "Das vierte 'Ebed-Jahwe-Lied: Is 52,13–53,12." *BZ* 14 (1917) 140-146.

Zwaardemaker, H. *De eenheid der eschatologische Voorstellingen in het boek Jesaja,* Utrecht 1910, 92-97.

2. Ancient Judaism, Ancient Versions, Jewish Interpretation

Ådna, J. "Herrens tjener i Jesaja 53 skildret som triumferende Messias. Profettargumens gjengivelse og tolkning av Jes 52,13–53,12." *TTKi* 63 (1992) 81-94.

Aejmelaeus, A. "Herran palvelija Septuagintassa ja kristillisessä tulkintatraditiossa." *Teologinen Aikakauskirja* 92 (1987) 199-205.

Aytoun, R. A. "The Servant of the Lord in the Targum." *JTS* 23 (1922) 172-180.

Bachl, G. "Zur Auslegung der Ebedweissagung (Is 52,13–53,12) in der Literatur des späten Judentums und im Neuen Testament." Diss. Univ. Gregoriana Rome, 1974.

Bastiaens, J. C. *Interpretaties van Jesaja 53. Een intertextueel onderzoek naar de lijdende Knecht in Jes 53 (MT/LXX) en in Lk 22:14-38, Hand 3:12-26, Hand 4:23-31 en Hand 8:26-40* (TFT-Studies 22), Tilburg 1993, 95-194.

Betz, O. "Die Übersetzung von Jes 53 (LXX, Targum) und die Theologia Crucis des Paulus." In idem, *Jesus. Der Herr der Kirche. Aufsätze zur biblischen Theologie II* (WUNT 52), Tübingen 1990, 197-216.

Black, M. "Servant of the Lord and Son of Man." *SJT* 6 (1953) 1-11.

Brierre-Narbonne, J. J. *Le Messie souffrant dans la littérature du rabbinisme,* Paris 1940.

Brown, R. E. "The Messianism of Qumrân." *CBQ* 19 (1957) 53-82, esp. 75ff.

Brownlee, W. H. "The Servant of the Lord in the Qumran Scrolls." *BASOR* 132 (1953) 8-15; 135 (1954) 33-38.

―――. "Messianic Motifs of Qumran and the New Testament." *NTS* 3 (1956-57) 12-30, 195-210.

―――. *The Meaning of the Qumrân Scrolls for the Bible with Special Attention to the Book of Isaiah,* New York 1964, esp. 204-216, 292-296.

Bruce, F. F. *Biblical Exegesis in the Qumran Texts,* Grand Rapids 1959, 50-58.

Bundy, D. D. "The Peshitta of Isaiah 53:9 and the Syrian Commentators." *OrChr* 67 (1983) 32-45.

Carmignac, J. "Les citations de l'Ancien Testament, et spécialement des poèmes du Serviteur, dans les hymnes de Qumran." *RevQ* 2 (1959-60) 357-394.

―――. "La théologie de la souffrance dans les Hymnes de Qumrân." *RevQ* 3 (1961-62) 365-386.

Chilton, B. *The Theology and Provenience of the Isaiah Targum* (JSOTSup 23), Sheffield 1983, esp. 91ff.

Dalman, G. *Jesaja 53. Das Prophetenwort vom Sühnleiden des Gottesknechtes mit besonderer Berücksichtigung der jüdischen Literatur,* Schriften des Institutum Judaicum in Berlin 13, Leipzig ²1914.

Déaut, R. le. "Aspects de l'intercession dans le Judaïsme ancien." *JSJ* 1 (1970) 35-57, esp. 55-56.

Dip, G. "Problema del Mesías paciente." *EE* 43 (1968) 155-179.

Duarte Lourenço, J. "Humilhação no judaismo antigo." Diss. Studii Biblici Franciscani Jerusalem, 1985.

―――. "A 'Humillação-Exaltação' do Servo de Is 53 no Targum e na Literatura Rabínica." *Itinerarium* 31 (1985) 302-359.

―――. "Targum de Is 52:13–53:12. Presupostos históricos e processos literários." *Did(L)* 20 (1990) 155-166.

―――. "Sofrimento e glorificação en Is 52:13–53:12. Sua interpretação judaica e crista." *Did(L)* 22 (1992) 17-38.

Escande, J. "La traduction dans sa relation au corpus juif et/ou chrétien." *SémBib* 31 (1983) 34ff.

Euler, K. F. *Die Verkündigung vom leidenden Gottesknecht aus Jes 53 in der griechischen Bibel* (BWANT 66), Stuttgart 1934.

Fascher, E. *Jesaja 53 in christlicher und jüdischer Sicht,* Berlin 1958.

Fischel, H. A. "Die Deuterojesaianischen Gottesknechtslieder in der juedischen Auslegung." *HUCA* 18 (1944) 53-76.

Gärtner, B. *The Temple and the Community in Qumran and the New Testament* (SNTSMS 1), Cambridge 1965, 123-130.

Ginsberg, H. L. "The Oldest Interpretation of the Suffering Servant." *VT* 3 (1953) 400-404.

Guillaume, A. "Some Readings in the Dead Sea Scrolls of Isaiah." *JBL* 76 (1957) 40-43, esp. 41f.

Haag, H. "Der 'Gottesknecht' bei Deuterojesaja im Verständnis der Judentums." *Jud* 41 (1984) 23-36.

Hegermann, H. *Jesaja 53 in Hexapla, Targum und Peschitta* (BFCT.M 56), Gütersloh 1954.

Hillyer, N. "The Servant of God." *EvQ* 41 (1969) 143-160, esp. 148-151.

Hofius, O. "Kennt der Targum zu Jes 53 einen sündenvergebenden Messias?" In *Private Freundesgabe für Prof. Peter Stuhlmacher zum 50. Geburtstag am 18. Januar 1982,* 215-254.

―――. "Zur Septuaginta-Übersetzung von Jes 52,13b." *ZAW* 104 (1992) 107-110.

Hooker, M. D. *Jesus and the Servant: The Influence of the Servant Concept of Deutero-Isaiah in the New Testament,* London 1959, 25-61.

Hruby, K. "Die rabbinische Exegese messianischer Schriftstellen." *Jud* 21 (1965) 100-122.

Humbert, P. *Le Messie dans le Targum des Prophètes,* Lausanne 1911, esp. 26-31.

Hutterer, N. *Die mittelalterlichen jüdischen Kommentare zu den Ebed-JHWH-Liedern des Jesaja,* Berlin 1938.

Jeremias, J. "Erlöser und Erlösung im Spätjudentum und Urchristentum." In *Der Erlösungsgedanke. Bericht über den 2. deutschen Theologentag in Frankfurt a.M. (Herbst 1928),* ed. by E. Pfenningsdorf, *Deutsche theologie* 2, Göttingen 1929, 106-119.

―――. "Zum Problem der Deutung von Jes. 53 im palästinischen Spätjudentum." In

Aux sources de la tradition chrétienne. Mélanges offerts à M. Maurice Goguel à l'occasion de son soixante-dixième anniversaire, Neuchatel 1950, 113-119.

Kleinknecht, K. T. *Der leidende Gerechtfertigte. Die alttestamentlich-jüdische Tradition vom "leidenden Gerechten" und ihre Rezeption bei Paulus* (WUNT II/13), Tübingen ²1988, 83-166.

Koch, K. "Messias und Sündenvergebung in Jesaja 53-Targum." *JSJ* 3 (1972) 117-148.

Koenig, J. *L'herméneutique analogique du Judaïsme antique d'après les témoins textuels d'Isaïe* (VTSup 33), Leiden 1982, esp. 274-283.

Kooij, A. van der. *Die alten Textzeugen des Jesajabuches* (OBO 35), Fribourg 1981, 70ff.

Lagrange, M.-J. *Le Judaïsme avant Jésus-Christ* (EBib 5.01), Paris 1931, esp. 368-381.

Lohse, E. *Märtyrer und Gottesknecht. Untersuchungen zur urchristlichen Verkündigung vom Sühntod Jesu Christi* (FRLANT 64), Göttingen ²1963, 94-100.

Moo, D. J. *The Old Testament in the Gospel Passion Narratives,* Sheffield 1983, 79-86.

Morrow, F. J. "The Text of Isaiah at Qumran." Diss. Catholic University of America, 1973, 141-144.

Neubauer, A., and S. R. Driver. *The Fifty-Third Chapter of Isaiah According to the Jewish Interpreters,* 2 vols., Oxford 1876-77 (repr. New York 1969).

Page, S. H. "The Suffering Servant between the Testaments." *NTS* 31 (1985) 481-497.

Pavoncello, N. "L'esegesi rabbinica del cap. 53 di Isaia." In *Gesù e la sua morte: Atti della XXVII Settimana biblica,* by Associazione Biblica Italiana, G. Boggio, A. Bonora, S. Cipriani et al., Brescia 1984, 237-251.

Rembaum, J. E. "The Development of a Jewish Exegetical Tradition Regarding Isaiah 53." *HTR* 75 (1982) 289-311.

Rese, M. "Überprüfung einiger Thesen von Joachim Jeremias zum Thema des Gottesknechts im Judentum." *ZTK* 60 (1963) 21-41.

Rowley, H. H. "The Suffering Servant and the Davidic Messiah." In idem, *The Servant of the Lord and Other Essays on the Old Testament,* Oxford ²1965, 63-93.

Ruppert, L. *Der leidende Gerechte. Eine motivgeschichtliche Untersuchung zum Alten Testament und zwischentestamentlichen Judentum* (FB 5), Würzburg 1972, esp. 59-62.

Sacchi, P. "Ideologia e varianti della tradizione ebraica: Deut 27,4 e Is 52,14." In *Bibel in jüdischer und christlicher Tradition. Festschrift für Johann Maier zum 60. Geburtstag* (BBB 88), ed. by H. Merklein, K. Müller, and G. Stemberger, Frankfurt 1993, 13-32.

Seeligmann, L. *The Septuagint Version of Isaiah* (MEOL 9), Leiden 1948, 70ff., 90ff.

———. "ΔΕΙΞΑΙ ΑΥΤΟΙ ΦΩΣ (Jes 53,1)." *Tarbiz* 27 (1957-58) 121-141 (Hebrew).

Seidelin, P. "Der 'Ebed Jahwe und die Messiasgestalt im Jesajatargum." *ZNW* 35 (1936) 194-231.

Skehan, P. W. "The Text of Isaias at Qumran." *CBQ* 17 (1955) 158-163.

Soloff, R. "The 53rd Chapter of Isaiah According to the Jewish Commentators, to the Sixteenth Century." Diss. Drew University, 1967.

Staerk, W. "Zur Exegese von Jes 53 im Diasporajudentum." *ZNW* 35 (1936) 308.

Suggs, M. J. "Wisdom of Solomon 2:10-5: A Homily Based on the Fourth Servant Song." *JBL* 76 (1957) 26-33.

Syrén R. "Targum Isaiah 52:13–53:12 and Christian Interpretation." *JJS* 40 (1989) 210-212.

Varo, F. "El cuarto canto del Siervo (Is 52:13–53:12). Balance de diez años de investigación (1980-1990)." *Scripta Theologica* 22 (1990) 517-538.

———. "El Siervo Sufriente (Is 52:13–53:12) en la exégesis hebrea, según Don Isaac Abrabanel." In *III Simposio Bíblico Español*, ed. J. Carreira das Neves, Fundación Bíblica Española, Valencia-Lisboa, 1991, 597-608.

———. "Los canticos del Siervo en la exegesis hispano-hebrea." Córdoba 1993.

Wittenberg, M. "Zum jüdischen Verständnis des Gottesknechts." *ELKZ* 11 (1957) 310-313.

Ziegler, J. *Untersuchungen zur Septuaginta des Buches Isaias* (ATA 12/3), Münster 1934.

Zillessen, A. "Jesaja 52,13–53,12 hebräisch nach LXX." *ZAW* 25 (1905) 261-284.

3. New Testament and Early Christianity

Allen, W. C. "The Old Testament Quotations in St. Matthew and St. Mark. II. St. Matthew." *ExpTim* 12 (1900-01) 281-285.

Amsler, S. *L'Ancien Testament dans l'église*, Neuchâtel 1960.

Anderson, H. "The Old Testament in Mark's Gospel." In *The Use of the Old Testament in the New and Other Essays: Studies in Honor of William Franklin Stinespring*, ed. by J. M. Efird, Durham (N.C.) 1972.

Argyle, A. W. "1 John 3:4f." [Cf. LXX version of Isaiah 53.] *ExpTim* 65 (1953) 62-63.

Audet, J. P. *La Didache. Instructions des Apôtres*, Paris 1958.

Bachl, G. "Zur Auslegung der Ebedweissagung (Is 52,13–53,12) in der Literatur des späten Judentums und im Neuen Testament." Diss. Univ. Gregoriana, Rome 1974.

Barrett, C. K. "The Lamb of God." *NTS* 1 (1954-55) 210-218.

———. "The Old Testament in the Fourth Gospel." *JBS* 48 (1947) 155-169.

———. "The Interpretation of the Old Testament in the New." In *The Cambridge History of the Bible*. Vol. 1: *From the Beginnings to Jerome*, ed. by P. R. Ackroyd and C. F. Evans, Cambridge 1970, 377-411.

Barrick, W. B. "Rich Man from Arimathea (Matt 27: 57-60) and 1QIsaᵃ." *JBL* 96 (1977) 235-239.

Barth, M. *Was Christ's Death a Sacrifice?* (SJT Occasional Papers 9), Edinburgh and London 1961.

Bartsch, H. W. "Jesu Schwertwort. Lukas XXII.35-38. Überlieferungsgeschichtliche Studie." *NTS* 20 (1973-74) 190-203.

Bastiaens, J. C. *Interpretaties van Jesaja 53. Een intertextueel onderzoek naar de lijdende Knecht in Jes 53 (MT/LXX) en in Lk 22:14-38, Hand 3:12-26, Hand 4:23-31 en Hand 8:26-40* (TFT-Studies 22), Tilburg 1993, 195-354.

Benoit, P. "Jésus et le Serviteur de Dieu." In *Jésus aux origines de la christologie*, ed. by J. Dupont, Louvain 1975, 112-140.

Betz, O. "Die Übersetzung von Jes 53 (LXX, Targum) und die Theologia Crucis des Paulus." In idem, *Jesus. Der Herr der Kirche* (WUNT 52), Tübingen 1990, 197-216.

————. "Der gekreuzigte Christus: Unsere Weisheit und Gerechtigkeit (Der alttestamentliche Hintergrund von 1 Kor 1–2)." In *Tradition and Interpretation in the New Testament: Essays in Honor of E. Earle Ellis for His 60th Birthday*, ed. by G. Hawthorne and O. Betz, Grand Rapids and Tübingen 1987, 195-215.

Beutler, J. "Greeks Come to See Jesus (John 12:20f)." *Bib* 71 (1990) 333-347.

Bieringer, R. "Traditionsgeschichtlicher Ursprung und theologische Bedeutung der ὑπέρ-Aussagen im Neuen Testament." In *The Four Gospels 1992: Festschrift Frans Neirynck*, 3 vols., ed. by F. Van Segbroeck et al., Leuven 1992, 1:219-248.

Black, M. "Servant of the Lord and Son of Man." *SJT* 6 (1953) 1-11.

————. "The Christological Use of the Old Testament in the New Testament." *NTS* 18 (1971-1972) 1-14.

————. "The Theological Appropriation of the Old Testament." *SJT* 39 (1986) 1-17.

Bock, D. L. *Proclamation from Prophecy and Pattern. Lucan Old Testament Christology* (JSNTSup 12), Sheffield 1987.

Braun, H. "Das Alte Testament im Neuen Testament." *ZTK* 59 (1962) 16-31.

Brooks, R. "A Christological Suffering Servant? The Jewish Retreat into Historical Criticism." In *Hebrew Bible or Old Testament? Studying the Bible in Judaism and Christianity*, ed. by R. Brooks, Notre Dame 1990, 207-210.

Bundy, D. D. "The Interpretation of Isa 53 in East and West." *Eichstätter Beiträge* 4 (1983) 54ff.

Childs, B. S. *Biblical Theology of the Old and New Testaments*, Philadelphia 1993, esp. 513-514.

Chilton, B. "John XII 34 and Targum Isaiah LII 13." *NovT* 22 (1980) 176-178.

Collins, A. Y. "The Suffering Servant: Isaiah Chapter 53 as a Christian Text." In *Hebrew Bible or Old Testament? Studying the Bible in Judaism and Christianity*, ed. by R. Brooks, Notre Dame 1990, 201-206.

Coppens, J. "Phil 2:7 et Is 53:12, le problème de la 'kénose.'" *ETL* 41 (1965) 147-150.

————. *Le messianisme et sa relève prophétique. Les anticipations vétéro-testamentaires, leur accomplissement en Jésus* (BETL 38), Leuven ²1989.

Corbin, M. "Connais-tu ce-que tu lis? Une lecture d'Actes 8, v. 26 à 40." *Christus* 93 (1977) 73-85.

Craig, C. T. "The Identification of Jesus with the Suffering Servant." *JR* 24 (1944) 240-245.

Cullmann, O. *Die Christologie des Neuen Testaments*, Tübingen ⁵1975, 50-81 = *The Christology of the New Testament*, translated by S. C. Guthrie and C. A. M. Hall, London and Philadelphia 1959, 51-82.

Davies, P. E. "Did Jesus Die as a Martyr Prophet?" *BR* 2 (1957) 19-30.

Dautzenberg, G. "ἀμνός, ἀρήν, ἀρνίον." *EWNT* 1:168-172 = *EDNT* 1:70-72.

Decock, P. B. "The Understanding of Isaiah 53:7-8 in Acts 8:32-33." *Neotestamentica* 14 (1981) 111-133.

Derrett, J. D. M. "Midrash in the New Testament: The Origin of Luke 22:67-68." *ST* 29/ 2 (1975) 147-156.

Descamps, A. *Les justes et la justice dans les évangiles et le christianisme primitif hormis la doctrine proprement paulienne*, Louvain 1950.

Dodd, C. H. *According to the Scriptures: The Sub-Structure of New Testament Theology*, London 1952.

―――. *The Apostolic Preaching and Its Developments*, London 1936.

Durand, G. M. "Sa génération, qui la racontera? Is 53,8b: L'éxégèse des Pères." *RSPT* 53 (1969) 638-657.

Ekenberg, A. "'Det var om honom han talade': Jes 53, Jes 6 och Joh 12." *SEÅ* 59 (1994) 119.

Elliot, J. H. "Backward and Forward 'In His Steps.' Following Jesus from Rome to Raymond and Beyond. The Tradition, Redaction and Reception of 1 Peter 2:18-25." In *Discipleship in the New Testament*, ed. by F. Segovia, Philadelphia 1985, 184-208.

Ellis, E. E. *Paul's Use of the Old Testament*, Edinburgh 1957.

Escande, J. "La traduction dans sa relation au corpus juif et/ou chrétien." *SémBib* 31 (1983) 34ff.

Evans, C. A. "Obduracy and the Lord's Servant: Some Observations on the Use of the Old Testament in the Fourth Gospel." In *Early Jewish and Christian Exegesis*, ed. by C. A. Evans and W. Stinespring, Atlanta 1987, 221-236.

Fascher, E. *Jesaja 53 in christlicher und jüdischer Sicht*, Berlin 1958.

Fekkes, J. *Isaiah and Prophetic Traditions in the Book of Revelation: Visionary Antecedents and Their Development* (JSNTSup 93), Sheffield 1994, 153-158.

Feuillet, A. "Le logion sur la rançon." *RSPT* 51 (1967) 365-402.

Fjärstedt, B. "The Use of Isaiah 53 in the NT — Recent Scandinavian Research." *IJT* 20 (1971) 109-116.

Flesseman-van Leer, E. "Die Interpretation der Passionsgeschichte vom AT aus." In *Zur Bedeutung des Todes Jesu. Exegetische Beiträge*, by H. Conzelmann et al., Gütersloh 1967, 237-265.

Gelio, R. "Isaia 52:13–53:12 nella patrologia primitiva." In *Sangue e antropologia biblica nella patristica. Atti della settimana: Roma, 23-28 novembre 1981*, 2 vols., ed. by F. Vattioni, Rome 1982, 1:119-148.

Ghiberti, G. "Il modello del 'giusto sofferente' nella passione di Gesù." In *La storiografia della Bibbia: Atti della XXVIII Settimana biblica*, by Associazione Biblica Italiana, G. L. Prato, J. A. Soggin, R. Gelio, et al., Bologna 1986, 153-168.

Goppelt, L. *Theologie des Neuen Testaments*, Göttingen ³1991, esp. 238-247 = *Theology of the New Testament*, 2 vols., translated by J. E. Alsup, Grand Rapids, 1981-1982, 1:195-199.

Green, J. B. "Jesus on the Mount of Olives (Luke 22:39-46): Tradition and Theology." *JSNT* 26 (1986) 29-48.

Grimm, W. *Weil ich dich liebe. Die Verkündigung Jesu und Deuterojesaja* (ANTJ 1), Frankfurt am Main and Bern ¹1976. Second edition under title: *Die Verkündigung Jesu und Deuterojesaja*, ²1981.

Gryglewicz, F. "Das Lamm Gottes." *NTS* 13 (1967) 133-146.

Guillaume, A. "Mt 27:46 in the Light of the Dead Sea Scroll of Isaiah." *PEQ* 83 (1951) 78-80.

Gundry, R. H. *The Use of the Old Testament in St. Matthew's Gospel* (NovTSup 18), Leiden 1967.

Hampel, V. *Menschensohn und historischer Jesus. Ein Rätselwort als Schlüssel zum messianischen Selbstverständnis Jesu*, Neukirchen-Vluyn 1990.

Heimerdinger, J. "La foi de l'eunuque éthiopien. Le problème textuel d'Actes 8:37." *ETR* 63 (1988) 521-528.

Hengel, M. "Der stellvertretende Sühnetod Jesu. Ein Beitrag zur Entstehung des urchristlichen Kerygmas." *IKaZ* 9 (1980) 1-25, 135-147.

⸻. *The Atonement: The Origins of the Doctrine in the New Testament*. London and Philadelphia, 1981.

Hofius, O. "Das 4. Gottesknechtslied in den Briefen des Neuen Testamentes." *NTS* 39 (1993) 414-437. [Translated as pp. 163-188 of the present volume.]

Holtz, T. *Untersuchungen über die alttestamentlichen Zitate bei Lukas* (TU 106), Berlin 1968, 41-43.

Hooker, M. D. *Jesus and the Servant: The Influence of the Servant Concept of Deutero-Isaiah in the New Testament*, London 1959.

Houston, W. "Today, in Your Very Hearing: Some Comments on the Christological Use of the Old Testament." In *The Glory of Christ in the New Testament: Studies in Christology in Memory of George Bradford Caird*, ed. by L. D. Hurst and N. T. Wright, Oxford and New York 1987, 37-47.

Hughes, R. K. *Mark: Jesus, Servant and Savior*, Westchester, Ill., 1989.

Jeremias, J. "παῖς θεοῦ im Neuen Testament." In idem, *Abba. Studien zur neutestamentlichen Theologie und Zeitgeschichte*, Göttingen 1966, 191-216.

⸻. *Die Abendmahlsworte Jesu*, Göttingen ⁴1967 = *The Eucharistic Words of Jesus*, translated by N. Perrin, London and New York 1966.

⸻. "ἀμνός, ἀρήν, ἀρνίον." *TWNT* 1:342-345 = *TDNT* 1:338-341.

⸻. *Neutestamentliche Theologie*, Gütersloh ³1979 = *New Testament Theology*, New York 1971.

⸻. "παῖς θεοῦ, C-D." *TWNT* 5:676-713 = *TDNT* 5:677-717.

⸻. "Erlöser und Erlösung im Spätjudentum und Urchristentum." In *Der Erlösungsgedanke. Bericht über den 2. deutschen Theologentag in Frankfurt a.M. (Herbst 1928)*, ed. by E. Pfenningsdorf, *Deutsche Theologie* 2, Göttingen 1929, 106-119.

⸻. "Das Lösegeld für Viele (Mk 10,45)." In idem, *Abba. Studien zur neutestamentlichen Theologie und Zeitgeschichte*, Göttingen 1966, 216-229.

Johnson, S. E. "The Biblical Quotations in Matthew." *HTR* 36 (1943) 135-153.

Jones, D. L. "The Title 'Servant' in Luke-Acts." In *Luke-Acts: New Perspectives from the*

Society of Biblical Literature Seminar, ed. by C. H. Talbert, New York 1984, 148-165.

Katz, P. *Justin's Old Testament Quotations and the Greek Dodekapropheton Scroll,* Studia Patristica 1 (TU 63), Berlin 1957.

Kertelge, K. "Der dienende Menschensohn (Mk 10,45)." In *Jesus und der Menschensohn,* ed. by R. Pesch and R. Schnackenburg, Freiburg, Basel, Vienna 1975, 225-239.

Kleinknecht, K. T. *Der leidende Gerechtfertigte. Die alttestamentlich-jüdische Tradition vom "leidenden Gerechten" und ihre Rezeption bei Paulus* (WUNT II/13), Tübingen ²1988.

Kim, Y. B. "Justice, Participation and Peace." In *Out of Control,* ed. by C. Tremewan, Singapore 1985, 122-132.

Kränkl, E. *Jesus, der Knecht Gottes* (BU 8), Regensburg 1972.

Krinetzki, L. "Der Einfluss von Is 52,13–53,12Par auf Phil 2,6-11." *TQ* 139 (1959) 157-193, 291-336.

Lamau, M. L. "Exhortation aux esclaves et hymne au Christ souffrant dans la Première Epître de Pierre." *MSR* 43 (1986) 121-143.

Lampe, G. W. H. "The Two Swords (Lk 22:35-38)." In *Jesus and the Politics of His Day,* ed. by E. Bammel and C. F. D. Moule, Cambridge 1984, 335-351.

Larkin, W. J. "Luke's Use of the Old Testament as a Key to His Soteriology." *JETS* 20 (1977) 325-335.

Leonardi, G. "Venuti per servire, non per essere serviti." In *Parola e Spirito: Studi in onore di Settimio Cipriani,* 2 vols., ed. by C. C. Marcheselli, Rome 1982, 1:163-194.

Levoratti, A. J. "La lectura non sacrificial del evangelio en la obra de René Girard." *RevistB* 47/3 (1985) 159-176.

Litwak, K. D. "The Use of Quotations from Isaiah 52:13–53:12 in the New Testament." *JETS* 2 (1983) 385-394.

Lohmeyer, E. *Gottesknecht und Davidssohn,* Göttingen ²1953.

Lohse, E. "Die alttestamentliche Sprache des Sehers Johannes." In idem, *Die Einheit des Neuen Testaments,* Göttingen ²1973, 329-333.

———. "Die alttestamentlichen Bezüge im neutestamentlichen Zeugnis vom Tode Jesu Christi." In idem, *Die Einheit des Neuen Testaments,* Göttingen ²1973, 111-124.

———. *Märtyrer und Gottesknecht. Untersuchungen zur urchristlichen Verkündigung vom Sühnetod Jesu Christi* (FRLANT 46), Göttingen ²1963.

Maillot, A. "Notule sur Romains 7,7-8ss." *FoiVie* 84 (1985) 17-23.

Marshall, I. H. "Son of God or Servant of Yahweh? A Reconsideration of Mark 1:11." *NTS* 15 (1968-69) 326-336.

Maurer, C. "Knecht Gottes und Sohn Gottes im Passionsbericht des Markusevangeliums." *ZTK* 50 (1953) 1-38.

Milne, D. J. W. "Mark — The Gospel of Servant Discipleship." *RTR* 49 (1990) 20-29.

Moo, D. J. *The Old Testament in the Gospel Passion Narratives,* Sheffield 1983, 86-172.

Moule, C. F. D. "Fulfilment-Words in the New Testament: Use and Abuse." *NTS* 14 (1967-68) 293-320.

Mussner, F. "Der Messias Jesus." In *Jesus — Messias? Heilserwartung bei Juden und Christen,* ed. by H. Greschat, S. Talmon, and R. Werblowski, Regensburg 1982, 89-107.

Pastor-Ramos, F. "'Murio por nuestros pecados' (1 Cor 15:3; Gal 1:4): Observaciones sobre el origen de esta formula en Is 53." *EE* 61 (no. 239) (1986) 385-393.

Patsch, H. "Zum alttestamentlichen Hintergrund von Röm 4,25 und 1Petr 2,24." *ZNW* 60 (1969) 273-279.

Pavoncello, N. "L'esegesi rabbinica del cap 53 di Isaia." In *Gesù e la sua morte: Atti della XXVII Settimana biblica,* by Associazione Biblica Italiana, G. Boggio, A. Bonora, S. Cipriani et al., Brescia 1984, 237-251.

Porter, R. J. "What Did Philip Say to the Eunuch?" *ExpTim* 100 (1988) 54-55.

Radl, W. "Alle Mühe umsonst: Paulus und der Gottesknecht." In *L'Apôtre Paul: Personalité, style et conception du ministère,* ed. by A. Vanhoye (BETL 73), Leuven 1986, 144-149.

Reim, G. *Studien zum alttestamentlichen Hintergrund des Johannesevangeliums,* Cambridge 1974.

Rese, M. *Alttestamentliche Motive in der Christologie des Lukas* (StNT 1), Gütersloh 1969.

Ricoeur, P. "From Proclamation to Narrative." *JR* 64 (1984) 501-512.

Rodgers, P. R. "Mark 15:28." *EvQ* 61 (1989) 81-84.

Roloff, J. "Anfänge der soteriologischen Deutung des Todes Jesu (Mk 10,45 und Lk 22,27)." *NTS* 19 (1972-73) 38-64.

Rosenberg, R. A. "Jesus, Isaac and the 'Suffering Servant.'" *JBL* 84 (1965) 381-388.

Ruppert, L. "Jesus als der leidende Gerechte? Der Weg Jesu im Lichte eines alt- und zwischentestamentlichen Motivs (SBS 49), Stuttgart 1972.

Ryan, W. F. J. "The Church as the Servant of God in Acts." *Scripture* 15 (1963) 110-115.

Schinzer, R. "Die Bedeutung des Prozesses Jesu (Mk 14,63)." *NZSTh* 25 (1983) 138-154.

Schwager, R. *Brauchen wir einen Sündenbock? Gewalt und Erlösung in den biblischen Schriften,* Munich 1978 = *Must There Be Scapegoats? Violence and Redemption in the Bible,* translated by M. L. Assad, San Francisco 1987.

Selvidge, M. J. S. "And those who followed feared (Mark 10:32)." *CBQ* 45 (1983) 396-400.

Smith, D. M. "The Use of the Old Testament in the New." In *The Use of the Old Testament in the New and Other Essays. Studies in Honor of William Franklin Stinespring,* ed. by J. M. Efird, Durham, N.C. 1972.

Soards, M. "The Silence of Jesus before Herod: An Interpretative Suggestion." *ABR* 33 (1985) 41-45.

Spencer, F. S. "The Ethopian Eunuch and His Bible: A Social-Science Analysis." *BTB* 22 (1992) 155-165.

Stanks, T. "The Servant of God in John 1:29, 36." Diss. Louvain, 1963.

Stanley, D. M. "The Theme of the Servant of Yahweh in Primitive Christian Soteriology and Its Transposition by St. Paul." *CBQ* 16 (1954) 385-425.

Stuhlmacher, P. *Biblische Theologie des Neuen Testaments*, 2 vols., Göttingen, vol. 1: ¹1992; ³2004; vol. 2: ¹1999 = *Biblical Theology of the New Testament*, 2 vols. in 1, translated by Daniel P. Bailey, Grand Rapids 2005.

————. "Sühne oder Versöhnung?" In *Die Mitte des Neuen Testaments*, Festschrift für E. Schweizer, ed. by U. Luz and H. Weder, Göttingen 1983, 291-316.

————. "Existenzstellvertretung für die Vielen." In idem, *Versöhnung, Gesetz und Gerechtigkeit. Aufzätze zur Biblischen Theologie*, Göttingen 1981, 27-42 = "Vicariously Giving His Life for Many, Mark 10:45 (Matt. 20:28)." In idem, *Reconciliation, Law, and Righteousness: Essays in Biblical Theology*, translated by E. R. Kalin, Philadelphia 1986, 16-29.

————. "Der messianische Gottesknecht." *JBTh* 8 (1993) 131-154.

Syrén, R. "Targum Isaiah 52:13–53:12 and Christian Interpretation." *JJS* 40 (1989) 201-212.

Ternant, P. *Le Christ est mort "pour tous": Du serviteur Israël au serviteur Jésus*, Paris 1993.

Thyen, H. *Studien zur Sündenvergebung im Neuen Testament und seinen alttestamentlichen und jüdischen Voraussetzungen* (FRLANT 46), Göttingen 1970.

Torrey, C. C. "The Influence of Second Isaiah in the Gospels and Acts." *JBL* 48 (1929) 24-36.

Wagner, G. "Le scandale de la croix expliqué par le chant du serviteur d'Esaïe 53: Réflexion sur Philippiens 2:6-11." *ETR* 61/2 (1986) 177-187.

Wilckens, U. *Die Missionsreden der Apostelgeschichte* (WMANT 5), Neukirchen-Vluyn ³1974.

Wolff, H. W. *Jesaja 53 im Urchristentum*. Mit einem Vorwort von P. Stuhlmacher, Giessen ⁴1984.

4. Updated Bibliography

Albrecht, R. "Sühne und Stellvertretung in Jesaja 53." *Jahrbuch für evangelikale Theologie* 12 (1998) 7-24.

Bailey, Daniel P. "Concepts of *Stellvertretung* in the Interpretation of Isaiah 53." In *Jesus and the Suffering Servant*, ed. W. H. Bellinger and William R. Farmer, pp. 223-250, Harrisburg, Pa., 1998.

Bailey, Daniel P. "The Suffering Servant: Recent Tübingen Scholarship on Isaiah 53." In *Jesus and the Suffering Servant*, ed. W. H. Bellinger and William R. Farmer, pp. 251-259, Harrisburg, Pa., 1998.

Bailey, Daniel P. "The *Wirkungsgeschichte* of the Bible in Recent Research." *Currents in Biblical Research*, forthcoming (2005).

Barré, Michael L. "Textual and Rhetorical-critical Observations on the Last Servant Song (Isaiah 52:13–53:12)." *Catholic Biblical Quarterly* 62, no. 1 (Jan. 2000) 1-27.

Batnitzky, Leora. "On the Suffering of God's Chosen: Christian Views in Jewish Terms." In *Christianity in Jewish Terms,* ed. John C. Cavadini et al., Boulder 2000.

Bellinger, William H., Jr., and William R. Farmer, eds. *Jesus and the Suffering Servant: Isaiah 53 and Christian Origins,* Harrisburg, Pa., 1998.

Benzi, G. "Il Servo sofferente, figura di Cristo. Linee per una lettura esegetica e teologica dei Canti del Servo di Isaia." *Riv. di Teolog. dell'Evangelizzazione* 3, no. 6 (1999) 211-229.

Bergey, R. "The Rhetorical Role of Reiteration in the Suffering Servant Poem (Isa 52:13–53:12)." *JETS* 40, no. 2 (1997) 177-188.

Betz, Otto. "Jesus and Isaiah 53." In *Jesus and the Suffering Servant,* ed. W. H. Bellinger and William R. Farmer, pp. 70-87, Harrisburg, Pa., 1998.

Bingham, D. Jeffrey. "Justin and Isaiah 53." *Vigiliae christianae* 54, no. 3 (2000) 248-261.

Cavadini, John C. "The Meaning and Value of Suffering: A Christian Response to Leora Batnitzky." In *Christianity in Jewish Terms,* ed. Tikva Simone Frymer-Kensky et al., Boulder 2000.

Clements, R. E. "Isaiah 53 and the Restoration of Israel." In *Jesus and the Suffering Servant,* ed. W. H. Bellinger and William R. Farmer, pp. 39-54, Harrisburg, Pa., 1998.

Dunn, James D. G. *Christianity in the Making,* volume 1: *Jesus Remembered,* Grand Rapids 2003, pp. 809-818.

Eynikel, E. "De liederen van de lijdende dienaar van Jahwe." *Collationes* 22 (1992) 115-127.

Farmer, William R. "Reflections on Isaiah 53 and Christian Origins." In *Jesus and the Suffering Servant,* ed. W. H. Bellinger and William R. Farmer, pp. 260-80, Harrisburg, Pa., 1998.

France, R. T. "Servant of Yahweh." In *Dictionary of Jesus and the Gospels,* ed. Joel B. Green et al., pp. 744-747, Downers Grove, 1992.

Frymer-Kensky, Tikva Simone, et al., eds. *Christianity in Jewish Terms.* Boulder 2000.

Gertel, E. B. "Isaiah Fifty-Three: A Test of Jewish Education." *Conservative Judaism* 45 (1993) 38-49.

Goulder, Michael Douglas. "'Behold My Servant Jehoiachin.'" *Vetus Testamentum* 52, no. 2 (2002) 175-190.

Groves, J. Alan. "'For He Bore the Sins of Many': Atonement in Isaiah 53." In *The Glory of the Atonement: Biblical, Historical, and Practical Perspectives. Essays in Honor of Roger R. Nicole,* ed. Charles E. Hill and Frank A. James III, Downers Grove 2004.

Hanson, Paul D. "The World of the Servant of the Lord in Isaiah 40–50." In *Jesus and the Suffering Servant,* ed. W. H. Bellinger and William R. Farmer, pp. 9-22, Harrisburg, Pa., 1998.

Henning-Hess, Heike. "Bemerkungen zum ASCHAM-Begriff in Jes 53,10." *ZAW* 109, no. 4 (1997) 618-626.

Holman, J. "De Lijdende Dienaar (Jesaja 53) in het Nederlandse verzoeningsdebat." In

Exegeten aan het werk, Hertogenbosch, Katholieke Bijbelstichting, ed. P. H. M. Welzen, pp. 201-212, 1998.

Hooker, Morna D. "Did the Use of Isaiah 53 to Interpret His Mission Begin with Jesus?" In *Jesus and the Suffering Servant,* ed. W. H. Bellinger and William R. Farmer, pp. 88-103, Harrisburg, Pa., 1998.

Hooker, Morna D. "Reply to Mikeal Parsons." In *Jesus and the Suffering Servant,* ed. W. H. Bellinger and William R. Farmer, Harrisburg, Pa., 1998.

Hugenberger, G. P. "The Servant of the Lord in the 'Servant Songs' of Isaiah." In *The Lord's Anointed: Interpretation of the Old Testament Messianic Texts,* ed. P. E. Satterthwaite et al., pp. 87-104. Carlisle, 1995.

Kabasele Lumbala, F. "Isaiah 52:13–53:12: An African Perspective." In *Return to Babel,* ed. J. E. Levison and P. Pope-Levison, pp. 101-106, Louisville 1999.

Knohl, Israel. *The Messiah before Jesus: The Suffering Servant of the Dead Sea Scrolls,* trans. David Maisel, Berkeley 2000.

Leske, Adrian M. "Isaiah and Matthew: The Prophetic Influence in the First Gospel." In *Jesus and the Suffering Servant,* ed. W. H. Bellinger and William R. Farmer, Harrisburg, Pa., 1998.

Likins-Fowler, Deborah G. "Sociological Functions of the Servant in Isaiah 52:13–53:12." *Proceedings — Eastern Great Lakes and Midwest Biblical Societies* 21 (2001) 47-59.

Lindström, Fredrik. "Han bar de mångas skuld: profetia och uppfyllelse utifrån Jes. 53." *Svensk teologisk kvartalskrift* 75, no. 3 (1999) 98-109.

Lourengo, J. D. "Sofrimento e glorificaçâo em Is 52,13–53,12. Sua interpretaçâo na exegese judaica e cristâ." *Didaskalia* 22 (1992) 17-38.

Mayhue, R. L. "For What Did Christ Atone in Isa 53:4-5?" *Master's Seminary Journal* 6 (Fall 1995) 121-141.

Melugin, Roy F. "On Reading Isaiah 53 as Christian Scripture." In *Jesus and the Suffering Servant,* ed. W. H. Bellinger and William R. Farmer, pp. 55-69, Harrisburg, Pa., 1998.

Menken, Martinus J. J. "The Source of the Quotation from Isaiah 53:4 in Matthew 8:17." *Novum Testamentum* 39 (1997) 313-327.

Menken, Martinus J. J. "The Use of the Septuagint in Three Quotations in John: Jn 10,34; 12,38; 19,24." *Scriptures in the Gospels,* ed. Christopher M. Tuckett, pp. 367-393, Louvain 1997.

Meynet, R. "Le quatrième chant du serviteur: Is 52,13–53,12." *Gregorianum* 80 (1999) 407-440.

Moon, C. H. S "Isaiah 52:13–53:12: An Asian Perspective." In *Return to Babel,* ed. J. E. Levison and P. Pope-Levison, pp. 107-113, Louisville 1999.

Pagán, Samuel. "La iglesia hispana es sierva del Señor: una lectura exegética de Isaías 52.13–53.12." *Apuntes* 22, no. 1 (Spring 2002) 4-28.

Parsons, Mikeal C. "Isaiah 53 in Acts 8: A Reply to Professor Morna D. Hooker." In *Jesus and the Suffering Servant,* ed. W. H. Bellinger and William R. Farmer, pp. 104-119, Harrisburg, Pa., 1998.

Pixley, J. V. "Isaiah 52:13–53:12: A Latin American Perspective." In *Return to Babel,* ed. J. E. Levison and P. Pope-Levison, pp. 95-100, Louisville 1999.

Reventlow, Henning Graf. "Basic Issues in the Interpretation of Isaiah 53." In *Jesus and the Suffering Servant,* ed. W. H. Bellinger and William R. Farmer, pp. 23-38, Harrisburg, Pa., 1998.

Sapp, David A. "The LXX, 1QIsa, and MT Versions of Isaiah 53 and the Christian Doctrine of Atonement." In *Jesus and the Suffering Servant,* ed. W. H. Bellinger and William R. Farmer, pp. 170-192, Harrisburg, Pa., 1998.

Schenker, A. *Knecht und Lamm Gottes (Jesaja 53). Übernahme von Schuld im Horizont der Gottesknechtlieder,* Stuttgarter Bibelstudien, 190, Stuttgart 2001.

Schreiner, J. "Theologie der Passion: Jes 52,13–53,12." *Klerusblatt* 81, no. 2 (2001) 25-26.

Scobie, Charles H. H. *The Ways of Our God: An Approach to Biblical Theology,* Grand Rapids 2003, pp. 403-440.

Varoni, G. "Erwählung, Leiden, Stellvertretung im 'Gottesknecht' verdichtete Erfahrung Israels." In *Christliche Glaube in der Begegnung mit dem Buddhismus,* ed. A. Bsteh, pp. 125-138, Mödling 2001.

Volgger, D. "Das 'Schuldopfer' Ascham in Jes 53, 10 und die Interpretation des sogenannten vierten Gottesknechtliedes." *Biblica* 79, no. 4 (1998) 473-498.

Wagner, J. Ross. "The Heralds of Isaiah and the Mission of Paul: An Investigation of Paul's Use of Isaiah 51–55 in Romans." In *Jesus and the Suffering Servant,* ed. W. H. Bellinger and William R. Farmer, pp. 193-222, Harrisburg, Pa., 1998.

Watts, Rikki E. "Jesus' Death, Isaiah 53, and Mark 10:45: A Crux Revisited." In *Jesus and the Suffering Servant,* ed. W. H. Bellinger and William R. Farmer, pp. 125-151, Harrisburg, Pa., 1998.

Welch, John W. "Isaiah 53, Mosiah 14, and the Book of Mormon." In *Isaiah in the Book of Mormon,* by Donald W. Parry and John W. Welch, pp. 293-312, Provo 1998.

Wendland, Ernst R., and Salimo Hachibamba. "'Do You Understand What You Are Reading (Hearing)?' (Acts 8:30): The Translation and Contextualization of Isaiah 52:13–53:12 in Chitonga." In *The Bible in Africa,* ed. Gerald O. West and Musa W. Dube, pp. 538-556, Leiden 2000.

Wright, N. T. "The Servant and Jesus: The Relevance of the Colloquy for the Current Quest for Jesus." In *Jesus and the Suffering Servant,* ed. W. H. Bellinger and William R. Farmer, pp. 281-297, Harrisburg, Pa., 1998.

Index of Primary Sources

Citation of a page implies that a reference may be found either in the text or in the foot-notes on that page. Occasionally specific note numbers are given. A few subject entries pertinent to the translation and interpretation of the fourth Servant Song may be found under Isaiah 52:13–53:12. **Boldface** indicates more extended or detailed discussion.

Index of Modern Authors

In addition to the authors of the modern secondary literature, this index selectively includes the editors and translators of ancient texts, especially for matters such as textual criticism, translation alternatives, and annotations. More prominent mentions, including critical discussions (or corrections) of an author's work, are occasionally marked by **boldface**. Similarly marked are several of the more substantial additions to the German essays in the Translator's notes: see Bailey, D. P. (translator).